北京的城墙和城门

[瑞典] 喜龙仁 著

赵晓梅 佟怡天 译

学苑出版社

图书在版编目（CIP）数据

北京的城墙和城门 /（瑞典）喜龙仁著；赵晓梅，佟怡天译. — 北京：学苑出版社，2016.11
ISBN 978-7-5077-5128-4

Ⅰ.①北… Ⅱ.①喜… Ⅲ.①古建筑-北京 Ⅳ.① K928.71

中国版本图书馆 CIP 数据核字 (2016) 第 268788 号

责任编辑：战葆红
装帧设计：徐道会
出版发行：学苑出版社
社　　址：北京市丰台区南方庄 2 号院 1 号楼
邮政编码：100079
网　　址：www.book001.com
电子信箱：xueyuanpress@163.com
联系电话：010-67601101（销售部） 67603091（总编室）
经　　销：新华书店
印　刷　厂：北京京华虎彩印刷有限公司
开本尺寸：787×1092　1/8
印　　张：66.75
版　　次：2017 年 4 月北京第 1 版
印　　次：2017 年 4 月第 1 次印刷
定　　价：980.00 元

中译本序

熟悉国际汉学史的我国读者，都会知道瑞典在汉学界的突出地位。瑞典拥有一系列知名的汉学家，而其间如果要举出对中国考古文物的研究作出重要贡献的学者，相信大家一定会讲到高本汉（Bernhard Karlgren）。其实同高本汉并时，盛誉和影响都堪相比肩的，还有喜龙仁，由于他的著作很少介绍到中国来，就恐怕很少有人知道了。

喜龙仁（Osvald Sirén），1879年诞生于芬兰，毕业于赫尔辛基大学。自20世纪初年在瑞典斯德哥尔摩国家博物馆任职，同时于斯德哥尔摩大学教授美术史。1930年，被选为芬兰科学院院士。他原本专攻欧洲美术史，后对东方美术史产生浓厚兴趣，从1920年到1956年，曾多次来访中国，撰著了多部关于中国的作品，逝世于1966年。

1921年，喜龙仁得到当时中国北洋政府准许，对北京的城墙和城门做了两年系统的考察和测量，其成果编纂为《北京的城墙和城门》一书，1924年于英国伦敦出版。这部书印数甚少，却使喜龙仁的大名在汉学界播传遐迩。其后喜龙仁有关中国的作品很多，但《北京的城墙和城门》仍不失为他汉学方面的代表作。

《北京的城墙和城门》这部书，既是美术史的专题，又是考古文物研究的论著。大家了解，西方的考古学和中国的考古学，究其渊源颇有不同。起源于欧洲的考古学，继承了中世纪的所谓古物学，本来便是同美术史密不可分，而中国的考古学，虽受西方的影响，却是以"证经补史"的传统金石学为基础的，从而一直同典籍文献的研究互相结合。我们看喜龙仁的这部《北京的城墙和城门》，其自序一开头就说"我撰写这本书，是源于北京城门之美丽；源于城门具有的非凡意义，它具有京城最美景致的典型特征"，即可认识到他是站在美术史的立场上，去从事考古文物研究的，这部书所显示的特色，也正在于此。

请允许我在这里絮谈一点个人的感想。我生于1933年，在北京成长工作已80余年，算得是北京的一名老市民了。少年时，我还有机会比较完整地瞻望北京的各处城门、城墙。回忆新中国成立前的几年，我在汇文中学念书，学校的南方即是崇文门迤东的城墙。我和几个同学都对巍峨的城墙深怀好奇而又敬畏之感。一天，我们由马道攀爬上了城墙，一起走向崇文门城楼。我们钻进门楼,仰面观看,顿觉楼体雄伟壮观,充满了美的魅力,几个人都震撼得说不出话来。此情此景,是我永不能忘的。

《北京的城墙和城门》中译本出版,使大家重观古老北京的壮丽风貌,更有助于北京历史文化的深入探究,值得向读者推荐,而对于我这样的市民来说,尤其激发了感触和忆念,这是我乐于写几句话的缘由。

李学勤

2016年9月2日于北京清华园

中译本序

19世纪的中国，正值社会动荡与变革的时代，留存的文化遗产正在以惊人的速度毁坏和消亡，当时的国人无意也无力进行文物和建筑遗产的整理和保护工作。20世纪初，一些外国学者出于不同的目的竞相来华对中国建筑进行考察研究，如英国人钱伯斯、叶慈，法国人沙畹，德国人艾克、鲍希曼，瑞典人喜龙仁，日本人关野贞、伊东忠太、田边泰、塚本清和村田治郎等，他们搜集资料，著书立说，其中较有影响的就有喜龙仁及他的这本《北京的城墙和城门》。

近年随着中国经济的腾飞，国人对文化遗产价值的认知有了极大提升，对文化遗产保护的力度也逐年加大，一些以前不被人们关注的历史建筑及遗迹都进入了保护的视野，抢救、记录、修缮、展示都进入保护范畴。然而，早年那些价值连城的珍贵建筑遗产或文化遗存或因认知空洞，或因无力回天，已然灰飞烟灭，踪迹难寻，令人唏嘘，明清北京旧城的倾废或拆毁即为其一。北京城门和城墙的倾废可追溯至喜龙仁调查之时，他在书中写道："北京如此壮丽如画之美还能延续多少年？每年有多少鎏金雕花的店面被毁掉？为建造三四层高的半现代砖房，多少座带有前廊的旧式庭院以及布满亭台楼阁的大花园被夷为平地？为了铺设有轨电车，多少古老街道被拓宽？多少宏伟的皇城粉墙被拆除？老北京正遭受迅速的破坏。北京已经不再是帝王之都，当局也无力保护这座城市中最值得骄傲、最珍贵的遗址。"文中流露出作者对当时北京城墙正面临的自然倾塌和人为拆除的痛惜和忧虑。作者似乎已经预见到古城最终消失的命运："这些美妙的城墙与城门，这些北京最美丽、最辉煌的无言的历史记录者，它们的美还能够延续多久呢？"由此产生的紧迫感和使命感督促他要记录下这座人类丰碑的有关文字和图象，完成自己"对这座伟大的中国帝都履行了些许义务"的承诺。面对今日已荡然无存的古城风貌，喜龙仁的这部著作无疑显得尤其珍贵。

作者在书中有很多即景描写："宽阔如运河的护城河是整幅风景的动脉……近处，孩子们像青蛙似的在芦苇中游戏，成群的白鸭在水面游荡，溅起水花，发出嘎嘎叫声，回应着各自主人的呼唤。拿着锡桶来河边取水的人，往往要在那里蹲一会儿，凝望着这幅田园诗歌般的画面，沉浸于寂静的欢愉中。"这些每每勾起我童年的记忆，我幼时曾住在朝阳门内烧酒胡同里的南弓匠营胡同，那里其时早就没有什么烧酒酿造和弓箭制作的匠人及痕迹。当年每逢周日，我们用自制的小车拉着废旧书报出城卖废品，朝阳门城楼的门洞乃是必经之路，每次都要先跑到护城河边，用废报纸折叠成纸船放入河中，希冀将自己莫名的愿望承载其中，目送小船随波逐流消失远方。书中的一些细致的观察和记载也让我感同身受："连续的城砖层层叠砌，状若阶梯。收分最大的北城墙自然最明显，这些阶梯的宽度足以让人直登城头。外立面自然要顺滑得多，因为从防卫的角度来看，在外立面建造这样宽的阶梯是非常危险的。"我还清楚地记得和小伙伴们沿着砌缝攀爬城墙而翻越城头的场景。近年来，北京市政府希望重振古都风貌，恢复了外城的永定门城楼和左安门角楼，但毕竟是假古董而难有历史价值。

中国自己对建筑史的研究始于 1930 年成立的营造学社，当时曾任北洋政府内务总长的朱启钤召集同好，创办了营造学社，知名学者梁思成、刘敦桢分别任法式部主任和文献部主任，开中国人系统调查研究古代建筑的先河，此前中国旧时文人的研究多为钩稽章句，迻录掌故，缺少现代科学意义上的实证研究，梁思成曾感叹说："我国古代建筑，征之文献，所见颇多，《周礼考工记》《阿房宫赋》《两都》《两京》，以至《洛阳伽蓝记》等等，固记载详尽，然吾侪所得，则隐约之印象，及美丽之辞藻，调谐之音节耳。明清学者，虽有较专门之著述，如萧氏《元故宫遗录》及类书中宫室建筑之辑录，然亦不过无数殿宇名称，修广尺寸，及'东西南北'等字，以标示其位置，盖皆'闻'之属也。读者虽读破万卷，于建筑物之真正印象，绝不能有所得。"这种状况一直持续到近代早期，如乐家藻所著《中国建筑史》，其内容仍是以旧时文人的考据观点写成，很少触及建筑艺术及技术问题。

喜龙仁是瑞典著名的艺术史家，著述颇丰，对中国古代艺术情有独钟，撰写了多部有关中国文化的著作，这本《北京的城墙和城门》是其中比较有价值的一部，也是近代外国学者研究北京历史建筑和风物的代表作品。归纳起来，这本著作的特点有三：一是对中国古代文明的敬重，对古代艺术与文化遗产的热爱之情充盈全书之中；二是科学严谨，记录详实，一丝不苟，为后学演示了科学的研究方法，留下了珍贵的测绘资料；三是不畏辛苦，以苦为乐，在十分困难的条件下坚持不懈，完成了全城的测绘调研和文献采集工作。著作于 1924 年出版，调查过程中所用实地测绘与艺术考古方法，对当时中国的相关学术研究有启发和借鉴意义。梁思成在其《蓟县独乐寺山门考》中就对这种方法予以了特别的强调："搜集实物，考证过去，已是现代的治学精神"，"研究建筑非作遗物之实地调查测绘不可"。

当年喜龙仁撰写这部书籍是带着一种强烈的冲动和感动的："我撰写这本书，是源于北京城门之美丽；源于城门具有的非凡意义，它具有京城最佳景致的典型特征。"正是这种感情和感触使一部本来可能枯燥干涩的调查报告变得如此真切而生动:"薄薄的白雪取代绿色的枝叶,覆盖着屋脊和檐口,如泡沫般熠熠闪烁。晨雾笼罩下的城市,像是一片冰冷的灰色海洋,奔涌向前的波浪戛然而止,波涛起伏的节奏仍然可见,但运动已然止息,仿佛被施了魔法。难道大海也被冻结了古老的中国文明生命力的寒魔所震慑了吗?"作者还以其特有的艺术敏感和浪漫情怀阐述了北京城墙作为休憩游赏场所的可能性:"从长长的坡道(中国人称之为"马道",因为可以骑马登城)爬到城墙之上,我们便来到世界上最有趣的散步之地。在这里,人们可以漫步好几个钟头,目不暇接地欣赏全景图画:万绿丛中掩映着的金灿灿的皇宫与庙宇,铺设着蓝绿琉璃瓦的王府宅院,带有开敞前廊的朱红色房子,半掩在百年古树之下的灰色小房屋,宽敞而繁荣的街道,这些街道两侧还布满商店和装饰华丽的牌楼,以及一片片有牧童放羊的开阔场地——所有这些景致都呈现在脚下这轴展开的长卷之上。"20世纪50年代,梁思成和陈占祥两先生提出了著名的北京城墙环城公园方案,畅想了包裹在曲水、绿茵之中的璀璨如项链般的环城公园诱人景象,不知两位先生是否受到喜龙仁的灵感启发。

此书1985年曾由著名历史学家侯仁之先生推荐而有过译本,但当时译文有所删节,加之开本缩小,致使测绘图比例失效,照片也因纸张和印刷技术原因不甚清晰,今由学苑出版社重出新本,弥补了缺憾与不足,也说明此书对于当代相关领域的学术研究和古迹保护仍有重要的价值。

刘 托
2016年8月8日于中国艺术研究院

译者的话

从未间断的城市建设让我们早已难觅北京城的昔日风貌，千篇一律的现代建筑掩盖了这座城市的精髓，只能在残存的遗迹中想象往日北京城的模样。幸有这样一本书，作者用他欣赏艺术品般的目光和对北京城的热爱，并凭借深厚的专业知识，在90多年前的民国初期，记录下了当时已然开始遭受破坏的北京城墙和城门的一砖一瓦，还拍摄了大量照片，请匠人绘制了数十张建筑图纸。那细致详尽的记载、优美而诗意的语言、精美的图片与测绘图，在今天看来，仍令人叹服不已，至今仍可被视为北京城墙和城门最翔实、最优美的资料。而这本书的作者，便是享誉中国艺术史学界的瑞典学者喜龙仁。

喜龙仁，原名 Osvald Sirén，1879年生于芬兰，毕业于赫尔辛基大学，历任瑞典斯德哥尔摩国家博物馆助理、斯德哥尔摩大学艺术史教授等职，早年从事西方近代艺术史研究，1920年前后在日本讲学、旅居中国，开始对中国古代艺术产生浓厚兴趣，并进行了深入的研究。

喜龙仁是他的中文名字，与他的姓氏音译颇似，但并非音译。之前，Osvald Sirén 曾被翻译为"奥斯伍尔德·喜仁龙"，乃是将音译与中文名混淆，并且他的中文名并不叫"喜仁龙"，应为"喜龙仁"。民国十八年（1929）八月十日，内政部内政公报上的一则指令明确称其为"喜龙仁"；最早刊行于民国时期的《中国营造学社汇刊》也称其为喜龙仁；与他有多次往来的，在中国近现代绘画史上与齐白石并称"南黄北齐"的黄宾虹先生，在书信中一直称呼他为"喜龙仁"……可知，喜龙仁确是其汉名。

喜龙仁著有多部关于中国古代艺术的著作，如《中国雕刻》（*Chinese Sculpture*，1925年）、《北京故宫》（*The Imperial Palace of Peking*，1926年）、《中国绘画史》（*Histoire de Art Anciens*，1929—1930年）与《中国花园》（*Gardens of China*，1949年）等，《北京的城墙和城门》（*The Walls and Gates of Peking*，1924年）则是他最早出版的关于中国的著作，他的著作为西方人了解中国的古代文化艺术提供了独一无二的资料。

本书正文根据喜龙仁于1924年由约翰·兰恩－柏德利·海德出版社（*John Lane The*

●內政部指令

呈一件 呈爲瑞典人案祝仁顧請在天壇內考查測量請飭示遵由

令北平檔案保管處

呈悉據呈稱護瑞典人入國請在天壇內考查測量並據七年前（民十一）北京內務部曾准許在三殿等處測量給圖等語惟查民十一舊卷護瑞典人只請拍照測量似與來呈不符再據民二外交部通咨以外人遊歷不准測繪險要曾經外務部於光緒三十四年四月通照各使禁阻在案嗣後遇有外人測繪情形即可將測繪器具及圖稿扣留以爲交涉證據俟由領事將該測繪人處分後再將測繪器具交還圖稿沒收及民四七月外交部復江西遇按使日生拍照古蹟風景有關險要地點自應設法禁阻二條則測繪險要已通知各使禁阻在案拍照古蹟名勝似微有不同應飭禁阻測量准此拍照風景仰即知照此令

中華民國十八年八月十日

內政部長趙戴文

民國十八年（1929）八月十日內政部內政公報，公報中明確稱其為：喜龍仁

Bodley Head Limited）出版的 *The Walls and Gates of Peking* 进行翻译，全书共分八部分，详细介绍了中国北方筑墙城市、北京城址上的早期城市、内外城城墙及其内外侧壁以及内外城城门等内容。在翻译过程中，遵循下列原则：

1. 翻译过程中一般不轻易改动原版文字，一律全录，不加删除，以存全貌。若遇有原文有误，必须做校改之处，以及需做进一步解释说明之处，均以译者注形式标出。

2. 正文中加括号的注释，非特别说明是译者注外，均为作者注。

3. 本书中年号纪年甚多，在英文原版中的年号纪年之后，作者有的加注了公元纪年，有的没有，全书并未统一。本书译文尊重原文照录。

4. 原书附有英汉对照索引，主要针对行文中涉及的中国人名、地名及专有名词给出中英文对照，并标识出该词出现的页码。本书译文中人名、地名与专有名词的翻译，一般据原书的英汉对照表翻译，少量名称经考证错误的进行修正，或调整为中文惯用词汇，均以译者注的形式标出，以便读者理解。

5. 原书中数字的表达，既有采用小数点的形式（如 20.75 米等），又有用半或几分之几的表达（如 1 里半、$1\frac{1}{4}$ 等），译文尽量尊重原文数字表达方式进行翻译。

6. 原书计量单位既有公制，也有英制，还有古代中国的"里"、"步"等。如果都统一为公制，势必造成混乱，故译文尊重原文照录。

7. 本书行文中提及多位西方汉学家（包括作者本人），他们大多有中文名字，译文直接使用其中文名字，用译者注的形式注释出其外文名字及其中文音译。

8. 本书正文中插有大量由中国工匠绘制的建筑图纸，图纸本身有绘图者撰写的中文图名，作者又为它们加上了英文图注。译文在翻译过程中仅对英文图注进行翻译，但翻译后的图注与中文图名又不尽相同，如"切面图"与"剖面图"、"内楼"与"城楼"及"外楼"与"箭楼"等。此种情况，翻译的图注与译文正文用词保持一致。

9. 本书插图均带有比例尺，本书按原比例印刷。但由于排版等问题，难免出现误差，以图中所绘比例尺为准。

赵晓梅[1]　佟怡天[2]

---

[1] 赵晓梅，复旦大学文物与博物馆学系讲师。2012 年 7 月博士毕业于清华大学建筑学院建筑历史与理论专业，曾于 2010 年 3 月 –8 月在罗马 ICCROM 访学、2015 年 2 月 –8 月在荷兰莱顿大学亚洲研究中心访学。研究方向包括建筑遗产保护、遗产社区与管理及建筑历史等。

[2] 佟怡天，瑞典哥德堡大学硕士，主要从事博物馆及文化遗产方面的工作，亦为文化艺术类新媒体撰稿，在文化领域有较丰富的经验。

英文版序

我撰写这本书，是源于北京城门之美丽；源于城门具有的非凡意义，它具有京城最佳景致的典型特征；源于城门绝好地衬托着古老的房屋、荫翳的树木和倾圮的城壕；亦源于城门那充满装饰意味的建筑特质。无论从历史亦或风土的意义上讲，有几座城门至今依然称得上是北京的地标。城门与毗连的城墙一起，反映出这座伟大城市的很多早期历史。城门亦与其周边的街道、景观一同，构成了一道道紧密相关又独具特色的优美风景。

如此这般的印象，促使我花费数月时间，对北京的城门展开专门研究，以期借助一系列照片，再现城门之美。此愿望究竟能在多大程度上得以实现，当留给读者来评判。本书的图版包括从中遴选出的109张凹版印刷照片。

着迷于城门的艺术特质，使我渐渐产生一个愿望——希冀知晓城门作为历史古迹的重要意义，渴求更深入地洞察不同年代中城门营造与变迁的历史。不单单是城门，还有城门周围的环境以及附属于城门的绵长的城墙，它们都成为历史与建筑的研究材料，激发着我的研究兴趣；对它们的研究愈深入，愈感到其中蕴含着一些理解中国历史重要篇章的关键因素；本书虽然对此表述不多，但透过其中的零碎信息，读者依稀可以领略到北京的城门和城墙同过去的密切联系，尽管它们因多处翻新而形成了新的联系，但主体依然古老，布满逝去岁月的斑驳痕迹与印记。

本书中的历史文献主要引自中国地方志，这些地方志包含大量有关前朝城墙和城门的信息，此前从未如此大规模地翻译成任何外文并出版。除这些有印刷文字可循的记录之外，其他信息大都来自文物本身，主要是城砖铭文和镶嵌在城墙和城门各处的石碑碑记。将上述材料仔细收集起来，或用于历史研究，或用于对文物进行断代。虽然，所有这些文献仅仅是分析工艺与建筑的佐证，但在很多没有任何文献记载的情况下，它们就成为历史研究与考证的主要依据。

诚然，这项工作是在有限的条件下完成的。我们无法在建筑上进行材料检测，也不能凿开城墙，亦不能搭建脚手架来仔细研究城墙的上部。不过，我们得到内务部的许可，测绘了多座城门。这些测绘图都是在作者的指导下由中国工匠绘制的，无疑，它们不仅成为研究北京城门的最珍贵、精确的数据，同时对中国建筑的整体研究亦具有价值。毕竟，城门是体现中国建筑基本原则的典型范例。

在此书的编写过程中，本人得到了各方人士的协助，甚为感激。文中引用的诸多中文史料由北京培华学校的包哲洁[1]小姐（A.G.Bowden-Smith）及其助手翻译，此部分的贡献应归功于她，也由其担负文责。

本人的中国老师周谷城先生耐心、细致地记录下大部分石碑碑记与城砖上的铭文，其中一部分铭文由英国公使馆的萨允格[2]先生（Mr.Scott）翻译。

著名的鲍迈斯特·蒂勒先生（Baumeister Thiele）曾多次给予我可贵的实际帮助，正是他为我联系了中国制图师。他们在我指导下绘制的图纸，在本书中以彩绘与线图的方式呈现。

几年前，建筑师罗特凯格尔[3]先生（Rothkegel）主持了前门的改造工程。在我的请求下，他为我们提供了前门箭楼图纸与前门总平面图。

本人还应感谢英国皇家建筑师学会（R.I.B.A）的贾普先生（Mr.Jupp），承蒙他校对了文中有关建筑的一些描述。

本书撰写中的最大困难是不可避免地涉及大量中文词汇与名称。理想的方法当然是给出每个词汇对应的中文，然而由于种种原因未能实现。东方研究学院的叶先生为我们将重要的中文词汇编汇成表，聊补正文未录汉字的缺憾。

英文拼写一般据韦氏拼音法，不过本人也注意到存在一些微小的偏差，如用 e 代替 é 之类，我也很清楚在中文复合名称中使用大写字母有失严谨，但这在涉及邮政式拼音的名字时难以避免。本书尽管存在省略或不规范之处，但我希望并没有给真挚的读者留下任何难解之处。

希望本人的付出最终能为对汉语和中国历史更为精通的人在同领域开展进一步的研究提供些许便利。假若本人能够唤起人们对北京城墙和城门的新兴趣，唤起人们对那些曾经壮观但却正在消逝的文物的兴趣，多少反映出城墙和城门的瞬息之美，那么，本人也就心满意足了，亦感到对这座伟大的中国帝都履行了些许义务。

喜龙仁
1924 年 5 月于巴黎

---

[1] A.G.Bowden-Smith，A.G 鲍登-史密斯，中文名包哲洁，英国女教士，曾来华办学。
[2] Mr.Scott，全名 James Scott，詹姆斯·斯科特，中文名萨允格，晚清时英国驻广州领事。
[3] Rothkegel，全名 Curt Roth Kegel，戈尔·罗特凯格尔，德国建筑师。

目 录

图版目录/1

一、中国北方筑墙城市——概述/1

二、北京城址上的早期城市/9

三、内城的城墙/21

四、内城城墙的内侧壁/31

五、内城城墙的外侧壁/57

六、外城的城墙/65

七、内城的城门/77

八、外城的城门/117

照片/141

附：《北京的城墙和城门》英文版/249

英汉对照索引/495

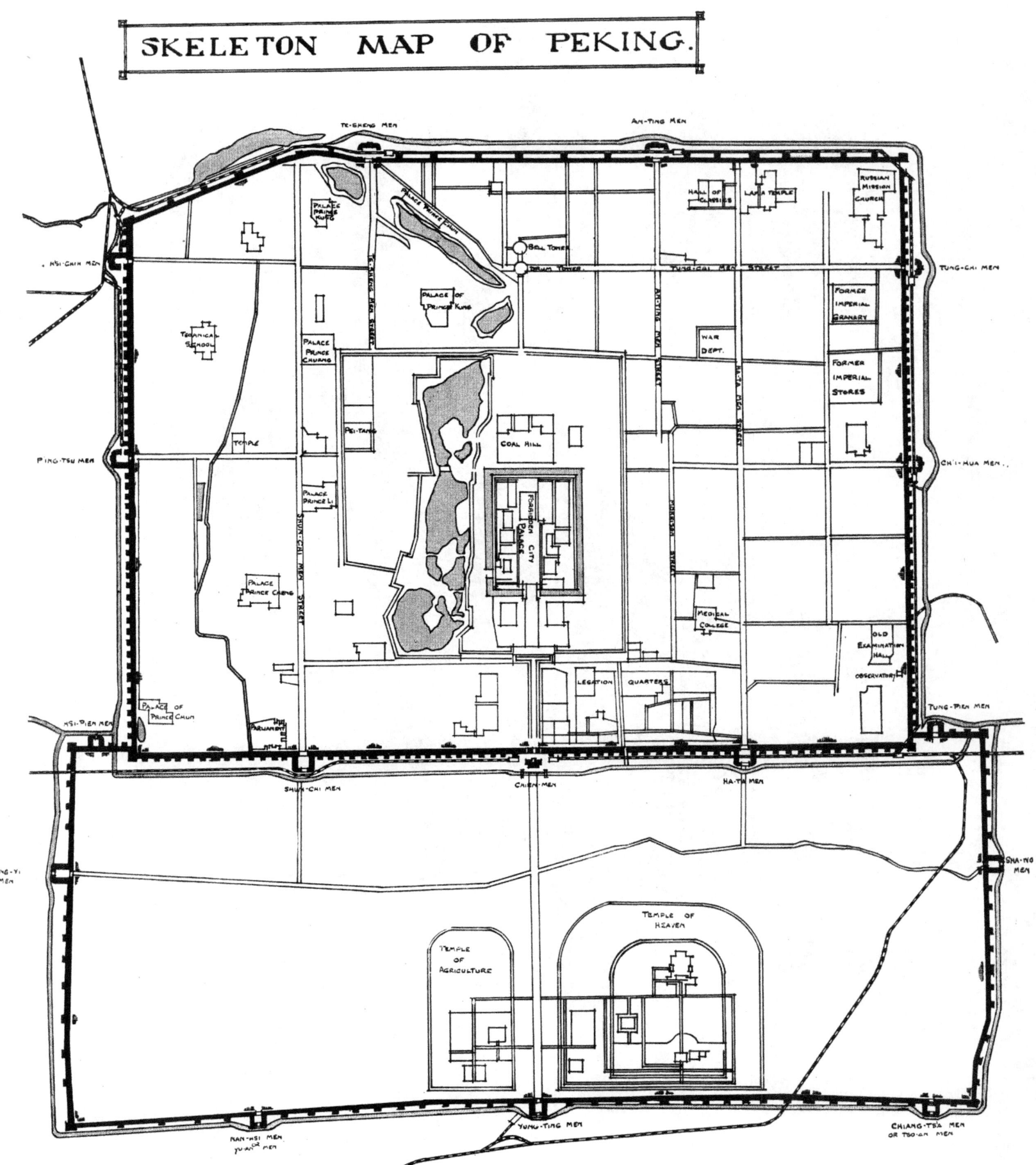

沙窝门：透过箭楼门洞所见景象

Sha Wu Men
View through the outer gate

图版目录

照片

沙窝门：透过箭楼门洞所见景象
西安府：西南隅的城墙/141
青州府：北城墙/141
北京：外城中的街道/142
青州府：老商业街/142
山东潍县的石牌楼/143
西安府：从鼓楼上远眺/144
西安府：西城门与城墙/144
外城西南隅城墙外的景象/145
北城墙下的古井/146
前门与顺治门之间的南城墙/147
西南隅附近分段修缮的南城墙/148
顺治门与前门之间南城墙外的景象/148
观象台处的东城墙/149
东城墙上不同年代的墙段/150
一段保存完好的东城墙/150
东直门处的东城墙/151
东城墙上的大洞和露出的多层砖面/152
齐化门与东直门之间的长马道/152
北城墙下吃草的羊/153
北城墙下休憩的驼队/154
北城墙内侧壁的新、老墙段/155
德胜门以西的北城墙外侧壁/155
北城墙处积水潭的河道/156
西城墙南段城墙外的景象/157
西直门附近的西城墙内侧壁/157
平则门以南分三段修缮的马道/158
平则门望向主城墙外所见景象/158
西城墙南端/159
内城东南隅城墙上的角楼/160

东南角楼及内、外城城墙之间的衔接处/160
外城城墙西北隅/161
西城墙上墙面砖脱落之处/161
西南角楼/162
东南角楼/162
外城东城墙内侧壁修补不当、严重残损的部分/163
外城东城墙的内侧壁/163
从彰义门箭楼城台眺望外城城墙/164
外城南城墙的内侧壁/164
外城东城墙外的景象/165
外城城墙东北隅/165
外城西南角楼/166
东便门外老路上的送葬队伍/167
东便门附近城门桥与水闸/167
东便门处的外城城墙/168
平则门：两座城门楼与瓮城局部/169
平则门：城楼与瓮城局部/170
平则门：从城墙望至城楼北端/171
平则门：箭楼侧面/172
平则门：从城墙望向箭楼/173
平则门：箭楼与沿瓮城城墙而立的摊位/174
西直门：从南侧看城门全景/175
西直门：城楼侧面/176
西直门：瓮城关帝庙中栽有柏树的院子/177
西直门：关帝庙庭院/178
西直门：透过箭楼门洞看到的景象/179
西直门：瓮城边门之上的谯楼及附近的商铺/180
西直门：城门外老商铺林立的街道/181
齐化门：城楼侧面及附近的建筑/182
齐化门：城楼正面/183

从南侧眺望东直门/184
东直门护城河的景象/184
东直门：城楼正面/185
东直门：透过城楼门洞所见景象/186
东直门：城楼侧面/187
东直门：箭楼与护城河/188
东直门：箭楼与现代平台/189
东直门：白鸭游弋的护城河/190
哈达门：站在街上望向城楼/191
哈达门：城楼侧面/192
哈达门：城楼以及在瓮城中等待火车通过的人群/193
顺治门：最近修葺的城楼/194
顺治门：城楼与瓮城中央/195
顺治门：箭楼无存的城台上的老铁炮/196
顺治门：堆满陶器的瓮城主街/196
前门：从南侧看到的城楼/197
前门：透过城楼门洞所见景象/198
前门：瓮城关帝庙山门入口处/199
前门：关帝庙中的香客/200
前门：从箭楼上望新建的城门桥和外城主街/201
安定门：城楼与原有瓮城内部/202
安定门：箭楼与护城河/203
安定门：箭楼与瓮城中的真武庙/204
安定门：一段经过修葺的瓮城城墙/205
安定门：真武庙庭院/206
德胜门：瓮城的残存部分与箭楼/207
德胜门：透过城楼门洞所见景象/208
德胜门：原瓮城内的大椿树/209
德胜门：瓮城中的流动剃头匠/210
德胜门：瓮城中的真武庙/211
德胜门：箭楼侧面/212
西便门：通向城门的街道/213
西便门：所谓的"城楼"/214
西便门：瓮城中的大洋槐/215

西便门：瓮城中的椿树/216
西便门：正在穿过箭楼门洞的驼队/217
西便门：城门外树荫笼罩的街道/218
东便门：城楼景象/219
东便门：箭楼门洞/220
东便门外的城门桥/221
西便门外的骆驼/222
东便门外休憩的驴子和牛/222
东便门外、东运河终点处/223
沙窝门：瓮城侧面及两座城门楼侧面/224
沙窝门：城楼/225
沙窝门：透过瓮城所见景象/226
沙窝门：城门外的送葬队伍/227
彰义门：城门楼及瓮城侧面/228
彰义门：部分瓮城与城楼/229
彰义门：城楼侧面/230
彰义门：瓮城与城楼/231
彰义门：箭楼/232
右安门：透过瓮城与城楼门洞所见景象/233
右安门：瓮城及箭楼/234
右安门：冬日的驼队/235
右安门：箭楼与护城河/236
右安门：城门外的垂柳/237
右安门外护城河中的芦苇与孩童/238
右安门：城楼及长着椿树的城台/239
左安门：瓮城及城楼/240
左安门：已成废墟的马道，1922年9月/241
左安门：箭楼侧面/242
左安门：箭楼与护城河/243
永定门：两座城门楼及瓮城正面/244
永定门：从瓮城望向城楼/245
永定门：从瓮城望向箭楼/246
永定门：横跨护城河的城门桥上的车马/247
永定门：从侧面望城门全景及护城河/248

平面图、立面图和剖面图

图1　前代都城与今北京城址的大致位置关系／10

图2　中都——金国女真人的都城。
　　　汗八里——元朝皇帝的都城／12

图3　平则门以南西城墙的两个剖面／27

图4　北城墙的两个剖面；上图选取于临近东端的位置；
　　　下图选取于临近安定门的位置／28

图5　西南角楼平面／55

图6　平则门（又称阜成门）总平面／80

图7　平则门城楼平面／81

图8　平则门城楼纵剖面／82

图9　平则门城楼横剖面／83

图10　平则门城楼正立面／85

图11　平则门城楼侧立面／86

图12　平则门箭楼平面／87

图13　平则门箭楼横剖面／88

图14　平则门箭楼纵剖面／90

图15　平则门箭楼侧立面／91

图16　平则门箭楼正立面／92

图17　西直门城楼平面／93

图18　齐化门城楼平面／96

图19　东直门城楼平面／97

图20　哈达门城楼正立面／99

图21　哈达门城楼平面／100

图22　顺治门城楼平面／101

图23　重建前的前门广场总平面／103

图24　重建后的前门广场总平面／105

图25　修缮前的前门箭楼正立面／107

图26　修缮前的前门箭楼平面／108

图27　修缮前的前门箭楼侧立面／109

图28　前门城楼正立面／110

图29　前门城楼平面／111

图30　安定门城楼平面／113

图31　德胜门城楼平面／114

图32　西便门总平面／118

图33　西便门城楼正立面／119

图34　西便门城楼横剖面／119

图35　西便门城楼平面／120

图36　西便门箭楼平面／121

图37　西便门箭楼横剖面／122

图38　西便门箭楼正立面／122

图39　彰义门（也称广安门）总平面／126

图40　彰义门城楼正立面／127

图41　彰义门城楼平面／128

图42　彰义门城楼横剖面／128

图43　彰义门箭楼平面／129

图44　彰义门箭楼横剖面／130

图45　彰义门箭楼正立面／130

图46　永定门总平面／133

图47　永定楼城楼正立面／134

图48　永定门城楼平面／136

图49　永定门城楼纵剖面／137

图50　永定门城楼横剖面／137

图51　永定门箭楼平面／138

图52　永定门箭楼纵剖面／139

图53　永定门箭楼正立面／140

地图

北京简略地图

一、中国北方筑墙城市——概述

中国的长城举世闻名，不过多数人仅仅将其视作历史遗迹，由一位头脑狂热的古代皇帝所兴建的一项巨大工程的雄伟废墟。人们对长城的普遍印象是它已然垮塌，一如中国的许多其他建筑一样，而且，千百年来它发挥过的实际作用也仿佛不足称道。这完全是误解。长城是中国为数不多的得到适当保护的建筑之一，它屡经修葺、重建，数世纪以来，不论是作为防御工事还是分界线，其重要作用一直持续到近年。当然这是中国人自己的观点。实际上，长城充分地表达了中国人根深蒂固的筑墙观念。

墙垣，墙垣，仍然是墙垣，可以说是它们构成了每一座中国城市的骨架或结构框架。它们围绕着城市，将其划分为若干地块与场院，比其他任何建筑构造更能凸显中国住区所共有的基本特点。在中国北方，没有城墙围绕，便不能被视为真正的城市。中文里的"城"字既可表示城市，又可表示城墙，这一用法就已经表明了不存在没有城墙的城市，这就如同没有屋顶的房子一样不可思议。一个聚落，在中国人的传统观念中，其规模、重要性及治理的好坏等因素都无足轻重，只要没有城墙为其确定范围并把它围绕起来，就算不上一座中国传统意义上的城市。因此，譬如上海（位于"原住民城镇"之外）这个现代中国最重要的商业中心，对于老派的中国人而言，并不是一座真正的城市，而仅仅是由渔村发展起来的聚落或大型贸易中心。同样，其他几个类似的现代商业中心也没有城墙环绕，无论当今的民国官员如何称呼它们，按照中国人的传统观念，也不能称之为"城"，或者城市。

的确，城墙是中国城市最基本、最引人注目、最稳定的组成部分。除了省城或其他的"府"，中国的每一座住区，即使是小村镇，都筑有城墙。中国北方的村庄，无论规模大小，历史长短，它的草房或者牲圈都至少有一道土墙或其他类似的东西。无论这个地方多么贫穷，多么不显眼；无论土坯房多么寒酸，庙宇多么破败，坑洼不平的道路多么脏乱、泥泞，围墙却一直屹立不倒，通常比村镇中的其他任何建筑保存得都要完整。我曾经到过西北省份的一些城市，它们已完全被战争、饥荒和火灾摧毁，房倒屋塌，人迹罕至，然而，带有雉堞的城墙、城墙上的城门与望楼却都保留了下来。它们能够比城中的其他建筑更顽强地承受无情烈火与野蛮士兵的破坏。城墙留存下来,成为纪念着昔日荣光的纪念碑,在无尽的荒凉与孤寂中显得格外触目。

裸露的砖墙与其城台、城门楼一同耸立于城壕之上,或是从空旷的平地上拔地而起,这些空地上没有树木或高大的建筑遮挡住视野,它们要比城中的任何房屋、庙宇更能显示出这些城市昔日的荣光与显要。尽管这些城墙的修造年代并不久远(中国北方现今已难觅明代之前的城墙),然而那些破旧的城砖和残损的城垛却给人一种历经沧桑的印象。一般来说,修缮与重建很少会改变城墙的总体形态和规制。砖墙出现之前,中国北方的许多城镇由土墙围绕,这种情况至今仍可在一些偏僻的小地方见到。在城镇兴建之前,则是由临时性的篱笆或土墙环绕着村庄或一片片的茅草土屋。

可以通过陕西的西安府和山东的青州府这两个例子来阐释中国北方筑墙城市的类型。西安府现存的城墙是明代第一位皇帝于14世纪末建成的,有好几处后代修补过,但从整体来看,城墙出色地抵御住了时间与战火的摧残。城墙围绕着一座近乎正方形的城市,由于周边是开阔的黄土高原,其整体轮廓从远处即可辨认。从北侧或西侧远远地走向该城,可以看到绵延数里的城墙。再走近一些,双重城门楼、方形城台以及巨大的圆形角楼逐渐呈现在眼前;建筑的线条和体块的韵律渐趋明显——缓慢凝重、强劲有力。城市好似巨型要塞般矗立于黄土高原之上,同时又通过城墙绵长的水平线条与之融为一体,统摄着黄土高原。

走近青州府,景观则大不相同。乍看起来,这座城市的外观和西安府不同,无论如何也谈不上雄伟和引人注目。然而,愈是靠近,景色就愈发有趣,城墙在如画般的自然环境中愈发令人震撼。这座城市坐落在一片肥沃的溪谷间,周围是富饶的农田和果园,树木掩映着城墙,打破了它的单调与沉闷。一条清澈的小河取代了城市西、北两侧的护城河。到城市北门和西门,得穿过结实的古老石桥。城墙顺着蜿蜒的河道延伸,形成一系列的转角,也把河岸切分成不规则的台地。一些砖、石因势堆砌成一级级的台阶,自然得体,浑若天成。例如,穿过城西低矮的石桥,踏上蜿蜒向上的石板路,你会看到河岸边呈现为一层层台地,宛如层层阶梯,样子十分有趣。局部以砖块砌边,绿荫笼罩。城墙很高,且有巨大的扶垛加固,墙顶生长着繁茂的灌木和树木,枝条都攀附缠绕到了锯齿状的雉堞之外。此处有一种浪漫之美,使人联想到意大利北部某些筑墙之城,好像眼前倒不是中国的城市了。

穿过这些城市中比较冷清的城门,人们通常会惊讶于自己并未置身于两旁都是商铺和房屋的繁华街道,而是来到了一片开阔的田野或大片的空地,其间除了垃圾堆和污浊的泥塘,别无他物。比如,尽管新进城的人很难找到一间屋舍或窝棚作栖身之所,但青州府的西部和南部城区仍将大片土地用作农田和菜园。而在西安府,东、西、北面的城墙内,则有大片的空地,其间丞有鸭子、乌龟生长栖息的宁静的泥塘。这些中国古城大多可以追溯到明朝甚至更早，自上世纪（19世纪——译者注）以来，虽然城市人口并没有减少，但古城开始衰落、缩小。人们被迫居住得越来越拥挤，或是栖身于郊外的棚屋。毫无疑问，同在城墙内修建新屋相比，这是解决住房问题更低廉、更简便的方法。当然，也有例外。不断发展的商业和新型交通工具的使用，或者某些地方政府的积极态度，都推动了一些城市新式建筑的兴建。山西的太原府就是其中一例。不过这样的城市十分罕见，那些遍布装饰的新建筑实在称不上美观，以至于我们更希望看到这片地方再次变为菜园。

在这里，我们没有必要对导致众多中国北方城市衰退、面积缩减的原因做进一步调查。毫无疑问，这些原因与当时中国的政治、社会和经济状况密切相关。总的来说，这样的状况不利于对老城和历史文物的保护。不幸的是，官方既缺乏进取精神，又缺乏必要的财力。当战争、革命和随之而来的掠夺、大火和饥荒席卷城市时，他们几乎没有为恢复城市的原貌而做什么努力。人们更愿意聚居于半洋式房屋构成的新兴聚落之中，南京、西安府和洛阳等古都，是上述情况最为突出的例子，它们如今只剩下苍白、萎缩的昔日旧影。而许多较小的城市也呈现出类似的倒退趋势：建筑面积缩减，房屋破败不堪。在很多城市中，这一趋势不仅表现在城市建筑面积和空地面积比例的失衡，还表现在许多房屋造价低廉、质量低劣。

在中国北方的普通城市中，具有建筑学价值的建筑物寥寥无几。当然，有些庙宇可能因其雕饰的门楼和巨大屋檐下的开敞柱廊而别具一格。但严格来说，它们算不上是建筑杰作，尤其是经过近些年的重建。从建筑学角度来看，更重要的是那些造型相当奇特而略显怪诞的古老石塔或砖塔，还有至今仍屹立在许多古城之中的钟鼓楼，它们的宏大身躯与曾经伟大的过去紧密地联系在一起。不过，城中大多数的建筑都是些不起眼的小房子，它们都以漆为红色的木梁柱为框架，用青砖砌成。在商业区，店面或多或少都有面向街道的敞开的门廊和成排的柱子。只有在较富裕的地方，才能见到饰以雕刻、黄铜挂件或华丽招牌的店面。在普通的城市，雕饰镀金的店面并不多见，很大程度上是由于自民国以来，人们对砖和水泥的喜爱像传染病一样广泛蔓延。自从"中华"[1]成为"民国"之后，古老文明的艺术繁花便开始迅速凋零。

城市中的住宅区，常常将房屋空荡荡的外墙朝向路人。多数的房屋只能看到高低不一、大小各异的翘曲屋顶和掩映其间的树木。人们几乎看不到房子的其他部分，它们全都隐身于单调的青砖墙或涂以暗红色的墙垣之后，墙壁因年久和污垢而变色。在狭长而空荡的墙壁上，除了简朴的门头或由几级台阶和一个鞍型[2]小屋顶构成的小门廊外，别无其他间隔或

---

1 此处英文原著中为 Flowery Middle Kingdom，中花之国。根据文意，译为"中华"。
2 本书中的鞍型屋顶（saddle roof）大多指中国传统建筑的歇山式屋顶。

装饰。其建筑风格之千篇一律无以复加。有时给人的感觉就像是从监狱或修道院的街道上穿过，只有光影的变换和偶尔出现在墙角晒太阳的乞丐，才使画面鲜活起来。走街串巷的小贩们摇铃的叮咚声或阵阵的锣声，不时地传入耳中，但当他们走过之后，一切又陷入深邃的寂静。活力与美感仿佛躲在墙后，了无踪迹。中国人的家是守卫森严的地方，每个家庭自成一个小社区（通常人口很多，成家的儿子继续与父母同住），围绕家屋的墙垣既有效地界定了家人的亲密关系，又保护他们免遭闯入者的侵扰。特别值得一提的是，女性被严格地禁闭在这些高墙大院中，就如同中世纪的修道院一样严格。

只有进入大门，绕过所谓的"影壁"[1]之后，才能感受到这种住宅的独特之美。如果这是一座大宅，里边有两三进以上的院子。那么，第一进院一般较为平常：简单铺设的地面，被三面低矮的房屋围绕。但之后的另一进院遍植花木，或用池塘、假山和亭榭布置出一座真正的花园。当然，庭院的考究程度取决于住宅的规模和地位。建筑全都是统一的样式，只是大小和细节有所不同。最重要的房屋坐落于主院的尽头，耸立于石台基之上。建筑正面是敞廊或露台，这种前廊类似"前厅"，是由两侧突出的山墙和立于其间的一排木柱构成。高大而翘曲的鞍型屋顶延伸到前廊之上，屋檐由廊柱支撑，在所有比较精美的古老宅邸上，檐下都有彩绘的斗栱。墙体的构造有些许不同，但立面的框架通常都是由立柱支撑起横向的梁枋。立柱之间，下部砌砖，上部则是制作精致的隔扇窗，糊着代替玻璃的透明纸。立面中央是正门，门前有登上台基的宽阔的踏步石，门上有雕饰的裙板，有的门上部也做成隔扇窗，糊着透明纸。其他不太重要的结构细节就不再赘述了，但对中国房屋的外观效果影响最显著的色彩，尚需补充几句：所有的木构件都被漆成深红色，而砖瓦则是灰色的，门板上的雕饰用金色，以增强其效果。如果建筑规模宏大，那么柱上的斗栱则饰以蓝、绿彩绘。中国人敢于使用浓墨重彩，尤其是当房屋置于鲜花绿叶之中时，远观效果非常精彩。不过装饰的细节不够精致，经不起近距离的观赏。

现在回到街上，我们可以步行到城市的商业区。此处的街景大不相同，总体来讲，较居住区而言，要更有活力且有趣得多。房屋不再躲在整齐划一的封闭的围墙之后，而是以隔扇门窗的形式直接向街道敞开，透明窗纸也被窗玻璃所取代。屋顶倒是同那些住宅一般高且出檐深远，不过店铺门前通常没有木立柱。因为外立面相对较窄，檐口的挑檐檩可以由两侧突出的山墙支撑。有时店铺的入口上方还架着用于遮阳的倾斜的小屋顶或顶棚，由斗栱或立柱支撑。炎热的季节，店铺前都用竹竿搭架覆以草席，或者遮挡阳光；倘若街道狭窄，遮阳棚便会搭到对面的店面上，或者至少把人行道遮上。事实上，这些人行道大多被商户

---

[1] 影壁（spirit-wall）一种类似屏风的墙，位于门内正中，以抵挡恶魔。据传说，恶魔总是直线行走。——作者注

而非行人占用。在街上，店家或小贩做着各种买卖，特别是食品店，会在店外摆放出他们的美味佳肴。有时，店铺前的街道俨然成为一个真正的市场，西安府有条满是粮店的街道便是如此。每天早上都在那里进行粮食交易，熙熙攘攘的顾客和商贩，手推车、运粮车到处都是，令人难以通过。实际上，位于狭小的老式房屋中的店铺内部，与其说是经营场所，倒不如说是起居空间，店主、店员在这里吃饭、睡觉、吸烟、饮茶。或许只能从外观上才能明确地分清这是小商铺还是住宅。

店铺一家接着一家，它们的内外样式差异明显，这不但取决于地段的繁华程度，还取决于当地的风俗以及他们所销售的商品类型。干货铺总是不同于药铺、金匠铺或茶店。而且通常来说，店铺外观的装饰在某种程度上反映出所售商品的质量与品质。在这里描述店铺的细节和错综复杂的店铺类型，未免离题太远，因为我们在此处主要是讨论中国街道的建筑问题。这方面最为重要的是，在一些保存较好的古城中，这种高大的雕饰铺面还能得以一见。在北京，这样的店铺曾经在许多重要的商业街上比比皆是，但近年来由于对半洋式水泥建筑的狂热而数量锐减。这些水泥建筑的立面上挂着飘扬的装饰彩带和民国旗帜，它们凌驾于屋脊之上，在商铺入口处形成华盖或牌楼，其结构框架由极高的牌楼柱构成，横向由枋木连接，枋上的多跳斗栱承托着一层或两层的鞍型楼檐。楼檐之下是类似华版的板面，上面饰有人物浮雕或花卉图案的镂空雕，店铺的牌匾嵌入其中。底部错综复杂的叶子图案被刻成镂空的浮雕，像是整个牌楼的宽大花边，所有雕刻都用鎏金装饰，有的还点缀以其他颜色。此外，还有小的华盖或顶棚，从牌楼柱伸出的龙头上还悬挂有鲜艳的丝带和流苏（有些为木制）。

两边林立着这种雕饰、鎏金店面的街道，景观一定极为富丽堂皇，在三五十年以前，这样的景象在省会城市中绝不少见。而今却逐年减少，因为人们无意保存这些，大多数人情愿见到它们被水泥混合建筑或单调的砖房所取代，这些建筑除了在入口上方或门旁挂上写着几个大字的招牌之外，别无装饰。因此，把中国北方普通城市商业区的街景当作一个建筑群来看，倒不如把它看作一幅光影交错、人群熙攘、车水马龙的画卷更为吸引人。尤其是如果街上还保留着古树的话，这幅图景则会更为生动别致，虽然它缺乏建筑艺术的重要特色。

街道的情形一般就是这样，但也有例外——有些街道上有装饰性的纪念物、纪念碑、拱门或门楼。这些例外却很重要，其中最重要的就是牌楼——一种横跨街道（包括人行道）、三开间（或更多开间）的装饰性门楼。立牌楼的目的通常是为纪念当地的杰出人物或这个地方的重要历史事件，但是，它们对于后人和外来者的吸引力，则主要在于其非同一般的装饰特征。牌楼多为木制，涂以鲜艳的红漆，除了鎏金雕饰外，还点缀有蓝、绿色的装饰物。支撑立柱的数目或4根，或8根，亦或有12根的，取决于牌楼的体量和重要性。牌楼柱立于夹杆石之上（有时饰以石狮），柱间横跨着两三排宽大的枋木，间以雕板、华版或刻有颂词的牌匾。顶部是翘曲的鞍型屋顶，每间牌楼上都有一个独立的屋顶，由多跳斗栱承托，并覆有蓝色或绿色的筒瓦，屋脊上饰有仙人像和脊兽，即所谓的"夔龙字"。这些牌楼蕴含着中国传统建筑最突出的特点，例如，支柱、由出两三跳斗栱承托的翘曲的鞍型屋顶、装饰考究的梁枋、雕花的栏板以及喜庆富丽但略显粗杂的彩绘。牌楼基本都是木结构的，除去屋顶上的装饰物以外，整体特征和装饰均是根据这种材料性质的特殊要求发展演变的，石牌楼明显地印证了这一点。石牌楼的各部分构件都是直接参照木牌楼复制而来，各部分构架的连结实际上更适合木结构，而非石结构（与日本石"牌坊"非常相似，同样显现出由木结构演变为石门的痕迹）。当然，在某些特定部位，如屋顶（无曲线）和斗栱（有时变为曲线托座）等处，还是会做出一些必要的调整：梁枋上饰有浮雕而非彩绘，方柱或八角牌楼柱用石墩予以加固——低矮的石基上设一面巨型石鼓，鼓上栖有一只小狮子。如果仔细研究这些文物，就会发现各种石牌楼的结构有很多细小的差异，但自明代以来其结构与装饰部分的一般特征未发生大的变化。迄今发现的最古老的石牌楼都是位于寺庙花园中，它们比在街道上的牌楼保存得要好。然而，我确实不曾知道哪座牌楼是明代以前修建的。我见过的最漂亮且数目最多的街景牌楼是在山东潍县，主街上横跨着六座高大的三间五楼的牌坊。它们大概始建于乾隆年间。不过并非所有的牌楼都是横跨街道的，也有立于旷地或顺沿街道而立的，可作为寺庙或衙门的入口标志，其作用不外乎纪念某个令人尊敬的人物，或彰显某人某地的荣耀。

在许多中国古城里，主要街景就是两座高大宏伟的建筑——钟楼和鼓楼，它们总是占据着城市的中心位置。城市的主要街道往往从钟楼、鼓楼或者其中之一的脚下延伸出去，或交汇并横穿楼下。钟楼、鼓楼宽大的台座上贯穿着类似城门的筒形拱门，拱门正下方便是城市的交通枢纽或交通隧道，经常拥堵不堪。因为这里不仅是各种交通工具和行人的必经之路，也是流浪汉和乞丐避雨遮阳之地。砖砌的台座有城墙那么高，在其顶部矗立着真正的高楼——两三层高的殿阁，通常是木构框架结构，梁柱间以砖填充，楼身一、二层由围廊环绕，顶层是封闭的。出檐深远的翘曲屋顶由精糙不一的"三头"[1]（日语为"斗组"[2]）系统承托，"三头"即檐下出挑三、四跳的复杂斗栱。其建造和装饰的细节，自然会因建造的年代和建筑的重要性的不同而有所不同，但是，一般说来，相对于建筑的主体构成——高耸的楼阁与厚重的基座，这些细节对钟楼、鼓楼的总体效果影响甚微。这类建筑在中文里被称作"台"，它们在很久之前就有多种用途，例如瞭望台、黄金台和观象台。鸟瞰中国城市，

---

[1] "三头"为英文原版索引中"san tou"的对应中文；1985年出版的中文版将其翻译为"散斗"；本书按原版英文直译，但根据上下文，这里应当指支撑屋檐的斗栱体系。

[2] "斗组"的英文原版单词为"masugami"，系作者笔误，应当为masugumi，表示斗组、枡组、斗栱的意思。

大多只见低矮的墙垣和屋顶，而"台"鹤立其上，为整幅图画添加了古朴与庄严的注脚。

除钟楼、鼓楼外，中国北方的古城还有一些重要的宗教建筑，即"佛塔"，或称寺塔，但它们大多坐落于城墙之外而非城内。这些宝塔的修筑总是与重要的宗教神殿（用于保存珍贵的圣物）有关，而且通常来说，最好的佛寺并不修建在拥挤的城市中央，而是建在郊外景致旖旎的地方。从建筑角度来看，根据时代、建材及当地宗教的不同需求，塔的样貌呈现出明显的差异。因此，几乎无法总结出这些塔的共有特征，只能说，这些塔的平面呈方形或多边形，高度从50到350英尺不等，层数为3、5、7、9、11或者13。年代久远一些的大都是砖塔，近代的则多是木结构。不过，也有完全由石或铁建造的塔。在地势平坦开阔的乡村，这样的高塔常常成为重要的地标，它们不仅为百姓指引方向、提示距离，更是风水观念下的一种庇佑和好运的象征。与杭州、苏州这样的南方城市不同，极少见到塔在北方城市景观中占据重要的地位。如果北方城市中出现了塔，给人的印象就如同某种异邦宗教的建筑物一样显得怪诞，虽然它们与这一古老城市的周边环境和历史氛围的协调程度高于基督教大教堂或教堂钟楼。后者外观庄严而僵硬，在一片片低矮的古旧建筑和残垣中，仿佛是最突兀的闯入者。

中国的古城，虽然外表看上去单调乏味、千篇一律，但里面却扑朔迷离，或许有使人惊叹的古迹。比如一些残破的老房或半毁的纪念物，没有出现在街道上，而是隐藏于有着阴沟和下水道的肮脏巷子中。这些隐秘的昔日辉煌有待发掘，普通的游客或只经行城市主街的路人是不可能看到的。一直以来，我们的目标不是驻足去详查历史，而是要勾勒出中国城市、街道和建筑物的典型外貌特征，进而更好地阐述城市内部和四周城墙的关系。据我们所见，整体来讲，中国城市就是一片隐蔽在翘曲大屋顶之下的低矮房屋和墙垣。

鸟瞰全城，常常只能看到覆盖着灰瓦的鳞次栉比的屋顶，一排连着一排。温暖的季节里，高出屋顶的树木点缀着这片单调的风景，有的树甚至穿透屋顶。（在城里，中国人不惜以建筑为代价来保护树木，可在乡间，树木却被任意砍伐）到了冬季，大部分树木同屋顶一样，灰蒙蒙、光秃秃的。薄薄的白雪取代绿色的枝叶，覆盖着屋脊和檐口，如泡沫般熠熠闪烁。晨雾笼罩下的城市，像是一片冰冷的灰色海洋，奔涌向前的波浪戛然而止，波涛起伏的节奏仍然可见，但运动已然止息，仿佛被施了魔法。难道大海也被冻结了古老的中国文明生命力的寒魔所震慑了吗？春日再来之时，它会伴随着老树上鲜翠欲滴的绿叶和盛开的花朵而消融吗？生命还会带着美丽和喜悦归来吗？我们能否再度见证新生力量的波涛冲破古老中国的残败墙垣？抑或，内部的运动已经停滞——灵魂已经永冻？

晨雾慢慢消散，眼前的幻影逐渐消失——站在城墙上的士兵吹起号角，向街头熙攘而瑟缩的人群宣告：民国十一年的又一个忙碌的日子就这样开始了。

二、北京城址上的早期城市

在进行北京城墙和城门的专门研究之前，对曾坐落在如今北京城的那些小城的遗址与边界，有必要做一简略叙述。关于这些早期城市，中国元、明两代留下了大量的历史记载，其中收录信息最多的是《顺天府志》。此书即是对顺天府的描述，初版于万历年间（1593年），上世纪末（1885年）又经历了大规模修订和重编。全书凡130卷，内容涉及京师与京畿的地理、历史、考古、统计、艺文、宗教和其他相关主题，但是主题分类不甚合理、明晰，有几卷对同一事物的叙述存在较大分歧甚至矛盾，因此出现了不少令人疑惑的问题。例如，第一卷关于北京城墙的论述与第二卷中的记述就大相径庭。必须非常审慎地参考这些内容，并以批判的眼光予以阐释。下面的补充说明主要建立在《顺天府志》前两卷的基础上，同时还参考了《日下旧闻考》（日光之地的旧历史）中的零星记载，该书1658年初版，1744年进行了较多的修订而再版，以及贝勒博士（Bretschneider）[1]的极具价值的历史研究著作，该书1876年上海出版英文版，1879年巴黎发行法文版[2]。

中国史学家提到过的北京旧址上最早的城市叫做"蓟"。它曾是蓟州[3]最重要的城镇，据传早在舜帝的时代（公元前2400年）便已存在。史书说这座城市"固若金汤"。公元前723年蓟成为燕国都城，公元前221年被秦始皇帝的军队摧毁。这座城位于如今北京城的西北角。汉代以前，它似乎并非战略要地。

直到汉代晚期，公元70年前后，才在前代蓟城以南约10里的地方，即今鞑靼城[4]的西南

---

[1] Bretschneider 原名 Emil Bretschneider，埃米尔·布雷特施耐德，中文名贝勒，俄国汉学家。

[2] 此处指贝勒所著的 *Archaeological and historical researches of Peking and its environs*. Shanghai: American Presbyterian Mission Press. 1976.

[3] 英文原版索引中 Chi Chou 对应中文为"冀州"，当为作者笔误或翻译之误，因蓟城为西周蓟国之都。

[4] 即明清北京内城，因清代只允许旗人（以满族人为主，有部分蒙古族人）居住而得此名。以后我们将此译为内城。鞑靼人在我国一般指北方游牧民族，更多指向蒙古族人或塔塔尔族人。

角一带，建起一座新的城市，占据了所谓汉人城[1]的西北部一大片区域。这座新城叫做"燕"，三国时期更名为"幽州"。除去唐朝皇帝曾派驻一支由鞑靼将军率领的精兵强将外，直到936年被契丹人占领，这座城市似乎没有发生什么重大事件，当契丹人建立统治中国北方的辽国时，他们认为这座雀城规模的小城不符国都之制。他们在幽州城原址上建起一座规模更大的新国都，新城向西、向南扩张了很大一片区域。因为辽代在辽东已有一座北方的都城，故它被称为"南京"（南方的都城），不过更为人所熟知的名字是"燕京"（燕子的都城）。

贝勒曾探寻过燕京城的南墙，约在今北京外城以南约二里半的地方，南墙的西端约在今北京外城以西约4里的地方，从而确定了燕京城的西南角。燕京城的东墙在今琉璃厂（前门西南，因书籍古玩店铺林立而闻名的一条街）西面一点，据《顺天府志》所引《辽史·地理志》载，这里曾出土一块墓碑，标注该地为燕京东门外的"海王"村，就在燕京东门以外。燕京城的北墙很可能与北京内城的南墙一致。

城市的平面呈四边形，周长36里。城墙高30英尺，厚15英尺，建有城门楼和弓箭手用的楼橹，有八座城门，即东墙上的安东门（安宁的东方之门[2]）和迎春门（迎接春天之门），南墙上的开阳门（显示力量之门），丹凤门（红色凤凰之门），西墙上的显西门（光辉的西方之门）和清音门（清晰声音之门），北侧墙上的通天门（通往天堂之门）和拱辰门（致敬黎明之门）。

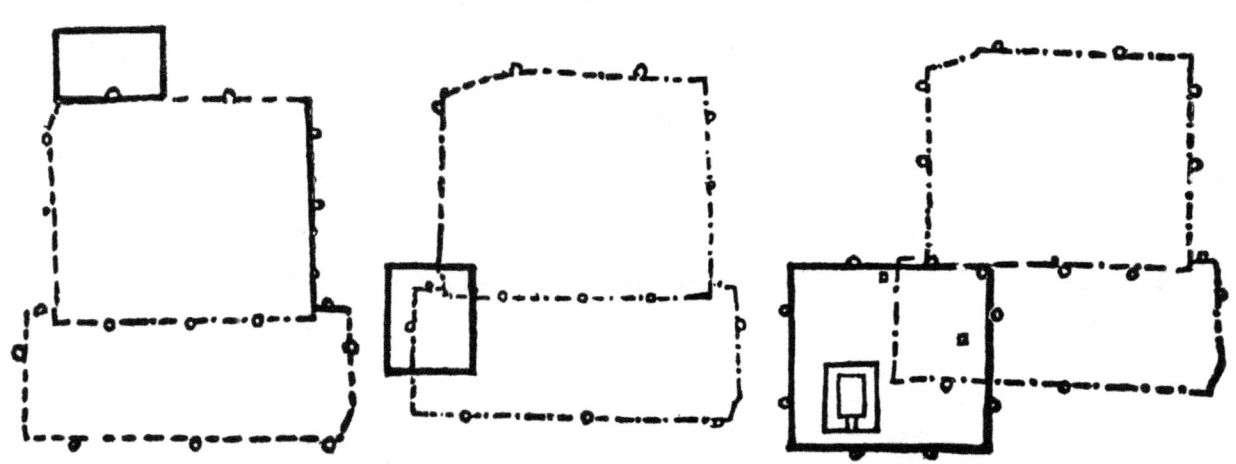

图1 前代都城与今北京城址的大致位置关系

（第一幅图是蓟城，第二幅图是燕城，或称幽州，第三幅图为燕京。这几张草图是根据《马特罗列旅行指南》和1914年《北京天主教会通报》中发表的平面图而绘制的。）

---

[1] 即明清北京外城，因清代不允许汉人居住在内城，仅能居住在外城而得名，以后我们将 Chinese City 皆译为外城。但外城居住的不仅只有汉人，还包括其他未纳入八旗体系的民族人口。

[2] 本书中对城门名称的注解均为作者个人观点，特此说明。

辽代统治者的宫殿位于城市的西南部，平面为矩形，有两重围墙环绕。

当辽王朝被其曾经的藩属金国（金色的）女真人击败（1125年），这座都城再次经历了重大的变化。《顺天府志》中虽有大篇幅的文字叙述，却语焉不详，对于不同资料来源的各种叙述未能进行考订。不过其中一部分倒颇为有趣，引述如下：

> 金太祖天会三年（1125年），宗望取燕山府。因辽人宫阙，于内城外筑四城，每城各三里，前后各一门，楼橹墉堑，悉如边城。每城之内立仓廒甲杖库，各穿复道，与内城通。时陈王兀室及韩常笑其过计。忠献王（宗望的别名）曰："百年间当以吾言为信"。[1]

从这段叙述来看，似乎宗望（后称太宗）曾于燕京城内或近郊的地方建立一座环有城墙的营地或军事堡垒。直到几年后的海陵王统治时期（1149—1160年），才扩建燕京城，建造了一座包括新宫殿在内的真正的都城。

> 及海陵（1135—1149年之间有两位统治者）立，有志都燕，而一时上书者争言燕京形胜。梁汉臣曰：'燕京自古霸国，虎视中原，为万世之基。'何卜年曰：'燕京地广坚，人物蕃息，乃礼义之所。'天德三年（1151年），始图上燕城宫室制度。三月，命张养浩等增广燕城，城门十三：东曰施仁（施予仁爱），曰宣曜（宣告荣耀），曰阳春（春之力量）；南曰景风（清泽之风），曰丰宜（充足公道），曰端礼（确立仪典）；西曰丽泽（光荣政策），曰灏华（灿烂之美），曰彰义（伸张正义）；北曰会城（团结城市），曰通元（沟通原则），曰崇智（崇尚知识），曰光泰（崇高的光芒）。遂以燕为中都，府曰大兴，定京邑焉。都城之门，每一面分三门，一正两偏。其正门旁又皆设两门。正门常不开，惟车驾出入，余悉由旁两门焉。周围二十七里，楼壁高四十尺。楼计九百一十座，地堑三重。[2]

上文所述城墙周界的长度，明显不适用于全城，因为燕京旧城部分，周长就有36里，如果是仅指后来扩建的部分，那么旧城是完全由新城墙包围，还是只有三面筑有新墙，其余一面是利用旧城原有的城墙，仍然不清楚。根据同书中后文的另一处陈述，全城墙垣周长75里，明显是严重的夸张或印刷错误。应当补充的是，明初敕命测量所谓的南城（原来

---

[1] 参见《光绪顺天府志·京师志一》。
[2] 参见《光绪顺天府志·京师志一》。

的金中都）时，其周长为53280英尺（近30里）。或许那时，旧城的一部分已经无存。依据上面的描述，几乎不可能推断出金中都（中央都城）城的确切规模，不过可以肯定的是，它的规模要远大于辽代的燕京，并且金中都是以辽燕京为基础向东延伸扩建的。史书在这一点上倒是十分肯定："辽金故都当在今外城迤西，以至郊外之地。其东北隅约当与今都城西南隅相接。又考元王恽中堂事记载，中统元年赴开平，三月五日发燕京，宿通玄（东便门）北郭。"[1]还引用一些碑文以佐证某些寺庙曾经地处金都城市范围之内，例如白云观、天宁寺、土地庙和其他坐落于今北京内城西部和南部的寺庙。我们得出结论，中都城包含了旧燕京城，城市范围延伸至今北京外城以西约4里处，东城墙延伸至东便门。其南城墙大概是沿用燕京城的南墙（内城以南约2里半处），北城墙则在今北京内城南墙以北1里处。倘若这些推断无误，城墙总长应当为54里左右。

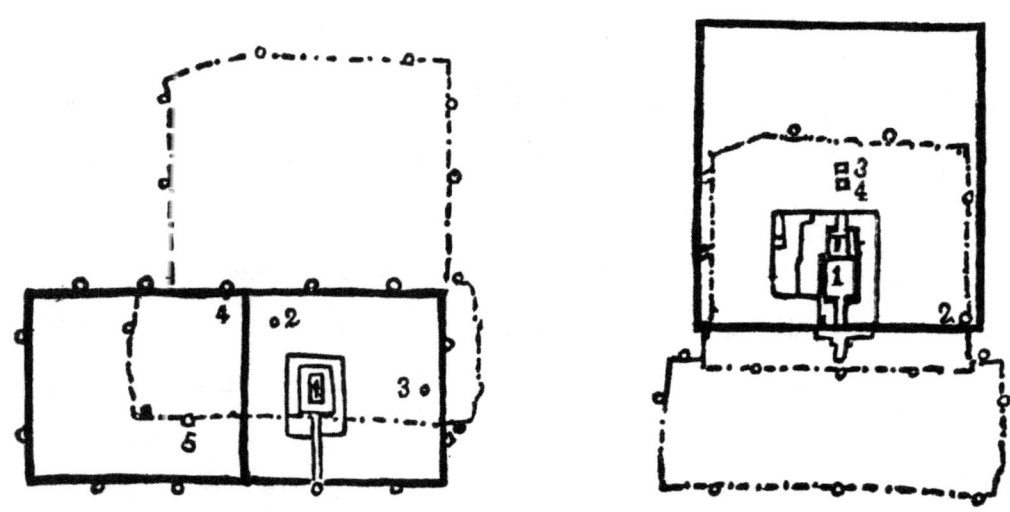

图 2　中都——金国女真人的都城。汉八里——元朝皇帝的都城

这些城墙仅是土墙，如果中国史书下述记载可靠的话，可知这些筑墙土是从若干里之外的地方用人工运来的："筑城用涿州土，人置一筐，左右手排立定，自涿至燕传递，空筐出，实筐入，人止土一畚，不日成之。"[2]（但令人费解的是，为什么要从那么远的地方把土运过来？！）

1　参见《钦定日下旧闻考》。
2　参见《光绪顺天府志·京师志一》。

"至卫绍王（1209—1213年[1]）时，蒙古军至。乃命京城富室迁入东子城，百官入南子城，宗室保西城，戚里保北城，各分守兵二万[2]。大兴尹乌陵用章命京畿诸将，毁各桥梁，瓦石悉运入四城，往来以舟渡运，不及者，投之于水。拆近城民屋为薪，纳之城中。蒙古兵攻城，四城兵皆迭自城上击之。蒙古兵凡比岁再攻，不能克。……"事实上，金中都这次（1213年）没有沦陷，是由于金朝皇帝按照成吉思汗提出的条件迅速签订了和约，金朝皇帝丧失了对北方的控制权，并迁都汴梁，或称南京（南方的都城），也是现定都杭州的宋朝皇帝的旧都。金朝统治者离开中都不久，蒙古人就发起了第三次进攻（1215年），不但占领了城市，还放火烧毁了皇宫。据史载，大火整整烧了一个月。大批官民被杀，大片区域被毁，然而整个元朝时期还留有旧宫的重要遗迹。"是金故城遗迹，明初尚有存者。逮嘉靖时筑外罗城（1554年）而后，辽、金故城遗址，遂茫昧不可复识矣。"忽必烈汗于1260年开始统治中国北方，他似乎有意恢复旧朝金都，不过这项设想很快便被一个更宏大的规划所替代。《顺天府志》对此描述道："世祖中统二年（1261年[3]），修燕京旧城。至元元年（1264年），都中都。四年（1267年[4]），始于中都之北建今城而迁都。九年（1272年），改大都。城方六十里。"[5]

这一记载，可以由如《元史》等其他类似的文献印证，它极简练地概述了北京城的起源和早期历史：正是帝国的伟大缔造者忽必烈汗意识到位于哈拉和林（乌兰巴托西南）的成吉思汗旧营地并不适合作为一个世界帝国的首都。这样一个都城应该建在中国，而非世界上任何其他地方，因为中国文化最发达，自然资源最丰富。虽然这个地方位于蒙古帝国的东缘，但这样的地理位置无关宏旨。的确，当时的中国是唯一可能建设世界中心的国家。

新城建于1267或1268年，称"大都"（伟大的都城）或"汗八里"（可汗之城）。"时，诏旧城居民之迁京城者，以赀高及有官者为先；仍定制，以八亩（1亩为260步，相当于769平方米）为一分，其或地过八亩及力不能筑室者，皆不得冒据，听他人营筑。筑城已周，乃于文明门外向东五里立苇场，收苇以蓑城。每岁收百万，以苇排编，自下砌上，恐致摧塌。"[6] 环绕元大都的城墙，明显是一种在苇草篱笆或苇栅之间夯土而筑成的土墙。很可能直到明代，才开始在城墙上使用城砖。

根据前面的引文，新都城址位于"中都之北"，《顺天府志》中另一段描述则更加详尽："至

---

1 卫绍王去世于1213年，英文版写做1312年，系误做。

2 英文版此处为2000年，系误做。

3 英文版此处为1262年。

4 英文版此处为1268年。

5 本段参见《光绪顺天府志·京师志一》。

6 参见《光绪顺天府志·京师志一》。

元（忽必烈的年号）四年（1267年——译者注），筑新城，城方六十里。……新城分十一门：正南曰丽正（美丽正义），南之右曰顺承（喜爱传承），南之左曰文明（文化高度发达）；北之东曰安贞（安宁纯真），北之西曰健德（蓬勃美德）；正东曰崇仁（珍惜仁义），东之右曰齐化（联合影响），东之左曰光熙（光荣闪耀）；正西曰和义（和谐正义），西之右曰肃清（庄重纯净），西之左曰平则（安定与公正）……大都达今安定门、德胜门（今北二门）外，其时围有城墙。"

如果我们认可北京以北约5里处部分残留的土墙是元城墙遗址的话，那么关于元大都向北延伸至多远的问题，就有了最合理的答案。这段城墙，民间至今还称为"元城"——除此之外也很难有其他的解释。明代文献曾提到1368年元大都的北城墙收缩了5里，从而进一步印证了这一推测。《顺天府志》记载："洪武初，改大都路为北平府。缩其城之北五里，废东西之北光熙、肃清二门（即东、西城墙上最北面的各一座城门），其九门俱仍旧。"这样的叙述应该理解为：新建的北墙建有与旧城墙上对应的两座城门，剩下的七座城门仍保留在原先的位置。《顺天府志》中的另一段文字印证了新北墙的位置（引自《元志》）："元之都城，视金之旧城拓而东北。至明初改筑，乃缩其东西迤北之半而小之。今德胜门外有故土城关，隆然坟起，隐隐曲抱，如环不绝，传为北墙遗址。"东、西城墙各被缩短一半的说法实则应更正为缩短了五分之二，这一记载虽有些夸张，仍然不失其重要性，因为它对于起伏的土墙和原先的两座城门，给出了最佳说明。

大致可以肯定，元大都的东、西城墙与明代的东、西城墙一致。两座城门的名称——平则门和齐化门也沿用下来，只是和义门改称西直门，崇文门[1]更名为东直门。如果这几段城墙的位置发生变化，肯定会被记录在册，就像城市北边界的变化那样。但是元大都的南城墙却与完整的明代城市（即今北京内城）的南城墙位置不大相同，因为实际上元大都南城墙是位于旧金都北界内的一大段城墙，元代时金中都北城墙尚存，被称为"南城"。我们应该还记得诸如白云观（白色云彩之庙观）坐落于金中都城中。如果该城的北城墙不在今北京内城南城墙以北至少1里的地方，这种情况就不可能成立。又据《日下旧闻考》曾引用《元一统志》（元王朝的地理）的记载，当蒙古人建元大都时，下令在庆寿寺（今双塔寺）以南30步之处修建南城墙，寺中的双塔至今还耸立于现在的南城墙以北约1里半处。此外，根据记载，观象台坐落于元大都的东南隅，现仍可见其遗迹位于今城东南角以北约1里半的东城墙上。从以上证据来看，几乎可以确定的是，元大都的南城墙是沿着今内城南墙以北1至1里半处修筑，并且极有可能与金都北城墙重合（或在其几步开外）。这座南城墙的位置

---

[1] 此处的崇文门（Ching Wen men）即上文所述"崇仁门"Chung Jen men，东直门起源确有崇文门一说，但此处当为英文版笔误或印刷错误，因英文版索引中提示本页出现"CH'UNG JEN MEN"一词。

在 15 世纪初的永乐年间以前，一直未曾改变，而北城墙则在此前 50 年左右的时候，由洪武皇帝下令改建。明代关于这部分的记载非常详尽，下一章将会引用到。但是在把历史翻到下一个时代之前，有必要进一步收集元大都的资料。元大都只存在了约一个世纪，但在这段时间里，显然开展过大量的建造和整修工程。《顺天府志》中的两条记载值得一读：

"（至元）二十年（1283 年）修大都城。二十一年（1284 年）五月丙午，以侍卫亲军万人修大都城。"元大都先后于 1292 年和 1322 年进行了整修。

"至正十九年（1359 年）冬十月庚申朔，诏京师十一门皆筑瓮城，造吊桥。"直到那时，城门似乎尚无永久性的防御设施，可能蒙古人当年使用的是史书记载的辽金两代所用的可移动的"楼橹"。不过，当时在城门前修建起瓮城，即一种平面为 U 型的墙垣。北京现在这种风格独特的翁城就是由此建立起来的——有着马可·波罗曾特别提及的深深的庭院和高大的城楼。然而城壕上架起的桥梁依然是木制的，石制桥梁直到后来的明代才开始使用。

元朝的首都汗八里，规模远大于现在的北京内城，然而却不可能像前述《元史》中记载的那般庞大，书中称城墙全长 60 里。假若我们所述的城墙位置大致正确，则城墙周长不会超过 50 里，中国史书的记载要么是印刷错误，要么就是夸大其词。这种夸张在马可·波罗对汗八里的描述中更加突出，且看以下这句：

"此城之广袤，说如下方：周围有二十四英里，其形正方，由是每方各有六英里。"[1] 根据尤尔的推测，马可·波罗家乡意大利的 1 英里相当于 2.77 里，照此计算，整个城墙的周长超过了 66 里，显然是不可能的。还应注意的是，城市的平面决然不是规则的正方形，而是北缘呈圆角的矩形。马可·波罗显然是倾心于汗八里的宏伟壮观，而对各方面极尽描绘之能事。他的描述总体来说是夸张的，不过同时，其中也不乏值得注意之处，尤其是他为我们提供了关于元大都街道与建筑物的仅有的信息。例如，他对城墙和城门有着一段精彩的描述：

环以土墙，墙根厚十步，然愈高愈削，墙头仅厚三步。遍筑女墙，女墙色白。[2]

城墙从上到下有显著的收分，由于城墙没有完整的砖面包砌（尽管当时城墙顶部的城垛已经用砖或石筑成），这样的收分是不得已而为之。

"全城有十二门，各门之上有一大宫，颇壮丽。四面各有三门五宫，盖每角亦各有一宫，

---

[1] 参见冯承钧译：《马可波罗行纪》，第二卷，2001 年上海书店出版社出版。
[2] 参见冯承钧译：《马可波罗行纪》，第二卷，2001 年上海书店出版社出版。

壮丽相等。宫中有殿广大，其中贮藏守城者之兵杖。"[1] 马可·波罗记忆中的城门大概也有些偏差。实际上，三面城墙各开三座门，而第四面城墙上仅有两座门。中国各种文献的记载完全一致，总共只有11座城门。另外，被马可·波罗称为宫殿的城门楼和角楼很可能与现存的那些没有什么不同，即亦为四面有回廊的木架构砖楼，出挑三重檐，向外挑出。这种建筑的形制也体现在鼓楼上，其构造的主要部分是元代建造的，也是根据前代同类建筑的式样仿建的。中国建筑的延续性，使我们可以通过研究现存建筑来了解已不复存在的前代建筑的大致特征。因此我们可以基本断定，汗八里的城门楼同明代修建的城门楼相似，但诸如瓮城是否有箭楼等问题尚不明确。

关于汗八里城市规划和街道的总体特征，马可·波罗也提供了一些信息：

> 街道甚直，以此端可见彼端，盖其布置，使此门可由街道远望彼门也。城中有壮丽宫殿，复有美丽邸舍甚多。各大街两旁，皆有种种商店屋舍。全城中划地为方形，划线整齐，建筑房舍。每方足以建筑大屋，连同庭院园圃而有余。以方地赐各部落首领，每首领各有其赐地。方地周围皆是美丽道路，行人由斯往来。全城地面规划有如棋盘，其美善之极，未可言宣。[2]

城市规划严整规则，街道笔直、纵横交错，把城市划分为方形街区，中国古代皇都的城市格局或多或少都具有这样的特征，特别是伟大的隋唐帝都长安，将这种设计手法运用到极致。根据带有插图的长安古方志，这座城市的平面看上去俨然一副棋盘，主干道将城市分割成方格，或称"坊"，每个坊又由狭窄的街道将其划分为四个更小的方格。一座宫邸或衙门有时占据整整一个"坊"，而一般的民居则只占一个坊的四分之一。汗八里城中，每个方格占地约8亩（约1.25—1.5英亩），由一个家庭使用，空间足以建造豪华深宅，宅内还有若干屋宇环绕着的重重院落和花园，外面环以围墙。很难判断元大都在多大程度上达到了这种理想的城市规划体系，不过肯定具备了其主要特征，正如我们在今北京内城中仍可看到的那样，二道均为正南正北或正东正西走向。特别是在城市北部，仍留存大量的老住宅区，呈现出规则的坊式划分。但与此同时，我们仍然应对马可·波罗所说的规则的棋盘格城市规划格局持审慎之态度，毕竟，鉴于政治或地形条件的限制，这座城市的规划格局难免存在着大量的不合规则之处。并且，伴随着经年累月的战乱、革命或各种缘由的毁坏，这些不规范之处与年剧增。大部分重建和修缮都是随意进行的，许多小巷修得像蜿蜒

---

[1] 参见冯承钧译：《马可波罗行纪》，第二卷，2001年上海书店出版社出版。

[2] 参见冯承钧译：《马可波罗行纪》，第二卷，2001年上海书店出版社出版。

的小路，而不像分隔方形街区的笔直道路。尽管如此，原有的城市规划的主要特征依然可辨，并且值得进行更深入的研究。应当指出的是，长安城和元大都的规划，更接近于以宽阔大街将城市划分为整齐地段的西方现代城市，而不同于房屋狭窄、道路蜿蜒的欧洲中世纪城市。这些中国古城面积宽广，视野开阔，房屋低矮，树木花园众多，尽管它们大都隐藏在建筑群的围墙之内。

马可·波罗曾谈到"带有庭院和花园的宏伟宫邸"，但遗憾的是，他没有进一步描述那些建筑。他似乎想当然地认为这种建筑的大体外观是尽人皆知的。并且，见过一两座这样的中国宅邸，确实也可以举一反三。这些宅邸之间的区别不大，仅房屋、院落的数量或花园的精致程度有所不同，其中花园是中国人理想家园的核心。马可·波罗唯一提到的元大都建筑是钟楼，他这样写道：

> 城之中央有一极大宫殿，中悬大钟一口，夜间若鸣钟三下，则禁止人行。鸣钟以后，除为育儿之妇女或病人之需要外，无人敢通行道中。纵许行者，亦须携灯火而出。每城门命千人执兵把守。把守者，非有所畏也，盖因君王驻跸于此，礼应如是，且不欲盗贼损害城中一物也。[1]

北京城中至今可见一座钟楼和一座鼓楼，矗立于皇城以北一段距离开外，恰好位于东、西城墙正中。因此，钟鼓楼现今的位置不再是城市中心，不过马可·波罗关于钟楼方位的描绘可以用前文提及的事实来解释：元大都的北墙比现在的北墙向北远出5里，南墙也比现在的南墙向北远出1里。如果考虑到城市规划的这些变化，可以发现，钟鼓楼实际上正好位于汗八里中心的位置，正如大多数至今仍保留有钟鼓楼的中国古城一般。此外，《元一统志》还记载："至元九年（1272年）……建钟鼓楼于城中。"

具备些许历史知识的人便可发现，如今的钟楼、鼓楼两座建筑是在不同年代建造的。比起庞大笨重的鼓楼，钟楼要灵秀得多，通体砖构，汉白玉门券、栏杆，还有乾隆时代风格的装饰性雉堞。这是1745年火灾后彻底修缮的结果。其前身是15世纪初永乐皇帝时修建的钟楼，取代了元初位置略偏东的钟楼。鼓楼面阔比钟楼宽两倍还多，建筑风格迥然。下半部分是巨大的土筑墩台，表面包砖，两个券门从中穿过；上半部分为一座两层高的大殿，四周有敞廊，双重檐。整体构造属于比较传统的类型，在这里表现为纪念碑式的巨大体量。鼓楼虽然经过局部修缮、翻新，但大概还可算是一座元代鼓楼。倘使将鼓楼与北京其他类

---

[1] 参见冯承钧译：《马可波罗行纪》，第二卷，2001年上海书店出版社出版。

似的建筑相比，比如建于明代和清初的紫禁城主城门，便能发现鼓楼细部结构（如斗栱）较为精简，并且体量笨重，显示出早期建筑的特征。由于鼓楼矗立于直通皇宫的道路尽头的小高地上，营造出了气势恢宏的建筑效果。所以极有可能这就是北京现存最古老的宫殿式建筑（与中国人称为"台"的建筑极为类似）。此外，北京城中或近郊的元代建筑也就只有几座佛塔了。

然而最使马可·波罗和鄂多立克[1]（他曾在忽必烈汗去世后到访过汗八里）等欧洲游历家赞叹不绝的建筑是皇宫。尽管他们来自拥有不朽建筑的国度，但仍视大汗的宫殿为世间奇迹之一：宫殿占地广袤，戒备森严，重门广院，殿宇亭阁连绵不绝，无止尽的城墙似乎隐含着许多不可探知的秘密。这里确实是世界大帝国的心脏：掌控着广袤的帝国疆域，威慑四方，而宫殿建筑之宏伟、装饰设计之华丽，同样摄人心扉。我们在此不展开对元代宫殿的专项研究，不过可引述马可·波罗对宫殿外观的描述作为参考，来展现元大都最重要的建筑：

> （大宫殿）周围有一大方墙，宽广各有一英里。质言之，周围共有四英里。此墙广大，高有十步。周围白色，有女墙。此墙四角各有大宫一所，甚富丽，贮藏君主之战具于其中，如弓箙弦、鞍、辔及一切军中必需之物是已。四角四宫之间，复各有一宫，其形相类……此墙南面辟五门，中间一门除战时兵马甲仗由此而出外，从来不开。[2]

以上描述指的是皇城（黄色之城[3]），元朝时也称"宫城"（宫殿之城）。该城大概也没有那么方正，而是一个矩形，由高墙围起，四角有精美壮丽的角楼，城门上亦有城门楼。不过该城周长不是4意大利里（约11里）长，而在如元、明诸史料记载的6至7里之间。马可·波罗后来提及的"大墙"是更外一道边界，大约与今北京"皇城"宫墙一致。根据元代史料记载，这道城墙全长20里，而现今的"皇城"周长18里。如果对相关史料和现存遗迹进行细致研究，无疑可以断定，元明两代皇城的范围基本相同。对于宫城之中的建筑，马可·波罗仅有只言片语提及：

> 此墙之内……别有一墙，其长度逾于宽度。此墙周围亦有八宫，与外墙八宫相类，其中亦贮君主战具……此二墙之中央，为君主大宫所在，其布置之法如下：君等应知此宫之大，向所未见……

---

[1] 鄂多立克（Friar Odoric），意大利圣方济各会托钵僧，著名的旅行家，著有《鄂多立克东游录》。
[2] 参见冯承钧译：《马可波罗行纪》，第二卷，2001年上海书店出版社出版。
[3] 英文版如此，当为作者理解有误。

后面接着描述内部陈设，此处省略即可，因为我们这里只考虑城市的外貌概况。蒙古人统治时期，这座内宫被惯称为"大内（伟大的内部）"，这个名字至今仍有时被用来指代"紫禁城"。

马可·波罗的描述由鄂多立克一段简短的观察评论所印证，后者还补充道，内、外两道城墙之间的距离约为半个箭程——"两墙之间则有着他的库藏和他所有的奴隶，同时大汗及他的家人住在内层，他们极多……"[1]

读着这样的文字，叫人不禁想起筑墙的兵营，周围是戒备森严的层层防线。大汗的居所似乎在向人们表示，他对中国的统治并非神授，而应归功于武力。中国没有哪座前朝的都城拥有如此防卫严密、重墙环绕的宫殿。唐朝皇帝的大明宫坐落于长安城的北端，宫城平面为矩形，突出于城墙外，宫城南面与之相邻的是"皇城"，皇城内坐落着各类政府机构等。开封的宋朝宫殿也不是防卫等级如此之高的军事机构。当然，那里也建有城墙，上有角楼和坚固的城门，不过，如此强调宫殿的军事意义，却是蒙古统治者独有的特征。

其他方面，元大都的规划以旧时长安城为蓝本，正方形的平面格局，朝向东、西、南、北四个正方向，以及规则的街区划分和笔直的街道设计为元大都所效仿。一些官署建筑可能亦然。大汗雄心勃勃，要将他的都城建成史上最固若金汤、最华美壮丽的城市，这座城市要能够显示出他无尽的财富、雄厚的军力与强大的组织能力。自公元1280年始，当中国的正统王朝——为尊严而顽抗的南宋朝廷彻底崩塌后，元大都成为囊括整个中华帝国及大片西亚乃至东欧地区的国都。忽必烈的统治疆域不断扩张，从朝鲜到波兰边境均是其领土。当时在这片广袤的大陆上，没有哪座城市能与宏伟壮丽的汗八里相媲美。公元1368年，蒙古帝国崩溃，国都亦遭受大规模的破坏，不过主体部分随即得以修复。重建后的城墙更加坚不可摧，防御能力进一步提升。也是从那时开始，它以"北京"这个名字示人，成为整个"中央之国"的国都。

---

[1] 参见何高济译：《海屯行纪 鄂多立克东游录 沙哈鲁遣使中国记》，2002年中华书局出版。

三、内城的城墙

　　北京城中任何一座宏大建筑都无法比及内城城墙的伟大和不朽。初看城墙，它并不如古老街道两旁或围墙之内的宫殿、寺庙与店面等这些遍身彩绘、构造精致的木构建筑那般吸引人，然而，当我们慢慢熟悉了这座大城市，城墙反而成为最动人心魄的古迹——它规模庞大并以无声而有力的韵律主宰着这方土地。也许因为有着古朴的外观和绵延不断的水平线条，城墙初看起来单调无趣，但如果仔细观察，我们就会发现城墙的建筑材料与工艺多种多样，也因它承载着前代的历史而具有重要的意义。城墙朴素的灰墙面由于年岁久远而破败，它们被树根拱起、裂开，被雨水侵蚀、破坏，在城墙上留下斑斑痕迹。墙面破碎后又不断被修补，但它仍然统一于主体旋律，连绵而悠长。城墙外侧，每隔一段距离便筑有大小不尽相等的坚固墩台，一座座坚固的墩台增强了城墙整体的韵律感。城墙内侧，各段城墙之间极不平整的接缝，以及由于雨水与树根压力而造成的墙体弯曲、膨胀，使得此段旋律的变化趋于缓慢，也更加不规则。徐缓的韵律在城门处突然加快，由渐弱到渐强过渡为有力的重音——这正是昂然耸立在绵延不绝的城垛之上的两座城门楼，较大的那座仿佛是建造于高台之上的宫殿，堡垒般的大角楼构成整个乐章的壮丽终曲。令人遗憾的是，这样的角楼仅有两座留存至今。

　　当然，不同的季节、不同的时间、不同的天气以及不同的观赏角度，城墙给人的整体感受也是不同的。远观城墙，它呈现为一条条完整的长线，高耸的城门楼间或突出于线上。气候温暖的时候，墙头上长出一簇簇灌木树丛，使得线条更加富有生机。一年中秋高气爽的十月早晨是景色最美的时候，尤其是当你向西眺望时，深蓝的西山映衬于澄澈无比的蓝天之下，共同构成了城墙的背景。一旦在北京城墙上享受过一个完美的秋日，就没有人可以忘记那光之美。每个细节都是如此不同，五彩斑斓的色彩和谐地交汇在一起！近观城墙，许多地方则有些煞风景，因为在三面城墙的城根处，林立着煤栈或其他肮脏的仓库，更不要说那些不雅观的小房子与垃圾山了。不过，也有一些地段沿着护城河或运河栽植了垂柳，或者是在护城河与城墙之间的地带种植了椿树与槐树。春季是造访这些地方的好时节，那时，浅绿色的柳枝交织在一起，形成半透明的帷幔，倒映在如镜般的水面上。或者略晚一些时节，槐树枝头缀满了花串，空气中弥漫着淡淡的素雅清香。只要懂得如何寻找合适的观赏点，我们就能够在这些古老城墙附近发现极好的景致。

从长长的坡道（中国人称之为"马道"，因为可以骑马登城）爬到城墙之上，我们便来到世界上最有趣的散步之地。在这里，人们可以漫步好几个钟头，目不暇接地欣赏全景画卷：万绿丛中掩映着的金顶灿灿的皇宫与庙宇，铺设着蓝绿琉璃瓦的王府宅院，带有开敞前廊的朱红色房子，半掩在百年古树之下的灰色小房屋，宽敞而繁荣的街道，这些街道两侧还布满商店和装饰华丽的牌楼，以及一片片有牧童放羊的开阔场地，所有这些景致都呈现在脚下这轴展开的长卷之上。只有那些西洋风格或半洋式的现代建筑才敢高于古老的城墙。这些建筑像傲慢的入侵者，破坏了画面的和谐，蔑视着城墙的庇护，而且其数量还在迅速地增长。北京如此壮丽如画之美还能延续多少年？每年有多少个鎏金雕花的店面被毁掉？为建造三四层高的半现代砖房，多少座带有前廊的旧式庭院以及布满亭台楼阁的大花园被夷为平地？为了铺设有轨电车，多少古老街道被拓宽？多少宏伟的皇城粉墙被拆除？老北京正遭受迅速的破坏。北京已经不再是帝王之城，当局也已无力保护这座城市中最值得骄傲、最珍贵的遗址。中华已经成了"民国"，人们又怎么会去关心旧王朝之美呢？

如果对北京城城墙进行仔细的考察，将其无声的见证转译为文字，毫无疑问，与任何有关这座北方都城的文字记录相比，城墙讲述的故事将更为有趣和准确。城墙以土石之身构筑了一部编年史，这部历史还在不断地被改写、添加，它直接或间接地反映了北京城从始建至清末的兴衰变化。都城历史上的大变革大多在城墙上留下了烙印——毁灭性的战争时期或和平建设时期，或好或坏的政府，无所作为或积极进取的官员，贫困或富饶的时代，以及以不同方式参与到防御工程宏大建设之中的个人。然而这条围绕着都城的长达14英里的砖作画卷，如果想要探究其经历的所有时代以及人的活动，就必须铲开覆土，挖穿城墙的不同地方，但现在完全不可能展开这项考古挖掘工作。也许这样的时机会在未来，但是在此之前，我们不得不停止对这个古迹进行外部考察，并参考其在中国史书中的早期文献。下面我们将先引用《顺天府志》中的相关记载，做以简短陈述，再描述城墙的现状。

《顺天府志》第一卷简要地记述道："明初缩城之北面，而元之规制以改。永乐中，重拓南城，又非复明之旧矣。"[1]（也就是说，在南面扩建。）

该书第二卷又更细致地阐述如何造成的这一变化：

---

[1] 参见《光绪顺天府志·京师志一》。

洪武（1368—1398年）初，改大都路（即燕京）为北平府，缩其城之北五里。废东西之北光熙、肃清二门，其九门俱仍旧。大将军徐达命指挥华云龙经理故元都，新筑城垣，南北取径直，东西长一千八百九十丈（即每边长10里半）。又令指挥张焕计度故元皇城，周围一千二百六丈（约6里半）。又令指挥叶国珍计度南城（即旧金都），周围凡五千三百二十八丈（约32.4里）。南城，故金时旧基也。改元都安贞门为安定门（确保和平之门），健德门为德胜门（道德胜利之门）……创包砖甃，周围四十里（测量大致准确，因为南城墙没有任何加建）。其东南西三面各高三丈有余，上阔二丈；北面高四丈有奇，阔五丈。濠池各深阔不等，深至一丈有奇，阔至十八丈有奇。城为门九（除新新筑北墙上两座城门的变化如前所述外，其他城门的名称与位置与元代完全相同）。……各门仍建月城（瓮城）外门十座[1]。（丽正门有两座箭楼，因此共计十座，而不是九座。）

14世纪末，明洪武年间，在北平尚未成为大明都城之前，其城市的边界和城墙大致如此。东、西、南三面的旧土墙原先似乎只是在土墙外用砖包砌，但厚度仅为现存的一半，也略低矮些。北面的新城墙未必比其他城墙更坚实厚重。我们有理由认为，北城墙在后期才有所改造，这一点将在后文中加以说明。

那时的北平并不是一个安全、宜居的帝国新都。蒙古人在中国北方的势力仍十分强大，洪武皇帝的武将历经苦战才从宿敌的手中重新夺回这座城市。明朝最初选择定都南京，完全是为军事形势所迫，其后差不多半个世纪，中国北方的蒙古敌对势力才被完全击溃。史书简要地记录了北平如何逐渐成为首都：

永乐元年（1403年）正月，礼部尚书李至刚等言：'自昔帝王或起布衣平定天下，或由外藩入承大统，其于肇迹之地（北平），皆有升崇。窃见北平布政司实皇上承运兴王之地，宜遵太祖（洪武）高皇中都之制，立为京都'。制曰：'可，其以北平为北京（北方的都城），府为顺天府'。[2]

（永乐）四年（1406年），闰七月，建北京宫殿，修城垣。十七年（1419年末）十一月，拓北京南城，计二千七百余丈（15里）。[3]

末句的意思似乎是指城墙南面新扩建的城墙总长为15里。如果从中减去原南城墙的长

---

[1] 参见《光绪顺天府志·京师志一》。

[2] 从1403年到1421年，北京被称为"行在"，即"走在"或"暂时的居所"。南宋时杭州也被称为同样的名字，并被马可波罗抄录。——A.D.W.——作者注

[3] 参见《光绪顺天府志·京师志一》。

度11.64里，仅剩余3.46里，再平均分到东、西两侧城墙上，则每边各有1.75里，基本与我们判定的元故都南城墙的位置相符。这个位置与现在南城墙位置之间的距离大约为1.5—1.75里。

上述南城扩建年代与《顺天府志》第一卷的记载不符："永乐十五年（1417年），营建北京宫殿，十五年（1432年）拓城之南面、共周围四十里。"[1]

如果这个记录是准确的，那么城南的扩建，不可能在永乐年间完成，而是在他死后的八年。但是事实并非如此，城墙修建工程在永乐时期已大规模展开，有多个文献可以佐证。最有趣的记载来自于一位阿拉伯大使——沙哈鲁，他们在1420年来到北京。据大使记载：当他们来到汗八里的城门时，他们看到"一座完全用石头（！）建造的伟大壮丽的城市！但是城墙仍在建设之中，埋没在数千座脚手架之下"。《明史·地理志》中记载，城墙工程于永乐十九年（1421年）完工，又补充说明城墙包砌砖面的工程完工于1437年——此前是否将砖用于城墙，还是在这一年首次使用？为了明确回答这个问题，我们需要有比中国史书上的记载还更为详尽的资料。然而从中至少可以看出，在明正统年间包砌砖面还没有成为常规做法。当然永乐时期城墙内部也有可能使用几层砖来粘合墙体内芯的泥土、石灰与砂砾的，但是在外部使用砖包砌则是后来的发明。还需要说明的是，我们已发现在现存城墙砖石结构中，最早的城砖是成化年间（1466-1487年）的。

《顺天府志》中有一段模糊的记载，很有可能提及的就是这一包砌砖面工程："正统十年（1455年）元月，命太监阮安、都督同知沈青、少保工部尚书吴中，率军夫数万人修建（或为改造）京师九门城楼。四年四月，修建京师门楼、城壕、桥闸完。正阳门正楼一，月城（瓮城）中左右楼各一，各正楼一，月城楼一。各门外立牌楼，城四隅立角楼。又深其濠，两涯悉砌以砖石。九门旧有木桥，今悉撤之，易以石。两桥之间各有水闸，濠水自城西北隅环城而东，历九桥九闸，从城东南隅流出大通桥而去，自正统二年（1437年）正月兴工，至是始毕。"[2]

这两个年代的叙述相当紊乱，因为先说到后一个年代，之后才提及前面的年代，又没有很清楚地说明两个年代的具体工程。护城河、运河与桥梁可能是最先建设的，然后才是城墙、城门与角楼等，亦或不同的工程是同时开展的。所有这些工程的总工期大约为十二年（1437-1449年），役使的人力甚众，完成的工程总量想必也是庞大的。

城墙的修缮或改造工程，似乎向我们表明30年前的筑造并没有妥善完成，也没有包砌

---

[1] 参见《光绪顺天府志·京师志一》。
[2] 参见《光绪顺天府志·京师志一》。本段第一句原文为"正统元年十月"，可能是作者参照的英文译文之误。

砖面。这期间没有发生使城墙遭受破坏的战争或革命，也没有发生对永乐年间完成的工程造成不良影响的大灾害。在正常情况下，城墙应当可以延续几百年，而不是短短几十年。只有假设原先工程中尚有未竣之处，才能解释为何在新城墙建成后不久又大兴土木。可能是当初没有完成砌砖面，包砌之后的城墙就变得既坚固又美观。于是，在明正统年间，城墙首次具有了现在宏伟壮丽的外观。

与外包砖面同样重要的是当时城门楼与角楼上的工程。至少四座城门（东、西两侧城墙上各两座）基本上自元代以来没有变化，而新建的南城墙城门显然当时并没有完全竣工。现在所有的城门都建有瓮城，都有外侧的箭楼与内侧的城楼。箭楼是为弓箭手射击准备的，城楼是供鼓手使用的，他们敲打振奋的鼓点来激励战士击退敌人。南城墙正中的城门比其他城门更高大，建造有三座箭楼，而不是一座。令人遗憾的是，这座城门的城楼与城门上很多其他设施的命运一样，均已被改建，下一章我们会更详细地对此加以描述，也会涉及现存的两座角楼。

除城墙与城门工程外，护城河与城门桥也开展了大规模的修整工作，以确保它们运转良好。石桥与护城河的石砌堤岸的确是新建砖面城墙不可或缺的补充。然而整体来看，它们的衰败状况比城墙其他部分都更为严重，但却无人问津。有好几处护城河河段看上去就像小水沟，而另外一些河段又像死水塘。目前的水量远比先前更加稀少和不稳定。因为铁路建成后，护城河已经失去作为水道的使用价值，所以对它缺乏有效的管理。城墙下仍然可看到古老的水关，现在仅仅作为城市排水系统的组成部分来使用。水闸的栅栏经常被污物堵塞。目前仅东边护城河水流较为充沛，在其东南角，我们仍然可以看到上文所述的漂亮石桥，桥身上有石雕栏杆，券洞上饰以兽首。这座大通桥水闸仍有拦水的作用，可以调节通惠河的水位。

修缮完工后，其中几座城门便被正式命名。南面正中的城门原称丽正门，现在改称正阳门（直对艳阳之门），这个名称一直沿用至今，也俗称为前门。南城墙西边一座城门原先称顺治门，现称宣武门（宣扬威武之门），但旧名称比新名字更流行。南城墙东边一座城门原称文明门，现在改称崇文门（崇尚文化之门）——可以说是与东边的宣武门相对应，虽然其官方名称至今未变，但哈达门之名更为人所熟知。东城墙南城门齐化门被改称朝阳门（迎接日出之门），但人们普遍使用早先的名称，而不是新的官方名称，西城墙南城门也有相同的情况，平则门被改称为阜成门（意为堆成），但人们不大使用这个新名称。其他四座城门，即西直门（正对西方之门）、东直门（正对东方之门）、安定门（确保和平之门）与德胜门（道德胜利之门），没有变更名称，想必认为它们的名称依然合适。

历史文献中记载的竣工后的明北京城墙长度各不相同。前面引用的文献号称城墙长 40

里，(明代)工部也记录了同样的数字："永乐中，定都北京，建筑京城周围四十里，为九门。"[1]《明史·地理志》则称城墙长度为45里。

这些数据均不精确。城墙的实际长度在41—42里之间，严格地说是41.26里或23.55公里[2]。其平面也不是历史文献中所说的规整的正方形。东、西两侧的城墙要比南、北城墙短不少，并且西北角还有一个缺角。根据现代精确的勘察，各边城墙长度如下：

南城墙长6690米，合11.64里；北城墙长6790米，合11.81里；东城墙长5330米，合9.27里；西城墙长4910米，合8.54里。

中国各种文献所记录的城墙高度与厚度也有很大出入，这并不奇怪，因为城墙各处的高、厚有很大的变化。《顺天府志》中有如下记载："下石上砖，共高三丈五尺五寸。堞高五尺八寸，址厚六丈二尺，顶阔五丈（中国尺为十四又八分之五英寸）。设门九，门楼如之，角楼四。城垛一百七十二，旗炮房九所，堆拨房一百三十五所，储火药房九十六所。雉堞一万一千三十八，炮窗（豁口）一万二千一百有八。"[3] 在其他历史记载中，城墙高度为33.5尺。

如今想要精确地说明城墙高度几乎是不可能的，因为每隔几步就有变化，这不仅仅是因为城墙历经毁坏与修缮，而且也是因为城根的地面发生了很多变化，以致在很多位置无法确定墙基的确切位置或高度。测量城墙高度时，我们自然选择了一些地平高度没有变化或变化很少的地方，然而这些测量结果也只能被视为近似值。城基厚度的测量也如此。数据只是近似值，因为这是通过从顶部测量立面倾斜度计算出来的（如图所示）。我们无法用测杆穿透古城墙，唯一准确的测量（约有1—2英寸的误差）是对城墙顶宽以及女儿墙、城垛的测量。尽管有些偏差，下列数值，对四面城墙平均高度来说却是最适用的：

南城墙（水门以东），城墙外侧高10.72米，内侧高度也是10.72米；顶宽15.20米，基厚18.48米。往东邻近哈达门的位置，城墙高度相同，但顶部稍窄，宽14.80米，基厚18.08米。往西接近顺治门的位置，外侧高11.05米，内侧高10.15米；顶宽14.80米，基厚18.40米。

东城墙（顺治门与齐化门之间），城墙外侧高11.10米，内侧高10.70米；顶宽11.30米，基厚16.90米。齐化门以北：城墙外侧高11.40米，内侧高10.48米；顶宽12.30米，基厚18.10米。（附近的城墙受雨水侵蚀，顶平面向内塌陷，由此形成孔洞。）

---

[1] 参见《钦定日下旧闻考》。

[2] 参见第六章，1里等于640米，但此处核算为1里等于571米，下一段又合575米。

[3] 参见《光绪顺天府志·京师志一》。

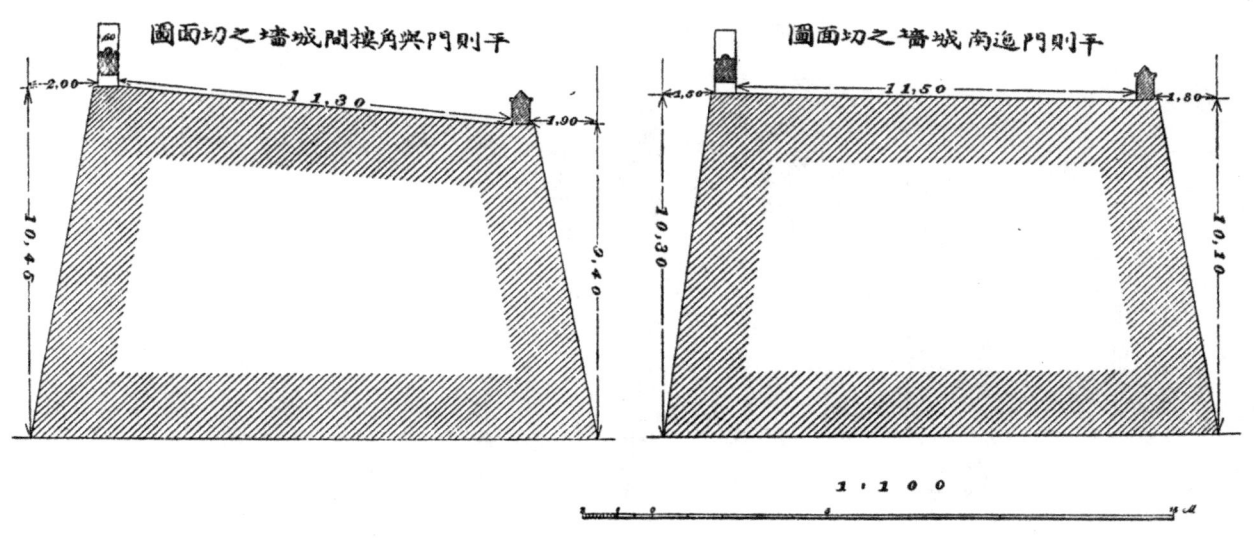

图 3 平则门以南西城墙的两个剖面

西城墙（平则门以南），外侧高 10.30 米，内侧高 10.10 米；顶宽 11.50 米，基厚 14.80 米。靠近平则门的位置：外侧高 10.50 米，内侧高 9.40 米；顶宽 11.30 米，基厚 15.20 米。平则门与西直门之间：外部高 10.95 米，内部高 10.40 米；顶宽 14 米，基厚 17.40 米。

北城墙（靠近东北角），外侧高 11.92 米，内侧高 9.20 米；顶宽 17.60 米，基厚 22.85 米。安定门以东的位置：外侧 11.90 米，内侧高 10.40 米；顶宽 17.63 米，基厚 21.72 米。德胜门与西北角之间：外侧高 11.60 米，内侧高 11 米；顶宽 19.50 米，基厚 24 米。

南城墙顶部平均宽约 15 米，城墙外侧平均高约 10.70 米，内侧比外侧低几厘米。

东城墙顶部平均宽约 12 米，或更少一些，外侧平均高约 11 米，内侧比外侧低 0.5 米。

西城墙平均宽度约 11.50 米，外侧高约 10.40 米，内侧比外侧低几厘米。

北城墙顶宽在 17.60—19.50 米之间变化，外侧高在 11.50—11.93 米之间，内侧高度在 11—9.20 米之间。

因此可以说，东、西城墙的高、宽基本相同，而西城墙整体较薄、较低。东、西城墙可能是在元代城墙基础上建造的，但我们还没有充分的证据来确定这一观点。

南城墙比东、西城墙要厚 3 米（甚至更多），而高度大致相同。北城墙的高度、宽度均比其他城墙都要大不少，其宽度比南城墙多出 3—4 米，立面的倾斜度也要比其他城墙大得多。由此可见，彻底重建的城墙要比那些在原有基础上扩建的城墙远为坚固厚重。由此看来：城墙厚度逐渐的增加（从南城墙到北城墙），也许暗示了建造年代的先后关系。东、西两边的城墙可能是基于原有元代城墙，经过加宽、加高扩建而成。南城墙大体新建于永乐年间，其后又增加了砖包砌的外墙。而那时北城墙可能仍保持着 15 世纪的原始形态，也就是说，比现状要低矮、单薄得多，这个变化归究于约 16 世纪初的后期营造，这个假设可由城墙的

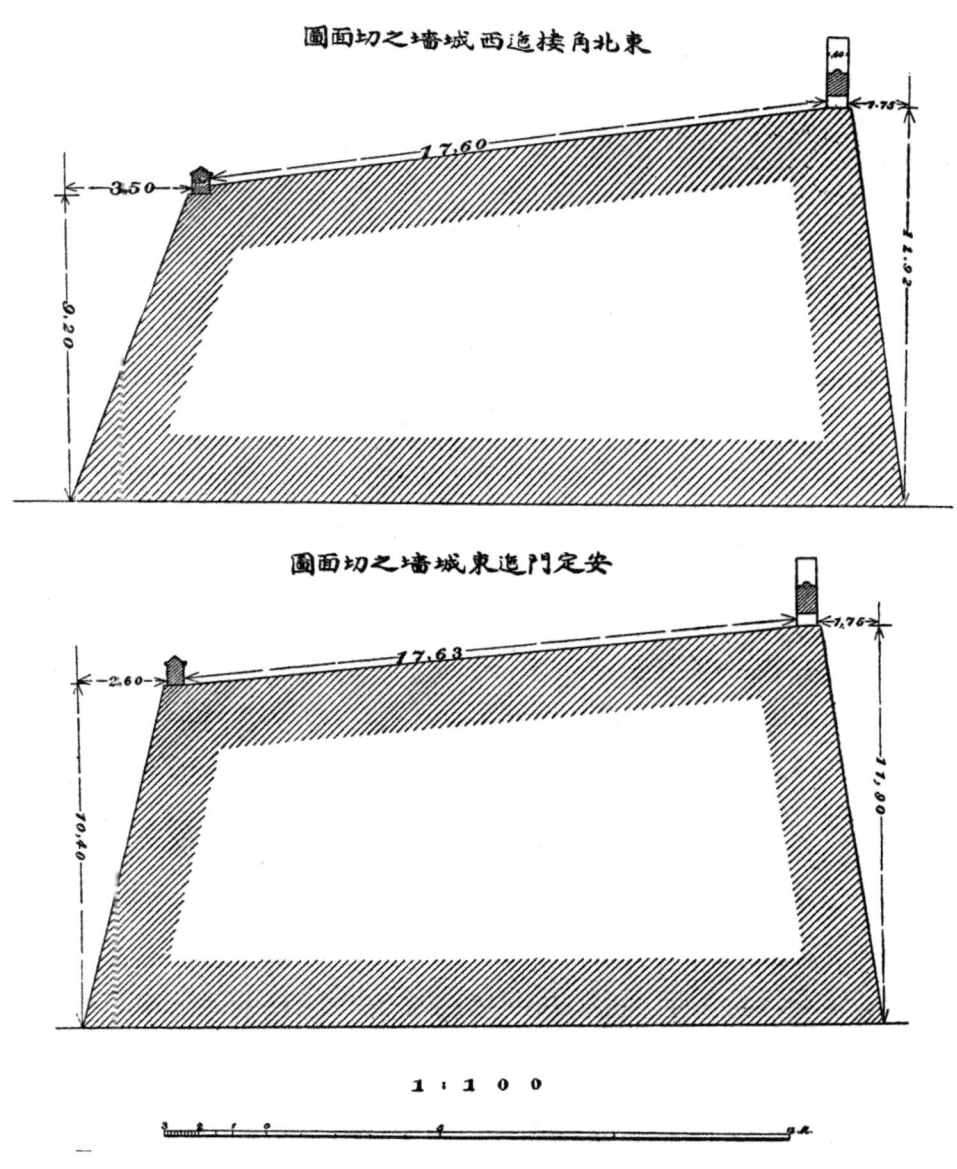

图 4 北垣墙的两个剖面：上图选取于临近东端的位置；下图选取于临近安定门的位置

砖构来证实。

我们没机会探究城墙的内部结构，但有人目睹过城墙被打穿，例如在建造前门新的边门时。我们从他们那里收集到了一些信息。这些信息表明，城墙由一系列夯土层、砂砾层与石灰层构成，间或穿插有砖层来粘合夯土或黏土。据说在某些位置可以看到在大墙中有更小的土墙，至于这一说法的可靠程度如何，适用于哪些地方，只有剖穿城墙才能判定，而这样的工作只能留给未来的调查者了。

我们多次提及城墙外部有砖包砌，砖面不只是薄薄的一层壳，而是由几层，甚至多达七八层砖构成的。城墙某些地方因树根或流水浸蚀而开裂，我们由此可以看到那些砖层。厚砖层内部较为粗糙、不平整，这是因为使用了过量的灰泥，而且砖砌得又非常不规整。表面的砖层砌得比较仔细，广泛采用荷兰式砌筑法，但并非始终都使用该砌筑法。如果更细致地检视实际工程，我们就会发现城墙现有表面是不断修补和修缮的产物，很难从中发现最初的砖作工程。城墙底部是一层低矮的砂岩板底座（有时是双层），其下是石灰三合土地基，厚约 2 米或更多。在一些地点，砂岩基层与石灰三合土地基完全被砂土所覆盖，另一些地点的地基又被水侵蚀，导致城墙内部塌陷或砖层下滑，很难找到保存完好的地基。如有之，我们可以看到石灰三合土地基大约伸出底座外一米半，由此沿着城墙内侧形成了一条极好的人行步道。

墙面从底座升起，有不同坡度的倾斜，一般内侧要比外侧更平缓一些。北城墙的斜度为 3.5 米的底宽与不足 10 米的墙高之比，其他各面城墙是仅 1.5—2 米的底宽与 10 米的墙高之比。连续的城砖层层叠砌，状如阶梯。收分最大的北城墙自然最明显，这些阶梯的宽度足以让人直登城头。外立面自然要顺滑得多，因为从防卫的角度来看，在外立面建造这样宽的阶梯是非常危险的。在外立面每隔一段距离就建造一座墩台，也增强了城墙的防卫作用，墩台的厚度与城墙一致，类似方形扶壁。在北城墙上，所有的墩台规模相同，其间距为 200 多米。而其他几面城墙的城台间距只有 80—90 米。并且除了普通大小的墩台，还有对应城墙内侧马道的形体较大一些的墩台。

城墙的顶平面以大砖海墁，内侧边缘砌筑女儿墙，外侧砌筑城垛。内侧的女儿墙只是简单的一道砖砌屏障，60 厘米厚，80—90 厘米高，上部抹圆。外侧的城垛没有女儿墙厚，但高度至少为女儿墙的两倍。城垛高 1.80 米，城垛之间的宽大射击口（有时被错称为"观察孔"）仅 0.5 米。城垛与女儿墙下部，与城墙顶面相平的高度有方形的孔洞。城垛的孔洞可能用于防卫目的，而女儿墙的孔洞仅作排水之用。从这些孔洞伸出一些排水石，但这些石条太短，不足以避免水落到低处的城墙表面。实际上水都是由内侧壁排出的，城墙顶平面或多或少向内侧壁倾斜（参见前文数据），仅在很少的地方，城墙顶面从中间也向外侧壁稍作倾斜。这种排水体系对城墙的危害很大。雨季中，城墙内侧壁被来自顶部的水流冲刷，大量雨水渗入城砖缝隙，尤其是在那些因树根与灌木已形成缝隙的地方。结果是外层砖大多松动、跌落，不得不一遍一遍地反复修补砖面。另一种对城墙的较大危害是墙根处的积水没有办法顺畅地排出。最初石灰三合土地基一侧有石砌的小壕沟或阴沟，然而现在大多被废。这些城壕，有的变为深深的泥土路，有的则以沟渠替代了运河，但是缺乏适当的排水口。在雨水充沛的时节，水会漫过城墙基座，造成城墙底部的石板和城砖的松动；当这些底部基础承受不住来自上部的压力时，后果就非常严重了，城墙内侧大面积砖面因此而坍塌。我们顺着城墙内侧走，时常能见到这些坍塌，以及历史上城墙的其他毁坏状况。

《顺天府志》记载的城垛和"观察孔"（可能是豁口或用作射击孔）的数量基本正确，我们没有必要去数城墙顶上曾经有多少哨所，当然也不可能，因为现存数量很少，仅在城门与角楼处有几座，且呈非常破败的状态。清代城墙防守分配给八个不同的"旗"，或称守卫部门，旗杆上高挂他们的旗帜。城门附近仍可看到不少插旗杆的夹杆石，但已然没有旗杆了。"镶黄旗居安定门内，正黄旗居德胜门内；正白旗居东直门内，镶白旗居朝阳门内；正红旗居西直门内，镶红旗居阜成门内；正蓝旗居崇文门内，镶蓝旗居宣武门内"。[1] 根据中国传统的象征体系，北城墙由黄色庇护，黄色代表土；西城墙由白色庇护，白色代表金；东城墙由红色庇护，红色代表火；南城墙由蓝色庇护，蓝色代表水。土、金、火与水是城市防卫必需的四元素，中国人也认为这些元素能够相互制衡，防止某一旗试图反叛或占领整个城市。

中国人在都城的平面布局以及不同街区、城门的设计中都赋予了丰富的象征意义。他们将城市设计为方形并对应四个主要方向不仅仅是出于实际需要。星象位置是设计的基础，一座坚固的城市必须遵守天则。就我们所知，城市的布局要和谐一致、要均分为方形的主要思想在元代已经形成（虽然没有完全实施），而明代帝王试图使其更加完美，将城市建成正方形而不是长方形。但这一意图也不得不根据实际情况而变通。整个城市与皇宫的正面都是向南的，即"朝向太阳"——上天的统治者。在阳光最少的地方，即西北角，正方形平面被削掉一大块。与之相对的东南角，按中国人的说法此处地面是"下沉"的，实际上由于水道的关系它的确如此，但在中国人看来，这表明太阳在东南角是至高无上的。观象台就是位于这个角落，天坛也在相同的方向。

我们没有必要对中国人的传统象征体系作深入探讨，因为对我们西方人来说，其意义是非常含糊、不明确的。但是需要记住的是，中国人从来不仅仅根据美学或实用需要来规划设计建筑作品，无论是住房、寺庙，还是一座城市，他们总是有更深层次的目的以及更重要的象征意义。然而，天子的忠实臣民虽然从未忽略这些事情，但也从未能充分理解和领会。

---

1 参见《光绪顺天府志一·京师志一》。

四、内城城墙的内侧壁

现存的北京城墙，决非统一而同质的结构。四面城墙在规模及外观上的主要差异已在前文提及。此外，对于频繁进行的修缮，我们也略有一些调查。目前正在开展的进一步考察清晰地表明，城墙内侧壁的砖面是一段段拼接而成的，各段修筑时期、质量、工艺各不相同。很多城段的修建年代，可以通过城墙顶部镶嵌的石碑碑记来推断。这些碑记上不仅记录着修缮的时间与范围，还记载着监修官员的姓名。

如果工程质量好，那么这些碑记就成为表彰官员勤勉的光荣榜，而一旦工程质量低、不耐用，这些官员便会被置于公众的批评与谴责之下。遗憾的是，这种激励监修官员的体系，直到乾隆年间才开始推行。这些官员大都是工部、礼部、刑部等一些政府机构的侍郎或员外郎。早期修缮、建造的内城城墙上并无这样的石碑，砖文便成为仅有的早期记录。这些砖文上至明成化年间（1465—1487年），下迄清道光年间（1821—1850，译者注）。其内容各异，通常会列出砖窑名称和工匠姓名，有时则只有如"停泥城砖"、"新大城砖"等文字的简单描述。不过，城砖上可能刻有比表面所见更多的砖文，提供的信息也更多，现在已经看不到了，即使能看到，由于风雨侵蚀与尘土覆盖等原因，字迹也难以辨认了。

我们真正寻找的是那些载有修建年代的砖文，因为它们与城墙的历史有着最直接的关联。砖文所载的年代可能未必是所在城段城墙竣工的确切年份，但造砖时间与城墙建造年代应基本吻合，因为将早期的砖用于后期修葺工程的情况是极为罕见的，即使有，也往往与其他材料混用。倘若某段城墙上既无碑记亦无砖文，那么断代只能根据城墙的特征和质量来推测了，这是一种通常的做法。一般来说，区分明初和嘉靖年间的工程，甚至更晚的万历或崇祯时期的工程并不难做到。而且，明代工程与清代工程的区别明显，因为用料与工艺均有所不同。清代的乾隆时期在城墙营建历史中占据着极为重要的地位，这是由于该时期是中国艺术的最后一个黄金时代，其工程规模和质量均远超其他时期。

遗憾的是，我们无法判定康熙年间的城墙，因为并未发现那段时间的碑记或砖文。不过，我们有理由相信，那些特征上早于乾隆时期而又不同于明朝晚期做法的小段城墙，应当是清初的工程。乾隆时期的辉煌传统在嘉庆时得到了较好的传承，但是到了道光年间，材料特征与建造工艺都发生了变化。到更晚的时期，城砖变得更小、更轻，城墙在18世纪时那样精美的外表已不复存在。如今，城墙内侧壁多处均需大规模修缮，尤其是东城墙，其中几处状况极差。过去二十年间，除前门城台的重建和几条马道的局部修缮外，便没有其他保养城墙的举措了。现在的政府显然并未采取任何措施以保护北京城的老城墙，他们甚至连这样做的兴趣都没有。如果继续放任雨水和树根对城墙的侵蚀破坏而不加以控制，就像过去二十年间那样，部分城墙将处于危险状态。

一旦意识到北京城城墙那卓然的长度和变化多样的建造工艺，便不会有人要求对城墙进行逐尺的详细阐述，我们也不打算这样做。只要沿着城墙观察，注意到各段城墙由于凹凸不平的衔接和材料的差别而有所区别，就已足够。嵌入城墙的石碑或砖文上记载的年代，只要从地面上可见的（有时借助小望远镜）便可一一记载下来。如果并未发现这样的城砖或碑记，则可根据城砖的特征判定其年代。下文中所列的各段城墙长度，仅为基于粗略估算或步测的近似值，这些测量有时也受城墙下房屋或其他障碍的影响。尽管测量不够精确，但它们仍应被当作确定各段城墙与马道、城门位置的辅助手段而被记录下来。自然，有些城段由于多次修缮，不同时期的修补痕迹纵横交错，很难为它们断代。对这类情况，我们会根据主要材料和工艺特征来断代。我们对城墙的研究确实是在严格的限制和相当困难的条件下开展的，除非能花费重金来攀登、清理和挖掘城墙，否则这些限制和困难便无法消除。数世纪以来，这座雄伟的建筑一直守卫着北京的历史和城市，因此我们的工作成果决不应该被视作最终结果，仅是为其历史研究做的一些贡献而已。

1. 南城墙

南城墙可以说是由两个近乎均等的部分组成的：前门东侧的一半和西侧的一半。中间那座宏大的城门不仅是城墙上的最大开口，而且是城墙与毗邻街区间风貌发生重要转换的标志。城门以东，是有着高大西洋建筑和整洁街道的使馆区。这里的城墙墙面修葺得较好，部分墙壁上长满了爬山虎。城门以西，是风格不中不西的民国建筑的杂乱的内城街区，道路泥泞，煤棚和垃圾堆一直蔓延到城墙边上。这个西南区域实际上是城市中最不引人注目的角落之一，有些地方的垃圾堆至城墙一半的高度，这些地方成了秃鹫和野狗肆意猎食的地方，更不用提附近那些不考虑邻里氛围与环境卫生的住户。再向西行，到顺治门的另一边，这座城市的西南地带才有了相对整洁的道路和体面的房屋，民国政府的国会议场巍然耸立其间。

不过新修的路仅延伸到国会议场的拐角处，便转向北面了，而沙沟（作为道路使用）和垃圾堆则继续沿着城墙蔓延到草木丛生的西南城角。

邻近使馆区的这片区域，尤其是前门至哈达门一带，确实干净整洁，不过从城市历史的角度来看却少了些许趣味。城墙的砖砌面在爬山虎的遮盖下若隐若现，墙根下的道路十分狭窄，路面高高隆起，甚至埋没了城墙的基础，城墙也因此变矮。对城墙风貌更不利的是，使馆区的一些欧式建筑十分扎眼，高度与城墙呈竞争之态。结果自然是不和谐的。这些傲慢的初来乍到者，完全无视古老的城墙，建起了众多高过城墙的塔楼和山花。

经使馆区往东，穿过哈达门之后，城墙与相邻区域就变得较为协调了，景观也变得更加有趣。在这几处城段，城墙结构的全貌包括城基、三合土人行道及其前面的小运河，均可一览无余。附近的建筑物不多，几片空地中间，坐落着意大利人、奥地利人和德国人的墓地，墓园草木葱郁，犹如美丽的绿岛。

第1段：东南角在1915年建设环城铁路时被毁，铁路在此处转弯，将城角两边的城墙截断。故，此处的砖作结构在近期历经修补。

第2段：长约90米（以下所有测量数值均为粗略估算）。18世纪下半叶重修，所用城砖为乾隆与嘉庆时期常用的样式。其中一些城砖上刻有印文"停泥细砖"，一些刻有"通丰窑大城砖"，亦有"工部监督桂"。所有的城砖都为工部监制，乾隆时期的砖上常能见到监工的名字。这一时期，其他砖窑亦有烧制的类似城砖，这将在下文中提及。这些砖的平均尺寸为：长48厘米，宽23厘米，高12.5厘米；标准重量为48市斤。明代以及明之后的城砖普遍偏小，以下的观察报告中将会提及。

第3段：长50米。约筑于明中期，后期有些许修葺。

第4段：长190米（或更长）。筑于明中期，砖文为嘉靖三十二年（1553年）。

第5段：长80米。砌筑精细，根据墙上镶嵌的石碑记载，筑于乾隆五十三年（1788年）末，砖由永成窑烧造。

第6段：长200米。用大型城砖砌成，砌筑精细，根据墙上镶嵌的石碑记载，筑于嘉庆二十年（1815年）。该段城墙正前方为一块墓地，妨碍了进一步的观察。

第7段：南墙最东边的马道。包括四个不同的组成部分：第一部分，明初工程（无砖文）；第二部分，1907年地震后修缮部分，但大部分使用旧材料，系乾隆时期的城砖；第三部分，明初工程，城砖上有砖文"成化十八年"（1482年）；第四部分，马道最西面的一部分，是新砌筑的。

第8段：长14米。可能筑于18世纪，无砖文。

第9段：长3米。该段很短，由中型砖砌筑，无砖文。此段所用城砖尺寸大约为乾隆时期城砖的四分之三。自道光时期开始广泛使用这种尺寸的城砖，不过清初时也使用类似样式的城砖，可惜那时（顺治与康熙年间）的城砖上没有砖文。

第 10 段：长 14 米。年代与材料同第 8 段。

第 11 段：长 10 米。年代与材料同第 9 段。

第 12 段：长 30 米。18 世纪晚期的工程。砖烧造于乾隆时期的力丰窑，砖文曰："工部监督桂。"

第 13 段：长 60 米。年代与材料同第 9 段。

第 14 段：长 30 米。筑于 18 世纪末。砖烧造于乾隆时期，上书"停泥新城砖"。

第 15 段：长 10 米。约筑于明晚期，无砖文。这段城墙下有水闸，城墙已经严重起鼓。

第 16、17 段：长 45 米。两段皆用中型砖筑成，无砖文。

第 18 段：长 20 米。筑于明中期。有砖文"嘉靖二十八年"（1549 年），或"嘉靖三十二年（1553 年）窑户孙传为造"，亦有"嘉靖三十三年（1554 年）窑户符居为青州府（山东）造"。可能还有许多其他嘉庆年份的不同砖文。

第 19 段：长 150 米。筑于明中期。砖文载有嘉靖时期不同的年份，如"嘉靖三十一年（1552 年）窑户李奇威为南阳府（河南）造"。

第 20 段：长 120 米。砌筑平整，工程质量精良，根据城墙上镶嵌的石碑，当为乾隆四十一年的工程。砖文为常见的"停泥细砖"。

第 21 段：长 20 米。筑于 18 世纪末。砖出自乾隆年间的永成窑。

第 22、23、24 段：长 80 米。这三段（或可分为更多城段）似为明代遗存，因墙根有其他建筑，无法进一步考察。

第 25 段：哈达门马道上部的城墙，有砖文曰："嘉靖三十三年（1554 年）窑户符居造。"

第 26 段：马道本身，在后期用中型砖重筑。

第 27 段：长 60 米。可能筑于清早期，用中型砖。

第 28、29 段：长 75 米。这两段城墙似为明代工程，但城砖较大且无砖文。

第 30 段：长 60 米。筑于 18 世纪晚期，砖文曰："东河窑细泥新城砖。"

第 31 段：长 60 米。筑于明中期，砖文曰："嘉靖二十八年（1549 年）窑户孙紫东造。"

第 32 段：长 40 米。筑于明中期。砖文曰："嘉靖二十八年（1552 年）窑户刘钊造。"也有嘉靖三十一年的砖文。此段城墙上部曾于 18 世纪用"停泥细砖"重修。

第 33、34 段：长 60 米。两段均为明中期的工程，大城砖，印有嘉靖年间的年款。

第 35 段：长 20 米。筑于 18 世纪晚期，用大型砖，上有乾隆年款，如"恒顺窑新停细城砖"。

第 36 段：长 90 米（或更长）。筑于明中期，砖文曰："嘉靖二十九年（1550 年）窑户何宗造。"

第 37 段：长 90 米。根据墙顶部碑记，为乾隆三十八年（1773 年）重筑。

第 38 段：哈达门与水门之间的马道，至少包括四个部分：第一部分，用乾隆年间城砖，有普通砖文；第二部分，明初砌筑工程，用大型砖，无砖文；第三部分，约清初砌筑工程，用中型砖，无砖文；第四部分，最西一段，年代和材料与第一部分相同。

第 39 段：长 60 米。筑于明中期。有"正德六年（1514 年）作头李环造"、"成化十八年（1482 年）"、"嘉靖三十二年（1553 年）"等砖文。此段城墙似于 16 世纪重筑，局部采用旧材料。

第 40 段：长 60 米。城墙顶部碑记表明此段为嘉庆十二年（1807 年）重修。乾隆年间样式的城砖上有砖文"停泥细砖"。

第 41、42 段：长 80 米。两段均为近期（可能为光绪年间）修葺。

第 43 段：水门，为 1900 年义和团运动之后所建。周围城墙大多较为古旧，但经多次修葺。

第 44 段：长 20 米。城墙下部的年代较为久远，大部为明中期筑，有的城砖有砖文曰："嘉靖三十一年（1552 年）。"上部由中型城砖筑于 17 世纪或更晚。

第 45 段：长 30 米。明末筑，上有多处新的修补，砖文曰："万历三十二年（1604 年）。"

第 46 段：水门与前门之间的马道，包括三个不同的部分，根据墙顶碑记，中间的主体部分于嘉庆十六年（1811 年）重修，但城墙本身的年代明显更早。

第 47 段：长 60 米。筑于 18 世纪晚期。碑记显示为嘉庆二年（1797 年）重修。

第 48 段：长 50 米。筑于明中期，砖文曰："嘉靖三十一年窑户李志高造。"

第 49 段：长 80 米。城墙顶部碑记显示为光绪十年（1884 年）重建。

第 50 段：长 14 米。明代砌筑工程，用大型砖，无砖文。

第 51 段：前门东侧马道处的城墙，主要为乾隆年间修建。城墙顶部有两块相距不远的碑记，一块为乾隆五十二年（1787 年），另一块为乾隆四十六年（1781 年）。

第 52 段：前门城台似乎为同时期所建，但于 1914—1915 年开辟新门时修葺。

我们对南城墙东半部分的考察情况大致如此，如果要冒昧地总结出一般性的结论，可以说这段城墙罕有明初遗留的城垣。约 16 世纪中叶的嘉靖时期及乾隆末年，对城墙进行过大规模的修缮，19 世纪嘉庆和光绪年间修缮规模较小。其中，最平整、细致的工程显然是乾隆时期所筑，不过一些嘉靖时期砌筑的亦极佳。明初的城砖大都饱受风雨侵蚀，已不再平整贴合，灰泥的使用量比后来要多。从前门向西，考察工作变得愈发困难，因为此处的棚屋和垃圾堆全都紧贴城墙，多处墙壁上也积满了厚厚的灰尘。不过我们很快就发现，这边的修缮工作并不少于东边。

第 53 段：前门西边马道处的城墙，大多是新筑的。

第 54 段：长 35 米。据墙顶碑记记载，于乾隆四十七年（1782 年）重修。

第 55 段：长 70 米。筑于明中期，砖文记载年代为嘉靖三十二年（1553 年），城墙上部经后代修葺。

第 56 段：长 35 米。筑于明晚期，砖文曰："万历三十二年（1604 年）。"

第 57 段：长 50 米。筑于乾隆时期，砖文曰："工部监督永。"

第 58 段：新墙，约光绪时期筑。

第 59 段：长 35 米。筑于乾隆时期，砖文曰："工部监督永。"

第 60 段：长 30 米。筑于 18 世纪晚期，用乾隆时期的大型砖，城墙顶部的石碑无字。

第 61 段：长 5 米。筑于明晚期，砖文曰："万历三十二年。"

第 62 段：同第 60 段。碑上字迹模糊。

第 63 段：长 20 米。筑于明晚期，砖文曰："万历三十二年。"

第 64 段：长 38 米。新墙，据墙上碑记，为光绪十七年（1891 年）重筑。

第 65 段：长 150 米（或更长）。筑于明中期，砖文曰："嘉靖戊子年（1528 年）。"

第 66 段：马道，根据碑记，为嘉庆七年（1802 年）修缮。

第 67 段：筑于 18 世纪末期的一小段城墙。用乾隆时期砖，有砖文"工部监督桂"。

第 68 段：长 38 米。新墙，根据碑记，光绪十九年（1893 年）修缮。

第 69 段：长 35 米。筑于明中期，城砖严重残损，无可辨砖文。城墙被树根拱起。

第 70 段：长 35 米。筑于 18 世纪。根据镶嵌的石碑记载，为乾隆五十四年（1789 年）修葺。

第 71 段：约筑于 19 世纪初。砖文曰："新样大城砖。"

第 72、73、74 段：长 200 米。三段均为 16 世纪末期的城墙。用乾隆时期的砖，上有砖文"工部监督桂"及"工部监督永"。

第 75 段：第二条马道，下部为明代筑，而上部，据镶嵌的石碑记载，为乾隆五十二年（1787 年）重筑。

第 76 段：马道西端的城墙，根据镶嵌的碑记，为乾隆三十年（1765 年）重筑。

第 77 段：长 30 米。据壁上嵌入的碑记所载，为乾隆四十二年（1777 年）重筑。

第 78 段：长 75 米。据壁上嵌入的碑记所载，为光绪十年（1884）年重筑。

第 79 段：一小段明代古城墙，墙面因有树根长出而鼓起、破裂。

第 80 段：筑于 18 世纪末期。根据碑记，为乾隆五十六年（1791 年）重筑。

第 81 段：较长，多用明代材料，但修葺年代可能较晚。

第 82 段：筑于 18 世纪末期。用乾隆时期砖，上有砖文"工部监督永"。

第 83 段：约筑于明中期，无砖文。

第 84 段：此段的下部为明时修筑，有砖文曰："嘉靖三十四年。"上部用乾隆时期城砖筑，砖文曰："工部监督永。"

第 85 段：顺治门东侧马道，主要修筑于明中期。

第 86 段：顺治门西侧马道及相邻城墙，根据碑记，为乾隆四十九年（1784 年）重修。

第 87 段：长 65 米。筑于 18 世纪末期。用乾隆时期的城砖，上有砖文"工部监督桂"。

第 88 段：一小段用明代城砖的城墙，但可能经后代重筑。

第 89 段：筑于明中期，无砖文。

第 90 段：根据城墙顶部碑文，为嘉庆二十年（1815 年）重筑，砖文记"新样大城砖"。

第 91 段：长 65 米。年代、材料均与第 87 段相同。

第 92 段：一小段似为明初筑造的城墙。

第 93 段：可能筑于 17 世纪末期。用中型砖，无砖文。

第 94 段：另一小段由中型砖筑成的城墙。可能为清初所筑。

第 95 段：筑于 18 世纪末期。用乾隆时期城砖，砖文记"工部监督永"。

第 96 段：一小段明中期的城墙，无砖文。

第 97 段：年代、材料均与第 95 段相同。

第 98 段：年代、材料均与第 96 段相同，不过可能经后代修葺。

第 99 段：长 5 米。筑于明末期，有砖文"万历三十二年"。

第 100 段：长 35 米。根据城墙顶部碑记，为乾隆五十四年（1789 年）修缮。

第 101 段：较长，筑于明中期。有砖文"嘉靖二十八年（1549 年）"。

第 102 段：明代旧城墙，局部乾隆时期重筑。有砖文"嘉靖三十二年"，亦有后代砖文"大通成窑造，工部监督永"。

第 103 段：南墙最西侧的马道，大部分为明代所筑，但中段的一部分可能为光绪时期修葺。马道东端有砖文"嘉靖二十八年（1549 年）"。

第 104 段：新筑。筑于光绪时期，有砖文"官窑造停泥新砖"。

第 105 段：明代旧筑，无砖文。

第 106 段：长 25 米。根据嵌入的碑文记载，为乾隆四十四年（1749 年）修葺。有砖文"官窑造新样大城砖"。

第 107 段：时代、材料均与第 105 段相同。

第 108 段：长 11 米。根据嵌入的碑文记载，为乾隆二十八年修葺。有常见的砖文。

第 109 段：筑于明中期，砖文曰："嘉靖三十二年窑户高尚义造。"

第 110 段：长 75 米。根据嵌入的碑文记载，为乾隆二十八年（1763 年）修葺。参见第 108 段。

第 111 段：长 38 米。根据嵌入的碑文记载，为乾隆九年（1744 年）修葺。有砖文"工部监督永"。

第 112 段：一小段明城墙，无砖文。

第 113 段：长 18 米。根据嵌入的碑文记载，为乾隆二十八年修葺。参见第 110 段。

第 114 段：长 20 米。根据嵌入的碑文记载，为乾隆三十年（1765 年）修葺。砖文曰："工部监督桂。"

第 115 段：城角的马道，主要为明中期筑造，一些城砖上有嘉靖等字样砖文，但亦经后代修葺。

我们对南墙西半部的考察，毋庸置疑表明其保养不善的程度与东半部相同。在这段城墙中，主要是 18 与 19 世纪修葺的部分，旧时明城墙的部分则很短。有些明城墙的修补，部分用旧料，部分厌新料。我们还发现这一带有几处墙貌颇为独特：墙面被沉重的树根拱起、破裂，但这样的损毁在东边的城墙上更为常见；可辨的砖文极少，这是因为大段大段的城墙被北风带来的灰尘层层覆盖，北风还侵袭着墙根的土路，也将城墙下的垃圾堆刮得乱七八糟。只有国会议场（原城隍庙）前的一段城墙相对干净，墙根没有垃圾堆积。再往西边一些，旧日风貌至今尚存：一排美丽的槐树在贯穿古城壕河道的路上投下树影，城墙上生长着的椿树和枣树枝繁叶茂。

自从新种上柳树和椿树之后，西南角附近一处空地的景致便更为幽雅怡人了，嫩绿的枝桠在黑色城墙的映衬下青翠欲滴。此段城墙古旧而苍老，加之至今犹存的古老角楼，从看不到角楼瓦楞铁屋顶的侧面看去，气势恢弘，成为北京城墙中最迷人、最别致的一段。

2. 东城墙

就某些方面来看，东城墙是内城四面城墙中最有趣的一段。它包括相当数量的明初城墙，虽然保存状况极差，却也为其平添了几分美感与历史底蕴。如果现今的北京政府能对首都历史古迹的维护有一丁点儿的兴趣和资金投入，这里便是急需关注的第一批文物之一。

然而由于这并不可能发生，几段城墙不久后的坍塌便可想见。有几处墙基逐渐遭水侵蚀，砖墙也因树根的侵害而开裂、剥落。结果可想而知，在我们的照片中也可窥见一二。

如前文所述，东南城角被铁路线截穿，铁路前面又新建有一道围墙，这直接破坏了原有城角的结构，也严重损害了角楼的景观。只要立于城外或城墙之上，这样的景象便可尽收眼底。城角处的空地上随意堆放着垃圾，一条明沟蜿蜒流过平地，穿过城墙下的水栅，流入城外的护城河。雨季时节，它会涨成一条宽阔的溪流，而在其他时间，沟内夹杂的泥土要比水多。

这一带原来有一座贡院[1]，它即便不是东南城区的建筑中心，至少也是其文化中心，自它被废弃以来，这片区域的旧时风貌与重要功能丧失殆尽，已变得单调而荒凉。古观象台也已被一座十分平庸的半洋式砖楼所取代。不过，从城角至古观象台以北30米处之间的一段城墙，基本仍保留着古色古香的气息，尽管从各段衔接处能明显看出它是分段筑成的。如前文提及，明初时曾对元代旧城进行扩建，这段即为当时增建的城墙。

第1段：长70米。筑于明中期，有砖文：嘉靖十年。这段墙体下部有一半进行过翻新。

第2段：长35米。新筑，无砖文。

第3段：长18米。筑于明中期，有砖文："嘉靖二十八年（1549年）。"

第4段：很短一段城墙。上部为明末期所筑，下部为近世修葺。

第5段：长180米。筑于明中期，有砖文："嘉靖二十七年。"墙上有五处后世的修葺。

第6段：长150米。筑于明中期，有砖文"嘉靖二十一年（1542年）"及"嘉靖三十二年（1553年）"。

第7段：长120米。筑于明中期，有砖文"嘉靖二十年（1541年）"及"嘉靖二十七年（1548年）"。

第8段：长35米。筑于明中期，有砖文"嘉靖十八年（1539年）窑户孙文传造"。

第9段：观象台马道，在乾隆年间经过大规模重筑。南侧的城砖有砖文"停泥细砖"。之后为一小段由薄砖砌成的明代城墙。北侧亦为乾隆时期砌筑。马道上的城墙年代悠久，但无砖文。

第10段：长64米。筑于明初。这段城墙是饱经风雨的古城墙的最后一截，与新修建的观象台城台形成对比，十分显眼。

第11段：长150米。筑于明末，有砖文"万历三十二年及万历三十三年（1604–1605年）"。

---

[1] 贡院：举行科举考试的地方。

第 12 段：长 24 米。根据嵌入的碑记，为嘉庆十八年（1813 年）修葺。

第 13 段：长 36 米。根据嵌入的碑记，为乾隆八年（1743 年）修葺。

第 14 段：长 100 米。筑于明中期，有砖文"嘉靖三十二年（1553 年）东河窑造"。

第 15 段：长 20 米。根据嵌入的碑记，为嘉庆七年（1802 年）修葺。有砖文"停泥新城砖"。

第 16 段：长 50 米。筑于明初，城砖损毁严重，无砖文。

第 17 段：长 60 米。可能为 17 世纪末期筑成，用中型砖，无砖文。

第 18 段：长 50 米。筑于明末期，有砖文"万历三十二年"。

第 19 段：长 90 米。时代与材料同第 17 段。

第 20 段：长 60 米。筑于 18 世纪，碑上无铭文。有砖文"乾隆辛巳年（1761 年）"。

第 21 段：长 60 米。筑于明末期，有砖文万历三十一年及万历三十二年（1603-1604 年）。

第 22 段：长 5 米。筑于明中期，有砖文"嘉靖二十八年窑户林永寿造"。

第 23 段：长 5 米。筑于明末期，有砖文"万历三十二年窑户吴玉造"。

第 24 段：长 30 米。可能为 17 世纪末期所筑，同第 17 段。

第 25 段：长 2 米。筑于明中期，有砖文"嘉靖三十二年窑户卜天贵造"。

第 26 段：长 5 米的一小段。根据碑记记载，为嘉庆十八年修葺。

第 27 段：长 5 米。所用城砖与第 26 段相同，但属不同的墙段。

第 28 段：长 5 米。筑于 18 世纪中期（参见第 20 段）。有砖文"乾隆辛巳年（1761 年）"、"乾隆甲午年（1774 年）"及"乾隆丙申年（1776 年）"。

这些段的城墙被巨大的树根顶开，好几层砖因此而塌落。靠近地面的几处大洞，因城砖被肆意盗用而进一步扩大，甚至已经露出了三合土的墙芯。

第 29 段：长 30 米。明代旧城墙，城墙上部有砖文"嘉靖二十三年（1544 年）窑户林贵造"。

第 30 段：马道，主要为明代修建。有砖文"嘉靖二十三年及嘉靖三十三年"。根据嵌入的碑记，南端为嘉靖四年（1525 年）修葺，目前已残破不堪。马道前的垃圾一直堆到城墙半腰。

第 31 段：长 70 米。明代旧城墙，无砖文。

第 32 段：长 30 米。筑于 19 世纪初。有砖文"停泥新城砖嘉靖年间窑户居正耀造"。

第 33 段：长 60 米。筑于明中期。有砖文"嘉靖十年（1531 年）"，以及"任威南、卜通威、宋文明'等窑户的名字。

第 34 段：长 40 米。筑于 19 世纪初。有砖文"东河窑停泥新城砖"。参见第 32 段。

第 35 段：长 60 米。筑于明中期，有砖文"嘉靖三十八年（1559 年）窑户曹春造"。

第 36 段：长 30 米。明初筑，砖大都残损严重，无砖文。

第 37、38 段：长 70 米。两段均筑于 18 世纪末。据嵌入的碑记记载，其中一段于乾隆三十一年（1766 年）进行过修葺。

第 39 段：长 150 米。据嵌入的碑记记载，为嘉庆十二年（1807 年或之后）修葺，用"停泥新城转"。

第 40 段：长 25 米。筑于 18 世纪末。用乾隆年间的城砖，有砖文"停泥细砖"。

第 41、42 段：长 130 米。两段均为明初城墙，城砖残损严重，无砖文。

该段城墙外观古旧，衔接处参差不齐，特别是靠近墙基的部分，基石和石灰三合墙基被水浸没，尤为明显。

第 43、44 段：长 35 米。两段城墙上均有带砖文的城砖，上记：万历三十二年（1604 年），但显系乾隆时期重修。

第 45、46、47 段：长 100 米。三段约为明末期的城墙，有砖文"万历三十二年"。

第 48 段：长 9 米。约筑于明末。使用的是一种流行于崇祯时期的非常薄的砖。

第 49 段：长 9 米。通向城门马道的一段乾隆时期的城墙。

第 50 段：齐化门处城墙，主要为明中期修筑。有的砖上带有嘉靖年款，但城门的城台和马道为 18 世纪末期重筑，城砖上有乾隆和嘉庆的年款。

第 51 段：长 6 米。筑于 18 世纪末期。乾隆时期的城砖，有砖文"工部监督萨"。

第 52 段：长 30 米。筑于明中期，有砖文：嘉靖二十四年及嘉靖二十六年（1545–1547 年）窑户段洲及张宝钞造。

第 53 段：长 30 米。可能为清初所筑，用中型砖，无砖文。

第 54 段：长 3 米。明代旧墙，砖残损严重，无砖文。

第 55 段：长 12 米。筑于明中期，有砖文"嘉靖三十三年（1554 年）窑户高尚义造"。

第 56 段：长 40 米。根据嵌入的碑记，为嘉庆四年（1799 年）修葺。

第 57 段：长 40 米。根据嵌入的碑记，为道光二十三年（1843 年）修葺。

第 58 段：长 100 米。这是两段 19 世纪的城墙。根据两块嵌入的石碑记载，分别为光绪二年（1876 年）和同治九年（1870 年）修葺。不过使用的城砖年代更早，有些城砖有砖文"永定官窑造新大停细砖"和"咸丰元年（1851 年）作头王泰立造"。

第 59 段：长 50 米。根据嵌入的碑记，为乾隆四年（1739 年）修葺。

第 60 段：长 60 米。根据嵌入的碑记，为乾隆八年（1743 年）修葺。

第 61 段：长 9 米。筑于明中期，有砖文"嘉靖十六年（1537 年）窑户林永寿造"。

第 62 段：长 25 米。可能为清初所砌，用中型砖，无砖文。

第 63 段：长 22 米。城墙的下部为明代所砌，有砖文为证：嘉靖十五年（1536 年）；城墙上部为清初或更晚用中型砖重筑。

第 64 段：齐化门与东直门之间的马道，包括至少三个部分：最南边的一段城墙，下部为明代所砌，砖文有"嘉靖三十二年（1553 年）"；而上部则是后期砌筑的。中段与此类似，城墙下部的砖文写道"嘉靖十六年（1537 年）窑户林永寿造"，而上部为 19 世纪砌筑。北段城墙的下部有砖文：嘉靖二十三年（1544 年）。

马道目前的保存状况令人堪忧，砖与三合土构筑的支撑台座因水流的侵蚀而残损。马道有多处已经坍塌，还带出了基石。马道的上部曾经反复修缮，然而如果听任下部基础结构坍塌，这种修缮也无济于事。这种情形之所以在东城墙上出现得比南、西、北三面更为频繁，是因为东墙一带水量相对更大。原本沿城墙内侧修筑的砖砌城壕，如今已经损毁殆尽，甚至有几处变成道路。雨季时节，积水常常没过城墙的基石。

第 65 段：长 20 米。此段城墙与前处马道的状况相似：城墙下部用明代砖，上部则是后期用中型砖重筑的。

第 66 段：长 60 米。上半部分当为明中期砌筑，下半部分经后代修葺。有砖文：大停细砖。

第 67 段：长 24 米。筑于明中期，有砖文：嘉靖二十八年（1549 年）。

第 68 段：长 7 米。据嵌入的碑记记载，为道光五年（1825 年）重筑。

第 69 段：长 14 米。明代旧墙，无砖文。

第 70 段：长 7 米。据嵌入的碑记记载，为道光四年（1824 年）修葺。有砖文"瑞顺窑造大城砖"。

第 71 段：长 50 米。筑于明末，有砖文：万历三十二年（1604 年）。墙上有数处经后代修补。

第 72 段：长 14 米。筑于 18 世纪末期。有砖文"大停细砖"。

第 73 段：长 9 米。此段城墙主要为明末砌筑，但亦有几处用"大停细砖"修补。

第 74 段：长 30 米。该段城墙上部为新修，可能修造于光绪年间；下部修于明中期，所用城砖含有嘉靖（？）年款。嵌入的石碑字迹模糊，似乎为光绪时期的遗存。

第 75 段：长 100 米（或更长）。根据嵌入的碑记记载，该段城墙的上部为光绪二十年（1894 年）修葺；下部为明末所筑，有砖文：万历三十年（1602 年）。

第 76 段：长 60 米。筑于明末期，有砖文：万历三十二年。

第 77 段：长 10 米。这是两小段明代所砌的城墙，多处用新砖。

第 78 段：长 55 米。可能为 19 世纪初所砌（嵌入的石碑字迹不清）。有砖文"新城砖"。

第 79 段：长 45 米。筑于 18 世纪末，墙顶端嵌有一方明显为乾隆时期的石碑。

第 80 段：长 25 米。筑于明末，有砖文：万历三十二年。

第 81 段：东直门马道及相连的城墙，根据嵌入的碑记，为嘉庆八年（1803 年）修葺。城砖与乾隆时期的城砖相同，有砖文"大停细砖"。

值得注意的是，相较于东城墙的南段，东直门附近的城墙保存状况更好。基石和石灰三合土筑起的宽阔便道至今尚存，城墙砖面平整。墙面收分不大，因而显得格外高大庄严。东直门以北的城墙亦然，修葺得十分规整。

第 82 段：长 24 米。筑于明中期。砖为嘉靖二十四年（1545 年）苏州府分官窑烧造。其他还有一些同年代的砖，为扬州府造。

第 83 段：长 20 米。据嵌入的碑记记载，为嘉庆四年（1799 年）修葺。

第 84 段：长 24 米。筑于 18 世纪末期。乾隆时期城砖，有砖文：工部监督永及工部监督桂。嵌入的石碑上无文字。

第 85 段：长 80 米。筑于 18 世纪末期。有砖文"永定官窑造大停细砖"，碑上文字涣漫不清。

第 86 段：长 26 米。据嵌入的碑记记载，为乾隆六年（1741 年）修葺。有砖文"通钦窑造大城砖"。

第 87 段：长 60 米。据嵌入的碑记记载，为嘉庆八年（1803 年）修葺。城砖产于瑞盛窑。

第 88 段：长 3 米。上部用崇祯时期的薄砖砌成，下部用大型砖。

第 89 段：长 9 米。上半部分用中型砖砌成，可能为清初的工程；下半部分用永顺窑造大砖。

第 90、91 段：长 30 米。均筑于明末，局部使用乾隆砖修葺。

第 92 段：长 20 米。筑于明中期，有砖文：嘉靖二十八年。

第 93 段：长 6 米。筑于 18 世纪末，有砖文：工部监督永。

第 94 段：长 6 米。筑于 19 世纪初，砖烧造于瑞顺窑。

第 95 段：长 12 米。明代城墙，局部用乾隆砖修葺。

第 96 段：长 9 米。据嵌入的碑记记载，为乾隆三十年（1765 年）修葺，有砖文"永通官窑造新停泥大城砖"。

第 97 段：长 3 米。筑于 18 世纪末，砖为乾隆时期常见的样式，无砖文。

第 98 段：长 3 米。筑于 19 世纪初，有砖文"王府用砖"。

第 99 段：长 12 米。筑于 18 世纪末，明代旧城墙，大部分用乾隆时期的材料重筑。

第 100 段：长 50 米。据嵌入的碑记记载，为乾隆四年（1739 年）修葺。

第 101 段：长 20 米。筑于明末，有砖文：万历三十二年，亦经后代修葺。

尽管踏勘时我们留意到大量修葺，东城墙的北段与南段相比，外观仍更为和谐统一。18 世纪及 19 世纪初的修葺与明代城墙衔接得比一般情况要好，对脱节部分的修补也不如南城墙那样多，也没有那么多坑洞。城墙较好地留存下原貌，这可能是因为城市的北部正处冷清、空旷之地，人为破坏相对较少的缘故。

城角部位已经因为环城铁路而被损毁，铁路贯穿城墙铺设的情况与东南城角如出一辙。一道平整的新墙遮蔽了铁路的弯道，而古老的角楼则已荡然无存，城角处昔日的特质与美丽被剥夺殆尽。

城墙周围的街区虽然非常安静而偏僻，但并不因此而枯燥无趣。这里仅有的一些建筑，都坐落在俄国教会区内。除了北京最早的东正教堂和教士住所，还有墓园、菜园、牛圈，以及欧洲小规模教会庄园中常有的其他类似的基础设施。我们仿佛置身于异国，其历史也许不像中国那样悠久。但在神职机构中，这样的传统却更为持久。

3. 北城墙

北京所谓的"北城"，与这座满人都城的其他区域相比确实不同。这里坐落着那些显赫的满族亲王的大型王府建筑群，其中，别致的花园与壮丽的古树占据了比房屋更多的空间。在贴近北墙的地带，还有几座北京最大的庙宇，如雍和宫与孔庙，皆为黄、蓝的琉璃瓦屋顶，庭院宽敞，古杉掩映。除去这些大规模的建筑群，还有一些小型的宅邸，它们曾经是满清显贵的居所。随着户主家境的败落，这些屋舍也日渐倾颓，但它们典雅依旧，透露着一抹昔日荣光的浪漫情调。这里曾经是北京城的圣日耳曼区[1]（Faubourg Saint Germain），如今仍保留着与世隔绝的氛围，因此，与南墙、东墙处的普遍特征不同。越往北，城市的活力越弱。房屋与建筑群之间的距离逐渐拉大。城墙附近有很多开阔的旷地、沙土地和草地，再向西面一些，名为"西海"[2]的一大片湖泊几乎伸到了城墙根。因为这一区域不易受到强劲的北风的侵袭，城墙内侧的道路便成了北京城内最好的漫步场所。

---

[1] 位于巴黎市郊，是以前的法国王室区域之一。

[2] 英文版原文为 North Lake（北海），应系作者误解或笔误。按照书中描述的地理位置，此处是什刹三海最北端的西海，即后文所说的积水潭。

不过北墙附近人迹罕至。即便在这条路上走一天，可能都见不到一辆马车或人力车，至多遇到遛鸟的独行者或靠着城墙晒太阳的人。旱季，在仍残存有些许青草的地方，常有一小群绵羊啃食青草，纯朴活泼的孩童在一旁守着，他们看上去与市中心那些冒失的顽童大不一样。路上偶尔会有骆驼商队经过，朝着德胜门或者安定门方向前行。无声的队伍在柔软的沙土路上安静地走过，只有领头骆驼颈上的驼铃发出的叮当声响，才能显示出这支气宇轩昂的动物部队的缓慢节奏。一旦骆驼商队走远，孤寂便再次笼罩这里，仿佛一团沉甸甸的乌云，即便偶尔会被光束穿破，也仅能维持几分钟而已。

北城墙与北京内城其他三面城墙差异较大。正如之前指出的，它的规模更大，内立面收分也比东墙或南墙更大。一般来说，北墙保存得相对较好，这可能是因为其建造年代更晚，不过更大程度上是得益于其从未直接暴露于具有破坏性的北风的吹袭之下。外立面却因风吹雨打和敌兵攻击而破损严重，并经不断修补，下文中我们还将谈及。

沿着截断城墙东北角的铁轨修有一道新墙，走过这道墙后，面前便是以下各段城墙：

第1段：长75米。用乾隆时期大型砖重砌，砖文漫漶不清。

第2段：长40米。筑于明末，有砖文：万历四十六年（1618年）窑户刘松作头刘能造。

第3段：长60米。据嵌入的碑记记载，为道光十年（1830年）修葺，上有砖文"停泥新城砖"。

第4段：长20米。一小段明城墙，上有后代砖砌修补。

第5段：长35米。用"恒顺窑造停泥城砖"筑成。

第6段：长9米。据嵌入的碑记记载，为道光九年（1829年）修葺。

第7段：长100米。根据碑刻记载，为乾隆辛巳年（1761年）修筑。有砖文：工部监督永与工部监督桂。

第8段：长40米。于嘉庆年间（19世纪初）用"大停细砖"修葺。

第9段：长100米。为相连的两段城墙，可能建于清初，用中型砖。

第10段：长25米。可能建于18世纪末期，用乾隆时期大型砖，无砖文。

第11段：长50米。同第9段。

第12段：长9米。一小段城墙，据嵌入的石碑碑文，为乾隆时期由工部监督永督造。

第13段：长50米。两小段明代城墙，以新砖修补。

第14段：长25米。据嵌入的石碑记载，为道光十四年（1834年）修葺。

第15段：长75米。根据嵌入的石碑，为乾隆四十年（1775年）修葺。

第16段：长55米。两小段明末城墙，含砖文：万历三十二年。

第17段：雍和宫后面的长马道，主体部分为明末工程，有砖文"嘉靖三十年分窑户杨造"。马道上部经后代修补。

第18段：长15米。一小段明代城墙，包含砖文"嘉靖三十一年（1552年）分窑户林高造"。

第19段：长20米。筑于18世纪末，用乾隆时大型砖。

第20段：长25米。可能为17世纪末（或更晚）修筑，用中型砖，无砖文。

第21段：长45米。两小段明代城墙，经后代修补。

第22段：长30米。明末筑成，其中有使用万历三十二年烧造城砖。根据嵌入的石碑，为乾隆四十年（1775年）修葺。

第23段：长40米。两小段明末城墙，有砖文：万历三十二年（1604年）。

第24段：长50米。城墙的下部为明末修筑；根据嵌入的石碑，上部为咸丰十年（1860年）修葺。

第25段：长35米。两小段与前一段特征相似的城墙。

第26段：长50米。明末修筑，所使用的砖与崇祯年间（1628-1643）的薄砖相同。

第27段：长40米。据嵌入的石碑，为乾隆二十年（1755年）砌筑。

第28段：长25米。可能为17世纪末或18世纪的城墙，用中型砖，无砖文。

第29段：长150米。这段城墙的下部为明代工程，严重失修。根据碑刻记载，城墙的上部为道光二十年（1840年）重筑。

第30段：长115米。乾隆十九年（1754年）使用工顺窑烧造的城砖修葺。

第31段：安定门马道和城台主要为明末工程。城台的上部由崇祯时期常用的薄砖筑成，下部则用乾隆时期的大型砖修补。

第32段：长10米。用中型砖修葺。

第33段：长20米。明末修筑，有砖文：万历三十二年。

第34段：长25米。这段明代城墙的下部有砖文：嘉靖戊子年（1528年）；上部为乾隆时期修建。

第35段：长18米。下部为明代修筑，上部年代更晚。均使用中型砖。

第36段：长10米。筑于明末，无砖文。

第37段：长60米。下半部为明末修筑；根据镶嵌的碑刻记载，上半部为道光四年（1824年）重筑。

第38段：长40米。明代修筑，有修补。

第39段：根据镶嵌的碑刻记载，这是一大段嘉庆八年（1803）修葺的城墙。

第40段：长20米。筑于18世纪末，有砖文"通顺窑造大停细砖"。

第 41 段：长 30 米。根据嵌入的石碑，为道光四年（1824 年）修葺。有砖文"大停细砖"。

第 42 段：一小段明中期修筑的城墙，有砖文：嘉靖二十一年（1542 年）窑户王林造。

第 43 段：长 40 米。筑于 18 世纪末，有砖文：东河窑。

第 44 段：长 15 米。筑于明初，有砖文：成化十三年（1477 年）——这是我们迄今发现的年代最久远的砖文年款。

第 45 段：长 50 米。可能为清初修筑，用中型砖，无砖文。

第 46 段：长 36 米。筑于 18 世纪末，用大型砖，无砖文。

第 47 段：长 20 米。与第 45 段的年代、材料相同。

第 48 段：长 20 米。筑于明初，有砖文：正德四年（1509 年）。

第 49 段：长 25 米。与第 45 段的时代、材料相同。

第 50 段：一小段明代城墙，上部用薄砖重建。

第 51 段：长 30 米。根据嵌入的碑记，为乾隆八年（1743 年）重筑。

第 52 段：一小段清代城墙，用中型砖，无砖文。

第 53 段：长 20 米。筑于明中期，有砖文：嘉靖十一年（1532 年）。

第 54 段：长 35 米。筑于明中期，有砖文：嘉靖二十八年窑户张明造。

第 55 段：长 60 米。根据城墙顶部嵌入的石碑，为咸丰年间（1851-1861 年）修葺。

第 56 段：长 40 米。可能为清初所筑，用中型砖，无砖文。

第 57 段：长 25 米。这段城墙用各种材料混合砌筑，可能于 19 世纪初修葺。墙顶部的碑记文字无法辨认。

第 58 段：长 30 米。上半部用中型砖砌成，可能为 19 世纪所修；下半部为明末工程，有砖文：万历三十二年。

第 59 段：长 12 米。筑于明中期，无砖文。

第 60 段：根据嵌入的碑记，这是一大段乾隆七年到乾隆八年（1742-1743 年）修葺的城墙。

第 61 段：长 40 米。筑于明中期，用大型砖，无砖文。

安定门至北城墙中部长马道之间的城墙保存状况相对较好，后代重修部分不像其他城墙那样多。墙面坡度徐缓，城砖层层叠起，踏面很宽，可使人攀爬而上（这在南、东、西城墙是不可能的）。这样的缓坡使得该段城墙看上去比其他陡峭的城墙要低矮一些。

第 62 段：这段长长的马道在不同时期均经过修葺，其修补也不尽均衡，可区分出的至少有十二处，大部分修于明代，即嘉靖、万历和崇祯年间，亦有修补于 18 世纪与 19 世纪初的部分。对于这些细碎的修修补补，似乎没有必要一一列举。

从这段马道而出至德胜门延伸的城墙也进行了大规模修葺，特别是城墙的上部，下部的年代基本都较早。

第63段：长12米。筑于明末，有砖文：万历三十二年。

第64段：长12米。筑于19世纪初，用中型砖，无砖文。

第65段：长12米。筑于明末，无砖文。

第66段：长10米。年代与材料均同第64段。

第67段：长20米。年代与材料均同第63段。

第68段：长45米。这段城墙的下部为明末修筑，上部于19世纪用中型砖重筑。

第69段：长12米。上部为明代修筑，下部为乾隆时期修葺。

第70段：长50米。筑于明末，有砖文：万历三十四年。

第71段：长20米。下部为明代所筑，其中有嘉靖十七年的城砖；上部于19世纪用中型砖重筑。

第72段：长40米。可能为19世纪初筑成，墙顶部的碑文载有道光年号（部分文字被树枝遮挡）。

第73段：长35米。两小段城墙，用19世纪中期的中型砖砌筑而成。

第74段：长20米。两小段明末城墙，有些砖上有砖文：万历二十九年。

第75段：长10米。时代、材料均与第73段相同。

第76段：德胜门的马道和城台于明末用薄砖重筑。根据嵌入的石碑，"部分城门马道"（约54米）为嘉庆七年（1802年）修葺。

德胜门与西北城角之间的城墙，呈连续的不规则的曲线，衔接处极不平整，外观奇特。这段别致的城墙，在其建造时似乎并未严格遵循任何规范的规划图纸或设计方案。

第77处：长50米。根据嵌入的碑记，为道光二十年（1840年）重筑。

第78段：长40米。根据嵌入的碑记，为嘉庆三年（1798年）重筑。

第79段：长30米。筑于18世纪末或19世纪初，用乾隆时期的大型砖。

第80段：长75米。筑于明末，有砖文：万历三十二年。

第81段：长40米。可能为19世纪初所筑，用大型砖，墙顶部有碑记。

第82段：长20米。筑于19世纪末，用中型砖。

第83段：长25米。筑于明末，用薄砖，与崇祯时期常用的砖相似。

第84段：长12米。筑于18世纪末或19世纪初，用大型砖，无砖文。

第85段：长40米。可能为清末所筑，用中型砖，无砖文。

第 86 段：长 40 米。与上段城墙特征相似。

第 87 段：长 40 米。乾隆时期砌成，有砖文：工部监督萨。

第 88 段：长 40 米。筑于明末，用崇祯时期的薄砖。

第 89 段：长 30 米。上半部为明末砌成，用薄砖；下半部多处使用乾隆时的城砖进行修补。

第 90 段：长 20 米。下半部为明中期砌成，有砖文：嘉靖十四年；上半部用崇祯时的砖砌筑。

第 91 段：长 40 米。下半部为明中期工程，有砖文：嘉靖十一年（1532 年）"常州府造"；上半部用中型砖重筑。

第 92 段：长 350 米。一大段非常平整的城墙。筑于乾隆或嘉靖时期，有砖文："辛巳年（1761 年）造"或"福金窑造"。

第 93 段：这段马道与前一段城墙的特征相似，马道之上的城墙顶部有两块碑记，文字漫漶不清。

第 94 段：长 60 米。根据嵌入的碑记，为嘉庆八年（1803 年）修葺。有砖文：大停细砖。

第 95 段：长 24 米。可能为清末所砌，用中型砖。

第 96 段：长 30 米。筑于明末，有砖文：万历三十一年。

第 97 段：长 9 米。19 世纪初砌成，用嘉庆时城砖。

第 98 段：长 12 米。可能筑于乾隆年间，无砖文。

第 99 段：长 40 米。可能筑于清末，用中型砖。

第 100 段：材料与上段城墙相似。

第 101 段：长 100 米。筑于明末，用崇祯时期薄砖。

第 102 段：长 75 米。筑于 18 世纪末，有砖文：广成窑甲午年（1774 年）造。

第 103 段：长 24 米。筑于明末，用薄砖。

第 104 段：两小段用中型砖砌筑的城墙。（参见第 99 段）

第 105 段：长 200 米。根据嵌入的碑记，为嘉庆四年（1799 年）修葺。有砖文"永定官窑新大城砖"。

第 106 段：长 15 米。筑于明中期，用大型砖，无砖文。

第 107 段：长 90 米。根据嵌入的碑记，为嘉庆四年（1799 年）修葺。有砖文"停泥新城砖"。

第 108 段：这段通达角楼城台的马道修葺于 18 世纪。城墙顶端西侧有一块无字石碑。

显然，北城墙的最西段比其他城段修缮得更加频繁，这可能是因为这段城墙蜿蜒曲折，不如其他部分坚固耐久。它包含一小段16世纪的工程，略多一些的是17世纪的，不过主要的几大段还是18世纪至19世纪初的修缮。无论是从技术角度还是历史角度看，这段城墙都要比前一段（北墙两座城门之间的那一段）逊色一些，不过从自然之美的角度来欣赏，此处的吸引力远高于前者。为了完整地领略这段城墙及其周边城区的美景，你最好选择一个十月的晴朗清晨，登上德胜门的马道眺望。向西，可以看到不规则的蜿蜒的城墙，墙头草木丛生。墙脚下的道路被高大的椿树笼罩着，南行数步便是北海的延伸部分——"积水潭"，湖畔一棵棵垂柳舞动着柔嫩的枝叶。纵目远眺，越过开阔的空地，西山构成了熠熠发光的背景，特别是在夜间，当山顶覆盖上一层薄雪之时。空气是难以名状的清新，苍穹仿佛一口巨大的透明的玻璃钟罩，似乎只要用魔槌一敲，便可发出声响。

4．西城墙

西北城角之所以特殊，是由于两段城墙在此并未以直角相交。我们已经指出，北城墙向西南方向略有偏折，这个城角因此而成为一个钝角，西城墙实际上比东城墙短520米。角楼已毁，取代这座坚固的砖构建筑的是一座用于城市观测的小型木构建筑。城角与第一座城门——西直门之间，是一段不足300米的城墙，由若干小段的修补组成，衔接处极不平整，其中很多城段可以追溯到明代。我们对城墙上相连城段的简短说明，将能大致描述出它们的年代与基本特征，然而需要注意的是，我们的目的不是研究每一寸的城墙，而是对其重要的部分、独特的特征进行考察。城墙上的修补过多，且往往混杂于一处，不易分辨，故难以详查。通常来说，乾隆时期修筑的城墙最为精心、坚固，不过嘉庆和道光年间也修筑出不少优秀的工程。北城墙上常见的嘉靖、万历时期遗留下来的质地优良的明代城墙工程，在这里却极为罕见。但此处有几段年代更久远的城墙，只不过大都因风吹日晒而损毁严重了。因此，西城墙未经修葺之处，给人一种比北城墙更加古老的印象。同东城墙一样，它的厚度与收分均小于北城墙。

第1段：角楼城台，主要以明末常用的薄砖砌筑。马道及其毗连的城墙均修葺于乾隆时期，有砖文：工部监督桂及工部监督福。

第2、3段：两小段明初城墙，损毁严重。

第4段：长54米。根据碑记，城墙上部于嘉庆二年（1797年）修葺；下部有砖文：永定官窑造。

第5段：长15米。可能为明中期砌筑，无砖文。

第 6 段：长 30 米。似为明初所筑，无砖文。

第 7 段：长 24 米。筑于明中期或末期，无砖文。

第 8 段：长 18 米。筑于明初，无砖文。

第 9 段：长 22 米。明代修筑，后代有修葺。

第 10 段：长 26 米。年代与筑法同第 9 段。

第 11 段：长 24 米。年代与材料均同第 9 段。

第 12 段：长 11 米。筑于明初，无砖文。

第 13 段：长 20 米。可能为明中期修筑，无砖文。

第 14 段：西直门的两条马道由薄砖砌筑，所用城砖与明末使用的薄砖相同。马道后面的城墙与城楼处的城台均用较大的城砖，同样为明代修筑。

第 15 段：长 38 米。筑于明中期或末期，无砖文。

第 16 段：长 22 米。可能为 19 世纪中期修筑，用中型砖。

第 17 段：长 15 米。筑于 18 世纪末，用"停泥城砖"。

第 18 段：长 15 米。筑于明中期或末期，无砖文。

第 19 段：长 38 米。上部用薄砖（可能是崇祯时期的）砌成，下部用中型砖修葺。

第 20 段：长 20 米。筑于明初，无砖文。

第 21 段：长 15 米。似为明末工程，无砖文。

第 22 段：长 38 米。根据嵌入的石碑，为乾隆四年（1739 年）修葺，然而局部使用明代城砖，有砖文：嘉靖三十一年。

第 23 段：长 24 米。根据两块石碑记载，为道光二十一年（1841 年）修葺，城砖为乾隆时期的大型砖。

第 24 段：长 8 米。筑于 19 世纪初，有砖文：甲申年（1824 年）造。

第 25 段：长 26 米。筑于 19 世纪中期，有砖文："同治（1862–1874 年）万万岁"。

第 26 段：长 20 米。可能筑于 19 世纪，用中型砖，无砖文。

第 27、28 段：长 38 米。两段明末城墙，无砖文。

第 29 段：长 22 米。筑于明末，有砖文：万历十九年。

第 30 段：长 15 米。筑于明初，有砖文：成化十九年（1483 年）高唐州窑造。

第 31、32 段：长 26 米。两段明代城墙，经后代修葺。

第 33 段：长 30 米。使用瑞盛窑烧造的城砖重筑，石碑上的文字漫漶不清，可能为 19 世纪初的工程。

第 34 段：长 15 米。筑于明中期，有砖文：嘉靖十六年（1537 年）窑户刘钊造。

第 35 段：长 7 米。可能为 19 世纪初工程，有砖文：永和窑造停泥城砖。

第 36 段：长 15 米。嘉庆时期（1796-1820 年）修葺，有砖文：瑞盛窑造城砖、永定官窑造停泥细砖。

第 37 段：长 20 米。年代与材料均同第 36 段。

第 38 段：长 22 米。可能筑于 19 世纪初，用河盛窑烧造的城砖。

第 39 段：长 70 米。乾隆时期修葺，石碑上文字漫漶不清，包含砖文：辛巳年（1761 年）造。

第 40 段：长 11 米。筑于明末，有砖文：万历三十二年。

第 41 段：长 11 米。可能筑于 18 世纪末或 19 世纪初，有砖文：源泉窑新大城砖。

第 42 段：长 38 米。乾隆时期修葺，砖系东河窑烧造，亦有砖文：德顺窑造大停细砖。

第 43 段：长 38 米。可能筑于 19 世纪，用中型砖，无砖文。

第 44 段：长 38 米。根据嵌入的石碑，为乾隆二年（1737 年）修葺。

第 45 段：长 22 米。根据嵌入的石碑，为乾隆四十一年（1776 年）修葺。有砖文：工部监督萨。

第 46 段：马道保存状况良好，上方城墙损毁较多。根据碑文描述，为乾隆三十一年（1766 年）修葺。有砖文：内府官办裕成窑造。

第 47 段：长 22 米。年代与材料均同第 43 段。

第 48 段：长 19 米。筑于明末，有砖文：万历三十二年（1604 年）。

第 49 段：长 38 米。乾隆时期修葺，石碑文字不可辨识。有砖文：工部监督萨。

第 50 段：长 7 米。筑于明末。有砖文：万历三十二年窑户张九志造。

第 51 段：长 22 米。筑于明中期，有砖文：嘉靖十六年窑户陈举造及嘉靖十六年（1537 年）窑户姜同造。

第 52 段：长 7 米。一小段经各代修葺的城墙。

第 53 段：长 70 米。筑于明末，砖上年款有万历三十年、三十一年、三十二年。底部有几处经后代修葺。

第 54 段：长 50 米。筑于明中期，无砖文。底部有三段不同的城段，应为乾隆时期修葺。

第 55 段：长 40 米。上部用明代薄砖重筑，下部用多种城砖修葺。

第 56、57 段：长 80 米。两段保存相对较好的明代城墙。用大型砖，无砖文。

第 58 段：长 200 米。明末用薄砖砌成，所用砖为崇祯时期的样式。

第 59 段：长 15 米。根据石碑记载，为嘉庆二十年（1815 年）修葺。

第60段：长10米。乾隆时期修葺，有砖文：东河窑造停泥新城砖、工部监督桂。

第61段：长50米。该段通达平则门，明显是乾隆时期修葺的。有砖文：广盛窑大城砖。城台上的城砖有砖文：停泥城砖、工部监督桂。南侧的马道上方有一块乾隆二十七年（1762年）的石碑。

西城墙的北面半段，尽管自15世纪末至19世纪中期经历了不断的修补，但很多城段都相当完整，不仅包括带有女儿墙的城墙，还包括城墙附近的三合土人行便道和架设有大石板的小城壕。城壕两岸不远处排列着大槐树，城墙顶部长有高大的枣树和椿树，砖面因而被拱起，甚至断裂。整体来说，西城墙北半段比与之对应的东城墙北段显得更古老，墙上也没有那么多的乾隆或后期修缮的痕迹。

从平则门向南行不久，我们便感到顺沿城墙漫步不那么令人愉悦了：眼前的城区人口众多，随之而来的必然是更多的垃圾、更臭的地方、更多的夜间清洁工、更多的街头流浪儿、更多乞丐、更多游手好闲的人，更多的猪、狗，更不用说很多其他小动物。城北的宁静与荒凉在平则门戛然而止，忽然便转换成喧闹而拥挤的、半欧化的商业中心地带。平则门以南的城墙似乎为明末重筑。

第63、64、65段：120米。三段城墙，连接完好，均使用崇祯年间（1628–1643年）流行的黑色薄砖砌成。无砖文。

第66段：长56米。可能为清初修建，用中型砖，无砖文。

第67段：长19米。年代、材料均与第63–65段相同。

第68段：长45米。年代、材料与第66段相同。

第69段：长22米。筑于明中期（可能为嘉靖时期），无砖文。

第70段：长15米。明末筑成，有砖文：万历三十二年。

第71段：长45米。筑于明中期，有砖文：嘉靖二十九年（1550年）窑户陆造及嘉靖二十四年（1545年）造。

第72段：长25米。与前段类似。

第73、74段：长50米。两段均以中型砖砌筑而成，可能为清初所砌，无砖文。（参见第66段）

第75段：长20米。根据碑记记载，为乾隆三十年修葺，但局部使用老城砖，上有砖文：万历三十年窑户孙宝造。

第76段：长38米。筑于明中期（可能为嘉靖时期），无砖文。

第77段：平则门南面的第一条马道，筑于明代，由三部分构成：第一段系用嘉靖二十九年的城砖；第二段系用正德三年（1508年）的城砖；第三段（北京城墙中年代最早的城段之一）系用成化年间（1465-1487年）的城砖。

第78段：长80米。筑于明中期，有砖文：嘉靖三十一年（1552年）窑户张钦造。

第79段：长175米。筑于明末。砖文上记有万历二十三年、二十九年和三十二年的诸多窑户姓名。

第80段：根据嵌入的碑记，这是一大段（近100米）乾隆二十八年（1763年）修葺的城墙。

第81段：长40米。可能为清初修葺，用中型砖，无砖文。

第82段：长10米。筑于明末，城砖上有年款：万历三十二、三十三年。

第83段：长50米。筑于明中期，砖文上记有嘉靖三十一年、三十三年、三十六年及三十九年（1552-1560年）的诸多窑户姓名。

第84段：一小段用中型砖砌筑的城墙，可能为清初所筑。

第85段：长60米。根据嵌入的碑记，为乾隆三十二年（1767年）修葺。有砖文：工部监督永。

第86段：一小段由嘉靖二十四年（1545年）和嘉靖二十七年（1548年）的城砖砌筑而成的明代城墙。

第87段：一段用乾隆辛巳年（1761年）和壬午年（1762年）城砖修葺的城墙。

第88段：平则门与城隅之间的第二条马道，主要筑于明朝不同时期：马道北端及所连的城墙用正德二年（1507年）、嘉靖二十二年与二十三年（1543-1544年）的城砖。马道的中段与南端大部分重修于明末或之后不久，用薄砖。

第89段：长8米。筑于明末，有砖文：万历三十二年。

第90段：长15米。筑于明中期，无砖文。

第91段：根据嵌入的石碑，为乾隆三十年（1765年）修葺。砖文写明为甲午年（1754年）由工顺窑烧造。

第92段：长22米。筑于明初，有砖文：成化十九年（1483年）。

第93段：一小段18世纪末或19世纪初修葺的城墙。上有砖文：大停细砖，嘉庆二年（1797年）。

第94段：一大段（60-70米）明初城墙。城砖损毁严重，无砖文。

第95段：一段明中期的城墙，用嘉靖三十二年（1553年）窑户林永寿烧造的砖，此外还有嘉靖二十二年（1543年）窑户张钦所造城砖，亦有嘉靖二十六年（1547年）永义兴窑户王瑞烧造的城砖。

第96段：一小段可能为明末筑成的城墙，无砖文。

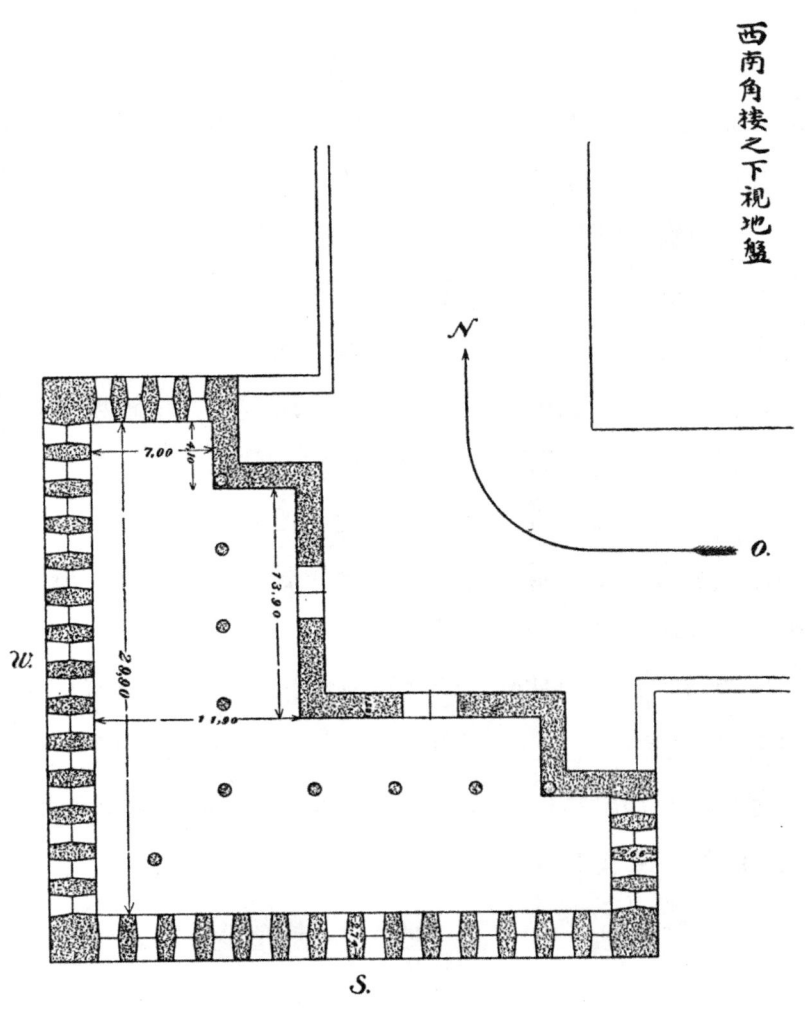

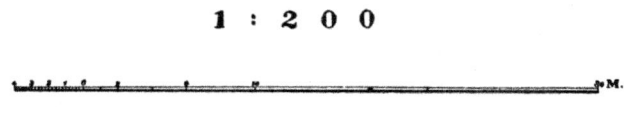

图 5 西南角楼平面

第 97 段：一小段（10–12 米）明中期城墙，有砖文：嘉靖十六年（1537 年）。

第 98 段：根据碑记，这一小段城墙于乾隆十九年修葺。有砖文：丙申年（1776 年）。

第 99 段：非常短的一段，用万历三十二年城砖。

第 100 段：一小段乾隆统治初期修葺的城墙，砖系兴泰窑烧造。

第 101 段：一小段用嘉靖二十六年城砖的明中期城墙。

第 102 段：西南城角的北缘似乎为乾隆时期修葺，但使用大量更早的城砖，有些砖文上有嘉靖二十六年、嘉靖三十二年的年款。无疑，使用前代城砖的情况不在少数，砖文上的年代不能代表这段城墙的确切修筑时间，不过倒是提供了可靠的上限年代。

西城墙的南段比北段更加协调统一。城墙从开阔的平地上拔地而起，高大而陡峭，给人留下相当雄伟的印象。城墙表面相对平滑，不像北城墙那样可以攀援而上。角楼至今保存完好，唯古老的琉璃瓦顶缺失，大部分竟然为瓦楞铁所替代！使这座堡垒样式的巨大角楼从正面看上去呆板而乏味，幸好从侧面观察时，该建筑分四个层次逐层升高，构成了一幅生动的景观。北京城墙上的角楼，仅有南城墙的两座留存至今，它们均采用与主城门箭楼相同的样式，不同之处在于城角的城台之上有两个长长的立面。在内侧一面，建筑各部分以越来越小的变化逐层下降，进而逐渐伸出城墙。

毗邻南城隅的城西地带是一块非常幽静而独立的区域。主要建筑是一座古老的满族王府——"老七爷庑"，后被废弃。府墙之外是著名的"太平湖"，如今则更像是一处池塘而非湖，不过湖上仍有几只肥鸭游嬉，岸边的古柳投出大片树荫。城市距此处仿佛遥不可及，这里无人居住亦无人经过，空气中飘荡着凄凉与没落王朝的旧梦。

五、内城城墙的外侧壁

　　总体来说，北京城墙的外侧壁较其内侧壁在外观上更加整齐划一和平整。由于外壁对于城防更为重要（这毕竟是这类建筑物的主要功能），历代皇帝与官员不断对它修缮。直到近20年，城墙外侧壁的一些部位开始损毁，特别是在西墙，可以发现由于表面砖层渐渐剥落而形成的大洞。诚然，即使是这些部位，其损坏程度也不及内侧壁最糟糕的地方。其中主要原因之一，无疑是雨水总是从内侧排出，不经过外侧壁。再者，外侧壁比内侧要陡直得多，灌木和树木不像我们在南城墙和东城墙内侧看到的那样茂盛。

　　必须承认的是，城墙外侧壁在美观和历史价值方面都不及内侧壁，但作为建筑文物却更引人注目，更饶有趣味。城墙外侧壁更高耸、陡峭，墙脚下的地面也不像城墙内侧常见的那样隆起，城墙或多或少向护城河倾斜，为高耸的城墙平添了雄浑的气势。遗憾的是，在城墙与护城河之间，沿着铁路线常常建满了各种各样肮脏的屋舍、煤棚、仓库和作坊，破坏了城墙的景观，东面与南面的城墙外尤为严重。

　　对于建筑外观来说，最为重要的是方形城台（或称墩台），它们间隔均匀，突出于城墙之外。无论从哪个角度来看，墩台都使城墙显得格外雄劲和庄严。墩台的视觉效果总是非常显著，特别是当你伫立在城门楼上眺望城墙时，墩台之间的间隔渐次减小，直到除却城门楼和城门，所有建筑都变得模糊。旧时，墩台上曾有过铺舍、储存火药的小仓房，但这些建筑现在都已被毁，仅存几座布局分散的供城门守卫使用的小砖房。甚至在某些城墙段落上，连供射击用的城垛都已损毁，即便不说是使得城墙掉了脑袋，也至少是不再完整。

　　之前的章节已经提到墩台的规制及其布列。它们的平面基本为方形，边长大致与城墙等宽。除了这些普通的墩台外，还有一些较大的墩台，不仅建于城角和城门处，城墙内侧登城马道之上亦有。显然，在马道顶部设置这种宽阔的平台很有必要，因为马道不仅可以供人步行、骑马登城，还可供马车运送枪炮、弹药。南城墙上有六条这样的马道和六座较大的墩台，东城墙上有四座，而西、北城墙上仅有三座。同样值得注意的是，这些大型墩台亦不尽相同，大小也不统一，特别是北城墙上的墩台，与其他墩台相比差异明显，因为整面北墙为后世所筑。

我们对外侧壁的说明会比内侧壁更为简短。通过在城门之间或两城角之间数墩台的简单方法，就能够指出哪些地方有石碑或者其他砖文。仅在涉及这些碑记依附的墩台或墩台之间的城墙时，才简单叙述这些大量碑记的所在位置。遗憾的是，没有哪块石碑是早于乾隆年间的，而且只有两三块属于乾隆之后的嘉庆年间。其他的修缮将依据砖作的特征去推断，不过不会再辨读大量的砖文了。实际上，因为城墙前面都建有房屋，大段大段的城墙都无法靠近。尽管如此，鉴于我们已经对不同朝代的建筑及其基本工艺风格有所了解，大部分城砖的年代即使从远处也是可以辨认的。

1. 东城墙

从东南城角开始，最先遇到的是城墙外侧壁最古老的一段。东城墙上最初6座墩台，包括为观象台马道配置的墩台，残破不堪的城砖表明这段城墙可能为15世纪末期所筑。第1座墩台仅北侧壁在近代进行过修缮。前文曾提及，同段城墙的内侧壁同样为早期样貌，没有清代修缮的痕迹。但当我们刚一走过第6座墩台，乾隆时期的修葺工程便赫然出现。在第6与第7座墩台之间的城墙上嵌有一块无字石碑，不过一看就是常见的乾隆时期风格。第7座墩台经过修缮，但无碑记。第7座墩台毗连的城墙得到过修缮，根据石碑记载，为乾隆三十三年重修。

第8座墩台，根据碑文记载，为乾隆四十六年重建。

第9座墩台经翻修，石碑文字无法辩读，与之毗连的墙壁亦经翻修。

第10座墩台于乾隆三十六年修缮，与之毗连的墙壁亦然。

第11座墩台一部分老旧，另一部分连同毗连的墙壁一道进行过修缮，根据墙上嵌入的石碑记载，为乾隆三十一年。

第12座墩台于乾隆三十六年修缮，与之毗连的墙壁亦然。

第13座墩台于乾隆三十六年修缮。

第14座墩台于乾隆三十一年（？）修缮，与之毗连的墙壁为乾隆三十六年修缮。

第15座墩台于乾隆三十六年修缮，与之毗连的墙壁为同年所修。

第16座墩台于乾隆三十六年修缮，与之毗连的墙壁亦然。

第17座墩台及其毗连的城墙均进行过修缮，尽管上面没有任何碑文记载。

第18座墩台于乾隆三十一年修缮，根据碑文记载，与之毗连的墙壁为同年所修。

第19座墩台于乾隆三十六年修缮，与之毗连的墙壁可能修于乾隆三十七年（碑文几乎无法辨认）。

第 20 座墩台于乾隆三十七年（？）修缮，与之毗连的墙壁有块类似的石碑。

第 21 座墩台为翻新的，不过没有任何碑记，毗邻的墙壁亦然。

第 22 座墩台同样为翻新的，不过没有任何碑记。

第 23 座墩台在修建齐化门小火车站时拆毁。根据齐化门城台转角处的石碑所记，毗连的城墙于乾隆三十一年翻修。

齐化门以北的第 1 座墩台同样被拆毁。

第 2 座墩台于乾隆十八年修缮，毗连的墙壁较老旧，残损严重，杂木丛生。

第 3 座墩台于乾隆十八年修缮，与之毗连的墙壁仅翻新了一半，另一半依然老旧。

第 4 座墩台于乾隆三十六年修缮，与之毗连的墙壁更老旧，不过多处已得到修补。

第 5 座墩台修缮过，不过没有任何石碑记载，与之毗连的墙壁局部得到修缮，根据嵌入的石碑记载，为乾隆三十六年。

第 6 座墩台古旧，多处砖作已进行修补，与之毗连的墙壁有相似特征。

第 7 座墩台古旧，第 8 座与第 9 座墩台及其毗连的城墙亦然。

第 10 座墩台于乾隆三十二年修缮，毗连城墙老旧，仅最北端与第 11 座墩台于乾隆三十二年进行过修缮，毗连的城壁亦已修缮。

第 12 座墩台于乾隆二十八年修缮，与之毗连的城壁为乾隆三十一年所修。

第 13 座墩台古旧，保存较好，与之毗连的城壁于乾隆三十六年修缮。

第 14 座墩台只有南侧壁于乾隆四十九年进行过修缮，与之毗连的城壁于乾隆三十六年修缮。

第 15 座墩台翻修过，不过没有任何碑记，与之毗连的城壁于乾隆三十一年修缮。

第 16 座墩台于乾隆三十一年修缮，与之毗连的城壁亦已翻修。

第 17 座墩台翻修过，不过没有任何碑记，与之毗连的城壁局部为乾隆二十八年所修。城墙连接到东直门。城门上的石碑无文字。城门北侧壁于乾隆三十二年修缮。

东直门以北的第 1 座墩台于乾隆三十一年修缮，毗连城壁为乾隆三十六年所修。

第 2 座墩台修缮于乾隆三十年，与之毗连的城壁则为乾隆三十一年所修。

第 3 座墩台翻新过，但碑文无法辨认，与之毗连的城壁年代稍早。

第 4 座墩台于乾隆三十年修缮。

第 5 座墩台于乾隆三十一年修缮，与之毗连的城壁亦然。

第 6 座墩台古旧，不过保存较好，与之毗连的城壁于乾隆五十一年修缮。

第 7 座墩台，因修建环城铁路时由此穿过，故遭拆毁，与之毗连的城壁于乾隆三十一年修缮。

东北城角的大型墩台使用深色薄砖精心砌筑，此种城砖在明末使用广泛。

以上这些考察无疑表明，东城墙只有极少段落为乾隆之前所修，现存的这段城墙墙壁大部分都是乾隆三十年至三十六年（1765–1771年）所修。这一时期的工程质量上乘，应当比后世的修缮保存更长久。各个墩台及其邻壁的断代，可以通过砖文得以印证，然而对我们来说，那些极为枯燥的记录，对城墙历史或各城段断代没有提供更多重要信息，多费笔墨去引用似乎实无必要。

倘使你取道城墙和护城河之间铁道的斜坡前行，那么沿着东城墙走过的路程是十分轻松且令人愉悦的。但是靠近城根走，却满是新近栽种的洋槐与刺槐，步行颇受干扰。在东城墙的南半段，观象台和齐化门之间，依然留存着一些皇家粮仓，它们是几座简朴的低矮房屋，几乎都建于墩台之间，不过这些历史上的"太平仓"，现在大都被不太简朴、有点扎眼的火药库和兵营所取代。愈向北走，像运河一般的护城河变得愈发宽阔而优美。齐化门与东直门之间，河岸遍栽垂柳，成群的白鸭游弋而过。时而有作为大型渡船的方型平底船缓缓撑过混浊的水面，船上用四根竿子搭起遮阳棚，不过同上代人的时代相比，这里的交通不再那么重要了，那时，北京的粮食和其他物资都是经由这条运河从北边和东边运送而来的。然而，这里依然是城墙附近最为风景如画的地点之一，从图版中东直门附近的照片可以看到这一点。

2. 北城墙

北城墙比其他三面城墙上的墩台都要少，规模却更大。墩台的间距从200米到350米不等，而其他三面城墙墩台的平均间距不超过90米，有些仅为65或70米。靠近东北城角处，也就是我们出发的地方，墩台的间距最短，城墙样貌也最规整。

城角与第1座墩台之间的这段城墙，局部为乾隆五十六年所修，第1座墩台的一部分亦然。第2、3、4、5座墩台及其台间的城壁，明显为明代中期所修，砖作损毁严重，墙体多处冒出树丛、灌木，唯一翻修过的部分是城垛。

第6座墩台于乾隆四十七年修缮，与之毗连的城壁年代更早。

第7座城台年代较早，为明代所筑，与之毗连的城壁连通安定门，城壁为乾隆二十八年修缮。

第8座墩台及其毗连的城墙（安定门以西）为明代旧作，已严重残损。

第8和第9座墩台之间的城壁分两部分修缮，墙壁上有两块石碑，年代分别为乾隆四十二年和乾隆五十一年。

第 9 座墩台于乾隆五十一年修缮。第 10、11 和 12 座墩台及其之间的城墙大都古旧，不过墙上面有多处是后世修补。第 12 和 13 座墩台间的城壁，分三部分翻修，均为乾隆五十一年，墙上三块石碑年代相同。

第 13 座墩台于乾隆四十七年翻修。该墩台与德胜门之间的城墙损毁严重，明显不晚于明中期，城门楼下的城台亦然，仅拐角处翻修过。

德胜门以西的城墙于乾隆三十七年修缮。

第 14 座墩台部分翻修过，石碑文字已不可辨认。与之毗连的城壁分三部分修缮：两处碑记显示为乾隆五十二年，第三部分的碑文不可辨。

第 15 座墩台的修缮年代明显早于乾隆年间，与之毗连的城墙呈长长的曲线，为乾隆五十一年修缮。

第 16 座墩台及其毗连的城墙均年代较早。

第 17 座墩台两面均修缮于乾隆四十八年。蜿蜒的城墙亦经翻修过，但石碑上没有日期。

第 18 座墩台及其相连的城墙翻修过，根据上面的三块石碑记载，分别修于乾隆四十七年、乾隆五十一年和乾隆五十六年。

第 19 座墩台年代较早，不过与之相连通往城角的城墙为乾隆五十六年所修。

城角处的墩台用明代薄砖精心修筑。

概括来说，北城墙的外侧壁是所有城墙中最引人注目、最雄伟的一段。北城墙自始至终比另外三面城墙的规模更为宏大，墩台更宽厚，城垛更高，墙体本身也更有气势。城砖的特征同样相当古老，被沙尘暴染黑，由于年久而残损，墙壁多处冒出树丛、灌木。

靠近城墙的地方栽种有一些小树，一条铁轨铺设于护城河内侧，不过火车不多，交通量总体来说不大，只是到了两座城门处，才看到主路两侧均有商铺。这里的乡村荒凉、单调，一片开阔的沙地上少有房子以及可以阻挡沙尘的植被，一旦起风，霎时间灰尘漫天。然而也正是这块土地，城墙以北 5 里的范围，曾经是蒙古帝国的首都——汗八里的一部分。

3．西城墙

我们从西北城角继续往南行进。虽然这段城墙比另外三座都要短，却还建有 44 座墩台，其中大多数重建于乾隆后期。城角与第 1 座墩台之间的城壁已修缮，上面有石碑，但无铭文。

第 1 座墩台年代古老，为明中期所筑，与之毗连的城壁为乾隆五十年所修。

第 2 座墩台年代古老，与之毗连的城壁亦然，除了靠近西直门的部分为 1895 年所修。

第 3 座墩台较为古旧，明显为明代所筑。

第 4 座墩台于乾隆四十七年修缮，与之毗连的城壁可能是同时期所修。

第 5 座墩台修缮过，墙上有石碑，但碑文漫漶。与之毗连的城壁为乾隆四十七年所修。

第 6 座墩台及其毗连的城壁进行过修缮，上面的石碑无碑文。

第 7 座墩台相当古旧，残损严重。与之毗连的城壁分两段进行了修缮，有石碑，无铭文。

第 8 座墩台于乾隆四十六年修缮，与之毗连的城壁古老而衰败。几段垛墙已坍塌。

第 9 座墩台于乾隆五十二年修缮，与之毗连的城壁局部进行过修缮。

第 10 座墩台上部进行过修缮，下部老旧，与之毗连的城壁有多处修补，保存状况较差。

第 11 座墩台的两侧均于乾隆四十七年进行过翻修（但中间部分没有翻修）。

第 12 座墩台较老旧，保存状况较差。

第 13 座墩台多处于乾隆二十九年修缮，毗连的城壁亦然。

第 14 座墩台分几段进行修葺，其中一段的石碑为乾隆四十七年。

第 15 座城台主要为乾隆五十二年所修，与之衔接的中间部分有年代更早的修复。

第 16 座墩台北侧壁进行过修缮，但无石碑，与之毗连的城壁保存较差，无城垛。

第 17 座墩台部分进行过修缮，但城垛已残破，与之毗连的城壁大多经翻修，有碑记，但文字已不可辨。

平则门的城台较老旧，其南侧壁于乾隆五十二年进行过翻修。

平则门以南的第 1、2、3 座墩台及其毗连的城墙年代古老，均为明中期所筑。

第 4 座墩台可能在光绪时期翻修过，但无任何碑文记载，与之毗连的城壁为乾隆五十二年所修。

第 5 座墩台的两侧均修缮过，北侧壁有石碑，但无碑文。与之毗连的城壁有一半为嘉庆四年所修，其余一半年代古老。

第 6、7 座墩台为明代所筑。第 7、8 座城台之间的城壁局部于乾隆三十九年翻修。

第 8 座墩台规模较大，使用明代薄砖筑造，目前已年久失修。与之毗连的城壁于乾隆四十六年修缮。

第 9 座墩台整体较古老，不过北角处于乾隆四十六年进行过修缮。

第 10 座墩台年代较早，不过与之毗连的城壁为乾隆三十七年修缮。

第 11 座墩台部分经翻修，但无石碑。

第 12 座墩台部分经翻修，但石碑上的文字已不可辨。第 13、14、15 座墩台及其与之毗连的城壁均古旧。最后一段的城壁有些大城砖已剥落，之后一段，即第 15、16 座墩台之间的城壁为嘉庆二年所修。

第 16 座墩台年代较早，与之毗连的城壁分两部分进行过修缮，碑文显示分别为乾隆五十一年和嘉庆二年。

第 17 座墩台于乾隆四十七年所修，与之毗连的城壁保存现状极差，表面砖层大片大片地剥落。

第 18 座墩台整体较为古老，修缮的状况不佳，城垛亦残破。北面经翻修，嵌入的石碑上无碑文。

随后的四座墩台：即第 19 至第 22 座年代古老，很可能为明中期所筑，略经修缮。

第 23 座墩台于乾隆三十六年修缮，与之毗连的城壁年代较早。

第 24 座墩台年代较早。附近有一座大型城台，台上为一座方楼，是外城城墙与主城墙的衔接处。根据嵌入的石碑，该城台为乾隆四十九年修缮。

西城墙上修缮部分的一般分布情况，与东城墙的情况十分相似。包含 6 座墩台的最南段是最古老、变化最少的一段（恰如东城墙的最南段）。这段城墙似乎比其北面的部分修筑得更加坚固，大抵是由于它新建于 15 世纪，而其余部分则建造在元代土墙的基础之上。西城墙上 18 世纪的修缮部分不如东城墙那般多，不过在现存城墙中占绝大部分，修缮年代一般略晚，为乾隆四十七至乾隆五十二年，有些甚至是嘉庆二年的。凡未经过这种精心修整的地方，墙表砖层的保存状况比内城四面城墙的其他部分更差，砖面大片剥落，如果不采取任何补救措施，这种趋势无疑将继续恶化。

4．南城墙

南城墙外侧壁的建筑形制和规模，同我们在东、西城墙所见到的一样，在所有城墙中，只有南墙受到妥善的保护，因而修缮较少。它没有成为首都的外城墙，只是作为外城与内城之间的城中界墙。再者，应当记住的是，较其他立面，中国北方城市或建筑的南立面往往较少遭受雨水和风暴的侵袭。因此，南城墙外侧壁相比其他城墙，保留下更多的明代城壁。乾隆时期修缮的城墙同早期城墙相比要短很多，仅有的 4 块纪年石碑，年代为 18 世纪，而后期较为重要的修缮，也只不过有两三处。

从西南城角到顺治门的全部 13 座墩台似乎都较为古老，没有发现记载后世修缮的石碑。第 4、5 座墩台之间的城墙顶部，可以看到一小块汉白玉浮雕，图案为莲花，立于底座之上，周围饰有云纹。在同一段城墙，再往东，还有 4 块类似的浮雕，纹饰略有差别，不过，原有的应当是一组 8 块，构成一整套"八宝"。这种吉祥的图案是佛寺中常见的象征性装饰，也是佛教徒与喇嘛教徒的随身饰物。[1] 它们可能是为表示对保护神的虔敬而被安放于城墙上，大抵与乾隆时期喇嘛教的复兴有关。

顺治门与前门之间有 19 座墩台，多为明代修筑。根据嵌入的石碑，第 9、10 座墩台之间的城壁为嘉庆四年修缮。然而，不太可能对这一段城墙进行更详尽的观察，因为靠近城根密布着大型煤棚和诸如此类的障碍物。靠近前门的地方是京汉铁路车站的大片建筑，前门另一面则是更大的京沈铁路车站，它占据了前门与水关之间的整个地面。在这个城墙上新开辟的通道东侧，墙上有一块石碑，根据碑文，城墙修缮于乾隆五十一年。前门与哈达门之间仍有 15 座墩台，（水关西面的）一座已荡然无存，其余的进行过不同程度的修缮，然而大多数看起来还是十分古旧。

哈达门以东，沿着城墙走下去，行程开始变得更加轻松愉快，铁道斜坡与城墙之间没有建筑，只有茂密生长的小树。第一座墩台外观颇新，显然是光绪年间所修。与之毗连的城壁古旧，残损严重。

第 2 至第 9 座墩台间的城墙外侧壁有许多微小的修缮痕迹，例如，墩台的转角或城垛完全是翻新过的，而主体部分还是明代的。

第 10 座墩台，根据嵌入的石碑，为乾隆四十六年所修。

第 11 座墩台，位于东便门车站，大部分修葺一新。为给环城铁路开辟道路，拆毁了最后一座墩台，穿过铁路通道，人们可以看到城墙内侧有一块石碑，记载着城角这段为乾隆五十四年所修。

与其他几面城墙相比，要确知南墙外侧壁城砖的情况更加困难，因为墙脚下的空地几乎都盖上了房屋，有车站、火药库以及铁路干线的工厂，前门以西还有北京最大的煤市。显然，这些设施与古城墙极不协调。这些设施意味着现代因素的渗入，在这样的新时代，城墙更像是一种障碍，而非防御设施。

总体来说，必须承认的是，铁路及其各类附属建筑对北京城墙和城门风格与美感所起的破坏作用，比起维护保养这些珍贵文物时的忽视或草率的态度更为有害。

---

[1] 关于浮雕的解释以及原有数量的说法由钢和泰男爵（Baron Stael van Holstein）（即 Baron Alexander von Staël-Holstein，亚历山大·凡·斯坦因－候斯泰因，爱沙尼亚（当时还属于俄国）梵文学者，译者注）在北京热情提供。——作者注

六、外城的城墙

北京，作为中国伟大的首都，不仅仅有一座住着满族人或鞑靼人的内城，我们在前两章已对它进行过介绍。北京还包括一座"外城"，或将其称为"汉人城"，它与主城南城墙相接。这一区域的俗称让我们记起这样的历史：满族征服者将大部分当地人口从主城赶到郊区，尤其是已被城墙包围的南郊。由于该地区的地理位置与形状像是主城上的一顶帽子，于是汉人称之为"外城"或"帽子城"。

京城的外城地区，大体上由喧闹的集市、乡村的田野和庞大的寺庙群组成。其中，仅北半部分看上去像城市，三条主要街道从内城的三座南城门笔直地向南延伸出去，在这三条主路之间的街区是繁荣的现代商业中心，人群熙熙攘攘，喧闹无比。

但稍稍向南走远一点，在天坛与先农坛建筑群之间，或者朝东、西两边的城墙再走一段，就能够从繁闹的商业城市进入到车马稀少、安静清幽的乡村，越向西南或东南方向走，房屋越稀少，旷野也越多。外城最多有三分之一的土地建有房屋，而很多房屋又是极不显眼的那种。这不禁让人质疑为什么要把南城墙建在这么远的地方？唯一合理的解释似乎是：在规划设计城墙时，认为有必要将天坛与先农坛的神圣祭祀区囊括在城墙之内。最初想要在内城东、西城墙外再建一道城墙，将东郊、西郊像南郊外城那样包裹进来，因此外城的东、西城墙建在了现在的位置上。但这个工程未能完成，因此外城的城墙仅仅在主城东南、西南两城角与之相接，并以直角形状包裹住内城城角。我们可以在《顺天府志》（我们在内城城墙叙述中相当广泛地引用到该书中的内容）中了解到最初是如何规划这项包围内城的外城城墙的大工程，皇帝如何颁布谕旨实施以及最终如何由于缺乏资金而放弃该计划。尽管其测量数据并不准确，但这段叙述是对外城城墙最完整的记录了，因此我们在这里加以引用。

描述完内城城墙与城门之后，该书又有以下陈述：

> 嘉靖二十一年（1542年），掌都察院毛伯温等言宜筑外城。二十九年（1550年），

命筑正阳、崇文、宣武三关厢外城，既而停止。[1]

继这个简短的说明后，下面补充道："（嘉靖）三十二年（1553年），给事中朱伯辰言：城外居民繁伙，不宜无以圉之。臣尝履行四郊，咸有土城故址，环绕如规，周可百二十余里（？）。若仍其旧贯，增卑补薄，培缺续断，可事半而功倍。乃命相度兴工。闰月丙辰，兵部尚书聂豹等上言：臣等……相度京城外，四面宜筑外城，约七十余里。自正阳门外马道口起，经天坛南墙外，及李兴、王金箔等园地，至荫水庵墙东止，约计九里。转北，经神木厂（神之木场院）、獐鹿房、小窑口等处，斜接土城旧广禧门基止，约计一十八里（在东面）。自广禧门起，转北而西至土城小西门旧基，约计一十九里（在北面）。自小西门起，经三虎桥（三只老虎之桥）村东、马家庙等处，接土城旧基，包过彰义门，至西南，直对新堡北墙止，约计一十五里。自西南旧土城转东，由新堡及黑窑厂，经神祇坛（神之圣坛，今名先农坛）南墙外，至正阳门外西马道口止，约计九里。大约南一面计一十八里，东一面计一十七里……。周围共计七十余里。内有旧址堪因者约二十二里，无旧址应新筑者约四十八里。其规制，臣等议得：外城墙基应厚二丈，收顶一丈二尺、高一丈八尺。上用砖为腰，墙基应垛口五尺，共高二丈三尺。城外取土筑城，因以为濠。"[2]

根据以上记载，外城墙最初规划的规模很宏大。如果上述记载的数据是准确的，最初的设计比现在的南城墙（仅长约13里）还要朝东、西方向各拓展3里，其西城墙将会与金中都古城墙相接。原计划北城墙沿用元大都城墙，但其西北角要被抹成钝角。因此外城与主城城墙之间的距离，在南、北两边约为5里，在东、西两边约为4里。然而由于计划沿用了原有的前朝城墙做基础，所以城墙最终的形状很可能会非常不规则。又由于上述地名多已不存，加之中国的"里"是很有弹性的长度单位，因此很难精准勾画出这一城墙扩建工程的轨迹。但显而易见的是，这个规划非常大胆。如果完全按照该方案实施，京城将会由三个同心城构成，也就是说，以紫禁城为中心，外面城郭层层环绕。后来证明这个规划太大了，并且需要耗费过多的帝国国库资金。《顺天府志》记载了该计划是如何被缩减的：

乙丑（1565年），建京师外城兴工，遣成国公朱希忠告太庙……。四月，上（嘉靖）又虑工费重大，成功不易，以问嵩等。嵩等乃自诣工所视之，还言宜先筑南面，俟财力裕时再因地计度以成四面之制。所以南面横阔凡二十里，今既止筑一面，第用十二三里

---

[1] 参见《光绪顺天府志一·京师志一》。

[2] 参见《光绪顺天府志一·京师志一》。

便当收结，庶不虚费财力。令拟将见筑正南一面城基东折转北，接城东南角，西折转北，接城西南角，并力坚筑，可以刻期完报。其东西北三面候再计度以闻报允。重城包京城南一面，转抱东西角楼止，长二十八里。为七门。[1]

我们注意到，在最后一段中，外城墙的长度与前段引文不一致。前文说 18–19 里长，现在又说四面城墙原规划各 20 里长，因此城墙周长为 80 里，而不是 73 或 74 里。较大的城墙长度与前文所述的城墙位置更为吻合（如果 1 里等同 640 米）。

似乎在当时，即嘉靖末年，南城墙建成为现在的长度，约 13 里，并且，从南城墙的两端向北延伸，在东、西两面还建造了城墙，这些都表明了原先的宏大计划已然被缩减。当时（1565 年），仅仅在外城城墙的端部修建了垂直的短墙，将它与主城城墙相连，从而完成了被缩减后的工程。连接部分的城墙在西面不足 1 里，在东面约 1 里半。因此外城城墙构成了主城的方帽子，恰如汉人称呼的"帽子城"。目前城墙总长度略大于 27 里，也正好与上述引文大致相同。

城墙的高度与宽度，据记载为："高二丈，垛口四尺；基厚二丈，顶收一丈四尺。"[2]

这些测量均不十分精确，例如，很明显城墙高度与城基厚度从来不会相同。实际上很多地方的其后测量显示，城基的厚度几乎是城墙高度的两倍。当然，与主城城墙一样，外城城墙的实际高度不可能在所有地方都一样，三边城墙的厚度也不一致，但与高度差异相比，厚度变化较少。根据对 3、4 个测量数据的取样，基本上能够推测出城墙的大致规制：

北侧短墙靠近东北角的地方：城墙外侧高 7.15 米（约 26 尺），内侧高 5.80 米（20 尺）。顶宽 10.40 米（36 尺），基厚 13.30 米（47 尺）。外侧雉堞高 1.72 米，内侧女儿墙高 1 米。接近东南角的东城墙：外侧高 5.80 米（20 尺），内侧高度相同。顶宽 10.30 米，基厚 12.40 米。各处雉堞与女儿墙的高度大致相同。

南城墙接近东端的位置：外侧高 5.80 米，内侧高 5.05 米。顶宽 9.82 米，基厚 12.20 米。

正中门（永定门）附近的南城墙：外侧高 6.18 米，内侧高 5.62 米。顶宽 9.90 米，基厚 11.80 米。

西城墙的规制大致与东城墙相同。

高度测量仅从城基边缘开始算起，北侧城基大多可见，但其他地方的城基，部分或全部被沙土掩埋。城基测量的数据受地面高度变化的影响不大。

---

[1] 参见《光绪顺天府志一·京师志一》。

[2] 参见《光绪顺天府志一·京师志一》。

根据《顺天府志》记载，东、西、南三面城墙的平均高度约为 20 尺，但是长度较短的北面城墙却要高得多。

城基的厚度在 41—47 尺之间，顶宽在 34—36 尺之间。如果不是排印错误的话，很难解释文献中所记载的厚度与宽度的数据值（20 尺与 14 尺）。

据记载，城墙外侧壁的城垛总数为 20772 个，"射击孔"或豁口的总数为 12602 个，这个数目大致是正确的，但是我们没有核对，当然我们也没有必要去核对。

据记载，城墙竣工于万历四十三年（1615 年）六月，墙土取自护城河，但当时护城河还有待修整，护城河是五年后才完成的。史书中这样记载："天启元年（1621 年）十月，给事中魏大中报京城濬濠工竣……崇祯己卯（1639 年）二月，内监曹化淳议京城外开河以通漕粮。自是年三月一九日起，至辛巳六月，所开河自土城广渠门（在北面）起至大通桥……共用班军二十三万二千余名，五城两县募夫二万九百余名。兵部侍郎吴姓视工以为劳费，无益且伤地脉，抗疏上之。"[1] 即使有如上记载，这项巨大的灌溉工程是否得以顺利施建，也是令人怀疑的。现在已经看不到多少这项工程的痕迹了，仅剩下连接东河的几条沟渠。在铁路修建之前，东河一直是京城与大运河之间的交通干道。

1. 城墙内侧壁

历史文献与城墙上的砖文、碑记较为一致，均倾向于证明城垣内侧壁始建于嘉靖（1522—1566 年）晚期，但在崇祯年间（1623—1643 年）经历了大规模的重建。在这两个时期，内侧城墙砖面均仅使用薄砖（这种薄砖的平均尺寸为：长 30 厘米，宽 15 厘米，厚 5 厘米）包砌，而后来在 18、19 世纪的修缮工程中采用的是如内城城墙上的那种较大的城砖。这些乾隆、嘉庆时期的城砖在南城墙墙面上使用广泛，而东、西城墙则几乎完全使用 16 世纪与 17 世纪初烧造的薄砖。

我们从东城墙开始考察，首先经过从主城墙垂直连向外城东北角楼的一小段城墙。城墙表面几乎完全由薄砖砌筑，没有砖文。仅东便门城门楼城台为大砖砌筑，砖上有嘉靖时期的砖文。在东便门与东北城隅之间，城墙上镶嵌有 3 块大石碑。其中一块石碑上的铭文字迹完全被侵蚀，但另外两块石碑铭文局部仍可辨识。根据这些石碑记载，修缮工程于崇祯八年（1635 年）由一位曹姓礼部官员出资赞助。这位曹姓官员出资修缮的工程还不止一处。东、西城墙上有很多相同年代的类似石碑，上面都有他的名字。这样的石碑总数在 30 块以

---

[1] 参见《光绪顺天府志一·京师志一》。

上。它们见证了这位曹姓官员的慷慨大度与热心公益的精神。根据中国人的观念，此举如果不是因为他触犯了法律而进行补偿，那么就是他从政府那里得到了很多好处。这些修缮工程全部采用与最初砌筑内侧壁一样的薄砖，工程质量很好。实际上，东城墙上仅很少的部分、很短的几段未采用这种较小的砖材，它们是在18世纪和19世纪早期添加上去的。

东北城角马道的下部由明中期的大城砖砌筑，上部则采用稍晚时期的薄砖砌筑。马道和城台均保存完好，但角楼已无存。

从城角向南延伸的城墙与上述城段情况相同。由此处到沙窝门，共有5块崇祯八年的石碑，其后修缮的城墙只有两三小段。沙窝门的城楼城台与瓮城上含有嘉靖时的大城砖，但城墙外侧为乾隆年间修缮。

沙窝门与东南城隅之间的城墙凹凸不平，修补较多。城墙上至少有13块石碑记载了崇祯八年的修缮工程，此外还有很多近期的修缮，采用了不同的材料。至于那些亟待修补的地方，就不再赘述。从沙窝门向南1公里左右，城墙目前的保存状态非常糟糕，没有女儿墙，墙面很大一部分年久失修，因恶劣的天气与战争的侵袭而伤痕累累。在此可以看到有一段城墙上满是枪眼，显然是最近几次发生在北京城门处的战争留下的痕迹。再往南一些，在到达东南角连接南城墙之前的一段，尽管城墙呈不规则的曲线，但其外观又重现了较为完整的状态，城角处的马道上有一座建于18世纪的精致角楼。

西城墙的情况基本与东城墙一致，但略长一些，因为西城墙在南端呈抹角。内侧壁砌面由通常采用的薄砖砌筑，崇祯八年用同一种材料进行过大规模修缮。然而这一侧城墙墙面在后期还进行过修缮，但相关碑记颇为罕见。其中第一段距西南城角约200米处，采用18世纪的大城砖修复，石碑记载的年代是1803年，即嘉庆八年。距此不远有两小段城墙与该段城墙特征相似，但没有任何碑刻记载修缮年代。西城墙南段的其余部分，在材料和砌筑工艺方面几乎没有任何差异，大多应为明代末期的工程。

西城墙中门是彰义门，曾于乾隆三十一年分两段修缮，但连接城门的城墙年代更早。彰义门与西北城角之间至少有8块普通样式的石碑，记载了该段城墙为崇祯八年由曹姓官员资助修缮。靠近京汉线铁路豁口处，有一小段乾隆四十一年（1776年）以大城砖砌筑的城墙，但这不过是个例外，大部分城墙都是明代晚期修筑，外观比东城墙更加统一。总体来说，西城墙的保存状况更好，但有几段城墙上的女儿墙已无存。西北角城台之上的角楼显系较晚时期翻新的结果，可能是18世纪末的工程。

西侧北部短墙，分为四五段修缮，其中两段采用18世纪的大砖。后期修缮工程中最长的一段位于西便门和内城之间，横跨连接西、南护城河的大沟渠（或称运河）之上。渠中的水量不如东城墙一侧护城河水量那般充沛，几乎任何船只都无法通过城墙下的小洞口，而倚着城墙内壁，建有一座大拱桥。内、外城墙的连接处筑有一座简朴的方形城楼。

外城南城墙上后期修缮的城段要比东、西城墙多得多。此面城墙上的几大段，特别是靠近两端城隅的城墙，均为乾隆三十、三十一年重筑。位于天坛与先农坛后面的南垣中间一段城墙则包含更多明代早期砌筑工程。

从东南城角开始，我们发现从此处到天坛东墙（最多1800米）不太长的城墙上有至少32块石碑，记载着自18世纪末开始的修缮工程，其中7块石碑年代为乾隆三十年（1766年），22块为乾隆三十一年，2块为乾隆四十七年（1782年），1块为嘉庆六年（1801年）。除上述石碑外，另有三块具有较早时期特征的石碑，记载的修缮年代似乎为崇祯八年。这几块早期石碑均为砂岩质地，碑面侵蚀严重，碑文几乎无法辨认。南城墙最东段城墙中仅有很少的几小段城墙为原有的明代工程。

天坛围墙后面可以看到更多的早期城墙。城墙情况更类似于东、西两侧的城墙，即用深色薄砖砌筑，砖缝间抹灰不多，因长期受风雨侵蚀而损毁严重。但此处也发现了一些重要的重修段落。有一大段、一小段（共计500米上下）重建于嘉庆四年（1799年），其余大概修于乾隆年间。有四块碑记，两块碑文已无法辨认，而另外两块的年代似乎为乾隆三十年。

天坛背后的这个街区是北京城墙以内最偏旷的地区。道路被柔软的沙土深深覆盖，少有车辆过往。一到雨季，道路两侧的枣树、大蓟和杂草因积水所滋养而高大繁茂。漫长的岁月与沙尘暴使城墙表面蒙上一层苔藓与尘埃混杂的"绒毯"。除此之外，城墙上各处还装点着从砖缝间生长出来的大把杂草与灌木丛。女儿墙大多已不存，整个城墙古色古香，与街区疏旷的氛围十分协调。

靠近永定门，城墙愈发破败，修补痕迹累累。此处有几小段修补，但没有任何碑记。根据城墙外侧的石碑记载，永定门城台重建于乾隆三十一年。

永定门以西的城墙也处于非常破败的状态。女儿墙无存，城墙基石被泥土掩埋，城墙因此看上去低矮而不显眼。距永定门不足100米的城墙重建于光绪十八年（1892年）。之后是一小段乾隆五十一年修缮的城墙。毗连的城墙处于废墟状态，部分墙基被水冲毁，表面砖层也开始剥落。实际上，这段城墙（先农坛背后）基本上未经任何修缮，只有一部分崇祯八年修葺过一次，其余墙段都是早期的明代城墙。但转过先农坛西角，城墙上乾隆年间的修缮工程又多了起来，就像在最东端城墙那般。从该处到西南城隅，共计30块石碑，其中只有一块为明代末期的，即崇祯八年，余均为18世纪末期的。乾隆三十年的石碑有10块，乾隆三十一年14块，乾隆三十六年1块，乾隆五十六年1块，嘉庆八年（1803年）3块。南城墙东、西两端的大部分墙段，看似几乎是同时修缮的，奇怪的是，乾隆三十年与其后一年的重修墙段迥然不同。前者只用最大号的城砖，后者却几乎停用这种大城砖（或许是为留给主城墙修缮使用），而采用小得多的城砖，砌筑风格沿袭乾隆年间一贯的精细、坚固。所有18世纪修缮过的城墙目前仍保存良好，而明代由曹姓官员资助的用薄砖砌筑的一些城墙段落已经开始崩坏、剥落，有待重新修葺。南西门与西南城角之间的南城墙西段大部分为乾隆三十一年重筑，这最后1公里的城墙目前比南城墙其他墙段的保存状态都要好一些。

2. 城墙外侧壁

显然，城墙外侧壁从建造之初就要比内侧壁更加坚固。外侧壁保存更好的另外一个原因是雨水的排水。同主城墙一样，此处的雨水是沿内侧壁排出的。外侧壁砖面用的不是内侧壁上常见的薄砖，而采用通常在明代主城墙上使用的那种大城砖。总体来看，砌筑工艺非常出色，外侧壁大多仍是始建时的墙面，修缮的墙段相对短而少。大多是18世纪晚期的修缮工程，只有两三段为光绪年间的翻新工程。

在外城连接主城墙的西北一段城墙上，一座简朴的矩形城楼守卫着通道。城楼不很高，但借助地形优势，可以方便地监视较低的城墙，有效地阻止从外城城墙上对内城的攻击。原先，在外城墙东北段与内城墙连接处，也建有一座类似的城楼，但该楼目前已毁。东、西两侧内外城墙交界之处，是检验城墙材料、工艺异同的最佳范例，考察结果发现，内城城墙的营造技术、建筑材料均占据绝对优势，令人印象深刻。

如内城城墙外侧壁一样，外城城墙的外侧壁也被方形墩台划分为若干段，墩台大小、规制基本相同，间距约200米。因而，此处墩台间隔的疏密程度与内城北墙（也是完全新建的城墙）基本一致，而内城南、东、西三面城墙上的墩台间距不足上述间距的一半。尽管外城南城墙是北京城最长的一面城墙，但由于间距很大，外城南墙也仅有30座墩台。东、西城墙上分别有14和13座墩台，其中不含角楼与城门城台。

从西侧开始，我们首先穿过西便门。城门处墙壁与城台墙壁是乾隆年间翻修的，但内、外两侧城墙表面年代均较早，且侵蚀严重。根据嵌入的石碑记载，城门西侧的墩台系乾隆四十一年翻新。毗连的城墙段落为后期重建，很可能为光绪年间。角楼城台的北侧壁年代较早，含有数块印文砖，如"嘉靖三十年（1551年）窑户李裕宝造"、"嘉靖三十年窑户刘金造"、"嘉靖三十年窑户楚祝造"、"嘉靖二十年（1541年）窑户孙馨造"。但根据嵌入的石碑，该城台的南侧壁为嘉庆二年（1797年）重建。

从这个城角向南，直到西城墙中间的城门——彰义门，其间没有任何重要的晚期修缮。根据几处砖文，这段城墙主要修于嘉靖年间，城墙上好几处砖面严重破损、剥落。砖文有："嘉靖三十六年（1557年）窑户楚琛造"、"嘉靖三十六年窑户吴济荣造"、"嘉靖二十二年造"、

"嘉靖三十六年窑户张钦造"。其后两处砖文表明的年代更晚，可能修于乾隆年间："新城砖"、"特制城砖"。再之后，又有明代砖文"嘉靖二十三年（1544年）窑户杨佩造"、"嘉靖二十年（1541年）窑户杨玉造"、"嘉靖二十二年窑户牛七造"、"嘉靖二十年窑户王兴造"、"嘉靖三十年窑户吴济荣造"、"嘉靖三十二年（1553年）窑户张楼造"、"嘉靖二十八年（1549年）窑户梁章造"、"嘉靖三十二年窑户周雪造"等。

彰义门箭楼城台重建于乾隆三十一年（1766年）。两块石碑均有记载，年代相同。由彰义门继续向南，这里的城墙与北城墙特征一致。大城砖上有不少嘉靖年间的砖文，其中有："嘉靖二十年窑户梁栋造"、"嘉靖二十三年窑户周钧造"、"嘉靖三十三年（1554年）窑户周新庐造"、"嘉靖三十二年窑户傅典造"。除明代城砖外，还有一些乾隆时期的城砖，表明经后代的小规模修缮。砖文有："新城砖"、"停泥城砖"。

彰义门以南第1座墩台很可能在乾隆年间进行过修整。有一块石碑记录了该工程，但其上的铭文已模糊不清。

根据石碑记载，第2座墩台曾翻修于嘉庆四年（1799年）。

第3座墩台为明代中期修筑，有一些记有年代的城砖，例如"嘉靖二十二年窑户杨金造"，以及"嘉靖二十九年（1550年）窑户曹荣造"。

第4座墩台年代较早，仅南侧被翻修过，但没有石碑记载年代。这座墩台与毗连的城墙上有很多砖文，引录如下：

"嘉靖二十年窑户侯六造"、"嘉靖二十年窑户常孟阳造"、"嘉靖十八年窑户杜充造"、"嘉靖二十年窑户常世荣造"、"嘉靖二十六年（1547年）窑户谭德政造"、"嘉靖二十四年（1545年）窑户刘茂造"、"万历戊申年（1608年）窑户蒋大顺造"。另有一些18世纪的"新城砖"和"停泥细砖"。

第5座墩台重建于嘉庆二年。毗连的城墙年代较早，已遭侵蚀，但临近下一座墩台之处有一小段嘉庆二年修缮的城墙。

第6座墩台年代较早，有一些嘉靖时期的砖文，例如："嘉靖二十六年（1547年）窑户李充造"。

第7座城台墩台的年代也较早，有类似的砖文，例如"嘉靖十四年（1535年）窑户李仁造"。

根据石碑记载，毗连的城墙局部翻新于乾隆五十一年（1786年）。

第8座墩台年代较早，但毗连的城墙南段修缮于嘉庆二年（1797年）。

城隅的墩台北侧壁和西侧壁年代较早，但南、东两侧曾于后代翻修。北侧城壁上的明代城砖发现了不少常见的嘉靖砖文，如"嘉靖二十八年窑户王瑞造"，以及其他的窑户姓名：

张增盛、胡永正、赵德辅与陆明阳。这些砖文的年代是嘉靖二十八年、二十九年（1549-1550年）的。

城隅与其南侧第 1 座墩台之间的部分城墙修缮于乾隆五十三年（1788 年）。

城隅与南西门之间的 4 座墩台的年代都较早，残损、侵蚀严重。其中含有一些说明工程年代的砖文："嘉靖二十六年窑户牛充造"、"嘉靖二十一年窑户张九造"、"嘉靖二十九年（1550 年）窑户张九造"。墩台间城墙的特征与建造年代都基本相同，仅在第 2、3 座城台之间有一小段（位于沟渠闸门之上）修于嘉庆二年（1797 年）。

南西门箭楼城台重建于乾隆五十一年，城台东、西两侧均有石碑记载。瓮城内部建造年代更早。

从南西门向东约一公里半的距离内（包含 6 座墩台），城墙上部大多曾翻修过，而下部比较古旧，包含一些明代的砖文，例如："崇祯？年窑户朱文造"，或"嘉靖二十六年（1547年）窑户李尚贵造"。

第 3 座墩台上有一块乾隆三十一年（1766 年）的石碑。这里的乾隆城砖常出现"工部监督桂"、"工部监督永"和"工部监督国"等字样。

走过第 6 座墩台，又能看到一些较早期的城墙，但这些墙段之间穿插有小段修缮，两块嘉庆二年的碑记记载了这些翻修工程。这几段城墙整体上与中间的城门并不相称。

第 7 座墩台总体年代较早，包含嘉靖时期的砖文。根据两块碑记记载，毗连的城墙修缮于嘉庆二年（1797 年）。

第 8 座墩台大体也年代较早。这里以及毗连的城墙上有很多嘉靖年间的砖文，例如"嘉靖三十二年（1553 年）窑户冯大昭造"、"嘉靖三十二年窑户林永寿造"。

走过第 9 座墩台，可以看到一些晚期的修缮工程，其中一处嵌有一块嘉庆二年的石碑。之后有一小段明代城墙，其中包含砖文"嘉靖三十二年窑户畅纶造"、"嘉靖三十二年窑户林永寿造"。

接着又有一小段 18 世纪的城墙，上有嘉庆二年的石碑。

根据碑记记载，第 10 座墩台与前一段城墙的修造年代相同。

毗连的城墙与第 11 座墩台年代较早。城墙砖面保存欠佳，上有几处嘉靖时期的砖文："嘉靖二十二年（1543 年）窑户孙标造"、"嘉靖三十一年（1552 年）窑户宋义造"、"嘉靖二十九年（1550 年）窑户陈福造"。临近城门的城墙曾被翻修。

永定门箭楼城墙、城台重建于乾隆三十一年，有两块石碑记载着该年代（1766 年）。

毗连的城墙翻修于乾隆四十七年，情况与城门西侧的城墙（1782 年）类似。

正门以东第 1 座墩台年代较早。其上有几处砖文，如"嘉靖三十二年窑户傅和造"、"嘉靖三十二年窑户赵丰玉造"。

第2座墩台情形同上，有着类似的砖文，以及"嘉靖二十三年东河窑窑户吴矩造"。

第3座墩台同上，砖文年代相同，如"嘉靖二十二年东河窑窑户李经造"。

第4座墩台同二，砖文相似："嘉靖三十二年东河窑窑户李林造"。

根据碑记记载，第5座墩台修缮于乾隆四十七年，但这段墙面上嘉靖年间的砖文表明，修缮工程使用的主要是早期的材料。

第6座城台年代较早，使用嘉靖时期常见的城砖砌筑，上有砖文："嘉靖二十二年窑户高尚义造"。

第7座墩台同上，城砖也类似，有砖文"嘉靖三十六年（1557年）窑户张钦造"、"嘉靖二十九年窑户薛香造"，以及"万历三十五年（1607年）窑户陈昌造"。最后这段砖文似乎能够表明，这部分城墙直到万历晚期才建造完成，或者是那时又有修缮。第二种可能性似乎更易为人所接受。

第8座墩台年代较早，采用常见的城砖建造，其中一些有砖文"嘉靖三十二年窑户陆明阳造"。

由于京津铁路穿过城墙，第9座墩台被拆毁。

与铁路通道毗连的东侧城墙年代较早，遭风雨侵蚀。从此处直到东南门（江擦门[1]），没有任何后期修缮工程。这段城墙砖文都是嘉靖年间的，引录几例如下："嘉靖三十一年窑户常增造"、"嘉靖二十三年窑户吴昌培造"、"嘉靖三十二年东河窑窑户陈贵造"、"嘉靖二十一年窑户李林造"、"嘉靖三十年窑户张孟昭造"。

铁路通道与江擦门之间的城墙上至少有5座墩台，而江擦门与城隅之间只有一座墩台，因此永定门以东的墩台总数为15座，与永定门以西墩台总数一致。实际上，外城的南城墙是北京城最长的一面城墙。长度超过7800米，如果东南城墙未被截断，东城墙南端未向内转弯，这个长度还应再增加200–300米。东南城门与城隅之间的距离非常短。城门城墙和箭楼城台重建于乾隆三十一年（1766年），但从此处到城隅之间的城墙（包含一座墩台）年代较早，其上有城砖，刻有嘉靖二十四年（1545年）的砖文。

城角的墩台已遭风雨侵蚀，目前亟待修缮。其上包含许多砖文，如"嘉靖二十四年窑户王瑞造"、"嘉靖二十六年窑户吴鲧造"、"嘉靖十五年工顺窑窑户任经造"、"嘉靖十八年（1539年）窑户孙龙造"。

可以看出，城角墩台上的砖文年代要早于城墙上的，由此推断砌筑工程可能始于城角。

---

[1] 江擦门即左安门，该俗名亦有多种解释，其中一种认为"江擦"乃"礓磜"的谐音，因为左安门箭楼外侧的门洞有石砌礓磜（台阶），所以俗称'礓磜门'；另一传说称有老和尚背塔经过该门，将将擦过城门之意。

与西城墙的情形相似，东城墙上的修缮工程比南城墙的更少。除下文将要说明的几小段例外的城墙，其余部分均以标准的嘉靖年间大城砖砌筑，很多城砖印有砖文。举例如下："嘉靖三十二年窑户张钦造"、"嘉靖三十一年窑户孙文葛造"、"嘉靖二十四年窑户吴良培造"、"嘉靖二十四年窑户杨中矩造"、"嘉靖二十二年窑户林永寿造"、"嘉靖三十四年窑户赵义造"、"嘉靖三十三年窑户蒋月造"、"嘉靖三十二年窑户吴矩造"等。

显然嘉靖年间不缺"窑户"，城砖烧造在当时也当是一种个人的工艺，而不同于其后的年代。没有哪个时期能像嘉靖年间那样，产生出这么多城砖烧造工匠。而其后的年代，中国是否烧造过更好的城砖，则颇令人怀疑。

根据碑刻记载，嘉靖时期的城墙上，间杂有重筑于乾隆三十一年的 6 座墩台以及两侧毗连的小段城墙。此处的城砖砖文没有造砖者的姓名，但刻有督造官员的名字：工部监督永、工部监督桂。二百年间，烧造城砖似乎已经失去了个人特质，而更多成为皇家官造。

走过这一段后，又是嘉靖年间的城墙，但在第 7 座墩台之前，有另一段 18 世纪的修缮工程，石碑年代为嘉庆二年。之后是一小段明代城墙。

第 7 座墩台经重筑，有碑记记载，但碑文漫漶不清（当为乾隆或嘉庆时期的）。毗连的一段城墙为嘉庆七年修缮。

第 8 座墩台年代较早，使用嘉靖年间城砖砌筑，其上有砖文"嘉靖三十六年窑户楚吴滨造"。

从此处到沙窝门的城墙（包括第 9、第 10 座墩台）年代较早，使用特征显著的嘉靖城砖砌筑，这种砖已多次提及并已引录砖文。

跟其他外城城门类似，沙窝门瓮城外墙和城台重建于乾隆三十一年。城门砖墙相对较新，尤其在城门两侧风雨侵蚀的明代老城墙陪衬下，显得格外醒目。明代老城墙一直向北延伸，包括邻近的两个墩台及其毗连的城墙，但（从沙窝门开始的）第 3 座重建于乾隆三十一年。毗连的城墙似亦修于同时，有石碑一块，但无碑文。

第 4 座墩台年代较早，顶部已毁。城角的城墙保存状态也很差，角楼已不存。

从城角到东便门的城墙上有两座墩台，重建于乾隆三十一年。记有该年代的石碑镶嵌于城门附近。城砖印有乾隆时期常见的砖文，有"工部监督桂"、"工部监督永"的字样。东便门瓮城城墙亦为同期所建，但另一侧可以发现使用了早期材料及砌筑工艺的迹象。

外城以外的近郊与所谓的城内情景极其相似——开阔的沙地上点缀有几处粮田，以及一片片环绕在住屋与寺庙周围的树丛。这种景象有时不禁使人纳闷，为何在此处建造城墙。实际上，比起城墙内侧一带，现在（城门附近的）城外地区住房和来往车辆更多，生活气息和活力也更浓一些。或许因为这里的生活成本更低，也更自由。东南方向上的几个地方，水源充沛，池塘与运河两岸芦苇丰茂，垂柳荡漾，景色宜人。西边田野的景致相对枯燥，但在一些受到保护的地区，仍能看到一些优美的柏树与椿树。整体来说，城市北部所特有的那种萧索、孤寂与单调，在此处并不多见。

七、内城的城门

引言

  城门堪称城市之口，城墙内五十余万生命体构成的庞大躯体正是通过它们来呼吸、说话的。整座城市的活力凝聚于城门处；进出城市的万物都必须途经这些狭窄的开口。往来穿梭于城门的，不仅仅有大批的车辆、牲畜与行人，更有思想与欲望、希望与绝望，以及象征着死亡与新生的丧礼与婚礼队列。在城门处，人们可以感知到全城的脉搏，因为全城的生命与意志都流经这些狭窄的通道，这一搏动赋予北京这个高度复合的有机体以生命与运动的节奏。

  夜幕降临，四处变得模糊不清难以辨识，市民在此时入眠，城门也随之关闭，至少曾经是这样。日出时分，第一批旅客驾着马车或骡车踏上漫长的旅程，厚重的木门被缓缓推开，像被惊醒的巨人一样发出不情愿的呻吟。陆陆续续进城的乡下人或推着小车，或肩挑扁担，扁担两头摇曳着装满土产的竹篮。太阳慢慢升起，城门处的交通与活动逐渐增多，种类也更加多样。挑夫、手推车与驴车的行列中混杂着黄包车与汽车，汽车不断地鸣笛，发出阵阵噪音。然而，汇集在这些狭窄通道上的人流车流却不为所动，此种情形可能愈演愈烈，但前进的速度却不会加快。当众多手推车与黄包车从相反的方向穿过城门时，交通甚至可能短暂停滞。主要城门处的交通在人们出门吃午饭时达到最高峰。接近傍晚时分，交通流量再次变小；从薄暮至深夜，车马人流便逐渐停止。（虽然现今北京主要城门的关闭时间已不受严格限制，但是很多地方城市仍然如此。）

  活跃在城门处的生活场面，不仅随着一天中的时辰变化而变化，也会因城区与郊区特征的不同而不同。南面是城市的门户，也有诸多交通中心与商业中心，其城墙上高耸着三座雄伟的城门。位于正中的正阳门（直面艳阳之门），比其他两座要高大得多，曾经仅供帝王出入，现在常被称为国门。尽管其雄伟壮丽的建筑与周边古色古香的环境均已饱受摧残，但它仍然是首都这一悸动着的生命体的心脏。正阳门东、西两侧不远处，分别耸立着为人熟知的哈达门与顺治门，虽然其官方名称并非如此。它们是两条南北通衢的入口。哈达门曾被俗称为景门，意为光明、昌盛之门，此门人人可以使用，皇帝有时也临幸至此。被称作顺治门的西侧城门正好与之相反，它被视为厄运与衰竭之门，以"死门"（死亡之门）著称。如今，仍有很多送葬队伍经由此门出城。南城墙上的这三座城门是调控内城与外城之间交通流量的闸门。它们是城与城之间的门户，因此不具备作为郊区进城入口的特征。尤其是现如今，双轨铁路戳穿哈达门瓮城，并围绕顺治门瓮城铺设，城门的原有韵味消失殆尽，两座城门的箭楼均已无存。

北城墙没有正门，仅有两座旁门，它们离城市中轴线较近，与南城墙的两座旁门并不对应。现在城门外是类似乡村模样的郊区，然而，如我们所知，这一带此前是元大都的一部分。北城门向来被视作北京最重要的城防大门，自然是因为对京城的攻击主要来自北方。如今，北城门处的军事物资运输仍最频繁，因为最大的兵营都位于城北。德胜门意为美德之门，也称"修门"（修饰之门）；安定门又称"生门"（丰裕之门），皇帝每年都要穿越此门，到地坛（土地之坛）祭祀以祈祷丰收。这两座城门外观雄伟，其瓮城（因修铁路而局部残缺）与城门楼在没有房屋与树木遮挡的光秃秃的地面上拔地而起。

在修建铁路环线时，两座东城门被毫无意义地改造，其瓮城已惨遭废弃。不过，城门外却引人入胜，护城河两岸遍植垂柳，为城门楼营造出美好的环境。在铁路修建之前，这条护城河，亦可以说是运河，对市民的主食——稻米的运输来说意义重大，这些稻米储存于东城墙下的粮仓中。东直门被称为"商门"（交易之门），平民百姓在此营生，帝王从不光顾。齐化门亦称"杜门"（休憩之门），显然是在对应有市场之名的东直门。

西城墙上的西直门与平则门是仅存的两座未遭铁路损毁的城门，如今它们依然能够完整地呈现出北京城门的旧日风光：不单有作防御和瞭望之用的双重城门楼，还有封闭严密的瓮城或市场，其间可以容纳小庙和很多摊棚。道路经由侧面开口，顺延瓮城城墙通向城外，道路两旁的粮店与食肆鳞次栉比。城门由此将城市与郊区以极其自然而别致的方式联系在一起。穿过城门的人群热闹非凡，我们可以从中窥见他们无忧无虑的幸福生活，就像很多中国北方的乡村旅店呈现出的那样，这同以汽车、摩托车方式表现出的现代文明的匆忙形成了强烈反差。平则门是安定与公正之门，据说，百姓在此听到皇帝的谕旨后，或因之雀跃，或受其惊扰，因此这座城门亦称"惊门"。下一城门是有"开门"（开放之门）之称的西直门，又称通晓之门，表示充分领悟皇帝谕旨的英明。

这些多少带有某种寓意、象征的城门别称究竟因何而起已不可确知，不过，这些称谓仍有记录的必要，因为它们仍旧存在于老北京人的记忆之中，并时常被引用以解释城门的传统用途或昔日特征。

内城各城门的规模与细节虽有不同，但都遵循相同的规划原则。它们最为显著的特征便是双重城门楼。城墙经拓宽加固形成城台，城楼便坐落其上，其外观近似于楼阁或殿堂，三重檐，上下两层均有敞廊。由长长的马道拾级而上，可以登上城台。箭楼是朴素的砖结构建筑，外墙由下至上逐渐收缩，除两层屋檐檐口与四排射击孔外，再无其他细部划分或设计处理。箭楼之下的宽大城台，凸出于U形瓮城城墙之外。

城门的整体规划设计完全是中世纪的，引入火炮后已不再适用。现存城门与元朝时期基本相同，之后虽有所改进，但其抵御炮火攻击的能力却并未得到提高。特别是木结构外露、砖墙单薄的城楼，事实证明，一旦面临现代武器的攻击，它自身便是危险重重，更遑论发挥保护作用了。值得庆幸的是，尽管如此，除了德胜门，其他城门的城楼仍存续至今。这些城楼一旦湮灭，北京的建筑将失去其最为别具一格而引人入胜的面貌。

从军事角度来看，随着现代战争手段的不断演变，城门作为军事瞭望点的实际功用已迅速丧失，不过它们仍因作为税收关卡而具有重要意义。城门处征得的过路税至今仍是北京政府最稳定的收入来源之一，而城墙、城门对首都的实际防御作用则变成虚幻的空中阁楼了。

1. 西城墙上的城门

平则门，官方名称为阜成门，是西城墙上的南城门。瓮城的城墙翻新于乾隆五十二年，但城楼下城台的年代显然要久远很多，应是明代后期所建，用薄砖精心砌筑而成。城楼给人以沧桑之感。木柱用铁箍加固。二层栏杆已不存，其下的平坐栏板上破了几个大洞。底层屋檐檐口已破碎，西北角也已完全塌毁。木构上的彩绘与装饰基本都剥落了，蒙着厚厚的灰尘。如果不及时更换腐朽的木构件，整个建筑就有坍塌的危险。城楼的主体结构可能是明代所建，但其后屡经修缮，不过每次修缮都要间隔三五十年以上的时间。

城楼屹立于略高于城身的石台基上，台基面阔33米，进深18.8米，楼身面阔27米，进深13米。环绕楼身的围廊面阔七间，进深三间，正面与山面的明间均略宽于两旁开间，城楼的四门开在此间。外廊檐柱直径约为半米，以包裹坚固内芯的若干木料拼接而成，立于方形石柱础之上，但未埋入台基。柱两侧设有方抱柱，用以加固柱子。

城楼墙体的构造框架也由木柱构成。柱子前后各两排，分别位于墙体的内外两侧，中间用砖填充，木柱表面几乎有四分之三砌于墙内。三排柱子[1]的柱间距完全相同，唯独角柱是按照对角线方向计算柱间距[2]。

---

[1] 指一排廊柱与两排随墙柱。
[2] 作者似乎想说的是柱子之间搭接的梁枋长度问题，角柱与金柱之间有斜向梁枋连接，其长度与其他纵横方向梁枋长度不同。

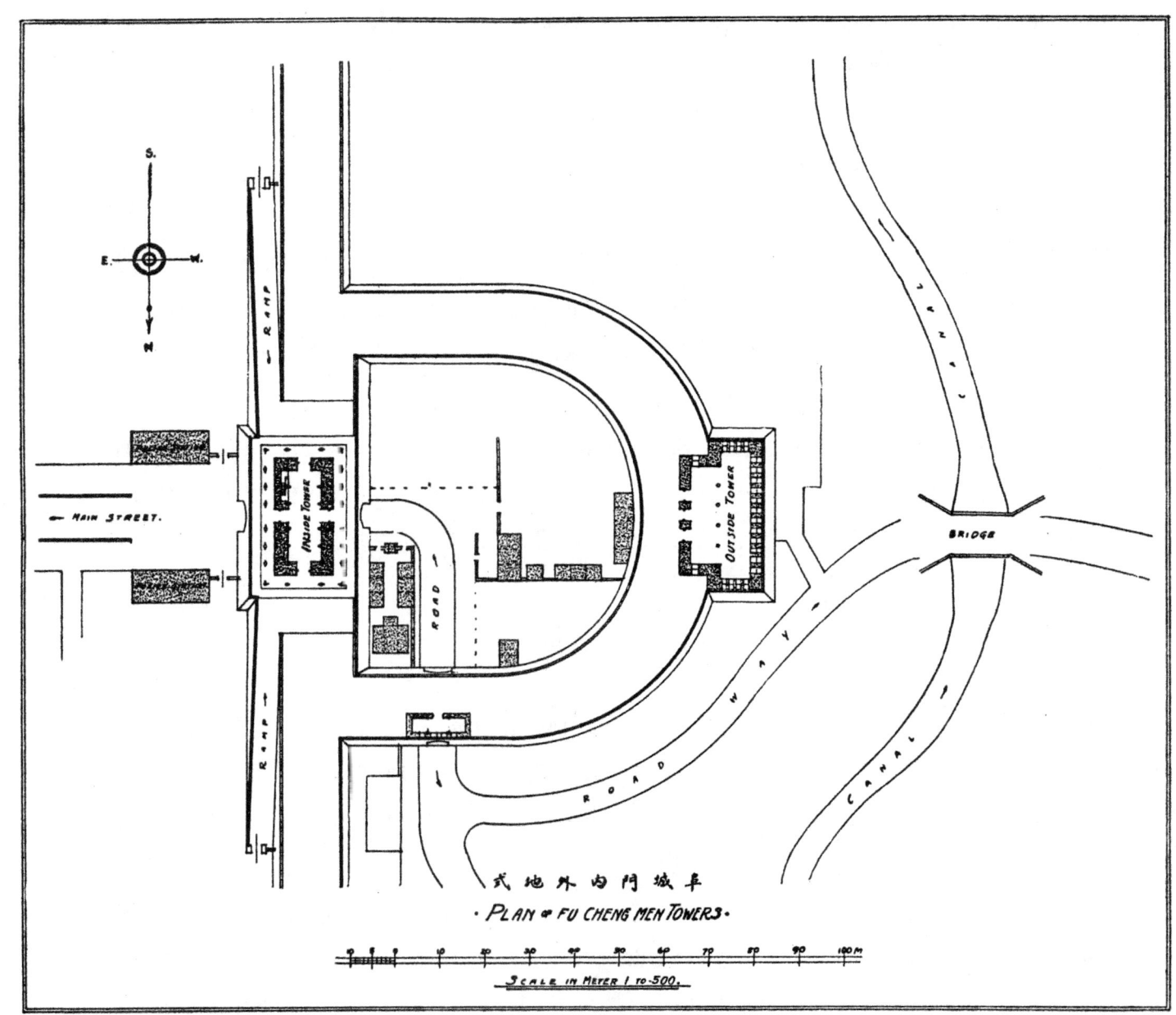

图 6 平则门（又称阜成门）总平面

显而易见，这种将双排柱局部嵌入墙内的排布方法并不常用，在其他大型城门上，内侧柱子往往脱离墙体，独立于室内，这表明平则门城楼可能建于相对较早的时代。

金柱高约 9 米，上承二层楼板梁。檐柱仅高 5 米，檐柱之间由嵌入柱端的额枋连接，檐柱与墙之间也有梁枋连接。檐柱不是直接承托斗栱，而是上承额枋，额枋之上设五踩斗栱，支撑着两根圆檩（檩的直径约为 0.30 米），檩承微微翘曲的椽、飞，再上为出挑深远的屋顶。连接墙体与檐柱的梁头外露，雕刻为花卉形状，相应地饰以彩绘。

相同特征的构造也用于第二层围廊处和顶层屋檐檐口下，不过这里并无空间容纳柱子，

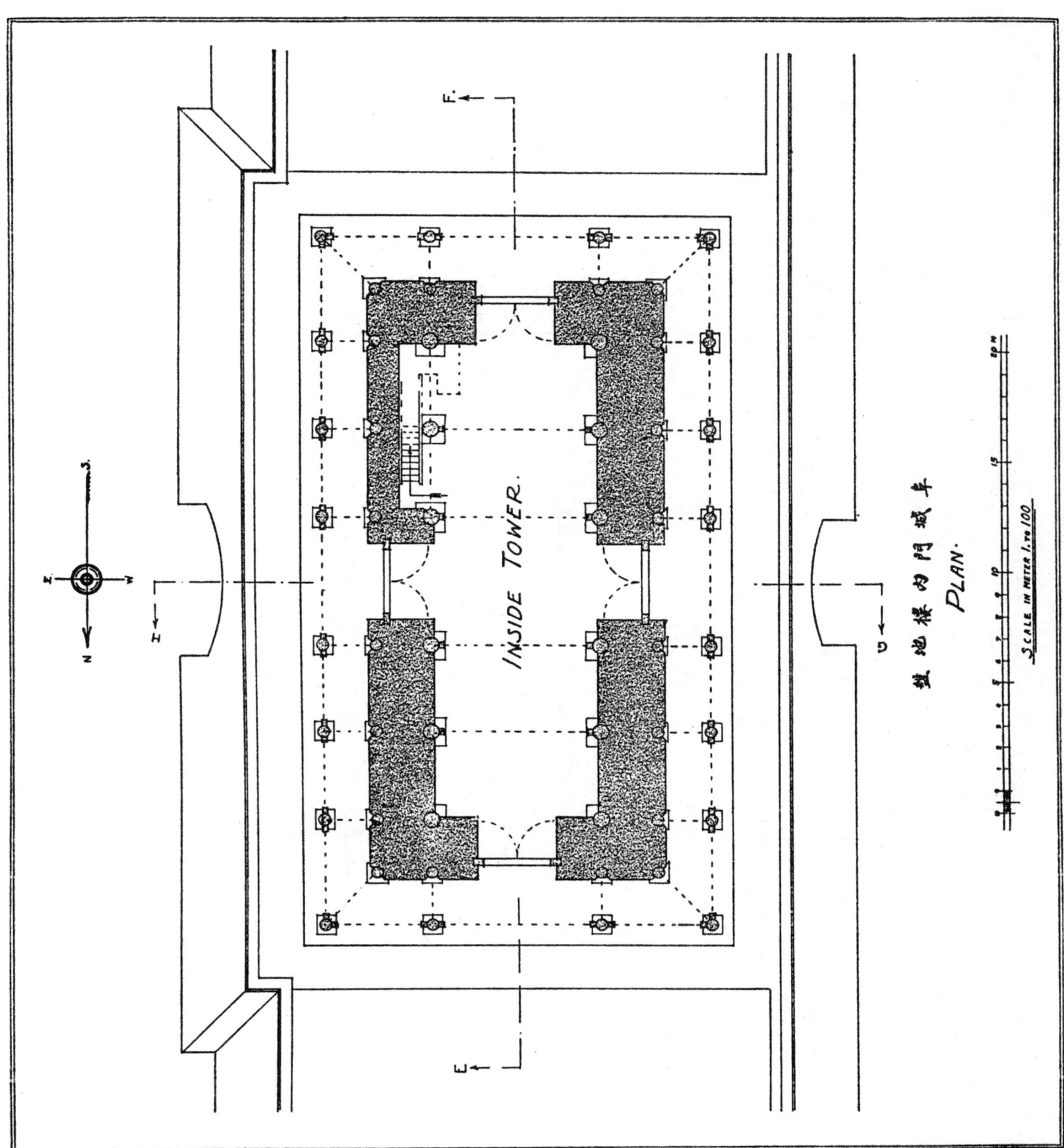

图 7 平则门城楼平面

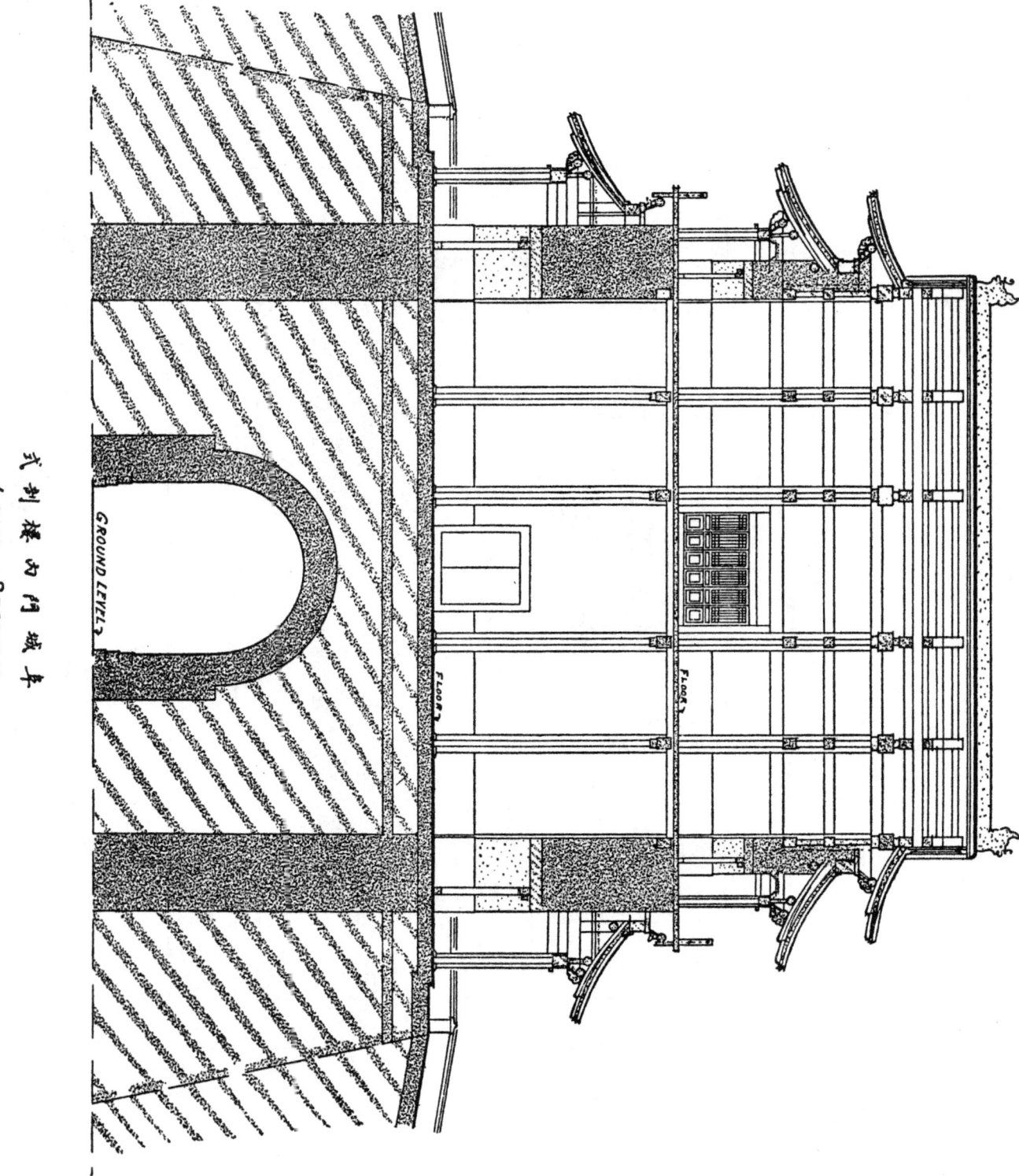

图 8 平则门城楼纵剖面

BEAM
FLOOR
JOIST
GROUND LEVEL
阜城門内樓剖式
·CROSS SECTION·
ON G--H.
10 5 10 15 20 M
SCALE IN METER 1 TO 100

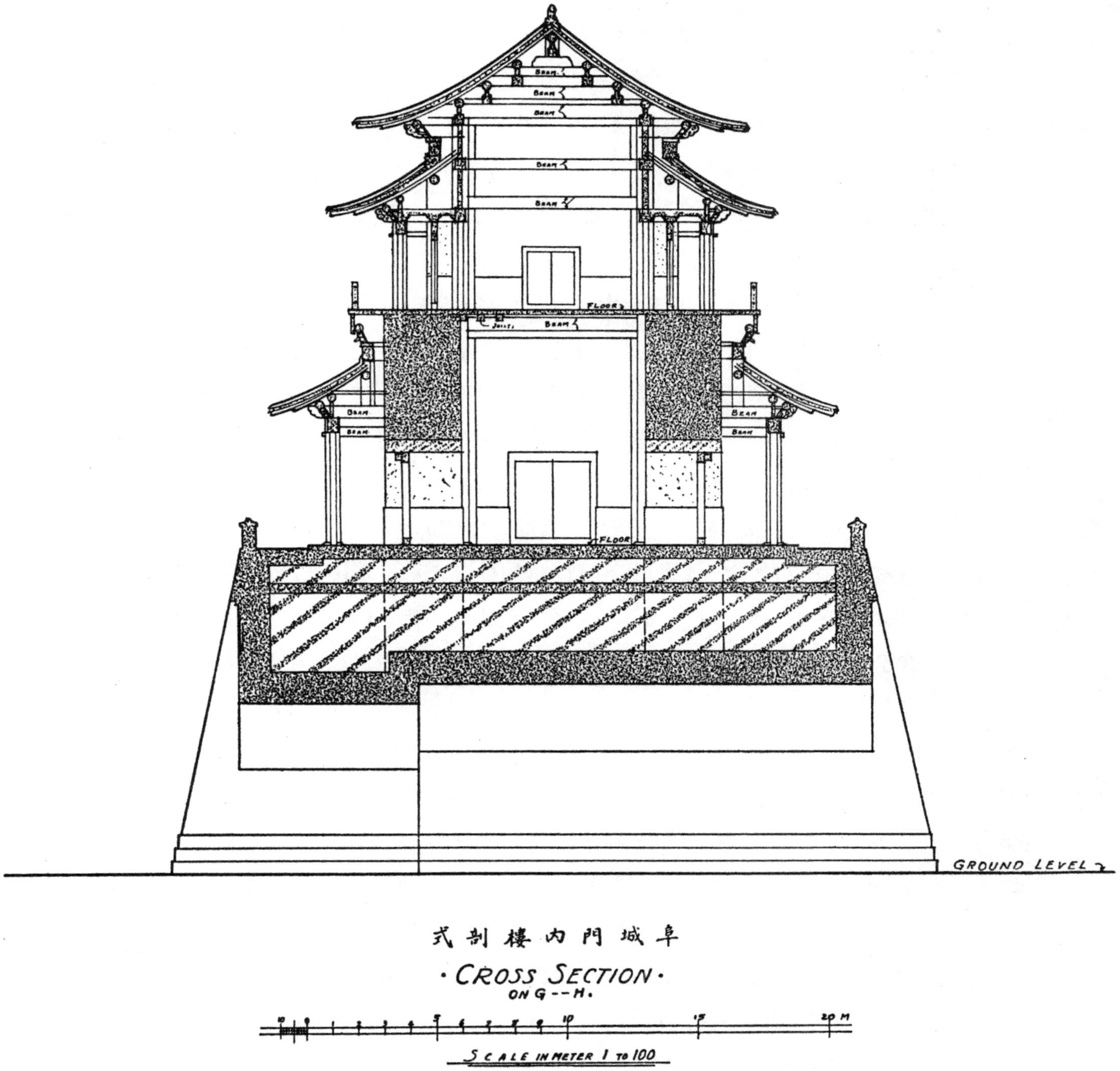

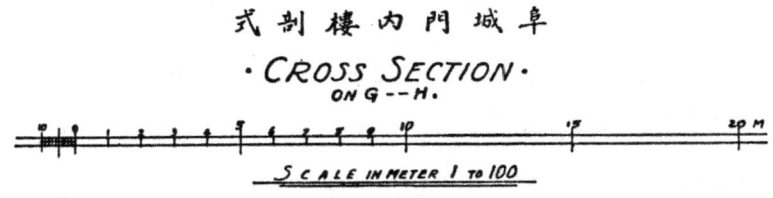

图 9 平则门城楼横剖面

仅以嵌入砖墙内的梁枋承托斗栱。二层室内长、宽与一层相同，但墙厚仅为一层的一半，因此其四周有敞廊。一层屋檐围脊上有枋，枋上置斗栱，斗栱上承平坐。二层柱高约 7.4 米，由处于不同高度的三层厚重梁枋纵横连接。第三层梁枋与主屋顶的檐口相平，未装天花板。因此屋顶结构一览无遗，它由两层纵横的梁枋构成，其中横向的梁是支撑屋顶上部尽端的三角山墙的必需结构。日语称这种常见的屋顶类型为歇山顶（irimoya），即指带有山墙的屋顶，其山墙向下延伸至屋檐一半处。椽下有三根檩，檩下为更厚重的方枋，脊檩由斗栱承接，斗栱坐于屋脊正下方的三架梁上。这里的梁枋用量巨大，后期重建的城门楼结构相对简化，但遵循相同的原则。包括主屋脊在内，城楼总高 21.2 米，最大面阔为 31.2 米。

通行的色彩曾以红色为主，但在风雨与岁月的共同作用下，现在已脱落殆尽。所有砖作都被施以朱红色抹灰，折叠门与柱子也涂成红色。外部的梁与斗栱饰以绿色与蓝色，平坐下的栏板可能曾有金色的装饰，这就是所有城门上的传统配色。筒瓦屋顶以仰俯瓦交替排列，原先可能全是绿琉璃瓦，但此瓦现在仅存于屋面边缘，其余都是灰瓦。正脊与翘曲的垂脊都很高，施用浇筑的琉璃瓦。屋脊末端饰以带有翅膀与犀角的兽首，此外戗脊上还有一排有趣的坐兽，即所谓的"夔龙字"，这无疑是为了保护房屋以破险恶的风水。

箭楼是一座状似堡垒的简朴建筑，由厚重的砖墙砌筑而成，但在结构方面砖墙并无实际作用，仅是木结构的附加物，亦可说是其厚重的外壳。不论箭楼外观如何，其内部构造和长长挑出、曲线优美的飞檐都与城楼基本相同。砖作的年代看似并不久远，根据镶嵌的匾额，瓮城城墙重建于乾隆五十二年（1787 年），箭楼不会比之更早。

箭楼包含两部分，主体部分坐落于凸出的城台上，正面对着城门桥，略为低矮的抱厦部分位于主体之后，坐落于瓮城城墙上，箭楼入口正在此处。主体部分在地平面处，面阔 40 米，城台顶（即箭楼的底部）面阔 35 米，箭楼顶（上层屋顶横梁下）面阔略少于 32 米。立面总高 30 米，其中城台高 13 米，楼高 17 米。山面进深仅 21 米，另有抱厦部分进深 6.80 米，山面墙体是连续砌筑的，但每边有 3.5 米长的转角。主体部分之后的抱厦总面阔 25 米，高 12 米，构成了主体空间的前厅，二者墙体相连，屋顶独立。

箭楼的构造框架与城楼相同，立柱也是由梁枋连接。六根大柱（直径 0.8 米）在屋内中线上排作一排，直抵高达 12 米的屋梁。柱间距为 3.8 米。与大柱对应的是四周镶嵌于砖墙中的较小柱子。独立的柱子与壁柱均由梁枋纵横拉接，以支撑现已毁弃的建筑主层楼板。

其上另有四层梁枋，上承圆檩，檩上为屋顶的椽、飞。出挑深远的翘曲檐口同样由斗栱上的檩枋支撑，斗栱则坐落于部分嵌入砖墙的额枋上。墙体很厚，底部厚度不少于 2.5 米，上部为应对外立面的收分而逐渐变薄，厚度为 1.2 米。底层屋顶与三层楼板相平，屋顶环绕着包括抱厦部分的整个建筑，抱厦部分为仅有三面的歇山顶，因为其第四面与主楼相连。

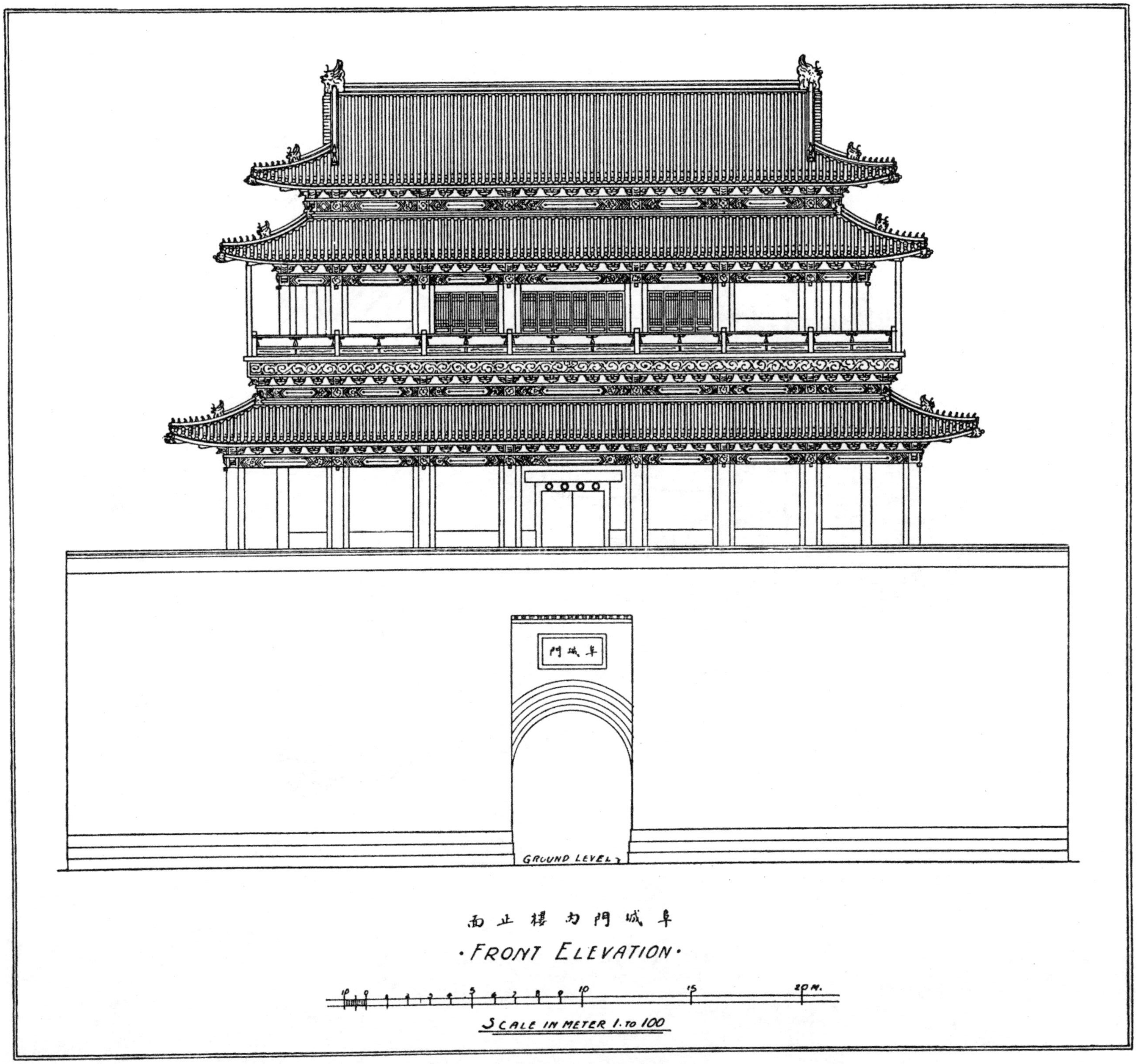

图 10 平则门城楼正立面

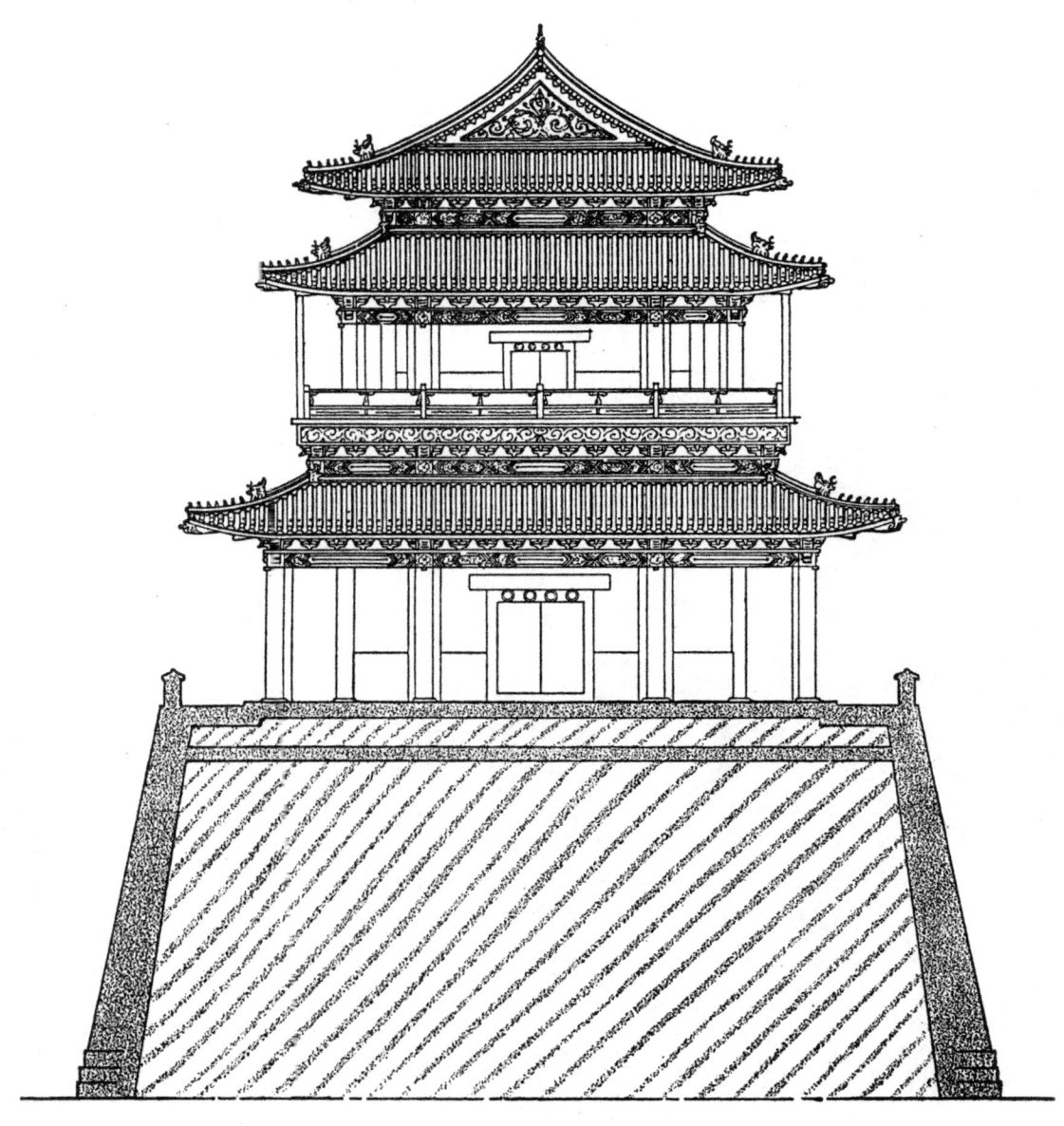

图 11 平则门城楼侧立面

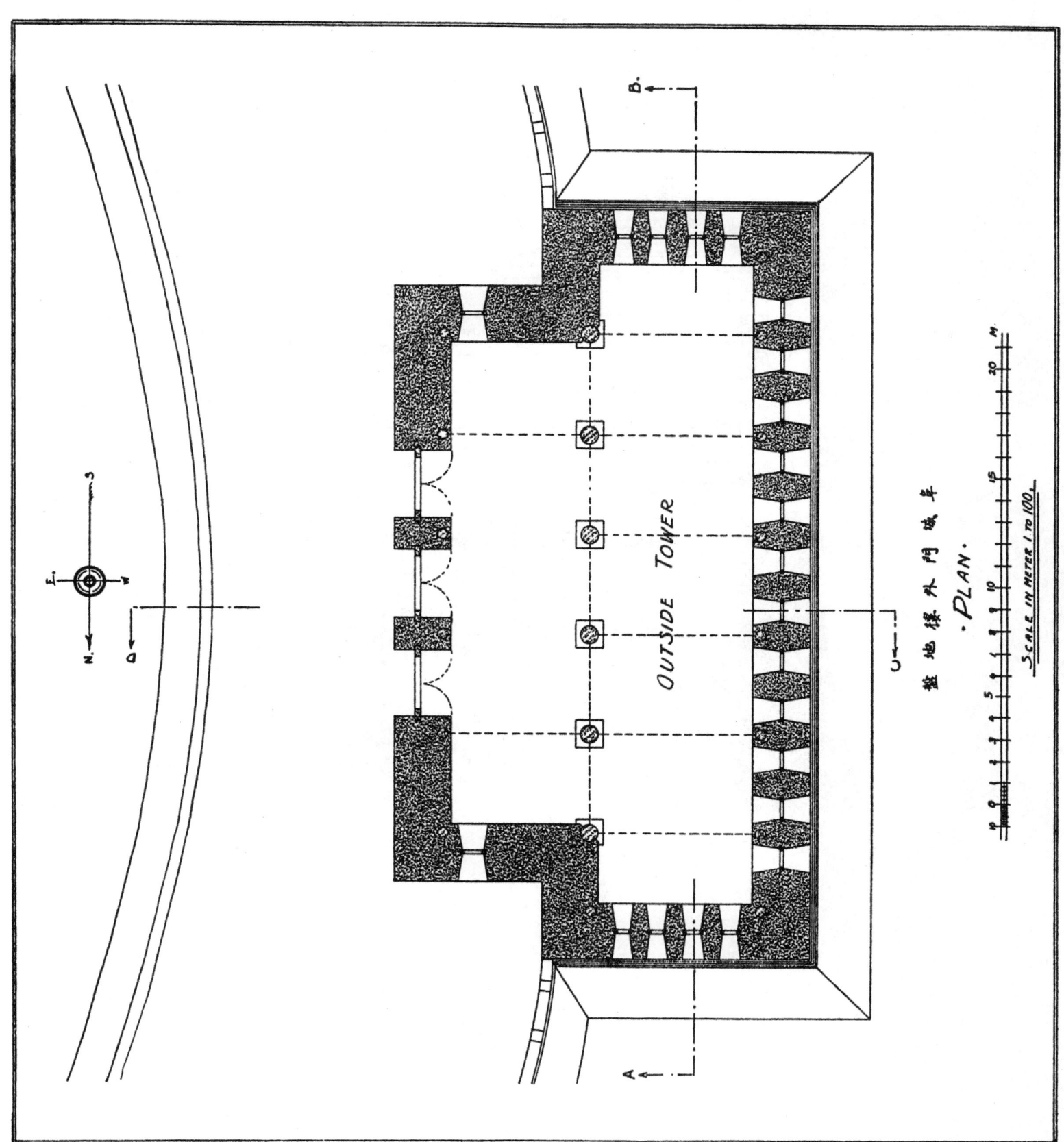

图 12 平则门箭楼平面

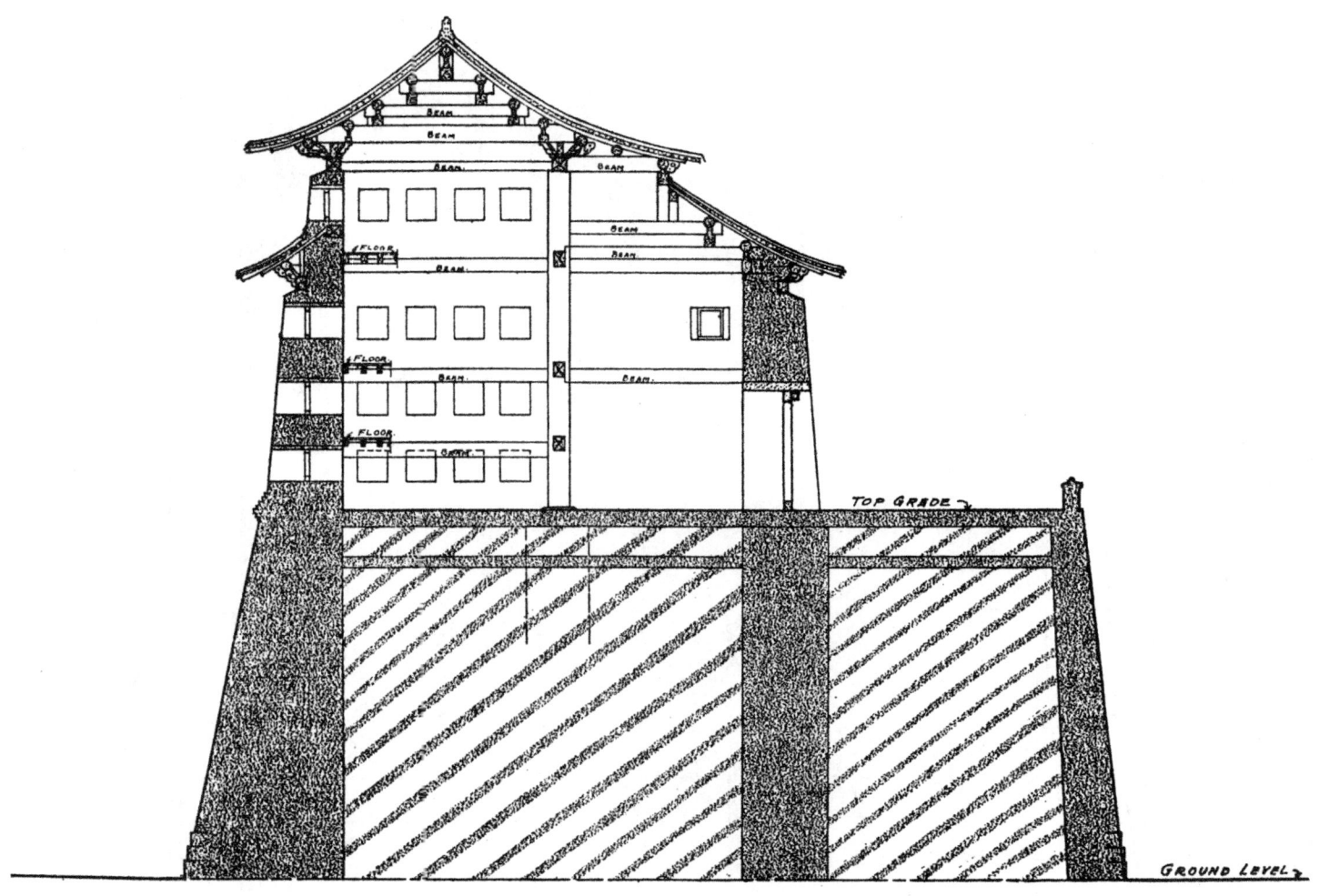

图 13 平则门箭楼横剖面

上层屋顶的构造、装饰与城楼上层檐完全相同。上层出挑的椽、飞照例比其下层的椽、飞略短些。

正面、山面的射击孔与内部大殿空间的划分一致，即一层屋檐之下有三排射击孔，之上有一排，正面每排有 12 个孔，山面每排 4 个。洞口从中间向内外均有扩张，状似纺锤，这种能使楼内弓箭手射击范围更广的安排极为实用。如果用枪炮防守，这样的设施就几乎没有必要了，我们甚至怀疑，沉重的枪炮除了可能在一层使用过之外，是否在箭楼上其他位置安置过。不过，在闭合的窗洞木板上绘制大炮炮口的这一设计，既有装饰效果，也与想象中的城门的防御价值相称。

这座箭楼的外观非常朴素。由于岁月与灰尘的侵染，加深了灰砖的色调，筒瓦也是灰色。只有木制梁枋、斗栱与山墙曾经有彩绘装饰，而如今大多已剥落了。但绘制在窗洞木板上的大炮炮口至今仍存，如同在警告可能出现的侵略者！

瓮城边门上有一座谯楼，比墙垛略高，其所在位置也没有突出于城墙表面。它是一座带有双坡屋顶的朴素砖作建筑，正面有两排射击孔。因其几乎完全隐没于墙垛与女儿墙之间，因此十分不显眼。

在主城墙上的城楼北面，有一座破旧的哨所。另有两个供街道巡警和守城卫兵使用的哨所，坐落于城门马道前街道的两侧，所幸为古树所遮掩。

平则门瓮城长 74 米，宽 65 米，其规模并不是最大的。其中，大部分场地都为煤栈与陶器铺所占，在东北角的道路与城墙之间，仍有属于小关帝庙的几座建筑，其外由院墙围绕。这个庙宇似乎现已不再用于宗教目的，在我参观之时，房间里堆满了陶罐和各种垃圾，但院落布局仍然完整。与之相对的瓮城东南角，堆着上过釉的色彩艳丽的瓷器，形成了更为亮丽的风景线。但瓮城后部却因充斥着煤栈与煤棚而变得肮脏而黑暗，商人就是在这里买卖各种由煤粉与黄泥混合制成的煤球、煤砖的。当春天到来时，内墙边的大桑树向黑色的地面舒展着新绿，小椿树也为堆满瓷器的角落增添了一抹艳丽。然而，最有活力的却是那些赶驴的人，一旦有人出现在瓮城之中，他们会立刻上前，不遗余力地劝说这些步行者，使其相信城外的道路不宜步行，只能骑驴——几乎没有哪个中国人会反对这一说法。

老式的铺面路从瓮城边门穿过，沿着北墙向外伸展，其两侧排列着小商店与乡村饭馆。世间再无比这更别致的风情画了。那些或驾着马车，或推着手推车，或用长扁担挑着两个晃晃悠悠的大篮子的乡下人，走在这里要远比走在其他城门外那些新近拓宽的碎石路上自在得多。商铺林立的街道与瓮城、城门楼浑然一体，构成了整个建筑群最恰当的引子，仿佛将我们置于数百年前的情景之中，让我们在走进城门深邃的拱洞之前便感染了与之相宜的情绪。

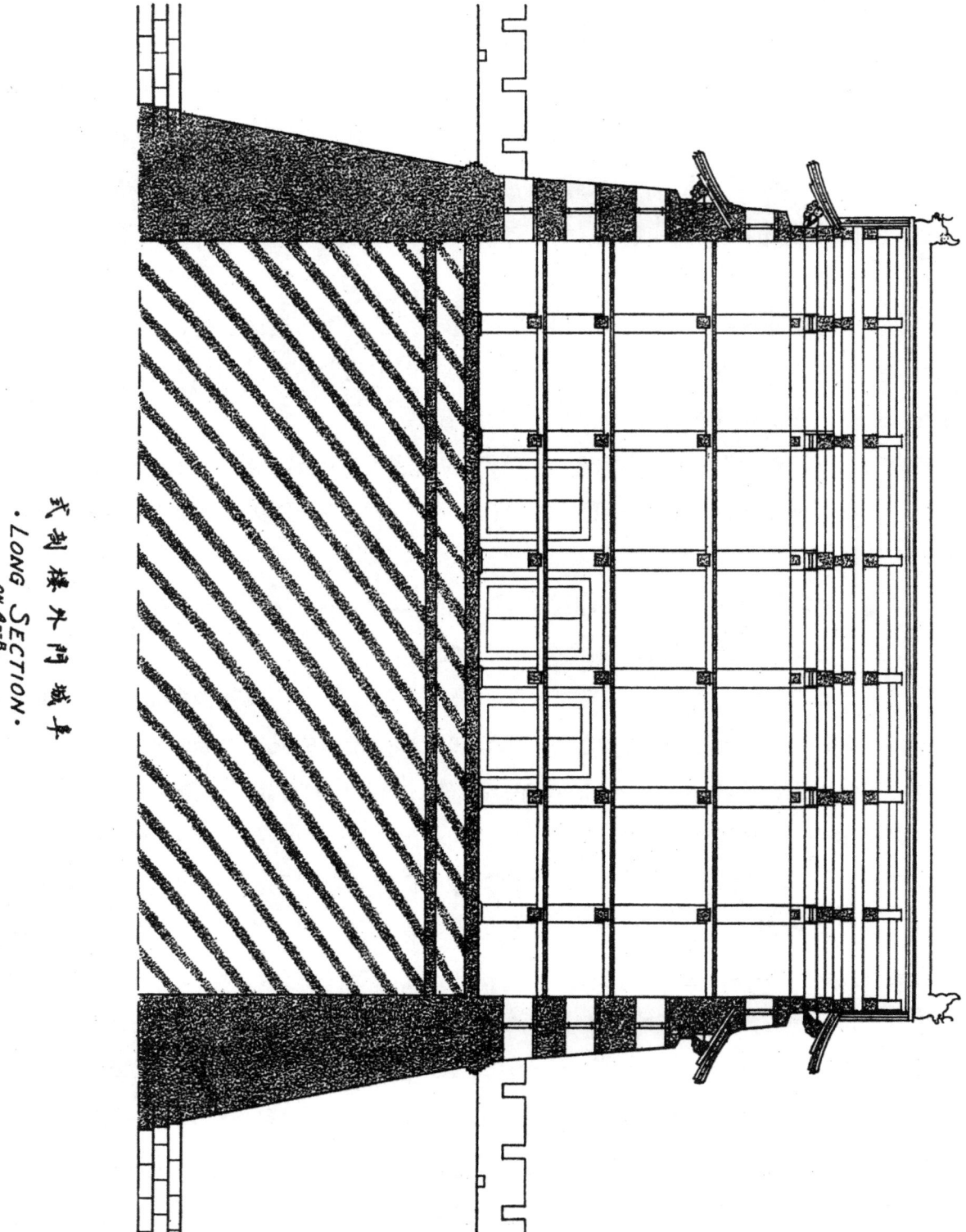

图 14 平则门箭楼纵剖面

图 15 平则门箭楼侧立面

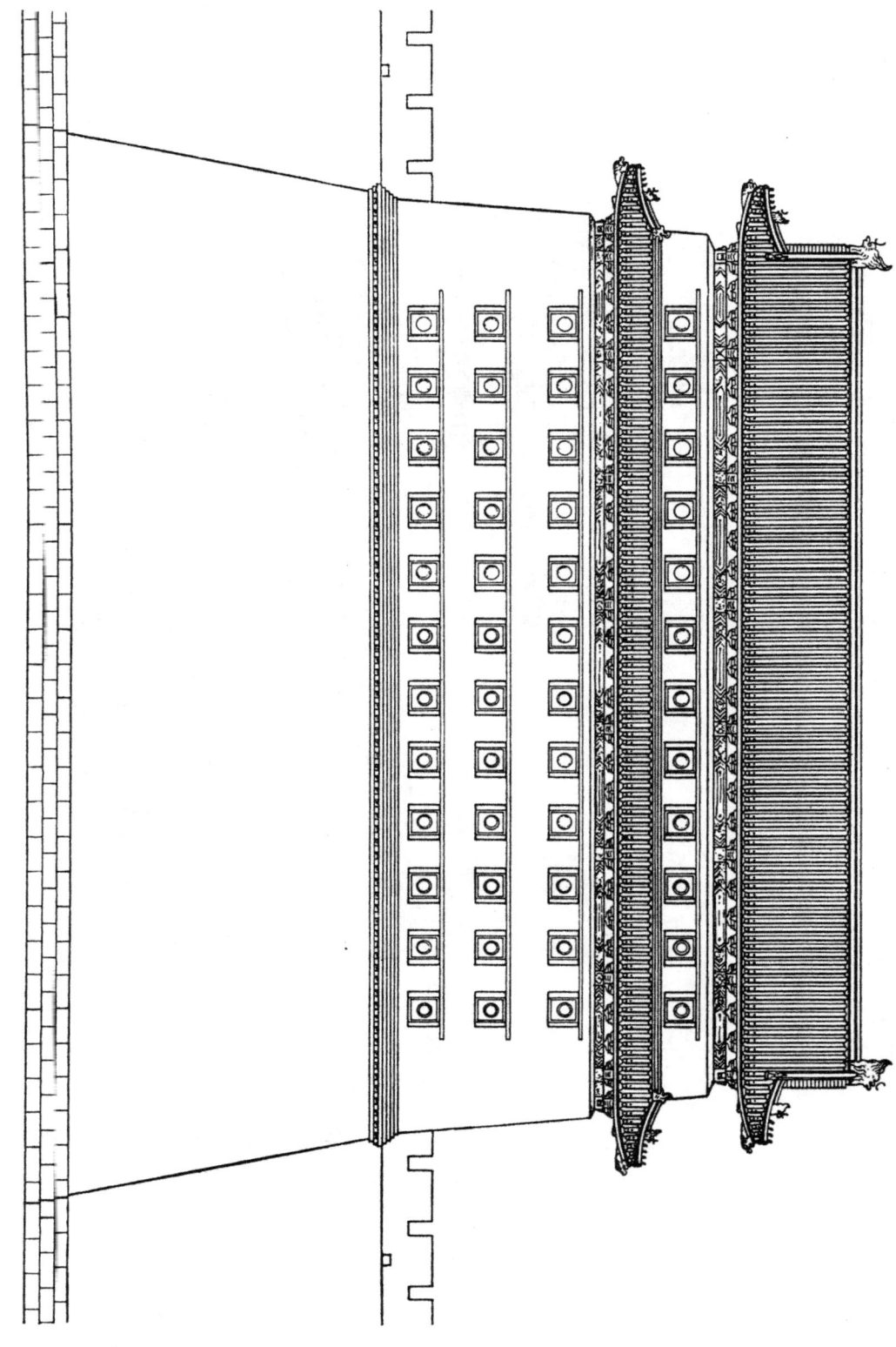

图 16 平则门箭楼正立面

西直门是西城墙上的北门,在很多方面与平则门相似,但其瓮城更大,转角几乎呈直角。整体来看,无论从哪个方向观赏,这座城门都宛如一幅壮观的画卷。沿着通向城门的宽阔道路走近城门,远远就能看到耸立于整齐划一的低矮建筑之间的巍峨城楼,道路两侧的这些老式建筑大多带有隔扇门窗,样式别致,因其规模较小,城楼便被映衬得格外高大、壮观。从城外走进来,最令人印象深刻的便是从荒地上拔地而起的方形瓮城和箭楼。瓮城的前墙长而直,有力地支撑着宽广的箭楼,与城角呈弧形的瓮城相比,它们给人的感觉是更加苍劲、厚重。从侧面看城门,特别是从南面,能够更好地体会到整组建筑的宏大规模。城楼与比之略矮的箭楼搭配协调,它们笔直的线条与鲜明的轮廓为建筑增添了韵律之美。两座雄伟的门楼倒映在城墙下的池塘里,显得更加气势磅礴。

城门的这座主体建筑目前保存相对较好。1894年重建颐和园并修通了穿过西直门通达颐和园的道路,同时也对该城门做了全面修缮。但是此工程尚未完工,便爆发了中日战争,因资金匮乏,工程不得不中断。彼时,城楼的大部分翻新工作已完成,而箭楼修得则比较少。西直门城楼的平面布局与平则门城楼大致相同,但比例有所差别,两座城楼总面阔相同,角柱之间的距离均为32米,楼身面阔27米多一点。但是西直门城楼进深较小,围廊进深15.8米,楼身进深11.2米。西直门城楼总高22.2米,仅比平则门城楼高1米。因此西直门城楼总体来说更为单薄。因此它外观看似更高,尤其是从山面看时。虽然山面较窄,但进

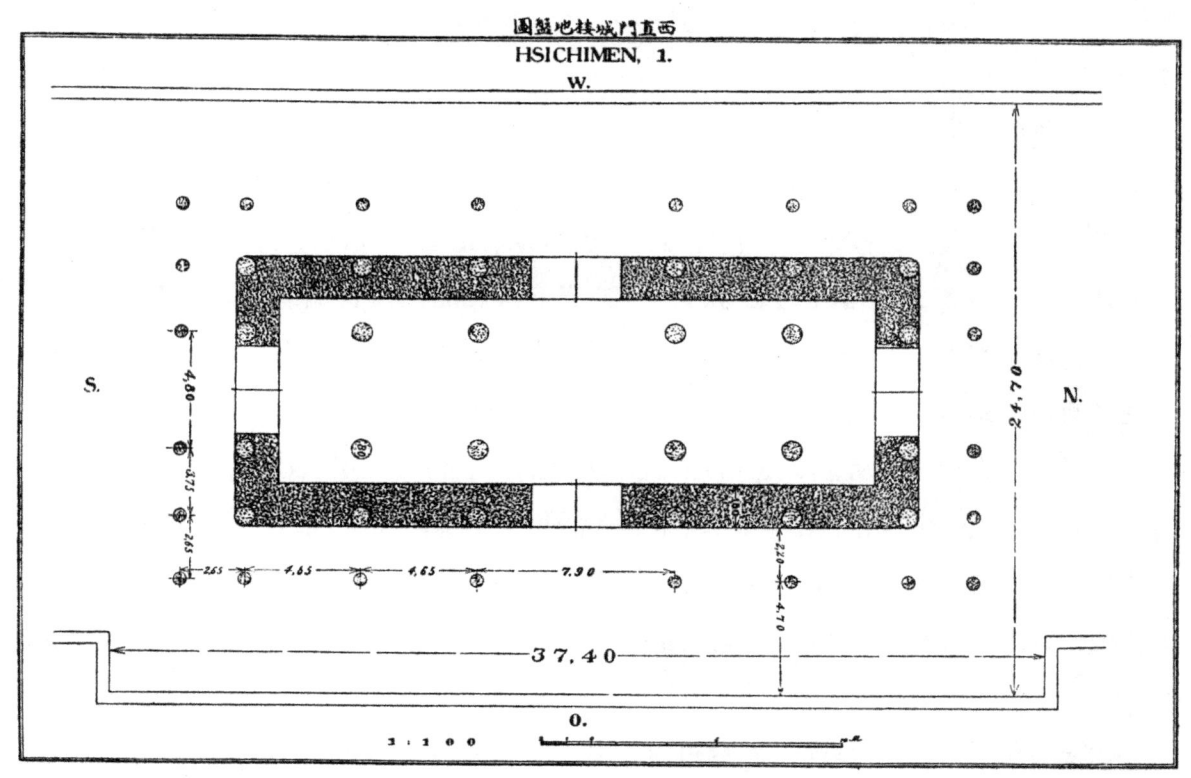

图17 西直门城楼平面

深是五间而非三间（平则门城楼的进深），面阔仍为七间。廊柱的排布很有韵律，柱间距从明间向稍间依次递减。各边明间面阔较大，上开楼门。第二排柱子完全嵌入砖墙中，最内一排柱子减少为每排4根，分立于室内。这些粗壮坚实的柱子（直径0.8米）支撑着主屋顶，但是柱身并未贯穿整个楼体，而是被二层楼板分为两部分，壁柱也是如此。上层柱与下层柱不完全对齐，而是略向中间靠拢，因此缩短了其横梁长度。三层翘曲的屋顶照例由圆檩承接，檩上为椽飞，檩下为出挑的斗栱。显而易见的是，西直门城楼的斗栱比平则门更为轻盈，这是晚期建筑的特征。中国建筑发展到晚期，降低了斗栱体系的结构功能，而增强了其装饰性，建筑绀构主要采用更为简洁的梁柱体系。另一区别于传统构造模式的做法是，二层平坐由立于围廊横梁、穿破屋面的瓜柱承接，不再由梁枋上出挑的斗栱承接，这样的构造可能更为坚固，但其与整体框架的融合度和之前的模式相比则相对偏低。出挑深远的二层屋檐，四角均由特殊的擎檐柱支撑。主屋顶由每侧两根檩子承托，而非早期城门楼的四根，因此梁的数量也减少了。设计者极尽全力简化了楼体构造，增大了其承重能力与强度。早期的构造方式自然更费工、费料，但它是否更为安全确实值得怀疑。

西直门城楼外部的装饰与彩绘，尽管已被北京的尘土侵蚀得有些模糊了，但仍完全可见。柱、门与窗框均被漆作朱红色，砖墙的抹灰也带有暖色调的红色。屋檐下与平坐下的梁枋均以蓝色与绿色的几何图案装饰。屋顶以绿琉璃瓦铺设，并饰有与平则门屋顶相同的脊兽与望兽。与平则门城楼相比，西直门城楼更窄，而屋顶更宽，因此其整体效果更为轻盈、典雅。

西直门箭楼修缮得不如城楼那般细致，其外观更为陈旧，背面的屋顶已开始塌陷。筒瓦显然是更新过的，伾墙体砖作应该已有几百年历史了。箭楼的规模、平面与立面，堪称平则门箭楼的副本，因此无需赘述。通过插图，就可以看出它的位置与宏大的规模。

瓮城很大，是个令人愉悦的地方。的确，它令人想起摆满货摊的嘈杂集市，那里充斥着人、畜、车的喧杂。与平则门相同，瓮城后部主要为煤栈所占，而在从正门向南转往边门的道路两边，则是陶器商贩的货摊以及人力车的泊车处。东北角被一圈独立的围墙隔开，墙内是一组很令人愉悦的寺庙，包括几间小屋（也有民居）、几棵大树以及一座精心培植的花园。寺庙曾用以供奉关帝，尽管它于1894年曾得到修缮，并保存完好，但似乎已被废弃。这组大型寺庙的前部原先是道士的住所，如今已被辟为商业性质的花园。园中几棵高大的椿树、柏树以其树荫遮住庭院，为盛夏带来一抹清凉与宁静，这与瓮城主区的烦乱嘈杂全然不同。

瓮城南边侧墙上有一座谯楼，穿过楼下的拱门，便来到了一条地道的中国老式街道，与其他城门外街巷两侧的简陋商店与临时货摊不同，这条街的两侧是一排排较为古老的老式房屋。倚靠瓮城城墙而建的是一排低矮建筑，从城门处一直延伸到箭楼城台，包围着瓮城西南角。这排长屋就像一个坐落于出挑深远的连续屋檐之下的市场，只不过这一市场由一个个商店组成，店主们把货品摆放在石头台阶上，或把食品摆放在门外的桌凳上。路的另一边大多是小旅馆与客栈，来此住宿的多为乡下人。房子同样是连续的一排，房屋式样千篇一律，但高度不同，有的仅一层，有的高两层。建筑物的天际线自然也是参差不齐的，中国传统街道的这一重要特征，并非出于审美的考虑，而是从风水的观点来看最适宜而已。这些房屋的正面由木柱与大的隔扇门窗构成，两层的房屋则在一层之上挑出雕饰鎏金的门楣。这条街显然是依照中国传统原则并按照统一规划布局的，也依然是正在迅速消失的风格独特的老北京最典型的风景之一。如今，那些从西直门飞驰而过、满载游客前往颐和园或西山的汽车，在驶过这些脆弱的老门面时应被强制减速，因为与颐和园或卧佛寺相比，这里毕竟展现了更真切的传统中国的日常生活图景。

2. 东城墙上的城门

东城墙的两座城门——齐化门与东直门，保存状况不如西城墙的城门，因此从建筑角度来看也就没那么吸引人了。环城铁路横穿瓮城，对此二门的破坏极大。城墙几乎全部被拆，这与修建穿过南城墙哈达门的京沈铁路时仅在墙上打孔的做法不同。东侧城墙瓮城原先如画般的景象自然消失殆尽，箭楼城门洞已不存，仅有一条道路顺沿铁路的低矮砖墙向外延伸，新建的带有月台的火车站侵占了原先由高大瓮城城墙庇护的场地。这样的改建，完全是对老城门的美与特质的漠视，如果仔细审视这些城门，就会发现新设计极度缺乏审美品位与建筑感知。

齐化门可能是北京城门中重建规模最大的一个。大约在20年前（1902年），这座城门的两座城门楼几乎全部翻新，因为义和团运动时期，日俄军队围攻北京，炮火对城楼造成了严重破坏。城楼虽尚未腐朽或衰败，但彩绘的装饰已有些许褪色，外部有几处干燥漆层也开始剥落。屋顶的绿琉璃瓦仍然保存完好，为建筑增添了一抹明亮。从街道远观城楼，前景中的绿树构成了画框，景色如画，极为怡人。

城楼的结构是通常的样式。楼高三层，由底层向上，每层的层高与面阔逐渐缩小。敞廊面阔七间，进深三间。建筑规模与平则门城楼（即与之对应的西侧城门楼）相同，但构造模式有所变化，类似于西直门城门楼以及其他几座重建的城门楼。与其他城门楼相比，这座城楼的特殊之处在于其不寻常的长宽比。楼身面阔27.5米，进深13米，围廊面阔32米，进深17米，虽然仅比平则门城楼相应的尺寸大一点，但墙体显然比早期城门楼薄很多，并

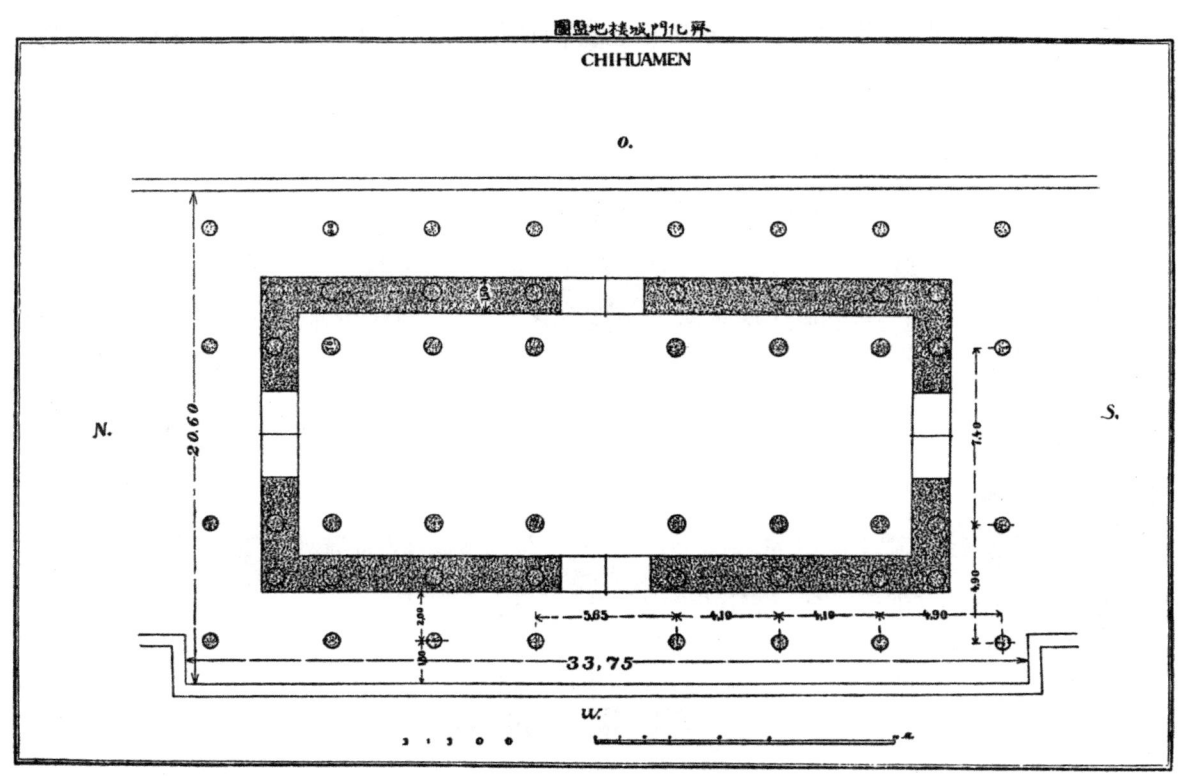

图 18 齐化门城楼平面

且，只有中间一排柱子嵌入砖墙。齐化门城楼最初与平则门城楼似乎并无二致，至于现在构造与细节上的不同乃是近代修缮的结果。

这两座城门的箭楼在平面与规模上非常一致，故对于前者的描述完全适用于后者。但齐化门箭楼的确保存稍好一些。平整的浅灰色墙砖看上去很新，与凹凸不平、风化严重的砖面城墙形成鲜明对照。城台显然更为古老，尽管其在乾隆三十一年（1766年）曾经局部修缮（据一块石碑的碑记）。

由城台处向外延伸的瓮城城墙有极少留存，而且端部以颇具异域风情的方式结束：蜿蜒的阶梯攀接着几个连续的平台，阶旁设有阶梯状的栏杆。其琐碎的的线条，似乎模仿了流行画册中的中世纪城堡，至少可以说，它与古城墙、城门肃穆庄严的风格格格不入。这种变化同样发生在或多或少受到铁路建设影响的其他城门瓮城上，只是变化稍有不同。

在这古老的瓮城中，唯一保留下来的是城楼门洞边上的一座小关帝庙。这组建筑虽然不显赫，但院中由其庇护的几棵树，却为被铁路所霸占的单调瓮城增添了一丝清新，与之相对的是位于门洞另一侧的火车站。门外的景象不甚有趣，狭窄的城壕上建有一座平淡无奇的城门桥，更不必提位于高大箭楼脚下不堪入目的房子。

正对东方的东直门与正对西方的西直门构成一对，二者遥相呼应。两门的城门楼形制相

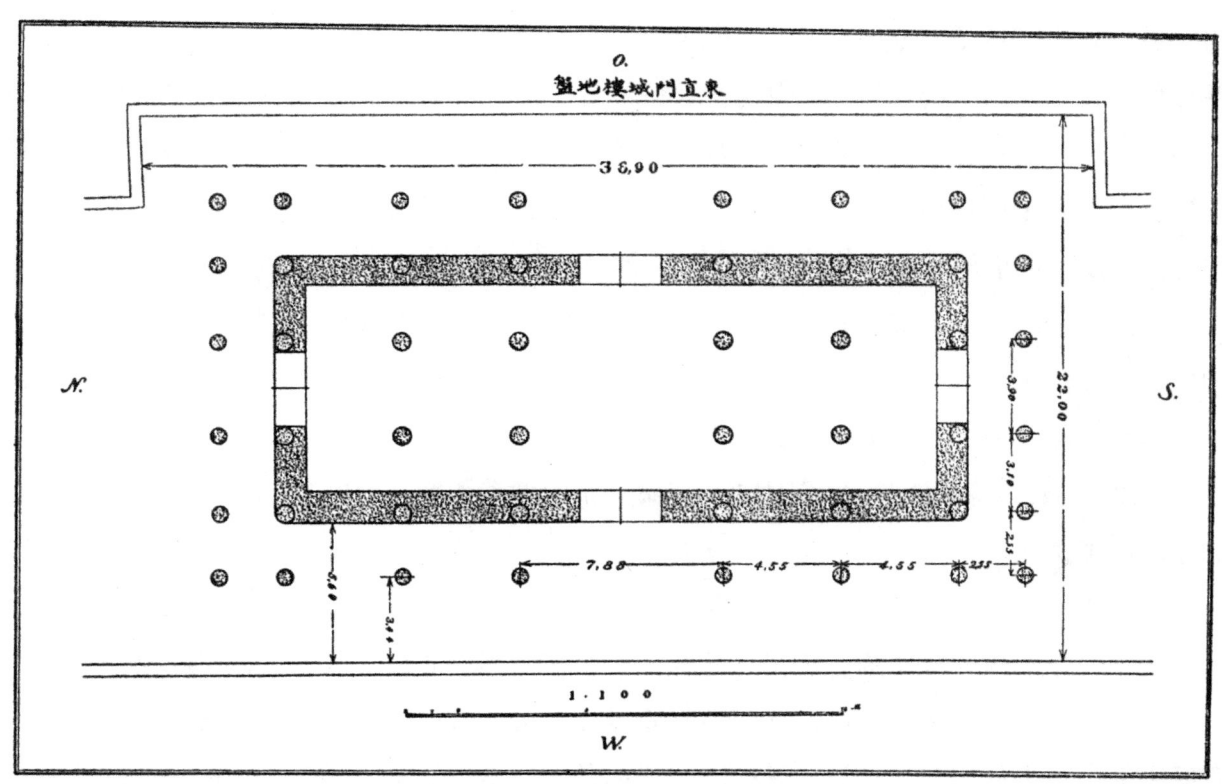

图 19 东直门城楼平面

同，规模也大致相同，因此与南边两座城门不同。但东直门保存不如西直门完整，其瓮城城墙已被拆除，瓮城基本被毁。两座城门楼保存状况也不佳。然而我觉得东直门城楼的历史恐怕不会超过百年。根据一款镶嵌在城墙上的石碑记载，通向城楼的马道重建于嘉庆八年（1803年），城楼很有可能也在此时翻修。墙体非常薄，表明其年代应该不会太早。箭楼可能有一部分年代更早，但不会早于乾隆末年，城台上嵌有石碑，但很遗憾的是其上并无铭文。

城楼的平面尺寸仅仅比对应的西直门城楼小一点点，楼身面阔26.7米，进深10.7米；墙厚1.2米；围廊面阔31.5米，进深15.3米。构造依旧为前后各三排柱，中间一排柱嵌入墙体，内、外两排柱以方抱柱支撑。其木作年代显然要早于西直门木作。平坐栏杆已基本被毁，其下的平坐栏板也是洞孔累累。屋顶已经开始腐朽、塌陷，倘若其上仍呈现为绿色，那并非来自于琉璃瓦，而是屋面上的一簇簇野草。柱子上累积着近几十年的尘土，遮蔽了原有的颜色及彩绘装饰。整座建筑看上去有种沧桑之美，别具风韵。

东直门城楼与箭楼之间的距离远比上述齐化门城门楼间距大。从侧面看，这座城门的规模与西直门差不多，是一组宏伟壮观的建筑，尽管两座城门楼之间现已失去连接部分。修建瓮城时参考的平面图，显然与西直门瓮城平面图类似，但城墙早已被毁，仅在箭楼城台边上有所残留。值得庆幸的是，留存部分比齐化门略长。箭楼残壁与主城墙之间的缺口似乎不像齐化门那般空洞，可能一部分原因是东直门瓮城植被较多，残墙端头尽管也有与齐化门完全一样的层层平台与锯齿状楼梯，但其斜坡处理似乎要略好一点。但是与前例中完全暴露于空旷单调环境之中的两座孤立城门楼和残缺城墙不同，东直门残留的建筑则掩映在周围丰茂的树丛与灌木之中。

因此这个地方除了前部有围绕着低矮砖墙与木栅栏的铁路穿墙而过之外，其原有特征还依稀可见。瓮城后部仍留存有一组别致的小建筑——关帝庙，几尊精美的雕塑被遗弃其中，因乏人问津而逐渐破败，几位老人将这座破庙当作他们的栖身之所。庙宇内外挺立着很多树木，有槐树、榆树与椿树，古老的瓮城城墙上散发着幽香的枣树，盛开着欢愉的花冠。如今，箭楼虽然并不古老，但其屋角已开始坍塌，它与装点在周围的生生不息的草木交相辉映、浑然一体。

瓮城残存部分的自然景色仅仅是城外美景的序曲——北京其他各大城门的风景是无法与之比拟的。观赏这幅美景的最佳时节是晚春或初夏，柳树清翠葱郁，护城河中的芦苇也翠绿如新。宽阔如运河的护城河是整幅风景的动脉；不论是从实用角度，还是从观赏角度来看，环境中所有的重要元素，均沿河岸而繁荣，亦或逐波而动。远离河岸处，黑猪用它们的长鼻子在肥沃的泥潭中翻腾；近处，孩子们像青蛙似的在芦苇荡中游戏，成群的白鸭在水面游荡，溅起水花，发出嘎嘎叫声，回应着各自主人的呼唤。拿着锡桶来河边取水的人，往往要在那里蹲一会儿，凝望着这幅田园诗歌般的画面，沉浸于寂静的欢愉中。向南走几步，有一个过河的小渡口，成为一条由对岸到火车站的捷径，水面不时划过一只方形平底船，载着身穿白色夏衣的乘客，游移于低垂的柳枝之间。组成这幅生动又宁静的和谐图景的各个要素无不倒映于水中，倒影又为其增添了意境之美与田园诗意，在铁路与汽车尚未出现之前，这种氛围在北京各城门处屡见不鲜。

3. 南城墙上的城门

如我们所知，南城墙上有三座城门，构成了内、外城之间的通道。由于处于中心位置，这三座城门都很知名，其宏大的规模和繁丽的装饰备受游客及初来乍到者的赞赏，但从历史与建筑学的角度来说，它们却是京城最无趣的城门。与其他几座城门相比，这三座城门在近代受创并重建的频率更高。正中央的前门改建最为彻底，两座旁门的改建规模也很可观。

哈达门与顺治门这两座城门是姐妹门。二者在规模与特征上都很相似，保存现状也相同。两座城门均于近期（1920—1921年）重建，或者说近期被毁，因为修复工程只涉及城楼，箭楼被简单地一拆了事。据称，之所以拆除是因为箭楼已然糟朽，岌岌可危，更有铁路从其下通过。但事实上，顺治门箭楼的梁枋仍然置于城台之上，看上去新而坚固。在被拆除之前，哈达门箭楼看似更糟糕一些，其屋角已然开始坍塌，但是倘若当局对它们稍微多花一点心思或兴趣的话，这两座箭楼其实是可以被保留下来的。当然拆掉箭楼，再卖掉建筑材料更加容易而且划算，并可以把重建计划推迟到更富财力且更稳定的政权时期（！）。因此，只有从内侧，或者说从内城的一侧，才能看到城楼高耸的壮观景象。从外侧，即外城的一侧观看就很枯燥乏味，因为瓮城里没有主体建筑能突出于主城墙的绵长水平线上。

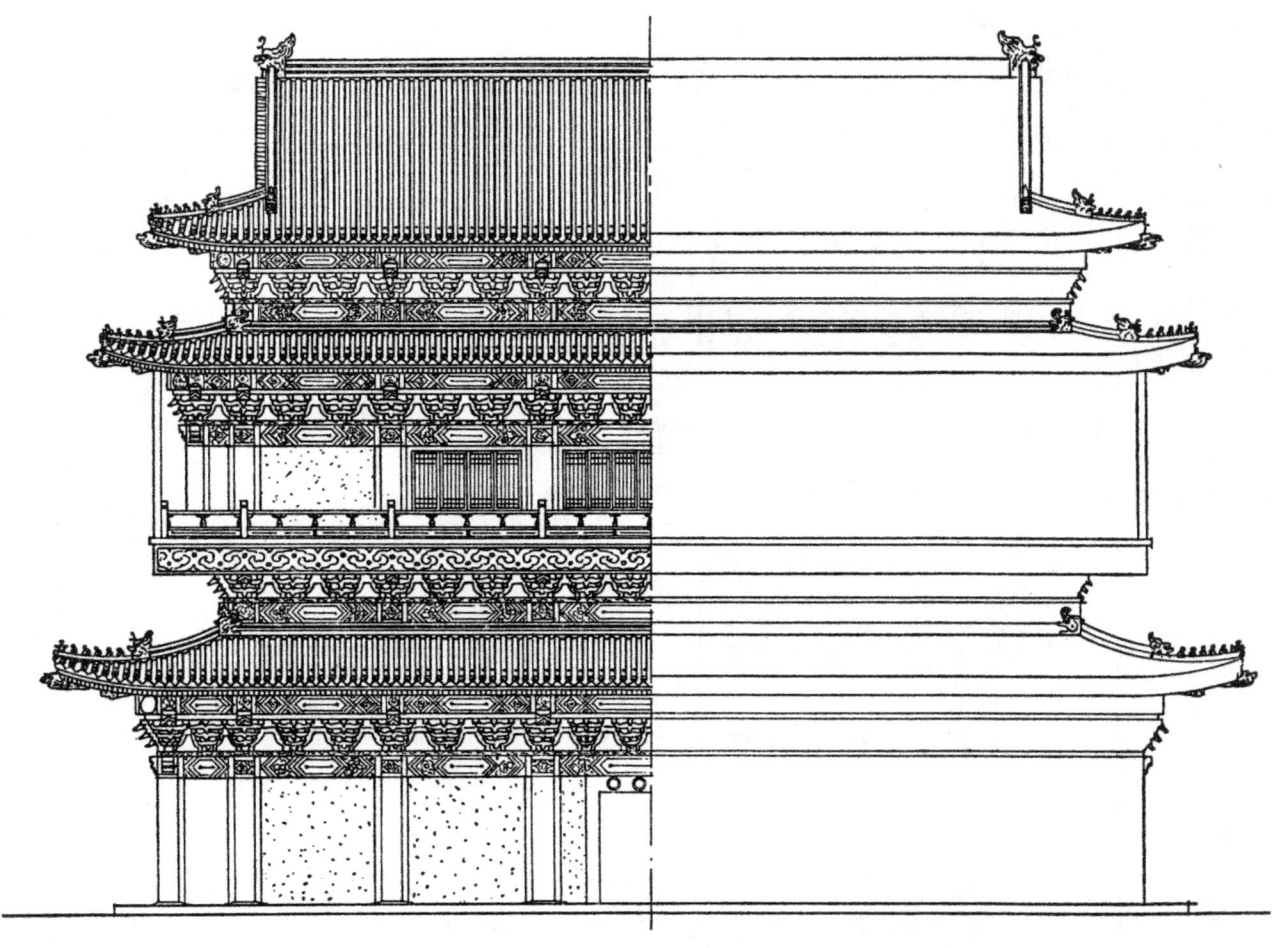

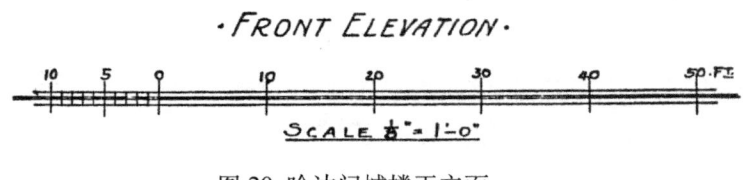

图 20 哈达门城楼正立面

外国人最熟悉的城门是哈达门，因为它靠近使馆区，并且横跨全城最热闹的商业街——哈达门大街。夏日傍晚，夕阳在红柱子与绿色琉璃屋瓦上撒下一抹余晖时，从此街眺望北门，装饰一新的城楼格外美丽动人。明亮而温暖的色彩泼洒于规模宏大的建筑上，其景象是如此令人愉悦，在装饰与工艺方面亦无可挑剔。城楼上的门楣、斗栱、栏杆与屋顶装饰等建筑部件都很完整，细部也无损坏或风沙侵蚀之处。

这座城楼规模比前述的任何一座都要大。楼身面阔28.7米，进深14.4米；柱廊面阔33.4米，进深18.8米。从城台到屋脊顶部的高度为25米；如果我们加上城台的高度，建筑总高接近40米。建筑上下两层面阔均为7间，进深5间。斗栱出三跳，然而其结构上的承重作用却不大。水平方向的梁枋非常宽厚，装饰繁复。承重结构照例由前后各三排柱构成，以梁枋横纵相连，并通过瓜柱与檩承托屋顶。与早期城门楼相比，其结构整体已经有所简化，屋顶梁枋数量不像平则门城楼那样多，但它仍是根据固有的原则营建，规模宏大。

街道穿过城楼城台高耸的拱门（很可能是后来扩建的），直贯巨大的瓮城，又从箭楼城台类似的拱门穿出。与这条街道垂直相交的是一条两边围着低矮砖墙的双轨铁路，穿过瓮城侧墙上的开口延伸开去。这条铁路上的火车来往频繁，因此城门处的交通常被关闭的铁路栅栏所阻断，此种设置时常导致马车与手推车的严重拥堵。然而，因为瓮城基本是空的，

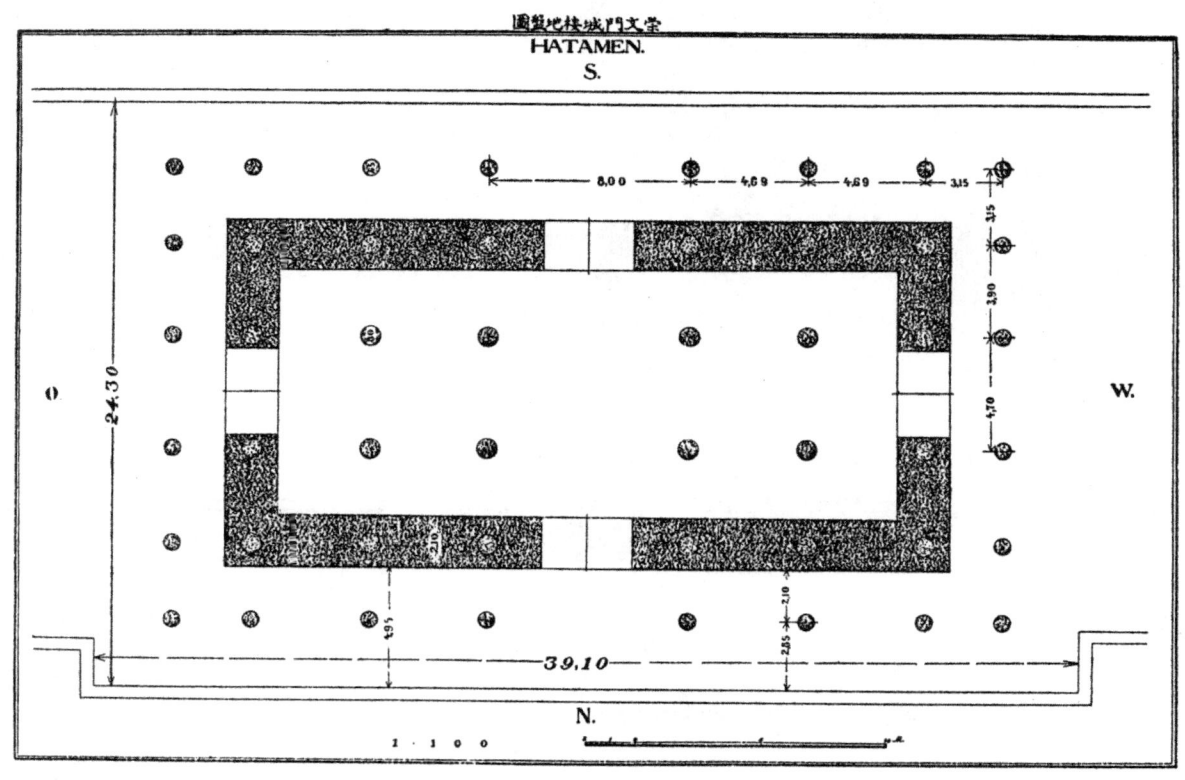

图21 哈达门城楼平面

所以道路两侧空间充裕。其中仅有的建筑物是一座毗邻铁路线的低矮哨所，及其对面的一间小平顶房。瓮城中庙宇无存，仅有几棵树。瓮城城墙与城台上，植被更为丰茂，这里有很多小槐树与枣树，雨季过后，便成为一片名副其实的丛林。

由于箭楼不存，城门外景变得单调而低沉。城壕很窄，其中只有一条混浊的小溪，城门桥也是普通的样式，附近最显眼的建筑要算铁路的煤棚了。只有沿着哈达门大街向南再走远一段，才能看到一些门面雕花鎏金的别致的旧式商店。

想要观赏城门本身，可以在主街正面仰视，也可以在顺城街从侧面去看，因为从此角度看去，马道周围有参天古树映衬着城门。

顺治门外观几乎与哈达门相同。瓮城城墙呈一条平缓的大弧形，箭楼已无存。箭楼遗址处，还能看到一些石柱础与大木料。此外，箭楼城台上，还留有五座生锈的高轮铁炮。其中三四座上标记着作为所有者的官员姓名，其中一位是崇祯时期的，其余均为康熙年间的。作为历史文物与法国耶稣教会铁炮铸造技艺的见证，这些铁炮本应被保存在更稳妥的地方。

新近修缮、重绘的城楼，规模几乎与哈达门城楼完全相同，仅比后者略窄、略低一点。因此我们可以忽略其装饰与构造，不再赘述。

尽管我们已多次谈及顺治门与哈达门之间的相似之处，但也不能以此推论两座城门是

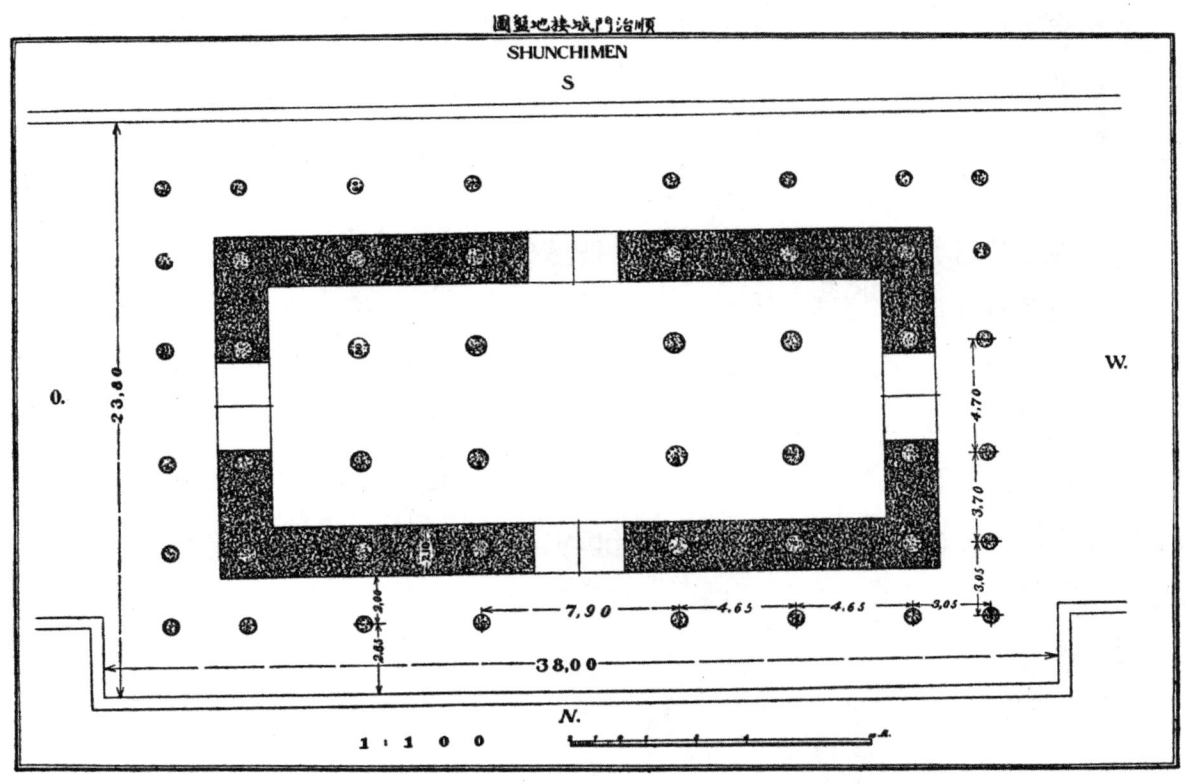

图 22 顺治门城楼平面

完全一样的。二者之间一个极其显著的区别便是顺治门仍然很好地保留了原来的瓮城。经过此门的铁路线没有穿透瓮城城墙，而是铺设于箭楼城台外侧。街道穿过主城楼下的拱门，没有沿直线向前延伸，而是陡然东转，从侧墙上一个较小的拱门穿出，就如前文所述的保存较好的那些西墙城门那样。因此，瓮城便成为一个由城墙隔绝起来的独具特色的场所。

这里主要的建筑当然是城门寺庙——小关帝庙，它坐落于道路与主城墙之间，由高大美丽的椿树环抱簇拥着。靠近小庙处，几位算命先生搭起了摊棚，收取很少的钱即可指导人们解决他们生活中的烦恼，这项服务比任何宗教服务都更受平民欢迎。在瓮城的另一侧，耸立着几座虽世俗却更为实用的小房子，其中大部分空间堆满了家用陶器，有些是上了釉的，在白棚与绿树的掩映下熠熠生辉。后部的煤棚不像平则门等城门处的煤栈那般显眼，占地面积也较小，并基本被大量木板、陶器堆与大树所遮挡，因而无损于此处的缤纷色彩与盎然绿意，这使得瓮城格外宜人。

一旦穿过边门门洞，这样独具魅力的景致便即刻消失了。古瓮城中安静祥和的氛围立即被现代中国城市的嘈杂所取代，这里有着宽阔而繁闹的大街，用砖和石膏建造而成的半洋式建筑，铁路轨道与煤栈，以及不断鸣笛以期强行穿过驼队与人力车群的福特汽车。

前门，又称正阳门，位于南城墙正中，是北京所有城门中最重要的一座。位于皇宫正前方的重要位置及其宏大规模，使之成为首都最重要的历史建筑地标。单就这座城门及与其相关的历史事件，就可以写厚厚的一本书。但在这里，我们仅能简略陈述其建筑特征与近年来实施的改建。这组宏伟的古城门建筑群曾是皇城的主要出口，连接着帝王禁苑与平民城市。然而事实上，现在的前门只是瑰丽的老城门建筑群在被毁后的临时替代物。

原先的建筑群包括一个巨大的 U 型瓮城，内有场院，四个主方向各有一门。北门位于巨大的城楼之下，面对宫城外门——大清门（现称中华门）[1]，并通过一道长方形围墙与之相连。与之截然相对的南门直穿箭楼城台，正对护城河上的城门桥和外城主街——前门大街。此门只为皇帝开启，其他老百姓只能从东、西侧的两个瓮城边门穿行而过。瓮城长 108 米，宽 85 米，环绕瓮城的城墙基厚 20 米，它是皇城最外一层院落，由城墙和城门与皇城连接。当然，这里以前主要被占为集市，但是，绕它而建的坚固瓮城和宽广的箭楼，最初无疑是为了防守内城而建造的。由于这座城门恰好位于首都中心，内、外城又在此紧密相连，因此这座伟大建筑的原有范围与特征已逐渐让位于更为新式的规划与理念，尤其关注大都市的交通问题。

最先，在瓮城两侧各修建了一座火车站，穿过城门的交通量随之剧增。之后，出现了民

---

[1] 大清门实际上是皇城城门，这里可能是作者理解有误或笔误。

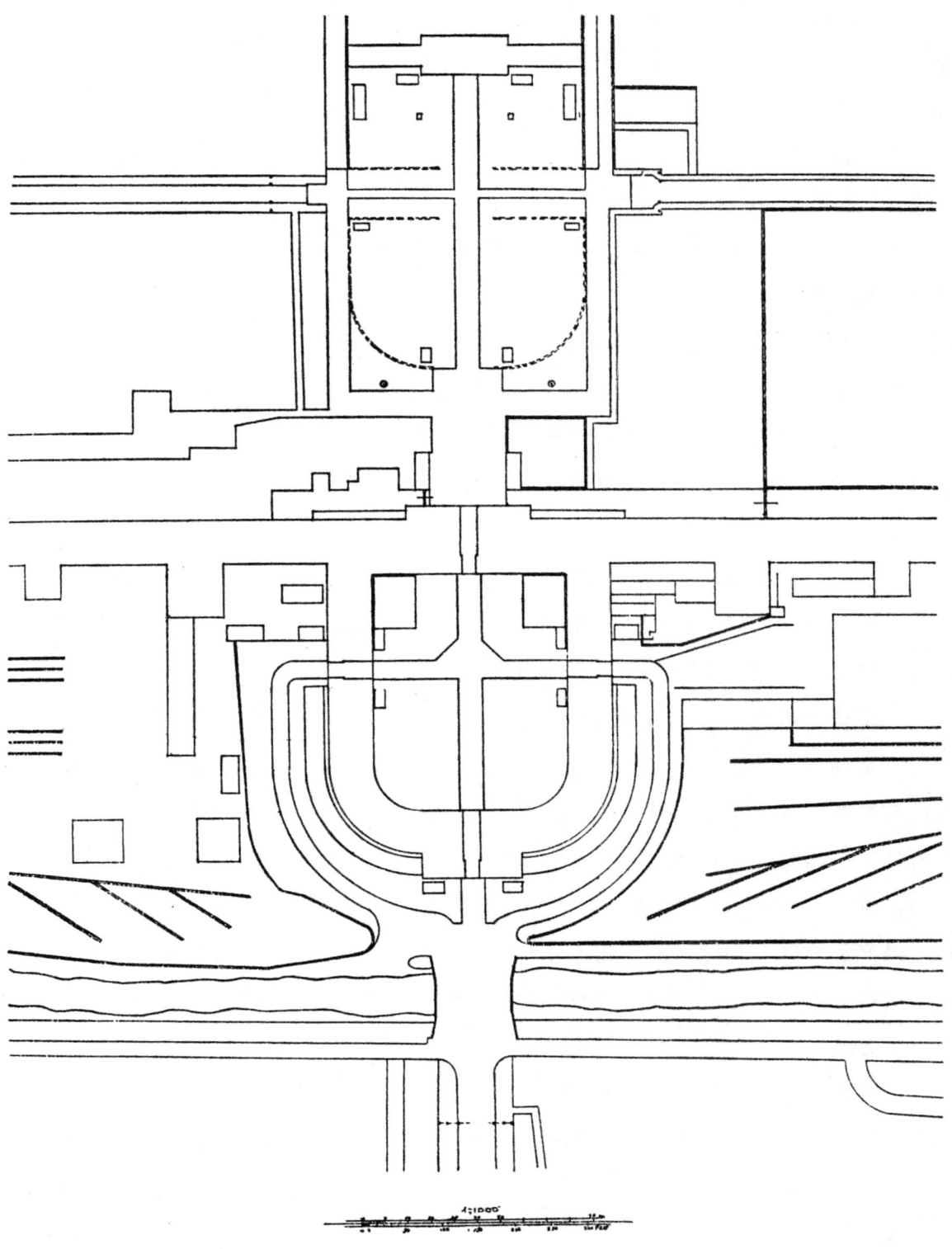

图 23 重建前的前门广场总平面

国政府，这个政府迫切要求剥夺皇权，将其交还民众。对于前门来说，这意味着将原先仅为皇帝专用的中心大门变为所有人都可使用的通道。由于经过城墙下唯一拱门往来内城的交通量飞速增加，这个通道很快就变得不能胜任，时常引发恼人的拥堵。为解决这一问题，政府委托德国建筑师罗特凯格尔（Rothkegel）制定改建前门的计划，以规范城门内及周边的交通。

北京中心城门的这一极为重要、影响深远的现代化规划于1915年筹备完成，并逐步开始实施，到1916年城门变为现在的样子。城门当初带有巨大的瓮城、边门与别致的场院，那些有幸看到过前门原貌的人，一致谴责这种大规模变动摧毁了众多老建筑，然而同时他们也承认，无论从卫生还是交通方面说，原先的状态都是不可忍受的。由于那位重新规划设计前门及与之相连的街道的欧洲建筑师备受责怪，我这里想要引用一下他自己对城门效果的评论，他认为他最初的设计方案并未得到中国当局的严格执行，其中很多细节被任意修改。然而这些修改很可能只关乎建筑装饰和箭楼改建的细节部分，而不涉规划布局的核心特质。这从罗特凯格尔先生自己的设计中便可看出，征得先生同意，我们得以将之展示于此。将前门彻底变化前后的平面图并置于此，即可为读者提供一个自行判断的机会，而我的任务则仅限于对其最重要的新特征加以简要说明。

瓮城城墙全部被拆，原先封闭的场院变为开放空间，或者说是一个在南端坐落着宽阔箭楼的矩形场地。老城楼城门两侧的主城墙上新辟了两个门洞，宽阔的街道由此穿过，为直通城门东西两侧的火车站提供了便利。两条大街紧贴原有瓮城城墙外侧而建，交汇于护城河大桥处。瓮城内外以及靠近主城墙的所有的小房屋与小商店均被清理拆除，仅有瓮城东南角与西南角的观音殿与关帝庙两座小庙得以保留。两组寺庙建筑未受影响，庙宇南侧不远处，矗立着两尊大石狮。原先瓮城范围内的其他地方依然很空旷，只有两条宽阔的铺面大路从东西、南北方向交叉而过，路两侧围有石墩与铁链，此种围栏同样被用于场地外边界，部分边界沿瓮城故墙而建。

与之相应的是，主城楼与中华门之间的北侧广场，亦铺有石板，并重新布局。原先位于广场北端的哨所，现已移近城墙，并以锁链环绕。在哨所北面一侧不远处，设置有一个装饰性的喷泉。广场另一边，直到中华门一带，一排排树木被以欧洲方式栽植，周围用铁链栏杆围起。

新规划的主要宗旨在于改善内城与外城之间的交通状况，从城门两侧的新通道穿过的两条大街贯穿南北，无疑使这一目的卓有成效地实现了。为达此目的，瓮城城墙被全数牺牲，原有的瓮城也基本湮灭不存。所有这些完全不顾及美学与历史的重建都是在中国政府的直接建议与监督下完成的，丝毫未受外国人所提顾虑的影响。

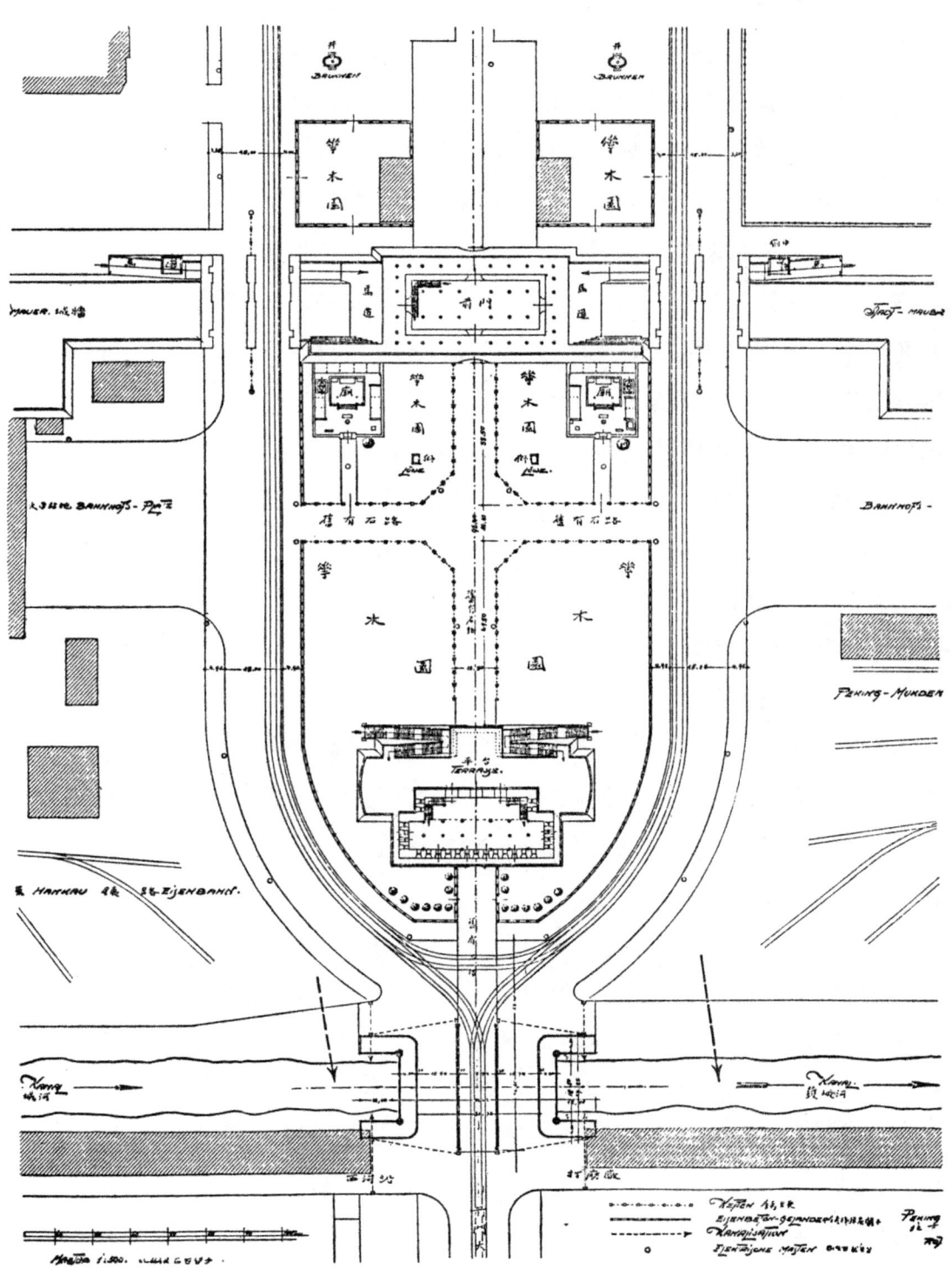

图 24 重建后的前门广场总平面

如今，中央大门给人的印象，不管从哪个方面看显然都是令人失望的。的确，城楼仍保有其原有形态，但通向城台的马道却被新开的两个拱门破坏了（看似损坏了马道的坚固性），楼前广场因过于西洋化而无法与城楼的建筑风格相协调。从南侧，包括原属于瓮城的一大片荒凉空地处看城楼，其景象更为糟糕。观赏箭楼时也有同样的感受，亦或更甚，至少可以这样说：箭楼被以一种与原有风格完全背离的方式装饰一新。箭楼孑然而立，两侧瓮城城墙遗迹所存无几。由两条之字型坡道拾级而上，可登上楼前的城台，台阶之间隔有数层平台，平台上饰有阶梯状汉白玉栏杆和凸出的挑台。此外，箭窗上还饰有弧形窗盖，弄巧成拙地仿照皇宫窗户的式样。箭楼的改造可以说是前门改造过程中最令人惋惜的一处，而且，这种改建并无实际价值或理由可循。

前门箭楼的形制与其他城门箭楼相同，但其规模要大得多。其主立面朝南，平台层面阔接近 50 米，最大进深 24 米，总高 38 米。因此，其构造部件的强度与数量均有增加。墙体收分，在底部厚约 2.5 米，前后各三排结实的柱子支撑起屋顶。外观照例有两层屋檐；上层屋檐较大，为歇山式，出挑的翘曲屋檐统领着整个建筑，下层披檐由第三层楼身上挑出。两层屋檐均铺有明亮的绿琉璃瓦。

整个建筑的历史不超过 20 年。它重建于义和团运动时期的毁灭性大火之后，火源来自瓮城中的店铺，民族主义狂热分子因店铺售卖外国商品而纵火。箭楼的墙体与屋顶显然是那时的，但其装饰特征，正如我们前文所讲，则属于更近的时期。

义和团运动结束后不久，城楼也遭遇了与箭楼相似的命运。裴丽珠（Bredon）[1] 所著的关于北京的书可供参考：

> 围城结束后的几个月，相同的场景再次上演：这次是城楼意外失火，有人将之归咎于印度军队的粗心。中国人担心厄运笼罩城市，急忙重建了这两座城门楼，这成为自乾隆时期（？）以来修缮的唯一古迹。城楼历时五年方才建成，建楼场景极为壮观：八层高的竹制脚手架震惊了西方建筑师。钉子、锯子或锤子全部不用，仅将木杆与竹子的端头捆扎在一起，便可达到任意高度，既不会造成材料的损坏或浪费，在搭建与拆除过程中也极为省力。[2]

在中国和日本，这种脚手架仍旧盛行。在日本，我见过搭建至令人晕眩高度的此种脚手

---

[1] Bredon，全名 Juliet Bredon，朱丽叶·布雷登，中文名裴丽珠，长期在华居住的女作家。

[2] 参见裴丽珠的《北京纪胜》(*Peking: A Historical and Intimate Description of Its Chief Places of Interest*)，第二章 *The Wonderful Walls of Peking*，1919 年由上海出版商别发洋行（Kelly and Walsh, Limited）初版。

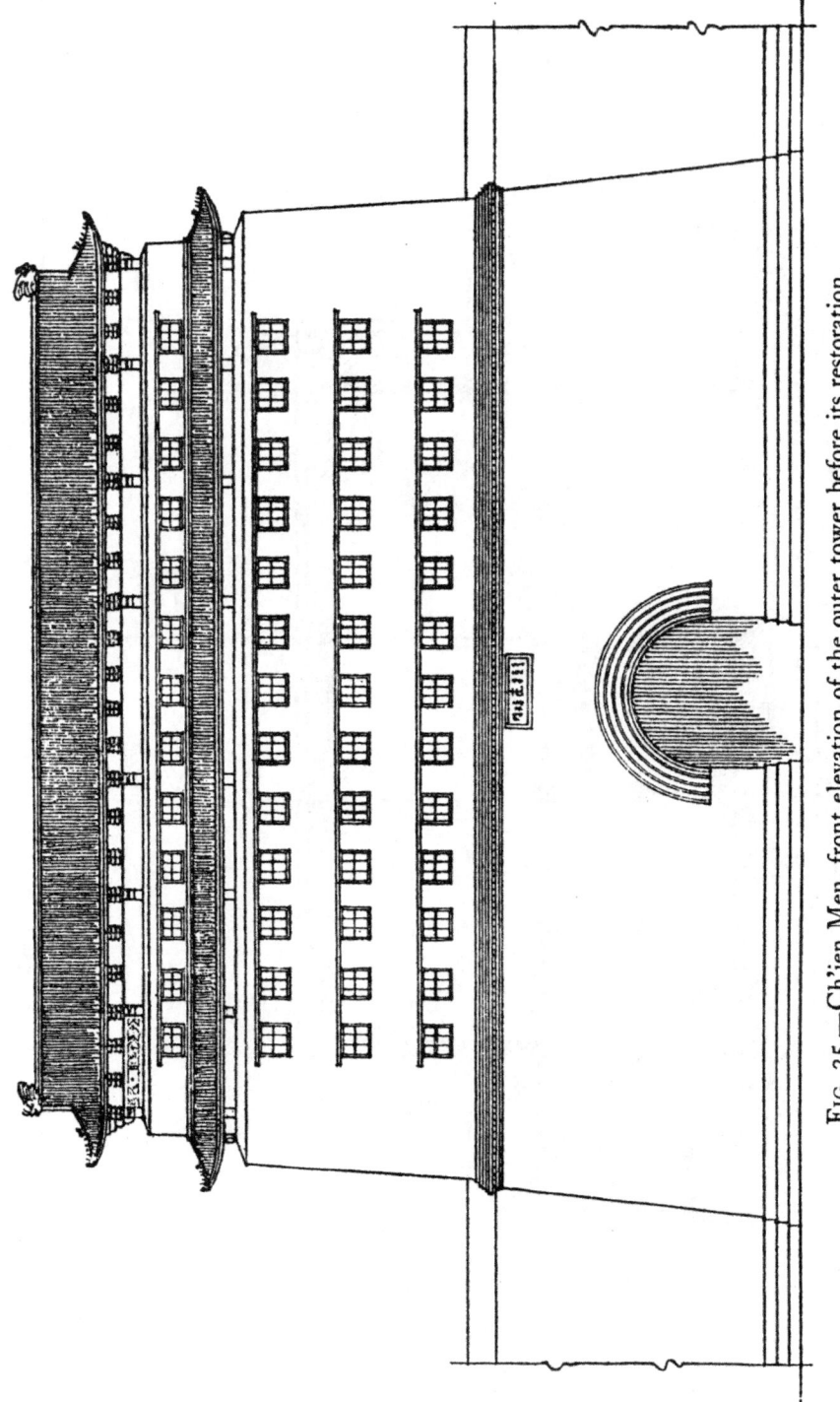

FIG. 25.—Ch'ien Men, front elevation of the outer tower before its restoration.

图 25 修缮前的前门箭楼正立面

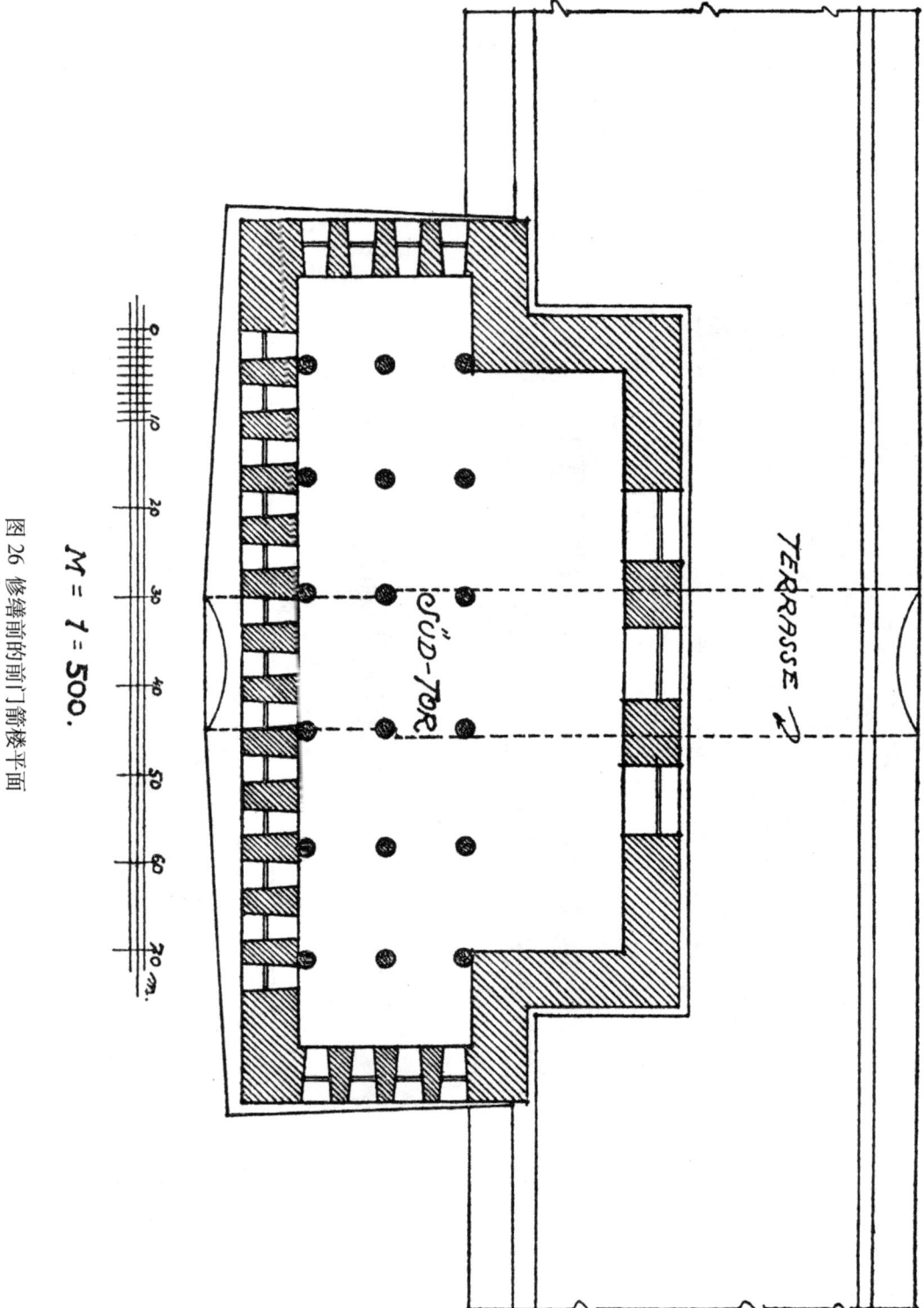

图 26 修缮前的前门箭楼平面

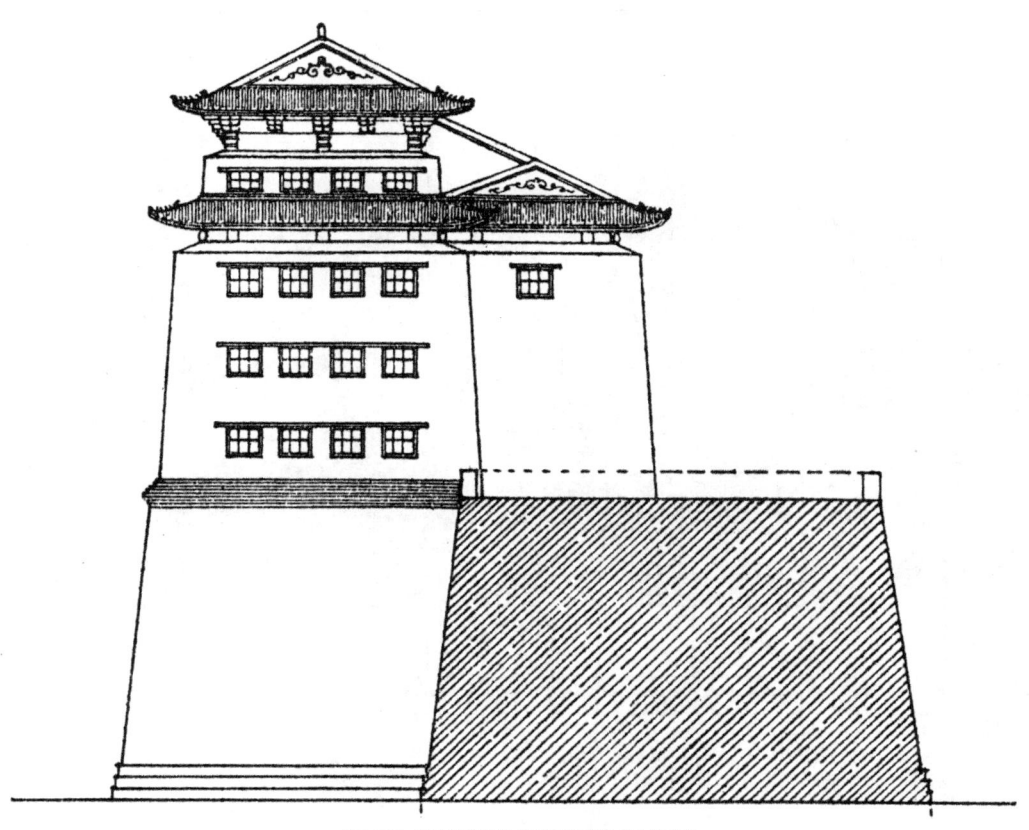

图 27 修缮前的前门箭楼侧立面

架,它们被用来建造极高的木塔。在那里,古老的传统工艺比在中国保存得好,木建筑仍很盛行,并保留着纯粹的形式。不幸的是,中国北方的木构工艺已日益罕见(部分原因是木材稀少),这可以从新建城楼上发现,例如,城楼之上的多层斗栱已失去其结构功能,变成了装饰构件。

前门新城楼上的斗栱非常繁复,在主屋檐下至少有五跳,但看其承载作用却似乎不大。栱很单薄,连接松散。这些斗栱与宋代及其以前建筑中结合牢固的斗栱之间的差别,是中国建筑发展到后期的重要特征之一。毫无疑问,前门城楼是北京在 20 世纪按照传统样式修建的最重要的建筑,尽管它绝非乾隆时期以来修缮的唯一大型建筑。在此期间,其他城门楼、宫殿与寺庙也有重建,但都不及前门城楼的规模之大。建筑围廊面阔 41 米,进深 21 米,楼身面阔 36.7 米,进深 16.5 米。从地面到屋脊通高 42 米,其中建筑高度为 27.3 米,其余为城台高度。建筑结构照例为前后各三排柱,以厚重的梁枋纵横相连,并以斗栱与檩承接椽子。当然,中间一排柱仍嵌于砖墙中,内外两排柱则以方抱框加固。外廊面阔达九间(进深五间),与其他小城门相比,屋顶坡度因其异常宽阔而显得相对较缓。必须承认的是,虽然整个建筑的尺度加大,但对于增强外观效果并没有什么补益。总体来说,小城门楼的比

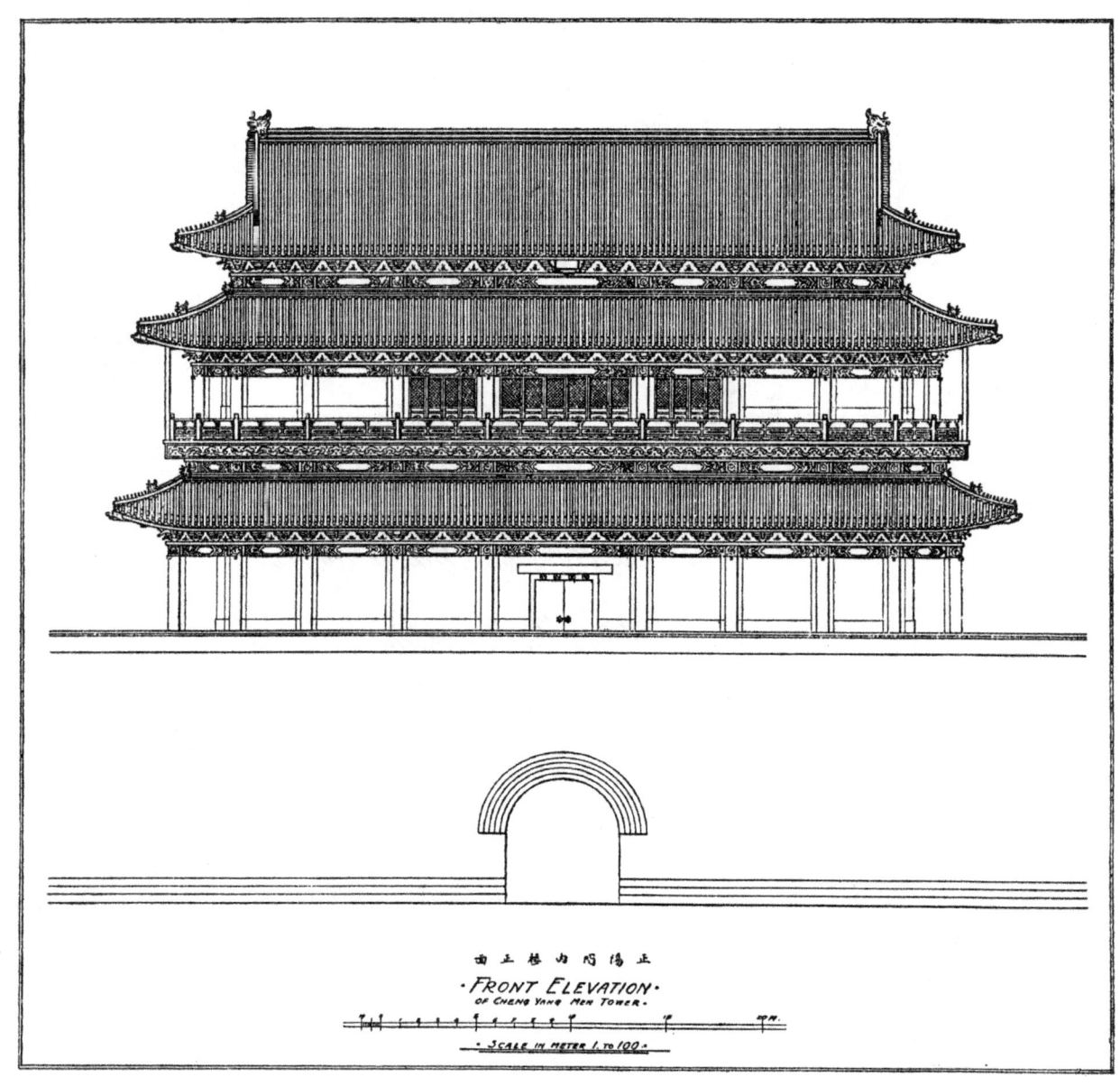

图 28 前门城楼正立面

例更为匀称，与城墙的关系也更为和谐。

前门建筑群中最别致的建筑当属主城门两侧的两座黄顶小庙。东为观音庙，西为关帝庙。关帝是北京很多城门与公共建筑的守护神，在历史上尤为著名，也很受北京人欢迎。与这座庙相关的历史记载与传统已被诸多杰出作家讲述（可参见1921年《新中国评论》中庄士敦（R.F. Johnston）[1]的《中国军事英雄崇拜》）。我只提醒大家注意这样的事实：皇帝每次经过前门时都会向关帝庙献上祭品，这成为一种惯例。庙中陈列的蟒袍与皇冠便是为

---

1 R.F. Johnston，R.F. 约翰斯通，中文名庄士敦，英国殖民地官员，曾在华任溥仪的英语老师。

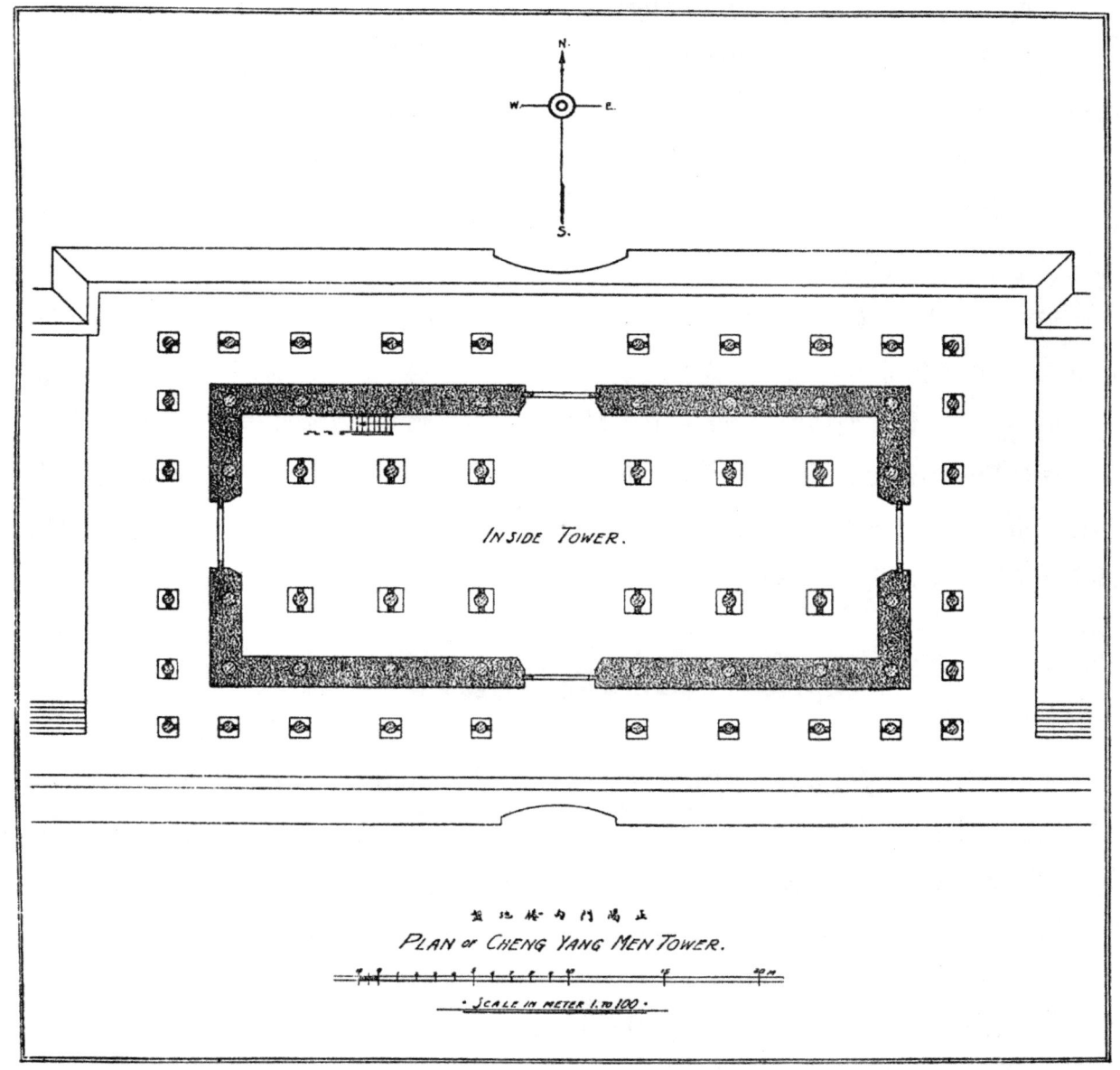

图 29 前门城楼平面

纪念这位"三界伏魔大帝"而设的,这正是这位大英雄的荣誉称号之一。这座小庙仍常被北京的有钱人所光顾,尤其是那些有钱但声誉不大好的女性,她们在关帝面前焚香、叩头。因此庙宇小院落中的大石碑与大树之下,常挤满穿着真丝刺绣衣裙的妇人,而院外门洞前的香炉周围,则常有一些抓住机会以慈善为名向富有的关帝信徒乞讨的乞丐。这组建筑的历史不超过百年,保存状况较好。以褐色城墙为背景的黄色屋顶与汉白玉石碑掩映于大树之间,景色宜人。

再往两侧一些,毗邻城墙处,是两条铁路的候车室。该建筑为传统样式,有着大大的翘曲屋顶与敞廊,它将城楼与火车站连接到一起,然而火车站却是与之格格不入的西洋样式。

它们之间的开放广场，原是瓮城，广场因环绕四周的铁索、两座孤独的石狮以及几棵枯萎的小树而倍显荒凉。因此处位于大道中间，且与马车、人力车隔绝，于是选择这处广场作为栖息地的那群肮脏乞丐与懒汉便成为这里仅存的还具有生机与活力的元素。箭楼城台深深的拱门处现已无交通通行，为他们提供了遮阳避雨的场地，城门外拥挤的商业街区则成为他们理想的猎场。我在北京见到过各色的乞丐与懒汉中，最丑、最脏的那些时常聚集在城市的正中心——前门老拱门之下。

箭楼南侧是北京最重要的交通中心之一。狭窄的护城河里只有一股浊流，河上横跨着一座非常宽阔的现代石桥，桥面形成一片方形广场。桥上的铁索与石墩将之分隔成四条大道，分别向南、东、西方向延伸出去，直达外城最重要的商业区。从箭楼远眺，前门大街掩映于婀娜多姿的垂柳与古老牌楼之下，构成首都最漂亮、最怡人的街景之一。此处交通熙来攘往，络绎不绝，马车、人力车、驴车、驼队等与汽车和自行车混杂在一起——旧事物已逐渐让位于繁闹不息的工业时代。

4. 北城墙上的城门

如今，北城墙上的两座城门中，安定门更为人熟知，也更重要。安定门是一条南北向大街的出口，大街南段叫莫里森大街（即以前的王府井大街），北段为安定门大街。安定门临近孔庙与雍和宫，它们可能仍是首都最大的两组寺庙建筑。此处交通繁忙，多是运载煤炭以及驻扎在城门外不远的士兵，其间也有一些喇嘛，以及由乡村来此拜谒雍和宫的蒙古朋友。

城门原有的建筑群已被横贯瓮城的环城铁路严重破坏。瓮城已有局部被毁，但箭楼两侧仍有相当长的弧形城墙留存，因此从北边看时，城门仍然相当完整，引人注目。此处最不协调的元素是一座两层高的半洋式哨所，它有着抹灰的墙面与曲线山花。箭楼本身气势磅礴，城台雄阔，朴素的墙面上仅有四排方形射击孔，上遮两层翘曲的屋檐。楼下的护城河相对较宽，箭楼倒映其中，使画面更加美丽。城台与瓮城城墙，或者说其残存部分均为明代中期建造，但箭楼显然是后代所建。与其他具有防御功能的箭楼类似，此楼应重建于乾隆年间，但其后无疑又经历过大规模修缮，因为在1861年北京受围时，它曾为英法炮火所毁。在和约签署之前，联军曾一度占领此门。

安定门城楼看上去更为古老，也更加残破。坡屋面与中间层平坐已开始坍塌。不少柱子已严重开裂，用铁箍加固着，木作上蒙着厚厚的灰土，因此只能隐约看到原有的彩绘装饰。雨季过后，松散的屋瓦之间便会长出丰茂的杂草、灌木。但事实上，与我们之前在南城墙

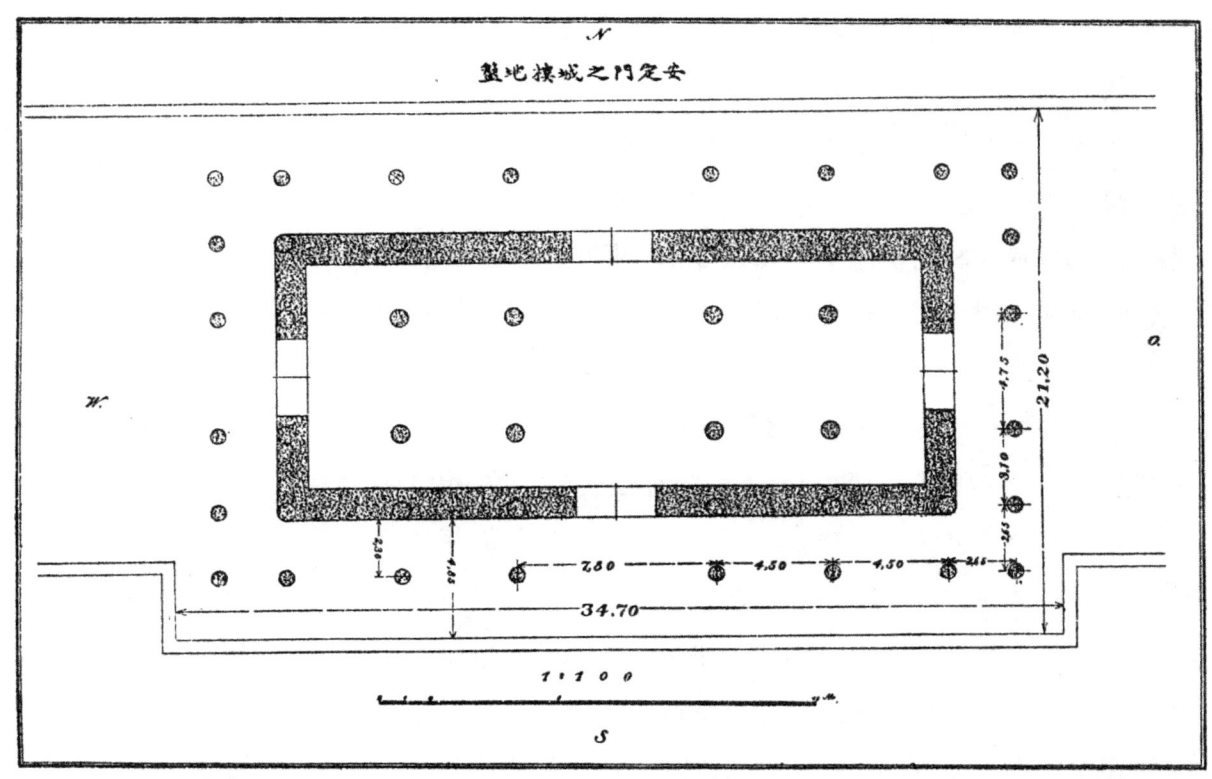

图 30 安定门城楼平面

上看到的那些光鲜亮丽的新城楼相比,这样的城楼与饱受风雨侵蚀的城墙更协调。

城楼的规制与东直门、西直门几乎完全一致,只是在建筑比例上略宽。楼身面阔 26.4 米,进深 11.5 米,外廊照例是面阔七间,为 31 米,进深五间,为 16 米。城台以上,楼高约 22 米。至于城楼墙厚,以及中间柱靠近墙面外侧的处理方式,都与东直门相同,细部亦如此,这似乎证明了两座城楼建造于同一时期——很可能为乾隆年间的假设。由于北京的木构建筑残损迅速,这两座城楼很可能在更晚时候亦有修缮。很遗憾我们没有找到关于这两座城楼建造年代的记录。

由于瓮城城墙大部分被毁,又有铁路横穿瓮城,因此瓮城内的景象颇令人失望。残存城墙的末端处理与东城门类似,即用一系列带有阶梯状栏杆的蜿蜒楼梯连接着各层小平台,这种细密精巧与城墙、城楼的简朴宏伟形成了鲜明对比。然而值得庆幸的是,残存的瓮城后部仍有一些老房子和树木,得以将人们的注意力从那些近代的不良设计上转移开去。在箭楼城台脚下依偎着一座小建筑群——真武庙,这是座田园般幽静的小庙,有六座独立的殿阁、门楼环绕着院子,院中浓郁的椿树掩映着大香炉与汉白玉石碑。对于充斥着荒凉砂原与单调泥屋的安定门街区来说,这是其中仅有的、富有魅力的风景点。

德胜门是北城墙上的西城门,城墙从这里开始折向西南方向。德胜门附近仍较为宁静,未受现代改造的侵扰，通向城门的大街两侧林立着一些高大的树木和旧式店铺，但一临近城门，街道陡然转了个弯，景象变得令人失望了。眼前出现的并非是一座带有敞廊的三重檐的高大城楼，而是略高于城墙的平坦城台，台下辟有一个大拱门。城台上的阁楼已荡然无存，只因1921年时该城楼被认为已进入腐朽的危险状态，故而将其拆除。截止1922年夏季，大部分建筑材料仍堆放在城台顶部，据我所见，梁、柱均未腐朽。柱础与墙基仍在原址，这使我们得以画出这座已毁城楼的平面图。这座城楼比安定门城楼更大：楼身面阔27米，进深12米，外廊面阔31.5米，进深16.6米。拱门尤其高大，顶部几乎已接近城台上沿，加之城楼的缺失，更显得格外高大。

穿过拱门，景象更引人注目。两侧围有栅栏与低矮砖墙的铁路穿过瓮城，造成了部分毁坏，就如在安定门瓮城中那样；然而与其他残破的瓮城相比，德胜门瓮城保存着更多的传统特征。这主要是因为它残留的弧形城墙较长，并且铁道分隔墙是沿对角线方向伸向瓮城城墙的阶梯式末端的。残存城墙与铁路围墙之间的通道仅够道路穿过。因此这条路便没有打破箭楼城台，而是分成两支，绕过瓮城与箭楼，汇合于北侧的城门桥上。老瓮城后部仍是一个相对独立且闭合的空间，并未被施以现代化的改动。这里有一处保存相当完好的寺庙群，庙前的椿树郁郁葱葱，使得整个环境十分宜人。树丛和灌木掩映着城墙末端的之字

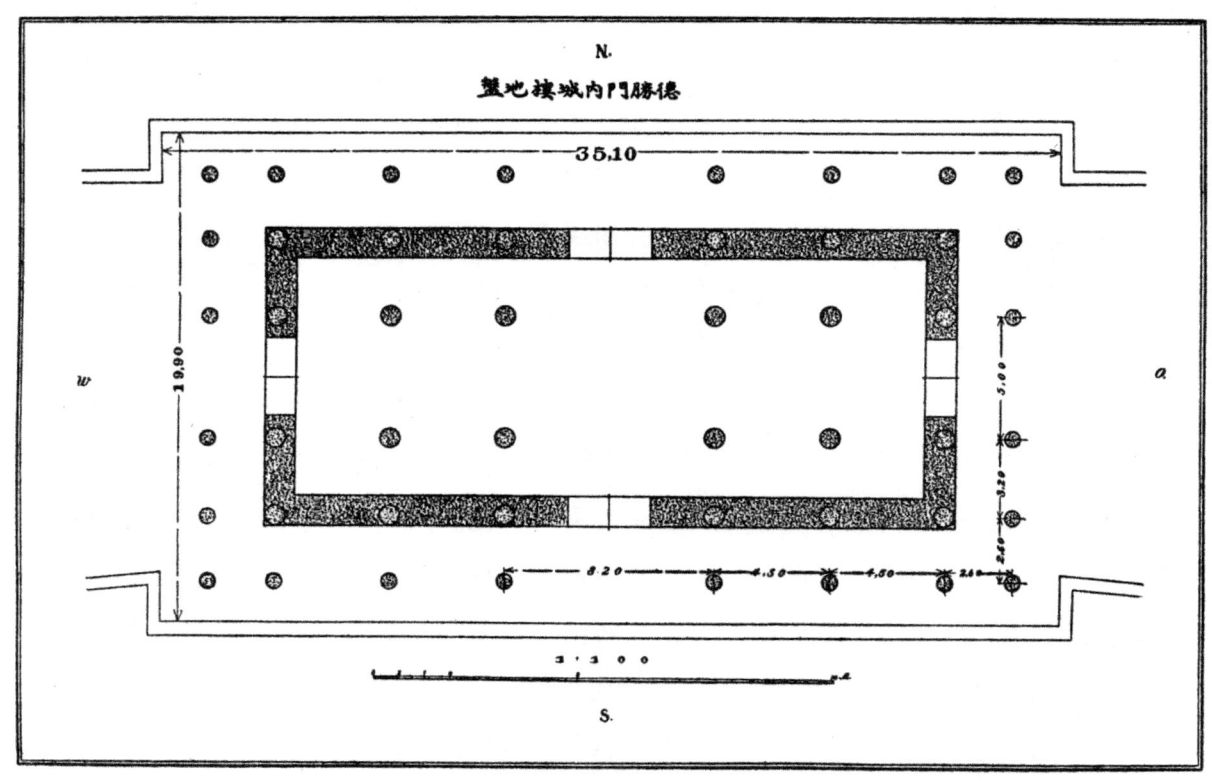

图31 德胜门城楼平面

形台阶与锯齿状栏杆，如此，树荫覆盖着的庙前空间挤满小吃摊贩、赶驴人、剃头匠和各色主顾也就不足为奇了。德胜门风光旖旎，恬静怡人，任何其他城门都无法与之相比。瓮城内的真武庙比大多数城门寺庙要大一些。山门两侧有钟鼓楼，还有几间亭阁和道士的住处。但我怀疑这里是否真的被用作宗教目的，因为我最后一次拜访真武庙时，其中的一两座精致的小房子里堆满了正在分拣的棉花，部分土地还种着白菜、土豆。

箭楼的规模与结构都很普通，显然是近二三十年修缮的结果。砖墙被涂以淡灰色，与其下城台老城砖形成了鲜明对比，令人不悦。毋庸置疑，箭楼底部建于嘉靖或万历年间，但与之相连的主墙面则是乾隆年间修复的。箭楼前的古老石桥已经开始破碎，护城河轮廓也变得参差不齐，然而从这个方向眺望，如果对城楼脚下破烂不堪的哨所不予注意的话，耸立于这片光秃秃的地带之上的德胜门还是非常壮观的。

德胜门瓮城中的奇珍，当属立于两条铁轨之间的碑亭。亭中是一座巨大的纪念石碑，上刻乾隆执政的六十二年[1]（1797 年）时的御制诗。这位当时的太上皇在诗中提到了德胜门（道德胜利之门），并说其威力足以在不冒犯别人的前提下，保证他的所有利益。

---

1 此系嘉庆二年，乾隆皇帝当时为太上皇，但作者认为他仍把持国政。

八、外城的城门

引言

　　外城，或者说汉人城的城门，比内城的城门要小很多。外城共有 7 座城门：3 座城门在南城墙上，一座在东城墙，一座在西城墙，东北角、西北角与内城相接的两侧短墙上也各有一座城门。尽管这几座城门规模较小，建筑特点也不突出，但它们的价值和趣味并不比内城城门低。一般说来，外城城门是按照大型城门的平面布局与建筑风格来建造的，但在构造方式与装饰细节方面有所简化。然而必须承认，在大多情形中，这非但没有减损，反而增强了城门建筑群的和谐一致的效果，较小的城门楼与城墙以及周边街道、景观的联系更亲密、更融洽。从画面效果来说，相比构成画面主体的大城门，与这些小城门交织起来的风景总是更精致。

　　我认为我的照片能够很好地体现出这一点。拍摄大型城门的照片大多表现的是建筑的主题，环境往往并不吸引人，而外城城门景象的生动之处时常是建筑与景观的完美融合，以及周边自然环境的独特之美。在一定程度上，这些照片可以成为建筑特征与保存现状的历史记录，但是我们希望城门可以揭示更多的内涵，表达一些难以言传的印象。至于这些印象所包含的意义，每位读者可以自行揣摩。我在这里只提示一点，那就是城门之美不仅仅取决于树木、房子与桥梁等具体的景物，更依赖于居民的生活气息、变幻的光线与氛围，任何一个在北京居住过的人都对此终身难忘。

　　西便门（西面方便之门）在西北城墙上，坐落于一条店铺林立、坎坷不平的老旧街道尽头，实际上街边的店铺远比不显眼的、低矮的城楼更引人注目，将其称为城楼实在是令人费解。它只是一座长方形的房屋，有着石灰砖墙，四面各有一门，既没有窗户，也没有外廊。除了屋顶上的望兽和脊兽外，别无其他装饰细节，但屋瓦之间杂草却生长茂盛。城楼坐落于城墙正中，城墙在城楼之处略突出墙面一点，构成城台之形，仅设一条马道。穿过城台的门洞不是拱顶，而是方顶，门洞天花由厚重的木板构成，下以横梁承托，横梁两端

N.
W.
E.
S.
POLICE STATION
POLICE STATION
RAMP
INSIDE TOWER.
OUTSIDE TOWER.
CANAL
BRIDGE
CANAL
西便門內外地式
• PLAN OF HSI PIAN MEN TOWERS •
10 5 0 10 20 30 40 50 M.
• SCALE IN METER 1.TO 200 •

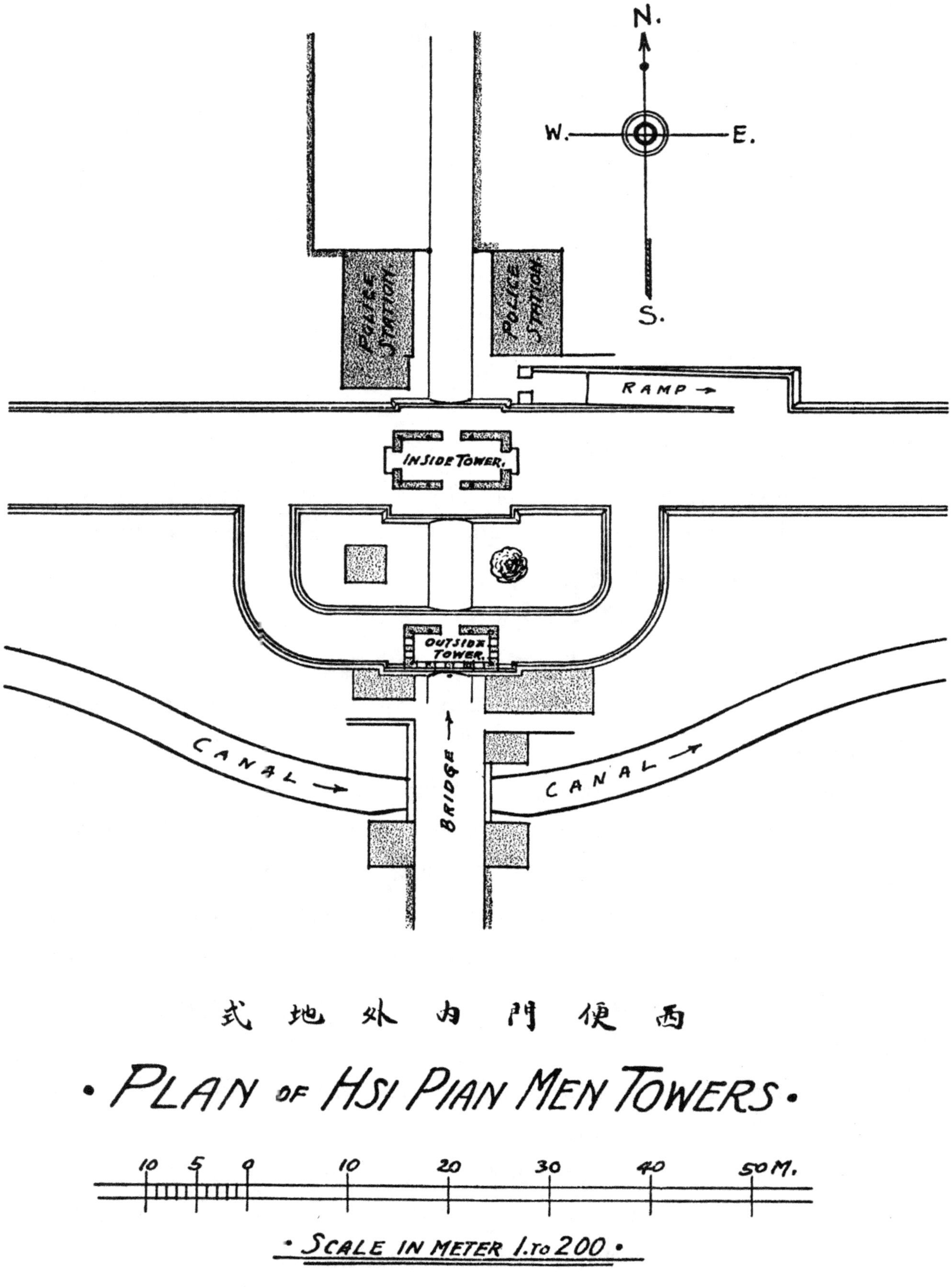

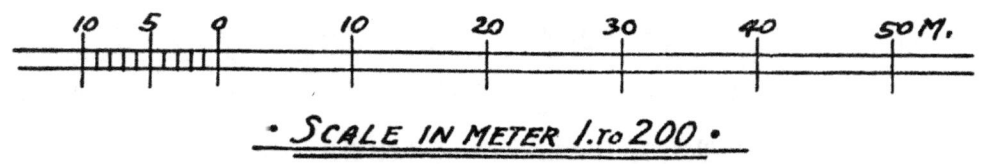

图 32 西便门总平面

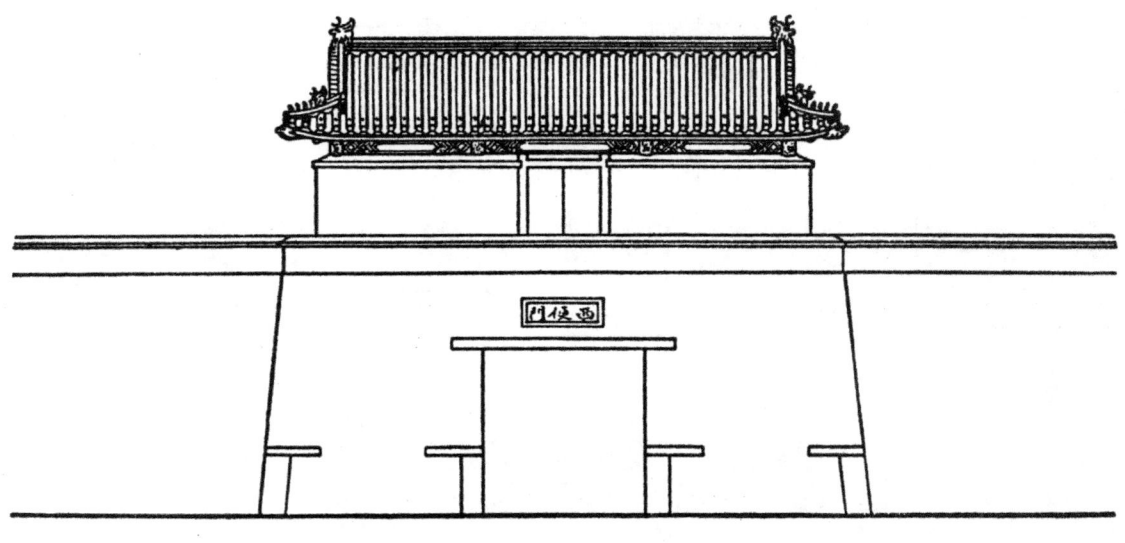

图 33 西便门城楼正立面

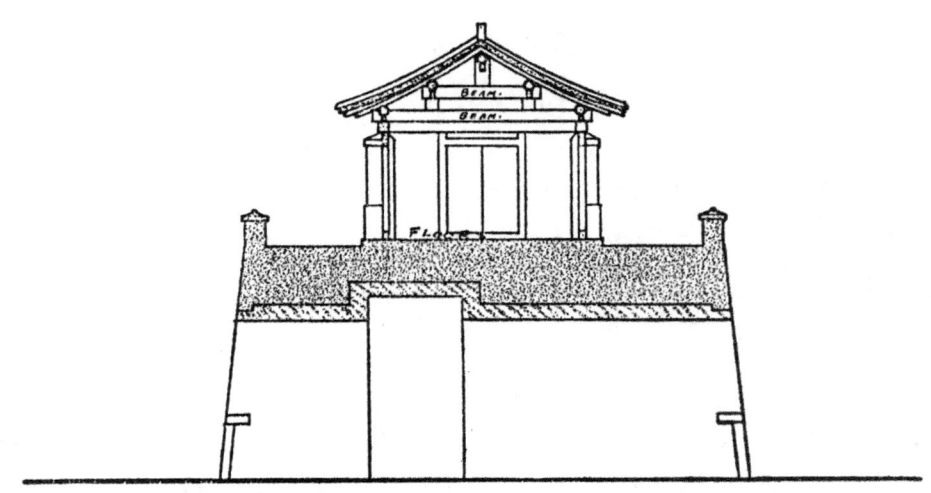

图 34 西便门城楼横剖面

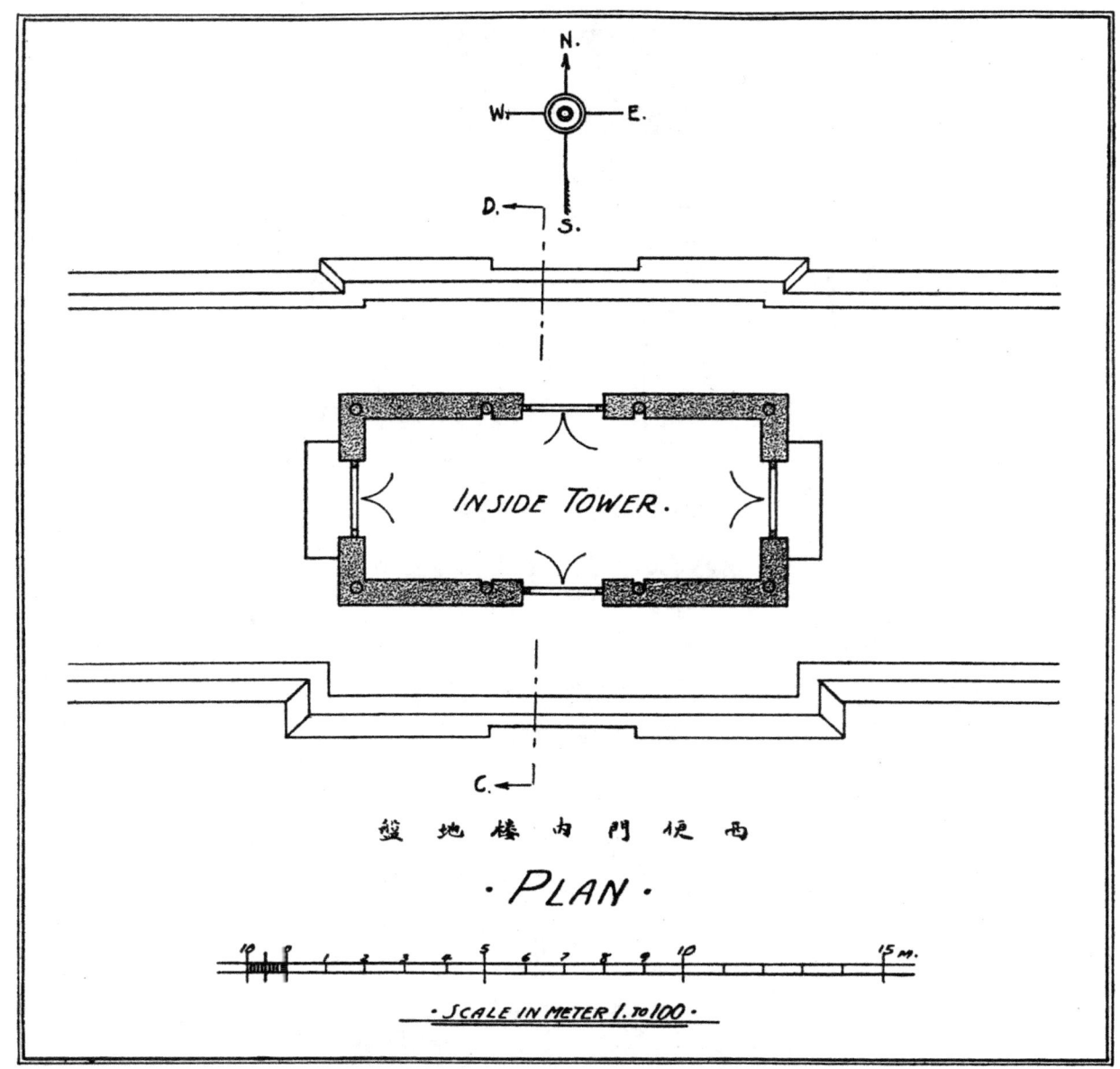

图 35 西便门城楼平面

嵌入砖墙之中。然而平顶门洞中间有一段更高、更宽的内券，其内设门轴，门扇挂于轴上，可以自由开合，也可以折入墙面凹处。城楼尺寸如下：面阔 11.2 米，进深 5.5 米，城台以上楼高 5.2 米，地面以上的通高为 11.2 米。城楼仅前后各一排柱，每排四根，嵌入砖墙中，共有两层梁枋，但既没有斗栱，也没有外廊柱。

瓮城极窄小，进深仅 7.5 米，宽 30 米。然而这里尚可容下一棵美丽的大树和一间小值房。这种树俗称"洋槐"，凡瓮城均可见到，它枝叶繁茂，树荫可覆盖半个瓮城。小值房则占据着另半边院子。瓮城城墙凹凸不平，残破不堪。城墙主体部分似乎是明代中期的，很多砖上有嘉靖三十九年（1560年）的砖文，但有些地方经后期补葺。瓮城外立面于乾隆年间重修。

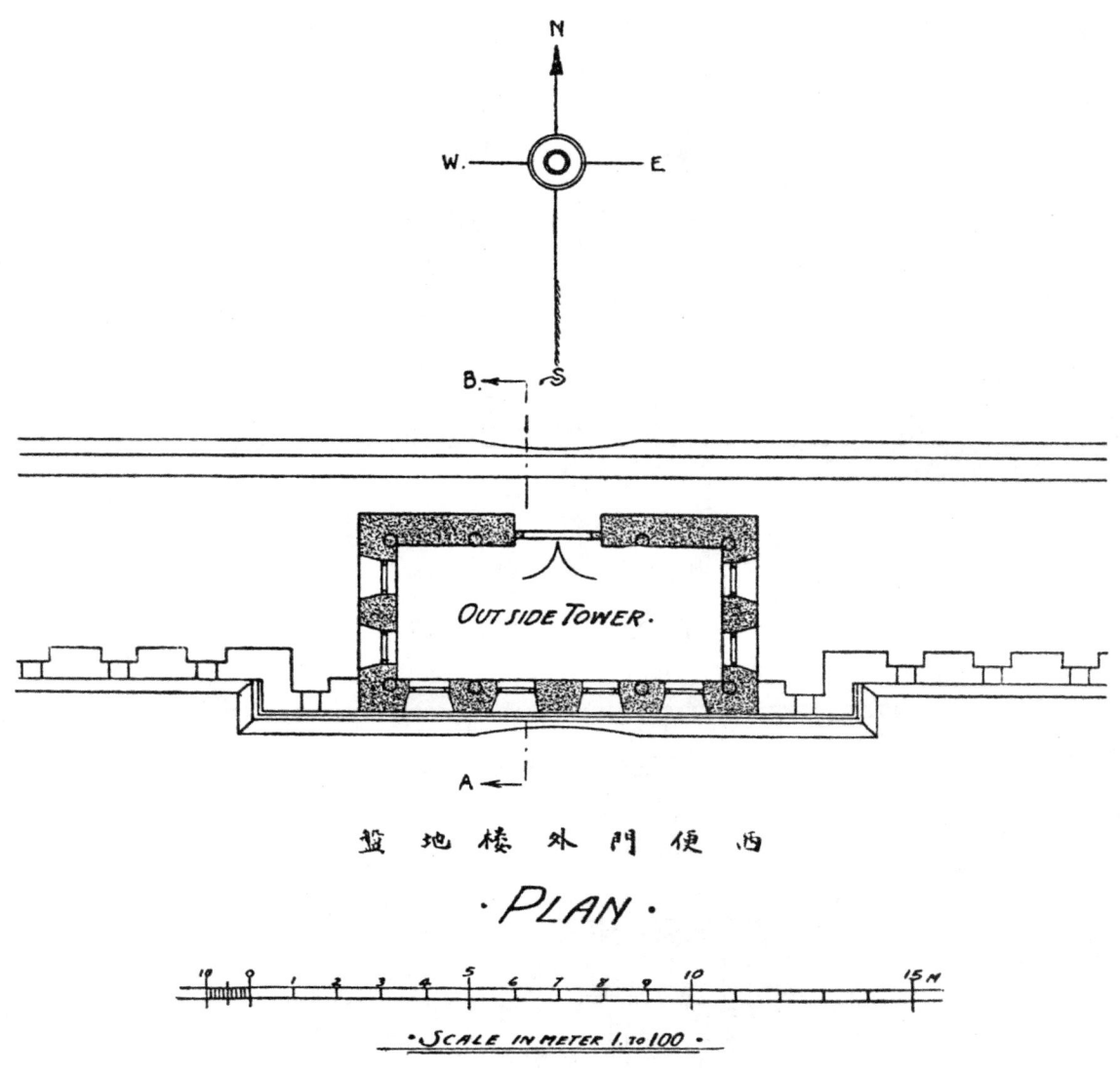

图 36 西便门箭楼平面

箭楼城台的门洞内侧为方形平顶,外侧为拱顶。门扇同样安置于门洞内较宽、较高的内券之处,因此既可以方便地合上门扇,打开门扇时又完全不妨碍交通。城台仅略突出瓮城城墙立面,但城台上缘施加檐口线来强化城台的形象。城台上即小箭楼,箭楼两侧为城垛。整个箭楼面阔仅9米,进深4.6米,城台以上楼高4.7米,从地面丈量的通高为10.5米。箭楼构造与城楼相同,前后各一列小柱嵌于砖墙内(每个立面各四根柱),外立面与两山面各有两排射击孔。这些射击孔与砖面墙比城楼更为有趣,但箭楼如此之小,以至于难以镇住楼下宽大的拱顶,这个大拱顶可以说是整个城门中仅有的大体量。

护城河深而窄,其上横跨一座小石桥。穿过石桥,道路即分为两支,一支笔直向北,另一支向西。后一条道路通往外国人尤为熟悉的赛马场。但向北那条路景色更美。道路两旁

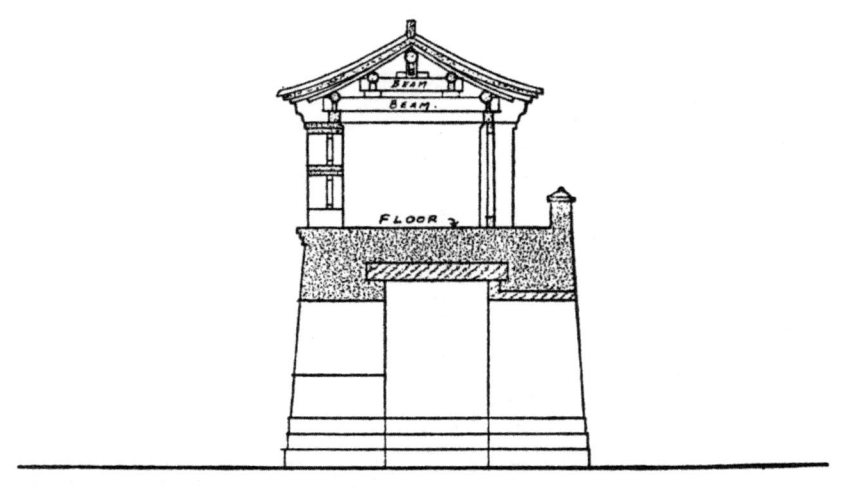

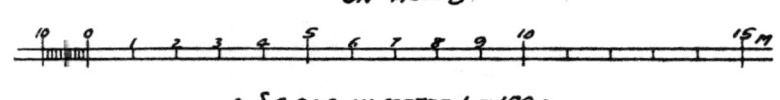

图 37 西便门箭楼横剖面

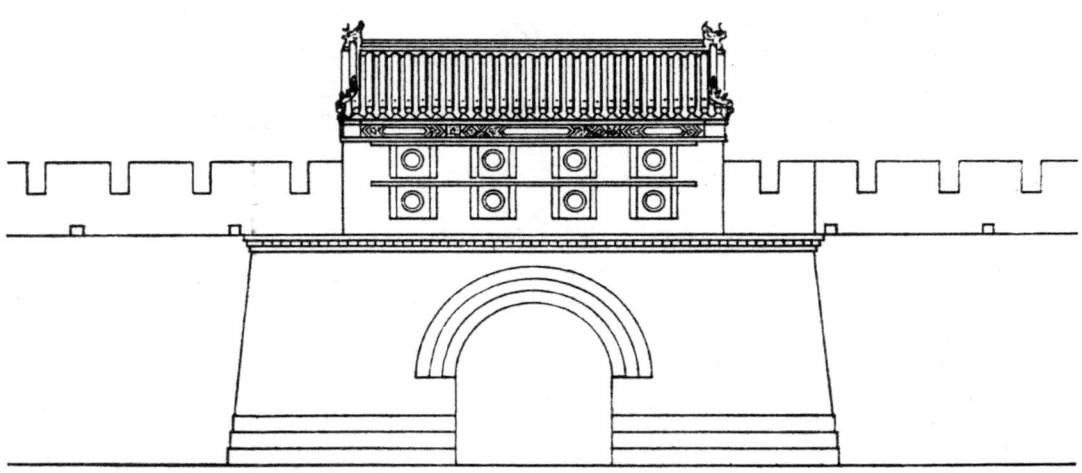

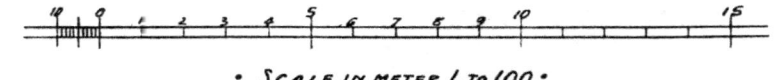

图 38 西便门箭楼正立面

是成排的小房子，房屋入口处有宽大的石阶，这些石阶原是赶驴人最便利的歇脚处，因为屋前有大槐树，树冠如伞，浓荫如盖，遮蔽着台阶、平台。在白墙与炙热的道路上投下婆娑的树影。在这里，没有必要像城里那样搭建竹棚或铺设草席，因为大自然以光影斑驳的树影和沙沙作响的绿叶提供了同样有效而又无比美丽的庇护。当然，树荫下"什么事也不做的美妙"仅限于春夏两季；寒冷的时节要萧索许多，周围都光秃秃的，只有驼队每天进出这座风雨侵蚀的老城门，才稍稍冲淡了这里单调的景象。

东北城墙上的东便门（东边方便之门）与西便门构成一对。在某些方面，东便门比西便门更朴素、更不显眼。城门楼的规模与西便门基本相同，东便门瓮城的大小虽也不比西便门大，但规制有所不同。城楼——如果仍可称之为楼的话，是一座小型砖作建筑，红色抹泥墙，城楼可能在上世纪（即19世纪——译者著）修缮过。

近观城楼，建筑几乎陷入城台之内，而不是从台上拔地而起。城楼的局部淹没于雉堞之后，仅露翘曲的大屋顶表明它的存在。楼前的值房与古老的城台比城楼本身更显眼，城台上有一些嘉靖时期的城砖，但显然后期又有修补。

东便门的门洞与西便门相同，都是方形的，上为横梁与木板。穿过门洞即到达小瓮城的内部。东便门的瓮城比西便门瓮城更深，但也更窄些。然而东便门瓮城却没有西便门那样别致。瓮城里没有树，也没有其他植物，只有一个小棚屋，或者说是守卫岗亭，它没有消减反而加重了瓮城的死气沉沉与空旷落寞的气氛。不时有人肩挑着扁担经过这座城门，扁担两端晃晃悠悠地吊着竹篮，但极少有人力车或马车经过此地。

与西便门相同，东便门箭楼城台的门洞同样在朝向瓮城的一边是方顶，在临城外的一侧为拱顶。此处的拱门没有西便门的那般大；因此拱门上的"箭楼"似乎略微显眼一点。箭楼照例是以厚重的砖墙包裹着由木柱木梁构成的结构框架，墙上有两排射击孔，使箭楼看上去具有防御建筑的肃穆气氛。但屋顶上覆盖着一层厚厚的、柔软而平滑的草。箭楼与城台城墙都是乾隆时期翻修的，很有可能是乾隆三十一年（1766年）。

就在城门外瓮城的转角处，有一个小型的牲畜市场，赶牛人与赶驴人经常光顾此地，时常可以看到健壮的公牛与无精打采的驴子在市场上待价而沽。再往东走几步，地面陡然下倾，城墙筑有双层台座予以加固。由于这个下部结构目前已局部坍塌，因此可以非常清晰地观察到其各个构成要素与构造方式，而屹立于层层台基之上的城墙也构成一幅令人印象深刻的图景。

由于临近东运河，东便门外的景观有着非常鲜明的特质与美感。护城河实际上被加宽，形成石砌堤岸的运河，水从北面经护城河源源而来，水量充沛。这里是东河的起点，它曾经是大运河上连接北京与天津的最重要的运输线。运河的终点，在城门西侧与内城护城河交汇的地方，形成了一个小湖泊，或者说是水塘，夏日里水面上覆盖着灯芯草与荷花，冬日里这里则成为滑冰的好去处。大柳树与大槐树映衬着背景中堡垒般雄伟的内城角楼，以及内外城交汇处的小城门楼残迹，构成美妙至极的景观。城门正前方横跨着一座精致的三孔石拱桥，桥上饰有虎首，桥下设有水闸，以调控河水流量。每当风和日丽之时，我们就会在桥墩上、石堤上看到喧闹的孩子，在闪闪发光的河水中漂洗着棉线与新染的蓝布。向东望去，又能看到油饰绚丽的蓬船载着无忧无虑的少男少女，沿着古老沉寂的运河，愉快地划向"公主坟"或者其他浪漫的所在。

沙窝门（大量尘土之门）又称广渠门，大概是北京最为孤寂的一座城门了。这座城门位于外城东城墙北段非常荒凉的街区中。想要抵达这座城门，我们需要走过一段旷地，这里无人居住，因此被肥料商人用来堆放不同品种的肥料。

城门矮小，但又不似西便门与东便门那般不起眼，沙窝门的瓮城要比上述两座城门的瓮城宽得多。城楼是一座单层的殿阁，前廊面阔五间，两山与背面无廊。由于部分隐藏于城台雉堞之后，城楼看上去很矮，极像西便门城楼，翘曲的屋顶目前处于危险状态，正脊坍塌，戗脊残缺。雨后的城楼屋顶看上去像是一个杂草覆盖的平台，而不是盖瓦屋顶。我认为这个城楼不会早于乾隆时期。城楼很可能与瓮城、箭楼同时重建于乾隆三十一年（1766年）。但是楼下的城台主要是用明代城砖砌筑而成。

城门门洞较大，呈尖拱型（很可能亦是乾隆时重建），与箭楼城台的门洞相似。与城台相比，两个门洞都颇为宽阔，透过拱门，可以清晰地看到瓮城内院以及城门外的乡村风光。

瓮城很大，足以容纳几间食肆，店面开敞，外设砖砌座椅，构成十分别致的建筑样式。这里虽然无树无庙，也没有其他特别之处，但仍然是一处布局匀称、保存完好的旧式瓮城。瓮城面积适中，恰好足以平衡内外两座低矮的城门楼，又不至于使城墙、店铺与城门楼一览无余，而这些共同构成了一幅和谐统一的画面，这样的图景在大瓮城中是看不到的。整个瓮城似重建于乾隆三十一年（1766年）。可以确定的是瓮城城墙建造于那一年，城楼的年代显然不会更早，只可能晚于此。

箭楼与城楼一样低矮，屋顶也同样破败。檐口残破，正脊残缺。箭楼仅设有两排射击孔。然而这座箭楼看上去却比上述东、西便门两座小城门的箭楼要好得多，坚固得多，这是因为它处于更为开敞的位置。箭楼城台犹如坚固的扶垛，高于并突出于瓮城城墙。城墙上的雉堞止于城台，城台之上施以扶手墙来支撑箭楼。这样的设计使箭楼看上去更高，巍然耸立并统领着与之毗连的城墙。

箭楼前的护城河较宽，砖砌堤岸，河上横跨一座古石桥，桥上也有几个小吃摊。河对岸的路原先好像铺以石板，但现在对于大车运输来说，障碍多于便利。其实极少有大车经过这里，出入城门的人，大多骑驴或步行，他们走在这条坑坑洼洼的道路上简直如履平地。某个吉日我去参观这座城门，恰好遇到一支婚礼队伍经过这里，一长队穿着白衣的人用抬杆和扁担挑着一担担嫁妆，跟随着装饰艳丽的新娘花轿。队伍一过城门，人们就无法保持稳健的步履，不得不跳过地上的坑石，放缓行进的速度，以适应这段坑坑洼洼的泥土路，但北京城的苦力早就对这种情形习以为常了。

彰义门（品行良好之门）又称广安门，是外城西城墙上的城门，对应东边的沙窝门。这座城门的规模与整体外观，最初可能与沙窝门完全相同，但经18世纪晚期彻底重建后，现在其城楼高大壮观，瓮城几乎呈方形（外侧拐角为曲度很大的弧形）。然而彰义门的箭楼与沙窝门箭楼基本相同。这座城门的平面总体呈现为乾隆时期非常流行的城门格局，彼时重建了很多城门与城墙。我们即将看到，永定门也采用了相同的设计。

与早期平则门的平面布局相比，这些较晚期的平面设计中堡垒式特征较少，因此防御功能显著降低。这不仅仅因为瓮城城墙变薄，也因为城墙更为平直。平则门的瓮城是呈完整的弧形，两端以很短的扶手墙与主城墙连接。箭楼城台突出很多，守卫者可以从两侧监视弧形的城墙。进入瓮城的通道也不是在箭楼下方，而是位于瓮城一侧，因此可以确保瓮城的安全。晚期城门的瓮城几乎都是方形的，但仅外侧的两个转角为抹角状，从城台上只能监视正面的城墙。入口恰好穿过城台，道路直穿瓮城。此外，装饰性城楼的高度几乎是箭楼的两倍，我们不难得出这样的结论：古时筑城御敌的宗旨已让位于商业、关税等更平和的目的。

广安门的瓮城深34米，宽39米。瓮城城墙基厚7米，顶宽5米。瓮城外壁有两块乾隆三十一年（1766年）的石碑，由此可确知瓮城的建造年代。铺面道路穿过瓮城正中，道路两边是小商店，主要兜售废铁、绳索和粗糙的家用陶瓷，这些东西再加上一些非常简单的食材，就是瓮城中兜售的传统商品了。几棵小槐树和几堆上了釉的陶器堆，为这座布局匀称、保存完好的瓮城增色不少。

无论从哪个角度看，城门建筑群的主体都是高大的城楼，这是一座真正的城楼，其高度令人惊叹。楼身面阔13.8米，进深6米，外廊面阔18米，进深10米。因此比起围廊，室内显得很小。城台以上楼高17.6米，从地面到屋脊顶端高度为26米。城楼外观照例被三重檐分为三层，而室内仅有一层楼板分隔上下，顶层是开放阁楼，仅容纳屋顶梁枋。支撑柱很少很细，每边仅有四根柱子埋入砖墙中。外廊由面阔五间、进深三间的细柱构成，仅四角多加一根柱子。建筑物各部分都保存完好，似乎在乾隆之后又有修缮。仅平坐栏杆与二层楼上的门不存。梁枋上的彩画依然清晰可见，屋顶完整，只是长满杂草。

箭楼的高度仅及城楼高度的一半。城台以上高7.8米，地面以上通高为16.6米。平面面阔13米，进深6.6米。每边墙由两棵埋入墙中的柱子支撑，正立面与山面上各有两排射

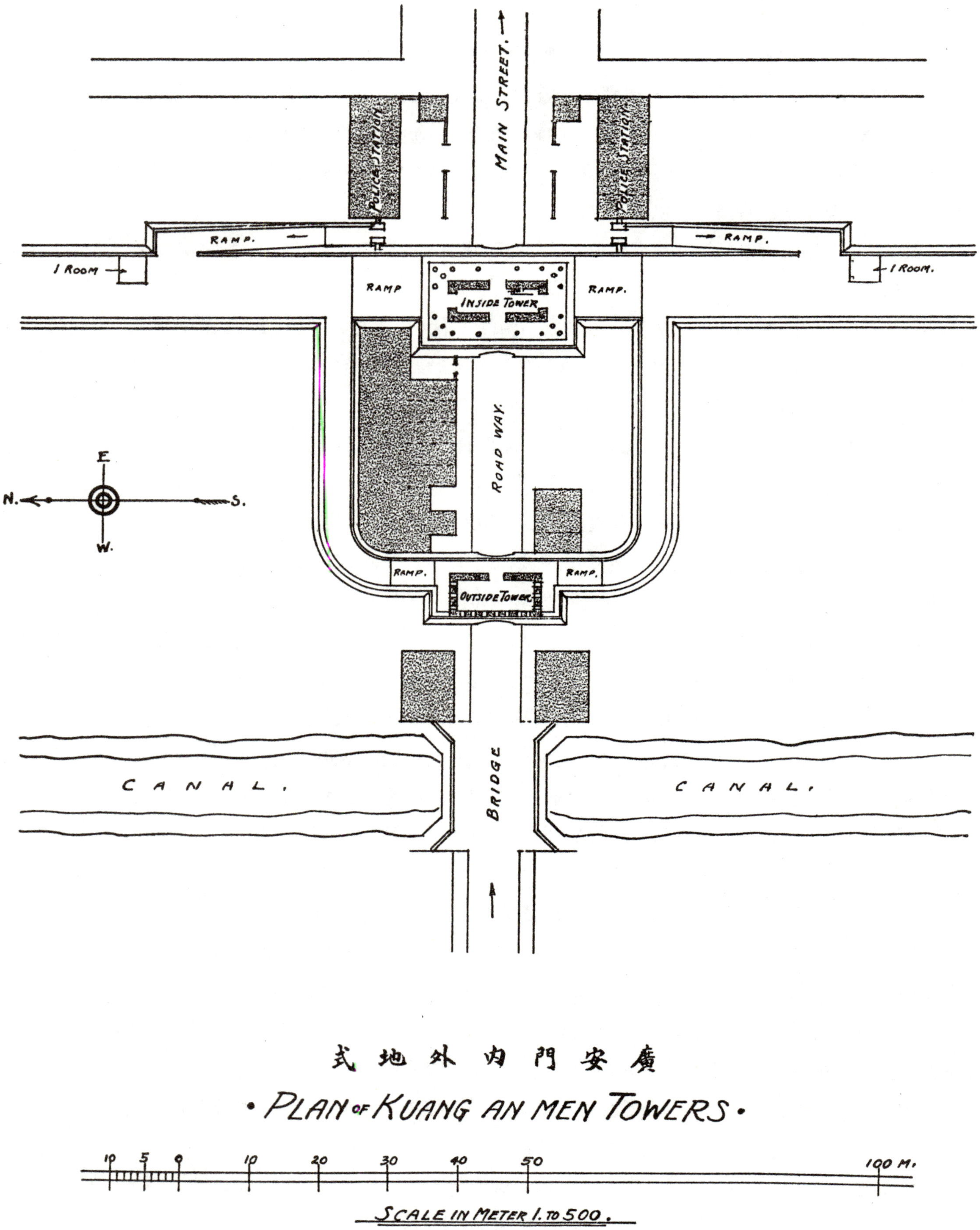

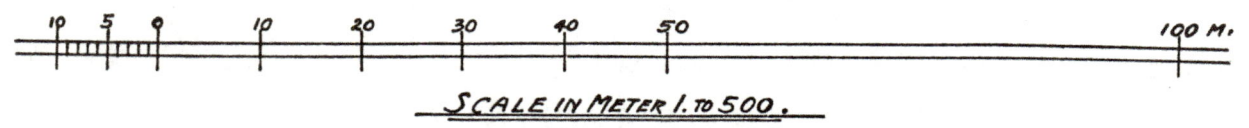

图 39 彰义门（也称广安门）总平面

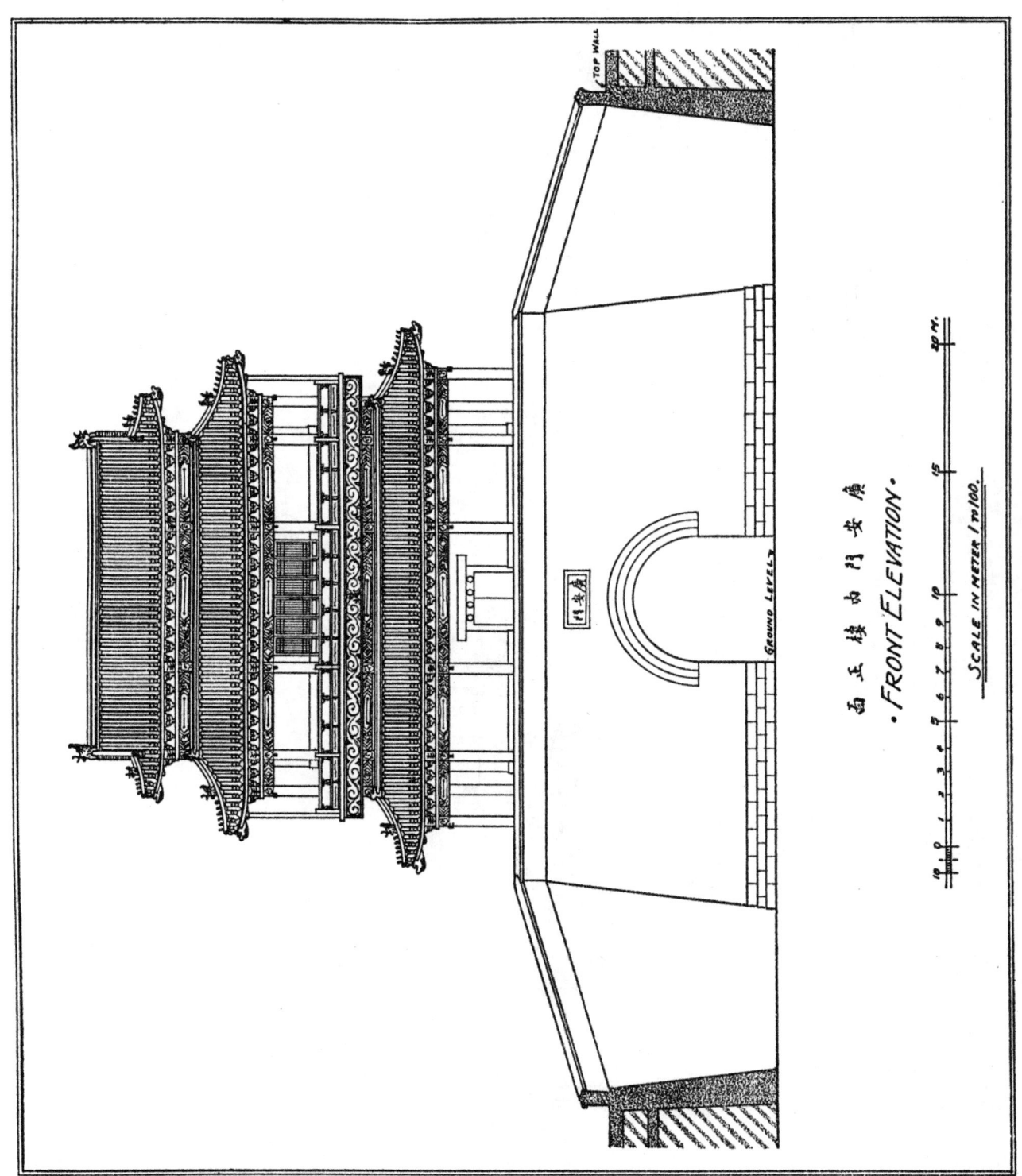

图 40 彰义门城楼正立面

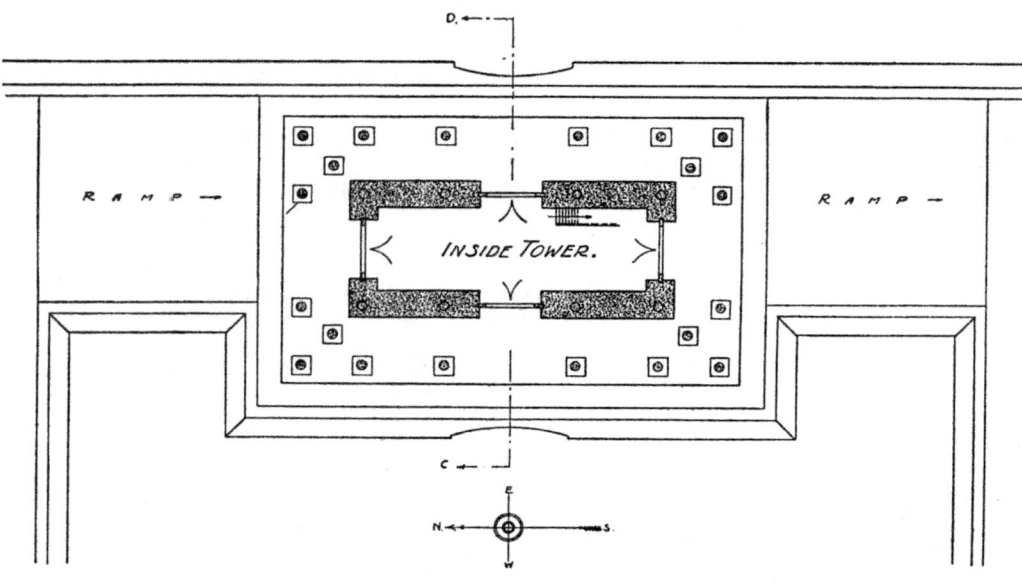

图 41 彰义门城楼平面

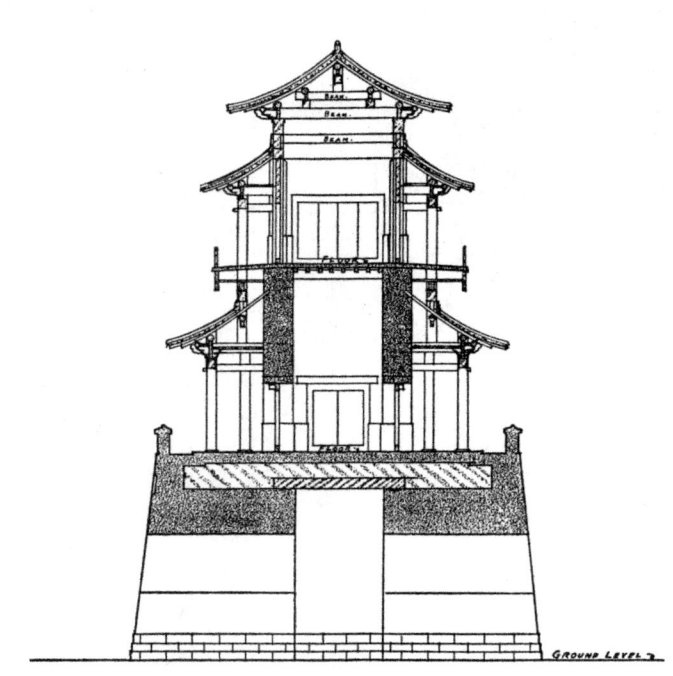

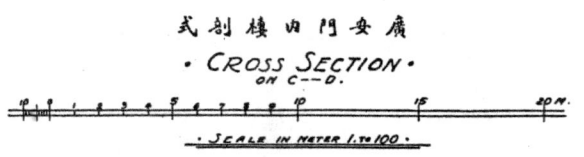

图 42 彰义门城楼横剖面

击孔,入口位于后部。就像沙窝门箭楼那样,广安门是一座简朴的方形砖楼,共同之处还包括两座箭楼,都坐落于高耸的城台之上,也都可以从两侧斜坡马道抵达城台。这两座箭楼真是无独有偶,唯一令人惊讶的是两座城楼的体量却不甚相似。其中一定有我们未知的特殊原因,才导致重建的彰义门城楼规模如此之大。

彰义门的两个门洞拱顶都十分宽大,而且略尖(比图中的还要尖一些)。城门楼正下方、门洞的中间,照例是更高一些的方顶,门扇可在其中开合。与更古老的内城城门不同,彰义门的拱门不是埋入墙体微微凹陷的地方,而是从收分的城台墙体表面开始砌筑的。拱由6到8列横纵相间的砖砌筑而成,但砖不是楔形的,因此很难称之为真正的拱。实际上是砖之间的泥灰使之成为拱,因此它的建造坚固性取决于泥灰的质量以及砌砖的精细度。在北京城城门中,这样的拱门很常见,其中大多数的拱门粗糙不平,但彰义门的拱砌筑得非常细致,经受住了时间的考验。

南城墙上的三座城门中,外侧的两座即左安门与右安门,也是一对姐妹门,城门楼和瓮城彼此很相似。正中的城门是永定门,相对更大、更重要。右安门和左安门大可称之为首都的"乡村之门"。两座城门所在的街区少有或几乎没有城市的景象,这两座城门的动人之处,主要不在于其建筑特色,而更多的是它们所处的自然环境。

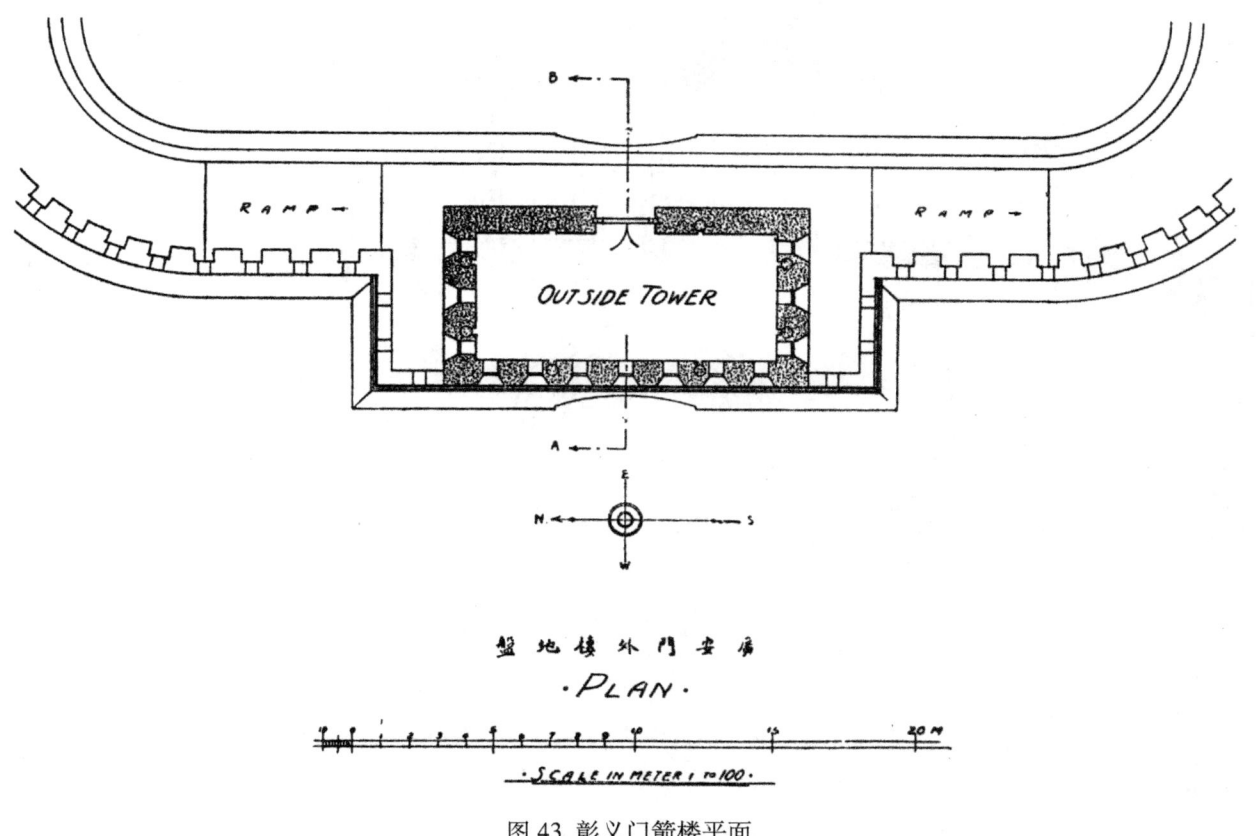

图 43 彰义门箭楼平面

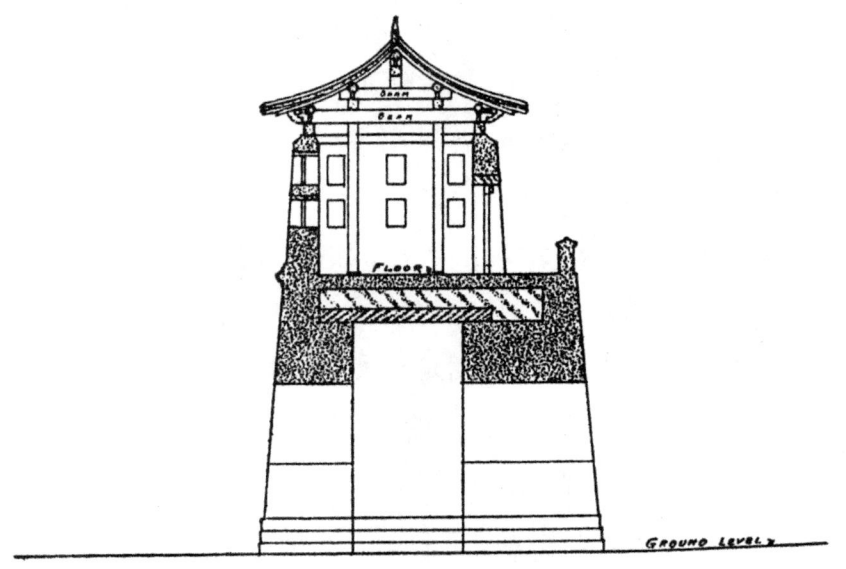

图 44 彰义门箭楼横剖面

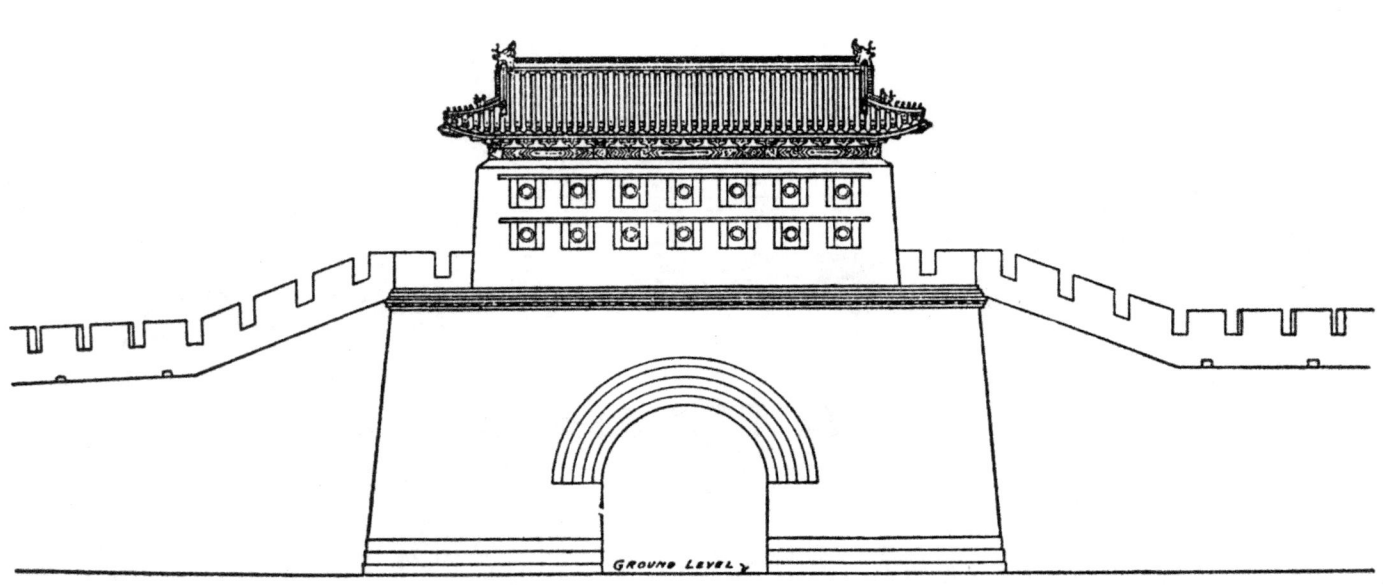

图 45 彰义门箭楼正立面

右安门（左边平安之门[1]），又称南西门，整体保存状态比左安门要好。由城门向外，逐渐进入一处罕见美景之中，没有铁路或汽车等现代设施的干扰，保持着静谧的乡村之美。参观这座城门，可以领略到独具魅力的老北京田园生活。我们需要穿过那些看上去像传统乡村的城市街区，还要穿过麦田和高粱地，才能抵达这座城门。这段旅行使人感觉在时间上和空间上都远离了中国首都的现代化街区。所谓"城楼"，是一座矮小的单层建筑，粉色的抹灰墙，四面均为敞廊，面阔约16米，进深约9米。整体保存完好，无疑是在近年重建的。城楼下的城台是明代建造的，风雨侵蚀，局部残损，还有几处由于树根的压力而膨胀开裂。大椿树从缝隙中生长出来，在敞廊前构成一道绿叶帷幕。

拱形门洞仍是常见的构造方式，如上所述，顶部微尖，相比城台、城楼，门洞显得尤其大。当阳光透过拱门前椿树与柳树的枝叶，洒向昏暗的拱门深处，视线穿过拱门看到瓮城，再穿过更远处箭楼城台上的拱门，看到门外的田野，一幅多么优美的景致。那景象和谐而宁静，未被繁乱的交通所打扰。马车和人力车也罕至此处。夏日，偶有形单影只的农民肩挑着新鲜的蔬菜经过，更增添了这世外桃源的梦幻情调。

瓮城的城墙，至少在内侧壁是非常古老而布满孔洞的，但根据两块嵌在墙上的碑记可知，箭楼城台曾在乾隆五十一年（1786年）翻建。城台上的建筑应当更晚。箭楼与城楼一样，崭新而保存完好，事实上箭楼构成这组建筑的主体，建筑似由缓慢升高的雉堞外轮廓线所托起，俯视着城台脚下的小棚屋与土房子。箭楼的体量几乎与沙窝门、彰义门的箭楼完全相同（面阔约13米，进深约6米），正立面上照例有两排射击孔，每排七个。巨大的翘曲屋顶比上述的外城城门箭楼保存得都要好。屋顶覆盖着简朴的灰瓦，檐口下的彩绘额枋上，为仅出一跳的斗栱。门洞的尺寸、构造方式，均与城楼门洞相似。

箭楼本身不大，大小恰到好处，在周边平庸无奇的建筑的反衬下，箭楼的景象超凡精美。当然箭楼旁边还有一个丑陋的、现代风格的值房，不过值房很小，城门外道路两旁的食品店与货摊的遮阳棚也遮盖住了一部分值房。狭窄的护城河上横跨着一座古石桥，桥两边的河道较宽，尤其在雨后，形成浅浅的池塘。南边几步外，另有一条壕沟，或者说是护城河支流，其上横跨着一座更小的桥。借由一座座石桥和依偎在城墙上的小土房，以及瓮城内外的树木，城门与自然之景紧密交织在一起。在这幅与其说是人类，毋宁说是自然创造的如画的美景中，两座城门楼仅是最后一笔，这幅风景画的魅力与特色，随着季节与光线的交替而变幻无穷，但无疑，最繁盛、迷人的时节是芦苇与荷花竞相盛放的炎夏。那时节，大柳树的"绿飘带"几乎要垂到尘土路面，椿树的枝叶轻扫墙面。即使有孤独的过客骑行穿过城门，

---

[1] 应当为右边平安之门，可能为作者笔误。

也是在驴子上昏睡。空气凝重，尘土路与石桥无比炙热。但凡能避开这暑热的人，没谁愿意出来走动。只有孩子们例外，他们的皮肤晒得黝黑，在护城河的泥水中与白鸭子一起玩闹。北京的夏天在这座老城门附近浓缩为一幅生机勃勃的图景，古朴的城门将衰败的城市与恬静的乡村浑然一体地联接起来。

左安门（右边平安之门[1]）又称江擦门（江中游泳之门），在建筑方面，左安门与右安门完全相同，但左安门给人的总体印象与右安门不同，因为城门附近的景观没有后者那么丰富、优美。相比右安门，想要抵达左安门，需要走更远的路。左安门是北京诸门中，距离人口稠密的市中心最远的城门。这里的路可以直抵东南城角，这条路穿过开阔的田野，田野中有的地方种植着谷子与蔬菜，有的地方长满了芦苇。这里除了远远可以望见的城墙，几乎没有什么城市的迹象。世界上有几个古都可以像这样，在其辖区中保留这么大一片未建之地，并保持着纯粹的田园生活呢？

左安门城门楼和瓮城均跟西南角的右安门极为相似，但左安门的保存现状不如右安门。虽然左安门很可能在乾隆三十一年（1766年）的时候进行过修葺——箭楼城台附近的石碑记录了修缮年代，但目前建筑荒废严重，急需维修。由于屋面上长满杂草，屋顶的檐口、垂脊等处已经开始塌陷。墙上的抹灰不断剥落，门扇与雉堞也遗失了。更糟糕的是，1922年夏天，城墙内侧通向城楼城台的马道完全坍塌。雨水渗入包砌的砖层之下，经由墙内的夯土层流走，导致整条马道塌方，这种情景可以在本书的一幅插图中看到。这个发生在最近的生动案例告诉我们，北京的城墙与城门马道一般是怎样损毁的，以及如果不认真地勘查城墙各处潜在的损毁威胁，它们未来的命运又会如何。

在叙述完右安门的城门楼之后，我们似乎没有必要再对左安门的城门楼予以特殊说明了。两座城门楼的基本特征高度相似，但在保存状态上十分不同，正如我们已经看到的那样。两座城门瓮城的规模与总体特征上也极相似，只是左安门的瓮城较空旷，不像右安门那样在其中栽植着美丽的大树。左安门瓮城中只有两个很小的老式商店，其中一个是马车铺，另一个是绳索五金店。瓮城中还有一个小吃摊，照例在室外凉棚下用砖做成桌椅。只有几个孤零零的赶驴人进出这座城门，偶尔也有大车。其他城门离首都中心更近，因此进出的交通量也更大。

城门外光秀秀的，到处落满尘土，几乎没有树木。在这个枯燥无聊的画面中，仅有的充满活力之物是羊与白鸭，羊群在护城河两岸稀疏的草地上吃着草，而白鸭则不知疲倦地在肥美的泥土中翻腾、啄食。这里几乎没有行人，甚至连儿童也不像其他城门那样多，他们

---

[1] 应当为左边平安之门，可能为作者笔误。

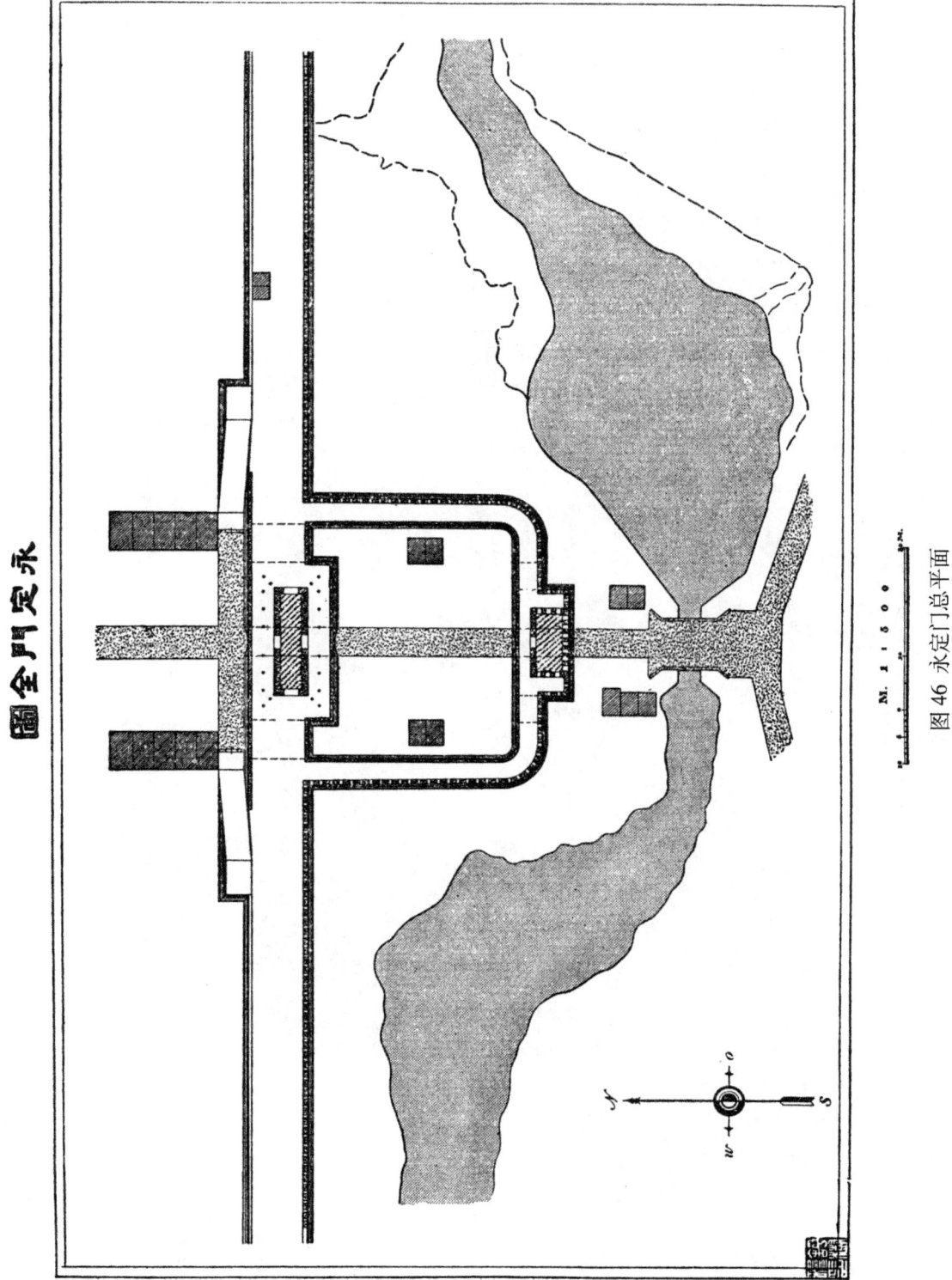

图 46 永定门总平面

图 47 永定门城楼正立面

怯生生地不愿说话，很不习惯见到外国人来此游览。

永定门（永远确定之门）是外城城墙上最高大、最重要的城门。它位于南城墙正中，城门也是从前门向南的大街的终点，长街两侧为一些知名的土产商店，街道南段位于天坛与先农坛建筑群之间。因此从很远的地方就可以望见永定门，城楼高耸，修缮完好，塑造出庄严宏伟的印象。城楼的总体印象与装饰效果可参见书中的彩绘图，然而图中表现的城门过于完美，忽视了北京尘土对建筑的消极影响，实际上，一旦刮起北风，位于城市南端的永定门附近便尘土漫天。

这座城楼的年岁应该不会很老，可能是在永定门外建小火车站之时重建，这座火车站是北京与马家铺之间的电力铁路线的起点，1900年之前，马家铺是北京—天津铁路线的终点。义和团运动末期，外国列强占领首都，火车站搬迁至天坛外，又过了大约四年，火车站搬到现址。如果我们的推测是正确的，那么永定门城楼可能也只有二十多年的历史，根据它的保存现状，城楼的年代应不会更早。城台与瓮城重建于乾隆三十一年（1766年），瓮城的形状与规制皆同彰义门，只是规模稍大。瓮城尺寸如下：深36米，宽42米，瓮城城墙厚度约6米，至箭楼城台处又增厚约5米[1]，因此箭楼城台厚9米，而城楼城台厚度接近15米。

城楼的比例较为特殊，进深很窄，但楼宽而高。楼体面阔19.8米，进深6.1米，围廊面阔七间24米，进深三间10.2米，通高26米，其中城台高8米，建筑本身高18米。它的结构很典型，但比早期城门楼要简洁一些。有三重檐，屋面仅在角部略呈曲线，檐下为柱、梁枋与斗栱，其上以檩为中介承托椽飞。二层向外伸出的平坐以柱支撑，柱下的梁枋连接着外廊与墙之间，这种构造不同于平则门城门楼，后者是以斗栱承托平坐。除通常的栏杆外，平坐四角的擎檐柱支撑着二层屋檐，这种擎檐柱在修缮过的城门楼上很常见。主屋顶由横纵两层梁枋与檩承接。二层、三层檐下的斗栱皆出三跳，但一层檐下的斗栱仅出两跳。斗栱饰以蓝绿相间的彩画，梁枋采用相同特征的彩画装饰，屋脊上有极好的兽首与夔龙字，皆可在图中看到。

永定门箭楼与外城其他几座较大的城门基本相同。然而它与城楼相比，箭楼显得很小。箭楼正面面阔12.8米，有两排射击孔，每排七孔，瓮城的雉堞高于下层射击孔，因此箭楼的高度看上去又低了些。建筑实际高度为8米，城台高7.8米。箭楼保存现状较好，屋顶与檐下梁枋彩画均完好无缺，射击孔上绘制的炮口也清晰可见。瓮城的后部照例是一面朴素的砖墙，上开双门。

瓮城景色优美，其间树木众多、商铺林立。除去肩挑扁担的行人，还有人力车、马车、

---

1 此处可能为作者笔误。根据图示，箭楼城台厚度约为9米，此处应当为增厚约3米。

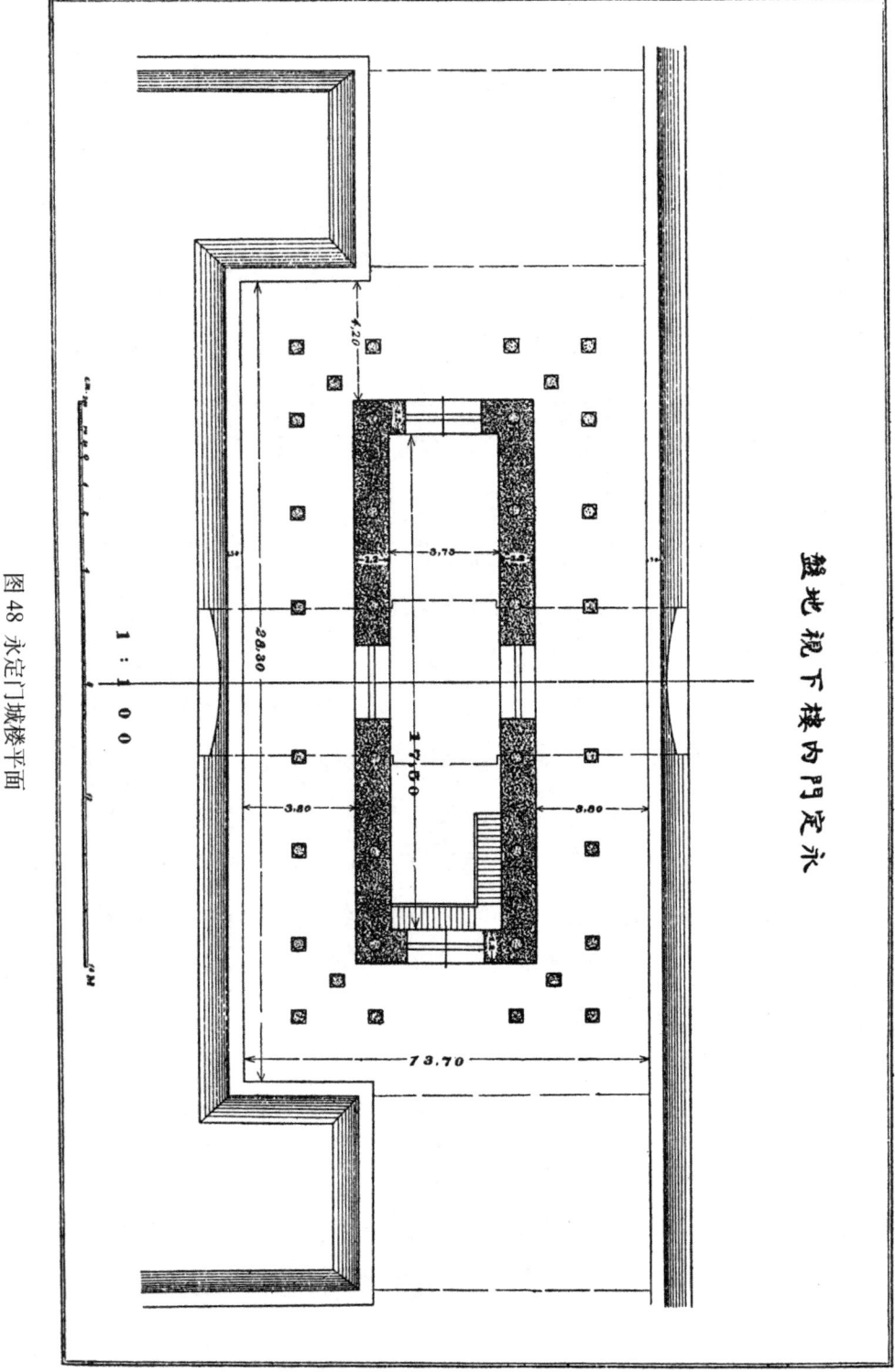

图 48 永定门城楼平面

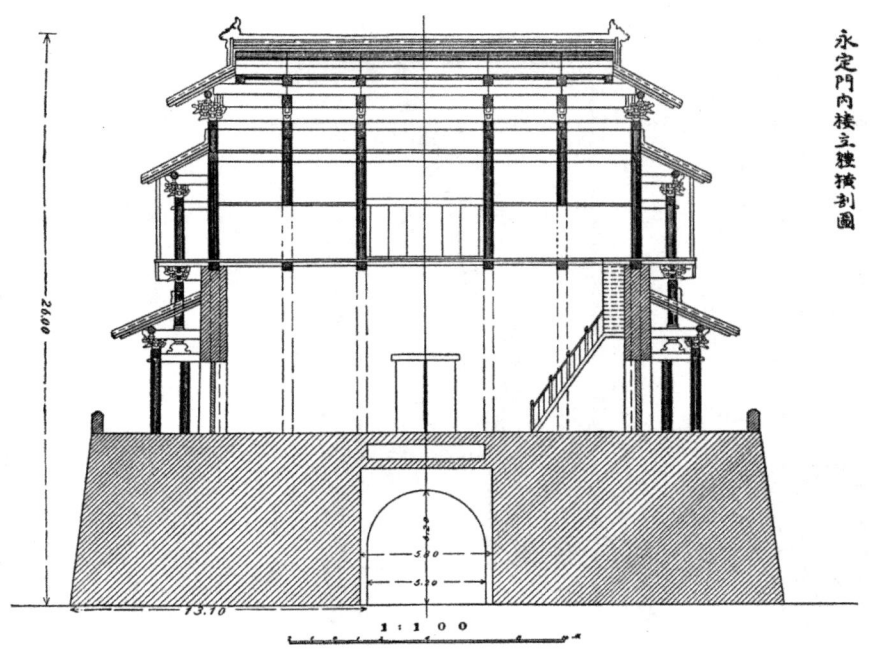

图 49 永定门城楼纵剖面

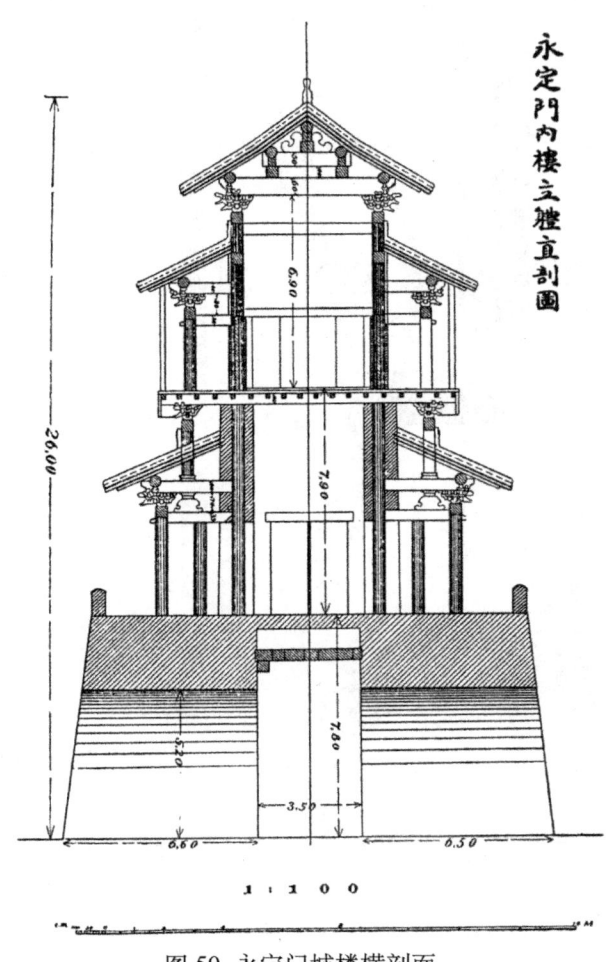

图 50 永定门城楼横剖面

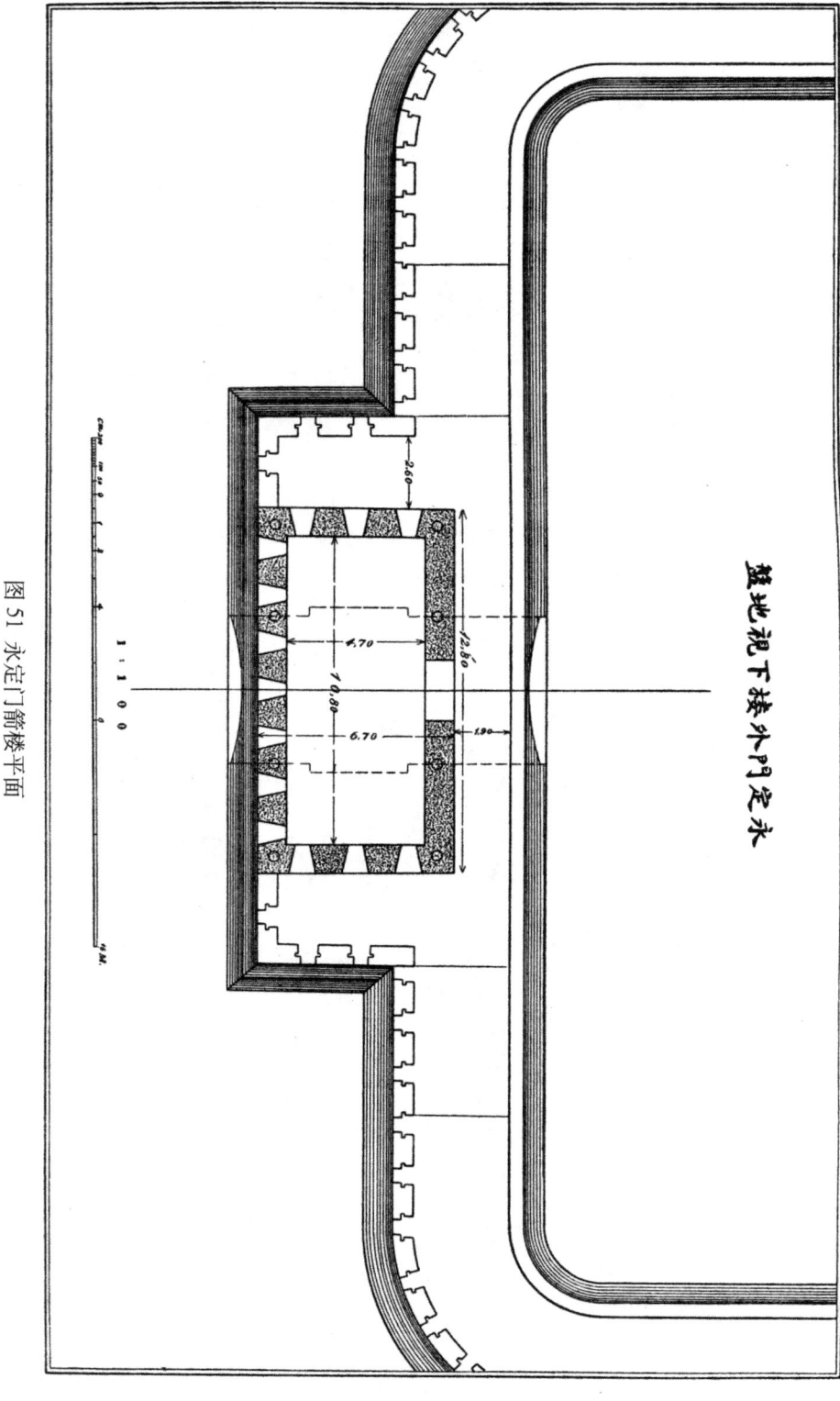

图 51 永定门箭楼平面

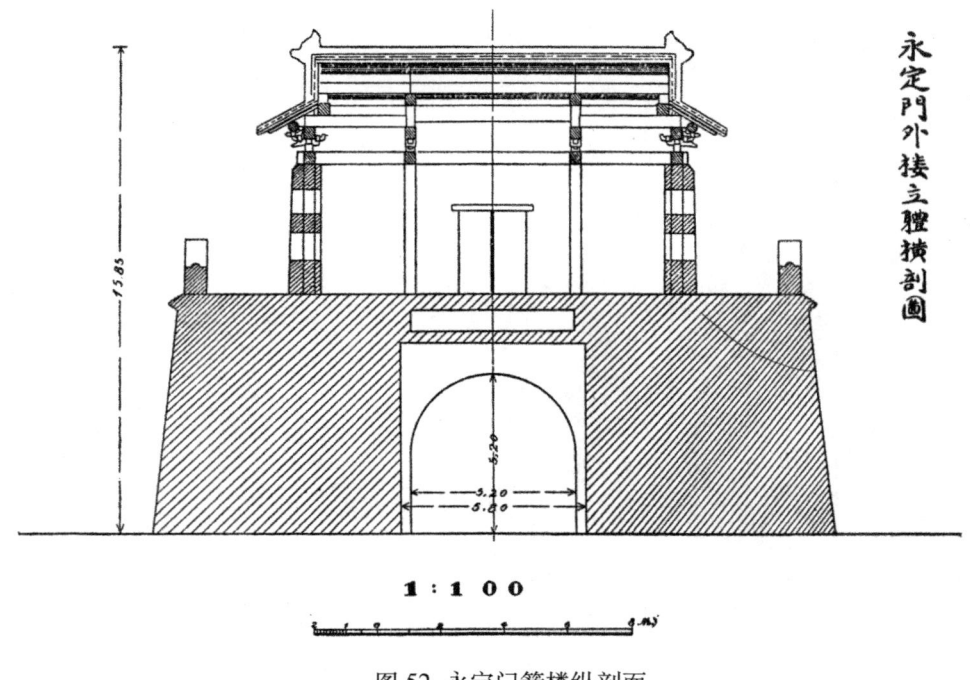

图 52 永定门箭楼纵剖面

手推车、驼队与军用运输（前往南边的兵营）源源不断地穿梭来往……人们有时在瓮城内外的小吃店稍作停留……又继续穿过深濠之上的大石桥，最终在桥头坡道处分道扬镳，向东、西两个方向继续他们的旅程。石桥上总是热闹非凡，与桥相连的道路两侧是老式商店，构成与这幅生动图景十分相称的背景。拥挤喧闹的城市生活在这里短暂地聚集，随后涌向城外，以及远方的宁静乡村。

从西边能够观赏到最美、最完整的永定门形象，而且整个建筑群一览无余。护城河非常宽广，河边满是芦苇与垂柳。两座城门楼以及弧形的瓮城城墙上的雉堞，在蓝天的映衬下呈现为黑色的剪影。城墙与瓮城的轮廓线一直延伸至主城楼，那如翼般的巨大屋顶似乎将城楼从厚重的城墙与城台上抬起，展翅欲飞。水中的倒影跟实物一样清晰。但当风拂过柔软的柳枝，城楼的倒影随即颤抖起来，垛墙也支离而摇曳起来……

这些美妙的城墙与城门，这些北京最美丽、最辉煌的无言的历史记录者，它们的美还能够延续多久呢？

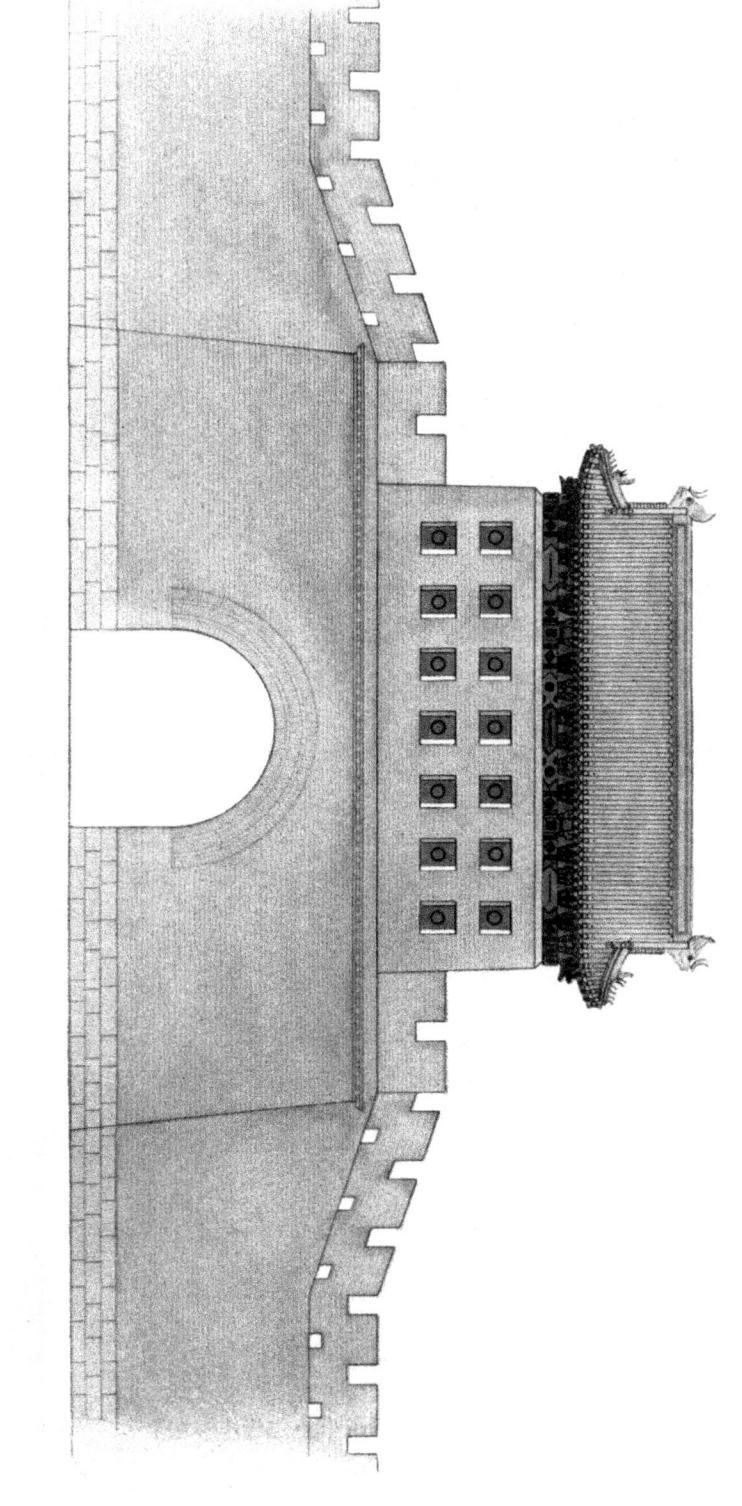

图 53 永定门箭楼正立面

西安府：西南隅的城墙

Sian-fu
The city wall at the south west corner

青州府：北城墙

Tsingchow-fu
The city wall on the north side

北京：外城中的街道
Peking. Street in the Chinese city

青州府：老商业街
Tsingchow-fu. Old business street

山东潍县的石牌楼

Stone p'ailou in Weihsien, Shantung

西安府：从鼓楼上远眺

Sian-fu
View from the drum tower

西安府：西城门与城墙

Sian-fu
The city wall and the west gate

外城西南隅城墙外的景象
Outside the Chinese City wall at the south west corner

北城墙下的古井
Old well at the north wall

前门与顺治门之间的南城墙

The south wall between Ch'ien Men and Shun Chih Men

西南隅附近分段修缮的南城墙
The south wall near the south west corner repaired in sections

顺治门与前门之间南城墙外的景象
Outside view of the south wall between Shun Chi Men and Ch'ien Men

观象台处的东城墙

The east wall at the Observatory

东城墙上不同年代的墙段
Sections of various age in the east wall

一段保存完好的东城墙
Well-preserved section of the east wall

东直门处的东城墙

The east wall at Tung Chih Men

齐化门与东直门之间的长马道

The long ramp between Ch'i Hua Men and Tung Chih Men

东城墙上的大洞和露出的多层砖面

A deep hole in the east wall revealing several layers of the brick coating

北城墙下吃草的羊

Grazing sheep at the north wall

北城墙下休憩的驼队
Resting camels at the north wall

德胜门以西的北城墙外侧壁

Outer side of the north wall west of Te Sheng Men

北城墙内侧壁的新、老墙段

Inner side of the north wall with old and new sections

北城墙处积水潭的河道

The water course - Chi Shui Tan - at the north wall

西城墙南段城墙外的景象
Outside view of the southern portion of the west wall

西直门附近的西城墙内侧壁
The inner side of the west wall near Hsi Chih Men

平则门望向主城墙外所见景象
Outside view of the main wall from Ping Tzu Men

平则门以南分三段修缮的马道
The ramp south of Ping Tzu Men, repaired in three sections

西城墙南端

At the south end of the west wall

内城东南隅城墙上的角楼
The tower on the south eastern corner of the inner wall

东南角楼及内、外城城墙之间的衔接处
The south eastern tower and the joint between the inner and the outer wall

外城城墙西北隅
The north west corner of the Chinese city wall

西城墙上墙面砖脱落之处
Portion of the west wall where the brick coating is falling down

The south west corner tower 西南角楼

The south east corner tower 东南角楼

外城东城墙的内侧壁

The inner east side of the Chinese city wall

外城东城墙内侧壁修补不当、严重残损的部分

Badly patched and decayed portions of the inner east side of the Chinese city wall

从彰义门箭楼城台眺望外城城墙

View of the Chinese city wall from the outer bastion of Chang I Men

外城南城墙的内侧壁

The inner south side of the Chinese city wall

外城城墙东北隅

The north east corner of the Chinese city wall

外城东城墙外的景象

Outside view along the east side of the Chinese city wall

外城西南角楼
Tower on the south west corner of the Chinese city wall

东便门外老路上的送葬队伍
Funeral procession on the old road outside Tung Pien Men

东便门附近城门桥与水闸
Bridge with water locks near Tung Pien Men

东便门处的外城城墙

The Chinese city wall at Tung Pien Men

平则门:两座城门楼与瓮城局部

Ping Tzu Men
The two gate towers and part of the barbican

平则门：城楼与瓮城局部

Ping Tzu Men
The inner tower and part of the gateyard

平则门：从城墙望至城楼北端

Ping Tzu Men
The northern end of the inner tower seen from the wall

平则门：箭楼侧面

Ping Tzu Men
Side view of the outer tower

平则门：从城墙望向箭楼

Ping Tzu Men
The outer tower from the wall

平则门：箭楼与沿瓮城城墙而立的摊位

Ping Tzu Men
The outer tower and stalls along the barbican wall

西直门：从南侧看城门全景

Hsi Chih Men
The complete gate from the south

Hsi Chih Men
Side view of the inner tower

西直门：城楼侧面

西直门：瓮城关帝庙中栽有柏树的院子

Hsi Chih Men
The outer court of the temple in the gateyard with a juniper tree

西直门：关帝庙庭院

Hsi Chih Men
The temple court

西直门：透过箭楼门洞看到的景象

Hsi Chih Men
View through the outer gate

西直门：瓮城边门之上的谯楼及附近的商铺

Hsi Chih Men
The small side tower over the barbican gate and adjoining shops

西直门：城门外老商铺林立的街道

Hsi Chih Men
The street lined with old shops outside the gate

Chai Hua Men
Interior of the inner tower and adjoining buildings

开化门：城楼侧面及附近的建筑

齐化门：城楼正面

Chih Hua Men
Front view of the inner tower

View of Tung Chih Men from the south 从南侧眺望东直门

View of the moat at Tung Chih Men 东直门护城河的景象

东直门：城楼正面

Tung Chih Men
Front view of the inner tower

东直门：透过城楼门洞所见景象

*Tung Chih Men
View through the inner gate*

东直门：城楼侧面

Tung Chih Men
Side view of the inner tower

东直门：箭楼与护城河

Tung Chih Men
The outer tower and moat

东直门：箭楼与现代平台

Tung Chih Men
The outer tower and the modern terraces

Tung Chih Men
The moat with the white ducks

东直门：白鸭游飞的护城河

哈达门：站在街上望向城楼

Hata Men
The inner tower from the street

哈达门：城楼侧面

Hata Men
Side view of the inner tower

Hata Men
The inner tower and the gateyard with people waiting for the train to pass

哈达门：城楼以及在瓮城中等待火车通过的人群

顺治门：最近修葺的城楼

Shun Chih Men
The inner, lately restored tower

顺治门：城楼与瓮城中央

Shun Chih Men
The inner tower and the central portion of the gateyard

顺治门：箭楼无存的城台上的老铁炮

Shun Chih Men
Old guns on the outer bastion which is divested of its tower

顺治门：堆满陶器的瓮城主街

Shun Chih Men
The road through the gateyard which is filled with stacks of pottery

前门：从南侧看到的城楼

Ch'ien Men
Inner tower from the south

前门：透过城楼门洞所见景象

Ch'ien Men
View through the inner gateway

前门：瓮城关帝庙山门入口处

Ch'ien Men
At the entrance to the temple in the gateyard

Ch'ien Men
Worshippers in the Kuan Ti miao

前门：关帝庙中的香客

前门：从箭楼上望新建的城门桥和外城主街

Ch'ien Men
View from the outer tower over the new bridge and the main street of the outer city

安定门：城楼与原有瓮城内部

An Ting Men
The inner tower and part of the former gateyard

安定门：箭楼与护城河

An Ting Men
The outer tower and the moat

An Tong Men
The outer tower and the temple in the gateyard

安定门：箭楼与瓮城中的真武庙

安定门：一段经过修葺的瓮城城墙

An Ting Men
A portion of the restored barbican wall

安定门：真武庙庭院

An Ting Men
In the gateyard of the Taoist temple

德胜门：瓮城的残存部分与箭楼

Te Sheng Men
The remaining bit of the barbican and the outer tower

德胜门：透过城楼门洞所见景象

Te Sheng Men
View through the inner gate

德胜门：原瓮城内的大椿树

Te Sheng Men
Old ailanthus tree in the former gateyard

德胜门：瓮城中的流动剃头匠

Te Sheng Men
The gateyard with the itinerant barbers

德胜门：瓮城中的真武庙

Te Sheng Men
The Taoist temple in the gateyard

德胜门：箭楼侧面

Te Sheng Men
Side view of the outer tower

Hsi Pien Men
The street leading up to the gate

西便门：通向城门的街道

Hai Tien Men
The inner gate tower

西便门:所谓的"城楼"

西便门：瓮城中的大洋槐

Hsi Pien Men
The old locust tree in the gateyard

西便门：瓮城中的椿树

Hsi Pien Men
The ailanthus tree in the gateyard

西便门：正在穿过箭楼门洞的驼队

Hsi Pien Men
Camel caravan passing through the outer gate

西便门：城门外树荫笼罩的街道

Hsi Pien Men
The shadowy street outside the gate

东便门：城楼景象

Tung Pien Men
View of the inner tower

东便门：箭楼门洞

Tung Pien Men
The outer gate

东便门外的城门桥

The bridge outside Tung Pien Men

Resting donkeys and oxen outside Tung Pien Men 东便门外休憩的驴子和牛

Camels outside Hsi Pien Men 西便门外的骆驼

东便门外、东运河终点处

Outside Tung Pien Men where the Tung Ho canal ends

Sha Wu Men
Side view of the barbican and the two towers

沙窝门：瓮城侧面及两座城门楼侧面

沙窝门：城楼

Sha Wu Men
The inner tower

Sha Wu Men
View through the gateyard

沙窝门：透过瓮城所见景象

Sha Wu Men. Funeral procession outside the gate

沙窝门:城门外的送葬队伍

Chang I Men
Side view of the towers and the barbican

彰义门：城门楼及瓮城侧面

彰义门：部分瓮城与城楼

Chang I Men
Part of the gateyard and the inner tower

彰义门：城楼侧面

Ch'ang I Men
Side view of the inner tower

彰义门：瓮城与城楼

Chang I Men
The gateyard and the inner tower

彰义门：箭楼

Chang I Men
The outer tower

右安门：透过瓮城与城楼门洞所见景象

Yu An Men
View through the gateyard and the inner tower

右安门：瓮城及箭楼

Yu An Men
The gateyard and the outer tower

右安门：冬日的驼队

Yu An Men
A camel caravan in winter time

右安门：箭楼与护城河

Yu An Men
The outer tower and the moat

右安门：城门外的垂柳

Yu An Men
The weeping willows outside the gate

Bulrushes and children in the moat, outside Yu An Men

右安门外护城河中的芦苇与孩童

右安门：城楼及长着椿树的城台

Yu An Men
The inner tower with ailanthus trees on the bastion

左安门：瓮城及城楼

Tso An Men
The gateyard and inner gate

左安门：已成废墟的马道，1922年9月

Tso An Men
The gate ramp in ruins, September 1922.

Tso An Men
Side view of the outer tower

左安门：箭楼侧面

左安门：箭楼与护城河

Tso An Men
The outer tower and the moat

Yung Ting Men
Front view of the two towers and the barbican

永定门：两座城门楼及瓮城正面

永定门：从瓮城望向城楼

Yung Ting Men
The inner tower from the gateyard

永定门：从瓮城望向箭楼

Yung Ting Men
View of the outer tower from the gateyard

永定门：横跨护城河的城门桥上的车马

Yung Ting Men
The traffic on the bridge over the moat

Yung Ting Men
Side view of the whole gate and the moat

永定门：从侧面望城门全景及护城河

北京的城墙和城门
(英文版)

This Edition is limited to eight hundred copies for sale, of which this is No._____

THE WALLS AND GATES OF PEKING

BY THE SAME AUTHOR
ESSENTIALS IN ART
THE BODLEY HEAD

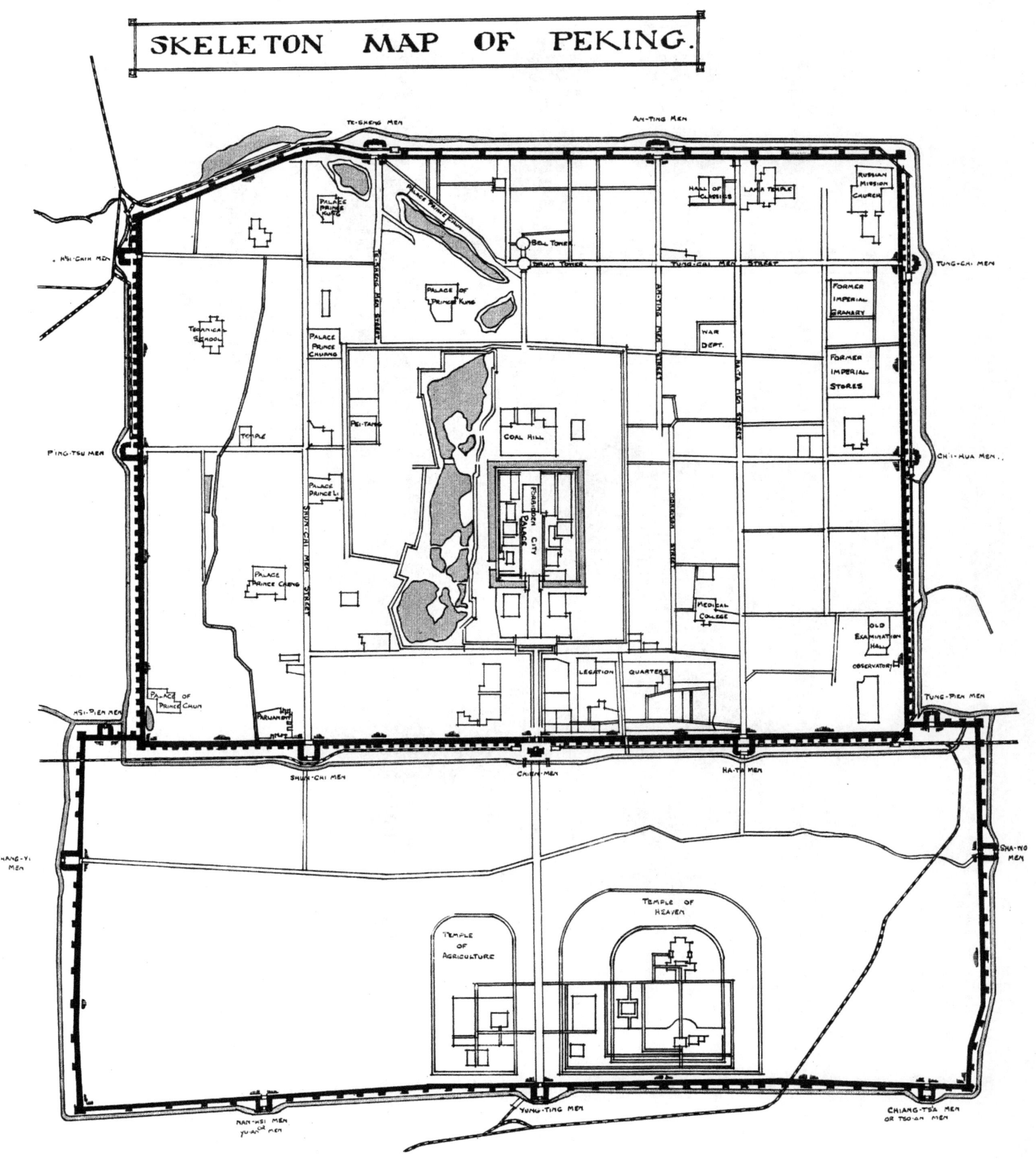

Sha Wu Men
View through the outer gate

THE WALLS AND GATES OF PEKING

RESEARCHES AND IMPRESSIONS BY
OSVALD SIRÉN
ILLUSTRATED WITH 109 PHOTOGRAVURES
AFTER PHOTOGRAPHS BY THE AUTHOR
AND FIFTY ARCHITECTURAL
DRAWINGS MADE BY
CHINESE ARTISTS

LONDON
JOHN LANE THE BODLEY HEAD LIMITED

First published in 1924

MADE AND PRINTED IN GREAT BRITAIN BY WILLIAM CLOWES AND SONS, LIMITED,
LONDON AND BECCLES

Photogravures engraved and printed by Frank C. Thomas, London

PREFACE

THE origin of this book is the beauty of the city gates of Peking; their importance as characteristic elements in some of the finest views of the Chinese capital; their wonderful setting amidst old buildings, fresh trees and decaying moats; their decorative architectural character. Some of these gates may still be called landmarks of Peking, historically as well as topographically; they reflect, together with the adjoining walls, much of the early history of this great city, and they form, together with the streets and landscapes in which they are set, the most relevant spots of characteristic and beautiful scenery.

Such were the impressions which led me to devote months of special study to the Peking gates with the aim of reproducing their beauty in a series of photographs. To what degree this has been accomplished may be left to the reader to judge; a selection of these photographs are reproduced in the present work on 109 heliogravure plates.

The interest in the artistic character of the gates gradually awakened the desire to know something about their importance as monuments of the past, to penetrate further into the history of their construction and their modifications in various ages. Not only the gates but their surroundings and the long walls of which they form parts attracted my interest as material for historical and architectural studies; and the more I dwelt on this material, the more I realized that it contained the keys to some important chapters of Chinese history. Very little of this is reflected in the text, but even the fragmentary information that I am able to offer may make the reader realize that the Gates and Walls of Peking form an unbroken chain with the past, renewed at many places with new links, but nevertheless mainly old and full of the marks and records of bygone days.

The historical part of the text is mainly based on the local Chinese chronicles, which contain much information about the city walls and the gates during earlier dynasties, and which never before have been published to the same extent in any foreign language. Besides these printed records others are to be found on the monuments themselves, mainly brickmarks and inscriptions on stone tablets inserted at various places on the walls and the gates. All these materials have been carefully collected and utilized for the historical discussion and dating of the various parts of the monuments. But all these documentary evidences form merely corroborations for the technical and architectural analysis which in many instances, where no written information was available, became the main basis for the historical study and definition.

The work had, of course, to be carried out within certain restrictions. It was not possible to make any material tests on the buildings, to dig into walls or to erect scaffoldings for a closer study of their upper parts, but permission was obtained from the Ministry of the Interior to make measured drawings of a number of the gates. These drawings, which were all executed by Chinese artists under the supervision of the author, will no doubt form a most valuable source of exact information, not only about the Peking gates but also about Chinese architecture in general, because the gates are, after all, highly representative examples of the general principles of Chinese architecture.

In preparing this work I have had the assistance of various persons to whom I rest under obligation. The Chinese chronicles from which long extracts are quoted in our text were translated by Miss A. G. Bowden-Smith

PREFACE

and some of her assistants, at the Pei Hua school in Peking; the credit and the responsibility for this part of the work thus rest with her.

Most of the inscriptions on the tablets and the bricks were taken down with great care and patience by my Chinese teacher, Mr. Chou Ku-chen, and some of these inscriptions were translated by Mr. Scott of the British Legation.

Valuable practical assistance was given me on various occasions by the well-known Baumeister Thiele, who also put me into communication with the Chinese draughtsmen. Their work, which was done under my direction, may be appreciated from the drawings reproduced in colour and line engraving in the present volume.

The drawings of the outer tower and the plans of Ch'ien men were kindly placed at my disposition by Architect Rothkegel, under whose supervision the great central gate was rearranged a few years ago.

I also owe special thanks to Mr. Jupp of the R.I.B.A., who kindly undertook to examine some of the architectural descriptions in the text.

The greatest difficulty in connection with the preparation of the text has been the unavoidable inclusion of a great number of Chinese words and names. The ideal way would, of course, have been to give every one of these words in Chinese characters, but as this proved impossible for various reasons, Mr. Yih, of the School of Oriental Studies, undertook to prepare a list of the more important of the Chinese words, which may, to some extent, atone for the lack of Chinese characters in the text.

The English transcriptions are generally in conformity with the Wade system, though I am conscious of certain slight deviations such as the use of *e* instead of *ê*, and I know only too well that the use of capital letters in Chinese compound names is somewhat arbitrary, which is almost unavoidable in reference to names codified by the Post Office; but I hope nevertheless—in spite of certain omissions and irregularities—that nothing remains unintelligible to the well-disposed reader.

PREFACE

My efforts may after all make it easier for some one further advanced than the author of this book in the intricacies of Chinese language and history to carry the researches on the same field a step further. If I have succeeded in awakening a fresh interest in the Walls and Gates of Peking, those wonderful but now decaying historical monuments, and in reflecting some glimpses of their transcient beauty, my ambition is satisfied and I feel that I have acquitted some of my obligation to the great capital of China.

OSVALD SIRÉN.

PARIS, *May*, 1924.

CONTENTS

		PAGE
I.	WALLED CITIES OF NORTHERN CHINA—SOME GENERAL IMPRESSIONS	1
II.	EARLIER CITIES ON THE SITE OF PEKING	15
III.	THE WALLS OF THE TARTAR CITY	34
IV.	NOTES ON THE INNER SIDE OF THE TARTAR CITY WALL	53
V.	NOTES ABOUT THE OUTER SIDE OF THE TARTAR CITY WALL	92
VI.	THE WALL OF THE CHINESE CITY	106
VII.	THE GATES OF THE TARTAR CITY	128
VIII.	THE GATES OF THE CHINESE CITY	188
	INDEX OF CHINESE WORDS	221

LIST OF ILLUSTRATIONS

PHOTOGRAVURES

	PLATE
Sha Wu Men: View through the outer gate . . . . *Frontispiece*	1
Sian-fu: The city wall at the south-west corner	2
Tsingchow-fu: The city wall on the north side	3
Peking: Street in the Chinese city	4
Tsingchow-fu: Old business street	5
Stone p'ailou in Weihsien, Shantung	6
Sian-fu: View from the drum-tower	7
„ The city wall and the west gate	8
Outside the Chinese City wall at the south-west corner	9
Old well at the north wall	10
The south wall between Ch'ien Men and Shun Chih Men	11
The south wall near the south-west corner repaired in sections	12
Outside view of the south wall between Shun Chi Men and Ch'ien Men	13
The east wall at the Observatory	14
Sections of various age in the east wall	15
Well-preserved section of the east wall	16
The east wall at Tung Chih Men	17
The long ramp between Ch'i Hua Men and Tung Chih Men	18
A deep hole in the east wall revealing several layers of the brick coating	19
Grazing sheep at the north wall	20
Resting camels at the north wall	21
Outer side of the north wall west of Tê Sheng Men	22
Inner side of the north wall with old and new sections	23
The water-course—Chi Shui Tan—at the north wall	24
Outside view of the southern portion of the west wall	25
The inner side of the west wall near Hsi Chih Men	26
Outside view of the main wall from P'ing Tzu Men	27
The ramp south of P'ing Tzu Men, repaired in three sections	28
At the south end of the west wall	29

LIST OF ILLUSTRATIONS

	PLATE
The tower on the south-eastern corner of the inner wall	30
The south-eastern tower and the joint between the inner and the outer wall	31
The north-west corner of the Chinese city wall	32
Portion of the west wall where the brick coating is falling down	33
The south-west corner tower	34
The south-east corner tower	35
The inner east side of the Chinese city wall	36
Badly patched and decayed portions of the inner east side of the Chinese city wall	37
View of the Chinese city wall from the outer bastion of Chang I Men	38
The inner south side of the Chinese city wall	39
The north-east corner of the Chinese city wall	40
Outside view along the east side of the Chinese city wall	41
Tower on the south-west corner of the Chinese city wall	42
Funeral procession on the old road outside Tung Pien Men	43
Bridge with water locks near Tung Pien Men	44
The Chinese city wall at Tung Pien Men	45
P'ing Tzu Men: The two gate towers and part of the barbican	46
,, ,, The inner tower and part of the gateyard	47
,, ,, The northern end of the inner tower seen from the wall	48
,, ,, Side view of the outer tower	49
,, ,, The outer tower from the wall	50
,, ,, The outer tower and stalls along the barbican wall	51
Hsi Chih Men: The complete gate from the south	52
,, ,, Side view of the inner tower	53
,, ,, The outer court of the temple in the gateyard with a juniperus tree	54
,, ,, The temple court	55
,, ,, View through the outer gate	56
,, ,, The small side tower over the barbican gate and adjoining shops	57
,, ,, The street lined with old shops outside the gate	58
Ch'i Hua Men: Sideview of the inner tower and adjoining buildings	59
,, ,, Front view of the inner tower	60
View of Tung Chih Men from the south	61
View of the moat at Tung Chih Men	62
Tung Chih Men: Front view of the inner tower	63
,, ,, View through the inner gate	64
,, ,, Side view of the inner tower	65
,, ,, The outer tower and moat	66
,, ,, The outer tower and the modern terraces	67
,, ,, The moat with the white ducks	68
Hata Men: The inner tower from the street	69
,, ,, Side view of the inner tower	70

LIST OF ILLUSTRATIONS

	PLATE
Hata Men: The inner tower and the gateyard with people waiting for the train to pass	71
Shun Chih Men: The inner, lately restored tower	72
,, ,, The inner tower and the central portion of the gateyard	73
,, ,, Old guns on the outer bastion which is divested of its tower	74
,, ,, The road through the gateyard which is filled with stacks of pottery	75
Ch'ien Men: Inner tower from the south	76
,, ,, View through the inner gateway	77
,, ,, At the entrance to the temple in the gateyard	78
,, ,, Worshippers in the Kuan Ti Miao	79
,, ,, View from the outer tower over the new bridge and the main street of the outer city	80
An Ting Men: The inner tower and part of the former gateyard	81
,, ,, The outer tower and the moat	82
,, ,, The outer tower and the temple in the gateyard	83
,, ,, A portion of the restored barbican wall	84
,, ,, In the gateyard of the Taoist temple	85
Tê Sheng Men: The remaining bit of the barbican and the outer tower	86
,, ,, View through the inner gate	87
,, ,, Old ailanthus tree in the former gateyard	88
,, ,, The gateyard with the itinerant barbers	89
,, ,, The Taoist temple in the gateyard	90
,, ,, Side view of the outer tower	91
Hsi Pien Men: The street leading up to the gate	92
,, ,, The inner gate "tower"	93
,, ,, The old locust tree in the gateyard	94
,, ,, The ailanthus tree in the gateyard	95
,, ,, Camel caravan passing through the outer gate	96
,, ,, The shadowy street outside the gate	97
Tung Pien Men: View of the inner tower	98
,, ,, The outer gate	99
The bridge outside Tung Pien Men	100
Resting donkeys and oxen outside Tung Pien Men	101
Camels outside Hsi Pien Men	102
Outside Tung Pien Men where the Tung Ho canal ends	103
Sha Wu Men: Side view of the barbican and the two towers	104
,, ,, The inner tower	105
,, ,, View through the gateyard	106
,, ,, Funeral procession outside the gate	107
Chang I Men: Side view of the towers and the barbican	108
,, ,, Part of the gateyard and the inner tower	109
Chang I Men: Side view of the inner tower	110
Chang I Men: The gateyard and the inner tower	111

LIST OF ILLUSTRATIONS

		PLATE
Chang I Men: The outer tower		112
Yu An Men: View through the gateyard and the inner tower		113
" " The gateyard and the outer tower		114
" " A camel caravan in winter-time		115
" " The outer tower and the moat		116
" " The weeping willows outside the gate		117
Bulrushes and children in the moat outside Yu An Men		118
Yu An Men: The inner tower with ailanthus trees on the bastion		119
Tso An Men: The gateyard and inner gate		120
" " The gate ramp in ruins, September, 1922		121
" " Side view of the outer tower		122
" " The outer tower and the moat		123
Yung Ting Men: Front view of the two towers and the barbican		124
" " The inner tower from the gateyard		125
" " View of the outer tower from the gateyard		126
" " The traffic on the bridge over the moat		127
" " Side view of the whole gate and the moat		128

PLANS AND ELEVATIONS

FIG.		PAGE
1.	Approximate situations of the earlier capitals in relation to the site of Peking	17
2.	Chung tu, capital of the Chin tartars. Khanbalic, capital of the Yüan emperors	20
3.	Two sections of the west wall, south of P'ing Tzu Men	45
4.	Two sections of the north wall; the upper one taken near the east corner, the lower one near An Ting Men	47
5.	Plan of the south-west corner-tower	90
6.	P'ing Tzu Men (also known as Fu Cheng Men), general plan	134
7.	P'ing Tzu Men, inner tower	135
8.	" " "	136
9.	" " "	137
10.	" " "	140
11.	" " "	141
12.	" " outer tower	142
13.	" " "	143
14.	" " "	146
15.	" " "	147
16.	" " "	148
17.	Hsi Chih Men, plan of the inner tower	151
18.	Ch'i Hua Men, plan of the inner tower	156
19.	Tung Chih Men, plan of the inner tower	158

LIST OF ILLUSTRATIONS

FIG.		PAGE
20.	Hata Men, inner tower	162
21.	Hata Men, plan of the inner tower	164
22.	Shun Chih Men, plan of the inner tower	166
23.	Ch'ien Men, general plan, before the reconstruction	168
24.	,, ,, ,, after the reconstruction	171
25.	,, ,, front elevation of the outer tower before its restoration	174
26.	,, ,, plan of the outer tower before its restoration	175
27.	,, ,, side elevation of the outer tower before its restoration	176
28.	,, ,, the inner tower	178
29.	,, ,, plan of the inner tower	179
30.	An Ting Men, plan of the inner tower	183
31.	Tê Sheng Men, plan of the inner tower	185
32.	Hsi Pien Men, general plan	189
33.	,, ,, inner tower	190
34.	,, ,, ,,	191
35.	,, ,, ,,	192
36.	,, ,, outer tower	193
37.	,, ,, ,,	194
38.	,, ,, ,,	195
39.	Chang I Men (also known as Kuang An Men), general plan	201
40.	,, ,, inner tower	203
41.	,, ,, ,,	204
42.	,, ,, ,,	205
43.	,, ,, outer tower	206
44.	,, ,, ,,	207
45.	,, ,, ,,	207
46.	Yung Ting Men, general plan	212
47.	,, ,, elevation of the inner tower	*To face* 212
48.	,, ,, plan of inner tower	214
49.	,, ,, ,, ,,	215
50.	,, ,, cross section of the inner tower	216
51.	,, ,, plan of outer tower	217
52.	,, ,, elevation of the outer tower	*To face* 218
53.	,, ,, cross section of the outer tower	218

MAP

Skeleton map of Peking . . . . *Between* pp. xviii *and* xix

THE WALLS AND
GATES OF PEKING

THE WALLS AND GATES OF PEKING

I

WALLED CITIES OF NORTHERN CHINA—SOME GENERAL IMPRESSIONS

EVERY one has heard of the Great Wall of China, but most people think of it as a mere historical relic, the stately ruin of an enterprise which sprang from an ancient emperor's overheated fancy. The prevailing impression about it is that it has fallen naturally into decay like other things in China, and that for hundreds of years past its practical importance has been largely a delusion. This is a complete misapprehension. The Great Wall is one of the few Chinese buildings which have been properly preserved. It has been repaired and reconstructed over and over again in the course of the centuries, and its importance both as a defence-work and as a boundary has been very considerable until quite recent years; certainly this is the opinion of the Chinese themselves. In it, in fact, the deep-rooted belief of the Chinese in walled enclosures finds its fullest and most enduring expression.

Walls, walls, and yet again walls form, so to say, the skeleton or framework of every Chinese city. They surround it, they divide it into lots and compounds, they mark more than any other structures the common basic features of these Chinese communities. There is no real city in Northern China without a surrounding wall, a condition which, indeed, is expressed by the fact that the Chinese use the same word *Ch'eng* for a city and a city-wall: for there is no such thing as a city without a wall. It is just as inconceivable as a house without a roof. It matters little how large, important, and well ordered a settlement may be; if not properly defined and enclosed by walls, it is not a city in the traditional Chinese sense. Thus, for instance, Shanghai (outside the "native town"), the most important commercial centre of modern China, is, to the old-fashioned Chinaman, not a real city, only a settlement or a huge trading centre, grown out of a fishing village. And the same is true of several other comparatively modern commercial centres without encircling walls; they are not *ch'engs*, or cities, according to traditional Chinese conception, whatever modern republican officials may choose to call them.

The walls are, indeed, the most essential, the most impressive, and most permanent parts of a Chinese city, and they belong not only to the provincial capitals and other *fu*-cities, but to every community, even to small towns and villages. I have seldom seen a village of any size or age in Northern China which has not at least a mud wall or the remains of something of the kind around its huts and stables. No matter how poor and inconspicuous the place, however miserable the mud-houses, however useless the ruined temples, however dirty and ditchlike the sunken roads, the walls are still there, and, as a rule, kept in better condition than any other buildings of the town or village. I have passed through cities in the north-western provinces which have been thoroughly demolished by wars and famine and fire, where no house is left standing and no human being lives, but which still retain their crenelated walls, their gates and watch-towers. These have withstood the ravages of fire and vandal soldiery better than the rest of the city buildings; they remain as monuments of a past glory, doubly impressive in the midst of a complete desolation and solitude.

The bare brick walls with their bastions and gate-towers rising over a moat or simply from the open level ground, where the view to a far distance is unblocked by trees or high buildings, often tell more about the ancient

WALLED CITIES OF NORTHERN CHINA

greatness and importance of these cities than any of the houses or temples. Even when these city-walls are not of a very early date (there are hardly any now standing in Northern China older than the Ming dynasty) they are nevertheless ancient-looking with their more or less battered brickwork and broken battlements. Repairs and rebuildings have, as a rule, done little to change their general shape and proportions. Before the brick walls there were ramparts around a good many of the cities and towns of Northern China, as still may be seen at smaller out-of-the-way places; and before the towns were built, there were villages or camps of mud and straw huts surrounded by fences or ramparts of a temporary character.

Two examples may be mentioned as illustrations of a whole class of walled cities in Northern China: Sian-fu in Shensi and Tsingchow-fu in Shantung. The present walls of Sian-fu were built at the end of the fourteenth century by the first Ming emperor: they have been repaired in places; but, as a whole, have withstood remarkably well the ravages of time and war. They enclose an almost square city which is visible in its completeness from far away, as the surrounding country is simply an open *loess* plateau. Approaching it from the north or from the west, one sees the walls as long unbroken lines stretching for miles and miles. Coming a little nearer, the double gate-towers, the square bastions, and the monumental round corner-towers begin to appear: the rhythm of the lines and of the masses becomes evident—a remarkably slow, heavy, and forceful rhythm. The city dominates the high *loess* plateau, rising over it like a huge fortress and at the same time blending with it by its own long horizontal lines.

The approach to Tsingchow-fu is quite different. The general view of the city is by no means as grand and impressive as the outer aspect of Sian-fu, but the nearer one approaches, the more interesting the view becomes, the more striking the effect of the monumental walls in the setting of a picturesque nature. The city lies in the midst of a fertile valley among rich grain-fields and orchards; there are plenty of trees to shade the walls and to break the monotony of their drab surface. A small river with remarkably clear water takes the place of the moat on two sides of the city; one has to pass over solid old stone bridges in order to reach the northern and the western gates. Following the windings of the river, the city-wall is broken up into a succession of angles and the river-bank is cut into irregular terraces. Bits of stone and of brickwork are thus piled up in successive steps as freely and fittingly as if they were placed there by nature. For instance, at the spot where the paved stone road winds up from the low stone bridge on the western side: the river-bank here has the most interesting formation of terraces and steps, partly lined with bricks and overshadowed by trees. The wall rises to an imposing height, strengthened by massive buttresses; the top of it is thickly clad with shrubs and trees which stretch their branches over the crenelated parapet. There is a touch of romantic beauty about this place which reminds us of certain walled cities in Northern Italy rather than of a Chinese town.

Passing through one of the less frequented gates in some of these cities one is often surprised not to find oneself in a busy street, lined with shops and houses, but in open fields or empty tracts with nothing but refuse heaps and stagnant muddy ponds. Thus, for instance, the western and southern portion of Tsingchow-fu is largely utilized for grain-fields and vegetable gardens, in spite of the fact that people who have lately moved into the city can hardly find a room or a shed to sleep in; and in Sian-fu there are large stretches of empty ground inside the walls on the western, northern, and eastern sides, and ponds of considerable size where ducks and tortoises thrive on the quiet mud-like water. Most of these old Chinese cities which date back to the Ming time, or before, have during the last century been decaying and diminishing in size, even if their population has not decreased. The people have simply been forced to crowd themselves more and more together or to settle in huts in the suburbs; which is no doubt a cheaper and easier way of solving the housing problem than to build new houses within the city walls. Exceptions may be quoted, cities where a quite modern building activity has been brought about by increasing business and new means of communication or by an unusually progressive local government, as, for instance, in Taiyuan-fu in Shansi ; but these cities are very rare, and the new buildings with which they have been adorned are such that we would rather wish to see the space again utilized for manure and cabbage-fields.

We have no occasion to enter here into any further investigations of the causes which led so many of these north Chinese cities to deteriorate, and decrease in size. The reasons are, no doubt, closely connected with the general political, social, and economic conditions of modern China, which, on the whole, have been unfavourable to the preservation of old cities and historical monuments. The spirit of enterprise as well as the necessary resources have been sadly lacking in official quarters, and when wars and revolutions with their sequels of pillage, fire, and famine have swept over a city, very little has been done to restore its previous status. The people have rather gathered in new settlements formed of semi-foreign houses. The most striking illustrations of such transformations are offered by ancient capital cities such as Nanking, Sian-fu, Loyang, etc., which now are only pale, shrinking shadows of what they used to be ; but a good many smaller cities show a similar backward tendency in their diminishing building-area and their architectural dilapidation. This tendency manifests itself in many cases not only in the disproportion between the wall-enclosed compass of the city and the ground actually covered by the buildings, but also in the cheap and poor quality of the houses.

It is a rare thing to find a building of architectural importance in any average city of Northern China. Some of the temples may, of course, be quite picturesque with their sculptured gateways and their open pillared porches under the enormous roofs, but they are, strictly speaking, no masterpieces of architecture, particularly if they have been rebuilt in recent years ; more important from an architectural point of view are some of the older stone or brick pagodas which represent a rather strange and artificial type, and the bell-towers and drum-towers which still stand in the midst of many of the old cities, forming by their monumental proportions the strongest link with a greater past. The majority of the buildings are, however, quite inconspicuous small houses built of grey bricks and on a framework of wooden pillars and beams which may be painted red. In the shopping district the façades are more or less open with porches and rows of pillars towards the street, but it is only in wealthier places that we find them decorated with carvings, brass hangings, and artistic signboards. Carved and gilt shop-fronts have become exceptional in the ordinary provincial towns, largely in consequence of the destructive modern fondness for brick and cement which has spread like an epidemic since the introduction of the republic. Since the " Flowery Middle Kingdom " has become the " People's Country," the artistic flowers of the old civilization have been withering very fast.

The residential sections of these cities usually turn the most blank and empty faces towards the passer-by. Here for the most part only roofs are to be seen, curved roofs of various height and size, and between them tree-tops; hardly anything of the houses. They are all hidden behind walls, plain grey brick-walls, or plastered reddish walls which may be tinted by time and dirt, long empty spaces with no divisions or ornaments except simple doorways or small porches marked by steps and small saddle roofs. The architectural monotony could hardly be more complete. It is sometimes like passing a street of prisons or monasteries; only the play of light and shade and some occasional beggar who basks in the sun at the foot of the wall animate the view. Once in a while the tinkling of a bell or the chiming of a brazen gong of some itinerant vendor may reach your ear, but when he has passed the silence again becomes deep and impenetrable. There are no indications of the life and the beauty that may be hidden behind the walls. The home of the Chinaman is an extremely well-guarded place. Every family forms a little community by itself—often quite a numerous one, as the married sons share the parental house—and the walls that enclose it are often just as effective for confining the inmates as for protecting them against intruders. The women, especially,

WALLED CITIES OF NORTHERN CHINA

used to be confined in these walled compounds as strictly as in a medieval monastery.

It is only after entering the gate and passing the so-called spirit-wall,* just behind it, that we may perceive something of the peculiar beauty of such a residence. If it is a large compound with two or three or more courtyards, the first one may not offer anything particularly interesting: it is simply a paved court, enclosed by low buildings on three sides. But behind this is another court, planted with trees and flowers, or arranged into a real garden with ponds and rockeries and pavilions. The arrangement depends, of course, on the size and importance of the place. The buildings are all of a uniform type, although varying in size and details; the most important one is situated at the end of the main court, raised on a stone platform. Along its façade runs an open gallery or patio formed by a row of wooden pillars between the protruding side-walls (which form a kind of "ante"). The high and curving saddle-roof extends over the patio, its eaves resting on the pillars which in all the finer old houses are provided with ornamented brackets. The construction of the walls may vary a little, but the framework of the façade consists usually of standing pillars supporting horizontal beams; the intervals between them in their lower part are filled out with brickwork, while the upper parts are treated as windows with more or less elaborate lattice-work and transparent paper instead of glass. The main door in the midst of the façade, where broad steps lead up to the terrace, has carved panels and sometimes also openings with lattice-work and transparent paper in its upper part. Other less striking details in the construction may here be passed over, but a word should be added about the colouring which is most essential for the outer effect of the Chinese house. All the woodwork is painted in a deep red tone while the brickwork and the pantiles are grey. The carved ornaments on the door-panels may be heightened with gold, and if it is a palatial building the brackets of the pillars

---

* A screen-like wall standing right in front of the inner gateway as a protection against the evil spirits, which always move in a straight line.

are adorned with green and blue ornaments. The Chinese are by no means afraid of using strong colours; the effect being very good at a distance, particularly when the house stands in a setting of green foliage or blossoming trees, but the ornamentation lacks refinement and will hardly stand closer inspection.

Returning to the street we may walk over to the business section of the town. The street views are quite different here, and, as a whole, much more animated and entertaining than in the residential quarters. The houses are not hidden behind uniformly closed walls but open into the street with latticed doors and windows, in which glass panes nowadays have taken the place of the transparent paper. The roofs are just as high and far-extending as on the dwelling-houses, but there are usually no wooden pillars in front of the shop; as the façades are comparatively narrow the beams of the eaves find sufficient support on the protruding side-walls. Sometimes the entrance is shaded by a small sloping roof or canopy, supported on brackets or pillars, and in the hot reason large sunsheds are arranged in front of the shops by means of bamboo scaffoldings covered with straw mats. If the street is narrow, these sheds may be built right across from one shop to another, otherwise they cover at least the sidewalks. These are, as a matter of fact, much more occupied by the traders than by the passers-by. A good deal of the business is transacted in the street, by the shopkeepers as well as by itinerant vendors, particularly at the food shops which display their delicacies outside. Sometimes the street in front of the shops becomes a veritable market, as was the case in a certain street of Sian-fu where most of the grain-shops were to be found. Something like a corn-exchange was established there every morning, and the throng and bustle of buyers and sellers, wheelbarrows and grain-carriers, was such that an outsider could hardly make his way through. The inner shop is, indeed, in many small old-fashioned houses, less of a business-place than a living-room where the proprietor and his assistants eat and sleep and smoke and sip their tea. It is only outwardly that a definite distinction may be made between simple dwelling-houses and small shops.

WALLED CITIES OF NORTHERN CHINA

There are, however, shops and shops; the variety both in their outward and inward appearance is very considerable, depending not only on the prosperity of the place but also on local customs and the kind of business for which they are intended. A dry-goods store is thus always different from a chemist's, a goldsmith's, or a tea-shop, and, as a rule, it may be said that the outer decoration to some extent reflects the quality and refinement of the goods offered for sale in the store. It would take us too far to go into a description of the details and intricacies of these various kinds of stores, particularly as we are here merely dealing with the architectural aspect of the Chinese street. Most important in this respect are, however, the high carved shop fronts which may still be seen in some of the better-preserved old cities. In Peking they used to line most of the important business streets, but have lately been much diminished in number by the modern craze for semi-foreign cement buildings with fluttering band-ornaments and republican flags in relief on the façade. They rise high over the roof-line of the houses, forming canopies or *p'ailous* in front of the shop entrances. The constructive frame consists of very tall masts joined by cross-beams with manifold rows of brackets which support small saddle-roofs of one or two stories. Under the roofs are frieze-like panels which may be ornamented with human figures in relief or with floral designs in open or pierced carving, into which the signboard of the shop is inserted. The bottom part is treated like a broad laced border to the whole canopy, its intricate leaf-pattern being carved in open relief. All these carvings are richly gilt, sometimes also accentuated by colours, and in addition to this there are small canopies or hats with brightly coloured ribbons and tassels (sometimes of wood) hanging from dragon-heads which protrude from the masts.

Streets lined with such carved and gilt shop fronts must have been gorgeous sights, and they were by no means uncommon in the provincial capitals a few generations ago. Now they are becoming rarer every year, as nobody appears to be interested in keeping them up, most people being contented to see them replaced by hybrid cement buildings or drab brick houses with no decoration except the large signboards with a few significant characters placed over or at the side of the entrance. The general view of a business street in an average North-Chinese town is thus much more enjoyable as a picture of light and shade, hustling people, wheelbarrows and donkey-carts, than as a composition of buildings. It may be very lively and quite picturesque, particularly if some old trees have been left standing in the street, but it has seldom any features of architectural importance.

Such is the rule, but there are important exceptions—streets with decorative monuments, memorial tablets, archways and towers. Most important in this respect are the *p'ailous*—decorative gateways with three or more openings spanning the whole street (including the sidewalks). The object of their erection is usually to commemorate some distinguished local character or some important event in the history of the place, but their main interest for posterity and for strangers depends on their unusual decorative character. The majority of these gateways are made of wood and brightly painted in red, with ornaments in green and blue besides gilt carvings. The supporting pillars or masts, which may be four, or eight, or twelve, according to the size and the importance of the monument, are placed on stone plinths (sometimes decorated with lions), and between them are spanned broad cross-beams in two or three horizontal rows, divided by sculptured panels, friezes or tablets with honorific inscriptions. At the top are curved saddle-roofs— a separate one for each gateway of the *p'ailou*—resting on manifold rows of brackets, covered with blue or green pantiles and decorated with human and animal figures on the hips, the so-called " *kuei lung tzŭ.*" These *p'ailous* contain some of the most characteristic features of traditional Chinese architecture, as, for instance, the supporting pillars, the curved saddle-roofs on double or triple rows of complex brackets, the highly ornamented cross-beams, the carved friezes, and a colouring which in its festal splendour might appear crude. They are essentially wooden structures. Their whole character and decoration have been developed in conformity with the special requirements of the material, except in the case of the ornamental figures on the roof. This is also strikingly confirmed when we see them executed in stone; the various parts of the stone *p'ailous* are simply copied from wooden models and joined together in a manner which, indeed, is more fitting for wooden than for stone construction (the case being quite parallel to the Japanese stone " torii," which also show wood-construction transferred to stone gates). Modifications are, of course, necessary in certain parts such as the roofs (which have no curve) and the brackets (which sometimes become curved consoles): the cross-beams are decorated with reliefs instead of with painted ornaments, and the square or octagonal pillars are strengthened by low buttresses, consisting of a large drum, rolled up on a low plinth with a small lion perched on its top. A good many lesser variations in the composition of stone *p'ailous* may be pointed out, if one goes into a detailed study of these monuments, but the general principles of construction and decorative arrangement have remained the same from the beginning of the Ming dynasty down to recent times. The oldest stone *p'ailous* are nowadays to be found in temple-gardens where they have had more protection than in the streets, but I do not know of any that could be ascribed to an earlier date than the Ming period. The most beautiful and numerous street *p'ailous* of stone that I have seen are at Weihsien in Shantung, where the main street is spanned by half a dozen tripartite archways of unusual height, having consoles and roofs in three different stories. They were probably constructed in the Ch'ien Lung era. But the *p'ailous* do not always traverse streets; they may stand in open places or alongside the street, marking the entrance to some temple-ground or to some official yamen, their object always being to accentuate the honorific character and distinction of a place or a person.

In a good many of these old Chinese cities the principal street views are dominated by the bell-tower and the drum-tower, two high and monumental buildings which always occupy a central position in the city. Very often important thoroughfares radiate from or intersect under one or both of these towers. Their broad terraces are pierced by barrel-vaults of the same kind as at the city gates, and right under them are created traffic-centres, or rather tunnel-crossings which often become highly congested, as they are used not only as passages by all sorts of vehicles and pedestrians but also as dwelling-places by the idlers and beggars who seek shelter from rain or a burning sun. On top of this brick-lined terrace, which may be as high as the city walls, stands the real tower, a large pavilion in two or three stories, usually constructed with a framework of wood with brick-filling between the pillars and beams. Around this are open galleries in the two lower stories, while the top story is closed. The far-protruding curved roofs are supported by a more or less elaborate system of "*san tou*" (Japanese: *masugami*), i.e. composite brackets arranged in three or four projecting rows under the eaves. The constructive and decorative details, of course, vary according to the age and importance of the building, but they are, as a rule, less essential to the general effect of the towers than the main proportions, the combination of the lofty pavilion and the massive sub-structure. Buildings of this type are called by the Chinese *t'ai*, and they have been used since the earliest times for different purposes, such as watch-towers, treasure-houses, and astronomical observatories. Whenever they rise out of the low masses of walls and roofs, which make up most of the Chinese city views, they add a note of ancient strength and dignity to the picture.

In addition to the bell-towers and drum-towers there are others with a religious significance in some of the old cities of Northern China, though the greater number of these "pagodas," or temple-towers, are situated not inside but outside the city walls. They were usually built in connection with some important shrine (to preserve some precious relics), and the finest of the Buddhist temples were, as a rule, not placed in the heart of a crowded city but at the most beautiful spots out in the country. Architecturally the pagodas show great variations, depending on period, material, and all sorts of local religious requirements, so that it is hardly possible to indicate any features which would be common to them all, except that they are towers on a square or polygonal plan, varying in height from about 50 to nearly 350 feet and divided into three, five, seven, nine, eleven, or thirteen stories. The older ones are usually built of brick, while the later ones are more often wooden structures. But there are also pagodas built entirely of stone or of iron. Many of these high towers are important landmarks in an open and flat country, signifying to the popular mind not only direction and distance but also a certain amount of protection and good luck, connected with the influences of *fêng shui*. It is quite rare to find them dominating a city view in the north, as they do in southern cities like Hangchow and Soochow; when they do appear in the midst of a city, they impress us as rather strange monuments of an imported religion, though they are in better keeping with the surrounding and the historical atmosphere of these old places than any of the Christian cathedrals and bell-towers which, in their rigid stateliness, are the most exacting and obtrusive strangers in these old clusters of inconspicuous small buildings and mouldering walls.

With all its apparent monotony and uniformity, an old Chinese city may be quite an intricate place, full of surprises, such as bits of old buildings or other half-ruined monuments tucked away in dirty alleys which often have the appearance of ditches or sewers rather than of streets. But those hid remnants of past glories have to be discovered; they are not seen by the ordinary traveller or the one who simply passes along the main streets of the cities, as we have been doing: our object not being to stop and investigate historical records or details, but simply to note some characteristic features in the appearance of the Chinese city, its streets and buildings, so as to give a better idea of the relation between the inner body of the city and its walled circumference. We have seen that the Chinese city, taken as a whole, is pre-eminently an extensive mass of low houses and walls, more or less hid under the large curved roofs.

Looking at such a city from some high point, there is often nothing to be seen but roofs, long rows of grey-tiled roofs, one behind another. In the warm season the drab monotony of the view is modified in places by the green trees that rise above the roofs, sometimes even piercing through them. (The Chinese protect the trees even at the expense of the buildings inside the cities, but exterminate them in the country.) But in the winter-time most of the trees are just as grey and bare as the roofs. Instead of green foliage there may be thin white snow, shining like foam, on the ridges and eaves. And when the morning haze envelops the city, it becomes like a grey wintry sea whose rolling waves have been suddenly arrested in their onward sweep. The regular rhythm of the rising and falling curves is still visible, but the movement has died, the sea become spell-bound. Has it been touched by the same magic frost that has congealed the vitalizing powers of the old Chinese civilization? Will it thaw again in a new spring-time with fresh leaves and flowers on the old trees? Will life come back with its beauty and joy? Are we once more to witness how waves of a new human energy break through the battered walls of Old China? Or is the inner movement congealed—the soul frozen for ever?

The morning haze is slowly dispersing, the vision fades—while shrill trumpet-sounds from the soldiers on the wall announce to the hustling and shivering people in the streets the advent of a new and toilsome day in the eleventh year of the Chinese Republic.

II

EARLIER CITIES ON THE SITE OF PEKING

BEFORE entering upon a special study of the actual walls and gates of Peking, it may be well to give a short account of the site and the boundaries of those smaller cities which preceded the present Peking. Chinese records of the Yuan and Ming dynasties contain a good deal of information about these earlier cities, and most of this recorded information has been collected in the *Shun T'ien fu chih*, the description of the prefecture of Shuntien, which was first edited in the Wan Li period (1593) and then thoroughly revised and re-edited at the end of the last century (1885). The work is divided into 130 chapters dealing with all sorts of geographical, historical, archæological, statistical, literary, religious and other subjects referring to the capital and the district in which it is situated, but the subjects are by no means well separated and classified; several of the chapters contain widely divergent or contradictory statements about the same things, and thus a certain amount of confusion is created. Thus, for instance, the statements about the walls of Peking found in Chapter I are not quite consistent with those of the second chapter; they have to be used with a certain amount of discretion and interpreted in the light of more critical observations. The following excursus is mainly based on the two first chapters of *Shun T'ien fu chih*, though special regard has also been had to scattered records in the *Jih Hsia Chiu Wen kao* (the Old History of the Place Under the Sun; first compiled in 1658 and re-edited in a larger revised edition 1744) and on

Dr. Bretschneider's most valuable historical researches (first published in English, in Shanghai, 1876; French edition, Paris, 1879).

* * * * *

The oldest city mentioned by Chinese historians on the site now occupied by Peking, was called *Chi*. It was the most important place in the prefecture of Chi Chou, and is said to have existed already in the time of Emperor Shun (2400 B.C.). According to the Chinese chronicle this city was " as strong as if defended by metal walls and a boiling moat." It became the capital of the Yen kingdom in 723 B.C. and was destroyed by the armies of Ch'in Shih Huang Ti in 221 B.C. This city was situated at the north-west corner of the present capital. The place seems to have been of no importance under the former Han dynasty.

Only in the later Han dynasty, about 70 A.D., a new city was built, some 10 li south of the former one, that is to say at the south-west corner of the present Tartar city, occupying a good bit of the north-western part of the so-called Chinese city. It became known as *Yen*, a name which in the Three Kingdom period was changed to *Yu chou*. Nothing of much importance is heard about it until its conquest by the K'itans in 936, except that the T'ang emperors had it occupied by a strong military garrison under a Tartar general. It was simply a small provincial town which the K'itans found quite insufficient for a capital when they established here the Liao dynasty as the ruling power in Northern China. A new and larger capital was built on the same site but stretching much further towards the west and the south than Yu chou. It was called Nan ching (southern capital), because the Liao had an earlier northern capital in Liao tung, but it became better known as *Yen ching*, the Swallow capital.

Bretschneider has traced the southern rampart of this city about $2\frac{1}{2}$ li south and its western limit some 4 li west of the present " Chinese city," thus determining the south-western corner of Yen ching. The eastern rampart was a little to the west of the present Liu Li ch'ang (the well-known street of

EARLIER CITIES ON THE SITE OF PEKING

book- and curio-shops to the south-west of Ch'ien men), because according to the geography of the Liao dynasty, as quoted in *Shun T'ien fu chih*, there used to be a tombstone in this street marking the place as the village " Hai Wang," outside the east gate of Yen ching. Its northern rampart coincided probably fairly well with the south wall of the Tartar city.

The plan of the city was quadrangular and measured 36 li in compass. The walls were 30 feet high and 15 feet wide. It had gate-towers and movable wooden towers for archers and eight gates, i.e. on the east side: An Tung men

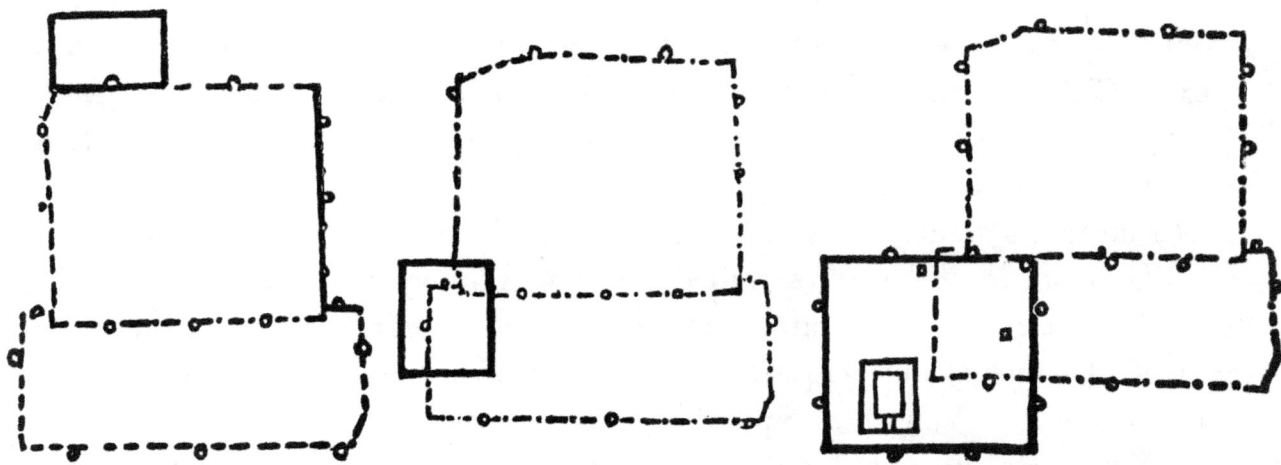

Fig. 1.—Approximate situations of the earlier capitals in relation to the site of Peking. The first is the city of *Chi*, the second *Yen* or *Yu Chou*, the third *Yen Ching*. These rough sketches are made on the basis of the plans published in the Guide Madrolle and in "Le Bulletin Catholique de Peking," 1914.

(Peaceful East gate) and Ying Ch'un men (Welcome Spring gate); on the south side: K'ai Yang men (Revealing Power gate) and Tan Feng men (Red Phœnix gate); on the west side: Hsien Hsi men (Glorious West gate) and Ch'ing Yin men (Clear Sound gate); on the north side: T'ung T'ien men (Reaching Heaven gate) and Kung Ch'en men (Saluting Dawn gate).

The palace of the Liao rulers was situated in the south-western section of their city forming a rectangle, surrounded by double walls.

When the Liao dynasty was defeated by its former vassals the Chin (golden)

Tartars (1125), the capital again underwent important modifications. The rather lengthy account of these in the *Shun T'ien fu chih* is somewhat confused, as no attempt has been made to reconcile divergent statements taken from different sources. But certain parts of it are interesting and well worth quoting:

" In the third year of T'ai Tsung (1125) Tsung Wang took Yen ching and used the Liao palaces. He built four new walls, each 3 li long, and each with two gates, a first and a second, gate towers, movable towers and battlements (as in the Liao city). Inside the walls he made granaries, store-houses, armouries, and covered ways leading to the inner city. This made O Shih, ruler of Ch'en and Han Chang, ridicule him for his extreme caution. Chung Hsien Wang (another name for Tsung Wang?), however, said: ' In less than two years you will find I was right.' "

From this statement it seems that Tsung Wang or T'ai Tsung, as he was called later on, built a kind of walled camp or military city somewhere within, or rather close by, Yen ching. It was not until several years later, in the reign of Hai-ling Wang (1149–1160), that a proper capital was arranged by a larger addition to Yen ching including new palaces.

" When Hai-ling succeeded Tsung Wang (there were two other rulers between them from 1135 to 1149) he wished to make Yen ching his capital and his officials presented a memorial pointing out its importance. Liang Ch'en said: ' Yen has ruled the country, from olden times, has commanded the central plain and for centuries has been the foundation of the State.' Ho Pu Nien said: ' The city of Yen ching is spacious and strong, it abounds in men and goods; it is a place of good manners and high morals.' In the third year of T'ien Tê (1151) the officials first proposed designs for palaces in Yen ching. In the third month Chang Yang Hao and others were ordered to enlarge the city and give it thirteen gates, i.e. on the east side: Shih Jen (Bestow Benevolence), Hsüan Yao (Proclaim Glory) and Yang Ch'un (Powers of Spring); on the south side: Ching Feng (Bright Winds), Feng Yi (Abundant Righteousness),

EARLIER CITIES ON THE SITE OF PEKING

and Tuan Li (Establish right Ceremonies); on the west side: Li Tse (Glorious Policy), Hao Hua (Splendid Beauty), and Chang I (Extend Righteousness); on the north side: Hui Ch'eng (Unite the City), T'ung Yüan (Communicating original Principles), Ch'ung Chih (Reverence Knowledge), and Kuang T'ai (Light Exalted). Each of the gates had three openings, one in the centre and one on each side. The centre gate was only opened for the passing of the Imperial chariot; everything else passed through one of the side gates. The circumference of the walls was 27 li; the wall towers were 40 feet high; altogether there were 910 towers and three sets of moats."

The statement about the circumference can evidently not be applied to the whole city, as the older part, Yen ching, measured by itself 36 li, and if it refers only to the additional new part, it still remains obscure whether this was enclosed all round by new walls or simply on three sides, adjoining on the fourth side the old city. According to another statement, quoted further on in the same chronicle, the circumference of the whole city was 75 li, which apparently is a gross exaggeration or a misprint. It should be added, that when the so-called South City (the former Chin capital) was measured by imperial order at the beginning of the Ming dynasty it was found to be 53,280 feet (almost 30 li) in compass. It may be that at that time a part of the old city was no longer in existence. It is hardly possible to deduce the exact size of the Chin capital, which became known as *Chung tu* (central capital) from the above statements, but there can be little doubt that it was considerably larger than Yen ching, the Liao city, and that it extended further east. The Chinese chroniclers are quite definite on this point: " Since the Chin capital was larger than the older one of the Liaos, its north-east corner must have joined the south-west corner of the present city. The biographer of Wang Hui, a Grand Secretary of the Yüan dynasty, mentions his sleeping one night at the Tung Yüan men (Tung Pien men) in the northern suburb. From other evidence it can be shown that the Chin capital lay south-west of the present city." Several inscriptions are quoted in proof of the fact that certain temples, like Po Yün kuan, T'ien Ning ssu, Tu Ti miao and others which are situated to the west and south of the present Tartar city, stood inside the capital of the Chins. We are thus led to the conclusion that the city of Chung tu included the old Yen ching, reaching about 4 li west of the present Chinese city and on the eastern side to a point near Tung Pien men. Its southern rampart was most probably a continuation of the south rampart of Yen ching (about $2\frac{1}{2}$ li south of the Chinese city) and the northern rampart would have been situated about a li to the north of the south wall of the present Tartar city. If these

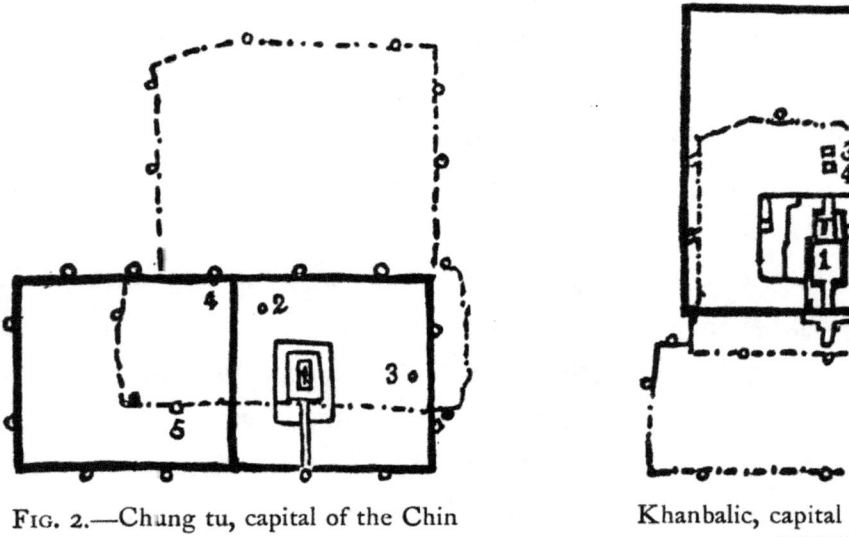

Fig. 2.—Chung tu, capital of the Chin tartars.

Khanbalic, capital of the Yüan emperors.

suppositions are correct, the whole length of the ramparts would have been about 54 li.

These ramparts were simply mud walls, and if we may believe the Chinese chronicle, the mud was transported from a place several miles off by hand power: "In building the city the people of Cho chou were impressed, making a chain and passing baskets from hand to hand from Cho chou to Yen ching, full baskets coming in and empty ones going back. By this simple means the work was finished in a very short time." (But it remains a mystery why the mud should have been transported such a long distance!)

EARLIER CITIES ON THE SITE OF PEKING

"In the time of Wei Shao Wang (1209–1312) the Mongol army came, and all the richer people were ordered to defend the eastern quarter; the officials protected the south, the Imperial clansmen the west, and the Imperial House undertook the north. In each (quarter) there were 2000 men. Wu Ling Yung Chang, the prefect, ordered all the commanders in the city to destroy the bridges, to bring all bricks and stone by boat inside the city, and if there was no time for this, to throw them into the water and to use the roofs of the houses near the city for fuel, bringing all inside. When the Mongols attacked the city, the defenders shot at them from the walls and beat them back. The next year the Mongols came again but failed to take the city." ... The fact is that the capital was saved this time (1213) by the speedy signing of peace on conditions prescribed by Ginghiz khan, and the Chin emperor was no more able to uphold his authority in the north, so he transferred his residence to Pien liang, or Nan king (southern capital), the old capital of the Sung emperors who now resided in Hang chow. Soon after the Chin ruler had left Chungtu the Mongols attacked the city for the third time (1215), conquered it and set fire to the imperial palaces, which, according to Chinese chronicles, burned for a whole month. A great number of officials and citizens were put to death and large tracts of the city practically destroyed, yet important ruins of the old palaces remained through the Yüan period. "At the beginning of the Ming dynasty the ruins of the Chin buildings could still be seen, but after the building of the wall around the outer (Chinese) city by Chia Ching (1554) all traces of them gradually disappeared." Kublai khan, who in 1260 became ruler of Northern China, seems to have had some intention of reinstating the old Chin capital, but this scheme was soon given up for mightier plans. The *Shun T'ien fu chih* reports about these: "In the second year of Shih Tsu (1262) the ancient city of Yen ching was repaired. In the first year of Chih Yüan (1264) from being the secondary capital it became capital of the state, and in his fourth year (1268) the present city was founded north of the old capital; the seat of government was moved thither, and in his ninth year (1272) this new city became the capital. It was a square measuring 60 li."

This statement, which may be corroborated by other similar ones, for instance from the chronicle of the Yüan dynasty, gives in the most condensed form the origin and earliest history of Peking: It was the great empire-builder Kublai khan who realized that the old camp of Ginghiz khan at Karakorum (south-west of Urga) was not a fitting capital for a world empire and that such a place should be built in China rather than in any other part of the world, because the country was the home of the highest civilization and the greatest natural resources. It mattered less that it lay on the eastern outskirt of the Mongol empire. China was, indeed, at that time the only country where it was possible to create a world centre.

The new city founded in 1267 or '68 was called T'ai tu (great capital) or Khanbalic (the city of the Khan). " At that time the inhabitants of the old city were ordered to remove to the new capital; the officials and the richer families first, eight *mou* (one mou is 260 pu, or square steps, equalling 769 sq. metres) being assigned to each. Had a family more than eight mou and was unable to build, others were allowed to settle on it. When the city had been built, a place for drying reeds was made about 5 li outside the Wên Ming men, so that there might be reeds to fence the walls. Every year 1,000,000 reeds were collected and woven into these ' shutterings,' and the space between was filled in gradually from the bottom." The enclosure around the Yüan capital was evidently a rampart of mud packed between fences or shutterings of reed. Most probably bricks were not used in the city walls until the Ming dynasty.

The site of the new capital, which in the above quotation is simply placed " north of the old capital," is more closely defined in another chapter of the *Shun T'ien fu chih*, where we read: " In the fourth year of the Mongol emperor Chih Yüan (a device of Kublai khan) another wall was added, extending for 60 li. The new part of the city had eleven gates, to wit on the south side:

EARLIER CITIES ON THE SITE OF PEKING 23

in the centre Li Cheng (Beautiful Justice), east of it, Wen Ming (High Culture), and west of it, Shun Ch'eng (Favourable Inheritance); on the east side: Chung Jen (Cherish Benevolence), Ch'i Hua (United Influence), and Kuang Hsi (Glorious Shining); on the west side: Ho Yi (Harmonize Right), Su Ch'ing (Solemn Purity), and P'ing Tzu (Just Rule); on the north side: An Chen (Peaceful Purity), and Chien Te (Vigorous Virtue). . . . The capital of the Yüan dynasty reached outside the present An Ting and Te Sheng gates (the two gates of the present north wall), but was then within the walls."

The question how far to the north the Yüan capital reached finds its most plausible answer, if we accept the partly visible mud rampart, about 5 li north of Peking, as the remains of the Yüan city wall. It is still popularly known as "Yüan ch'eng" and it can hardly be explained otherwise. This supposition is furthermore supported by records of the Ming dynasty in which it is stated that the walls of the Yüan capital were shortened by 5 li on the north in 1368. To quote from *Shun T'ien fu chih*: " In the first year of the Ming emperor Hung Wu, Hsü Ta was governor of the city. He shortened the walls by 5 li, and did away with the two northern gates, the Kuang Hsi and Su Ch'ing men (i.e. the most northern gate on the western and on the eastern side); the other nine gates were left "—a statement which must be taken to mean that the new north wall was provided with two gates corresponding to those in the old rampart, while the other seven gates were left in their old position. This position of the new north wall is confirmed by another passage in *Shun T'ien fu chih* (quoted from *Yüan chih*): " The capital of the Yüans extended north and east beyond the ancient capital of the Chins. It was the Mings who first shortened the walls east and west by one-half, so that outside the present Te Sheng men there are double gates of the old earth walls; these had no corners but were in a continuous curve, as is recorded of the north city wall." Excepting the exaggeration, that the east and west ramparts were shortened by one-half, which should be corrected to about two-fifths of their full length, this record is of particular importance, as it gives the best idea of the curving mud rampart and its two original gates.

There can be little doubt that the western and eastern ramparts of the Yüan capital followed the same lines as the west and east walls of the Ming city; the names of two of the gates, P'ing Tzu men and Ch'i Hua men, were kept unaltered, while Ho Yi men was renamed Hsi Chih men and Ching Wen men became Tung Chih men. If some alteration had been made in the position of these walls, it would surely have been recorded just as well as the change of the northern limit of the city. But the southern rampart of the Yüan capital can hardly have been at the same place as the south wall of the completed Ming city, i.e. the present Tartar city of Peking, because this is actually a good bit inside the northern limit of the old Chin capital which in the Yüan period still existed and was known as "the south city." We must remember that places such as Po Yün kuan (the White Cloud temple) lay inside the Chin capital (Chung tu) which could not have been possible if the northern wall of this city had not stood at least one li to the north of the present south wall of the Tartar city. It is furthermore recorded in the *Yüan I T'ung chih* (geography of the Yüan dynasty)—quoted in *Jih Hsia Chiu Wen kao*—that when the Mongol capital was built, order was given to make the southern rampart 30 pu (paces) south of the temple Ch'ing Shou ssu, now known as Shuang T'a ssu, whose two pagodas are still standing at a distance of about $1\frac{1}{2}$ li to the north of the present south wall. And it may be added, that the Observatory, according to recorded tradition, stood in the south-west corner of the Mongol city, while the remains of it that still exist are found on the east wall about $1\frac{1}{2}$ li north of the present south-east corner. From all these evidences it seems practically certain that the southern rampart of Khanbalic followed a line about 1 or $1\frac{1}{2}$ li north of the south wall of the present Tartar city, and it is quite possible that it was practically identical with the northern rampart of the Chin capital (or a few paces north of it). The position of this southern wall was not altered until the beginning of the fifteenth century, by emperor Yung Lo, while the north

EARLIER CITIES ON THE SITE OF PEKING

wall was changed some fifty years earlier by order of emperor Hung Wu. This becomes quite clear from the records of the Ming dynasty which will be quoted in the following chapter. But before passing to the later epoch, it may be worth while to see if any further information can be gathered about the Yüan capital. It lasted only for about a century, but during this time evidently a good deal of constructive and repairing work was carried on. Two records to this effect in the *Shun T'ien fu chih* are worth quoting:

"In the 20th year of Chih Yüan (1283) the capital was repaired, and in the 5th month of the 21st year 10,000 of the Imperial Guard were told off for the work. The city was successively repaired in 1292 and 1322.

"In the 10th month of the 19th year of Chih Cheng (1359) deep enclosures were ordered to be made for each of the eleven city gates with wooden bridges across the moats." Up to this time there seem to have been no permanent defensive arrangements at the gates; it may be that the Mongols used movable wooden towers, as is recorded of the Liaos and the Chins, but now some sort of barbicans, or walls forming U-shaped curves in front of the gates, were erected. The present characteristic gate type of Peking with deep yards and high towers (especially mentioned by Marco Polo) was thus finally established, but the bridges over the moat were still made of wood, not of stone, as they were later on in the Ming time.

The Mongol capital, Khanbalic, was considerably larger than the present Tartar city of Peking, yet hardly as large as stated in the above-quoted Yüan chronicle, where the full length of the walls was said to be 60 li. If the position of the walls that we have demonstrated is approximately correct, the whole compass could hardly have been over 50 li; the statement of the Chinese chronicle must be explained either as a misprint or as a gross exaggeration. The exaggeration, however, becomes still more accentuated in Marco Polo's description of Khanbalic, in which we read:

"As regards the size of this city you must know that it has a compass of 24 miles, for each side of it hath a length of 6 miles, and it is four square."

Accepting Yule's estimation of Marco Polo's Italian mile as equalling 2·77 li, the whole compass of the city would become over 66 li, which cannot have been the case. And it should further be remembered that the plan never was a real square but a rectangle with rounded corners at the northern end. Marco Polo, who evidently was deeply impressed with the grandeur and splendour of Khanbalic, has tried to make the most of it in every respect. His descriptions are as a whole exaggerated, but at the same time they contain points of great interest, particularly as they are the only ones that give us some information about certain streets and buildings in the Mongol capital. Thus, for instance, he gives a good description of the ramparts and the gates:

"It is walled round with walls of earth which have a thickness of full 10 paces at bottom, and a height of more than 10 paces, but they are not so thick at the top, for they diminish in thickness as they rise, so that at the top they are only about 3 paces thick. And they are provided throughout with loop-holed battlements which are all whitewashed."

The walls evidently sloped very much from the top to the bottom, which was the more necessary as long as they had no complete brick facing, though at the top provided with battlements of brick or stone.

"There are twelve gates, and over each gate there is a great and handsome palace, so that there are on each side of the square three gates and five palaces, for (I ought to mention) there is at each angle also a great and handsome palace. In those palaces are vast halls in which are kept the arms of the city garrison." Marco Polo's memory seems to have failed him also in reference to the gates; three of the walls have three gates each, but the fourth had only two. The Chinese chroniclers are quite unanimous in stating that there were only eleven gates in all. The gate and corner towers which Marco Polo calls palaces were probably not unlike those still in existence, i.e. brick buildings on a constructive frame of wood with open galleries around and projecting roofs in three stories. This type of building is also still preserved in the drum-tower which in its main parts is a construction of the Yüan dynasty, reproducing in its

EARLIER CITIES ON THE SITE OF PEKING

turn earlier buildings of a similar kind. The continuity in Chinese architecture is such as to make it possible to reach a good idea about the general appearance of buildings, no longer existing, through the study of their successors. Thus we may safely assume, that the gate-towers of Khanbalic were similar to those built by the Mings, though some uncertainty remains as to whether the barbicans were provided with special outer towers.

Marco Polo offers some information about the general character of the city plan and the streets of Khanbalic:

" The streets are so wide and straight, that you can see right along them from end to end, and from one gate to the other. And up and down the city there are beautiful palaces, and many great and fine hostelries and fine houses in great numbers. All the plots of ground on which the houses are built are four square, and laid out with straight lines; all the plots being occupied by great spacious palaces with courts and gardens of proportionate size. All these plots are assigned to different heads of families. Each square plot is encompassed by handsome streets for traffic; and thus the whole city is arranged in squares just like a chessboard, and disposed in a manner so perfect and masterly, that it is impossible to give a description that should do it justice."

The regularity of the city plan, its division into square lots by streets running straight in the four main directions, was a feature more or less characteristic of the old imperial cities of China, particularly of Ch'ang'an, the great capital of the Sui and T'ang emperors, where it had been developed to perfection. To judge from the old illustrated chronicles of Ch'ang'an, the plan of the city was truly like a chessboard, divided up by the main streets into squares, or " fangs," each one of these comprising four smaller squares, separated by narrower streets. A palace or a yamen sometimes occupied a whole fang, but ordinary residential compounds only a fourth part of it. In Khanbalic each square was supposed to be about 8 mou (about $1\frac{1}{4}$–$1\frac{1}{2}$ acre) and occupied by one family, the space being sufficient for fine large compounds with a number of houses placed around courtyards and gardens enclosed by walls. How far this ideal system was actually carried out in Khanbalic is difficult to tell, but the main features of it were certainly realized, as still may be observed in the Tartar city of Peking, where the principal streets run straight north-south and east-west and where a good many of the older house blocks, particularly in the northern section, reveal the regular fang-divisions. But at the same time we have to take Marco Polo's statement about the regular chessboard pattern of the city plan *cum grano salis*, because there must always have been considerable irregularities in the plan of this city owing to political and geographical conditions. And this element has been growing with the years as wars and revolutions and destructions of various kinds have rolled over old Khanbalic. Much of the rebuilding and repairing has been done in a quite arbitrary way, and many side streets have become more like winding paths than straight divisions between square blocks. But the main features of the original city plan are nevertheless still discernible and would merit a closer study than we are able to devote to this subject. It should only be pointed out that the plans of cities like Ch'ang 'an and Khanbalic show more affinity with some modern cities in the west where the regular lots are divided by broad streets, than with any medieval cities of Europe with their cramped houses and narrow, winding alleys. In these old Chinese cities which extend over such vast areas there is plenty of room, the views are long and open, the houses are low, and the trees and gardens plentiful, though largely hidden behind the walls of the compounds.

Marco Polo speaks about the " great and spacious palaces with courts and gardens," but unfortunately he does not give any further description of their architecture. He seems to take it for granted that their general appearance is known, and, of course, he who has seen one or two of these Chinese mansions knows practically all of them. They do not vary very much, except in the number of buildings and courts and in the elaboration of their gardens. The garden is the ideal centre of the Chinese homestead.

EARLIER CITIES ON THE SITE OF PEKING

The only building in Khanbalic which Marco Polo mentions specifically is the bell-tower, of which he writes as follows:

"Moreover, in the middle of the city there is a great clock—that is to say a bell—which is struck at night. And after it has struck three times no one must go out in the city, unless it be for a woman in labour or for the sick. And those who go about on such errands are bound to carry lanterns with them. Moreover, the established guard at each gate of the city is 1000 armed men; not that you are to imagine this guard is kept up for fear of any attack, but only as a guard of honour for the Sovereign, who resides there, and to prevent thieves from doing mischief in the town."

A bell-tower and a drum-tower are still to be seen in Peking, standing at some distance to the north of the imperial city and practically halfway between the east and the west wall. Their present position is thus hardly central, but Marco Polo's statement as to the situation of the bell-tower may be easily explained by the fact above mentioned, that the Mongol city extended some 5 li further north and had its southern rampart more than 1 li north of the present south wall. If these alterations in the plan are taken into consideration, one will find that the actual towers occupied a fairly central position in Khanbalic, just as they do in most of the old Chinese cities which still retain their drum- and bell-towers. In addition to these considerations may be quoted a statement in the *Yüan I T'ung chih* (Geography of the Yüan Dynasty) to the effect that "in the ninth year of Chih Yüan (A.D. 1272) a bell-tower and a drum-tower were erected in the midst of the city."

It needs little historical knowledge to see that the two towers, as they stand to-day, are of quite different periods. The bell-tower is a much more elegant and decorative structure than the larger and bulkier drum-tower. It is built entirely of brick with marble arches and balustrades and very ornamental battlements in a style well known from many Ch'ien Lung buildings. It is the result of a thorough restoration after a fire in 1745. The earlier tower was erected by Yung Lo at the beginning of the fifteenth century, replacing the original bell-tower of the Yüan dynasty which was situated a little further east. The drum-tower is more than twice as broad as the bell-tower and built in very different style. The lower half of it is a massive bastion of mud coated with brick and pierced by two tunnels; the upper half consists of a large hall in two stories surrounded by an open gallery and provided with double roofs. The whole structure is of a more old-fashioned, traditional type, here expressed on a very large scale with monumental proportions. It may well be the old tower of the Yüan period, partly restored and renewed. If one compares it with other buildings of a similar type in Peking, for instance, the main gates of the Forbidden City, which are works of the Ming and the early Ch'ing era, one may notice a greater simplicity in the structural details (such as the brackets) and a heaviness in the proportions that speak of an early origin. As it stands on a slight elevation at the end of a broad street that leads straight to the palace it makes a magnificent architectural effect. Most probably this is the oldest palatial building (closely akin to what the Chinese call a " *t'ai* ") now existing in Peking; the only other buildings of the Yüan time in or around the capital being temple pagodas.

The buildings, however, which aroused the greatest admiration from European observers, like Marco Polo and Friar Odoric (who visited Khanbalic some time after Kublai khan's death), were the imperial palaces. The palace of the Great Khan was to these travellers, in spite of the fact that they came from the classic land of monumental buildings, one of the marvels of the world, wonderful by its extension, its defensive arrangements, its succession of gateways, courts, halls, pavilions and towers and those endless walls which seemed to hide untold and unapproachable mysteries. It was indeed the innermost centre of a world empire, receiving just as much of its glamour from the extension of its influence as from its actual buildings and decorative arrangements. This is not the place to enter into a special

EARLIER CITIES ON THE SITE OF PEKING 31

study of the Yüan palaces, but Marco Polo's words about its outer appearance may be quoted, so as to convey some idea of the most important buildings in Khanbalic:

"It is enclosed all round by a great wall forming a square, each side of which is a mile in length; that is to say, the whole compass thereof is four miles. This you may depend on, it is also very thick, and a good ten paces in height, whitewashed and loopholed all round. At each angle of the wall there is a very fine and rich palace in which the war-harness of the emperor is kept, such as bows and quivers, saddles and bridles and bowstrings, and everything needful for an army. Also midway between every two of these corner palaces there is another of the like. . . .

"The great wall has five gates on its southern face, the middle one being the great gate which is never opened on any occasion, except when the Great Khan himself goes forth or enters." . . .

The above descriptions refer to the Huang ch'eng (Yellow city), or Kung ch'eng (Palace city) as it also was called in the Mongol time. The place was probably not quite square, but a rectangle, surrounded by high walls with fine palatial towers on the four corners as well as over the gates, nor was it four Italian miles (about 11 li) in compass but somewhere between 6 and 7 li, as stated in various chronicles of the Yüan and Ming periods. "The great wall," that Marco Polo mentions afterwards, was an outer boundary answering approximately to the wall of the "Imperial city" of Peking. It measured, according to the Yüan records, 20 li, while the compass of the present "Imperial city" is 18 li. A closer study of the records and the existing monuments leaves no doubt that the imperial cities of the Yüan and the Ming covered practically the same ground. Marco Polo has very little to say about the buildings within the enclosure of the palace city:

"Inside this wall there is a second, enclosing a space that is somewhat greater in length than in breadth. This enclosure also has eight palaces corresponding to those of the outer wall and stored like them with the

Lord's harness of war. . . . In the middle of this second enclosure is the Lord's great palace, and I will tell you what it is like.

"You must know that it is the greatest palace that ever was. . . ." Then follow some descriptions of the interiors, which here must be left out as we are concerned only with the general outer aspect of the city. The general name for this inner palace was in the Mongol time " Ta Nei " (Great Interior), a name which still sometimes is used for the " Purple Forbidden City."

Marco Polo's description is borne out by the shorter observations of Friar Odoric of Pordenone, who gives the additional information that the distance between the inner and outer ramparts was about half a bowshot. " In the midst between those two walls are kept his stores and all his slaves, whilst within the inner enclosure dwells the Great Khan with all his family who are most numerous."

Reading these descriptions one is indeed reminded of a walled military camp surrounded by successive lines of well-guarded defences. The dwelling-place of the Great Khan seems to have been an expression for the fact that he ruled over China not by the right of Heaven but by the might of the sword. None of the earlier Chinese capitals had had palaces so extremely well protected and walled in. The Ta Ming kung of the T'ang emperors in Ch'ang 'an was situated at the northern end of the city, forming a rectangle that projected outside the line of the city wall, bordering to the south on the " Imperial city " with all the government offices, etc. Neither was the Sung palace in Kaifeng such a strongly defended military establishment. It had, of course, its walls with corner towers and strong gates, but the accentuation of the military idea was a feature particularly characteristic of the Mongol conquerors.

In other respects their capital was planned after the model of old Ch'ang 'an. Its square form and orientation according to the four main directions, its regularity of divisions and straight streets were copied in Khanbalic, and so

EARLIER CITIES ON THE SITE OF PEKING

were probably several of the official buildings. The ambition of the Great Khan was to make his capital the strongest and finest that ever had been, a city that would reflect his enormous riches, military strength and power of organization. Since 1280, when the proud resistance of the Southern Sungs, who were the legitimate rulers of China, was finally broken, Khanbalic became the capital of the whole Chinese empire and of a good bit of Western Asia and Eastern Europe besides. Kublai khan's realm extended from Korea to the borders of Poland, and there was no other city on this wide continent that could vie with Khanbalic in greatness and splendour. When the Mongol empire fell, in 1368, a great deal of destruction took place in their capital, but the main parts of it were soon restored, its walls were rebuilt more solidly, its defences strengthened, and from that time onwards it has served, under the name of Peking, as the capital of the whole " Middle Kingdom."

III

THE WALLS OF THE TARTAR CITY

OF all the great buildings of Peking there is none which can compare with the walls of the Tartar city in monumental grandeur. At first sight they may not be as attractive to the eye as the palaces, temples and shop-fronts of those highly coloured and picturesquely composed wooden structures which still line the old streets or hide behind the walls, but after a longer acquaintance with this vast city, they become the most impressive monuments—enormous in their extension and dominating everything by their quiet forceful rhythm. They may appear monotonous and uninteresting to the newcomer in their severe simplicity and their continuity of horizontal lines, but on closer observation he will find that they are varied by many irregularities in material and workmanship, full of significance as records of past periods. Their plain grey surface is worn and battered by age, split and bulged by tree-roots, undermined and ruined in spots by dripping water, patched and restored over and over again, yet, still unified by a continuous rhythm. On the outer side of the walls this rhythm is accentuated by the powerful bastions which follow one another at regular intervals though somewhat varying in size. On the inner side the movement is slower and more irregular on account of the extreme unevenness of the joints between the sections and of the bends and bulges resulting from the pressure of water and tree-roots. This slow rhythm is suddenly quickened and changed into a powerful crescendo at the gates, where double towers rise triumphantly above the long horizontal lines of the battlements, the

34

THE WALLS OF THE TARTAR CITY

larger of these towers resembling palaces on high terraces. The corner towers, massive and fortresslike, form a magnificent finale of the whole composition. Unfortunately only two of them remain.

The general effect of these walls changes, of course, according to the season, the time of day, the weather and the standpoint of the spectator. Seen from a distance, they present a view of long unbroken lines, accentuated here and there by lofty gate-towers and—in the warm season—enlivened by clusters of trees and shrubs growing on the top. The clear atmosphere of an October morning brings out this view most beautifully, particularly if one looks towards the west where the background is formed by the deep blue Western Hills against an ineffably pure sky. No one who has enjoyed a perfect autumn day on the walls of Peking will be able to forget the beauty of the light, the distinctness of every detail, the harmony of all the transparent colours! A nearer view of the walls is at most places less attractive, because right close to them, on three sides of the city, are coal sheds and other kinds of dingy storehouses, not to speak of lesser buildings of a still more offensive character and hillocks of dirt and refuse. Yet there are also stretches where the moat or canal is lined with weeping willows, or the ground between the moat and the wall planted with ailanthus and locust trees. These are the places that should be visited in the spring-time, when the willows weave their light green, transparent draperies over the mirror-like waters, or a little later, when the locust trees are weighed down by clusters of flowers that fill the air with a balmy fragrance. If one only knows how to choose the spot, one can find perfect motives around these old walls.

Ascending some of the long ramps which lead to the top of the walls (called by the Chinese " horse roads " because they can be ascended on horseback) one arrives at one of the most interesting promenade-places in the world. Here one may walk for hours and hours enjoying a continuous panorama. Imperial palaces and temples with shining yellow roofs among thick green foliage, princely mansions covered with blue and green tiles, red houses with pillared open galleries in front, small grey huts half hidden under century-old trees, broad, animated streets lined with shops and spanned by brightly decorated *p'ailous*, and a good deal of open ground where boys may be seen watching the grazing sheep—all motives in the long vista that unrolls itself below one's feet. It is only the modern buildings in foreign or semi-foreign style which dare to raise their heads above the old walls. They look like arrogant intruders, destroying the harmony of the picture, despising the protection of the walls. . . . And they are increasing rapidly. How many years more will Peking be allowed to remain a city of monumental grandeur and picturesque beauty? How many of the gilt and carved shop-fronts are destroyed every year? How many of the old-fashioned residences with open patios and large gardens full of quaint rockeries and pavilions are levelled to the ground in order to give room for half-modern three or four-storied brick buildings? How many of the old streets are being widened, how much of the magnificent pink wall around the " Imperial city " torn down, in order to make room for electric street-car lines? The destruction of old Peking is going on very rapidly. It is no longer an imperial city, and there is no authority to protect its most proud and precious monument. China has become the " People's country," and what does the crowd care about the beauty of past ages?

If the city walls of Peking could be properly examined and their silent testimony translated into words, they would no doubt tell a story more interesting and accurate than any written records of the Northern Capital. They form a chronicle in clay and stone, repeatedly changed and added to, reflecting directly and indirectly, the various vicissitudes of Peking since the time when it received its present form and up to the end of the Ch'ing dynasty. Most of the transforming events in the history of the capital have left their marks upon the walls—destructive wars and constructive periods of peace, bad and good governments, careless and zealous officials, poor and prosperous times, besides the marks left by various indi-

THE WALLS OF THE TARTAR CITY

viduals who in one way or other have been concerned in the construction of these impressive defence works. But in order to interpret all that time and human endeavour may have written down in this brick scroll of 14 miles in length which encircles the capital, it would be necessary to put the spade into the earth and to cut through the wall at various places, which is absolutely impossible under present conditions in Peking. The time will perhaps come when archæological excavations can be started even in the capital of China, but until then we have to satisfy ourselves with observations of the outside of these monuments and with consultation of Chinese chronicles in which some records of their earlier history have been preserved. We will begin with a short report of the historical information collected in the *S'hun T'ien fu chih*, and then proceed to a description of the walls as they stand to-day.

In the first chapter of *Shun T'ien fu chih* it is simply stated: " When the Ming emperors shortened the North wall all the arrangements of the Yuans were altered. Under Yung Lo the city was enlarged but not on the old site " (that is to say, it was enlarged by adding a piece further south).

In the second chapter of the same chronicle some additional details as to how this change was accomplished are given:

" At the beginning of the reign of Hung Wu (1368–1398) Tai Tu lu (i.e. Yen ching) was called Pei P'ing lu (the Northern Peace road). The north wall was shortened by 5 li and the two northern gates in the east and west walls, the Kuang Hsi men and Su Ch'ing men, were demolished, the other nine being left. The general Hsü Ta ordered Hua Yün Lung to rule the ancient Mongol city and to build new walls running straight north and south, east and west. They were 18,900 feet long (i.e. 10½ li here given as the length measure of each side). Chang Huan was ordered to measure the circumference of the Mongol imperial city, which was found to be 12,060 feet (about 6⅔ li), and Yeh Kuo Ch'en found the South city (i.e. the old Chin capital) to be 58,280 feet (about 32·4 li). In the South city were the foundations of the ruins of the Chin city. The An Chen men of the Mongol capital was now changed to the An Ting men (Peace Assured gate) and the Chien Te men to the Te Sheng men (Righteous Victory gate). . . . Bricks were then used for the first time; the walls were now only 40 li round. (The measurement may be approximately correct as long as nothing had been added at the south end of the city.) The walls on the south, east and west side were 30 feet high and 20 broad at the top. The moat varied in breadth and depth; the greatest depth being 10 feet and the greatest breadth 180 feet. There were nine gates. (The names and sites of these gates correspond exactly to those of the Yüan city, except the two in the new north wall which were changed as stated above.) Each gate had a semicircular enclosure (barbican), and there were ten outer gates." (Ten instead of nine, because the central south gate, Li Cheng men, had two outer gates.)

Such was the city boundary and its wall at the end of the fourteenth century, under Emperor Hung Wu, before Pei p'ing had become the capital of the new Ming empire. The old mud ramparts on the east, west and south side seem to have been coated with bricks, but they were only half as thick and a little lower than the present ones. The new wall on the north side was hardly of a more substantial or heavy type than the other walls. We have good reason to assume that it was made over later, as will be shown in a following paragraph.

Pei p'ing was at this time by no means a safe and fitting residence for the new imperial house; the Mongols were still very strong in Northern China, and the generals of Hung Wu had a hard time in saving the city from renewed occupation by these ancient enemies. It was not from choice but in consequence of an absolute military necessity that the Ming emperors made Nanking their first capital, and it took about half a century before the resistance of the Mongols in Northern China was completely broken. How Pei p'ing gradually became the capital is shortly described in the Chinese chronicle as follows:

THE WALLS OF THE TARTAR CITY

"In the first month of the first year of Yung Lo (1403) the president of the Board of Rites, Li Chih Kang, and others respectfully reported to the emperor, that all rulers, whether risen from amongst the people themselves or coming from foreign conquerors, had always made their capital in this place (Pei p'ing) and they had always been powerful. The petitioners said they had seen the city treasury, and certainly emperors here would be in an auspicious and flourishing situation. It was fitting to follow the principles of government of the great emperor T'ai Tsu (Hung Wu) and establish the capital here. The emperor assented, and Pei p'ing became Pei ching (north capital) whilst in the prefectural system it was known as Shun T'ien fu.*

"In the seventh month of his fourth year, 1406, the imperial palaces were built in Peking and the walls repaired. In the 11th month of the 17th year (end of 1419) the South city was enlarged by more than 27,000 feet (15 li)."

The meaning of the last sentence seems to be, that the boundary of the new piece added to the city at its southern end was 15 li. If we detract from this measurement the length of the south wall, i.e. 11·64 li, only 3·46 li remain, which should be divided about equally on the east and west wall, each of these thus getting a length of about 1¾ li, roughly speaking the same measurement as the one we arrived at in our demonstration about the position of the south wall of Khanbalic. The distance between this and the present south wall of Peking must be estimated at 1½–1¾ li.

The date indicated above for the enlargement of the south city is contradicted by a statement in the first chapter in *Shun T'ien fu chih*: "In the 15th year of the Ming emperor Yung Lo, the imperial palaces were built (1417), and 15 years later (i.e. 1432) the south city was enlarged so that the whole was 40 li round."

If this time indication were correct, the enlargement of the city, at the

---

* From 1403 till 1421 Peking was known as *Hsing-Tsai*, "moving" or "temporary residence." The same name had been given to Hangchow by the Southern Sungs and is transcribed as Quinsay by Marco Polo.—A.D.W.

south end, would not have been accomplished in Yung Lo's reign but eight years after his death. But this was not the case; the work on the walls was pushed on with great energy in Yung Lo's time, as is borne out by the testimony from several sources. Most interesting is that of an Arab embassy—from Shah Rukh—which arrived in Peking in 1420; the recorder of the embassy tells that when they came to the gates of Khanbalic they beheld " a very great and beautiful city completely built of stone (!), but the walls were still under construction and hidden by thousands of scaffoldings." The Geography of the Ming dynasty records that the work on the walls was finished in Yung Lo's nineteenth year (1421), but it is added that they were coated with bricks in 1437. Had bricks been used before, or were they now introduced for the first time? To answer the question definitely we should need more detailed information than that available in the Chinese chronicles, but it seems at least highly probable that no regular brick coating had been attempted before the Cheng T'ung period. It is, of course, possible that layers of brick had been used in the Yung Lo walls to bind the mud, the lime and the gravel of which the inner body is made, but the regular outer appearance of the walls is a later product. It may be added that the earliest dated bricks that we have found in the masonry of the present walls are of the Ch'eng Hua period (1466–1487).

It is quite possible that the same brick coating work is hinted at in the following somewhat vague statement in the *Shun T'ien fu chih*: " In the first month of the tenth year of Cheng T'ung (1455) the tutor of the prince imperial Shen Ch'ung and others set an army of many thousand men to work at repairs (or improvements) on the city walls and towers. The work was finished in four years and four months and included the central gate-tower of Cheng Yang men, three archers' towers and one drum-tower, the semicircular enclosure (barbican) with towers and walls of all the other gates. Inscribed stone tablets were put up outside each gate and towers added to the four corners of the city. The moats were deepened and their sides lined with bricks or stone. The former wooden bridges of the moat were demolished and stone bridges built, and between each two bridges were water-locks. The water which filled the moat flowed from the north-west corner towards the east under the nine bridges and through the nine gratings. At the south-east corner of the city it flowed out under the Ta T'ung ch'iao (bridge of great communications). This work was begun in the fourth month of the second year of Cheng T'ung (1437) and was finished at the time mentioned."

It is rather confusing to find the two dates so arranged that the later is given first and the earlier afterwards without a definite statement as to how they should be applied. The moats, canals, and bridges may have been put in order first and the walls, the gates, and the corner-towers afterwards, or work may have been carried on contemporaneously at the different constructions. The whole time used for all these works was about twelve years (1437–1449), and as the number of workmen seems to have been very large, the amount accomplished must have been considerable.

The statement that repairs or improvements were made on the walls seems to us explicable only if we assume that those built some thirty years earlier had not been properly finished and brick coated. There had been no wars or revolutions by which the walls might have suffered, no great calamity to affect what already had been accomplished in Yung Lo's time. Under normal conditions a city wall ought to last for centuries, not only for a few decades. The only way in which this quite extensive building activity so soon after the construction of the new walls may be explained, is by assuming that something was lacking in the completion of the work. The outer coating was probably not finished; by adding this the walls became both stronger and finer-looking. Their present monumental aspect was thus first attained in the Cheng T'ung period.

No less important than the coating of the walls was the work now performed on the gate- and corner-towers. At least four of the gates (two on the east and two on the west wall) had probably remained practically unchanged since the Yüan period, and those in the new south wall had evidently not been completed. Now all the gate yards with their enclosing barbicans were established; each gate was provided with an outer tower for archers and an inner tower for the drum-beaters, who were supposed to encourage the soldiers and assist in driving away the enemies by their warlike music. The central south gate which was larger than the others was provided with three archers' towers instead of one. Unfortunately this, like so many other things on the gates, has been altered, as we shall have occasion to see in a following chapter, where also a closer description of the two remaining corner-towers will be given.

In addition to the work on the walls and the gates a great deal seems to have been done to put the moats and bridges in proper condition. Stone bridges and stone-lined moat banks were, indeed, necessary complements to the new brick-faced walls, but they have as a whole been allowed to fall into worse decay than any other parts of the wall. The moats have in some places become rather ditchlike, in other places like stagnant pools. The water supply is nowadays more scanty and uneven than it used to be; it is not properly regulated, since the moats, after the construction of the railways, have lost their practical importance as waterways. The old water-locks, which still can be seen at different places under the walls, serve mainly as sewers for the drainage of the city. Their gratings are often packed with foul matter. It is only on the eastern side that the water-flow is more abundant, and here, at the south-east corner, we find the beautiful bridge with sculptured balustrades and tiger heads over the arches, mentioned above. The water is still dammed at this Ta T'ung bridge, so as to regulate the level of the Tung Ho canal.

When the gates had been put in proper repair, new official names were adopted for some of them. The central south gate, which used to be called

THE WALLS OF THE TARTAR CITY

Li Ch'eng men, became Ch'eng Yang men (the gate Straight Towards the Sun), which is still its proper name, though it is commonly known as Ch'ien men. The western gate on the south side, which formerly was known as Shun Chih men, became Hsüan Wu men (Proclaim Military Strength); the older name of this gate, however, has remained more common than the new one. The eastern gate in the southern wall, Wen Ming men, became Ch'ung Wen men (Reverence Learning)—balancing, so to speak, the military gate on the east side—and it is still officially called by that name, though commonly known as Hata men. The southern gate in the east wall, Ch'i Hua men, was renamed Ch'ao Yang men (Facing the Rising Sun), but the older name has remained in more common use than the new official name, which also is true of the old name of the southern gate in the west wall, P'ing Tzu men, which received the official (but seldom heard) name of Fu Ch'eng men (Mound Formed). The other four gates, i.e. Hsi Chih (Direct West), Tung Chih (Direct East), An Ting (Peace Assured), and Te Sheng (Righteous Victory), received no new official names, and thus there is no doubt as to their proper appellation.

The length of the walls, when finally completed, around the capital of the Ming emperors is variously estimated in the old chronicles. In one of the quotations given above it was stated at 40 li, and the same figure is given in the Records of the Ministry of public work (of the Ming dynasty) where we read: "When Yung Lo decided to establish his residence in Peking, he built a wall around the capital which was 40 li long and pierced by nine gates." The Geography of the Ming dynasty puts the length down as 45 li.

None of these measurements is quite correct; the actual length of the walls is between 41 and 42 li—strictly measured, 41·26 li or 23·55 kilometres. Neither is the plan a regular square, as usually stated in the old chronicles; the east and west sides are a good bit shorter than the northern and southern walls, and the north-west corner is cut off. According to the most accurate modern surveys which have been published the different sides have the following lengths : south, 6·690 metres or 11·64 li ; north, 6·790 metres or 11·81 li ; east, 5·330 metres or 9·27 li ; west, 4·910 metres or 8·54 li.

The height and width measurements are also given differently in various Chinese books, which is quite natural, as they vary a great deal at different points of the walls. The *Shun T'ien fu chih* contains the following information : " The walls are of stone below and with brick above, and are 35·5 feet high, the parapet being 5·5 feet. At the bottom the wall is 62 feet wide, and at the top 50. (The Chinese foot is $14\tfrac{5}{8}$ inches.) There are nine gates with towers and there is also a tower at each corner, and 172 bastions. There are nine storehouses for banners and cannons and 135 guard-houses and 96 powder magazines. There are 11,038 merlons and 12,108 embrasures (or notches)." The height of the wall is in other old descriptions given as $33\tfrac{1}{2}$ Chinese feet.

It is nowadays practically impossible to state exactly the height of the wall, because this changes every few steps, not only in consequence of ruins and repairs but also because the level of the soil at the foot of the wall has undergone many changes ; it is at many places impossible to ascertain the exact position of the plinth or its height. In measuring the height of the wall, we have naturally chosen places, where the ground level seemed to be little or not at all altered, but these measurements should, nevertheless, be taken as only approximate. The same applies to the measurements of the wall at its base ; they are only approximations, arrived at by calculating the inclination of the wall faces from the top (as shown in our schematic drawings). We have had no facilities for piercing the old wall with a measuring rod. The only measurement which is exact (within one or two inches) is the one of the width of the wall at its top, besides those of the parapets and battlements. With these reservations the following figures may be taken as the best available indications of the average height of the walls on the four different sides :—

South wall, east of Water gate : height, outside 10·72 metres, inside also 10·72 m. ; width, at the top 15·20 m., at the base 18·48 m. Further east, near

THE WALLS OF THE TARTAR CITY

Hatamen, the height is the same but the width at the top somewhat less, i.e. 14·80 m., at the base 18·08 m. Further west, near Shun Chih men: height, outside 11·05 m., inside 10·15 m.; width, at the top 14·80 m., at the bottom 18·40 m.

East wall, between Tung Chih men and Ch'i Hua men: height, outside 11·10 m., inside 10·70 m.; width, at the top 11·30 m., at the base 16·90 m. North of Ch'i Hua men: height, outside 11·40 m., inside 10·48 m.; width, at the top 12·30 m., at the base 18·10 m. (In this vicinity the top plane of the

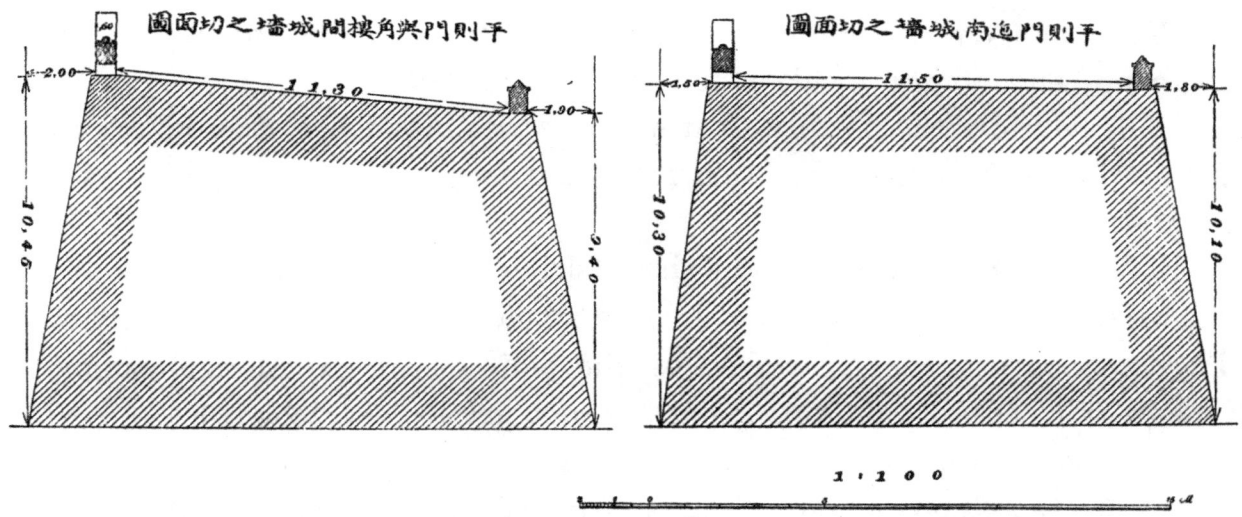

FIG. 3.—Two sections of the west wall, south of P'ing Tzu Men.

wall has sunk, forming holes, towards the inside owing to the effect of undermining water.)

West wall, at some distance south of P'ing Tzu men: height, outside 10·30 m., inside 10·10 m.; width, at the top 11·50 m., at the base 14·80 m. Near P'ing Tzu men: height, outside 10·5 m., inside 9·40 m.; width, at the top 11·30 m., at the base 15·20 m. Between P'ing Tzu men and Hsi Chih men: height, outside 10·95 m., inside 10·40 m.; width, at the top 14 m., at the base 17·40 m.

North wall, near the north-east corner: height, outside 11·92 m., inside

9·20 m.; width, at the top 17·60 m., at the base 22·85 m. East of An Ting men: height, outside 11·90 m., inside 10·40 m.; width, at the top 17·63 m., at the base 21·72 m. Between Te Sheng men and the north-west corner: height, outside 11·60 m., inside 11 m.; width, at the top 19·50 m., at the base 24 m.

The average width of the south wall at the top is about 15 m., its height, on the outside, about 10·70 m., and on the inside a few centimetres less.

The average width of the east wall, at the top, about 12 m. or less; its height, on the outside, about 11 m. and on the inside ½ m. less.

The average width of the west wall about 11·50 m., its height on the outside 10·40 m., and on the inside a few decimetres less.

The width of the north wall at its top varies between 17·60 and 19·50 m., the height on the outside between 11·50 and 11·93 m., on the inside between 11 and 9·20 m.

The east and west walls thus show fairly equal dimensions both in height and width, though the west wall is, as a whole, somewhat thinner and lower. They may have been constructed on the body of the old Mongol ramparts, though full certainty on this point has not yet been reached.

The south wall is 3 m. (or more) thicker than the side walls but approximately of the same height. The north wall is a great deal thicker and higher, exceeding the south wall in thickness by 3–4 m., and the inclination of its façades is much greater than the corresponding inclinations of the other wall façades. The entirely rebuilt walls are thus much stronger and heavier than those constructed on old foundations, and I should be inclined to think that the increasing thickness (from the south to the north wall) also may be taken as an indication of successive periods of construction. The side walls may have been the result of building over the Mongol ramparts, increasing both their height and their width. The south wall was built new from the ground mainly in Yung Lo's time, though brick-coated later. But the north wall was probably at this period still in the more

THE WALLS OF THE TARTAR CITY 47

primitive shape it had at the end of the fifteenth century, that is to say much lower and thinner than the present one, the difference being attributable

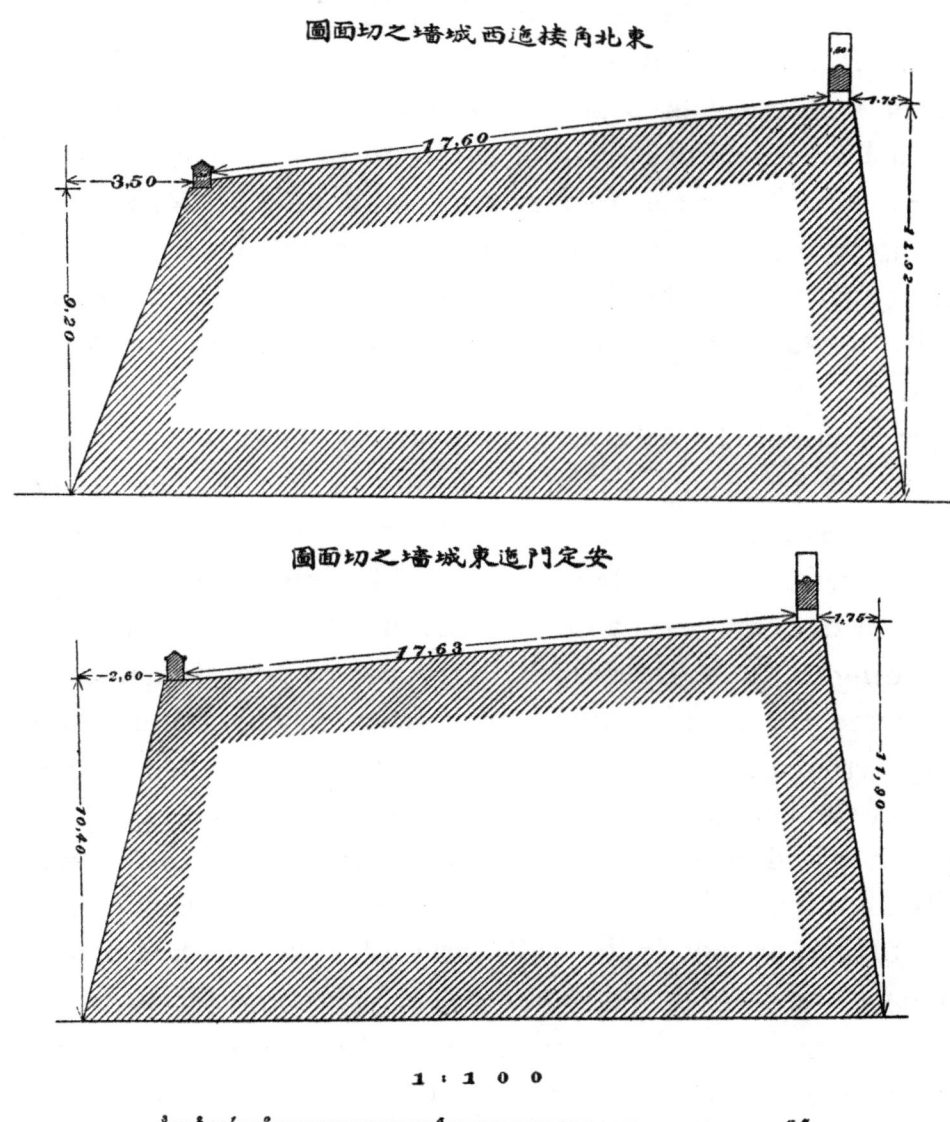

Fig. 4.—Two sections of the north wall; the upper one taken near the east corner, the lower one near An Ting Men.

to its later construction, probably at the beginning of the sixteenth century, an assumption which is borne out by the brickwork.

We have had no opportunity to examine the construction of the inner body of the wall, but have gathered some information about it from people who have actually seen the wall cut through, for instance, when the new side-openings at the Ch'ien men were constructed. According to these informants the wall consists of successive layers of mud, gravel and lime, and occasionally a layer of bricks to bind the mud or the clay. It has also been stated that at some places a smaller mud wall may be distinguished within the actual big wall. But just how far and at what places this statement as to the construction holds good is impossible to ascertain without making cuts through the walls, a work which must be left to future investigators.

The outer faces of the walls are, as repeatedly stated, coated with brickwork which does not form simply a thin shell but consists of several layers, sometimes as many as seven or eight, as may be seen at places where the outer shell has been destroyed by tree-roots or water. The inner parts of this thick brick casing are more or less rough and uneven: mortar has been used abundantly and the bonding is quite irregular. The surface coat is naturally executed with more care; the flemish bond is here prevalent, though by no means consistently carried out in all parts of the walls. We shall find on a closer examination of the actual work that the faces of the present walls are simply a series of patches and repairs among which it is difficult to discover any part of the original brickwork. A low plinth of sandstone slabs (sometimes in a double row) forms the foot of the wall, and under this is a bed of lime-concrete which reaches a depth of 2 metres or more. At some places both the plinth and the lime-concrete bed are entirely covered up by mud and sand, at other places they have been undermined by water which has caused depressions in the wall or brought the brickwork down. It is more unusual to find them completely preserved, but where this is actually the case, the lime-concrete bed extends for about $1\frac{1}{2}$ metre beyond the plinth, forming a splendid sidewalk along the inside of the wall.

The faces of the wall rise from the plinth at varying inclinations, the inside usually battering a little more than the outside. On the north wall this inclination is as much as 3½ metres to a height of less than 10 metres; on the other walls it is only between 1½ and 2 metres. The successive layers of brick are placed stepwise, an arrangement which naturally is most evident on the north wall, where the inclination is greatest. Here the steps are deep enough to make it possible to climb the wall right up to the top. On the outside the brickwork is naturally much smoother; it would indeed have been dangerous from a defensive point of view to make such deep steps here. The defensive value of the walls is also greatly increased on the outside by the bastions which follow at regular intervals like square buttresses of about the same thickness as the walls themselves. On the north wall all the bastions are of the same size and the intervals between them are over 200 metres; on the other walls the intervals are only 80–90 metres, and there are bastions not only of the regular size but also larger ones, corresponding to the ramps on the inner wall faces.

The top-plane of the wall is paved with large bricks and bordered, on the inner side, by a parapet and, on the outer side, by battlements. The inside parapet is a simple brick barrier, 60 cm. thick, 80–90 cm. high and finished at the top with a rounded moulding. The battlement on the outside is not much thicker but at least twice as high as the parapet. Its merlons are 1·80 m., while the broad embrasures between them (sometimes wrongly named "portholes") are only ½ m. Under the battlement and the parapet, on the level of the wall plane, are square holes; the former may have been used for defensive purposes but the latter serve simply as drains. Short stone spouts project from these holes, though not far enough to prevent the water dripping on the lower part of the wall surface. Practically all the water from the walls is drained over the inner side, the top level being more or less inclined this way (as shown by the measurements given above), only occasionally there is a slight slope from the middle towards the outer side as well. This arrangement of the water drainage has proved most destructive to the walls. During the rainy season the inner wall-face is washed by torrents of water from the top, and a good deal of this penetrates between the bricks, particularly where holes have been formed by the roots of trees and shrubs. Consequently large bits of the outer brickwork have been loosened and made to fall off, and the casing has had to be repaired over and over again. No less dangerous for the preservation of the wall is the lack of proper drainage for water that accumulates at its foot. There used to be a small stone-lined moat or sewer along the lime-concrete bed, but this is now mostly destroyed; it has at some places become a deep mud-road, at other places there is still a ditch in lieu of the canal, but the water has no proper outlet. When the rain is abundant it rises over the plinth of the wall and may loosen the stone slabs and the brickwork at the bottom of the wall, and when these lower strata give way under the pressure of the upper part the consequences are, indeed, very serious. Large sections of the inner wall casing have been made to slide down that way. We shall have abundant occasions to notice these slides and other more or less destructive vicissitudes in the history of the walls when we start on our walk along the inner façade.

The number of merlons and " portholes " (probably the notches or embrasures) mentioned in the *Shun T'ien fu chih* may be approximately correct; we have not made a point of counting them. Nor are we able to state how many guardhouses there used to be on the top of the wall, because very few of them now remain, except those at the gates and the corner-towers which are in a rather dilapidated condition. In the Manchu time, when the defence of the wall was allotted to the eight different " banners " or guard divisions, high flag-poles were erected for the hoisting of the banner-men's colours. The stone slabs where the masts were fastened may still be seen at various places near the gates, but the flag-poles are gone. " The men of the yellow-bordered banner were at An Ting men, the yellow at Tê Sheng men; the white were at Tung Chih men, the white-

THE WALLS OF THE TARTAR CITY

bordered at Ch'i Hua men; the red were at Hsi Chih men, the red-bordered at P'ing Tzu men; the blue were at Hata men, the blue-bordered at Shun Chih men." Thus the north wall was under the protection of the yellow colour, representing earth according to the old Chinese symbology, the west wall under protection of the white, representing metal; the east wall was protected by the red, representing fire, and the south by the blue, representing water. Earth, metal, fire, and water were the four elements most necessary for the defence of the city, and it was also thought that they could counterbalance each other in case any of them should try to rebel or dominate the whole city.

The Chinese attach a great deal of symbolical significance to the arrangement of the plan and to the different quarters and gates of the capital. They claim that it was not simply for practical reasons that the city was planned in the form of a square, oriented according to the four main directions. The position of the heavenly constellations lies at the root of it, a strong city could not be built without obeying the laws of Heaven. The main principles of this harmonious arrangement and perfectly equal square divisions of the plan were, as we know, already settled in the Mongol time (though never completely applied), but the Ming emperors tried to perfect it by making the city a real square instead of an oblong. Such was their intention, which, however, became modified by circumstances. The main front of the whole city as well as of the emperor's palace was towards the south, to " meet the sun," the heavenly ruler. Where the sun was supposed to be most wanting, i.e. at the north-west corner, a large piece of the square was cut off. In the diagonally opposite south-east corner the earth was said to " sink down," which it actually does, as proved by the watercourses, but the Chinese also claim that this saying infers that the sun is most supreme in the south-east corner. The Observatory was from of old in this corner and the Altar of Heaven was situated in the same direction.

It would be futile to follow the old Chinese symbolism into further details, as its meaning seems rather vague and nebulous to us westerners; but it is worth remembering that the Chinese never planned an architectural work, be it a house, a temple, or a whole city, simply from artistic or practical points of view. They had always a deeper purpose and a more significant object in view: things which though never forgotten were never fully explained or understood by the faithful subjects of the Son of Heaven.

IV

NOTES ON THE INNER SIDE OF THE TARTAR CITY WALL

THE present city wall of Peking is by no means a unified and homogeneous structure. Essential differences in the dimensions and the general appearance of the wall on the four sides of the city have already been pointed out, and we have also made some observations as to the very frequent repairs. The closer examination to which we are now proceeding will make it clear that the brick coating on the inside face of the wall is a continuous series of short stretches of varying dates, quality, and workmanship. Many of these stretches can be definitely dated by means of inscriptions on stone tablets inserted at the top of the wall and recording not only the time and the extent of the repairs but also the names of the officials who supervised them.

If the work was well done the tablet became an honorific record of the official's zeal, but if it was poor and non-lasting the official was thus exposed to the criticism and contempt of the public. But unfortunately this system of stimulating the zeal of the officials, who were mostly directors or secretaries of some government department such as the Board of Public Works, the Board of Rites, the Board of Justice, etc., was not introduced until the Kien Lung era. There are no stone tablets on the Tartar city wall of an earlier date; the only earlier records are those found on the bricks themselves. These marks go as far back as the Ch'êng Hua era (1465–1487) and as late as the time of Tao Kuang. Their contents are varying; very often they give the name of the brick-kiln and the master-potter, but sometimes they are simply such descriptions as "fine clay city-wall bricks," or "new-style large city-wall bricks," etc., but many of them may, of course, have more inscriptions than can be seen on the surface of the wall, where, furthermore, the corrosion and the covering dirt often make the reading difficult.

The only brick-marks that we have really been looking for are those containing dates, because they are of the greatest interest in connection with the history of the wall. They may not always indicate the exact year of the completion of the portion of masonry in which they occur, but the bricks are as a rule of the same period as the workmanship; it is quite exceptional to find early bricks used in later repairs, and in such instances they are usually mixed with other material. Where neither tablets nor brick-marks are to be found, the masonry must be dated simply on the basis of its particular character and quality. This can be done only in a very general way; as a rule it is possible to distinguish early Ming work from that done in the Chia Ching period, or still later, such as was done in the reigns of Wan Li and Ch'ung Chêng. And all the Ming work is quite distinguishable from the masonry of the Ch'ing dynasty period, because both the material and the workmanship are different. Within the Ch'ing period the Ch'ien Lung era stands out as by far the most important in the history of the wall both by reason of the extent and the quality of the work executed during this last golden epoch of Chinese art.

Unfortunately we have no means of dating definitely any portion back to the Kang Hsi era, as there are no inscriptions or marks of that time, but we have reason to believe that certain minor portions, which are earlier in character than the Ch'ien Lung work, and at the same time unlike the later Ming masonry, were executed in the early part of the Ch'ing dynasty. The splendid traditions of Ch'ien Lung's time were kept up pretty well during Chia Ch'ing's reign, but under Tao Kuang some change takes place both in the character of the material and in the workmanship. In still later times the bricks become smaller and lighter and the masonry has not the same excellent appearance as that of the

THE INNER SIDE OF THE TARTAR CITY WALL 55

eighteenth century. Nowadays there would again be plenty of room for repairs on the inner face of the wall, which at some spots, particularly on the east side, is in a miserable condition. Hardly anything has been done during the last twenty years to keep up the wall, except the rebuilding of the Ch'ien men bastion and the partial restoration of some ramps. The present government has certainly neither the means to take care of the old city walls of Peking nor the interest in doing so. If the gradual decay and destruction by water and tree-roots is allowed to go on unhampered, as it has been during the last two decades, some portions of the wall will soon be in a dangerous condition.

Realizing the extraordinary length of the Peking city wall and the great variety of its masonry, nobody will expect a detailed account of every foot of the work. We shall not attempt anything of the kind. It will suffice to pass along the wall and take notice of such portions of it as are to be distinguished by the uneven joints and the varying material. The dates of the inserted tablets and the brick-marks will be recorded as far as they are readable from the ground (sometimes with the aid of an opera-glass) and where no such marks or inscriptions are to be found the period is indicated only in so far as it is ascertainable from the character of the brickwork. The length given for the various sections is only approximate, based on a quite rough calculation or step-measuring which sometimes is difficult to carry out properly because of all the buildings and obstacles along the wall. Nevertheless it seemed to us that these measurements, however inaccurate, should be noted down as a help for ascertaining the situation of the various stretches in relation to the ramps and the gates. No doubt, there are portions in which various repairs are so closely mixed up that it is hardly possible to date them separately; in such cases we must simply keep to the prevailing character of the material and the workmanship. Our study of the wall has indeed been performed within strict limitations and under considerable difficulties which could not be removed without costly arrangements for climbing the wall, cleaning it and digging into it and consequently the results should by no means be taken as final, simply as contributions to the history of this great monument which for centuries has been the safeguard of Peking, historically as well as materially.

A. The South Wall

The south wall may be said to consist of two almost equal halves; the one to the east of Ch'ien men and the other to the west of it. The great middle gate is not only the largest opening in the city wall; it also marks a point where the general aspect of the wall and the adjoining quarters of the city undergo a complete change. Eastward from the gate is the legation quarter with its high foreign buildings and clean roads. The wall-face is here relatively in good repair and partly overgrown with Virginia creeper; to the west lies a rather disjointed bit of the Tartar city with some buildings in a sort of "republican" hybrid style, deep mud roads besides the coal sheds and garbage piles which are encroaching upon the wall. This south-western section is, as a matter of fact, one of the least attractive parts of the city adjoining the wall. The refuse heaps, which at some places reach almost half the height of the wall, form a hunting ground for scavengers and mangy dogs, not to speak of all the near-by lodgers who use the same places in a way still more offensive to the atmosphere and cleanliness of the neighbourhood. It is only further west, on the other side of Shun Chih men, that this south-western quarter of the city takes on a somewhat cleaner aspect with better roads and finer buildings, among which the assembly halls of the republican parliament stand out prominently.

But the new road does not extend further than the corner of the parliament house; here it turns northward, while the sandy ditch (which serves as a road) and the garbage heaps continue along the wall towards the south-western corner, where they finally become overgrown with grass and trees.

The part of the city which adjoins the wall inside the legation quarter—

THE INNER SIDE OF THE TARTAR CITY WALL

practically speaking, between Ch'ien men and Hata men—is indeed remarkably clean and well ordered, but hardly more interesting from a historical point of view. The masonry of the wall-face is more or less hidden under Virginia creeper; the road at the foot of the wall is quite narrow and so much filled out that it lies over the plinth of the wall, the height of which thus becomes diminished. Still more detrimental to the impressiveness of the wall are some of the European buildings within the legation quarter which actually vie with it in height. The effect is, of course, one of disharmony. These haughty new-comers have the air of completely disregarding the old wall, above which they raise their turrets and gables.

Further eastward, outside the legation quarter, and after one has passed Hata men, the wall is more in keeping with the adjoining city and becomes as a whole more interesting. There are stretches where the complete structure, including the plinth, the concrete sidewalk and the small canal in front of it can be fully seen. The ground near by is not much built over; in fact there are some empty tracts in the midst of which the thickly wooded cemetery of the Italians, Austrians, and Germans stands out as a beautiful green island.

1. The south-east corner has been destroyed by the construction of the Round-the-City railway line (in 1915), which makes a curve here cutting through the wall on both sides of the corner. There are consequently some quite recent repairs in the brickwork.

2. *Circa* 90 metres. (All the following measures are roughly estimated.) Repair executed in the latter half of the eighteenth century. The bricks are of the kind always used in the Ch'ien Lung period and also under Chia Ch'ing. Some of them are marked: "Fine clay lasting city-wall bricks," others: "Large size city-wall bricks from the Tung Fung kiln"; also: "Kung Pu inspector Kuei." Kung Pu is the Board of Public Works under the auspices of which all the bricks were made, and it is quite common to find the names of the board inspectors on the bricks of the Ch'ien Lung period. Similar bricks were made at various kilns during this epoch, as will be seen from our notes. Their average measurements are: length 48 cm., width 23 cm., height $12\frac{1}{2}$ cm.; their prescribed weight should be 48

Chinese pounds. The Ming bricks are as a rule smaller and so are the bricks of later times, as will appear from the following observations:—

3. 50 m. Probably Middle Ming period with some repairs of later date.

4. 190 m. (or more). Middle Ming period; bricks marked 32nd year of Chia Ching (1553).

5. 80 m. A stretch of fine masonry, executed according to an inserted tablet late in the 53rd year of Ch'ien Lung (1788); bricks from the Yung Chêng kiln.

6. 200 m. Good masonry made of large bricks, according to an inserted tablet, in the 20th year of Chia Ch'ing (1815). Right in front of this portion of the wall is the cemetery, which makes a closer examination difficult.

7. The most eastern ramp on the South wall. It consists of four different portions: I. Early Ming work (no brick-marks). II. Repaired after an earthquake in 1907, though mostly with the old material, i.e. Ch'ien Lung bricks. III. Early Ming work; bricks are dated: Chêng Hua, 18th year (1482). IV. The most western portion of the ramp is new.

8. 14 m. Probably eighteenth century; no brick-marks.

9. 3 m. Short stretch of middle-size bricks with no marks. These bricks are about ¾ the size of the Ch'ien Lung bricks; they seem to have been commonly used from the time of Tao Kuang onward, but it may well be that bricks of a similar pattern were also used at the beginning of the Ch'ing dynasty. Unfortunately there are no brick-marks of that period (Shun Chih and K'ang Hsi).

10. 14 m. Same date and material as 8.

11. 10 m. Same date and material as 9.

12. 30 m. Late eighteenth-century work. Ch'ien Lung bricks from the Li Fung kiln, marked: Kung Pu inspector Kuei.

13. 60 m. Same date and material as 9.

14. 30 m. Late eighteenth-century work. Ch'ien Lung bricks, marked: "Fine clay new style city-wall bricks."

15. 10 m. Probably late Ming period, no brick-marks. This stretch of the wall which is situated over a water-lock is now badly bulging.

16, 17. 45 m. Two stretches of middle-size bricks without marks.

18. 20 m. Middle Ming period; there are bricks marked: 28th year

THE INNER SIDE OF THE TARTAR CITY WALL 59

of Chia Ching (1549); others: Made by the master potter Sun Ch'uan Wei in the 32nd year of Chia Ching (1553); others again: Made by the master potter Fu Chü on behalf of the prefect of Ch'ing Chow fu (Shantung) in the 33rd year of Chia Ching (1554). And there are most likely still other dates of the Chia Ching era.

19. 150 m. Middle Ming period; bricks marked with various dates of the Chia Ching era, as, for instance, "Made by the master potter Li Chi Wei on behalf of the prefect of Nan Yang fu (Honan) in the 31st year of Chia Ching (1552).

20. 120 m. Very even and careful work executed, according to an inserted tablet in the 41st year of Ch'ien Lung. The usual brick-marks such as "Fine clay lasting city-wall bricks."

21. 20 m. Late eighteenth century. Ch'ien Lung bricks from the Yung Chêng kiln.

22, 23, 24. 80 m. Three or more stretches of what appears to be Ming work, but closer studies are here made impossible by the buildings along the wall.

25. The wall above the Hata men ramps contains bricks marked: "Made by the master potter Fu Chü in the 33rd year of Chia Ching" (1554).

26. The ramps themselves have been rebuilt in later times with medium-size bricks.

27. 60 m. Possibly early Ch'ing dynasty; medium-size bricks.

28, 29. 75 m. Two stretches of what appears to be Ming work, though the bricks are large and have no marks.

30. 60 m. Late eighteenth century; "Fine clay, new style city-wall bricks from the Tung Ho Kiln."

31. 60 m. Middle Ming period; bricks marked: "Made by the potter Sun Tzu Tung in the 28th year of Chia Ching" (1549).

32. 40 m. Middle Ming period; bricks marked: "Made by the potter Liu Chao in the 28th year of Chia Ching," and also in the 31st year of Chia Ching (1552). The upper part of this stretch has been rebuilt in the eighteenth century with "Fine clay lasting city-wall bricks."

33, 34. 60 m. Two stretches Middle Ming period work; large bricks with Chia Ching marks.

35. 20 m. Late eighteenth century; large bricks with Ch'ien Lung period marks, such as: "Fine new pattern city-wall bricks of the Hêng Shêng kiln."

36. 90 m. (or more). Middle Ming period; bricks marked: "Made by the master potter Ho Tsung in the 29th year of Chia Ching" (1550).

37. 90 m. Rebuilt, according to the tablet at the top of the wall, in the 38th year of Ch'ien Lung (1773).

38. The ramp between Hata men and the Water Gate contains at least four different portions of brickwork: I. Ch'ien Lung period bricks with the usual marks. II. Early Ming work, large bricks with no marks. III. Probably early Ch'ing work of middle-size bricks with no marks. IV. The most western portion is again of the same period and material as I.

39. 60 m. Middle Ming period; here are bricks marked: "Made by the workman Li Huan in the 6th year of Chêng Tê (1514)," and also: 18th year of Chêng Hua (1482), and again, 32nd year of Chia Ching (1553). This stretch seems to have been rebuilt in the sixteenth century with the partial use of older material.

40. 60 m. Rebuilt according to a tablet at the top of the wall in the 12th year of Chia Ch'ing (1807); bricks of Ch'ien Lung type marked: "Fine clay lasting city-wall bricks."

41, 42. 80 m. Two stretches of comparatively recent repairs (probably of the Kuang Hsü period).

43. The Water Gate was built after the Boxer rebellion in 1900; the wall around it is mainly old, but much repaired.

44. 20 m. The lower portion of the wall is old, mainly of the Middle Ming period, containing bricks marked: 31st year of Chia Ching (1552); the upper portion is made of middle-size bricks in the seventeenth century or later.

45. 30 m. Late Ming work with patches of new repairs, bricks marked: 32nd year of Wan Li (1604).

46. The ramp between the Water Gate and Ch'ien men consists of three different sections: the main, middle part was rebuilt, according to the tablets at the top, in the 16th year of Chia Ch'ing (1811), but the wall itself is evidently older.

47. 60 m. Late eighteenth century. Rebuilt according to the inscription on a tablet in the 2nd year of Chia Ch'ing (1797).

THE INNER SIDE OF THE TARTAR CITY WALL 61

48. 50 m. Middle Ming period; bricks marked: "Made by the master potter Li Chi Kao in the 31st year of Chia Ching (1552)."

49. 80 m. Rebuilt according to a tablet at the top of the wall in the 10th year of Kuang Hsü (1884).

50. 14 m. Ming period work of large bricks with no marks.

51. The wall at the east ramp of Ch'ien men is mainly of the Ch'ien Lung period. There are two tablets, close to each other, at the top of the wall, one of the 52nd year (?) of Ch'ien Lung, and the other of the 46th year of Ch'ien Lung (1781).

52. The gate bastion seems to be mainly of the same period, though repaired in connection with the construction of the new side openings in 1914–1915.

If we venture to draw any general conclusions from our observations on this eastern half of the South wall they would tend to prove that very little of the early Ming work remains here. Large repairs have been executed in Chia Ching's time, about the middle of the sixteenth century, and also towards the end of the Ch'ien Lung period; smaller repairs in the nineteenth century during the reigns of Chia Ch'ing and Kuang Hsü. The most even and carefully executed masonry is evidently that of the Ch'ien Lung period, but some of the Chia Ching work is also very good. The earlier Ming bricks are usually weather-worn and not particularly well laid or joined together, mortar being used more abundantly than in the masonry of later periods. Proceeding westward from Ch'ien men the observations on the masonry become rather more difficult, because of all the sheds and refuse heaps which are here encroaching upon the space in front of the wall and also because of the thick layers of dust covering the brickwork in many places; yet it soon becomes evident that the repairs are no less frequent on the western than on the eastern half of the South wall.

53. The wall at the west ramp of Ch'ien men is mostly modern.

54. 35 m. Rebuilt, according to the tablet at the top of the wall, in the 47th year of Ch'ien Lung (1782).

55. 70 m. Middle Ming period; bricks marked 32nd year of Chia Ching (1553). Later repairs in the upper part of the wall.

56. 35 m. Late Ming period; bricks marked: 32nd year of Wan Li (1604).

57. 50 m. Ch'ien Lung period; bricks marked: Kung Pu inspector Yung.

58. A stretch of modern work; probably of Kuang Hsü's time.

59. 35 m. Ch'ien Lung period; bricks marked: Kung Pu inspector Yung.

60. 30 m. Late eighteenth century; large Ch'ien Lung bricks; the tablet at the top of the wall shows no characters.

61. 5 m. Late Ming period; bricks marked: 32nd year of Wan Li.

62. Same as 60. Tablet with no visible characters.

63. 20 m. Late Ming period; bricks marked: 32nd year of Wan Li.

64. 38 m. Modern work, repaired according to an inscription on a tablet, in the 17th year of Kuang Hsü (1891).

65. 150 m. (or more). Middle Ming period; bricks marked: the Wu Tzu year of Chia Ching (1528).

66. The ramp was repaired, according to the inscription on a tablet, in the 7th year of Chia Ch'ing (1802).

67. A short stretch of late eighteenth-century work; Ch'ien Lung bricks, marked: Kung Pu inspector Kuei.

68. 38 m. Modern work, repaired, according to the description on a tablet, in the 19th year of Kuang Hsü (1893).

69. 35 m. Middle Ming period; bricks much corroded, no readable marks. The wall is bulging over tree-roots.

70. 35 m. Eighteenth century. Repair executed, according to an inserted tablet, in the 54th year of Ch'ien Lung (1789).

71. Probably early nineteenth century; bricks marked: New style large city-wall bricks.

72, 73, 74. 200 m. Three stretches of late sixteenth-century work; Ch'ien Lung bricks, marked: Kung Pu inspector Kuei and Kung Pu inspector Yung.

75. The second ramp is in its lower portion of the Ming period, while the upper portion, according to the inserted tablet, was rebuilt in the 52nd year of Ch'ien Lung (1787).

76. The wall at the western end of the ramp was rebuilt, according to an inserted tablet, in the 30th year of Ch'ien Lung (1765).

THE INNER SIDE OF THE TARTAR CITY WALL

77. 30 m. Rebuilt, according to an inserted tablet, in the 42nd year of Ch'ien Lung (1777).

78. 75 m. Rebuilt, according to an inserted tablet, in the 10th year of Kuang Hsü (1884).

79. A short stretch of old Ming work, bulging over the roots of the trees which are growing out of the wall.

80. Late eighteenth century. Rebuilt, according to an inserted tablet, in the 56th year of Ch'ien Lung (1791).

81. A long stretch built mainly of Ming material though possibly at a later time.

82. Late eighteenth century. Ch'ien Lung bricks, marked: Kung Pu inspector Yung.

83. Probably Middle Ming period; no brick-marks.

84. The lower part of this stretch is Ming work, containing bricks marked: 34th year of Chia Ching; the upper part is built of Ch'ien Lung bricks, marked: Kung Pu inspector Yung.

85. The east ramp of Shun Chih men is mainly of the Middle Ming period.

86. The west ramp of the same gate and the adjoining wall were rebuilt, according to an inserted tablet, in the 49th year of Ch'ien Lung (1784).

87. 65 m. Late eighteenth century. Ch'ien Lung bricks, marked: Kung Pu inspector Kuei.

88. A short stretch of Ming bricks though probably rebuilt at a later time.

89. Middle Ming period; no brick-marks.

90. Rebuilt, according to the tablet at the top of the wall, in the 20th year of Chia Ch'ing (1815); bricks marked: New style large city-wall bricks.

91. 65 m. Same period and material as 87.

92. A short stretch of what appears to be early Ming work.

93. Possibly late seventeenth century; middle-size bricks; no marks.

94. Another short stretch of middle-size bricks; possibly early Ch'ing period.

95. Late eighteenth century. Ch'ien Lung bricks, marked: Kung Pu inspector Yung.

96. A short stretch of the Middle Ming period; no marks.

97. Same period and material as 95.

98. Same period and material as 96, though with later repairs.

99. 5 m. Late Ming period; bricks marked: Wan Li 32nd year.

100. 35 m. Repair executed, according to the tablet at the top of the wall, in the 54th year of Ch'ien Lung (1789).

101. Long stretch. Middle Ming period; bricks marked: 28th year of Chia Ching (1549).

102. A stretch of old Ming wall which has been partly rebuilt in Ch'ien Lung's time. There are bricks marked: 32nd year of Chia Ching, but also later ones, marked: Made at the Ta Tung chêng kiln, Kung Pu inspector Yung.

103. The most western ramp on the southern wall is largely of the Ming period, but there is a repaired portion in the middle of it, probably of Kuang Hsü's time. At the eastern end of the ramp are bricks marked: 28th year of Chia Ching (1549).

104. Modern work. Kuang Hsü period; bricks marked: Fine clay city-wall bricks from the government kiln.

105. Old Ming work; no brick-marks.

106. 25 m. Repair executed, according to inserted tablet, in the 44th year of Ch'ien Lung (1779). "Large new style bricks from the government kiln."

107. Same period and material as 105.

108. 11 m. Repaired, according to the inserted tablet, in the 28th year of Ch'ien Lung (1749). Bricks with the usual marks.

109. Middle Ming period; bricks marked: Made by the master-potter Kao Shang Yi in the 32nd year of Chia Ching.

110. 75 m. Repair executed, according to the inserted tablet, in the 28th year of Ch'ien Lung. Cf. No. 108.

111. 38 m. Repair executed, according to the inserted tablet, in the 9th year of Ch'ien Lung (1744). Bricks marked: Kung Pu inspector Yung.

112. Short stretch of Ming work; no brick-marks.

113. 18 m. Repaired, according to the inserted tablet, in the 28th year of Ch'ien Lung. Cf. No. 110.

114. 20 m. Repaired, according to the inserted tablet, in the 30th year of Ch'ien Lung (1765). Bricks marked: Kung Pu inspector Kuei.

115. The corner ramp is mainly of the Middle Ming period; some bricks have Chia Ching marks but there are also later repairs.

*   *   *   *   *

THE INNER SIDE OF THE TARTAR CITY WALL 65

Our observations on the western half of the South wall have no doubt served to prove that this part is just as badly preserved as the eastern half. The repairs of the eighteenth and nineteenth centuries are predominant and the sections of old Ming work rather short. Some of them are repaired and patched up partly with old and partly with new material, and we have here also some characteristic spots where the brickwork has bulged and burst over heavy tree-roots, but such cases of destruction are still more frequent on the East wall. The readable brick-marks are comparatively few, because long stretches are covered with a black velvety coat of dust gradually accumulated by the north wind, which plays havoc with the mud roads and refuse heaps at the foot of the wall. It is only in front of the Parliament buildings, the old Ch'eng Huang miao, that the wall has a cleaner appearance and that the space in front of it is cleared of refuse. Further westward the old conditions remain practically undisturbed. A row of fine sophora trees shades the road which runs in the bed of the old moat, and the growth of ailanthus and jujube shrubs is quite abundant on the wall.

The open space near the south-west corner is a more pleasant spot since it has been planted with young willows and ailanthus, which stand out in fresh green against the dark colour of the brickwork. The wall is here of comparatively early appearance, and as the old corner-tower is still preserved, offering a very monumental view from the side where its corrugated iron roof remains invisible, this corner part is decidedly one of the most attractive and picturesque sections of the city-wall of Peking.

B. The East Wall

The eastern wall is in some respects the most interesting of all the four sides of the ramparts around the Tartar city. It contains a considerable portion of early Ming work and is to some extent in very bad repair, which indeed adds to its picturesqueness and also to its historical eloquence. If the present government of Peking had any interest and money left for the maintenance of the historical monuments of the capital, this would be one of the first structures requiring immediate attention, but as that is hardly the case, bits of the wall will probably soon be tumbling down. The foundations are at some places gradually undermined by water and the brickwork is cracked and flaked off by the tree-roots. The results of this can be easily imagined, and may also be observed in one or two of our pictures.

The south-east corner is, as already stated, pierced by the railway line, in front of which a new screen wall, which practically destroys the structural effect of the old corner, has been erected, also badly impairing the view of the corner-tower. This view can now be properly seen only from the outside of the city or from the top of the wall. The open space at this corner has been freely used for piling up refuse; an open sewer or ditch winds through the plain and finds its way through a grating under the wall into the outer moat. In the rainy season it swells into a broad stream, but for the rest of the year it contains more mud than liquid matter.

The adjoining quarter of the city has lost much of its old character and importance since the destruction of the examination halls, which formed, if not the architectural, at least the intellectual centre of the south-eastern city. The locality is now rather drab and desolate. The old Observatory has also been replaced by quite ordinary semi-foreign brick buildings. The wall from the corner to a point about 30 m. north of the Observatory is, however, mainly old, though built in sections which are easily distinguished at the joints. It is to be remembered that this stretch was newly constructed in the early part of the Ming period when a piece was added to the original Mongol city, as related in a previous chapter.

1. 70 m. Middle Ming period; bricks marked: Chia Ching, 10th year; half of this stretch is renewed in its lower part.
2. 35 m. Modern work; no marks.
3. 18 m. Middle Ming period; bricks marked: Chia Ching, 28th year (1549).

THE INNER SIDE OF THE TARTAR CITY WALL

4. Short stretch; upper part late Ming work; the lower part recently repaired.

5. 180 m. Middle Ming period; bricks marked: Chia Ching, 27th year. There are five patches of late repair.

6. 150 m. Middle Ming period; bricks marked: Chia Ching, 21st year (1542) and Chia Ching, 32nd year (1553).

7. 120 m. Middle Ming period; bricks marked: Chia Ching, 20th year (1541) and Chia Ching, 27th year (1548).

8. 35 m. Middle Ming period; bricks marked: Chia Ching, 18th year (1539); made by the potter Sun Wen Ch'uan.

9. The ramp at the Observatory has been largely rebuilt in the Ch'ien Lung period. The bricks in its southern part are marked: " Fine clay lasting city-wall bricks." Then follows a short section of Ming work made of thin bricks. The northern section is again of the Ch'ien Lung period. The wall above the ramp is old, but has no brick-marks.

10. 64 m. Early Ming period. This is the last section of the old weathered wall, which stands out in contrast to the newly built terrace of the Observatory.

11. 150 m. Late Ming period; bricks marked: Wan Li, 32nd and Wan Li, 33rd year (1604–1605).

12. 24 m. Repair executed, according to the inserted tablet, in the 18th year of Chia Ch'ing (1813).

13. 36 m. Repair executed, according to the inserted tablet, in the 8th year of Ch'ien Lung (1743).

14. 100 m. Middle Ming period; bricks marked: Made in the Tung Ho kiln, 32nd year of Chia Ching (1553).

15. 20 m. Repair executed, according to the inserted tablet, in the 7th year of Chia Ch'ing (1802). " Fine clay, new style city-wall bricks."

16. 50 m. Early Ming work, much corroded bricks with no marks.

17. 60 m. Possibly late seventeenth-century work; middle-size bricks, no marks.

18. 50 m. Late Ming work; bricks marked: Wan Li, 32nd year.

19. 90 m. Same period and material as 17.

20. 60 m. Eighteenth century. Tablet with no inscription. Bricks marked: Ch'ien Lung, Hsin Ssu year (1761).

21. 60 m. Late Ming period; bricks marked: Wan Li, 31st and Wan Li, 32nd year (1603–1604).

22. 5 m. Middle Ming period; bricks marked: Chia Ching, 28th year; made by potter Lin Yung Shou.

23. 5 m. Late Ming period; bricks marked: Wan Li, 32nd year; made by potter Wu Yü.

24. 30 m. Possibly late seventeenth-century work; same as 17.

25. 12 m. Middle Ming period; bricks marked: Chia Ching, 32nd year, made by the potter Pu T'ien Kuei.

26. 5 m. Short repair executed in Chia Ching's 18th year, according to the inscription on a tablet.

27. 5 m. Same bricks as 26, but the work is different.

28. 5 m. Middle of eighteenth century (cf. 20). Bricks marked: Ch'ien Lung, Hsin Ssu year (1761), Ch'ien Lung, Chia Wu year (1774) and Ping Shen year (1776).

At these sections of the wall big tree-roots have burst the masonry and forced various layers of brickwork to drop out. Some of the biggest holes near the ground have been wantonly enlarged by brick robbers and open now almost into the concrete core of the wall.

29. 30 m. Old Ming wall; the upper part of it contains bricks marked: Chia Ching, 23rd year (1544), made by the potter Lin Kuei.

30. The ramp is mainly of the Ming period; it contains bricks marked: Chia Ching, 23rd and 33rd year. According to an inserted tablet the south end of it was repaired in the 4th year of Chia Ching (1525); it is now in a miserable condition. In front of the ramp are refuse heaps reaching halfway up the wall.

31. 70 m. Old Ming wall; no brick-marks.

32. 30 m. Beginning of nineteenth century. Bricks marked: "Fine clay new style city-wall bricks," made by the potter Chü Chêng Yao in the reign of Chia Ch'ing.

33. 60 m. Middle Ming period; bricks marked: Chia Ching, 10th year (1531); and with the names of various potters such as Jen Wei Nan, Pu T'ung Wei, Sung Wên Ming.

34. 40 m. Beginning of nineteenth century. Bricks marked: "Fine clay, new style city-wall bricks, Tung Ho kiln." Cf. No. 32.

THE INNER SIDE OF THE TARTAR CITY WALL

35. 60 m. Middle Ming period; bricks marked: Made by the potter Tsao Ch'un in the 38th year of Chia Ching (1559).

36. 30 m. Earlier Ming work; much corroded bricks with no marks.

37, 38. 70 m. Two stretches late eighteenth-century work; one of them was repaired, according to an inserted tablet, in the 31st year of Ch'ien Lung (1766).

39. 150 m. Repaired, according to the inserted tablet, in the 12th (?) year of Chia Ch'ing (1807 or later), with "Fine clay new style city-wall bricks."

40. 25 m. Late eighteenth century; Ch'ien Lung bricks marked: "Fine clay lasting city-wall bricks."

41, 42. 130 m. Two stretches of early Ming work; corroded bricks with no marks.

The wall here is rather old in appearance and the joints between the successive sections are very uneven, particularly so towards the base of the wall at places where its plinth and the foundation of lime-concrete have been undermined by water.

43, 44. 35 m. Two sections containing bricks marked the 32nd year of Wan Li (1604), but evidently rebuilt in the Ch'ien Lung era.

45, 46, 47. 100 m. Three sections probably of the late Ming period containing bricks marked: 32nd year of Wan Li.

48. 9 m. Probably late Ming period; very thin bricks of a type that was mostly in use in Ch'ung Chêng's time.

49. 9 m. A stretch of Ch'ien Lung work leading up to the gate ramp.

50. The wall at Ch'i Hua men is mainly of the Middle Ming period; it contains bricks with marks of the Chia Ching era, but the gate bastion and the ramps have been rebuilt at the end of the eighteenth century; they contain bricks with Ch'ien Lung and Chia Ch'ing marks.

51. 6 m. Late eighteenth century. Ch'ien Lung bricks, marked: Kung Pu inspector Sa.

52. 30 m. Middle Ming period; bricks marked: 24th year and 26th year of Chia Ching (1545–1547), made by the master-potters Tuan Chow and Chang Pao Ch'ao.

53. 30 m. Possibly early Ch'ing period; middle-size bricks with no marks.

54. 3 m. Old Ming work, corroded bricks, no marks.

55. 12 m. Middle Ming period; bricks marked: 33rd year of Chia Ching (1554), made by the master-potter Kao Shang Yi.

56. 40 m. Repair executed, according to the inserted tablet, in the 4th year of Chia Ch'ing (1799).

57. 40 m. Repair executed, according to the inserted tablet, in the 23rd year of Tao Kuang (1843).

58. 100 m. Two stretches of nineteenth-century work. According to two inserted tablets the repairs were executed in the 2nd year of Kuang Hsü (1876) and in the 9th year of T'ung Chih (1870). The bricks used here are, however, somewhat older, some are marked: "Fine clay new style large city-wall bricks from the Yung Ting government kiln," others: "Made by the foreman Wang Tai Li in the 1st year of Hsien Fêng (1851)."

59. 50 m. Repair executed, according to the inserted tablet, in the 4th year of Ch'ien Lung (1739).

60. 60 m. Repair executed, according to the inserted tablet, in the 8th year of Ch'ien Lung (1743).

61. 9 m. Middle Ming period; bricks marked: Made by the master-potter of the branch kiln Lin Yung Shou in the 16th year of Chia Ching (1537).

62. 25 m. Possibly early Ch'ing period; middle-size bricks, no marks.

63. 22 m. The lower portion of this section is Ming work; it contains bricks marked: 15th year of Chia Ching (1536); the upper portion has been rebuilt with middle-size bricks in the early Ch'ing period or later.

64. The ramp between Ch'i Hua men and Tung Chih men consists of three or more sections. The most southern section is in its lower part of the Ming period; there are bricks marked 32nd year of Chia Ching (1553), but the upper part of this section is later. A similar division may be observed in the middle section which in its lower part contains bricks marked: Made by the master-potter Lin Yung Shou in the 16th year of Chia Ching (1537), while the upper portion is of the nineteenth century. The most northern section contains in its lower part bricks marked: 23rd year of Chia Ching (1544).

The present condition of this ramp is critical, as the supporting terrace of brick and lime-concrete is being undermined by water. It has already slid out at some spots, pulling bits of the plinth with it. Repairs have repeatedly been made in the upper portions of the ramp, but they are of little or no avail when the substructure is allowed to break down. The main reason why this has

THE INNER SIDE OF THE TARTAR CITY WALL 71

happened more frequently along the eastern wall than on the southern, western, or northern side, is that the water is most abundant here. The brick-lined moat, which originally followed the inside of the wall, is now practically destroyed and serves in some places as a road. In the rainy season the water sometimes rises over the plinth of the wall.

65. 20 m. The wall is here of the same kind as the preceding ramp; the lower part contains bricks of the Ming dynasty; the upper part is rebuilt later with medium-size bricks.

66. 60 m. Upper half probably of Middle Ming period, in the lower half later repairs; the bricks are marked: " Fine clay, large size city-wall bricks."

67. 24 m. Middle Ming period; bricks marked: 28th year of Chia Ching (1549).

68. 7 m. Rebuilt, according to an inserted tablet, in the 5th year of Tao Kuang (1825).

69. 14 m. Old Ming work; no brick-marks.

70. 7 m. Rebuilt, according to an inserted tablet, in the 4th year of Tao Kuang (1824); bricks marked: " Large size city-wall bricks from the Jui Shun kiln."

71. 50 m. Late Ming period; bricks marked: 32nd year of Wan Li (1604). There are also some later patches.

72. 14 m. Late eighteenth century; the bricks are marked: " Fine clay large size city-wall bricks."

73. 9 m. The main part of this stretch is late Ming work, but it also contains repairs of " fine clay, large size city-wall bricks."

74. 30 m. The upper part is modern; probably built in the Kuang Hsü period; the lower part is of the Middle Ming period containing bricks marked Chia Ching (?). The inserted tablet is illegible, but seems to be of the Kuang Hsü period.

75. 100 m. (or more). The upper part was repaired, according to an inserted tablet, in the 20th year of Kuang Hsü (1894); the lower part is of the late Ming period, containing bricks marked: 30th year of Wan Li (1602).

76. 60 m. Late Ming period; bricks are marked: 32nd year of Wan Li.

77. 10 m. Two short stretches of Ming work with new bricks here and there.

78. 55 m. Probably early nineteenth century (the inscription on the inserted tablet is illegible). Bricks marked: "New style city-wall bricks."

79. 45 m. Late eighteenth century; a tablet apparently of Ch'ien Lung's period at the top of the wall.

80. 25 m. Late Ming period; bricks marked: 32nd year of Wan Li.

81. The ramp at Tung Chih men and the adjoining wall are repaired, according to an inserted tablet, in the 8th year of Chia Ch'ing (1803). The bricks are the same as in the Ch'ien Lung period: "Fine clay, large-size city-wall bricks."

It should be noticed that the wall close to Tung Chih men is in a better state of preservation than the more southern section of the East wall. The stone plinth and the broad sidewalk of lime-concrete are still existing, and the brickwork is comparatively even. The inclination of the wall-face is not very great, which adds to its appearance of height and stateliness. The same is true of the wall northward from Tung Chih men, a stretch which is in remarkably good repair.

82. 24 m. Middle Ming period; bricks made by the Soo Chow fu branch government kiln in the 24th year of Chia Ching (1545). Other bricks with same date made at Yang Chow fu.

83. 20 m. Repair executed, according to the inserted tablet, in the 4th year of Chia Ch'ing (1799).

84. 24 m. Late eighteenth century. Ch'ien Lung period bricks marked: Kung Pu inspector Yung and Kung Pu inspector Kuei. The inserted tablet has no characters.

85. 80 m. Late eighteenth century; bricks marked: "Fine clay new pattern large city-wall bricks from the Yung Ting government kiln." The inscription on the inserted tablet is illegible.

86. 26 m. Repair executed, according to the inserted tablet, in the 6th year of Ch'ien Lung (1741); bricks marked: "Large city-wall bricks from the T'ung Ch'in kiln."

87. 60 m. Repair executed, according to the inserted tablet, in the 8th year of Chia Ch'ing (1803). Bricks from the Jui Shêng kiln.

88. 3 m. The upper part of this short stretch is made of thin bricks of the Ch'ung Chêng period; the lower part of large bricks.

THE INNER SIDE OF THE TARTAR CITY WALL 73

89. 9 m. Upper half built of medium-size bricks, possibly early Ch'ing period; the lower half of larger bricks made at the Yung Shun kiln.

90, 91. 30 m. Two stretches of late Ming work, partly repaired with Ch'ien Lung bricks.

92. 20 m. Middle Ming period; bricks marked: 28th year of Chia Ching.

93. 6 m. Late eighteenth century; bricks marked: Kung Pu inspector Yung.

94. 6 m. Early nineteenth century; bricks from the Jui Shun kiln.

95. 12 m. Ming work partly renewed with Ch'ien Lung bricks.

96. 9 m. Repaired, according to an inserted tablet, in the 30th year of Ch'ien Lung (1765): " Fine clay, new style large size city-wall bricks from the Yung Tung government kiln."

97. 3 m. Late eighteenth century; the bricks are of the usual Ch'ien Lung type, but have no marks.

98. 3 m. Early nineteenth century; bricks marked: " Bricks of the size used for the palaces of princes."

99. 12 m. Late eighteenth century; the old Ming wall is largely rebuilt with Ch'ien Lung material.

100. 50 m. Repaired, according to an inserted tablet, in the 4th year of Ch'ien Lung (1739).

101. 20 m. Late Ming period; bricks marked the 32nd year of Wan Li, but here are also later repairs.

The northern part of the East wall has, in spite of all the repairs that we have noticed during our walk, a more unified and homogeneous appearance than the southern part of the same wall. The repairs of the eighteenth and early nineteenth century blend better than usual with the Ming work and here are not so many patches of disjointed brickwork or actual holes as further south. The wall has been left more to itself, possibly because the city becomes thinner and emptier towards the north; the human destroyers have been fewer.

The corner portion is practically destroyed by the Round-the-City railway, which is here built through the walls in exactly the same manner as in the south-east corner. A very flat-looking new wall screens the railway curve.

And as the old tower is also completely demolished, the corner has been stripped of all its original character and beauty.

The adjoining quarter of the city is, however, by no means unattractive, thanks to its complete quietness and solitude. The only buildings here are those belonging to the compound of the Russian church, which comprises not only the earliest Christian church in Peking and dwelling quarters for the priests, but also a graveyard, vegetable gardens, cattle yards and similar essential elements of a small ecclesiastical estate in Europe. We almost seem to have stepped into a foreign country, perhaps not as ancient as China but hardly less immutable in its clerical institutions.

C. The North Wall

The so-called " North City " of Peking is really less like an ordinary city quarter than any other part of the Manchu capital. It includes some large palatial compounds belonging to the foremost Manchu princes, in which picturesque gardens and magnificent old trees occupy much more space than the actual buildings. In this part of the city, quite close to the North wall, are also some of the largest temples of Peking, such as the Lama temple and the Confucian temple, with yellow or blue tiled roofs and wide courts shaded by old cryptomerias. And besides these large compounds there are many smaller residential places which used to belong to prominent members of the Manchu aristocracy. They are now decaying, since the owners have become impoverished, but they are nevertheless beautiful, with a romantic touch of past grandeur. This was once the Faubourg Saint Germain of Peking, and it still retains an air of repose and exclusiveness, so unlike the prevailing character of the city quarters close to the South and the East wall. The life of the city seems to be gradually diminishing towards the north. The distances between the houses and the compounds increase. There is plenty of open space close to the wall, sandy plains and pasture, and further to the west, a large extension of the " North

THE INNER SIDE OF THE TARTAR CITY WALL

Lake" reaching almost to the foot of the wall. And as this neighbourhood is well sheltered against the sharp north winds, the road inside the wall has become one of the finest promenades of Peking.

But very few people go as far as the North wall. One may walk for a day along this road without meeting a cart or a rickshaw, only some solitary wanderer who is airing his cage-bird or simply enjoying the warmth along the sun-heated wall. Small flocks of sheep are grazing at places where some grass remains even in the dry season, watched by unspoiled happy children who have little in common with the obtrusive urchins in the centre of the city. Once in a while a camel caravan may pass this way towards Tê Sheng men or An Ting men. It moves on silently, almost soundlessly, along the soft, sandy road—only the tinkling of the leading camel's bell marking the slow rhythmic pace of the majestic animals. But when the caravan has passed, solitude closes once more over the neighbourhood like a brooding cloud which only for a few minutes lets through some rays of light.

The North wall is quite distinct from the three other sides of the Tartar city wall. Its measurements are greater, as was pointed out in a previous chapter, and its inner face is more battering than the sides of the East or the South wall. Generally speaking, it is in comparatively good repair, which may be a consequence of its later construction, but to a greater extent is due to the fact that its inner face was never exposed to the destructive northern winds. The outer face of this wall has indeed been severely battered, both by storms and the attacks of enemies, and repeatedly repaired, as we shall have occasion to observe in a subsequent chapter.

After we have passed the new wall along the railway line which cuts through the north-east corner we come to a stretch:

1. 75 m. Rebuilt of large Ch'ien Lung period bricks with undecipherable marks.

2. 40 m. Late Ming work; bricks marked: Made by Liu Sung master-potter, and his workman Liu Neng, in the 46th year of Wan Li (1618).

3. 60 m. Repaired, according to the inserted tablet, in the 10th year of Tao Kuang (1830): " Fine clay new style city-wall bricks."

4. 20 m. Short stretch of Ming work patched with later bricks.

5. 35 m. Made of "fine clay city-wall bricks from the Hêng Shun kiln."

6. 9 m. Repaired, according to the inserted tablet, in the 9th year of Tao Kuang (1829).

7. 100 m. Made, according to an inscription, in the Hsin Ssu year of Ch'ien Lung period (1761); bricks marked: Kung Pu inspector Yung and Kung Pu inspector Kuei.

8. 40 m. Repaired in the time of Chia Ch'ing (early nineteenth century) with "fine clay large city-wall bricks."

9. 100 m. Two adjoining stretches, possibly of the early Ch'ing period; made of middle-size bricks.

10. 25 m. Probably late eighteenth century; large bricks of the Ch'ien Lung period; no marks.

11. 50 m. Same kind of wall as No. 9.

12. 9 m. Short repair, executed, according to the inserted stone tablet, in the Ch'ien Lung period, by Kung Pu inspector Yung.

13. 50 m. Two short stretches of Ming work which have been patched with new bricks.

14. 25 m. Repaired, according to the inserted tablet, in the 14th year of Tao Kuang (1834).

15. 75 m. According to the inserted tablet, repaired in the 40th year of Ch'ien Lung (1775).

16. 55 m. Two short stretches of late Ming work containing bricks marked: 32nd year of Wan Li.

17. The large ramp, right behind the Yung Ho Kung, consists in its main parts of late Ming work; there are bricks marked: " Made by Yang, master-potter of the branch kiln in the 30th year of Chia Ching." The upper part has been repaired in later times.

18. 15 m. Short stretch of Ming work, containing bricks marked: " Made by Lin Kao, master-potter of the branch kiln in the 31st year of Chia Ching " (1552).

THE INNER SIDE OF THE TARTAR CITY WALL

19. 20 m. Late eighteenth century; large Ch'ien Lung bricks.

20. 25 m. Possibly late seventeenth century (or later) medium-size bricks; no marks.

21. 45 m. Two short stretches of Ming work with some later repairs.

22. 30 m. Late Ming work containing bricks from the 32nd year of Wan Li, repaired, according to the inserted tablet, in the 40th year of Ch'ien Lung (1775).

23. 40 m. Two short stretches of late Ming work with some bricks marked: 32nd year of Wan Li.

24. 50 m. Lower part late Ming work; upper part repaired, according to the inserted tablet, in the 10th year of Hsien Fêng (1860).

25. 35 m. Two more short stretches similar in character to the preceding one.

26. 50 m. Late Ming work of thin bricks as used in the Ch'ung Chêng period (1628–1643).

27. 40 m. Made, according to the inserted tablet, in the 20th year of Ch'ien Lung (1755).

28. 25 m. Possibly late seventeenth or eighteenth century; made of medium-size bricks; no marks.

29. 150 m. The lower part is Ming work and in a rather bad state of repair; the upper part rebuilt, according to a tablet, in the 20th year of Tao Kuang (1840).

30. 115 m. Repaired in the 19th year of Ch'ien Lung (1754) with bricks from the Kung Shun kiln.

31. The ramps and bastion at the An Ting men are mainly of the later Ming period. The bastion is in its upper part made of the thin bricks which were mostly used in the Ch'ung Chêng period, but in its lower section repaired with Ch'ien Lung large bricks.

32. 10 m. Repairs with medium-size bricks.

33. 20 m. Late Ming work, bricks marked: 32nd year of Wan Li.

34. 25 m. Lower part Ming work with bricks marked: Chia Ching Hsü Tzu year (1528); upper part of Ch'ien Lung work.

35. 18 m. Lower part Ming work; upper part of later date; made of medium-size bricks.

36. 10 m. Late Ming work; no marks.

37. 60 m. Lower half late Ming work; upper half rebuilt, according to the inserted tablet, in the 4th year of Tao Kuang (1824).

38. 40 m. Ming work repaired in patches.

39. Long stretch repaired, according to the inserted tablet, in the 8th year of Chia Ch'ing (1803).

40. 20 m. Late eighteenth century; bricks marked: " Fine clay large-size city-wall bricks of the T'ung Shun kiln."

41. 30 m. Repaired, according to an inserted tablet, in the 4th year of Tao Kuang (1824). " Fine clay large-size city-wall bricks."

42. Short stretch of the Middle Ming period; bricks marked: Made by the master-potter Wang Lin in the 21st year of Chia Ching (1542).

43. 40 m. Late eighteenth century; bricks marked: T'ung Ho kiln.

44. 15 m. Early Ming period; some bricks marked: 13th year of Chêng Hua (1477)—which is the earliest date we have found on any brick in the walls.

45. 50 m. Possibly early Ch'ing period; medium-size bricks, no marks.

46. 36 m. Late eighteenth century; large bricks with no marks.

47. 20 m. Same material and period as 45.

48. 20 m. Early Ming period; bricks marked: 4th year of Chêng Tê (1509).

49. 25 m. Same period and material as 45.

50. Short section of Ming work, rebuilt in its upper part with thin bricks.

51. 30 m. Rebuilt, according to the inserted tablet, in the 8th year of Ch'ien Lung (1743).

52. Short stretch of Ch'ing period; medium-size bricks; no marks.

53. 20 m. Middle Ming period; bricks marked: 11th year of Chia Ching (1532).

54. 35 m. Middle Ming period; bricks marked: Made by the master-potter Chang Ming in the 28th year of Chia Ching.

55. 60 m. Repaired, according to the tablet at the top of the wall, during the reign of Hsien Fêng (1851–1861).

56. 40 m. Possibly early Ch'ing period; medium-size bricks; no marks.

57. 25 m. A section of mixed material, probably repaired in the early nineteenth century. The tablet at the top of the wall is unreadable.

THE INNER SIDE OF THE TARTAR CITY WALL

58. 30 m. Upper half of medium-size bricks, possibly nineteenth century; lower half late Ming period; bricks marked: 32nd year of Wan Li.

59. 12 m. Middle Ming period; no marks.

60. Long stretch repaired, according to the inserted tablet, in the 7th and 8th years of Ch'ien Lung (1742–1743).

61. 40 m. Middle Ming period; large bricks; no marks.

The wall between An Ting men and the long ramp about the middle of the North wall is comparatively well preserved. The late repairs are not so extensive as on other sections. The wall-face has a considerable slope; the successive courses of bricks are laid in such deep steps that it is possible to climb the wall (which is not possible on the south, east, and west sides). This very marked slope makes the wall appear lower than at places where it rises more steeply.

62. The long ramp has been repaired quite extensively at different periods, and the patches are rather unequal. At least a dozen different sections may be distinguished in this ramp, most of them from the Ming period, i.e. Chia Ching, Wan Li, and Ch'ung Chêng, but there are also parts which were repaired in the eighteenth and early nineteenth century. It seems hardly worth while to enumerate all these small sections separately. The wall-stretch which extends from this ramp to Tê Sheng men has also been much repaired, particularly in its upper part, while the lower is mostly older.

63. 12 m. Late Ming period; bricks marked: 32nd year of Wan Li.

64. 12 m. Early nineteenth century; medium-size bricks; no marks.

65. 12 m. Late Ming period; no marks.

66. 10 m. Same period and material as 64.

67. 20 m. Same period and material as 63.

68. 45 m. Lower part of the wall is late Ming work; the upper part rebuilt in the nineteenth century with medium-size bricks.

69. 12 m. The upper part is Ming work, the lower part repaired in the Ch'ien Lung period.

70. 50 m. Late Ming work; bricks marked: 34th year of Wan Li.

71. 20 m. The lower part of Ming work, containing bricks of the 17th year of Chia Ching; the upper part rebuilt in nineteenth century with medium-size bricks.

72. 40 m. Probably early nineteenth century; the tablet at the top of the wall is of the Tao Kuang period (partly hidden by branches).

73. 35 m. Two short stretches of medium-size bricks from the middle of the nineteenth century.

74. 20 m. Two short sections of late Ming work; some bricks marked: 29th year of Wan Li.

75. 10 m. Same period and material as in 73.

76. The ramps and bastion of Tê Sheng men have been rebuilt in the late Ming period with thin bricks. According to an inserted tablet "a part of the gate ramp" (*circa* 54 m.) was repaired in the 7th year of Chia Ch'ing (1802).

The wall between Tê Sheng men and the north-west corner receives a peculiar character from its succession of irregular curves, which are very unevenly joined together. This very picturesque stretch seems to have been constructed without strict adherence to any regular plan or design.

77. 50 m. Rebuilt, according to an inserted tablet, in the 20th year of Tao Kuang (1840).

78. 40 m. Rebuilt, according to an inserted tablet, in the 3rd year of Chia Ch'ing (1798).

79. 30 m. Late eighteenth or early nineteenth century; large Ch'ien Lung bricks.

80. 75 m. Late Ming period; bricks marked: 32nd year of Wan Li.

81. 40 m. Probably early nineteenth century; large bricks, tablet at the top of the wall.

82. 20 m. Late nineteenth century; medium-size bricks.

83. 25 m. Late Ming period; thin bricks, such as were used in the Ch'ung Chêng period.

84. 12 m. Late eighteenth or early nineteenth century; large bricks, no marks.

85. 40 m. Probably late Ch'ing period; medium-size bricks, no marks.

86. 40 m. Another stretch of similar character to the preceding.

87. 40 m. Ch'ien Lung period work; bricks marked: Kung Pu inspector Sa.

88. 40 m. Late Ming period; thin bricks of the Ch'ung Chêng period.

THE INNER SIDE OF THE TARTAR CITY WALL

89. 30 m. Upper half late Ming period; thin bricks; lower half repaired in places with Ch'ien Lung period bricks.

90. 20 m. Lower half of the Middle Ming period; bricks marked: 14th year of Chia Ching; upper half thin bricks of the Ch'ung Chêng period.

91. 40 m. Lower half Middle Ming period; bricks marked: 11th year of Chia Ching (1532), "made for the prefect of Ch'ang Chow fu." The upper half is rebuilt with medium-size bricks.

92. 350 m. Long stretch of very even work; Ch'ien Lung or Chia Ch'ing period; the bricks are marked: Made in the Hsin Ssu year (1761), and also: "Made by the Fu Chin kiln."

93. The ramp is similar in character to the preceding wall-stretch, and there are two tablets at the top of the wall above the ramp, but their characters are invisible.

94. 60 m. Repaired, according to an inserted tablet, in the 8th year of Chia Ch'ing (1803). The bricks are marked: "fine clay large city-wall bricks."

95. 24 m. Probably late Ch'ing period; medium-size bricks.

96. 30 m. Late Ming period; bricks marked: 31st year of Wan Li.

97. 9 m. Early nineteenth-century work; Chia Ch'ing period bricks.

98. 12 m. Probably Ch'ien Lung period; no brick-marks.

99. 40 m. Probably late Ch'ing period; medium-size bricks.

100. Another stretch of similar material.

101. 100 m. Late Ming period; thin bricks of Ch'ung Chêng period.

102. 75 m. Late eighteenth century; bricks marked: Made in the Chia Wu year (1774) by the Kuang Ch'êng kiln.

103. 24 m. Later Ming period; thin bricks.

104. Two short stretches of medium-size bricks. (Cf. No. 99.)

105. 200 m. Repaired, according to an inserted tablet, in the 4th year of Chia Ch'ing (1799). Bricks marked: "New style city-wall bricks from the Yung Ting government kiln."

106. 15 m. Middle Ming period; large bricks with no marks.

107. 90 m. Repaired, according to an inserted tablet, in the 4th year of Chia Ch'ing (1799). Bricks marked: "Fine clay, new style city-wall bricks."

108. The ramp leading up to the corner bastion has been repaired in

the eighteenth century. At the top of it, on the western side, is a tablet without any inscription.

The westernmost portion of the North wall has evidently been more frequently repaired than any other section of it; it may have been less durable than the rest of this wall because of all its curves and windings. It contains only short bits of sixteenth-century work; a little more of the early seventeenth century, but mainly long stretches of eighteenth-century and early nineteenth-century repairs. Technically and historically this portion may be less interesting than the preceding section (between the two north gates), but from the point of view of natural beauty it is by far the more attractive. In order fully to realize the beauty of this section of the wall with its adjoining city quarter one has to climb the ramp at Tê Sheng men a clear October morning. Looking towards the west one may observe from here the irregular windings of the wall, which is richly overgrown with shrubs and small trees. The road at the foot of it is well shaded by large ailanthus trees, and only a few steps further south some weeping willows wave their soft foliage over the waters of " Ch'i Shui tan," an extension of the " North Lake." Further away, beyond the open plain, the Western Hills form a luminous background to the wide view, particularly if their summits have been strewn with light snow during the night. The air is indescribably clear and crisp, the sky like an enormous transparent glass bell. One almost feels that it would emit a sound if struck with a magic hammer.

D. The West Wall

The north-west corner takes its special character from the fact that the two adjoining wall-stretches do not here meet at a right angle. We have already remarked that the North wall curves or slants in a south-westerly direction, consequently the corner becomes blunt. The West

THE INNER SIDE OF THE TARTAR CITY WALL 83

wall is actually 520 metres shorter than the East wall. The corner tower is destroyed; instead of the solid old brick building there is a small wooden structure erected for the purposes of the city survey. The wall between the corner and the first gate, Hsi Chih men, a stretch of less than 300 metres, consists of a series of short repairs, very unevenly joined together, many of them dating back to the Ming dynasty. Our short notes about the successive portions of the wall will convey some idea as to their age and general appearance, though it should be remembered that we are not aiming at a definition of every inch of the brickwork but simply at some observations on prominent parts and special features. The repairs are too many and sometimes too confused and intermixed to be examined in their completeness. As a rule, those made in the Ch'ien Lung era are the most carefully and solidly executed, but a lot of good work has also been performed during the reigns of Chia Ch'ing and Tao Kuang. Very little of the good Ming work from the time of Chia Ching and Wan Li which is so abundant on the North wall is to be found here, but some stretches of still earlier brickwork which are now much corroded and weather-beaten. Thus at places where it is not rebuilt the West wall gives an impression of being older than the North wall, it is also thinner and less battering, being in these respects like the East wall.

1. The bastion of the angle tower is mainly built of thin bricks, such as were used in the late Ming period. The ramps and the adjoining wall have been repaired in the Ch'ien Lung era with bricks marked: Kung Pu inspector Kuei and Kung Pu inspector Fu.

2, 3. Two short sections of early Ming work in a rather decayed state.

4. 54 m. The upper section repaired, according to the tablet, in the 2nd year of Chia Ch'ing (1797); the lower section contains bricks marked: Made at the Yung Ting government kiln.

5. 15 m. Probably Middle Ming period; no brick-marks.

6. 30 m. Somewhat earlier Ming work; no brick-marks.

7. 24 m. Middle or late Ming period; no brick-marks.
8. 18 m. Early Ming work; no brick-marks.
9. 22 m. Ming work which has been repaired at a later date.
10. 26 m. Same period and workmanship as 8.
11. 24 m. Same period and material as 9.
12. 11 m. Early Ming work; no brick-marks.
13. 20 m. Probably Middle Ming period; no marks.
14. The two ramps of the Hsi Chih men are built of thin bricks such as were used in the late Ming period. The wall behind them and the gate bastion of larger bricks, though also of the Ming period.
15. 38 m. Middle or late Ming period; no brick-marks.
16. 22 m. Probably middle of nineteenth century; medium-size bricks.
17. 15 m. Late eighteenth century; made of "fine clay city-wall bricks."
18. 15 m. Middle or late Ming period; no brick-marks.
19. 38 m. Upper section built of thin bricks (probably in the Ch'ung Chêng period); the lower section repaired with medium-size bricks.
20. 20 m. Early Ming work; no brick-marks.
21. 15 m. Somewhat later Ming work; no brick-marks.
22. 38 m. Repaired, according to the inserted tablet, in the 4th year of Ch'ien Lung (1739), though partly with Ming bricks, marked: 31st year of Chia Ching.
23. 24 m. Repaired, according to inscriptions on two tablets, in the 21st year of Tao Kuang (1841). The bricks are the large ones of the Ch'ien Lung type.
24. 8 m. Early nineteenth century; bricks marked: Made in the Chia Shên year (1824).
25. 26 m. Middle of the nineteenth century; bricks marked: "May T'ung Chih live 10,000 times 10,000 years" (1862–1874).
26. 20 m. Probably nineteenth century; medium-size bricks, no marks.
27, 28. 38 m. Two stretches of late Ming work; no brick-marks.
29. 22 m. Late Ming period; bricks marked: 19th year of Wan Li.
30. 15 m. Early Ming work; bricks marked: Made by the Kao T'ang chow kiln in the 19th year of Chêng Hua (1483).
31, 32. 26 m. Two stretches of Ming work, repaired at a later date.

THE INNER SIDE OF THE TARTAR CITY WALL 85

33. 30 m. Rebuilt with bricks from the Jui Shêng kiln; the inscription on the tablet is unreadable. Probably early nineteenth century.

34. 15 m. Middle Ming period; bricks marked: Made by the master-potter Liu Chao in the 16th year of Chia Ching (1537).

35. 7 m. Probably early nineteenth century; bricks marked: Yung Ho kiln maker of fine clay city-wall bricks.

36. 15 m. Repaired in the reign of Chia Ch'ing (1796–1820); bricks marked: Jui Shêng kiln, city-wall bricks, and also: Fine clay city-wall bricks from the Yung Ting government kiln.

37. 20 m. Same period and material as 36.

38. 22 m. Probably early nineteenth century; bricks from the Ho Shêng kiln.

39. 70 m. Repaired in the Ch'ien Lung era; the inscription on the tablet is unreadable; some bricks are marked: Made in the Hsin Ssu year (1761).

40. 11 m. Late Ming period; bricks marked: 32nd year of Wan Li.

41. 11 m. Probably late eighteenth or early nineteenth century; bricks marked: Large new pattern city-wall bricks of the Yüan Ch'üan kiln.

42. 38 m. Repaired in the time of Ch'ien Lung; bricks from the T'ung Ho kiln, and also: Fine clay large-size city-wall bricks of the Tê Shun kiln.

43. 38 m. Probably nineteenth century; medium-size bricks; no marks.

44. 38 m. Repaired, according to an inserted tablet, in the 2nd year of Ch'ien Lung (1737).

45. 22 m. Repaired, according to the inserted tablet, in the 41st year of Ch'ien Lung (1776). Bricks marked: Kung Pu inspector Sa.

46. The ramp is in fairly good condition; the wall above it more corroded; according to a tablet it was repaired in the 31st year of Ch'ien Lung (1766). Bricks are marked: Yü Chên kiln, controlled by the palace officials.

47. 22 m. Same period and material as No. 43.

48. 19 m. Late Ming period; bricks marked the 32nd year of Wan Li (1604).

49. 38 m. Repaired in the time of Ch'ien Lung; the tablet is unreadable. Bricks marked: Kung Pu inspector Sa.

50. 7 m. Late Ming period. Bricks marked: Made by the master-potter Chang Chiu Chih in the 32nd year of Wan Li.

51. 22 m. Middle Ming period; bricks marked: Made by the master-potter Chên Chü in the 16th year of Chia Ching, and also Made by the master-potter Kiang Tung in the 16th year of Chia Ching (1537).

52. 7 m. A short section repaired at various times.

53. 70 m. Late Ming period. The bricks are dated in the 30th, 31st and 32nd year of Wan Li. At the bottom are some later repairs.

54. 60 m. Middle Ming period; no brick-marks. At the bottom are three different stretches which must have been repaired in Ch'ien Lung's time.

55. 40 m. Upper portion rebuilt of thin Ming bricks; lower portion repaired with bricks of various kinds.

56, 57. 80 m. Two stretches of comparatively well-preserved Ming work. Large bricks with no marks.

58. 200 m. Late Ming work built of thin bricks, as used in the Ch'ung Chêng period.

59. 15 m. Repaired, according to a tablet, in the 20th year of Chia Ch'ing (1815).

60. 10 m. Repaired in the time of Ch'ien Lung: New style fine city-wall bricks from the T'ung Ho kiln; Kung Pu inspector Kuei.

61. 50 m. The stretch leading up to P'ing Tzu men has evidently been repaired in the time of Ch'ien Lung; there are bricks marked: Large city-wall bricks of the Kuang Shêng kiln. On the gate bastion are bricks marked: Fine clay city-wall bricks; Kung Pu inspector Kuei. Over the ramp on the southern side is a tablet of the 27th year of Ch'ien Lung (1762).

In spite of the fact that the northern half of the West wall is a continuous succession of repairs varying in date from the end of the fifteenth to the middle of the nineteenth century, it is still at many places quite complete, that is to say, not only the wall with its parapet, but also the adjoining sidewalk of lime-concrete and the small moat which is bridged

THE INNER SIDE OF THE TARTAR CITY WALL 87

over by large stone slabs. Old locust trees line this moat for some distance, while jujube and ailanthus shrubs of considerable size are growing out of the upper part of the wall, making the brickwork bulge and burst. This northern half of the West wall is, as a whole, of a somewhat older appearance than the corresponding half of the East wall, and it does not contain so many and such extensive Ch'ien Lung or later repairs.

Proceeding southward from P'ing Tzu men we soon observe that the walk along the wall becomes less agreeable; we are approaching more populous quarters of the city, which means more dirt, more foul-smelling places, more night-cleaners, more street-urchins, more beggars, more loafers, more pigs and dogs, to say nothing of a good many smaller animals. The relative quietness and decay of the northern city changes at P'ing Tzu men into the noisy traffic and scramble of a half-Europeanized commercial centre. The wall south of P'ing Tzu men seems to have been rebuilt at the end of the Ming dynasty.

63, 64, 65. 120 m. Three stretches, well joined, all built of the thin dark bricks which were pre-eminently used in the Ch'ung Chêng era (1628–1643). They have no marks.

66. 56 m. Possibly early Ch'ing period; medium-size bricks, no marks.

67. 19 m. Same period and material as 63–65.

68. 45 m. Same period and material as 66.

69. 22 m. Middle Ming period (probably Chia Ching); no brick-marks.

70. 15 m. Late Ming work; bricks marked: 32nd year of Wan Li.

71. 45 m. Middle Ming period; bricks marked: Made by the master-potter Lu in the 29th year of Chia Ching (1550), and also: Made in the 24th year of Chia Ching (1545).

72. 25 m. Similar to the preceding.

73, 74. 50 m. Two stretches of medium-size bricks; probably early Ching period; no marks. (Cf. No. 66.)

75. 20 m. Repaired, according to tablet, in the 30th year of Ch'ien Lung, though partly with old bricks marked: Made by the master-potter Sun Pao in the 30th year of Wan Li.

76. 38 m. Middle Ming period (probably Chia Ching); no brick-marks.

77. The first ramp south of P'ing Tzu men consists of Ming work in three different sections. The first contains bricks of the 29th year of Chia Ching (1550); the second section contains bricks of the 3rd year of Chêng Tê (1508); in the third (one of the earliest sections), there are bricks from the reign of Chêng Hua (1465–1487).

78. 80 m. Middle Ming period; bricks marked: Made by the master-potter Chang Ch'in in the 31st year of Chia Ching (1552).

79. 175 m. Late Ming period. Bricks marked with names of various potters in the 23rd, 29th, and 32nd years of Wan Li.

80. A long stretch (nearly 100 m.) repaired, according to the inserted tablet, in the 28th year of Ch'ien Lung (1763).

81. 40 m. Probably early Ch'ing dynasty; medium-size bricks; no marks.

82. 10 m. Late Ming period; bricks marked: 32nd and 33rd year of Wan Li.

83. 50 m. Middle Ming period; bricks marked with names of various potters in the 31st, 33rd, 36th, and 39th years of Chia Ching (1552–1560).

84. Short stretch of medium-size bricks; possibly early Ch'ing dynasty.

85. 60 m. Repaired, according to a tablet, in the 32nd year of Ch'ien Lung (1767). Bricks marked: Kung Pu inspector Yung.

86. A short stretch of Ming work made of bricks from the 24th and 27th years of Chia Ching (1545 and 1548).

87. A stretch repaired with bricks made in the Hsin Ssu year (1761) and the Jen Wu year (1762) of the Ch'ien Lung era.

88. The second ramp between P'ing Tzu men and the corner is mainly Ming work, though of different times. The northern end of it and the adjoining wall contain bricks from the 2nd year of Chêng Tê (1507) and from the 22nd and 23rd years of Chia Ching (1543–1544). The middle part and the south end of the ramp were largely rebuilt at the end of the Ming period, or a little later, with thin bricks.

89. 8 m. Late Ming period; bricks marked: 32nd year of Wan Li.

90. 15 m. Middle Ming period; no brick-marks.

THE INNER SIDE OF THE TARTAR CITY WALL

91. Repaired, according to a tablet, in the 30th year of Ch'ien Lung (1765); bricks marked in the Chia Wu year (1754), made at the Kung Shun kiln.

92. 22 m. Early Ming period; bricks marked the 19th year of Chêng Hua (1483).

93. Short stretch repaired at the end of the eighteenth or beginning of the nineteenth century; there are bricks marked: Large fine city-wall bricks; 2nd year of Chia Ch'ing (1797).

94. A long stretch (60–70 m.) of early Ming work; the bricks are much corroded and show no marks.

95. A stretch of the Middle Ming period; it contains bricks made by the potter Lin Yung Shou in the 32nd year of Chia Ching (1553); others made by the potter Ch'ang Ch'in in the 22nd year of Chia Ching (1543); others made by the potter Wang Jui at the Yung Nien hsien kiln in the 26th year of Chia Ching (1547).

96. Short stretch, probably late Ming period; no brick-marks.

97. Short stretch (10–12 m.). Middle Ming period; bricks of the 16th year of Chia Ching (1537).

98. Short stretch, repaired, according to a tablet, in the 19th year of Ch'ien Lung; bricks marked: Ping Shên year (1776).

99. Very short bit containing bricks of the 32nd year of Wan Li.

100. Short stretch, repaired in the early part of Ch'ien Lung's reign; bricks from the Hsing Tai kiln.

101. Short stretch of the Middle Ming period containing bricks of the 26th year of Chia Ching.

102. The northern side of the south-west corner seems to have been repaired in Ch'ien Lung's time, though largely with old bricks, some of which have inscriptions of the 26th and 32nd years of Chia Ching. The use of earlier bricks in later repairs has, no doubt, been practised at many places; the brick-marks do not always indicate the exact date of the work, but they furnish generally a safe terminus *a quo*.

The southern part of the West wall is more unified and homogeneous than the northern part. It makes a rather fine impression as it rises very high and steep from the open and level ground. The surface is relatively smooth; it cannot be climbed in the same way as the North wall. The corner-tower is still mainly preserved with the exception of the old glazed tile roof, which is largely replaced by corrugated iron! This makes the

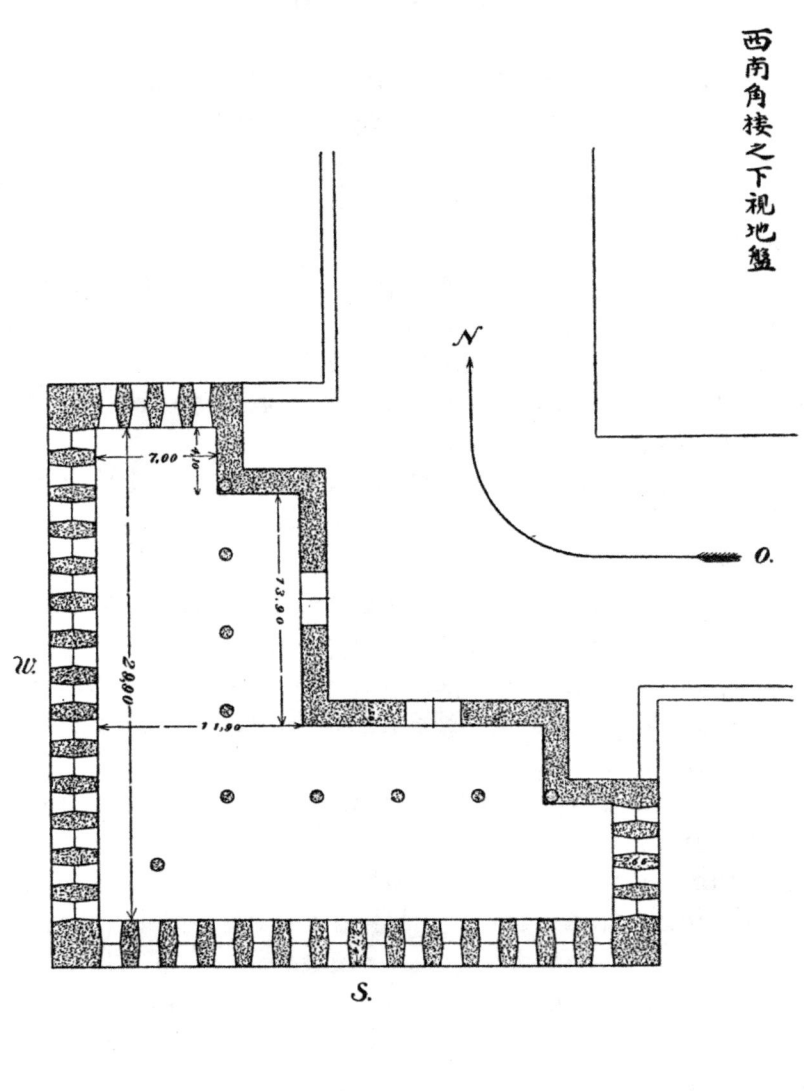

Fig. 5.—Plan of the south-west corner-tower.

front view of the broad fortress-like tower quite flat and dull, but from the side, where the four successive divisions of the building appear in a sort of rising scale, the view is decidedly interesting. These corner-towers, of which to-day only the two on the South wall remain, are built in the same style as the outer towers of the main gates, though with two long façades over the corner bastions. On the inner side the building descends step-wise by means of smaller divisions, thus growing gradually out of the wall.

The western quarter of the city, close to the south corner, is a very quiet and solitary neighbourhood. It is dominated by the large compound of one of the old Manchu princes' palaces, the so-called " Lao Chi Yeh fu," which in later years has been practically abandoned. The famous old lake outside the palace walls, known as Kung Pin hu, is now more like a big pond than a lake, but there is still room for a few fat ducks, and its banks are shaded by magnificent old willows. The city seems to be far away from this spot, where nobody lives and nobody moves, and the air is filled with solitude and dreams of decaying grandeur.

V

NOTES ABOUT THE OUTER SIDE OF THE TARTAR CITY WALL

THE outer face of the Peking city wall has, on the whole, a more unified and even appearance than the inner face. Being the more important for the defence of the city (which, after all, is the main purpose of such a structure), it has been kept in good repair by successive generations of emperors and officials. It is only during the last two decades that some portions of this outer face have been allowed to fall into decay, particularly on the west side where one may observe large holes caused by the gradual flaking off of the brick coating. Yet even at these spots the destruction is not as bad as at the worst places on the inner face, and one of the main reasons for this is, no doubt, the fact that the rain-water always was drained over the inner and not over the outer face of the wall. As, furthermore, the battering of the outer side is considerably less than that of the inner side, the growth of shrubs and trees has not been so abundant here as we found it at many spots on the inside of the South and the East wall.

It must be admitted that the outer wall-face is inferior to the inner in picturesqueness and historical significance, but it is more impressive and interesting as an architectural monument. It rises higher and more steeply, and the ground below is not filled out, as so often is the case on the inner side; but it slopes more or less towards the moat, which, indeed, adds to the monumental effect of the towering wall. Unfortunately, the

THE OUTER SIDE OF THE TARTAR CITY WALL 93

view is often badly impaired by all sorts of dingy buildings, coal sheds, store-houses, and workshops which crowd the space between the wall and the moat, following the railway line, particularly on the east and south sides.

Of the greatest importance for the architectural effect are the square bastions or buttresses which project from the wall at fairly regular intervals. They endow the view of the wall—from wherever it may be taken—with a very powerful and solemn measure. This is always very effective, but particularly so when the wall is seen in perspective from some of the gate-towers, the space between the bastions gradually decreasing in a sort of vanishing accelerando, until nothing else is distinguishable of the whole structure but the towers and the gates. In olden days there used to be pavilions and small store houses for arms and ammunition on the bastions, but these are now all destroyed and there are only a few scattered brick huts on the wall for the benefit of the guards. Even the crenellated battlement is destroyed along certain stretches, which makes the wall appear quite incomplete, not to say, headless.

Something has already been said in a previous chapter about the dimensions of the bastions and their arrangement. They are built on an almost square plan of approximately the same width as the wall. But besides these ordinary bastions there are a few larger ones not only at the corners and the gates but also in front of the ramps which facilitate the ascent of the wall on the inside. It was evidently found necessary to arrange broader terraces at the top of these ramps, which could be used not only for men on foot and on horseback, but also for carriages to draw up guns and ammunition. The South wall has six of these ramps and six larger bastions, the East wall four, but on the west and the north side there are only three. It is also worth noticing that these larger bastions are not all quite alike, or of uniform dimensions; in particular, those on the north side are different from the rest, the whole North wall being a later construction.

Our notes about the outer wall-face will be presented in a still shorter form than those referring to the inner side. It is possible to indicate where there may be a tablet or some other mark simply by numbering the bastions either between the gates or from corner to corner. The positions of the quite numerous inscribed tablets will thus be given simply in reference to the bastions or to the intervening spaces on which they are sometimes placed. Unfortunately none of these tablets is earlier than the Chi'en Lung era and only two or three are later, i.e. from Chia Ch'ing's reign. Other repairs will be mentioned according to the character of the brickwork, but we will not stop to read many of the brick-marks. Long stretches of the outer wall-face are, as a matter of fact, inaccessible, because of the buildings in front of them, but even so it is mostly possible to recognize the period of the brickwork at a distance, as soon as we have become familiar with the characteristics of the various dynasties and of the principal styles of workmanship.

A. The East Wall

Starting from the south-east corner we encounter first one of the oldest stretches of the outer wall-face. The six first bastions of the East wall, including the one which answers to the Observatory ramp, show much corroded brickwork which may well be from the end of the fifteenth century. Only the north side of the first bastion has been repaired in modern times. It should be remembered that the inner face of this same portion of the wall also has an early appearance and contains no Ch'ing dynasty repairs. The Ch'ien Lung repairs begin immediately after we have passed the sixth bastion; in the interspace between this and the seventh bastion there is a stone tablet with no inscription, though of the usual Ch'ien Lung type. The seventh bastion is repaired, but has no tablet. The following interspace was repaired, according to the tablet, in the 33rd year of Ch'ien Lung.

THE OUTER SIDE OF THE TARTAR CITY WALL 95

The eighth bastion was rebuilt, according to the tablet, in the 46th year of Ch'ien Lung.

The ninth bastion is renewed; the inscription on the tablet illegible; the adjoining interspace ditto.

The tenth bastion repaired in the 36th year of Ch'ien Lung; the adjoining interspace ditto.

The eleventh bastion is partly old and partly renewed in connection with the adjoining interspace which, according to the inserted tablet, was repaired in the 31st year of Ch'ien Lung.

The twelfth bastion repaired in the 36th year of Ch'ien Lung, and the adjoining interspace ditto.

The thirteenth bastion repaired in the 36th year of Ch'ien Lung.

The fourteenth bastion repaired in the 31st (?) year of Ch'ien Lung; the adjoining interspace repaired in the 36th year of Ch'ien Lung.

The fifteenth bastion repaired in the 36th year of Ch'ien Lung; the adjoining interspace repaired in the same year.

The sixteenth bastion was repaired in the 36th year of Ch'ien Lung; the adjoining interspace ditto.

The seventeenth bastion and the adjoining interspace are also renewed, though not marked by any tablet.

The eighteenth bastion repaired in the 31st year of Ch'ien Lung; the adjoining interspace is marked by a tablet of the same year.

The nineteenth bastion repaired in the 36th year of Ch'ien Lung; the adjoining interspace probably in the 37th year of Ch'ien Lung. (The tablet is almost illegible.)

The twentieth bastion repaired in the 37th (?) year of Ch'ien Lung; the adjoining interspace marked by a similar tablet.

The twenty-first bastion is renewed, though not marked by any tablet; the interspace ditto.

The twenty-second bastion also renewed, though without any tablet.

The twenty-third bastion was destroyed when the small railway station of Ch'i Hua men was built. The wall at the interspace was renewed in the 31st year of Ch'ien Lung, according to the tablet on the corner of the Ch'i Hua gate bastion.

The first bastion north of the Ch'i Hua men has also been destroyed.

The second bastion repaired in the 18th year of Ch'ien Lung; the adjoining interspace is old, much corroded and overgrown with trees.

The third bastion repaired in the 18th year of Ch'ien Lung; of the adjoining interspace only the one half is renewed, the other half old.

The fourth bastion repaired in the 36th year of Ch'ien Lung; the adjoining interspace is older but a great deal patched.

The fifth bastion is repaired, though without any tablet; the adjoining interspace was partly repaired, according to the inserted tablet, in the 36th year of Ch'ien Lung.

The sixth bastion is old; the brickwork is a great deal patched; the adjoining interspace is of a similar character.

The seventh bastion is old, and so are the eighth and the ninth bastions together with their interspaces.

The tenth bastion repaired in the 32nd year of Ch'ien Lung; the interspace is old, except for its northernmost end which was repaired in connection with the eleventh bastion in the 32nd year of Ch'ien Lung; the adjoining interspace also repaired.

The twelfth bastion repaired in the 28th year of Ch'ien Lung; the adjoining interspace was repaired in the 31st year of Ch'ien Lung.

The thirteenth bastion is old and fairly well preserved; the adjoining interspace was repaired in the 36th year of Ch'ien Lung.

The fourteenth bastion is repaired only on its south side in the 49th year of Ch'ien Lung; the adjoining interspace repaired in the 36th year of Ch'ien Lung.

The fifteenth bastion is renewed, though not marked by any tablet; the adjoining interspace repaired in the 31st year of Ch'ien Lung.

The sixteenth bastion repaired in the 31st year of Ch'ien Lung; the adjoining interspace is also renewed.

The seventeenth bastion is renewed, though not marked by any tablet; the adjoining interspace is partly repaired in the 28th year of Ch'ien Lung. It leads up to Tung Chih men. The tablet at the gate has no characters. The wall on the north side of the gate was repaired in the 32nd year of Ch'ien Lung.

The first bastion north of Tung Chih men was repaired in the 31st year of Ch'ien Lung; the interspace in the 36th year of Ch'ien Lung.

THE OUTER SIDE OF THE TARTAR CITY WALL

The second bastion repaired in the 30th year of Ch'ien Lung; the adjoining interspace in the 31st year of Ch'ien Lung.

The third bastion is renewed, but the tablet is illegible; the adjoining interspace is of somewhat earlier date.

The fourth bastion repaired in the 30th year of Ch'ien Lung.

The fifth bastion repaired in the 31st year of Ch'ien Lung; the adjoining interspace also in the 31st year of Ch'ien Lung.

The sixth bastion is old, though well preserved; the adjoining interspace repaired in the 51st year of Ch'ien Lung.

The seventh bastion has been destroyed by the Round-the-City Railway which here pierces the wall; the adjoining interspace was repaired in the 31st year of Ch'ien Lung.

The large bastion at the north-east corner is very carefully built of thin dark bricks such as were mostly in use towards the end of the Ming dynasty.

The above observations have no doubt served to make it clear that very small portions of the East wall are earlier than the Ch'ien Lung era; the major part of this wall-face as it stands to-day dates from the 30th to 36th year of Ch'ien Lung (1765–1771). The work performed at that time was of an excellent quality and will probably last longer than any later repairs. The dating of the various bastions and intervening spaces could be corroborated by some brick-marks, but it seems to us hardly necessary to devote more space to the quoting of such exceedingly dry records when they do not contain any important new items for the history of the wall or for the dating of its various portions.

The walk along the East wall is quite pleasant and easy, if one follows the railway bank, which runs between the wall and the moat, but closer to the wall it is obstructed by a dense growth of young locust and acacia trees which have been recently planted. At the southern half of it, between the Observatory bastion and the Ch'i Hua men, some of the old imperial storehouses for grain and rice still remain—simple, low buildings constructed almost between the bastions—but the majority of these historical " tai-ping tsang " have been replaced by less simple and less inoffensive magazines and barracks. The further one moves northward, the broader and more beautiful becomes the canal-like moat. Between Ch'i Hua men and Tung Chih men it is lined with weeping willows and animated by big flocks of white ducks. Sometimes large ferries in the shape of square flat barges with sunshades on four poles are punted slowly along the dark waters of the canal, but the traffic is now quite insignificant in comparison with what it used to be less than a generation ago when most of the grain and other provisions were brought to Peking by the canal transports from the north and the east. Still, this is one of the most picturesque bits of scenery adjoining the city wall, as may be observed on our plates from the neighbourhood of Tung Chih men.

B. The North Wall

This wall has fewer bastions than the three other walls, but they are of larger size. The distance between them varies from about 200 to 350 metres, while the average distance between the bastions of the other walls hardly exceeds 90 metres, and sometimes they are as short as 65 or 70 metres. Closest to the north-east corner, where we are starting, the distance between the bastions are shortest and the wall has its most regular appearance.

The wall between the corner and the first bastion was partly repaired in the 56th year of Ch'ien Lung, and so in part was the first bastion. The second, third, fourth, and fifth bastions and the intervening spaces are evidently of the Middle Ming period. The brickwork is much corroded and the wall-face is in spots well grown with trees and shrubs. The only portion that has been renewed here is the parapet.

The sixth bastion was repaired in the 47th year of Ch'ien Lung; the adjoining interspace is older.

The seventh bastion is old, i.e. of the Ming dynasty; the adjoining

THE OUTER SIDE OF THE TARTAR CITY WALL

interspace which leads up to An Ting men was repaired in the 28th year of Ch'ien Lung.

The eighth bastion and the wall leading up to it (west of An Ting men) are old, of the Middle Ming period, and a great deal corroded.

The interspace between the eighth and the ninth bastions is repaired in two portions, marked by two tablets, the one of the 42nd and the other of the 51st year of Ch'ien Lung.

The ninth bastion was repaired in the 51st year of Ch'ien Lung. The tenth, eleventh, and twelfth bastions together with the wall spaces between them are mainly old, though patched here and there with later work. The interspace between the twelfth and the thirteenth bastions was renewed in three different portions all from the 51st year of Ch'ien Lung, as confirmed by three tablets bearing the same date.

The thirteenth bastion was renewed in the 47th year of Ch'ien Lung. The wall between this bastion and the Tê Sheng men is badly corroded, evidently not later than the Middle Ming period, and so is the gate bastion, except for its corners which have been renewed.

The wall west of Tê Sheng men was repaired in the 37th year of Ch'ien Lung.

The fourteenth bastion is partly renewed and marked with a tablet which is illegible. The adjoining interspace is repaired in three portions; two of them marked by tablets of the 52nd year of Ch'ien Lung; the third tablet is illegible.

The fifteenth bastion has evidently been repaired at some earlier time than the Ch'ien Lung era; the adjoining interspace, which forms a long curve, was repaired in the 51st year of Ch'ien Lung.

The sixteenth bastion and the adjoining interspace are old.

The seventeenth bastion was repaired at both its sides in the 48th year of Ch'ien Lung. The curving interspace which follows this bastion is also renewed and marked by a tablet with no date.

The eighteenth bastion and the adjoining wall were renewed, according to three tablets, in the 47th, 51st, and 56th years of Ch'ien Lung.

The nineteenth bastion is old, but the adjoining wall which leads up to the corner was repaired in the 56th year of Ch'ien Lung.

The corner bastion is constructed with particular care of thin Ming dynasty bricks.

The outer face of the North wall is, broadly speaking, the most impressive and monumental of all the walls. It is all through of larger dimensions than the other three, its bastions are broader, its battlements are higher and the body of the wall itself is mightier. The brickwork is also to a large extent quite old in character, darkened by dust-storms, corroded by age, and in places grown over with trees and shrubs.

Close to the wall are planted some young trees, and a railway track runs inside the moat, but the trains are not very frequent and the traffic, as a whole, is very slight, except at the two gates where small suburbs with rows of shops cluster at the sides of the main roads. The country is bleak and drab, an open sandy plain with few houses and little vegetation to bind the dust, which rises in clouds as soon as the wind awakens. Yet this land, to an extent of 5 li northward from the wall, once formed part of the great Mongol capital, Khanbalic.

C. The West Wall

We continue our walk from the north-west corner southward. Though this wall is shorter than any of the other three, it has nevertheless forty-four bastions, most of which were rebuilt in the later part of the Ch'ien Lung period. The wall between the corner and the first bastion is repaired and marked by a tablet which, however, has no inscription.

The first bastion is old, i.e. of the Middle Ming period, the adjoining interspace repaired in the 50th year of Ch'ien Lung.

The second bastion is old and also the adjoining interspace, except for the portion closest to Hsi Chih men, which was repaired in 1895.

The third bastion is old, evidently of the Ming period.

The fourth bastion is repaired in the 47th year of Ch'ien Lung; the adjoining interspace probably of the same date.

The fifth bastion is repaired and provided with a tablet which is illegible. The adjoining interspace is repaired in the 47th year of Ch'ien Lung.

THE OUTER SIDE OF THE TARTAR CITY WALL

The sixth bastion and the adjoining interspace are repaired and marked with a tablet which has no inscription.

The seventh bastion is quite old and corroded. The adjoining interspace is repaired in two sections and marked by a tablet without inscription.

The eighth bastion was repaired in the 46th year of Ch'ien Lung. The adjoining interspace is old and decaying; bits of the parapet have fallen down.

The ninth bastion repaired in the 52nd year of Ch'ien Lung; the adjoining interspace partly repaired.

The tenth bastion is renewed in the upper part, but the lower portion is old; the adjoining interspace is a great deal patched and badly preserved.

The eleventh bastion is renewed on both its sides (but not in the middle portion) in the 47th year of Ch'ien Lung.

The twelfth bastion is old and in a poor state of preservation.

The thirteenth bastion was repaired in parts in the 29th year of Ch'ien Lung. The adjoining interspace likewise.

The fourteenth bastion has been repaired in different sections; one of them is marked by a tablet of the 47th year of Ch'ien Lung.

The fifteenth bastion is mainly renewed in the 52nd year of Ch'ien Lung; the adjoining interspace has some older repairs.

The sixteenth bastion is repaired on the northern side, but has no tablet; the adjoining interspace is badly preserved and has no parapet.

The seventeenth bastion is partly repaired, but its battlements are broken; the adjoining interspace is mainly renewed and marked by a tablet which is illegible.

The P'ing Tzu men bastion is old. The wall on its southern side was renewed in the 52nd year of Ch'ien Lung.

The first, second, and third bastions south of P'ing Tzu men together with their interspaces are old, of the Middle Ming period.

The fourth bastion is renewed, probably in the Kuang Hsü period, though not marked by any tablet. The adjoining interspace was repaired in the 52nd year of Ch'ien Lung.

The fifth bastion is repaired on both sides; the northern side is marked by a tablet with no inscription. Half of the adjoining interspace repaired in the 4th year of Chia Ch'ing; the other half is old.

The sixth and seventh bastions are of the Ming dynasty. The

interspace between the seventh and eighth bastions is partly renewed in the 39th year of Ch'ien Lung.

The eighth bastion, which is of large size and built of thin Ming dynasty bricks, is now in bad repair. The adjoining interspace repaired in the 46th year of Ch'ien Lung.

The ninth bastion is mainly old, but its north corner was repaired in the 46th year of Ch'ien Lung.

The tenth bastion is old, but the adjoining interspace was repaired in the 37th year of Ch'ien Lung.

The eleventh bastion is partly renewed, but has no tablet.

The twelfth bastion is partly renewed and marked by a tablet with an illegible inscription.

The thirteenth, fourteenth, and fifteenth bastions and their adjoining interspaces are old. In the last interspace some large bits of brickwork have slipped out. The next interspace, between the fifteenth and sixteenth bastions, was repaired in the 2nd year of Chia Ch'ing.

The sixteenth bastion is old; the adjoining interspace is repaired in two parts marked by tablets of the 51st year of Ch'ien Lung and the 2nd year of Chia Ch'ing.

The seventeenth bastion was repaired in the 47th year of Ch'ien Lung. The adjoining interspace is in a very bad state of preservation; large bits of the outer brick coating have fallen out.

The eighteenth bastion is mainly old and not in very good repair, the battlements being broken; it has been renewed on the north side where a tablet without inscription is inserted.

The following four bastions, Nos. 19–22, are old, probably of the Middle Ming period, only with minor repairs.

The twenty-third bastion was repaired in the 36th year of Ch'ien Lung; the adjoining interspace mainly old.

The twenty-fourth bastion is old. Close to this is a somewhat larger bastion supporting a square tower marking the joint between the Chinese city wall and the main wall. This bastion was repaired, according to the inserted tablet, in the 49th year of Ch'ien Lung.

The general distribution of the repairs is very much the same on the

THE OUTER SIDE OF THE TARTAR CITY WALL

West as on the East wall. The most southern section, including six bastions, is the oldest and least modified portion (exactly as it is on the East wall). It seems to have been constructed more solidly than the more northern stretches, possibly because it was made entirely anew in the fifteenth century, while the rest of these walls were built on the Mongol ramparts. The eighteenth-century repairs are not quite as frequent on the West wall as on the East, yet numerous enough to make up most of the actual wall space, and are generally a little later in date, i.e. of the 47th and 52nd years of Ch'ien Lung and even of the 2nd year of Chia Ch'ing. In places where these most careful repairs have not been executed, the brick coating is in a worse condition than anywhere else on the four sides of the Tartar city wall; it has flaked off in large bits and will, no doubt, continue to do so, if nothing is done to stop it.

D. The South Wall

The outer face of the South wall shows practically the same architectural arrangement and dimensions as we have seen on the East and the West wall, only it has been less frequently repaired owing to the fact that it is the most protected of all the walls. It does not form an outer rampart of the capital, but an inter-urban boundary between the Chinese and the Tartar city, and furthermore it should be remembered that the southern face of any building or city in Northern China is always less exposed to the ravages of rains and storms than any other side. Consequently it is not to be wondered at that the South wall contains more of the old Ming work on its outer face than the other walls. The Ch'ien Lung repairs are quite short in comparison with the earlier stretches; there are only four dated tablets of the eighteenth century and hardly more than two or three later repairs of any consequence.

All the thirteen bastions from the south-west corner to Shun Chih men seem to be old; there are no tablets marking later repairs.

Between the fourth and the fifth bastions, at the top of the wall, may be seen a small marble relief representing a lotus flower standing on a pedestal and overshadowed by a kind of cloud pattern. Four more similar reliefs with slightly varying patterns are to be seen on the same wall further east, but they may originally have been eight, forming a full set of the " eight jewels " or glorious emblems which are often used as symbolic ornaments in Buddhist temples and decorative paraphernalia designed for Buddhistic or Lamaistic use.* They may have been introduced on the city wall as a kind of symbolic dedication to protecting divine powers, probably in connection with the strong revival of Lamaism in the Ch'ien Lung era.

Between Shun Chih men and Ch'ien men there are nineteen bastions, mainly of the Ming period. The interspace between the ninth and the tenth bastions is repaired, according to an inserted tablet, in the 4th year of Chia Ch'ing. A closer examination of the wall at this stretch is, however, practically impossible because the space in front of it is crowded with large coal sheds and similar obstructions. Closest to Ch'ien men are the extensive station buildings of the Pekin-Hankow line. On the other side of Ch'ien men is the still larger station of the Peking-Mukden line, occupying practically the whole space between the great middle gate and the Water gate. On the east side of this new opening in the wall is a tablet, according to which the wall here was repaired in the 51st year of Ch'ien Lung. Fifteen bastions may still be counted between Ch'ien men and Hata men; one (west of the Water gate) has been demolished and others are more or less repaired, but the majority are mainly old.

East of Hata men the walk along the wall becomes easier and more pleasant; here are no buildings between the railway bank and the wall, only a thick growth of young trees. The first bastion is quite new,

* This explanation of the reliefs and suggestion as to their original number were kindly offered us by Baron Stael van Holstein in Peking.

THE OUTER SIDE OF THE TARTAR CITY WALL

evidently of the Kuang Hsü period; the adjoining interspace is old and much corroded.

From the second to the ninth bastion the wall shows many minor repairs; for instance, at the corners of the bastions and in the battlement, which is completely renewed; but the main part of it is of the Ming period.

The tenth bastion was repaired, according to an inserted tablet, in the 46th year of Ch'ien Lung.

The eleventh bastion, at the Tung Pien men station, is also largely renewed. The last bastion was destroyed when making the opening for the Round-the-City Railway. Passing through the railway opening one sees on the inside of the wall a tablet, according to which this corner section was repaired in the 34th year of Ch'ien Lung.

It is more difficult to form a correct idea about the brickwork on the outer face of the South wall than on the other walls, because the ground in front of it is so extensively built over. There are the stations, magazines, and workshops of the main railways, and also, to the west of Chi'en men, the greatest coal market of Peking. It need hardly be added that establishments of this kind by no means harmonize with the old wall; they mark the intrusion of a new age for which the wall is more of an obstruction than a protection.

On the whole it must be admitted that the railways with their various accessory buildings have done more to destroy the character and beauty of the Peking walls and gates than any amount of neglect, or carelessness in the upkeep, of these precious monuments.

VI

THE WALL OF THE CHINESE CITY

THE great capital of China does not consist simply of the Manchu or Tartar city, the walls of which were described in two previous chapters; it also includes an " Outer " or " Chinese " city, which adjoins the main city on the southern side. The name commonly used for this part of the capital reminds us of the fact that the conquering Manchus drove most of the native population from the main city into the suburbs, particularly the southern suburb, which already at that time was surrounded by walls. Among the Chinese this part of the city is known as " Wai ch'eng " (the Outer wall or city) or " Mao-tzŭ ch'eng " (the Cap city or wall), because of its situation and its shape, which is suggestive of a cap on the main city.

Taken as a whole, this outer part of the capital may be described as a combination of thronged bazaars, rustic fields and vast temple enclosures. It is only the northern half of it which gives the impression of a city; the quarters situated between the three main streets—running straight south from the three south gates of the Tartar city—are thronged with an extremely busy population, and resound with the hubbub of a modern commercial centre.

But one only needs to proceed a little further south, between the enclosures of the Temple of Heaven and the Temple of Agriculture, or still better, towards one of the side walls, in order to pass from the busy commercial city into a country village where the quiet air is seldom

THE WALL OF THE CHINESE CITY

disturbed by any noisy traffic. The further one moves towards the south-west or south-east, the fewer become the houses, and the larger the open fields. Hardly more than a third part of the Chinese city is built over with houses, and many of them are of a very inconspicuous kind. One wonders why the South wall has been placed so far off? The only reasonable explanation seems to be that it was found necessary to design it to include the sacred precincts of the Temple of Heaven and the Temple of Agriculture. The situation of the side walls is explained by the fact that they were intended to be continued all along the eastern and western sides of the main city, so as to enclose the lateral suburbs in the same way as the outer city on the south. But as this project was never accomplished, the side walls of the outer city were simply joined with the side walls of the main city just above the south-east and south-west corners, around which they form right-angled bends. How this great project of surrounding the whole city with outer walls was first conceived and put into execution by imperial command and then finally abandoned for lack of means may be read in the *Shun T'ien fu chih*, the county chronicle which we have quoted quite extensively in reference to the Tartar city wall. This account is worth quoting here as the most complete record of the building of the outer wall, even if it is by no means exact in reference to measurements and data.

After the description of the walls and gates of the Tartar city, the chronicle is continued with the following statement:—

"The censor Mao Po Wên and others reported that the city needed outer walls. They were ordered to be added in the 29th year of Chia Ching (1550) round the suburbs outside the three south gates, but the work was stopped before completion."

This short notice is further expanded in a subsequent paragraph: "In the 32nd year of Chia Ching (1553) Chu Po Chen, Secretary of the Inner Council, reported that it was not right that such numbers of people should be living outside the city without any protection; all the four suburbs had been explored, and for more than 120 li of the whole district (?) there were earth walls and ruins. These would only require some repairs and additions and thus save half of the work necessary. Orders were given for a survey and for the work to begin. In the intercalary month Nieh Pao, President of the Board of War, and others memorialized the throne, saying that all the suburbs had been surveyed and an outer wall of more than 70 li ought to be built from the opening of the Great East Road outside the Chêng Yang men, passing to the south wall of the Temple of Heaven and the private gardens of Li Hsing Wang, Chin Pu and others, to the east wall of the Yin Shui An, that is, about 9 li, and then running northward, passing the Shên Mu ch'ang (Shên's timber yard), Chang Lu fang and Hsiao Kao k'ou. From here it should continue, striking at a right angle the foundations of the old earth-wall and the ruins of the Kuang Hsi men, making a length of about 18 li (on the east side). From here it should run westward to the Hsiao Hsi men, the little west gate of the old earth-wall, measuring about 19 li (on the north side). From Hsiao Hsi men southward, passing San Hu ch'iao (Three Tiger bridge) and east of the village Ma Ch'iao miao to join the foundations of the old earth-wall. Thence south on the west side to Chang Yi men and to a point exactly opposite the north wall of Hsin Pao for about 15 li; thence south-west of the old earth-walls turning east from Hsin Pao and Hei Yao ch'ang, passing the south wall of the Shen Chih t'an (Spirits' altar, now known as the Temple of Agriculture) to the opening of the Great West Road, about 9 li, making altogether on the south 18 li and on the west 17 li, with a total length of more than 70 li. Within these limits might be traced for about 22 li the ruins of the old walls; the parts where there were no remains and entirely new walls would have to be erected amounted to about 48 li. The foundations of the new wall ought to be 20 feet wide, the width at the top 12 feet, and its height 18 feet. The wall was to be of

THE WALL OF THE CHINESE CITY

brick; the parapet five feet, making the total height 23 feet. The earth for the wall was taken from outside in order to make a moat."

According to the above statement, the outer wall was originally planned on a very large scale. If the measurements given are correct, the south wall was to extend nearly 3 li further both towards the east and the west than the present south wall (which is only about 13 li), and the western side wall would have coincided with the old rampart of the Chin capital. The northern wall was to follow the rampart of Khanbalic, but the north-west corner was cut off at an obtuse angle. The distance between the outer wall and the main city-wall would thus have been on the north and the south about 5 li, and on the west and the east about 4 li, though it may well be that the wall would have shown considerable irregularities, caused by existing older ramparts which were to be used as foundations. It is difficult to draw up the exact course of this projected wall as some of the places indicated no longer exist and also because of the somewhat elastic capacity of the Chinese li-measure. But it is quite evident that the plan was a very bold one; if it had been carried out completely, the Chinese capital would actually have consisted of three concentric cities, forming, so to say, successive shells around the imperial palace-city. No wonder that this project proved to be too big and costly for the imperial treasury. How it was curtailed is related in the following passage from *Shun T'ien fu chih*:

" In the year under the sign of Yi Ch'ou (1565) Duke Chu Hsi Chung was ordered to start work on the outer wall of the city, and the project was duly notified at the Great Temple. But in the fourth month the Emperor (Chia Ching) feared that the expenses would be too heavy and the work not easy. He consulted the officials, who enquired into the matter and recommended that the south wall should be first built and the others added, if funds, labour, and time sufficed. The south wall was accordingly built. The Throne was again memorialized and a report was made that the original estimate was to have been for all four walls, 20 li long, but now that the south wall was only 12 or 13 li, the whole work could be completed without too great cost either in money or labour. The foundation of the south wall had been laid where it turned north-east and west to join the actual city-wall at the south-east and south-west corners. Only the imperial sanction was needed to have the other three walls finished by an appointed day. The outer wall surrounds the city only on the south and stops where it rounds the towers at the east and west corners of the old city-walls. It is 28 li long with seven gates."

We notice that in this last paragraph the measurements of the outer walls are different from those in the previous quotation; there they were said to be 18–19 li long, and now the four walls are said to have been planned to be each 20 li long, which would have made the whole circumference 80 li instead of 73 or 74. These longer measurements answer more closely to the position of the walls indicated in our preceding comments (i.e. if the li is taken as being equal to 640 metres).

It also appears that at this time, namely, at the end of Chia Ching's reign, the south wall was constructed to its present length, about 13 li, and some side walls were built on the east and west straight northward from the ends of the wall—which all goes to prove that the original larger project had been already considerably reduced, a reduction which now (1565) was radically completed by simply joining the ends of the outer side walls with the main walls by means of short stretches running at right angles with these. This connecting stretch is just under one li in length on the west side and about a li and a half on the east side. Thus the outer city-wall took the shape of a kind of square cap on the main city, as emphasized in the Chinese name " Mao-tzŭ ch'eng." Its full length is at present a little more than 27 li, or approximately the same as indicated in the above quotation.

The height and the width of the wall are said to be: " 20 feet high

THE WALL OF THE CHINESE CITY   III

throughout, with a parapet 4 feet high; 20 feet through at the bottom and 14 feet wide at the top."

None of these measurements is quite correct; for one thing it is quite evident that the height and the width at the bottom could never have been equal; as a matter of fact the latter measures in many places nearly twice the height. It is, of course, true of the Chinese city-wall as well of the main wall that the actual height is by no means equal at all parts, nor is the width the same at every point along the three sides, though it varies less than the height. Three or four sample measurements may suffice to give an approximate idea of the dimensions of the wall:

The northern stretch, close to the north-east corner: Height, on the outside, 7·15 metres (about 26 Chinese feet), on the inside, 5·80 metres (20 Chinese feet). Width, at the top, 10·40 metres (36 Chinese feet); at the bottom, 13·30 metres (47 feet). On the outer side the parapet is 1·72 metres and on the inner side 1 metre high. The East wall, close to the south-east corner: Height, on the outer side, 5·80 metres (20 feet); on the inner side, ditto. Width, at the top, 10·30 metres, and at the bottom, 12·40 metres. The dimensions of the parapet are practically the same all through.

The South wall, near the east corner: Height, on the outside, 5·80 metres; on the inside, 5·05 metres. Width, at the top, 9·82 metres, at the bottom, 12·20 metres.

The South wall, near the middle gate (Yung Ting men): Height, on the outside, 6·18 metres, on the inner side, 5·62 metres. Width, at the top, 9·90 metres; at the bottom, 11·80 metres.

The West wall has practically the same dimensions as the East wall.

The height measurements are taken only to the rim of the plinth, which on the north side is mostly visible, but on the other sides partly or completely covered up with sand. They are thus not much influenced by the variations in the level of the ground below. The average height of the wall on the east, west, and south approximates 20 Chinese feet, the measurement indicated in the *Shun T'ien fu chih*, but the short northern stretches are considerably higher.

The width at the base varies between 41 and 47 Chinese feet, and at the top between 34 and 36 Chinese feet. The measurements of the width in the Chinese chronicle (20 and 14 feet) are hard to explain, if they are not misprints.

The total number of the merlons of the battlement on the outer wall is given as 20,772, and that of the " loopholes " or notches as 12,602, which may be approximately correct, although we can take no responsibility for these numbers, as we have not checked them.

The wall is said to have been completed in the 6th month of the 43rd year of Wan Li (1615), but the outside moat, which had yielded the mud for the walls, still remained to be properly built. It was accomplished within the next five years; to quote the chronicle: " In the tenth month of the first year of T'ien Ch'i (1621) Wei Ta Chung reported that the work of deepening the moat was completed. In the 2nd month of the year under the sign of Chi Mao (1639) T'sao Hua Shun proposed irrigation channels outside the city, and they were finished by the 6th month of the year Hsin Ssu. The channels ran from Kuang Chü men of the old earth-wall (in the north) to the Ta Tung ch'iao and the north bank of the Grand Canal. . . . The chief engineer, Yu Yao, was allowed to employ more than 23,000 soldiers on the work, and 20,900 coolies from five cities and two counties. A petition was sent up representing the work as too extravagant of money and labour and offering too little benefit and as harmful to the subsoil, but it was disallowed." Even so, it is doubtful whether this large irrigation project was ever properly carried out; there are not many visible traces of it to-day, except for some ditches connected with the Tung Ho canal, the main artery of communication between the capital and the Grand Canal until the railway was built.

THE WALL OF THE CHINESE CITY

A. Notes on the Inner Side of the Wall

The combined evidence of the historical records, the brick-marks and the tablets on the wall, tends to prove that the inner wall-face was first built during the latter part of the Chia Ching's reign (1522–1566), but largely rebuilt during the Ch'ung Chêng era (1623–1643) of the same dynasty. At both these periods only thin bricks were used for the inner wall coating (the average measurements of the thin bricks are: length 30 cm., width 15 cm., and thickness 5 cm.); but in the later repairs—those of the eighteenth and nineteenth centuries—larger bricks, such as we know from the Tartar city wall, were introduced. These Ch'ien Lung and Chia Ch'ing bricks are prevalent along the southern wall-face, while the East and the West walls are almost entirely made of thin bricks dating from the end of the sixteenth and beginning of the seventeenth centuries.

Beginning our observations on the eastern side, we pass first along the short stretch which runs at a right angle from the main wall to the north-eastern tower of the Chinese city. The wall-face consists almost entirely of the thin bricks, which have no marks, except at the inner bastion of the Tung Pien men, which is built of larger bricks with Chia Ching marks. Between this gate and the north-east corner there are three large stone tablets inserted in the wall; the inscription on one of them is entirely eaten away, but the two others are partly legible. According to these tablets the repairs were made at the expense of a gentleman called Ts'ao, who was Censor of the Board of Rites, in the 8th year of Ch'ung Chêng (1635). And these are not the only repairs executed at his expense; a great number of similar stone tablets with the same name and the same date are to be found both on the eastern and the western walls. More than thirty tablets in all bear witness to Censor Ts'ao's public spirit and generosity, which according to Chinese conception must have been caused by some very substantial benefits received from the government, if not exercised in atonement for some conflict with the law. These repairs are all executed with the same kind of thin bricks as those originally used in the building of the inner wall-face, and the work is fairly well done. On the East wall, there are, as a matter of fact, only a very few and short stretches which are not executed in this minor material; they were added in the eighteenth and early nineteenth century.

The ramp at the north-east corner consists in its lower part of large bricks from the Middle Ming period, but in its upper part of thin bricks of a somewhat later date. The ramp and the bastion are completely preserved, but the corner tower is gone.

The wall southward from the corner is of the same description as the stretch examined above. Up to the Sha Wu men there are five stone tablets of the 8th year of Ch'ung Chêng and only two or three short bits of later repairs. The inner bastion and gate yard of Sha Wu men contain large bricks of the Chia Ching period, but the outside was repaired in Ch'ien Lung's reign.

Between Sha Wu men and the south-east corner the wall is more uneven and patched. There are no less than thirteen tablets recording repairs of the 8th year of Ch'ung Chêng, and besides these a number of more recent repairs in different material, not to speak of all the spots which are now in great need of repair. About a kilometre or so south from the gate the wall is now in a very poor state of preservation, without a parapet, much eaten by time, and worn by hard weather and warfare. Thus one finds here a stretch full of holes caused by rifle bullets, evidently traces of some of the battles at the gates of Peking in fairly recent times. Further south the wall again takes on a more complete appearance, though it winds in a very irregular way before it reaches the corner and joins with the South wall at a ramp which is crowned by a picturesque eighteenth-century tower.

The western side practically corresponds to the eastern, although it is

THE WALL OF THE CHINESE CITY

a little longer, because it bends at an angle at its southern end. The inner coating is made of the usual thin bricks, and was largely repaired with the same material in the 8th year of Ch'ung Chêng. Yet, later repairs also occur along this side, but few of them are marked by dated tablets. The first of these may be observed about 200 metres from the south-west corner. The repair is executed with large eighteenth-century bricks and the tablet yields the date 1803, i.e. 8th year of Chia Ch'ing. Two shorter sections of a similar character may be seen quite near, but they are not marked by any tablets. For the rest there is very little variation in material and workmanship along this southern portion of the West wall; most of it seems to date from the latter part of the Ming dynasty.

The middle gate on the west side, Ch'ang I men, was repaired in two sections in the 31st year of Ch'ien Lung, but the adjoining wall is older. Between this gate and the north-west corner no less than eight tablets of the usual type mark repairs executed at the expense of Censor Ts'ao in the 8th year of Ch'ung Chêng. Just before one arrives at the railway opening for the Hankow line one may notice a short stretch built of large bricks in the 41st year of Ch'ien Lung (1776), but this is quite an exception; the wall is mainly late Ming work and has a more uniform appearance than the East wall. It is, on the whole, in a better state of preservation, though along certain stretches the parapet is lacking. The tower on the north-west corner bastion has evidently been renewed at a comparatively late period, probably at the end of the eighteenth century.

The short North wall on the west side has been repaired in four or five different portions, two of them being executed with large eighteenth-century bricks. The longest of these later repairs is between Hsi Pien men and the Tartar city wall over the big sewer or canal which forms the connection between the west and the south moat. The water is not so abundant here as on the east side, and the small opening under the wall would hardly make a passage for any kind of transport, yet there is a high camel-hump bridge, built against the inner side of the wall. The joint between the outer and the inner city-wall is marked by a simple square tower.

The South wall of the Chinese city shows a much greater number of late repairs than either the eastern or western side. Long sections of this wall, particularly towards the two corners, were rebuilt in the 30th and 31st years of Ch'ien Lung; the middle portion, behind the Temple of Heaven and the Temple of Agriculture, contains more of the old Ming work.

Starting from the south-east corner, we find that the comparatively short stretch from here to the east wall of the Temple of Heaven (no more than 1,800 metres) contains no less than thirty-two tablets marking repairs from the end of the eighteenth century, i.e. seven of the 30th year of Ch'ien Lung (1766), twenty-two of the 31st year of Ch'ien Lung, two of the 47th year of Ch'ien Lung (1782), and one of the 6th year of Chia Ch'ing (1801). Besides these tablets there are only three of an older type marking what seem to be repairs of the 8th year of Ch'ung Chêng. These older tablets, which are all made of sandstone, are so badly eaten away that their inscriptions are hardly legible. Only very short bits of the original Ming work remain on this easternmost section of the South wall.

Behind the enclosure of the Temple of Heaven more of the old work may be observed. The wall is here more like the eastern and western sides, i.e. built of thin dark bricks with little mortar between and rather worn by age and weather. But here are also found some important repairs; one long and one short stretch (amounting to about 500 metres) were rebuilt in the 4th year of Chia Ch'ing (1799) and the others were probably executed in the Ch'ien Lung period. They are marked by four tablets, two of which are illegible, while the two others seem to date from the 30th year of Ch'ien Lung.

This neighbourhood, behind the Temple of Heaven, is one of the most solitary places within the walls of Peking. The road lies very deep in soft sand and vehicles seldom pass over it. On both sides of it the jujube shrubs, thistles, and grass grow high and thick, because the water collects here in the rainy season. The wall-face is covered with a velvety carpet of moss and dust woven by age and sandstorms. In addition to this, it is decorated here and there with big patches of grass and clusters of shrubs which have forced their way through the mouldering brickwork. The parapet is mostly gone; the whole structure has an air of beautiful decay harmonizing with the lonely mood of this neighbourhood.

Close to the Yung Ting men the wall becomes still poorer and more patched. Here there are several short bits of repair, but none of them is marked by a tablet. The gate bastion was rebuilt in the 31st year of Ch'ien Lung, according to a tablet on the outside.

The wall westward from the gate is also in a very bad state; the parapet is missing and the plinth is covered up with mud, which all contributes to make the wall look low and insignificant. At a distance of hardly more than 100 metres from the gate the wall was rebuilt in the 18th year of Kuang Hsü (1892). Then follows a short repair dated in the 51st year of Ch'ien Lung. The adjoining wall-stretch is in a ruinous state; its foundations having been partly undermined and destroyed by water, the brick coating has begun to work its way out. There are, as a matter of fact, no late repairs on this section of the wall (behind the Temple of Agriculture) and only one of the 8th year of Ch'ung Chêng. The rest of this wall-stretch is earlier Ming work. But after we have passed the western corner of the Temple of Agriculture the Ch'ien Lung repairs become about as frequent as on the easternmost section. From this point to the south-west corner thirty tablets may be counted; of these only one dates from the end of the Ming period, i.e. the 8th year of Ch'ung Chêng; all the others are of the late eighteenth century; ten are dated in the 30th year of Ch'ien Lung, fourteen in his 31st year, one in his 36th, one in his 56th year and three in the 8th year of Chia Ch'ing (1803). For the most part the repairs seem to have been done almost simultaneously at the eastern and western ends of the South wall, and, curiously enough, those executed in the 30th year of Ch'ien Lung are quite distinct from the repairs of the following year. In the first year mentioned, only bricks of the largest size were used, but the next year this material was practically abandoned (or reserved for the main city-wall) and much smaller bricks came into use, the masonry being just as carefully and solidly built as ever in the Ch'ien Lung period. All the eighteenth-century repairs are still in good condition, while some of those which were made of thin bricks of the Ming period at the expense of Mr. Ts'ao have begun to moulder or to flake off and would require to be made over again. The westernmost section of the South wall between Nan Hsi men and the south-west corner was mainly rebuilt in the 31st year of Ch'ien Lung, and this last kilometre is now in a better condition than any other section of the same wall.

B. Notes on the Outer Side of the Wall

The outside of the wall was evidently more solidly built from the beginning than the inner side. Another reason for its better preservation must have been that the rain-water here, just as on the main wall, was drained over the inner wall-face. The brick coating was not done with the thin bricks, commonly used on the inner side, but with large bricks of the same type as we have found in the regular Ming work on the main wall. The workmanship seems on the whole to have been exceedingly good; most of the original work still exists along the outer side, the repairs being comparatively short and few. They are practically all of the late eighteenth century, with the exception of two or three stretches which were renewed in the reign of Kuang Hsü.

At the point where the north-western stretch of the Chinese city-wall abuts on the main wall a simple rectangular tower protects the passage. It is not very high, but offers a place of vantage from which the lower wall can easily be surveyed and an attack from the top of this wall against the main

THE WALL OF THE CHINESE CITY

city checked. Formerly also a similar tower stood at the point where the north-eastern stretch of the outer city-wall joins the inner wall, but this is now destroyed. The joints between these two walls, both on the east and west sides, afford the best opportunity for examining the differences of material and workmanship in these structures, an examination which inevitably leaves a strong impression of the technical and material superiority of the Tartar city wall.

This wall-face is divided up in the same way as the outside of the Tartar city wall by means of square bastions, all of practically uniform size and proportions and standing at intervals of about 200 metres. Thus the proportion between the bastions and the intervening spaces is here much the same as on the North wall of the main city (which also was an entirely new construction), while the intervals on the South, East and West walls are less than half as long. In consequence of these long intervening spaces there are only thirty bastions along the whole South wall, in spite of the fact that it is the longest wall in Peking. The East and the West walls have respectively fourteen and thirteen bastions, not counting those of the corners and the gates.

Beginning our observations on the western side we pass out through Hsi Pien men. The brickwork of the gate-wall and bastion was renewed in the Ch'ien Lung era, but the wall-face on both sides of it is old and eaten away. The bastion to the west of the gate was renewed in the 41st year of Ch'ien Lung, according to the inserted tablet. The adjoining wall-stretch was rebuilt at a later time, probably in Kuang Hsü's reign. The corner bastion is old on the north side; it contains a number of marked bricks, such as: "Made by the master potter Li Yü Pao in the 30th year of Chia Ching" (1551); "Made by the master potter Liu Chin in the 30th year of Chia Ching"; "Made by the master potter Ch'u Chu in the 30th year of Chia Ching"; "Made by the master potter Sun Hsin in the 20th year of Chia Ching" (1541). But on the south side this same bastion was rebuilt, according to an inserted tablet, in the 2nd year of Chia Ch'ing (1797).

Southward from this corner and up to the middle west gate, Ch'ang Yi men, there are no later repairs of any consequence. The brickwork, which is much worn and eaten in spots, is mainly of the Chia Ching period, as indicated by a number of brick-marks. To quote: "Made by the master potter Ch'u Ch'en in the 36th year of Chia Ching" (1557); "Made by the master potter Wu Chi Jung in the 36th year of Chia Ching"; "Made in the 22nd year of Chia Ching"; "Made by the master potter Chang Ch'in in the 36th year of Chia Ching." The two following marks indicate a later period, probably a repair of the time of Ch'ien Lung: "New style city-wall bricks"; "Special city-wall bricks." Then follow again marks of the Ming dynasty: "Made by the master potter Yang P'ei in the 23rd year of Chia Ching" (1544); "Made by the master potter Yang Yü in the 20th year of Chia Ching" (1541); "Made by the master potter Niu Ch'i in the 22nd year of Chia Ching"; "Made by the master potter Wang Hsing in the 20th year of Chia Ching"; "Made by the master potter Wu Chi Jung in the 30th year of Chia Ching"; "Made by the master potter Chang Lou in the 32nd year of Chia Ching" (1553); "Made by the master potter Liang Chang in the 28th year of Chia Ching" (1549); "Made by the master potter Chow Hsüeh in the 32nd year of Chia Ching."

The outer bastion of Ch'ang Yi men was rebuilt in the 31st year of Ch'ien Lung (1766); there are two tablets, both with this same date. Continuing southward from the gate one finds that the wall is here of the same character as the one on the northern side. The large bricks contain a number of Chia Ching marks, some of which may be quoted: "Made by the master potter Liang Tung in the 20th year of Chia Ching"; "Made by the master potter Chou Chün in the 23rd year of Chia Ching"; "Made by the master potter Chou Hsin Lu in the 33rd year of Chia Ching" (1554); "Made by the master potter Fu Tien in the 32nd year of Chia Ching." But beside these Ming bricks there are also some of Ch'ien Lung's time, indicating some minor later repairs; they are marked: "New style city-wall bricks" and "Fine clay city-wall bricks."

The first bastion south of the gate has been renewed, probably in the Ch'ien Lung period; it is marked by a tablet with an illegible inscription.

The second bastion was renewed, according to the inserted tablet, in the 4th year of Chia Ch'ing (1799).

THE WALL OF THE CHINESE CITY

The third bastion is of the Middle Ming period and contains some dated bricks, as for instance: "Made by the master potter Yang Chin in the 22nd year of Chia Ching," and also: "Made by the master potter Ts'ao Jung in the 29th year of Chia Ching" (1550).

The fourth bastion is old, except on the south side where it has been renewed, though not marked by any tablet. There are many brick-marks on this bastion and the adjoining wall-stretch; to quote:

"Made by the master potter Hou Lu in the 20th year of Chia Ching"; "Made by the master potter Ch'ang Mêng Yang in the 20th year of Chia Ching"; "Made by the master potter Tu Ch'ung in the 18th year of Chia Ching"; "Made by the master potter Ch'ang Shih Yung in the 20th year of Chia Ching"; "Made by the master potter Tan Tê Chêng in the 26th year of Chia Ching" (1547); "Made by the master potter Liu Mau in the 24th year of Chia Ching" (1545); "Made by the master potter Chiang Ta Shun in the Wu Shen year of Wan Li" (1608). There are also some eighteenth-century "New style city-wall bricks" and "Fine clay lasting city-wall bricks."

The fifth bastion was rebuilt in the 2nd year of Chia Ch'ing. The adjoining wall is old and eaten away, but just before one reaches the next bastion there is another short repair of the 2nd year of Chia Ch'ing.

The sixth bastion is old and contains some Chia Ching brick-marks, as for instance: "Made by the master potter Li Ch'ung in the 26th year of Chia Ching" (1547).

The seventh bastion is also old, with similar brick-marks; for instance: "Made by the master potter Li Jen in the 14th year of Chia Ching" (1535).

The adjoining wall was partly renewed in the 51st year of Ch'ien Lung, according to the inserted tablet (1786).

The eighth bastion is old, but the adjoining wall-stretch was repaired at its southern end in the 2nd year of Chia Ch'ing (1797).

The corner bastion is old on the north and the west sides, but renewed on the south and the east sides. The Ming bricks on the north side contain a number of the usual Chia Ching marks: "Made by the master potter Wang Jui in the 28th year of Chia Ching"; other master potters named here are: Chang Tseng Sheng; Hu Yung Cheng; Chao Tê Fu, and Lu Ming Yang. The dates are the 28th and 29th years of Chia Ching (1549-1550).

The wall between the corner and the first bastion on the south side was partly repaired in the 53rd year of Ch'ien Lung (1788).

All the four bastions which occur between the corner and the Nan Hsi men are old and rather worn and weathered. They contain several brick-marks indicating the period of the work: " Made by the master potter Niu Ch'ung in the 26th year of Chia Ching "; " Made by the master potter Chang Chiu in the 21st year of Chia Ching "; ditto in the 29th year (1550). The intervening wall-spaces are mostly of the same description and period except for a short repair between the second and third bastion (over the sewer lock) which was done in the 2nd year of Chia Ch'ing (1797).

The outer bastion of Nan Hsi men has been rebuilt and is marked both on the west and the east sides with tablets of the 51st year of Ch'ien Lung. The inner part of the gate yard is earlier.

Eastward from Nan Hsi men for a distance of nearly 1½ kilometres (including six bastions) the wall is mostly renewed in its upper part, while the lower section has an older appearance and contains brick-marks of the Ming dynasty, as for instance: " Made by the potter Chu Wên in the (?) year of Ch'ung Cheng "; or: " Made by the master potter Li Shang Kuei in the 26th year of Chia Ching " (1547).

On the third bastion is a tablet of the 31st year of Ch'ien Lung (1766). The Ch'ien Lung bricks are here marked by the oft-quoted names of the Kung Pu inspectors Kuei, Yung, and Kô.

After one has passed the sixth bastion some older bits may be observed, but they are interrupted by short repairs marked by two tablets of the 2nd year of Chia Ch'ing. The sections become on the whole more unequal towards the middle gate.

The seventh bastion is mainly old; it contains bricks with the Chia Ching marks. The adjoining wall was repaired, according to the inscriptions on two tablets, in the 2nd year of Chia Ch'ing (1797).

The eighth bastion is also mainly old; here and on the adjoining wall are many bricks with marks of the Chia Ching era; for instance: " Made by the master potter Fêng T'a Chao in the 32nd year of Chia Ching " (1553), and " Made by the master potter Lin Yung Shou in the 32nd year of Chia Ching."

THE WALL OF THE CHINESE CITY

Passing the ninth bastion we observe some bits of late repair, one of them dated by a tablet of the 2nd year of Chia Ch'ing. This is followed by a short stretch of Ming work, in which are some bricks marked: "Made by the master potter Ch'ang Lun in the 32nd year of Chia Ching"; and "Made by the master potter Lin Yung Shou in the 32nd year of Chia Ching."

Then again a short section of eighteenth-century work dated by the tablet in the 2nd year of Chia Ch'ing.

The tenth bastion was renewed in the same year as the preceding wall-stretch, as indicated on the inserted tablet.

The adjoining wall and the eleventh bastion are old. The brickwork, which is not in very good condition, contains several marks of the Chia Ching era: "Made by the master potter Sun Piao in the 22nd year of Chia Ching" (1543); "Made by the master potter Sung I in the 31st year of Chia Ching" (1552); "Made by the master potter Ch'ên Fu in the 29th year of Chia Ching" (1550). Close to the gate the wall has been renewed.

Yung Ting men outer wall and bastion were rebuilt in the 31st year of Ch'ien Lung; there are two tablets of the same year (1766).

The adjoining wall was renewed in the 47th year of Ch'ien Lung and is similar to the wall on the western side of the gate (1782).

The first bastion east of the middle gate is old. It contains several brick-marks such as: "Made by the potter Fu Ho at the Tung Ho kiln in the 32nd year of Chia Ching"; and "Made by the potter Chao Fung Yü in the 32nd year of Chia Ching."

The second bastion ditto; similar brick-marks and also: "Made by the potter Wu Chü at the Tung Ho kiln in the 23rd year of Chia Ching."

The third bastion ditto; brick-marks of the same period, for instance: "Made by the potter Li Ching at the Tung Ho kiln in the 22nd year of Chia Ching."

The fourth bastion ditto; brick-marks corresponding: "Made by the potter Li Lin at the Tung Ho kiln in the 32nd year of Chia Ching."

The fifth bastion was repaired, according to the inserted tablet, in the 47th year of Ch'ien Lung, but mainly with old material, as indicated by the Chia Ching brick-marks which also occur on this stretch.

The sixth bastion is old; built of the usual Chia Ching bricks, some of which are marked: "Made by the potter Kao Shang Yi in the 22nd year of Chia Ching."

The seventh bastion ditto; bricks marked correspondingly: "Made by the potter Chang Ch'in in the 36th year of Chia Ching" (1557); "Made by the potter Hsieh Hsiang in the 29th year of Chia Ching"; and also "Made by the potter Ch'ên Ch'ang in the 35th year of Wan Li" (1607). The last mark seems to indicate that this part of the wall was not finished until late in the Wan Li period or that a repair was executed here at that time. The latter alternative seems to us the more acceptable.

The eighth bastion is old, built of the usual large bricks, some of which are marked: "Made by the potter Lu Meng Yang in the 32nd year of Chia Ching."

The ninth bastion has been destroyed in the making of the opening for the Peking-Tientsin railway line.

The wall adjoining this railway gate on the eastern side is old and weather-worn. There are no later repairs until we reach the south-eastern gate (Chiang T'sa men). The brick-marks on this section are all of the Chia Ching period; to quote a few: "Made by the master potter Ch'ang Tseng in the 31st year of Chia Ching"; "Made by the master potter Wu Ch'ang Pei in the 23rd year of Chia Ching"; "Made by the master potter Chen Kuei at the Tung Ho kiln in the 32nd year of Chia Ching"; "Made by the master potter Li Lin in the 21st year of Chia Ching"; "Made by the potter Chang Meng Chao in the 30th year of Chia Ching."

The space between the railway opening and the Chiang Ts'a men includes no less than five bastions, but there is only one between the gate and the corner, the total number of the bastions east of the middle gate being thus fifteen, or equal to the number of the bastions west of the gate. The South wall of the Chinese city is actually the longest wall in Peking; it measures just over 7800 metres and should be 200–300 metres longer, had not the East wall been bent inwards at its southern end and the corner cut off. The distance between the south-eastern gate and the corner is quite short. The gate wall and outer bastion were rebuilt in the 31st year of Ch'ien Lung (1766), but the wall from here to the corner, including one bastion, is old. Some of the bricks bear marks of the 24th year of Chia Ching (1545).

THE WALL OF THE CHINESE CITY

The corner bastion is now in bad repair, much eaten away and weathered. It contains a great number of brick-marks, such as: "Made by the master potter Wang Jui in the 24th year of Chia Ching"; "Made by the master potter Wu Kun in the 26th year of Chia Ching"; "Made by the potter Jen Ching at the Kung Shun kiln in the 15th year of Chia Ching"; "Made by the potter Sun Lung in the 18th year of Chia Ching" (1539).

It may be observed that the dates here on the corner bastion are earlier than along the wall, which seems to indicate that the work started at the corner.

The East wall shows still fewer repairs than the South wall, corresponding in this respect to the West wall. With the exception of some short stretches which will be noted, it is built of the regular large Chia Ching bricks, many of which are marked. Some of these marks may be quoted as samples: "Made by the master potter Chang Ch'in in the 32nd year of Chia Ching"; "Made by the master potter Sun Wên Ko in the 31st year of Chia Ching"; "Made by the master potter Wu Liang Pei in the 24th year of Chia Ching"; "Made by the master potter Yang Chung Chü in the 24th year of Chia Ching"; "Made by the master potter Lin Yung Shou in the 22nd year of Chia Ching"; "Made by the master potter Ch'ao Yi in the 34th year of Chia Ching"; "Made by the master potter Ch'iang Yüeh in the 33rd year of Chia Ching"; "Made by the master potter Wu Chü in the 32nd year of Chia Ching."

There was evidently no lack of "master potters" in the Chia Ching era, and brick-making must have been regarded as more of an individual art than in later times. No other era has yielded us so many names of brick-makers, and it is doubtful whether better bricks have been made in China at any later time.

A short intermission in the Chia Ching work is marked by the sixth bastion and short stretches of the wall on both sides of it, which, according to an inserted tablet, were rebuilt in the 31st year of Ch'ien Lung. The bricks here are not marked with the names of the makers but with those of the supervising officials, the Kung Pu inspectors Yung and Kuei. It seems as if the brick-making had lost something of its individual character during the intervening two centuries and had become more of an imperial manufacture.

After this intermission the Chia Ching work begins again, but before we reach the seventh bastion there is another eighteenth-century repair dated by a tablet of the 2nd year of Chia Ch'ing. It is followed by a short stretch of Ming work.

The seventh bastion is rebuilt and marked by a tablet with an illegible inscription (Ch'ien Lung or Chia Ch'ing). A section of the adjoining wall-space was repaired in the 7th year of Chia Ch'ing.

The eighth bastion is old and made of Chia Ching bricks, some of which are marked: " Made by the potter Ch'u Wu Pin in the 36th year of Chia Ching."

The wall from here up to Sha Wu men, including the ninth and tenth bastions, is old and made of the characteristic Chia Ching bricks of which enough has been said and a sufficient number of marks quoted.

The outer barbican wall and bastion of Sha Wu men were, like the corresponding parts of the other gates of the outer city, rebuilt in the 31st year of Ch'ien Lung. This comparatively new brickwork of the gate stands out quite prominently against the much weather-worn old Ming wall on both sides of the gate. The old Ming work continues northward over the two nearest bastions and their adjoining wall-spaces, but the third bastion (from the gate) was rebuilt in the 31st year of Ch'ien Lung. The adjoining wall seems to have been renewed about the same period; it is marked by a tablet with no inscription.

The fourth bastion is old and ruined at the top. The corner bastion is also in a poor state of preservation and has lost its crowning tower.

The wall from the corner to Tung Pien men, including two bastions, was rebuilt in the 31st year of Ch'ien Lung. The tablet with this date is inserted close to the gate; the bricks here have the usual Ch'ien Lung period marks with the names of the Kung Pu inspectors Kuei and Yung. The barbican wall of the gate is of the same period, but on the other side of it may still be seen some of the older material and workmanship.

The country just outside this Chinese city wall is very much the same as the so-called city inside of it—an open sandy plain dotted with grain-fields and groups of trees around small houses and temples. One wonders sometimes why the wall has been built just where it stands.

As a matter of fact there are nowadays more houses, more traffic, more life and activity just outside the wall (near the gates) than along its inner side. Maybe it is because life here is cheaper and freer. Some spots towards the south-east, where the water supply is good, are very pretty, thanks to the abundant growth of bulrushes and weeping willows along the ponds and canals. On the western side the country is drier, but some fine cypresses and ailanthus trees may be seen at protected places, and on the whole one here finds little of that bleakness and desolate monotony which characterize the country on the northern side of the city.

VII

THE GATES OF THE TARTAR CITY

Introduction

THE gates may be called the mouths of the city; they are the openings through which this huge walled-in body of half a million or more organisms breathes and speaks. The life of the whole city becomes concentrated at the gates; everything that goes out of or in to it must pass these narrow openings. And that which passes in and out is not simply a mass of vehicles, animals, and human beings, but thoughts and desires, hopes and despairs, death and new life in the shape of marriage- and funeral-processions. At the gates can be felt the pulse of the whole city, as its life and purpose flows through the narrow openings—a pulse-beat which gives the rhythm of the life and activity of this highly complex organism which is called Peking.

At night it becomes faint and almost imperceptible; the gates are closed, or used to be so, during the sleeping hours of the citizens. At sunrise when the first travellers start on their long journeys in carts or mule-litters, the heavy wooden doors are slowly pushed back, groaning like giants unwillingly aroused. Gradually the country people begin to come in with their wheelbarrows or baskets filled with the products of the soil swinging from the ends of springy poles resting on their shoulders. And as the sun rises higher, the traffic and the movement at the gates gradually increase and become more varied; the stream of porters,

THE GATES OF THE TARTAR CITY

wheelbarrows, and donkey carts is mixed up with rickshaws and automobiles which keep up an excessive and futile noise with their sirens. The main rhythm of the movement focussed at these narrow passages is not to be disturbed by any threatening sounds. It may become highly intensified but not accelerated; it may even be brought to a temporary standstill when too many wheelbarrows and rickshaws are trying to push through in opposite directions. At the main gates the traffic reaches its culmination about the time of the midday meal, when everybody is out for a bite. Towards evening the stream grows thinner again, and as the twilight deepens into night the flow gradually ceases. (Though nowadays the closing of the main gates of Peking is by no means as strictly carried out as it used to be here and still is in most of the provincial towns.)

The life that pulsates through the gates varies not only with the hours of the day but also according to the different quarters of the city and the character of the suburbs. On the south side, which is the main front of the city and where the greatest centres of traffic and business are found, there are three monumental gates. The central one, Ch'eng Yang men (Straight to the Sun), is a good deal larger and higher than the others. It used to be the emperor's gate, now it is sometimes called "the Nation's gate" (Kuo men), and though much has been done to destroy its architectural grandeur and deprive it of its ancient characteristic surroundings, it is still the actual centre of the throbbing life of the capital. At some distance to the east and to the west stand respectively Hata men and Shun Chih men, as they usually are called, though their official names are different. They form the entrances to the main streets running straight through north-south. The former was sometimes popularly called Ch'ing men, the gate of brightness and prosperity; it could be used by everybody, even the emperor. In direct opposition to this the western gate, Shun Chih men, was looked upon as the gate of adversity and exhaustion, known as Ssǔ men, "the gate of the Dead." One may still observe that most of the funeral processions pass out through this gate. These three gates in the South wall are the sluices which regulate the flow of traffic between the Tartar city and the Chinese town. They are inter-urban gates and lack some of the characteristic features of the other gates which give access to the different suburbs. Particularly nowadays when double railway tracks pierce the gate yard of Hata men and skirt the barbican of Shun Chih men much of the original character is lost. Both have been deprived of their outer towers.

On the northern wall there is no central gate, only two side gates, and these do not answer exactly to the side gates of the South wall, being placed a little closer to the central axis of the city. Outside them are now village-like suburbs, but this neighbourhood was, as we have seen, formerly part of the Mongol capital. The northern gates have always been looked upon as the most important defensive gates of Peking, because most attacks on the capital have naturally come from this direction. The military traffic is also nowadays most considerable at those gates, as the largest barracks are situated north of the city. Tê Sheng men, which according to its name is the gate of moral excellence, was also known as "Hsiu men" (the gate of Adornment), while An Ting men was "Sheng men" (the gate of Abundance), through which the emperor passed once a year to sacrifice at Ti Tan (the Altar of the Earth) for a good harvest. The outside aspect of these gates is particularly imposing, their barbicans (partly spoilt by the railway) and towers rising from perfectly bare ground, unbroken by houses or trees.

The two eastern gates have been most senselessly modified in connection with the construction of the circuit railway, their barbicans are practically obliterated. But the neighbourhood outside the gates is rather attractive, as the moat is here lined with willows which give a beautiful setting to the towers. This moat or canal was in earlier days, before the construction of the railway, of great importance for the transportation of rice, the staple food of the city, which was stored in magazines along the eastern wall. Tung Chih men was known as "Shang men" (the gate of Bargaining), where common people carried on their daily business and where the emperor never went. Ch'i Hua men was sometimes called "Tu men" (the gate of Rest), which naturally followed after the marketing place at the previous gate.

The gates in the West wall, Hsi Chih men and P'ing Tzu men, are the only ones which have not been impaired or spoilt by the railway. They still offer complete pictures of what the city gates of Peking used to be: not simply double towers for defence and watch but also well-enclosed courtyards or market-places with room for small temples and numerous stalls. The road which leads out through a side opening and winds along the wall of the barbican is lined with foodshops and eating-houses. The gates thus connect in the most natural and picturesque way the city with the suburbs. The highly animated crowds at these gates offer glimpses of the care-free and happy life that we know from many country inns in Northern China, advantageously contrasting with the rush of modern civilization in the shape of automobiles and motor-cycles. P'ing Tzu men is the gate of quiet or just rule, and it was said that the people here became aroused or frightened by the decrees of the emperor, in consequence of which the gate was called "Ching men." The following gate, Hsi Chih men, was called "K'ai men" (the Open gate), the gate of understanding, symbolizing the full realization of the wisdom of the emperor's decrees.

It is difficult to say how these more or less significant and symbolical popular appellations for the different gates originated, but they are worth recording as they still live in the memory of the old Pekingese and sometimes are quoted to explain the traditional use or ancient character of one or other of the gates.

The gates of the Tartar city are all composed according to the same plan, though differing in scale and details. Their most conspicuous features are the two towers. The inner tower, which is placed on the city wall, here strengthened and broadened into a bastion, has the shape of a large pavilion or palatial hall with three successive roofs and open galleries in the two main stories. Long ramps facilitate the ascent to the terrace of the tower. The outer tower is a plain brick building with battering walls but no divisions or architectural treatment except the eaves of the double roofs and four rows of loopholes. It stands on a broad bastion-like substructure which projects from the outer curve of the U-shaped barbican.

The whole arrangement is thoroughly medieval and quite inadequate since the introduction of firearms. It is essentially the same gate type which was used already in the Mongol time; the improvements which may have been introduced since then have hardly served to increase its power of resistance to shells or gunfire. Particularly the inner tower, with its open woodwork and thin brick walls, has proved more dangerous than protective in the face of modern firearms. But fortunately it has, nevertheless, been kept up at all the gates, except one, the Tê Sheng men. When these towers are gone, Peking will have lost some of the most characteristic and beautiful features of its architectural ensemble.

The practical utility of the gates has thus rapidly decreased, from a military point of view, with the evolution of modern methods of warfare, but they have retained considerable importance as barriers for the levy of customs. The octroi of the gates is still to-day one of the surest sources of revenue to the Peking government, while the actual defence of the capital from the walls and gates has become merely imaginary.

* * * * *

THE GATES OF THE TARTAR CITY

A. The Gates of the West Wall

P'ing Tzu men, or Fu Ch'eng men, as it is officially named, is the southern gate on the west side. The wall of the barbican was renewed in Ch'ien Lung's 52nd year, but the terraces or bastions under the towers are evidently much older, dating probably from the latter part of the Ming dynasty; they are very carefully built with thin bricks. The inner tower gives the impression of considerable age; its wooden pillars are banded with iron; the balustrade of the second story is missing and the frieze-like panelling under it shows big holes. The eaves of the lowest roof are crumbling and the north-west corner has broken down completely. The paint and ornamentation of the woodwork is practically worn off and covered by thick layers of dust. There is danger of the whole structure falling to pieces if parts of the rotting woodwork are not soon renewed. The tower may be essentially of the Ming period, but it has been repaired several times since then, though hardly within a generation or two.

It stands on a stone platform slightly raised above the level of the wall, measuring 33 by 18·8 metres, while the outer measurements of the walls are 27 by 13 metres. The gallery around the walls has seven spans on the longer, and three on the shorter sides, the middle spans on each side being larger, as they correspond to the four doors of the tower. The columns of the gallery, which are built up of several pieces around a solid core, have a diameter of about $\frac{1}{2}$ metre; they stand on square stone plinths but have no bases. Reinforcing the columns on both sides are square balks or auxiliary posts.

The constructive frame of the wall consists also of wooden columns; there are two rows of them, one on the outside and one on the inside; the space between them is filled out with brickwork, and this covers nearly three-quarters of the face of the columns. The intercolumniations are exactly the same in all the three rows, except of course at the corners where the columns are arranged diagonally.

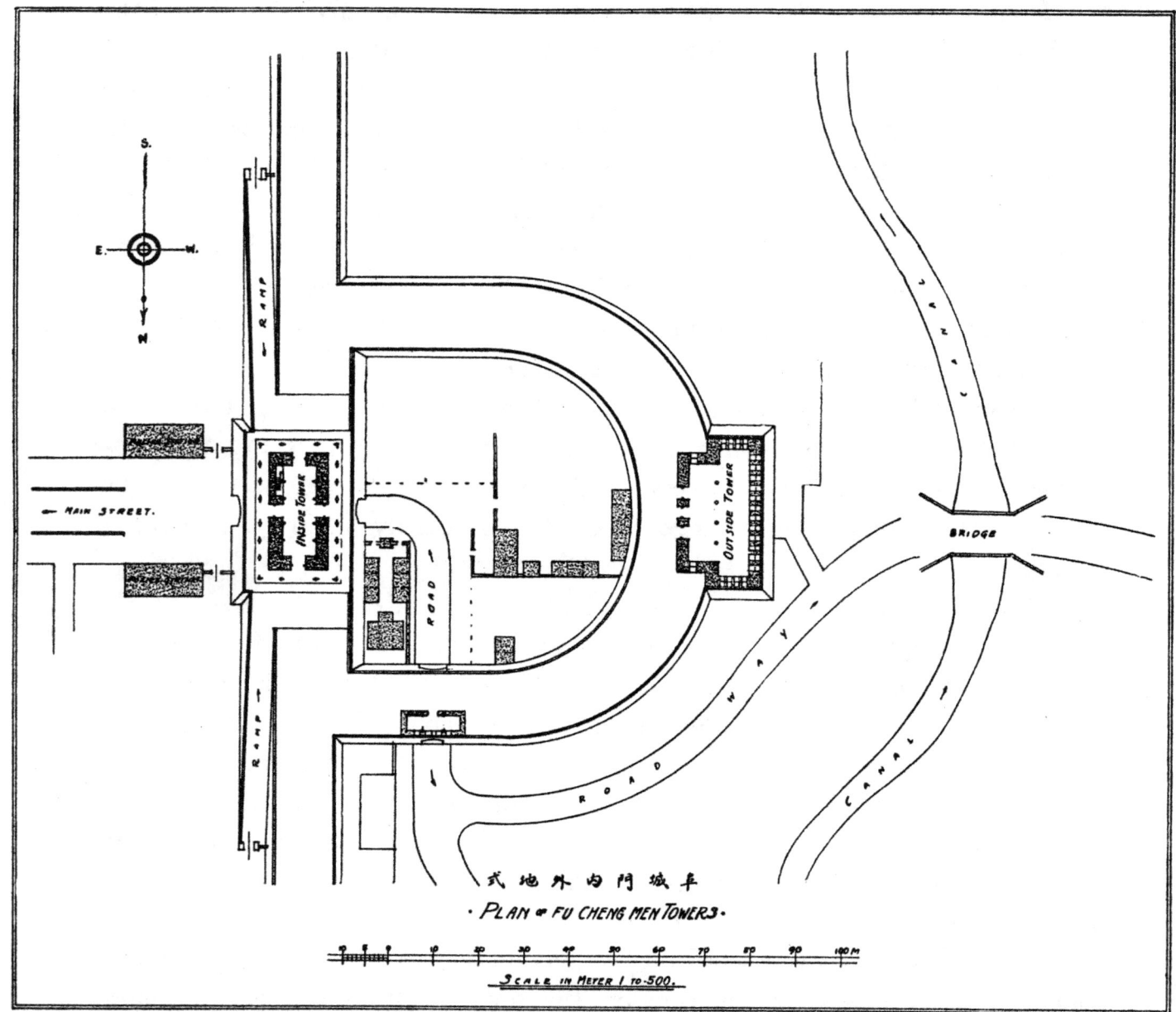

FIG. 6.—P'ing Tzu Men (also known as Fu Cheng Men), general plan.

It may be pointed out at once that this arrangement with double

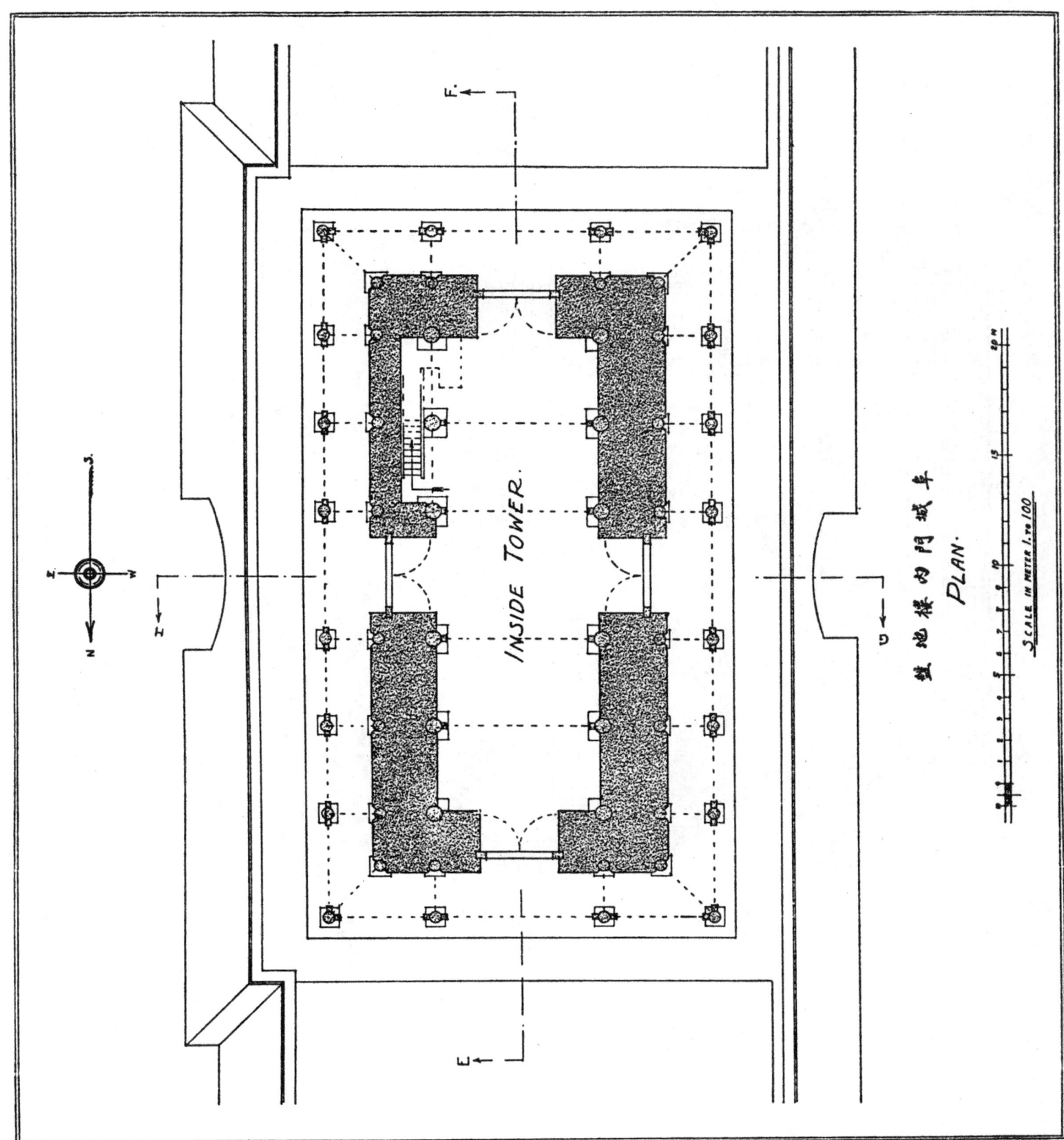

FIG. 7.—P'ing Tzu Men, inner tower.

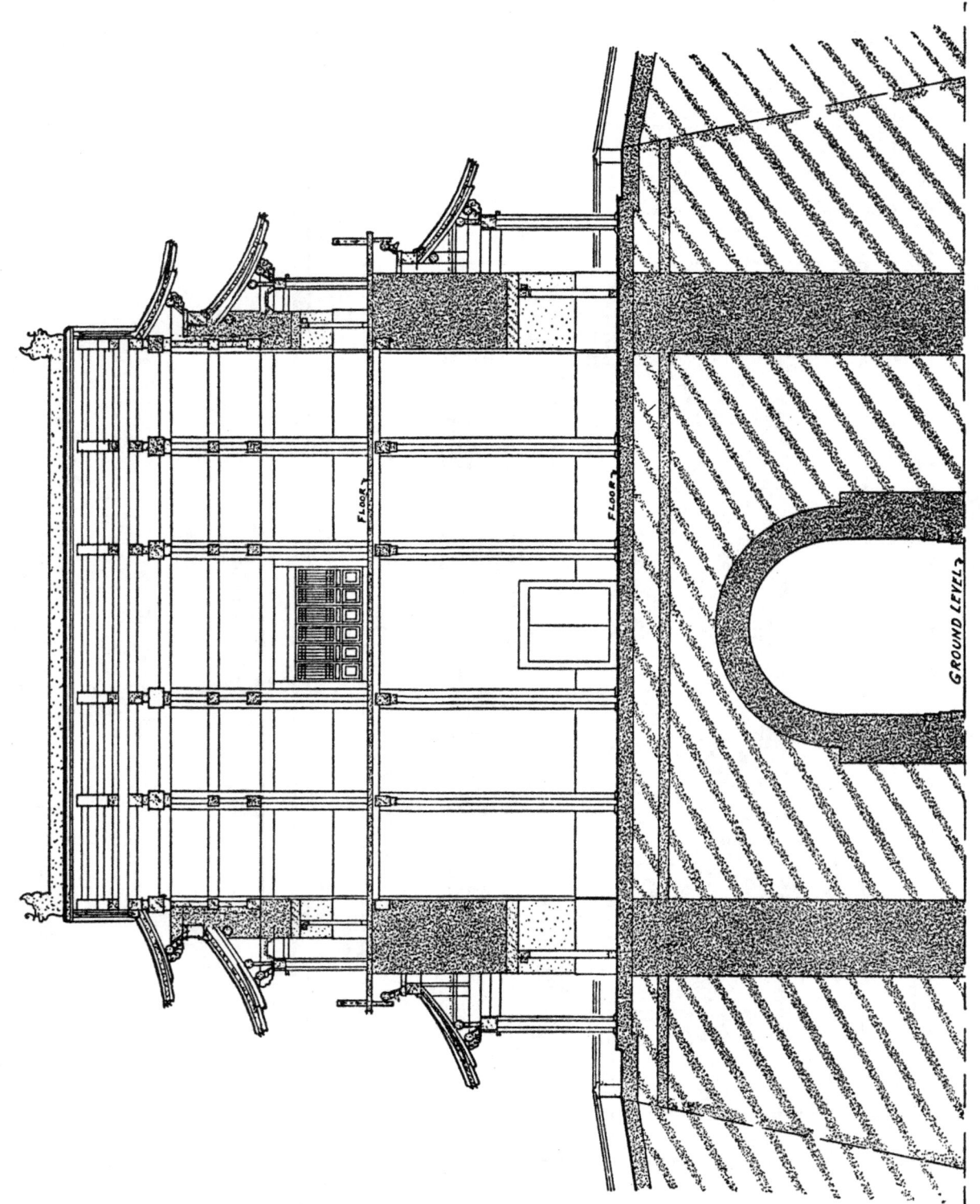

FIG. 8.—P'ing Tzŭ Men, inner tower.

THE GATES OF THE TARTAR CITY 137

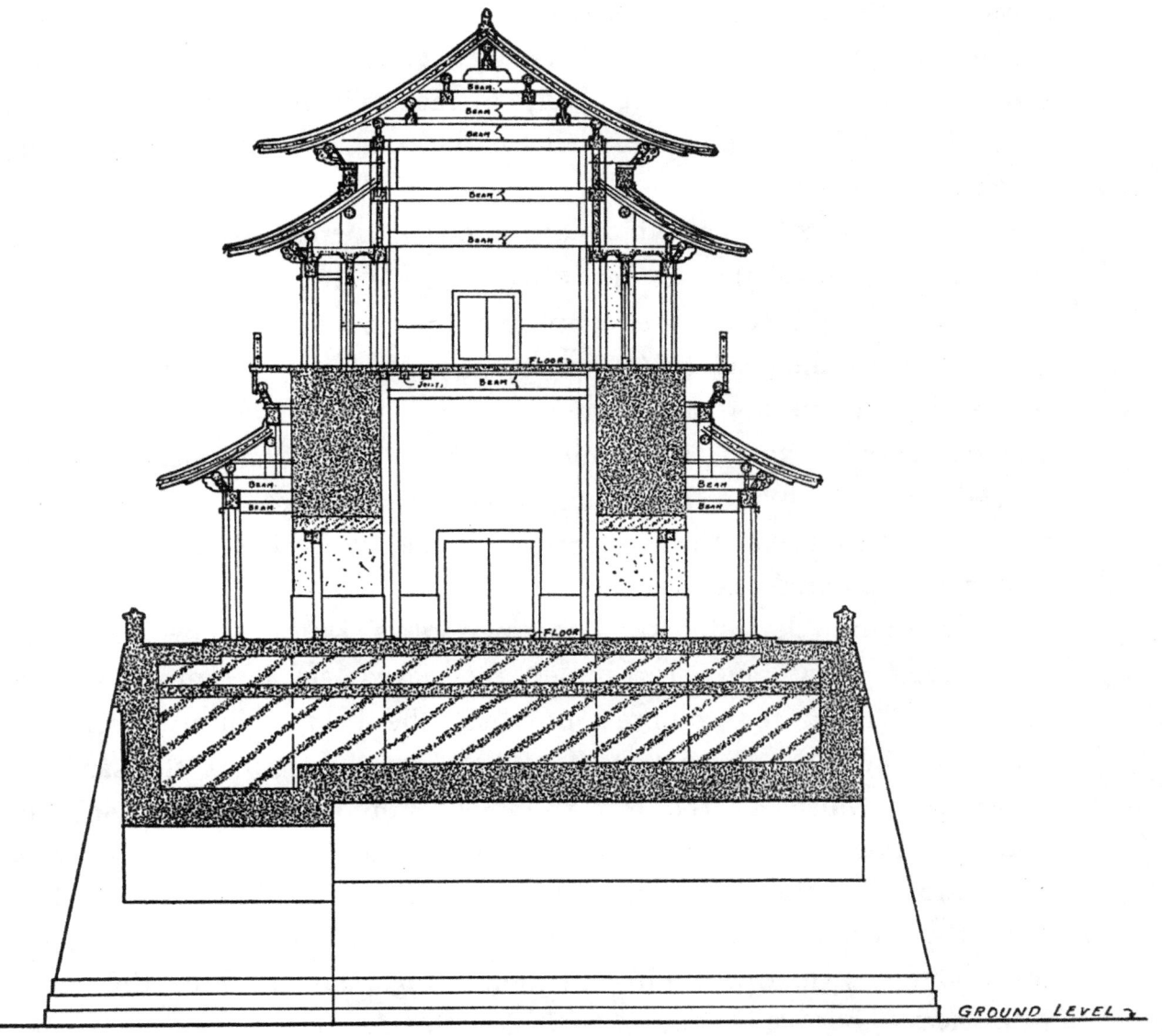

阜城門內樓剖式
· CROSS SECTION ·
ON G--H.

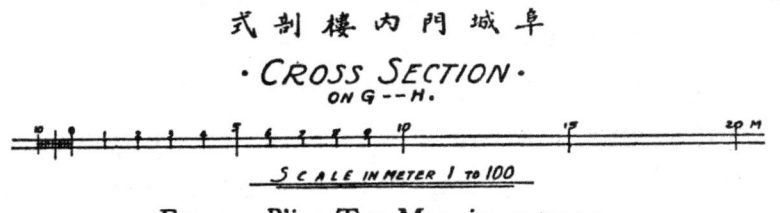

SCALE IN METER 1 TO 100

FIG. 9.—P'ing Tzu Men, inner tower.

138 THE WALLS AND GATES OF PEKING

rows of columns partly embedded in the brick wall is not the usual method employed; at the other large gates the inner row of columns stands detached, inside the hall, a fact which may be taken as an indication of the comparatively early date of the P'ing Tzu men tower.

The inner columns, which are about 9 metres high, serve to support the floor-beams of the second story. The columns of the gallery, which measure only 5 metres, are connected by tie-beams inserted at their top, and also with the wall by means of other beams. They have no capitals. From the crossbeams rise triple-armed brackets which support two round purlins (about 0·30 m. in diameter) which carry the double and slightly curved rafters of the projecting roof. The exposed end of the upper beam, that connects the column with the wall, is carved into a floral design and painted accordingly.

The same characteristic construction is repeated in the gallery of the second story and also under the eaves of the top roof, although here is no room for columns, only for the beams, inserted in the brick wall, on which the brackets rest. The second story has the same interior length and width as the ground floor, but its walls are only half as thick as those of the first story, thus making room for an open gallery all round. To this is added a balcony resting on brackets which project from the beams over the first roof. The columns of the second story are about 7·4 metres high and joined together at three different levels with heavy beams, running both lengthwise and crosswise. The third beam is at the level of the eaves of the main roof, but there is no ceiling. The roof construction is completely visible. It consists of two more layers of lengthwise and crosswise beams, the latter necessitated by the triangular gables which form the ends to the upper part of the roof. The Japanese term for this common roof type is *irimoya*, that is to say, a hipped roof with gables which reach only halfway down to the eaves.

THE GATES OF THE TARTAR CITY

The rafters are supported by three purlins resting on heavier square beams, while a top purlin supported by brackets on the uppermost crossbeams runs right under the ridge. The number of beams here is unusually large; in the gate towers which have been rebuilt in later times the construction is somewhat simplified, though carried out on the same principles. The full height of the tower including the main ridge is 21·2 metres and its greatest length is 31·2 metres.

The prevailing colour has been red, but this is now almost obliterated by the weather and by age. All the brickwork was coated with vermilion plaster and the folding doors and columns were painted red. The outer crossbeams and brackets were decorated in green and blue, and the panel under the balcony probably had some gold ornaments. Such is the traditional colour scheme on all the gates. The pantiles, which are alternately convex and concave, may have originally been green glazed, but such tiles are now to be seen only along the edges of the roofs, while the rest are unglazed. The main ridge as well as the curving hips are very high and made of moulded and glazed tiles. Their ends are decorated with monster heads having wings and horns, and in addition to these are rows of fantastic seated animals—the so-called Kuei Lung tzu—on the hips, no doubt in order to protect the building against dangerous Fêng Shui.

The outer gate tower is a simple, more fortress-like building with thick brick walls which, however, have no real structural importance, but simply form an addition to or a heavy coating of the wooden frame. The inner construction remains essentially the same, whatever the outer appearance of the building may be, and so do the elegantly curving, far-projecting roofs. The brickwork does not give the impression of great age; it is hardly older than the barbican wall which, according to an inserted tablet, was rebuilt in the 52nd year of Ch'ien Lung.

The tower may be said to consist of two parts, the main section,

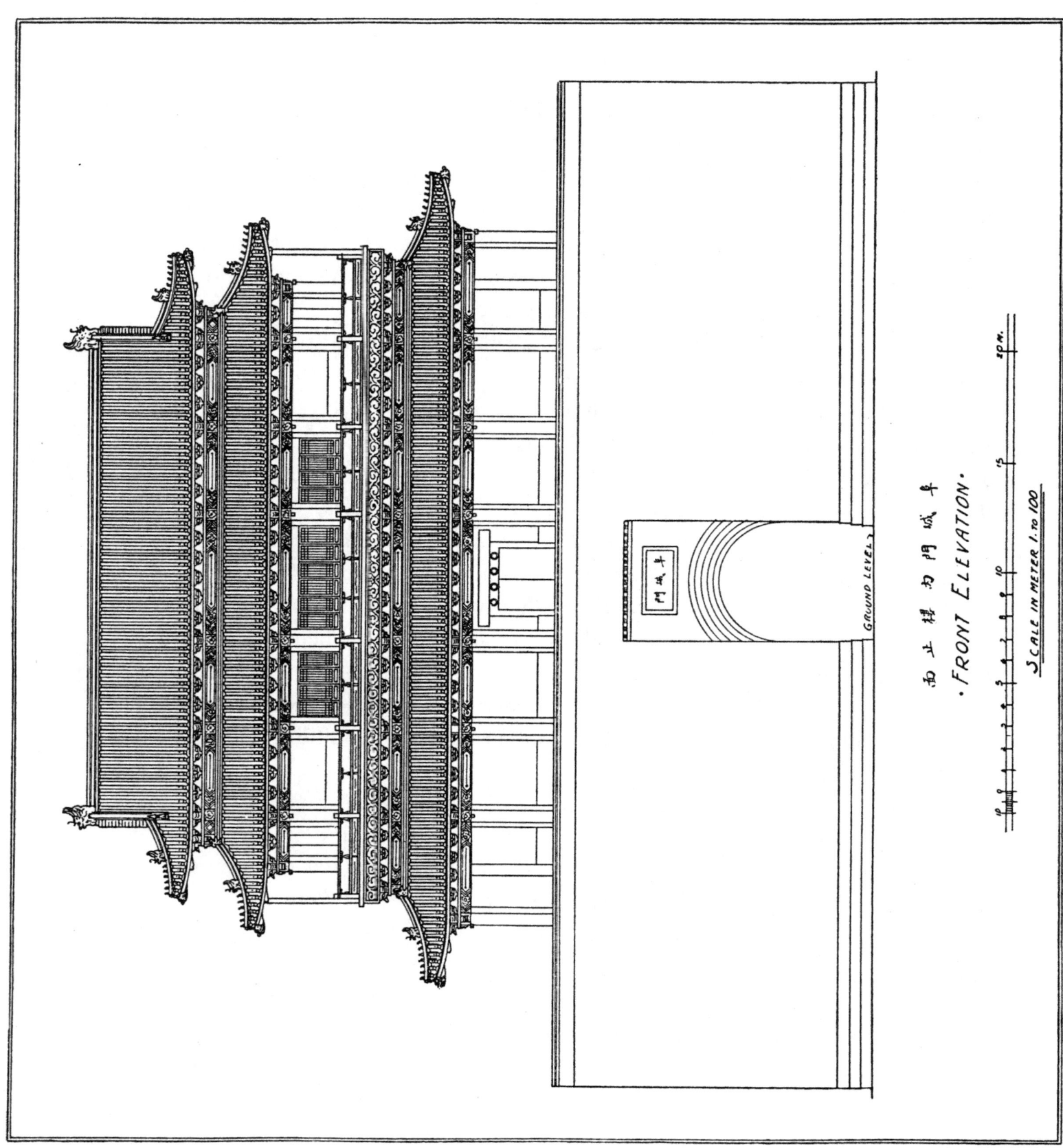

FIG. 10.—P'ing Tzu Men, inner tower.

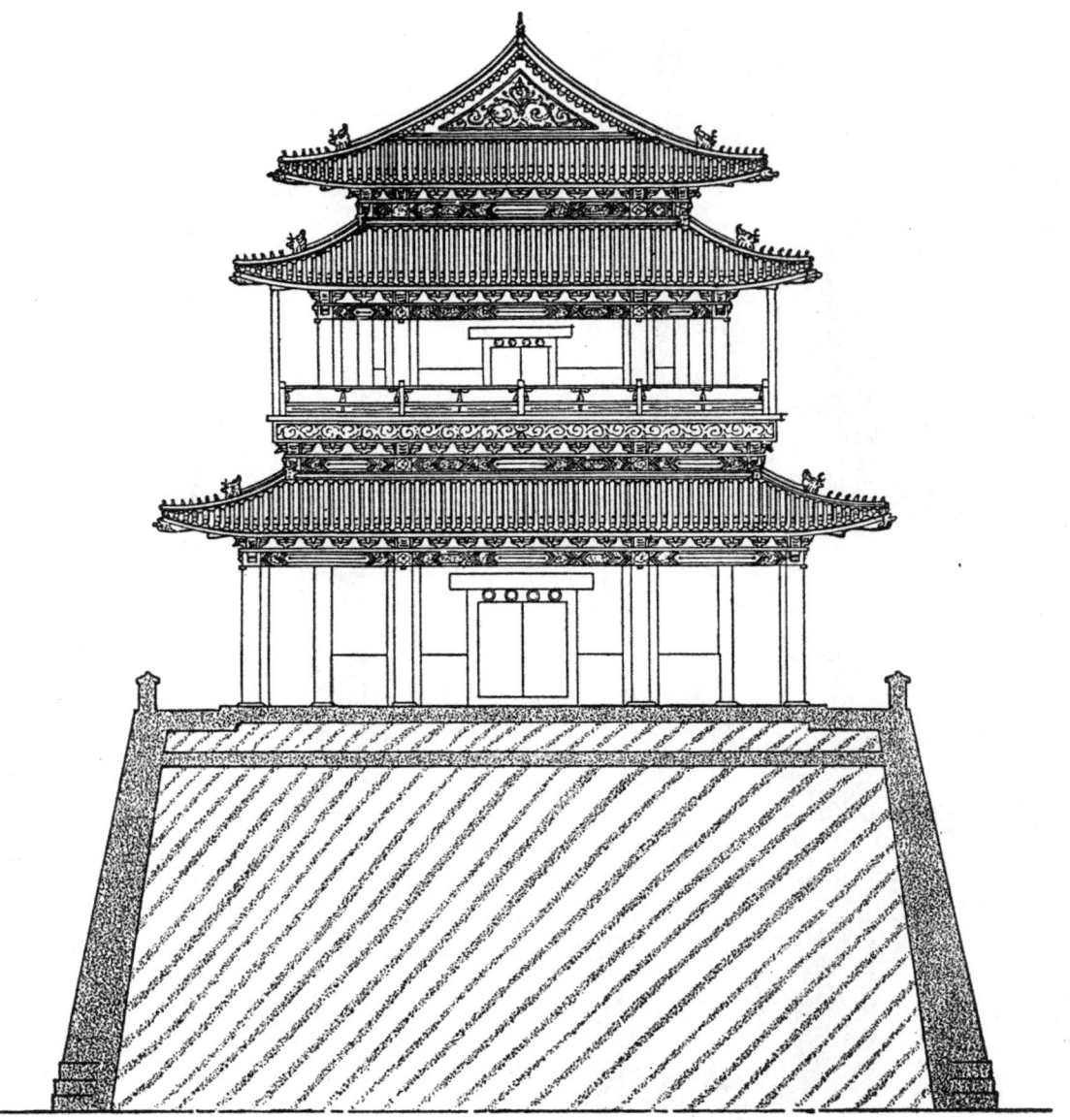

西面樓內門城阜
• SIDE ELEVATION •

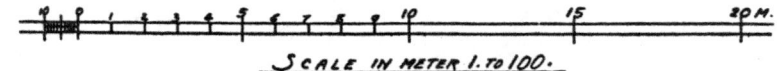
SCALE IN METER 1. TO 100.

FIG. 11.—P'ing Tzu Men, inner tower.

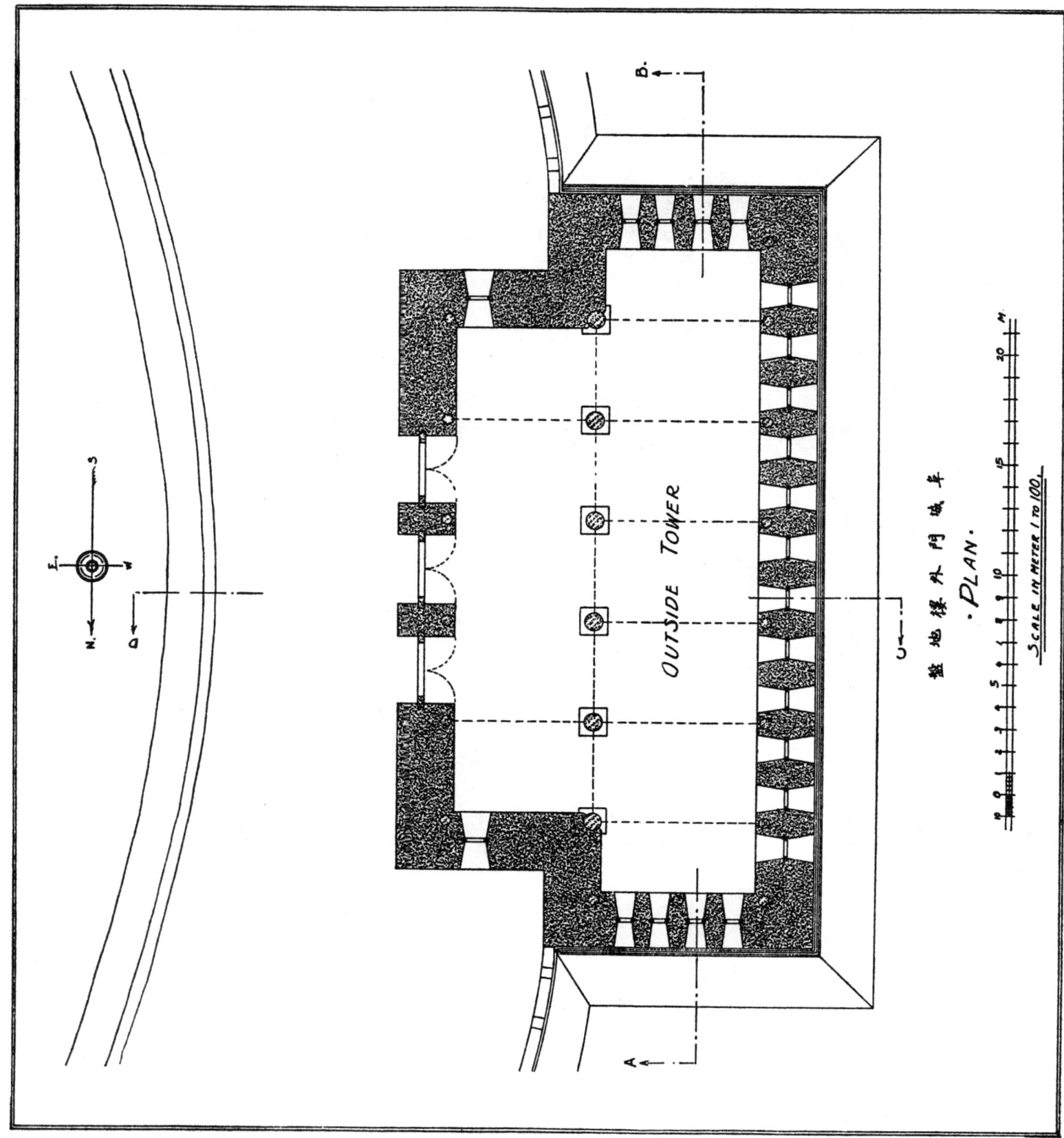

Fig. 12.—P'ing Tzu Men, outer tower.

THE GATES OF THE TARTAR CITY

which rests on the projecting bastion with its façade towards the bridge, and a smaller and lower section behind it, standing on the barbican wall,

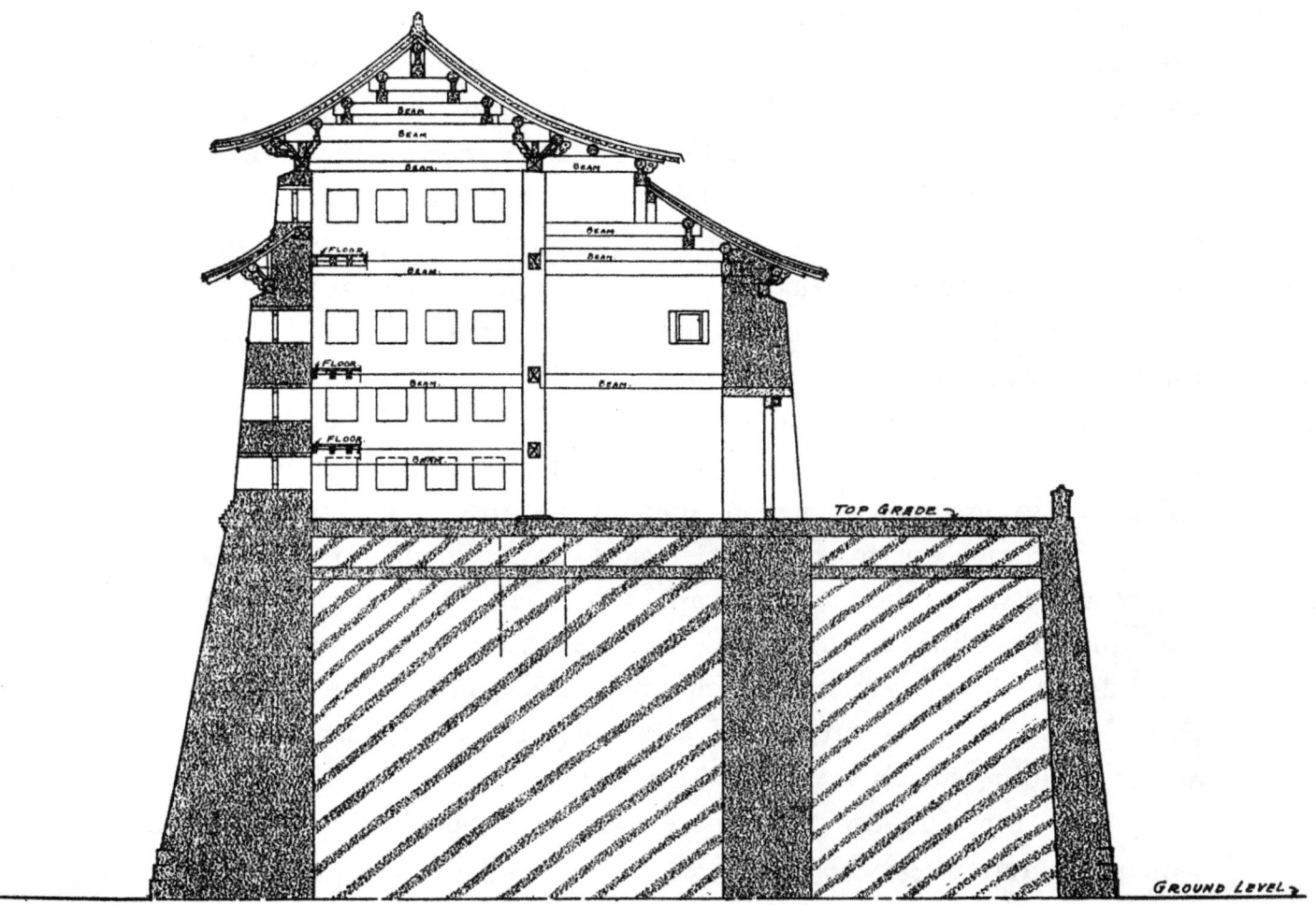

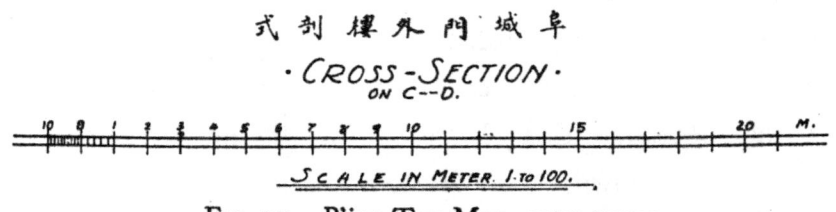

Fig. 13.—P'ing Tzu Men, outer tower.

from which the tower is entered. The façade of the main part is at the ground level almost 40 metres broad, at the top of the bastion the foot of the tower is 35 metres, and at the top (under the upper roof beam) a little less than 32 metres. The full height of the façade is 30 metres, the bastion being 13 metres and the tower itself 17 metres high. The two sides are only 21 metres broad, but to this may be added the breadth of the smaller hind section, i.e. 6·80 metres, the side walls being continuous, though forming a knee of about $3\frac{1}{2}$ metres width on each side. The whole width of the smaller section at the back of the main part is thus about 25 metres and its height is 12 metres. It forms a kind of vestibule to the main room; the walls are continuous, but the roofs are separate.

The constructive frame of the outer as well as of the inner gate tower is made of wooden columns connected by beams. Six large columns (80 cm. in diameter) stand in a row down the centre of the room, reaching up to the roof-beams at a height of 12 metres. The intervals between the columns are 3·80 metres. Corresponding to these are smaller columns embedded in the brick walls on all four sides. The detached and embedded columns are connected by beams running both lengthwise and crosswise, and serving to support the main floors of the building which are now destroyed.

Above these follow four more beams, supporting round purlins, on which the rafters of the roof rest. The far-projecting and curved eaves are, as usual, supported by stringers on triple-armed brackets projecting from beams which are partly embedded in the brick walls. These are very thick, measuring at the bottom no less than $2\frac{1}{2}$ metres and at the top, where they become narrower in consequence of the battering of the outer face, 1·20 metres. The lower roof is at the level of the third floor and is carried around the whole building including the annex, the latter having only a three-sided "irimoya" roof, as it joins the main tower on the fourth side. The upper roof is exactly like that of the

THE GATES OF THE TARTAR CITY

inner tower both in construction and decoration. Its projecting rafters are, as usual, a little shorter than those of the roof below.

The loopholes in the façade and the side walls correspond to the interior divisions of the big room. There are thus three rows below the first roof and one row above it; each row consists of twelve holes on the front and four on the side walls. The jambs of the openings are splayed both inside and outside—their plan being like a spindle—a practical arrangement which serves to give the arrows of the defenders in the tower a wider range. For a defence with guns such a form would hardly be required, and we may doubt whether heavy guns have ever been mounted in this tower except possibly on the ground floor, but nevertheless it has been found appropriate to paint muzzles of big guns on the wooden boards by which the holes are closed—a contrivance which is quite effective from a decorative point of view and in good harmony with the more or less imaginary defensive value of the gate as a whole.

The outer aspect of this tower is very plain. The grey bricks have taken on a dark hue with age and dust, the pantiles are grey; only the wooden beams, brackets, and gables have been painted and ornamented, a decoration which is now practically obliterated. But the cannon-muzzles on the boards in the loopholes are still preserved on the façade as threatening reminders to possible intruders!

The small tower over the side gate in the barbican wall rises only slightly above the battlements and does not project beyond the wall-face. It is a plain brick building with hipped roof and two rows of loopholes on the façade. It attracts no special attention, as it almost sinks into the wall between the battlement and the parapet.

On the main wall, to the north of the inner tower, is a rather shabby looking guard-house, while two other guard-houses, used by the street police and the soldiers who are in charge of the wall, stand on

阜城門外樓剖式

·LONG SECTION·
ON A.--B.

SCALE IN METER 1. TO 100.

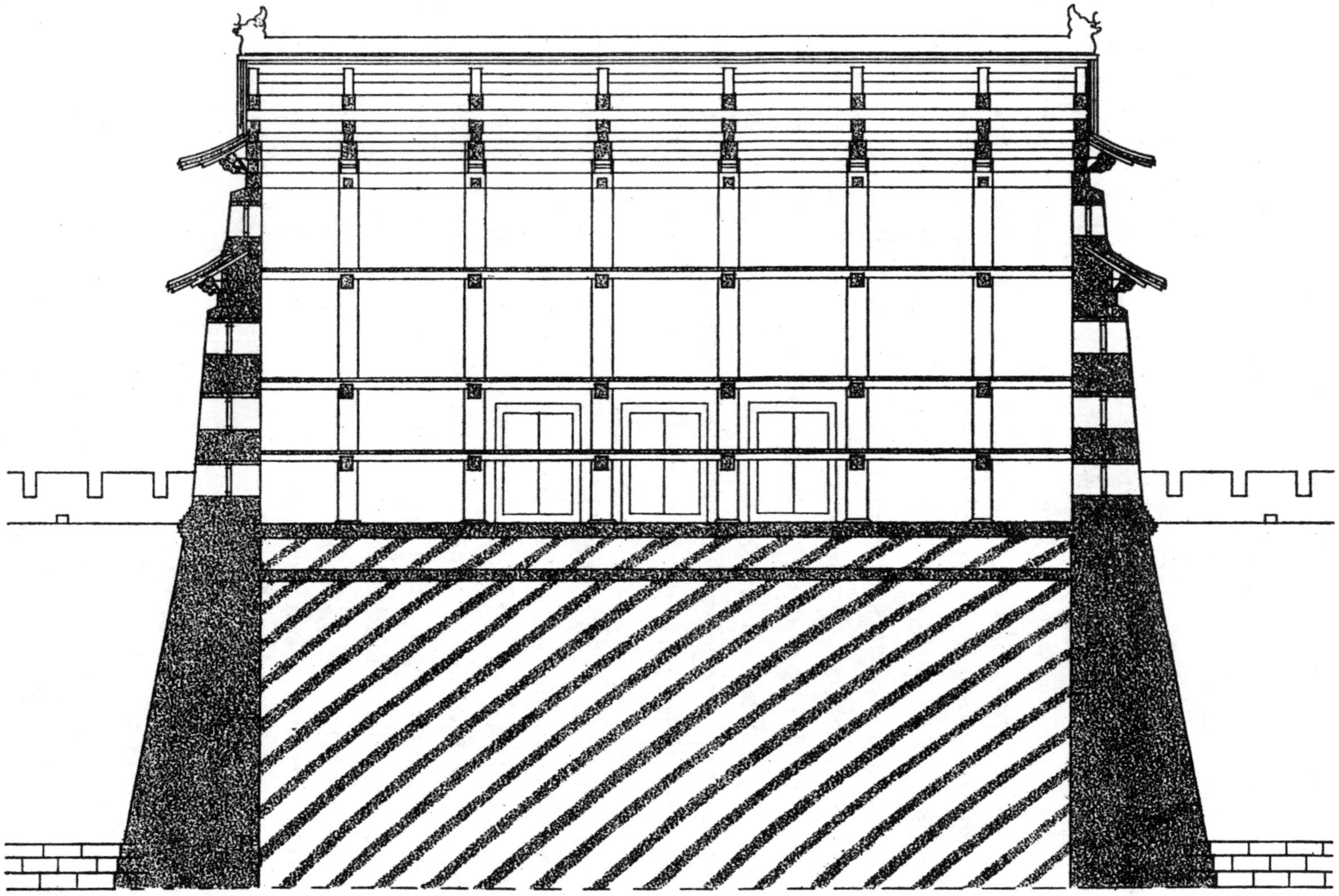

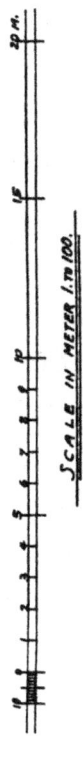

FIG. 14.—P'ing Tzu Men, outer tower.

THE GATES OF THE TARTAR CITY

either side of the street in front of the gate ramps, fortunately well obscured by old trees.

阜城門外樓旁面
· SIDE ELEVATION ·

SCALE IN METER 1. TO 100.

FIG. 15.—P'ing Tzu Men, outer tower.

The gate-yard of P'ing Tzu men is not one of the largest. It

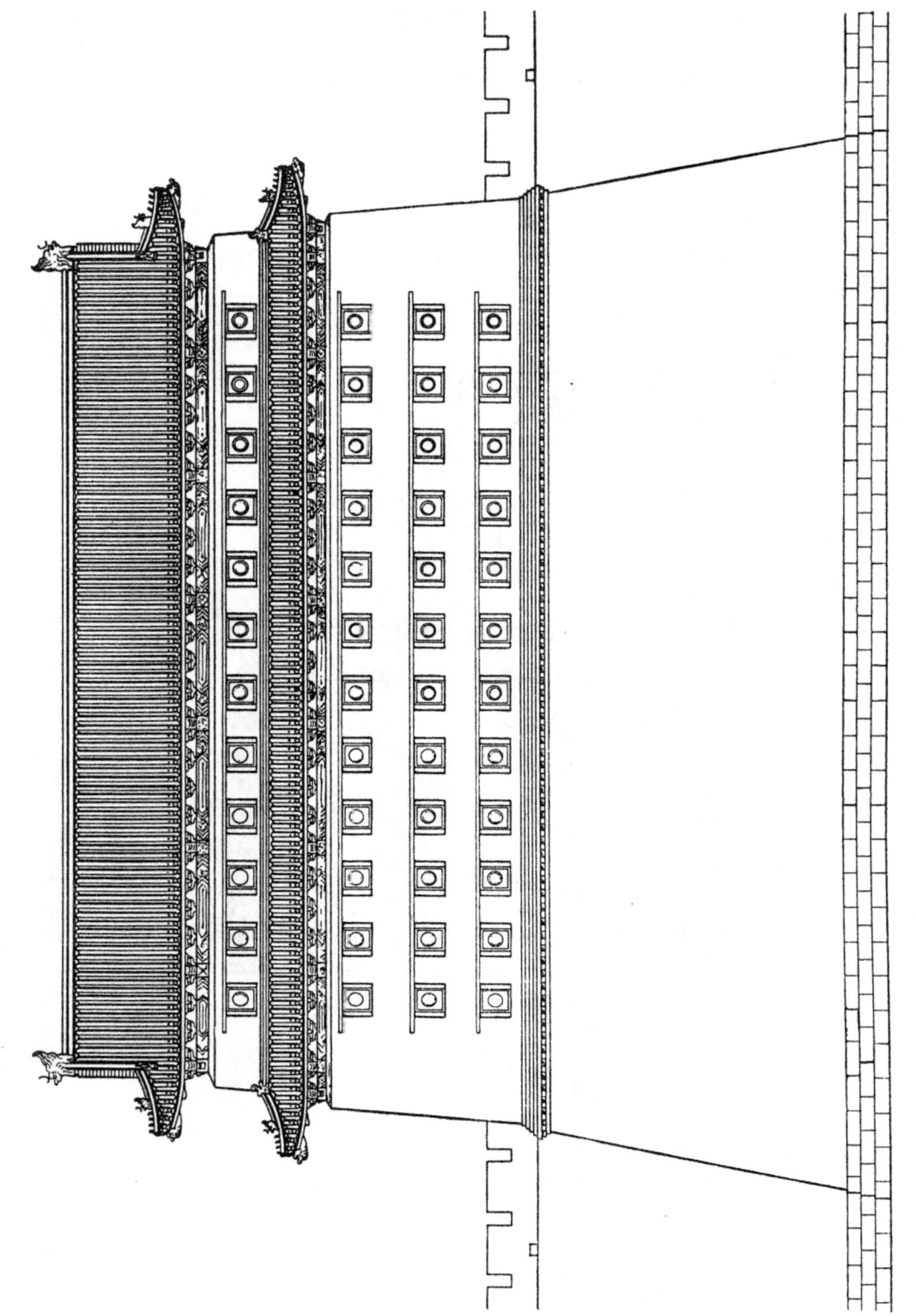

Fig. 16.—P'ing Tzu Men, outer tower.

measures only 74 metres in width and 65 metres in depth. The ground space is largely occupied by coal merchants and pottery dealers, yet, in the north-eastern corner, between the road and the wall, are still to be found the buildings forming a small Kuan Ti miao, enclosed by a wall. The temple seems to be out of use for religious purposes—at the time of my visit the rooms were filled with clay pots and all sorts of refuse —but the architectural composition is still complete. In the opposite, south-eastern corner of the gate-yard stacks of gaily coloured and glazed pottery form a prettier show, while the back part of the yard is dirty and black from the stores and sheds of the coal merchants who here carry on their trade with various mixtures of coal dust and mud baked into balls and bricks. But when spring comes the fine old mulberry tree, which stands close to the inner wall, spreads its refreshing green over the black ground, and some young ailanthus trees add to the colourful brilliancy of the corner where all the glazed pottery is stacked. The liveliest element is, however, formed by the donkey drivers who, as soon as a wanderer has emerged into the gate-yard, spare no efforts to convince him that the road outside the gate is not meant for walking but for riding on a donkey, an opinion which very few Chinamen are likely to contradict.

The old-fashioned paved road which passes out through the side gate and follows the northern side of the barbican is lined on both sides with small shops and rustic eating houses. Nothing could be more picturesque. The Chinese country-folk with their carts and wheelbarrows, or baskets swinging from long poles over the shoulder, are here much more at home than on the newly widened and macadamized roads outside some of the other gates. Such a shop-lined road is in perfect harmony with the barbican and the towers; it forms the right kind of prelude to the architectural composition, taking us a few hundred years back in time and putting us into the right mood before we enter the deep vault of the gate.

* * * * *

Hsi Chih men, the northern gate in the West wall, is in many respects closely akin to P'ing Tzu men, though it has a larger and almost right-angled barbican. As a whole this gate makes a very imposing picture from whatever side it is contemplated. Approaching it along the broad street that leads right up to the gateway, one sees at a distance the inner tower rising dominant over the uniformly low buildings which line the street—nice old-fashioned houses with latticed windows and doors which by their small scale make the tower look so much the larger and more monumental. Coming from the outside one is impressed by the fortress-like character of the square barbican and the outer tower which rises in startling contrast with the bare ground all around. The long straight front wall of the barbican gives effective support to the broad mass of the tower; the composition expresses more strength and massiveness than at gates where the corners of the barbican are rounded. The side view of the gate, especially from the south, gives the best idea of the extent of the whole composition. The two towers balance each other perfectly, the outer one being only slightly lower than the inner, their straight lines and sharp corners giving energy to the rhythm. The monumentality of the picture is enhanced by the reflection in the pool at the foot of the wall.

The main buildings of this gate are now in a comparatively good state of preservation. They were extensively repaired in 1894 in connection with the construction of the new Summer Palace and the road leading out to it through the Hsi Chih men. But before this restoration was completed the war with Japan occurred and the work had to stop, as no more funds for the purpose were available. The inner tower had then been largely renewed, but less had been done on the outer one. The plan of this inner tower is practically same as the plan of the P'ing Tzu men tower, though the proportions are somewhat different; the length of the whole façade is the same in both cases,

THE GATES OF THE TARTAR CITY

measuring 32 metres between the end columns and a little more than 27 metres over the wall. But the Hsi Chih men tower is not so broad, being only 15·8 metres between the colonnades and 11·2 metres over the brick wall. The full height of this tower is 22·2 metres, just one metre more than the height of the P'ing Tzu men tower. The Hsi Chih men tower is thus altogether a more slender building; this gives it the

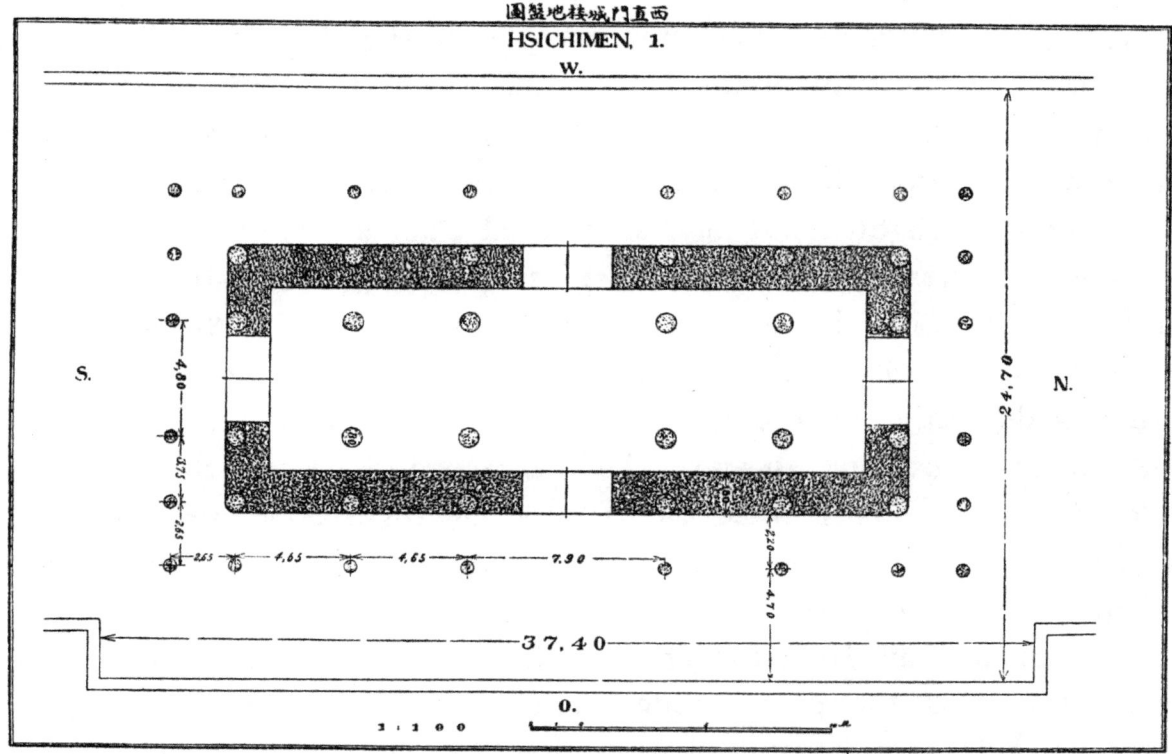

Fig. 17.—Hsi Chih Men, plan of the inner tower.

appearance of greater height, especially when contemplated from the gable side. Though these sides are comparatively short, they have, nevertheless, five spans instead of three (as on P'ing Tzu men's tower), while the façade has seven, as usual. The columns of the gallery are placed rhythmically, the intercolumniations gradually decreasing towards the corners. The large middle interval corresponds to the door on each side. The second row of columns is entirely embedded in the brickwork, while the innermost row, which is reduced to four columns on each side, is detached and stands inside the room. It serves to carry the main roof, yet these very thick and strong columns (diameter 80 cm.) are not continued through the whole height of the building, but are cut into two sections by the floor of the second story, and the same is the case with the embedded columns. The upper sections do not stand exactly on the top of the lower ones, but are placed slightly nearer the centre, thus shortening the span of the cross-beams. The three curved roofs rest, as usual, on round purlins placed on the rafters and splockets which are carried by the projecting brackets. It is, however, quite noticeable that the brackets are lighter and less substantial than at P'ing Tzu men, and this is a characteristic indication of a later period of construction. The general tendency of Chinese architecture in later years has been to lessen the constructive value of the bracketing system, treating it more and more as a decorative feature and relying mainly on the simpler construction with columns and cross-beams. Another deviation from the traditional mode of construction is that the balcony of the second story does not rest on brackets projecting from horizontal beams, but on short columns standing on the cross-beams of the gallery and piercing its roof. Such a construction may be stronger, but it does not fit as well into the general frame as the older mode. The very far-projecting curved roof of the second story is supported at the four corners by special slender poles. The main roof rests on two purlins on each side, instead of four, as in the older tower, and the number of cross-beams is also reduced. Here the utmost has been done to simplify the construction while giving it greater weight and strength. The older mode certainly required more labour and material, but whether it insured greater safety seems doubtful.

The outer decoration and colouring of the Hsi Chih men tower is still completely visible, though somewhat subdued by Peking dust. The columns, doors, and window frames are painted vermilion and the plaster on the brickwork has also a warm red hue. The beams under the eaves and the balcony are decorated with geometrical designs in blue and green. The roofs are laid with green glazed tiles, and provided with the same kind of fantastic winged heads and small seated animals as we saw on the P'ing Tzu men roof. The building being narrower and the roofs wider than in the previous instance, the general effect is remarkably light and elegant.

The outer tower of Hsi Chih men has not been so carefully repaired as the inner tower; it has altogether an older appearance and its roof is beginning to crumble at the back. The pantiles have evidently been renewed, but the brickwork of the walls may be several hundred years old. This tower is both in size, plan, and elevation almost a replica of the P'ing Tzu men tower and consequently need not detain us. Our illustrations will serve to give a sufficient idea of its position and monumental proportions.

The gate-yard is a very large and exceptionally entertaining place; indeed, it reminds one of a market-place with all its stalls and continuous clatter of all sorts of people, animals, and vehicles. The back part of it is mainly occupied by coal merchants, as is the P'ing Tzu men yard, but along the road which turns from the main gate towards the south to the small gate in the side wall are the stacks and stalls of pottery dealers and the stand of the rickshaw coolies. The north-eastern quarter is cut off by a separate wall, and inside this one finds a very pleasant temple compound consisting of several small buildings (also dwelling-houses), some fine trees and well-cultivated flower gardens. The temple itself, dedicated to Kuan Ti, seems to have fallen into disuse, though the buildings are still in a fairly good state since their restoration in 1894. The front part of this large temple enclosure is now mainly utilized as a commercial flower garden by the people who occupy the old priests' quarters. Some large ailanthus and tall junipers shade the place, giving it in the warm season a pleasant air of cool restfulness so different from the hustling and noisy life in the main gate-yard.

Passing out under the small tower which rises over the vaulted gateway in the southern side wall of the barbican one enters a genuine old-fashioned Chinese street which is not bordered simply by the plainest kinds of shops and temporary stalls like the streets outside most of the gates, but by rows of more permanent old-fashioned houses. Leaning against the barbican is a continuous low building which follows the wall from the gate to the outside tower bastion, rounding the south-west corner of the barbican. It is like a long bazaar under a continuous far-projecting roof, though divided into a series of shops, the owners of which display their goods on the stone steps or serve their eatables on tables and benches outside the doors. The buildings on the other side of the road are mostly inns and hostelries, much frequented by the country-folk. They also form a continuous row and their architectural type is fairly uniform, but the height varies, alternating from one to two stories. Consequently the skyline is considerably broken, an arrangement which used to be quite characteristic of the old Chinese streets, not for any æsthetic reasons, but because it was considered most desirable from the point of view of the Fêng Shui. The façades of these buildings consist of wooden columns and large latticed windows and doors; when they have two stories there is a carved and gilded frieze projecting over the ground story. This street has evidently been arranged on a unified plan according to traditional Chinese principles, and it is still one of the most characteristic views of that picturesque old Peking which is disappearing so rapidly. The automobiles, which nowadays rush out through Hsi Chih men to carry tourists on a flying visit to the Summer Palace or the Western Hills, should be forced to drive very slowly past these frail old façades, which, after all, give a truer impression of the *mise en scène* for the daily life in old China than either the Summer Palace or the Temple of the Sleeping Buddha.

B. The Gates of the East Wall

The two gates of the East wall, Ch'i Hua men and Tung Chih men, are less well preserved and consequently less interesting from an architectural point of view than those on the west side. They have been badly affected by the construction of the Round-the-City railway, which was carried right across the gate-yards. For this purpose it was deemed necessary to demolish the barbican walls almost entirely instead of simply cutting some opening through them as was done on the south side, at the Hata men, where the Peking-Mukden line passes through the barbican walls. Thus hardly anything remains of the picturesque old gate-yards on this side; there are no outer gateways, and the road simply winds along the low brick wall of the railway track, and the new stations with their platforms encroach upon the space formerly protected by the high walls of the barbican. The re-arrangement bears witness to a complete disrespect for the beauty and character of the old gates; it could hardly have been accomplished with greater lack of good taste and architectural sense, as will become evident from a closer scrutiny of these gates.

Ch'i Hua men is probably the most extensively rebuilt gate in Peking. Both the towers of this gate were practically renewed about twenty years ago (1902), as they had been severely damaged by the guns of the Russian and Japanese troops during the siege of Peking at the time of the Boxer War. They have not yet had time to become rotten or decay, though the painted ornaments have begun to look somewhat faded and the dry lacquer coating has started to flake off at certain spots. The roofs still have their green-glazed tiles well preserved, and this adds a note of brightness to the structure. The general view of the inner tower is quite effective at some distance from the street when framed by the verdant trees in the foreground.

The structure is of the usual type. It consists of three stories, gradually diminishing in height and width towards the top; the open galleries have seven spans on the façades and three on the shorter sides. The proportions are practically the same as on the P'ing Tzu men tower

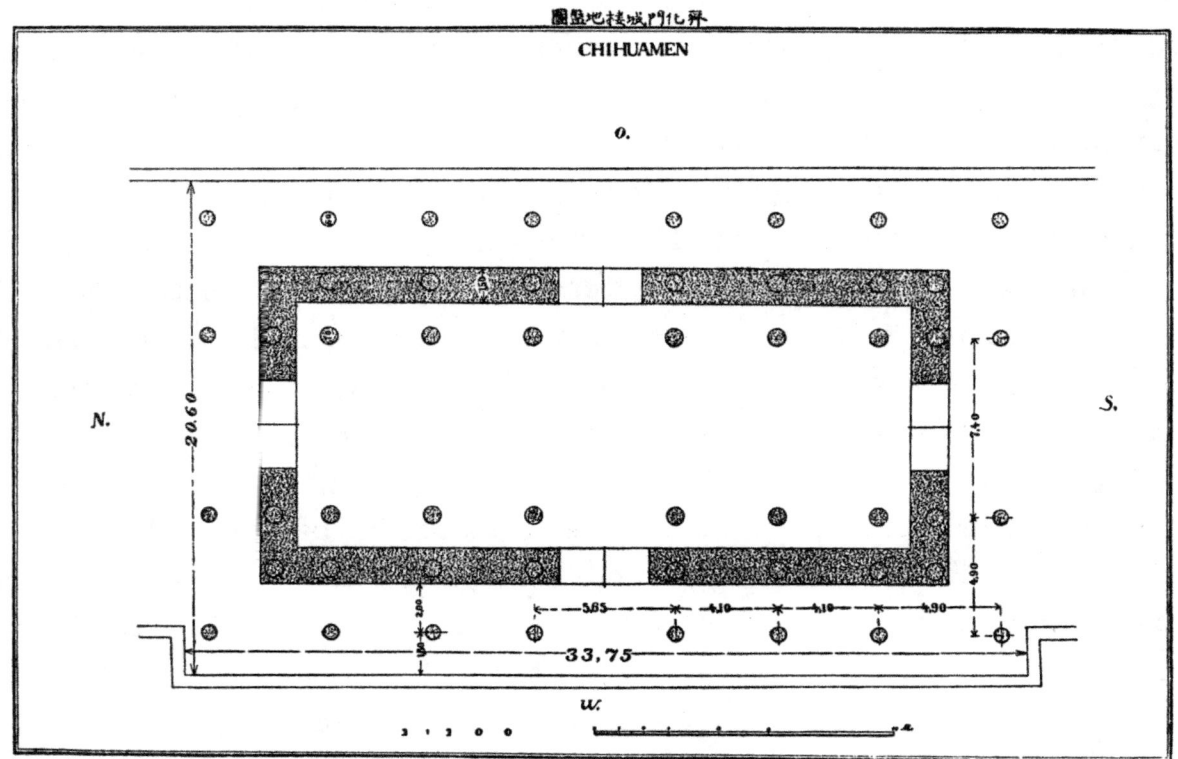

Fig. 18.—Ch'i Hua Men, plan of the inner tower.

(the corresponding one on the west side), but the principles of construction are modified in a similar way to those of the Hsi Chih men and some of the other rebuilt gates. The special characteristics of this tower as compared with the others depend on its unusual width in proportion to its length. The measurements of the walls are 13 by 27½ metres, and those of the outer gallery 17 by 32 metres, which is just a little

THE GATES OF THE TARTAR CITY

more than the corresponding measurements of the P'ing Tzu men tower, but the walls are of course much thinner than in the older building, and only the middle row of columns is embedded in the brickwork. It seems likely that the inner tower of Ch'i Hua men was originally almost identical with that of P'ing Tzu men, and that its present differences in construction and details are the results of modern restorations.

The outer towers of the two gates correspond also so closely in plan and dimensions that the description of the former may on the whole serve for the latter. But the Ch'i Hua men tower is indeed in a better state of preservation. The light grey smooth masonry of its walls looks quite new, particularly in contrast to the uneven and weathered brickwork of the bastion, which is evidently old, though partly restored in the 31st year of Ch'ien Lung (as stated on a tablet).

The remaining arms of the barbican wall which extend from the bastion are quite short and ended in a most outlandish fashion with winding staircases between successive terraces provided with stepped balustrades. The niggling lines of this composition—which seems inspired by some popular picture-book of semi-medieval castles—are, to say the least, entirely out of keeping with the quietly monumental character of the old walls and gates. Yet it is repeated with only slight variations at all those gate barbicans which have been more or less sacrificed to the railways.

The only thing that here remains of the old gate-yard is the small Kuan Ti miao at the side of the inner gate. It is of no particular importance, but it harbours a few trees inside its walls and marks a bright spot in the drab yard mainly dominated by the railway, the station of which is situated opposite the temple at the other side of the gateway. The outside view is impoverished by the very common-looking bridge over the narrow mound, to say nothing of the indescribable little house at the foot of the monumental tower.

Tung Chih men, the gate facing directly east, forms a pair with Hsi Chih men, the gate facing directly west, which lies exactly opposite. The towers of these two gates are of the same proportions and almost the same dimensions, being in this respect somewhat different from the two side gates further south, but Tung Chih men is not so completely preserved as its western counterpart; its barbican wall has been demolished

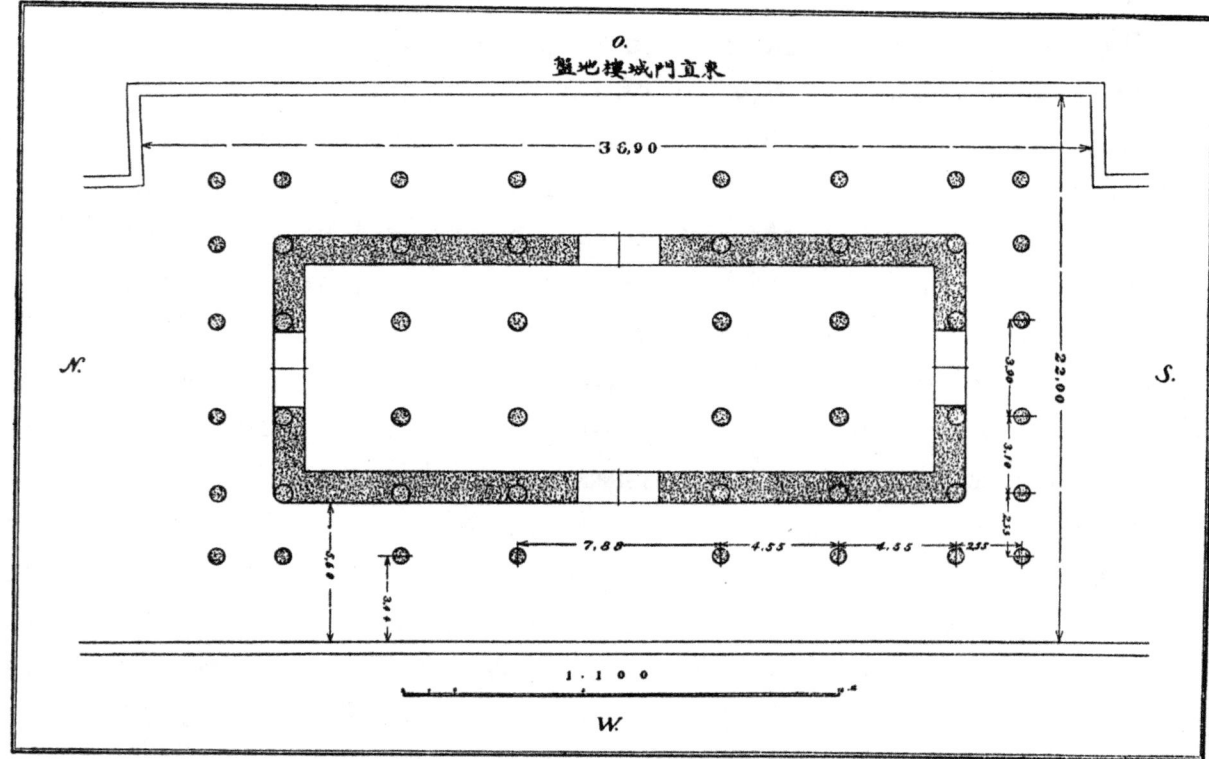

FIG. 19.—Tung Chih Men, plan of the inner tower.

and the gate-yard practically destroyed; nor are the towers in a very good state of preservation. Yet I should hardly think that the inner tower is much over a hundred years old. The ramps leading up to it were rebuilt, according to an inserted tablet, in the 8th year of Chia Ch'ing (1803), and it may well be that the tower was renewed at the same period. Its very thin walls do not suggest a much earlier date. The outer tower

THE GATES OF THE TARTAR CITY

may in part be a little older, though not before the latter half of the Ch'ien Lung period; the tablet on its bastion has unfortunately no inscription.

The plan dimensions of the inner tower are only slightly smaller than the dimensions of the corresponding tower on Hsi Chih men, i.e. walls: 26·7 by 10·7 metres; thickness 1·2 metres; outer gallery 31·5 by 15·3 metres. The construction is the usual one with three rows of columns, the middle row encased in the brick walls while the outer and inner columns are strengthened by square posts. The woodwork is evidently older than on Hsi Chih men; the balustrade of the balcony is practically destroyed and the panelling under it is full of holes. The roofs have begun to rot and break down, and if they now have a green hue it is not from any glazed tiles but from fresh tufts of grass. The original colours of the columns and the painted ornaments can hardly be distinguished under the thick layers of Peking dust which have accumulated here during a generation or more. The whole building has taken on a fine hue of age and seasoned beauty.

The distance between the inner and the outer tower of Tung Chih men is considerably longer than the corresponding distance at Ch'i Hua men, the gate described above. Seen in full side view this gate is about as extensive as Hsi Chih men—a truly imposing composition, though now lacking the connecting link between the two towers. The barbican wall, which evidently was built on a similar plan to that of the west gate, has been destroyed except for the stumps at the side of the outer tower bastion. Fortunately these are a little longer than at Ch'i Hua men. The gap between them and the main wall is not quite as empty as in the previous instance—partly owing to a richer vegetation—and the sloping ends are just a little less offensively arranged, in spite of the fact that the system with a series of terraces and zigzag staircases is the same as at Ch'i Hua men. But while in the former case the isolated towers and mutilated bits of the gate wall stood out in perfect nakedness amidst barren and drab surroundings, here at Tung Chih men they are partly overgrown and embedded in a rich foliage of trees and shrubs.

The original character of the place is thus not completely obliterated, except in the front part where the railway runs through, screened by a low brick wall and a wooden fence. The rear part of this old gate-yard contains also a very picturesque group of small temple buildings dedicated to Kuan Ti, in which some gaudy statues are left to moulder away and a few decrepit people find a gloomy shelter. Within and outside this temple enclosure stand a number of trees—locust, elm, and ailanthus—and at the top of the old barbican wall sweet-scented jujube shrubs form a festal garland. The present state of the outer tower, which although not very old has begun to break down at the roof corners, is in good keeping with the unhampered growth of nature's decorations.

The natural beauty of the half that remains of this gate-yard is, however, only the prelude to the richer scenery outside the gate—a view which is hardly equalled by the landscape at any other of the large city gates of Peking. The best time to see it is in the late spring or early summer, when the willows are fresh and glossy and the bulrushes in the moat still young. The broad canal-like moat is the artery of the whole landscape; everything that is of importance to this neighbourhood—either from a practical or a pictorial point of view—thrives along its banks or moves on its waters. Far up on the banks there are the black pigs ploughing the rich mire with their snouts; lower down children are playing like frogs among the bulrushes, and out on the water flocks of large white ducks splash and quack in response to the calls of their various owners. When the water-carrier comes down to fetch water in his tin pails he squats for a while on his heels contemplating the idyllic view in silent amusement. A few steps further south a small ferry crosses the canal, offering a short cut from the opposite bank to

THE GATES OF THE TARTAR CITY

the railway station, and now and again a square flat-bottomed vessel loaded with people in white summer attire comes gliding between the overhanging willows. And all these various elements of the animated and yet quiet and harmonious picture are reflected in the waters, a reflection which adds a note of more immaterial beauty, a touch of that idyllic mood which was more common at the gates of Peking before the existence of railways and motor-cars.

C. The Gates of the South Wall

On the southern side there are, as we have seen, three gates forming the thoroughfares between the Inner and the Outer city. They are all well known, thanks to their central situation, and much admired by tourists and new-comers to Peking for their large size and decorative gaudiness, but from a historical and architectural point of view they are the least interesting of all the gates of the capital. All three have been more dilapidated and rebuilt in modern times than any of the other Peking gates. The transformation has been most complete at the great middle gate, Ch'ien men, but quite considerable also at the side gates.

These two gates, Hata men and Shun Chih men, form a homogeneous pair; they correspond both in size and character and also in their present state of preservation. Both have been quite recently (1920–1921) rebuilt, or should we say ruined, as the restorations only concerned the inner towers, while the outer ones were simply demolished. The reason for this is said to have been that the outer towers were rotten and unsafe, especially in consideration of the railway at their foot, and yet the beams of the Shun Chih men tower, which may still be seen on the bastion, look quite fresh and safe. The tower of Hata men may have been in somewhat worse condition, as the roof corners had actually begun to break down, but no doubt both towers could have been saved, if the authorities had bestowed on them a little more care and interest.

But it was so much easier and cheaper to take them down and sell the material, postponing the rebuilding to a time of more prosperous

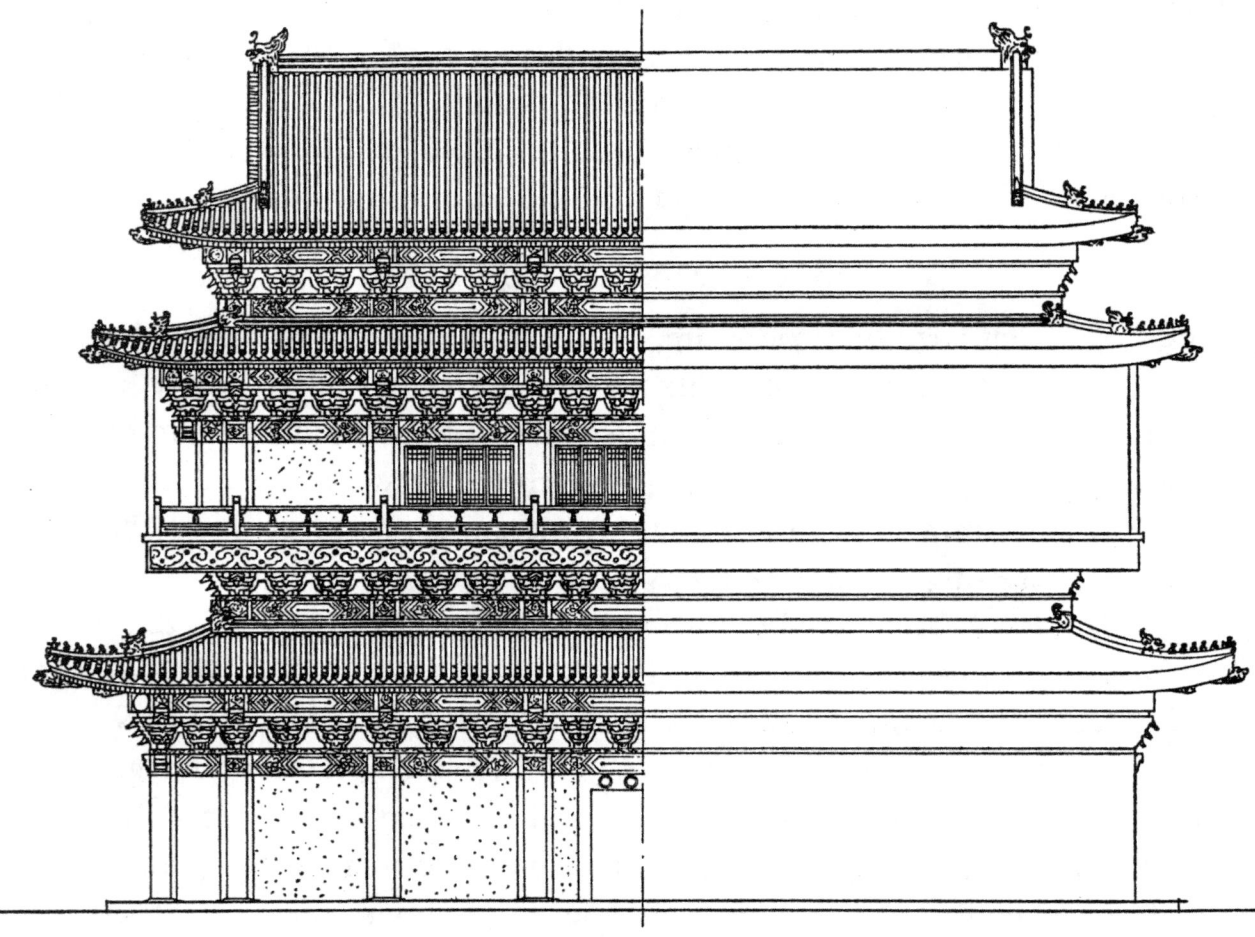

FIG. 20.—Hata Men, inner tower.

finances and better stabilized government (!). Thus it is only from the inner side, or the Manchu city, that these gates still offer imposing views,

THE GATES OF THE TARTAR CITY

dominated by high towers. The outer views, from the Chinese city, are quite monotonous, as the barbican has no concentrating central motive that would lift it over the horizontal flow of the main wall.

Hata men is especially popular among foreigners, as it stands close to the legation quarter and overspans the most frequented business street of the city: the Hata men ta chieh. Seen from this street on a summer evening, when the sun is shedding a warm light over the red columns and the green-glazed roof tiles, the newly restored tower makes a very effective picture. It is then enjoyable as a display of bright and warm colours over a monumental architectural frame, and one has no reason to look for refinement of ornament or technique. The tower is complete in all its parts with friezes, brackets, balustrades, and roof ornaments; no detail has yet been broken or weather-worn by dust-storms.

The dimensions are larger than in any of the previously examined towers. The walls measure on the outside 28·7 by 14·4 metres; the outer row of columns 33·4 by 18·8 metres. The height from the terrace to the top of the roof ridge is 25 metres; if we add to this the measure of the supporting bastion the full height of the building becomes nearly 40 metres. It has seven spans of columns on the façade in both the main stories and five on the short sides. The rows of brackets are tripled, though not of great constructive strength, and the horizontal beams are very broad and richly ornamented. The carrying frame is, as usual, made of three rows of columns connected lengthwise and crosswise by beams and supporting the roofs by means of consoles and purlins. The construction is on the whole somewhat simplified as compared with the earlier towers, the roof-beams not being quite so numerous, as for instance in the P'ing Tzu men tower, but it is carried out according to the old principles on a truly monumental scale.

The street that passes through the high vault of the inner bastion (which has probably been enlarged in later times), continues in a straight

164   THE WALLS AND GATES OF PEKING

line over the large gate-yard and passes out through a similar vault in the outer bastion. At right angles to this street, passing through openings in the side walls of the barbican, runs the double-tracked railway line between low brick walls. The trains on this trunk line are quite frequent, and thus the traffic through the gate has often to be stopped by the closing of the railway fences, an arrangement which sometimes causes a

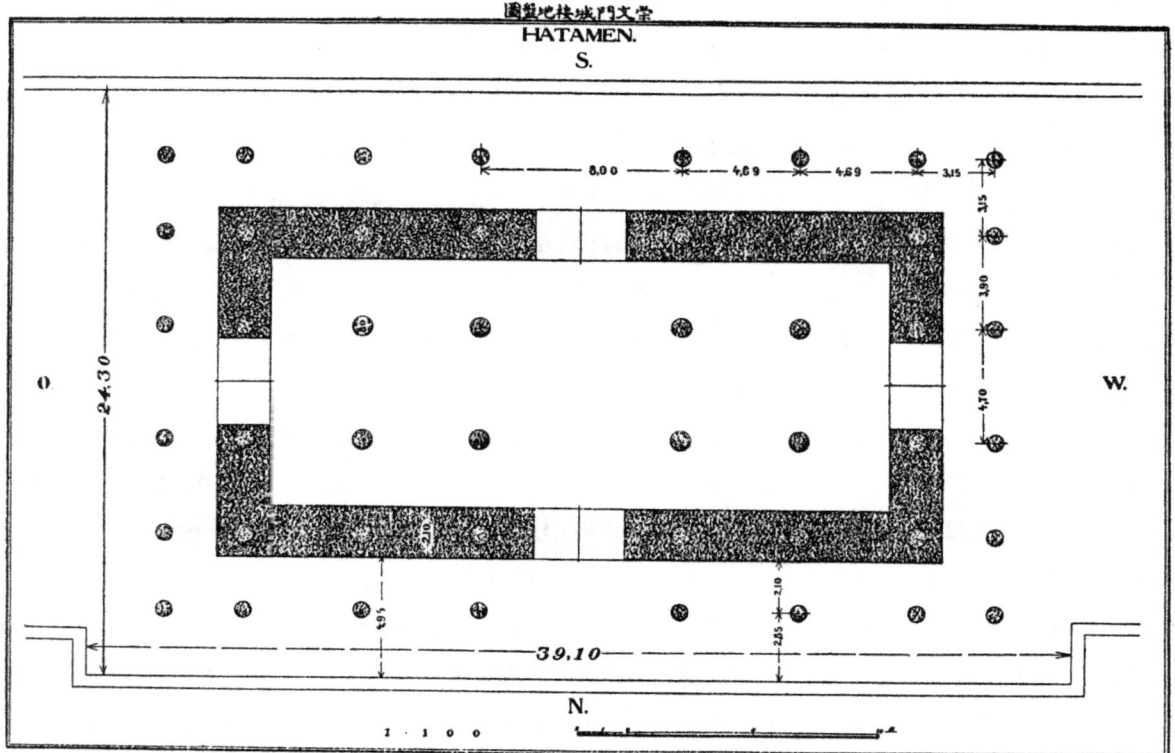

Fig. 21.—Hata Men, plan of the inner tower.

considerable congestion of carts and rickshaws. Yet there is plenty of room on both sides of the road, as the large gate-yard is practically empty. The only constructions here are a low guard-house adjoining the railway line and a small flat-roofed building on the opposite side. The temple is gone and only a few trees remain. On the top of the barbican wall and the bastions the vegetation is more abundant. Here are masses of young locust trees and jujube shrubs which after the rainy season grow into a veritable jungle.

Owing to the absence of the tower the outside view is quite flat and low. The mound is narrow with a shallow stream of dirty water, the bridge of a very ordinary type, and the most conspicuous buildings in the vicinity are the coal sheds of the railway. It is only after one has passed a little farther south along the Hata men street that one may observe some picturesque old-fashioned shops with carved and gilded façades.

The gate itself should be enjoyed either in full front view from the main street or in side view from the Rue de la Muraille, where some fine trees serve as a framing side-wing to the ramp.

Shun Chih men is outwardly almost identical with Hata men. Its barbican wall forms a large flat curve and has no crowning tower; only the stone plinths of the columns and some big timber may still be seen at the place of the tower. Besides these there remain five rusty iron guns on high wheels on the platform of the outer bastion. Three or four of these guns are marked with the names of the officials for whom they were cast; one is of the Ch'ung Chêng period and the others from Kang Hsi's reign. They would be well worth preserving in some safer place as historical relics and records of the French jesuits' skill in gun-foundry.

The newly repaired and redecorated inner tower is almost of the same dimensions as the Hata men tower, only a trifle shorter and lower. We may therefore pass it over without further descriptions either of its decoration or its construction.

However, from all that has been said about the close similarity between Shun Chih men and Hata men it should not be inferred that the two gates are exactly alike; a very considerable difference between them arises from the fact that Shun Chih men still has its old gate-yard well preserved. The railway line which passes this gate has not been cut through the barbican wall but laid just outside the outer bastion. The street which passes in through the vault under the main tower does not continue in a straight line but turns sharply towards the east and leads out through a smaller vault in the side wall, in the same way as in the still better preserved western gates described above. The gate-yard is

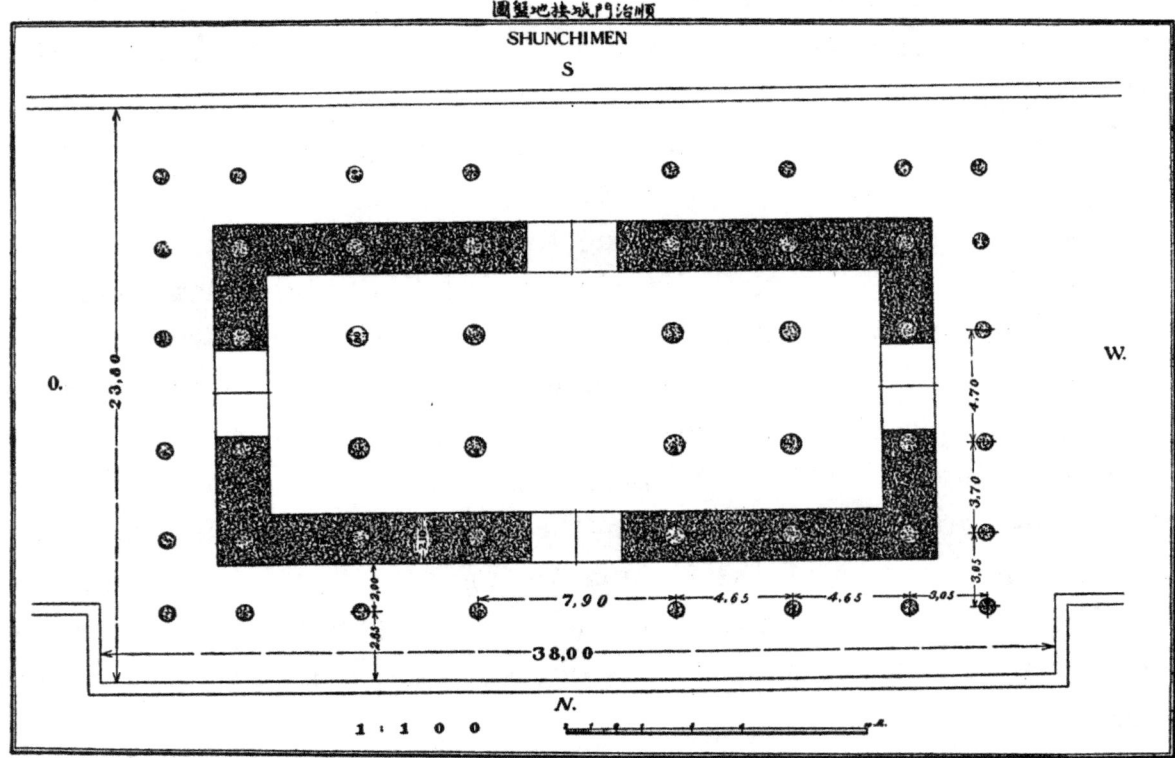

Fig. 22.—Shun Chih Men, plan of the inner tower.

thus a well-isolated, walled-in place with a very definite character of its own.

The main building here is, of course, the gate temple, the small Kuan Ti miao, which lies embedded among beautiful large ailanthus trees, between the road and the main wall. Close to the temple some fortune-tellers have established their stalls, offering for a small fee a guidance through the problems of life more appreciated by the common people than any kind of temple service. At the opposite side of the gate-yard some more profane, though highly useful, small buildings have been erected, but most of the space on this side is occupied by piles and stacks of household pottery, partly glazed and forming beautiful splashes of colour under the white sheds and the green trees. The coal yard in the rear is less visible and less extensive than, for instance, in P'ing Tzu men. It is fairly well screened off by planks, stacks of pottery, and large trees, so that it hardly interferes with the quaint colouristic charm and rich foliage which make this gate-yard quite attractive.

As soon as one has passed out through the gateway of the side wall this characteristic impression is gone. The rather quiet and harmonious air of the old gate-yard is changed into the clatter of a modern Chinese city, with broad and busy streets, semi-foreign buildings in brick and plaster, railway tracks and coal sheds and a few hooting Ford cars forcing their way through camel caravans and throngs of rickshaw coolies.

Ch'ien men, or Cheng Yang men, the great middle gate on the South wall, is by far the most important of all the Peking city gates. Its situation right in front of the Imperial palace and its extraordinary dimensions have made it one of the foremost historical and architectural landmarks of the capital. A whole volume could be written about this gate alone and the historical events connected with it, but here we have only the opportunity to say a few words about its architectural features and the transformation which it has passed through in more recent years. The present Ch'ien men is, as a matter of fact, only a mutilated makeshift for the magnificent old gate composition which formed the main outlet for the Imperial city—a monumental link between the secluded precincts of the rulers and the city of the vulgar crowd.

The original composition consisted of a very large U-shaped barbican enclosing a gate-yard with four openings towards the four main directions.

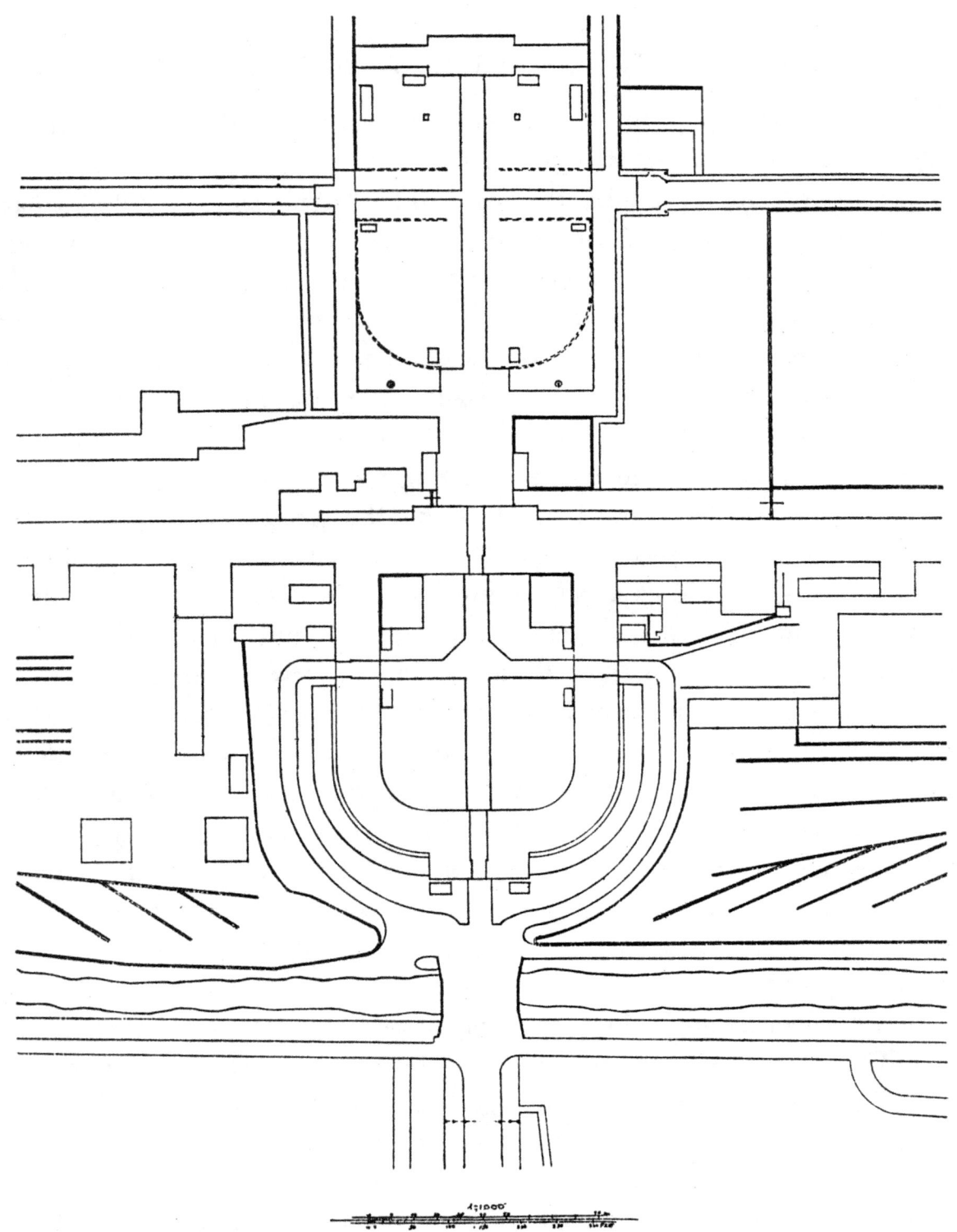

Fig. 23.—Ch'ien Men, general plan, before the reconstruction.

THE GATES OF THE TARTAR CITY

The north gate, under the great inner tower, faced the Ta Ch'ing men (now Chung Hua men), the outer gate of the Palace city, and was architecturally linked with this by means of a wall-enclosed oblong. The south gate, immediately opposite, pierced the bastion of the outer tower facing the bridge over the moat and Ch'ien men ta chieh, the main street of the Outer city. This gate was opened only for the Emperor; all other mortal beings had to pass through the two side gates which pierced the barbican walls to the east and to the west. The gate-yard, which was 108 metres long and 85 metres broad and surrounded by a wall 20 metres thick at its foot, formed a kind of outermost court to the Imperial city, connected with it by means of walls and gates. It was, of course, mainly utilized as a market-place, but the heavy barbican around it together with the very broad outer tower originally constituted, no doubt, a valuable asset to the defence of the Inner city. But as the gate happened to stand right in the centre of the capital where the Outer and the Inner city are most intimately knotted together, the original scope and features of this great construction were gradually outstripped by more modern aims and ideas especially connected with the traffic of the metropolis.

First came the railway stations, one on each side of the barbican, bringing with them a considerable increase of traffic through the gate. Then came the Republic with its dominant desire to lay hold on Imperial prerogatives and turn them to public use. In reference to Ch'ien men this meant a tendency to make the central gate, which had previously been opened only for the Emperor, a passage for everybody. And as all this rapidly increasing traffic from and to the Inner city had to pass through the one vault under the inner tower, this opening soon proved quite insufficient and often became the cause of a most annoying congestion. In order to remove this the government commissioned the German architect Rothkegel, to make plans for the rearrangement of Ch'ien men with the special view of regulating the traffic inside and around the gate.

These very important and far-reaching plans for the modernization of the great central gate of Peking were prepared in 1915 and gradually put into effect, so that the gate actually acquired its present appearance in 1916. Those who have been fortunate enough to see Ch'ien men in its original state with the huge barbican, the side gates and the picturesque yard, are unanimous in deploring the wholesale manner in which so much of the old structure was destroyed, but at the same time they admit that the old conditions were unbearable both from a hygienic point of view and from that of the traffic. As much blame has been bestowed upon the European architect who made the designs for the replanning of Ch'ien men and the adjoining streets, I should like to quote his own statement to the effect, that his original plans were not strictly followed by the Chinese authorities but arbitrarily modified in many details. Yet these modifications probably concerned architectural ornaments and details in the refashioning of the outer tower more than any essential features of the plan disposition. This becomes clear from Mr. Rothkegel's own designs, which we reproduce here with his kind permission. The juxtaposition of the plans of Ch'ien men before and after the radical change will give the reader an opportunity to judge for himself; my task must be limited to a few remarks about the most important new features.

The barbican wall was entirely demolished and the closed gate-yard became an open space or an oblong with a broad detached (outer) tower at its southern end. Two new openings were made through the main wall on both sides of the old inner gate and new broad streets were arranged here, facilitating access to the stations on the east and west sides of the gate. The streets run just outside the old barbican wall and join at the broad bridge which leads over the moat. All the small houses and shops

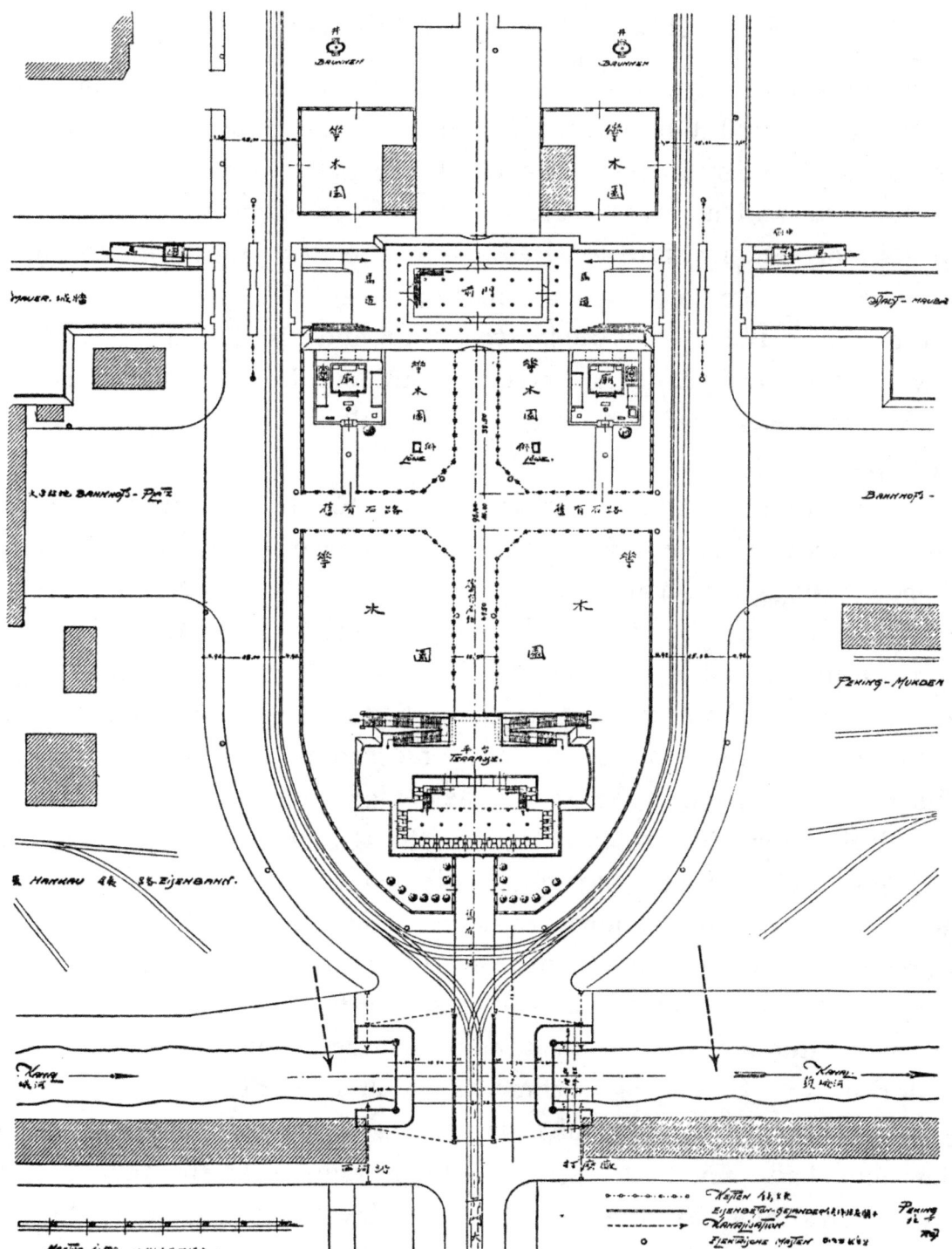

Fig. 24.—Ch'ien Men, general plan, after the reconstruction.

inside and outside the barbican or close to the main wall were cleared away except the two small temples, dedicated to Kuan Yin and Kuan Ti, in the south-east and south-west corners of the gate-yard. Their enclosures were untouched and at some little distance from them towards the south two large stone lions were erected. For the rest the grounds of the former gate-yard remained quite empty; only the broad paved roads which cross over them from north to south and from east to west were railed with stone posts and iron chains, and similar rails were also used along the outer edges of the place, partly following the line of the old barbican wall.

In conjunction with this, the square to the north, between the main gate tower and Chung Hua men, was paved with flagstones and rearranged. The guard-houses which used to stand at its northern end were moved nearer to the wall and enclosed by chain-rails, while decorative fountains were erected in front of them to the north. The further half of this square, up to Chung Hua men, was planted with rows of trees, in European fashion, and enclosed with chain-rails.

The main underlying idea of this new plan arrangement was to create better facilities for the traffic between the Inner and Outer city, and this was no doubt carried out quite effectively by means of two broad side streets running from north to south and passing through the wall by means of the double new openings on both sides of the gate. For this purpose the whole barbican wall was sacrificed and the old gate-yard practically obliterated. It was all done under the direct advice and supervision of the Chinese government, which certainly knew no æsthetic or historical scruples and would hardly have been influenced by such considerations had they been expressed by foreigners at the time.

The impressions that one receives nowadays of the great middle gate are certainly disappointing, from whatever side it is contemplated. It is true that the inner tower still exists in its original form, but the ramps leading up to its terrace are pierced by the double new vaults (which seems to impair their solidity), and the square in front of it is too foreign-looking to harmonize with the architectural character of the tower. Worse still, of course, are the views from the south side including more or less extensive bits of the quite desolate place which used to be the gate-yard. The same applies to the views of the outer tower, which, moreover, has been redecorated in a manner, to say the least, completely foreign to its original character. It stands quite isolated; hardly any stumps of the barbican wall have been left at the sides. The terrace in front of it is ascended by means of a double ramp arranged in zigzag fashion and divided up by a series of terraces decorated with stepped marble balustrades and bulging balconies. In addition to this, curving canopies have been applied over the loopholes with the somewhat inexpedient intention of making them look like palace windows. The transformation of this outside tower is indeed one of the most deplorable features in the refashioning of Ch'ien men, and it is hard to find any practical excuse or reason for it.

The shape and proportions of this tower are the same as of the corresponding towers at the other gates, but its dimensions are considerably larger. The main façade, towards the south, at the level of the terrace measures nearly 50 metres; its greatest width is 24 metres, and its full height is 38 metres. Consequently the constructive members have been strengthened and multiplied; the battering walls are about $2\frac{1}{2}$ metres thick at their base, and three rows of heavy columns support the roof. On the outside there are, as usual, two roofs; a large one with half-hipped ends spreading its curving wings over the whole building, and the slanting half-roof projecting from the notch over the third story. Both are laid with bright green-glazed tiles.

The whole building is hardly more than twenty years old. It was rebuilt after a destructive fire during the Boxer rebellion, when it was

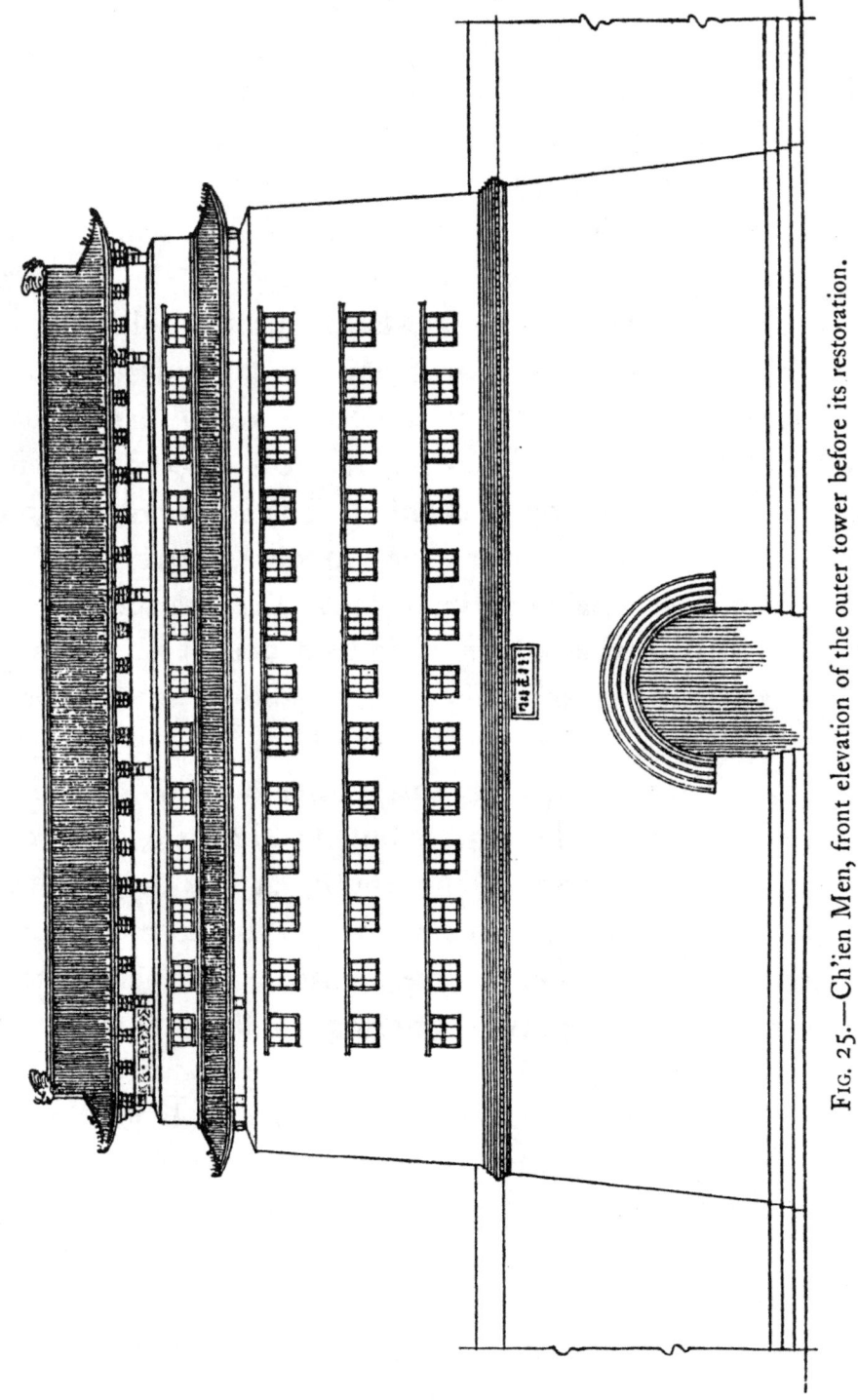

Fig. 25.—Ch'ien Men, front elevation of the outer tower before its restoration.

THE GATES OF THE TARTAR CITY

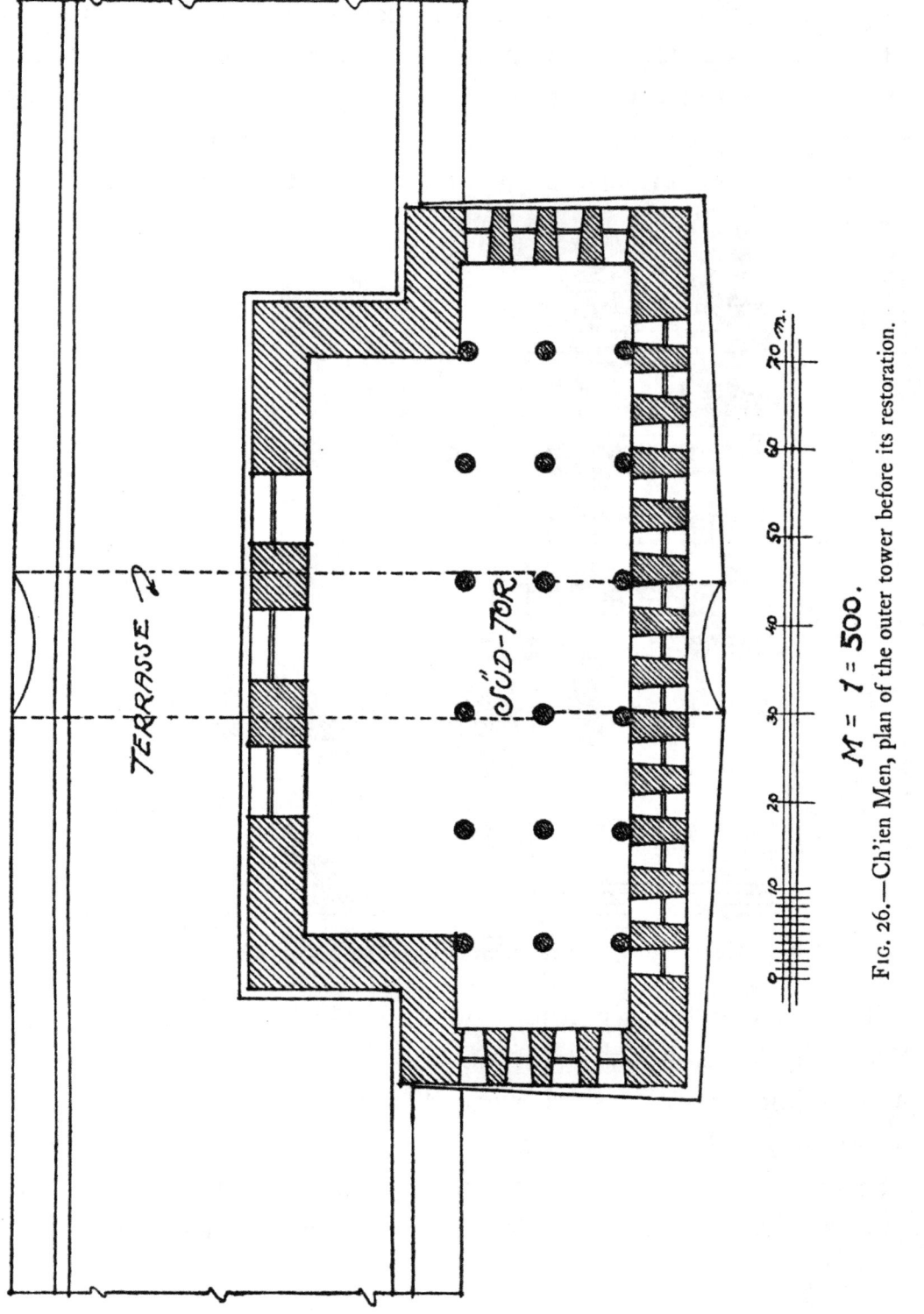

Fig. 26.—Ch'ien Men, plan of the outer tower before its restoration.

ignited by flames from the shops in the gate-yard which had been set on fire by those national fanatics, because foreign goods were sold there. The walls and roofs of the tower are evidently of that time, but the decorative features are, as we have pointed out, of a still more recent date.

The inner tower underwent a similar fate to that of the outer one,

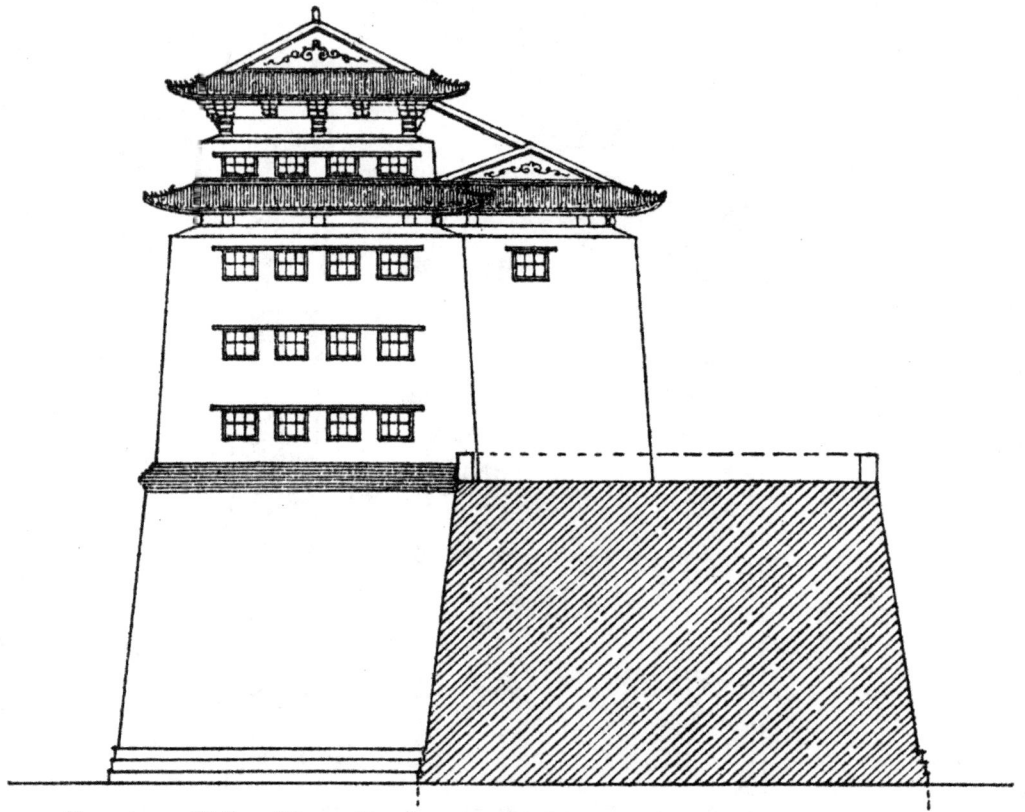

Fig. 27.—Ch'ien Men, side elevation of the outer tower before its restoration.

though it happened shortly after the end of the Boxer war. To quote from Mme. Bredon's book on Peking:

"A few months after the siege the scene was repeated when the inner tower accidentally caught fire, some say through the carelessness of Indian troops. The Chinese, fearful of ill-luck overtaking the city, hastened to rebuild both towers, which are practically the only monuments in Peking restored since Ch'ien Lung's time (?). The construction of the inner one—requiring nearly five years to complete—was a remarkable sight. Its eight-storied bamboo scaffolding astounded Western architects. Not a nail, saw, or hammer was used. Poles and bamboos were lashed together with overlapping ends, thus permitting any height to be reached without injury to or waste of lumber and with the minimum of labour in construction and removal."

This kind of scaffolding is indeed still in common use, both in China and in Japan. I have seen such scaffolding elevated to the most dazzling height in the construction of wooden pagodas in Japan, where the old craft-traditions have been better preserved than in China, and wooden constructions are still carried out in a very pure and strong manner. Unfortunately this is becoming more and more rare in Northern China (partly in consequence of the scarcity of wood), as also may be seen on the new gate-towers, on which, for instance, the multiple brackets have lost their constructive importance and become decorative accessories.

On the new tower of Ch'ien men the bracketing system is very rich, at least five-folded, under the eaves of the main roof, but it does not seem to have much carrying strength. The arms of the brackets are quite thin and they are joined together in a loose way. The difference between these and the firmly joined strong brackets of a building of the Sung period or earlier is highly significant for the general trend of Chinese architecture in later times. The tower is, no doubt, the most important building executed in the traditional manner in Peking during this century, though it is by no means the only large building restored since Ch'ien Lung's time. Other gate-towers, palaces, and temples have been rebuilt since then, but none of them is quite as large as the Ch'ien men tower. It measures along the outer gallery 41 by 21 metres and along the walls 36·7 by 16·5 metres. Its full height from the ground to the top of the ridge is 42 metres, of which 27·3 metres fall on the

2 A

178 THE WALLS AND GATES OF PEKING

building and the rest on the bastion. The constructive frame consists, as usual, of three rows of columns joined lengthwise and crosswise by

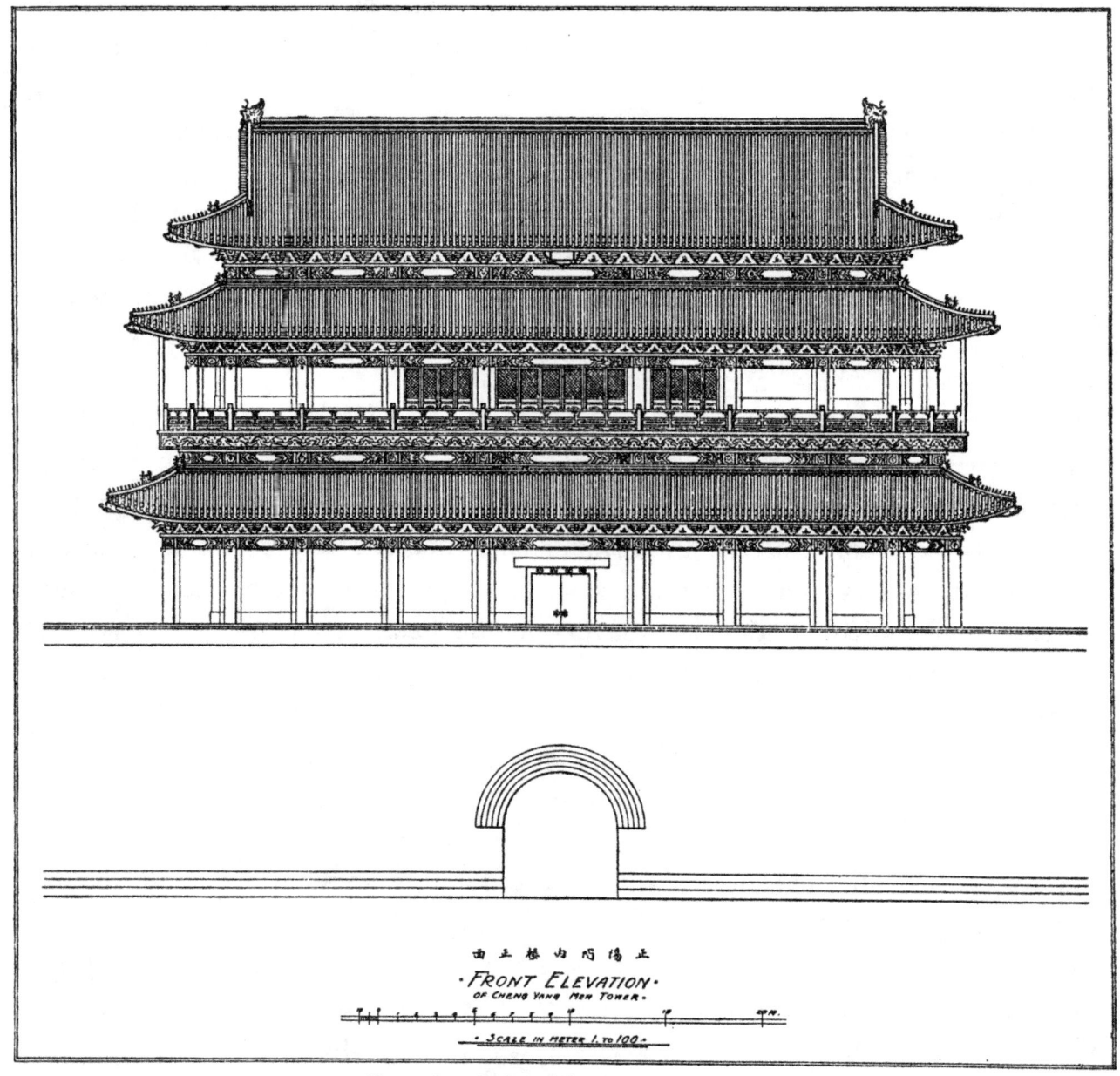

Fig. 28.—Ch'ien Men, the inner tower.

heavy beams and carrying the rafters by a system of brackets and purlins. The columns of the middle row stand, of course, encased in the brick walls, while those of the outer and innermost rows are

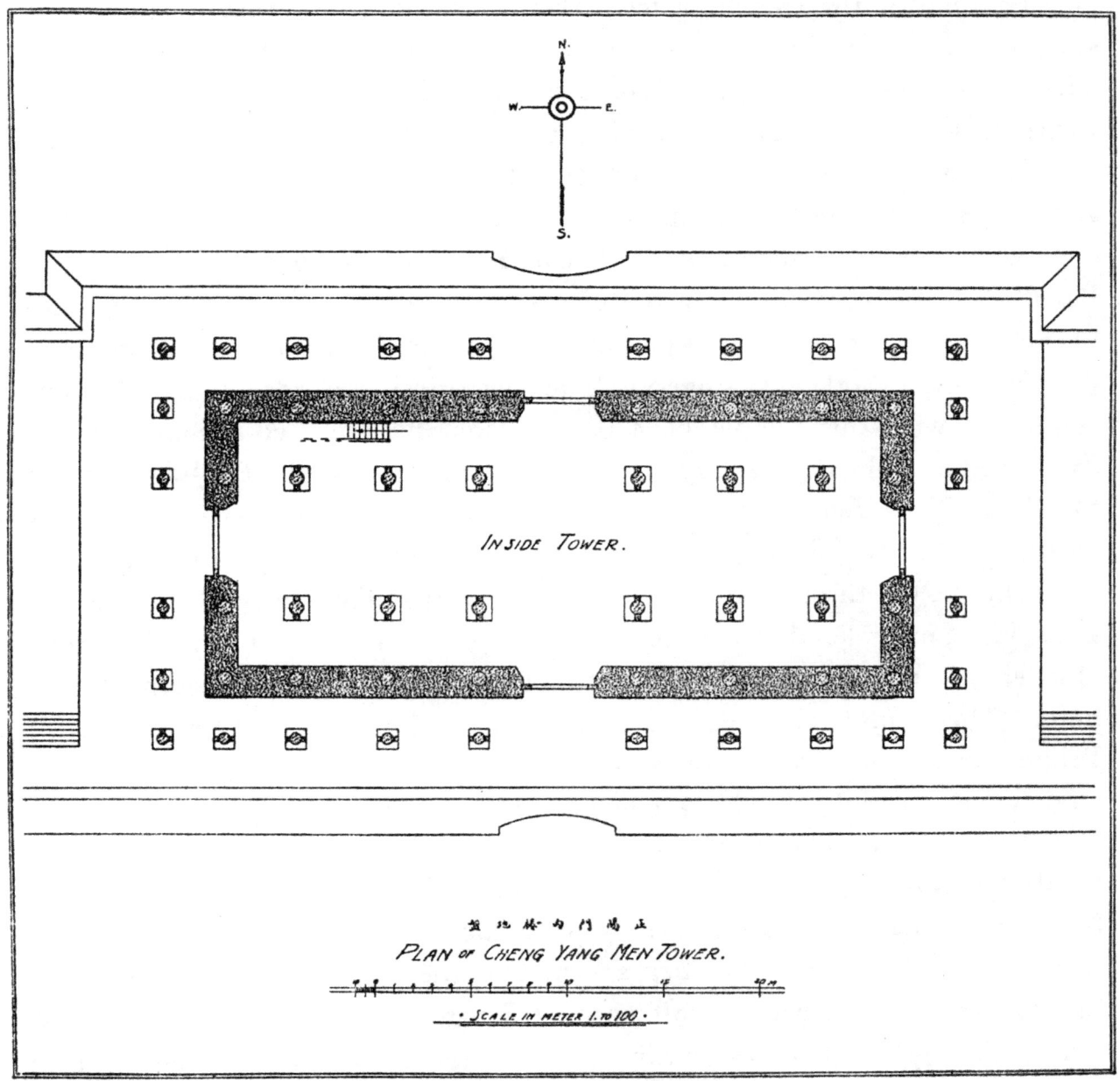

Fig. 29.—Ch'ien Men, plan of the inner tower.

strengthened by means of square posts. The outer gallery has no less than nine spans on the front (five spans on the short ends) and in consequence of this extraordinary extension the roofs seem to be less curving than at the smaller gates. It must be admitted that the increased scale of the whole building is hardly to the advantage of its architectural effect. The smaller gate-towers are generally better proportioned and stand in a more harmonious relation to the wall.

The most picturesque of all the buildings at Ch'ien men are the two small yellow-roofed temples at both sides of the main gate. The one to the east is dedicated to Kuan Yin and the one to the west to Kuan Ti, the protective patron of so many gates and public buildings in Peking, and it is especially this latter which is famous in history and popular among the Pekingese. The historical records and traditions connected with this temple have been related by more competent writers. (See "The Cult of Military Heroes in China," by R. F. Johnston, in the *New China Review*, 1921.) I would simply recall the fact that it was customary for the Emperor to offer small sacrifices at this Kuan Ti miao when he passed through the Ch'ien men, and that there were also deposited here an embroidered robe and state cap in honour of the "Demon Queller of the Three Worlds," one of the honorific titles of this great hero. The temple is still much frequented by the wealthy classes of Peking and especially by ladies of good means but less good reputation, who come here to burn joss-sticks and to kowtow before the great Demon Queller. There is often a fine array of embroidered silk dresses inside the tiny court with the large stone tablets and the beautiful trees, but right outside it, around the great incense burner which stands in front of the gateway, the beggars watch their chance to derive some benefit from the charitable influence of Kuan Ti on his wealthy adorers. The buildings, which are hardly over 100 years old, have been kept in good repair and form a very attractive picture with their yellow roofs and marble tablets among the trees against the background of the drab wall.

THE GATES OF THE TARTAR CITY

A little further towards the sides, adjoining the wall, stand the customs houses of the two railways. They are built in the traditional style with large curving roofs and open galleries, and architecturally form connecting links between the gate-tower and the railway stations which, however, are of an offensively foreign appearance. The open square between them—formerly the gate-yard—gives an impression of utter desolation with its iron chains, two isolated stone lions, and a few pining young trees. The only element of animation and life here is a horde of dirty beggars and idlers who have selected this square, which is so conveniently railed off against carts and rickshaws and yet in the midst of the thoroughfare, as a favourite dwelling-place. The deep vault of the outer tower bastion, where no traffic passes through nowadays, offers them shelter against sun and rain, and the thronged commercial quarters just outside the gate make an ideal hunting ground. Of all the rich varieties of beggars and loafers that I saw in Peking the ugliest and dirtiest specimens used to be gathered here right in the heart of the city under the old vaults of Ch'ien men.

The place to the south of the outer tower is one of the most important traffic centres of Peking. The narrow moat, which here only contains a thin stream of dirty water, is spanned by a very broad modern stone bridge forming a sort of square place. This is divided by means of chains and posts into four broad thoroughfares which radiate in southerly, easterly, and westerly directions leading to the most important business quarters of the Chinese city. The view from the tower along the Ch'ien men ta ch'ieh is one of the most beautiful and entertaining street views of the capital, framed as it is in the foreground by graceful willows and an old wooden p'ailou. The traffic here is often quite dense and highly variegated: Peking carts, rickshaws, pack mules, and camel caravans mixing with automobiles and bicycles—the old order of things slowly giving way to that of a more restless and mechanical age.

D. The Gates of the North Wall

Of the two gates in the northern wall *An Ting men* is nowadays the more popular and important one. It forms the outlet for the long street running from south to north, known in its southern section as Morrison Street (formerly Kung Fu Ching ta chieh, or the great street of the Princes Palace Wells), and in its northern part as An Ting men ta chieh. It is situated quite close to the Confucian temple and the Yung Ho kung, which probably still form the two largest temple compounds in the capital. The traffic here is considerable, and although it is made up mainly of coal transports and soldiers, who have their barracks not far outside the gate, it is also interspersed with lamas and their rustic Mongol friends who come to visit the Yung Ho kung.

The original gate composition has been badly impaired by the Round-the-City railway, which runs straight across the gate-yard. The barbican is partly destroyed, yet enough remains of its curving walls at the sides of the outer tower to make the view from the north fairly complete and impressive. The most disturbing element here is a two-storied guard-house in semi-foreign style with plastered walls and curving gable. The tower itself is severely monumental, with its broad bastion and plain brick walls divided only by four tiers of square loopholes and overshadowed by two curving roofs. As the moat is comparatively broad at the foot of the tower, the picture is often enhanced by a perfect reflection in the water. The barbican wall, or what remains of it, and the bastion seem to be of the Middle Ming period, but the tower itself is evidently of later date. It may have been rebuilt by Ch'ien Lung, as was the case with so many of these defensive gate-towers, but it was no doubt extensively repaired after the siege of Peking in 1861, when damaged by the English and French guns. The troops of the allies were for some time in possession of this gate before the treaty was signed.

THE GATES OF THE TARTAR CITY

The inner tower of An Ting men shows more signs of age and wear. The hips of the roofs as well as the balcony of the middle story are breaking down; some of the columns are badly cracked and iron-banded, and the woodwork is covered all over with a thick layer of grey dust, so that only faint traces of the original colouring are visible. After the rainy season the growth of grass and small shrubs is quite abundant

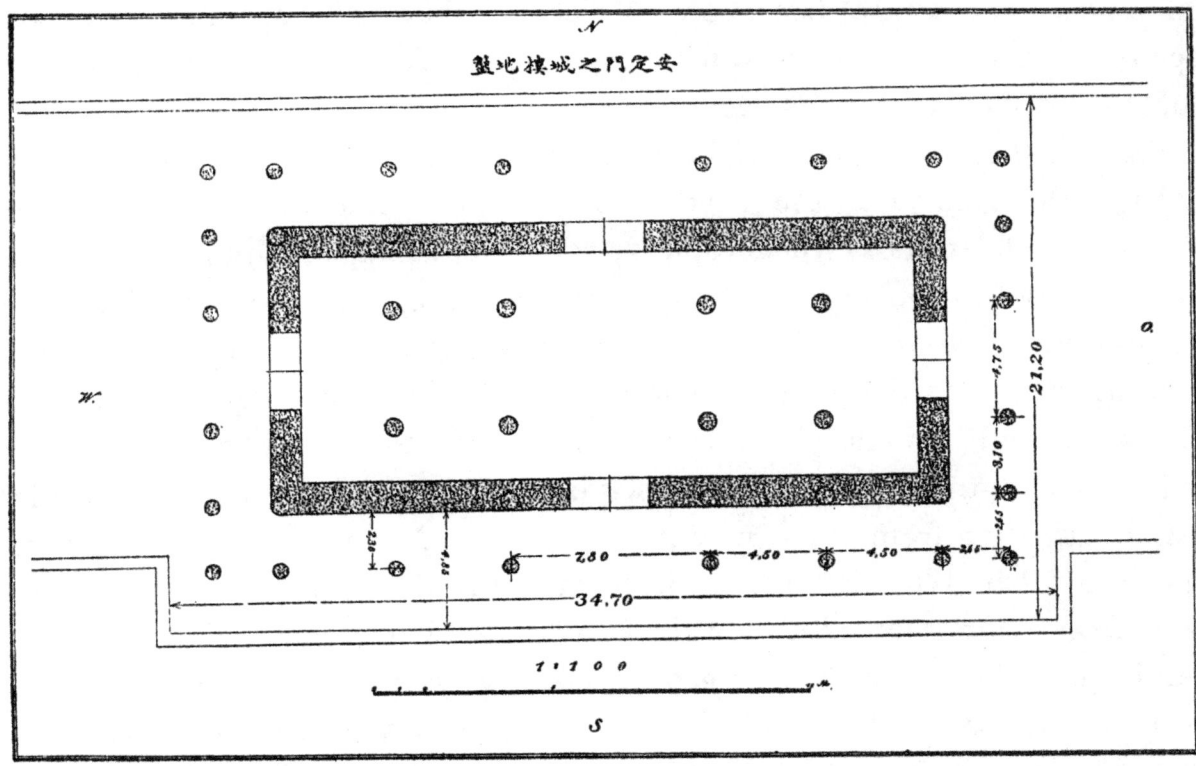

Fig. 30.—An Ting Men, plan of the inner tower.

between the loosening roof tiles. But as a matter of fact such a tower harmonizes better with the weather-worn walls than the brightly coloured new ones which we have seen on the south side.

The measurements are very nearly the same as on Tung Chih men and Hsi Chih men; the tower is only a little broader in proportion to its length. The walls are 26·4 by 11·5 metres, and the outer gallery, which as usual has seven by five spans, is 31 by 16 metres. The height over the terrace is about 22 metres. The thickness of the walls and the placing of the middle row of columns close to the outer face of the wall are exactly the same as at Tung Chih men, and so are various other details which seem to warrant the conclusion that these two towers were built in the same period, possibly in the reign of Ch'ien Lung. As wooden buildings very quickly deteriorate in Peking, they may possibly have been repaired even later. Unfortunately we have found no records with a clue to the date of these towers.

As the barbican wall has been largely destroyed and the railway runs through the gate-yard, the inside view is most disappointing. The ends of those wall stumps which still remain are arranged similarly to those on the east gates, i.e. in a series of winding staircases with stepped balustrades between small terraces, an arrangement which by its finicking elaboration stands in striking contrast to the monumental simplicity of the walls and towers. Fortunately, however, there are still some old buildings and trees within the preserved rear part of the gate-yard which distract attention from these modern misdeeds. A small temple compound, known as Chên Wu miao, nestles right at the foot of the bastion wall of the outer tower. It is an idyllic little place, consisting of half a dozen separate temple pavilions and gateways grouped around small courtyards with large incense burners and marble tablets overshadowed by dark ailanthus trees. It is a most rare and attractive spot in the An Ting men district, which is completely dominated by the bleak monotony of the sandy plain and the small mud houses.

Tê Sheng men, the western gate on the North wall, is situated at the point where the wall commences to bend in a south-westerly direction. The neighbourhood has remained comparatively quiet and undisturbed by modern improvement; the street leading up to the gate is lined with a few large trees and quaint old-fashioned shops, but just before one arrives at the gate it makes a sharp turn and from here the view is decidedly disappointing. Instead of a high tower with open galleries and curving roofs in three stories one sees simply a flat bastion slightly raised above the general level of the wall and pierced by a large vault. The crowning pavilion or tower is entirely demolished; it was taken down in 1921, because it was considered to be in a dangerous state of decay.

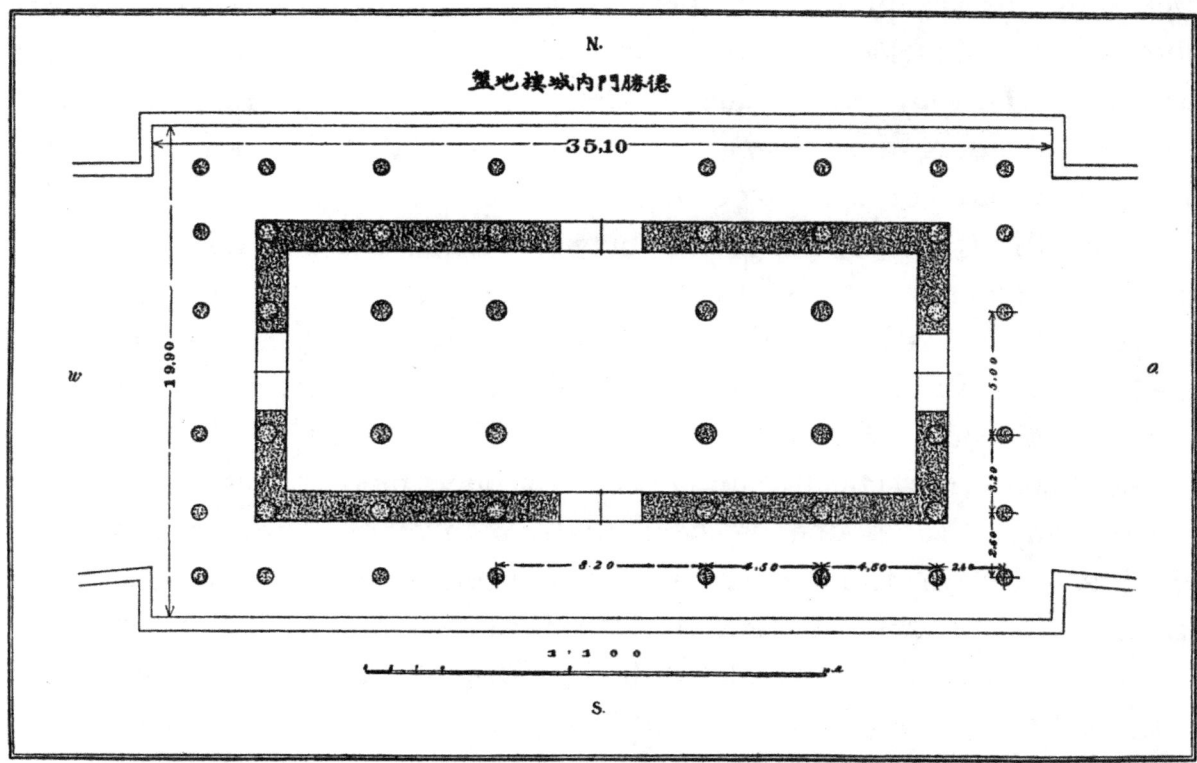

Fig. 31.—Tê Sheng Men, plan of the inner tower.

Much of the building material was still lying on the top of the bastion in the summer of 1922, and, as far as I could see, neither the columns nor the beams were rotten. The plinths of the columns and the wall were also *in situ*, which enabled us to make a plan of the destroyed building. This tower was still larger than that of An Ting men; the walls measured 27 by 12 metres, and the outer gallery 31·5 by 16·6 metres. The vault is uncommonly large and high; it reaches nearly to the upper edge of the bastion, appearing enormous in consequence of the absence of the tower.

After one has passed through this vault the view becomes much more interesting. The gate-yard is, indeed, partly destroyed by the railway which runs right through here, screened by a fence and a low brick wall, just as in the An Ting men yard, yet the place has retained more of its old character than any of the other gate-vats with broken barbicans. This is mainly due to the fact that the curving arms of the wall left standing are comparatively long and that the screen walls of the railway are drawn diagonally towards the terraced ends of these barbican arms. The openings left between them and the railway wall are only large enough for the roads to pass through. Thus the road does not pierce the bastion of the outer tower but is divided into two arms which wind around the barbican and the tower, uniting over the bridge on the north side. The rear part of the old gate-yard is still an isolated, enclosed space, practically untouched by any modern alterations; and as the temple compound is here uncommonly well preserved and the ailanthus trees in front of it are magnificent, the place makes a very attractive impression. A few trees and shrubs serve also to hide the curving staircases and crenellated balustrades of the barbican wall butts. It is not to be wondered at that this well-sheltered and shaded place in front of the old temple has become a popular resort for food vendors, donkey drivers, and barbers and their very picturesque clientele. None of the other gate-yards can compare with this in natural beauty and quiet country-like charm. The temple, known as Chên Wu miao, is larger than most of the gate temples; it comprises a bell-tower and a drum-tower at each side of the main gate, as well as several pavilions and living quarters for the taoist priests. But I doubt whether it is much utilized for religious purposes. At the time of my last visit one or two of the dainty small buildings were filled with raw cotton which was being sorted here, and the grounds were partly planted with cabbage and potatoes.

The outer tower, which is of the usual size and construction, has evidently been restored within the last generation. Its brick walls have been coated with a greyish colour contrasting rather unfavourably with the old masonry of the bastion below. This lower part of the tower dates no doubt from Chia Ching's or Wan Li's time, though the main wall adjoining it was restored in Ch'ien Lung's reign. The old stone-lined bridge in front of the tower is beginning to fall to pieces and the outlines of the moat are becoming irregular, yet the view from this side would be as a whole quite imposing in its bareness were it not for the wretched guard-houses at the foot of the tower.

A curiosity within the Tê Sheng men yard is the pavilion which has been left standing between the railway tracks. It harbours a large memorial tablet with a poem by Ch'ien Lung, written in his 62nd year (1797). The then ex-Emperor refers to the name of Tê Sheng men (Righteous Victory gate), and says that his might is great enough to protect all his interests without offending anybody.

VIII

THE GATES OF THE CHINESE CITY

THE gates of the Outer or Chinese city are much smaller than those of the Tartar city. They are seven in all; three on the South wall, one on the East, and one on the West wall, and one on each of the short wall-stretches which connect the north-east and north-west corners with the Inner city wall. Their comparatively small size and inconspicuous architectural features do not, however, make them less interesting or less significant. Broadly speaking, they are built according to the same plan and in the same style as the larger gates, though simplified both in construction and in their decorative details. It must be admitted, however, that the smaller dimensions are in most instances to the advantage rather than to the disadvantage of the harmonious effect of the gate compositions, and the smaller towers stand in a more intimate and perfect relation to the walls and to the adjoining streets and landscapes. The views connected with these smaller gates are almost invariably finer from a pictorial point of view than those in which the larger gates form the central motives.

This, I believe, is brought out quite clearly by my photographs; those of the large gates are in most cases mainly illustrative of architectural motives which sometimes do not present themselves in a particularly attractive setting, while the views of the gates in the outer wall more often derive their main interest from the perfect blending of the buildings and the landscape and the characteristic beauty of the natural surroundings.

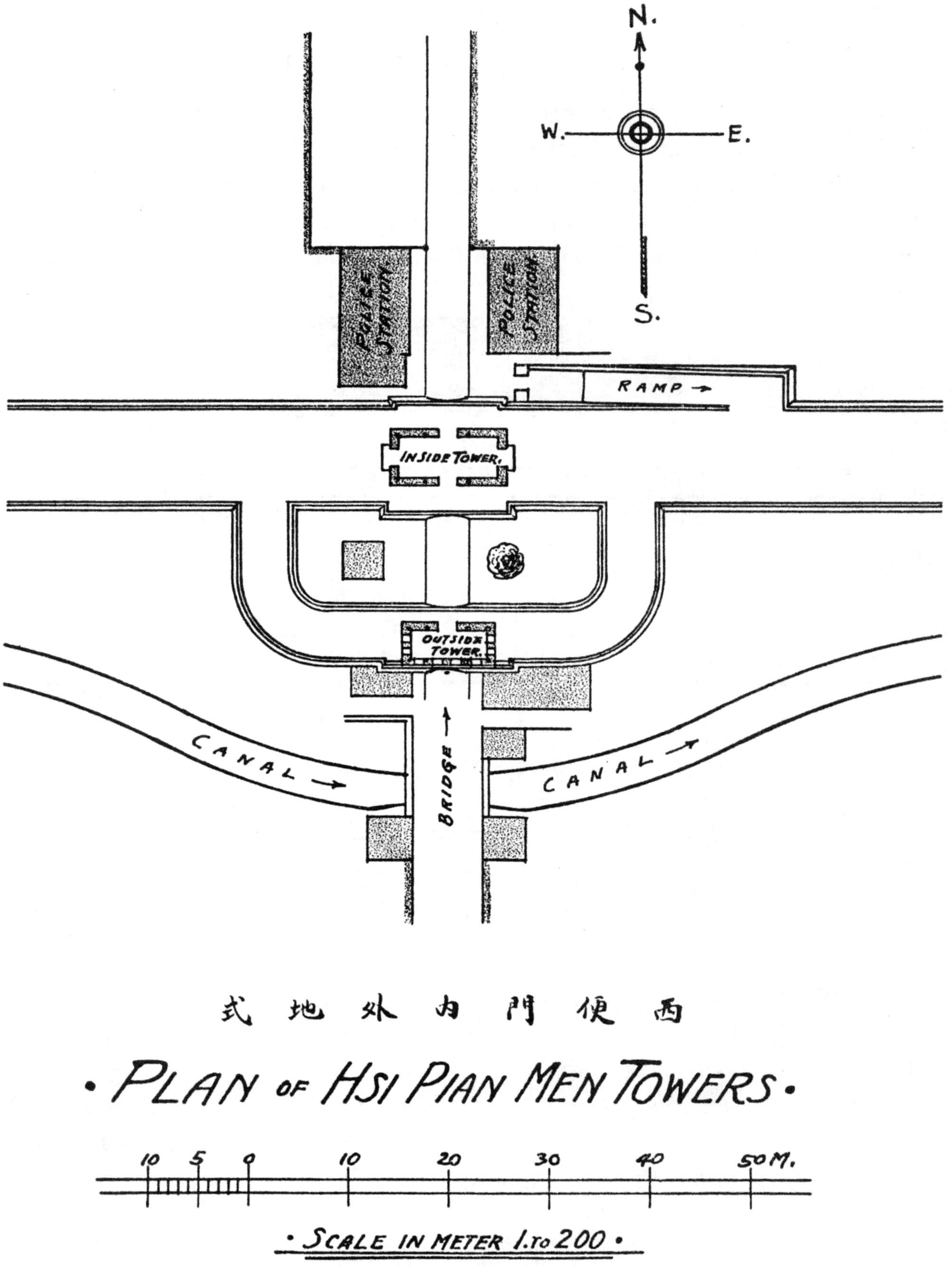

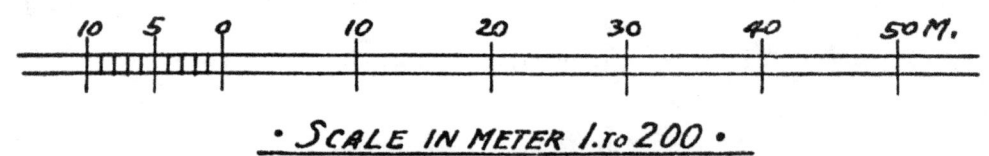

西便門內外地式

· PLAN OF HSI PIAN MEN TOWERS ·

· SCALE IN METER 1.TO 200 ·

FIG. 32.—Hsi Pien Men, general plan.

They may in part serve as historical records of the architectural character and present state of the gates, but it is hoped that they will reveal something beyond that and convey impressions which are not easily supplied by words. Just what these impressions consist of may be left to each reader to decide for himself. I should simply like to suggest

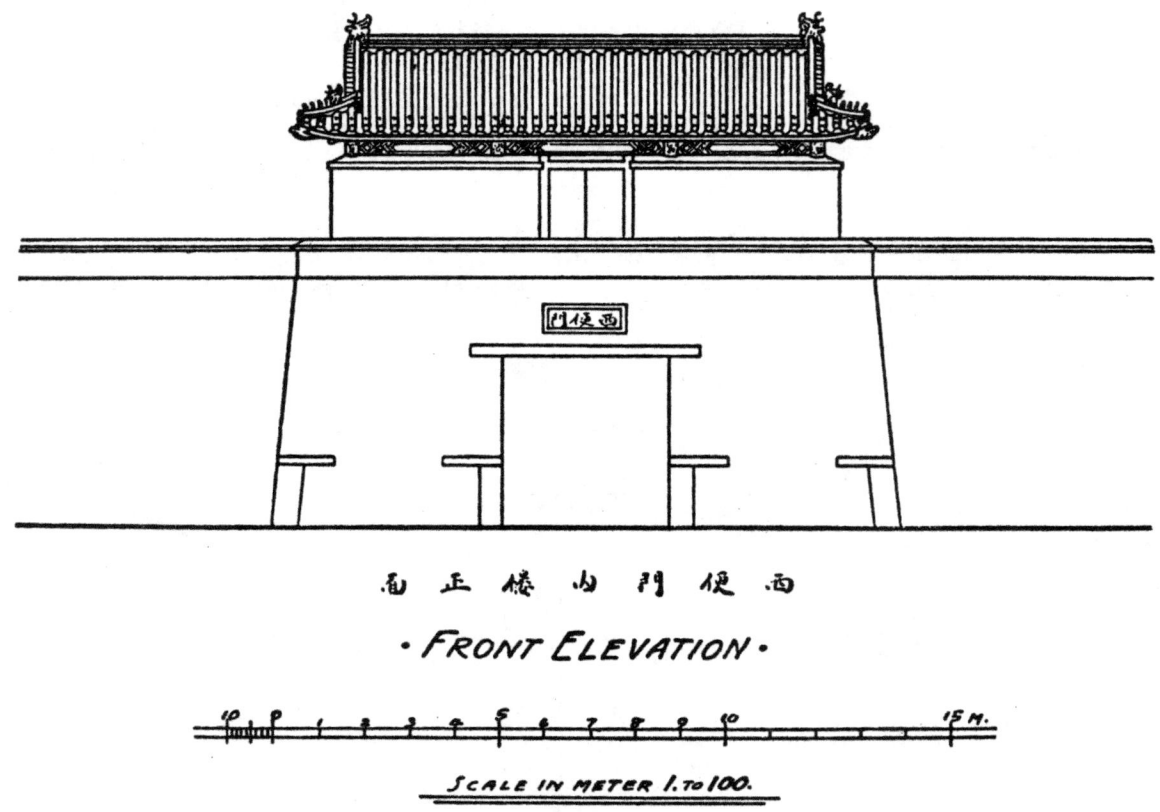

FIG. 33.—Hsi Pien Men, inner tower.

that the beauty of it all does not depend solely on the objects in the landscape, such as the trees, houses, and bridges, but just as much on the life of the people, the light and the atmosphere which nobody who has lived in Peking will ever forget.

Hsi Pien men (the western convenience gate) in the north-west wall lies at the end of an old-fashioned sunken street lined with shops which,

THE GATES OF THE CHINESE CITY

as a matter of fact, attract more attention than the low and inconspicuous inner gate-tower. To call it a tower is really misleading; the building is simply a rectangular house with plastered brick walls and a door on each side, but neither windows nor any outer gallery. It has no decorative details except the monster heads on the hips and on the roof ridge, but

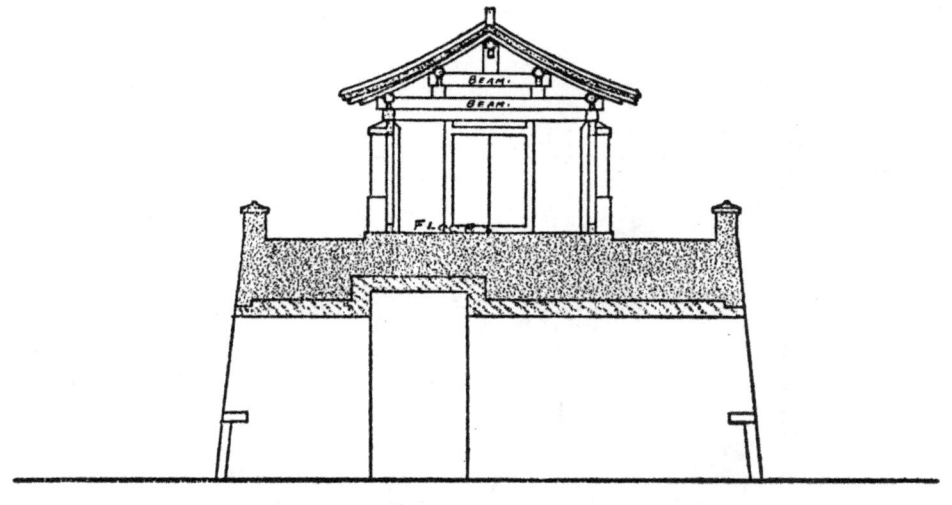

Fig. 34.—Hsi Pien Men, inner tower.

plenty of grass between the tiles. It stands on the middle of the wall, which is here only slightly accentuated in the shape of a bastion and provided with one ramp. The gateway which leads through this bastion is not vaulted but square, its ceiling being formed of heavy boards on beams which are encased in the brick walls on both sides. But in the middle of this flat-roofed corridor is a higher and broader compartment in which the doors, hung on pivots, move freely and may be folded into the walls. The dimensions of this tower are as follows: length 11·2

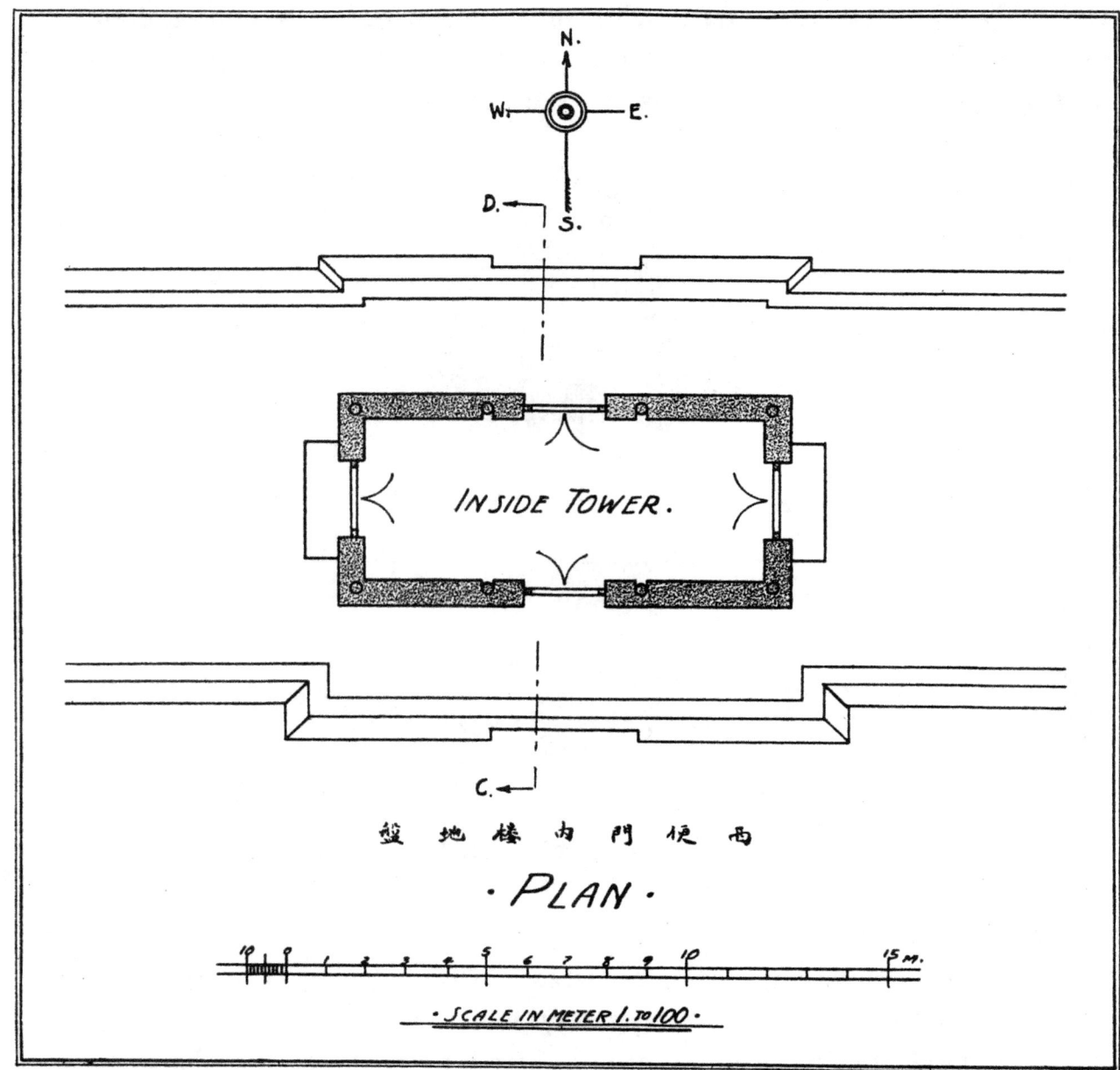

Fig. 35.—Hsi Pien Men, inner tower.

metres, width 5·5 metres, height over the bastion 5·2 metres and over the

THE GATES OF THE CHINESE CITY

ground 11·2 metres. It is constructed with a single row of columns, four on each side, encased in the brick walls, and with double roof-beams, but it has no brackets nor outer columns.

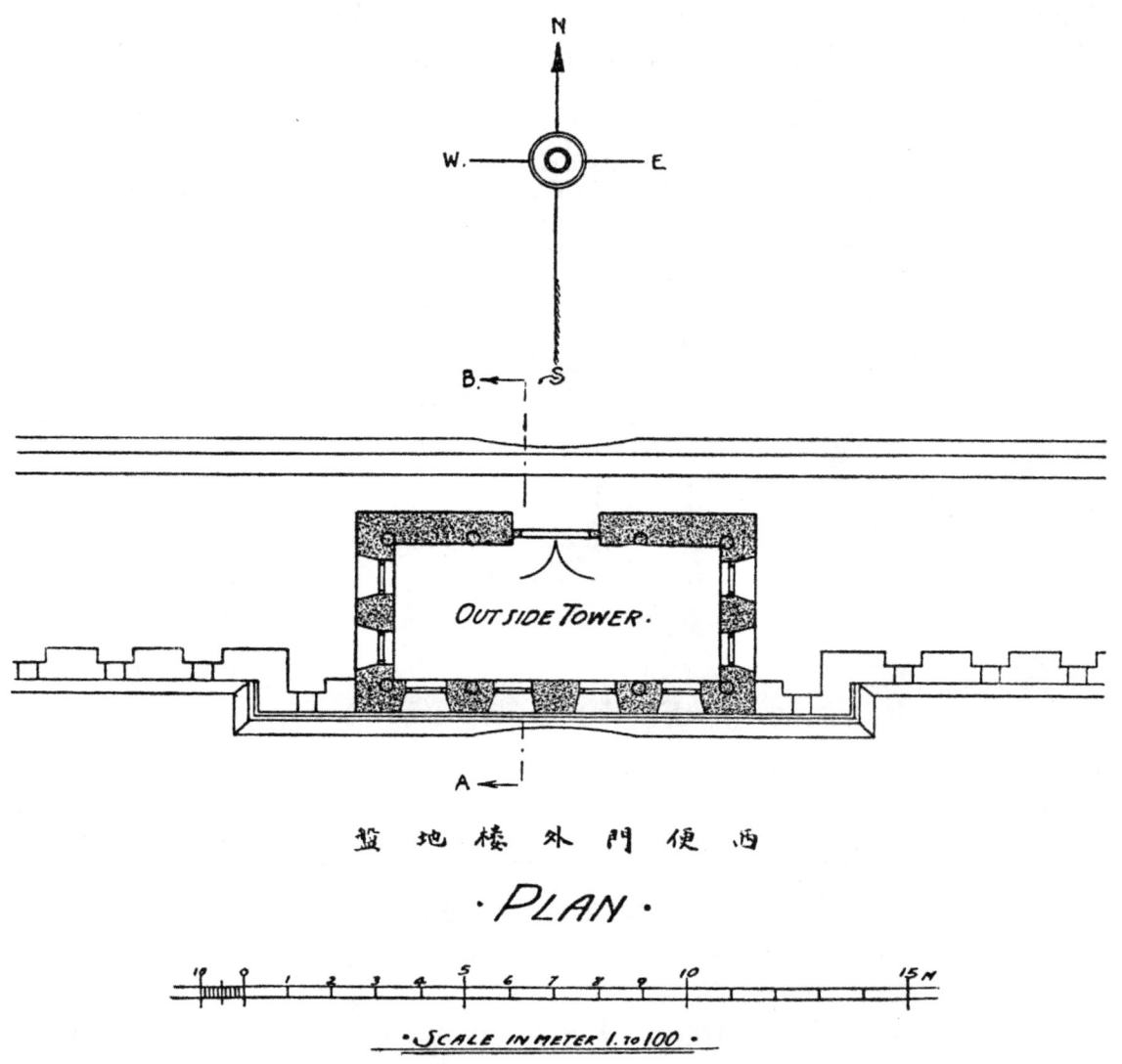

Fig. 36.—Hsi Pien Men, outer tower.

The gate-yard of the barbican is extremely short, measuring only 7·5 metres in depth by 30 metres in width. Yet there is room here for one of the finest trees that may be seen in any of the gate-yards, a large

Sophora japonica, popularly called "locust tree," which overshadows half of the yard, and also for a small guard-house which encroaches upon the other half. The barbican walls are quite rough and weathered; the main part of them seem to be of the Middle Ming period, and there are many bricks marked in the 39th year of Chia Ching, but some spots

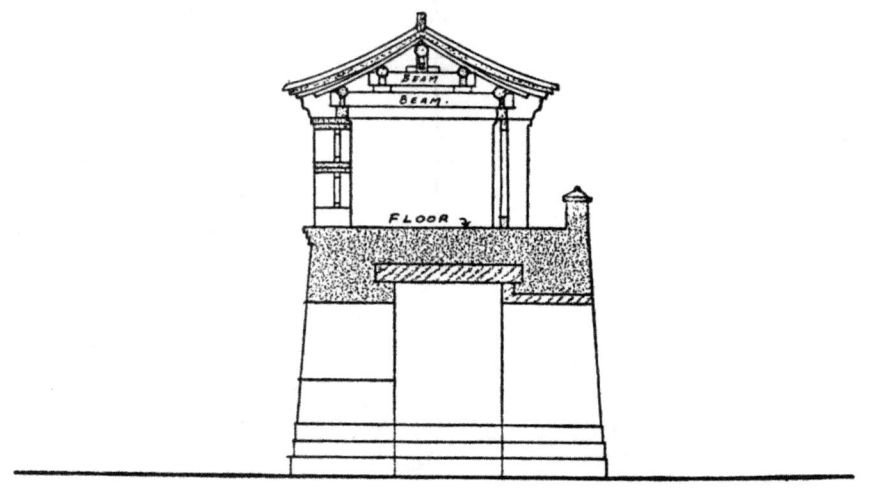

FIG. 37.—Hsi Pien Men, outer tower.

were patched at a later time. The outside face of the barbican was rebuilt in Ch'ien Lung's time.

The gateway through the bastion of the outer tower is square and flat-roofed towards the inside but vaulted towards the outside. The folding doors are here also fitted into a broader and higher section of the

THE GATES OF THE CHINESE CITY

corridor, which makes it possible to close them very effectively and fold them entirely out of the way when open. The bastion itself protrudes very little from the face of the barbican wall, but it is accentuated by a thin cornice at the top. Over this follows the small tower, and at the sides of it, the battlement. The whole tower is only 9 metres long,

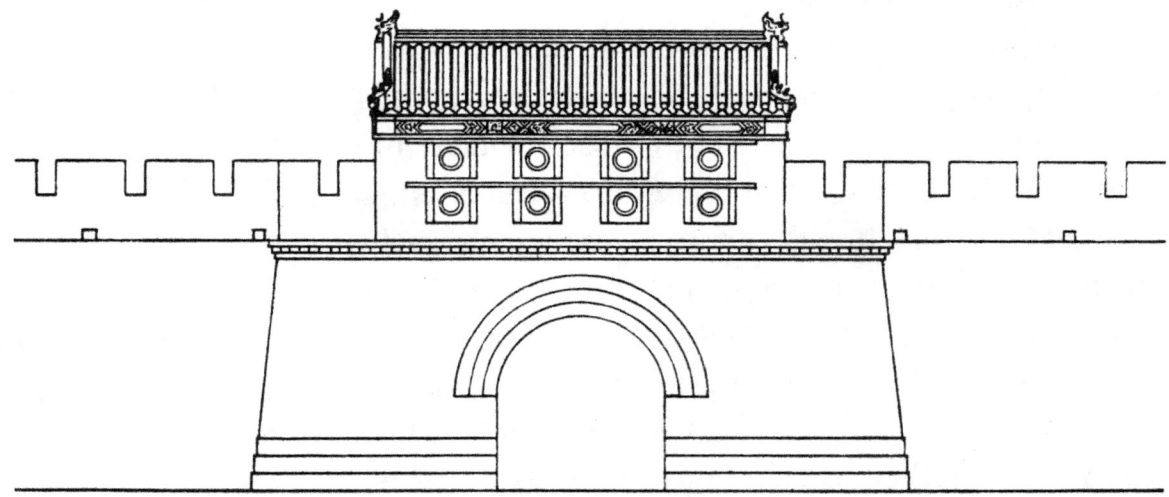

FIG. 38.—Hsi Pien Men, outer tower.

4·6 metres broad, 4·7 metres high over the bastion, and 10·5 at the ground level. It is built in the same way as the inner tower with a single row of small columns encased in the brick walls (four columns on both fronts) and provided with two rows of loopholes on the outer façade and on the two short sides. These loopholes in connection with the brick-coated walls give it a more interesting appearance than the inner tower, but it is so small that it can hardly vie with the broad arch underneath, which, after all, is the only monumental feature of the whole gate.

The moat is deep but quite narrow and is spanned by a small stone bridge. Directly one has passed this bridge the road branches off into two different directions, one straight north and the other westward, the latter being especially familiar to foreigners because it leads to the race-course. But it is the northern road which offers the most beautiful scenery. It lies quite deep between rows of small houses to which one has to mount on broad stone steps, which ordinarily are used by the donkey-drivers as their most convenient resting-places, because in front of the houses magnificent locust trees spread their dark foliage like huge umbrellas over the steps and terraces and paint vibrating silhouettes on the white walls and the sun-heated road. Here there is no need of building up bamboo scaffoldings with straw mats, as is usually done on the inner side of the gate, for nature has provided a protection just as effective and infinitely more beautiful with its quivering play of light and shade and soft rustle of fresh leaves. This dolce far niente under the shady trees is, of course, limited to the spring and summer season; during the colder part of the year the monotony of the bare landscape is relieved by the camel caravans which daily pass in and out through this weather-worn old gate.

Tung Pien men (the eastern convenience gate) in the north-east wall forms a pair with Hsi Pien men; it is, in some respects, even more humble and inconspicuous. The dimensions of the towers are practically the same as those of the western gate, and the barbican comprises no larger area, but it is of somewhat different proportions. The inner tower—if such it may be called—is a small brick building with red plastered walls probably renewed within the last century. Seen at a short

THE GATES OF THE CHINESE CITY

distance, it seems almost to sink into the bastion instead of rising above it; it partly disappears behind the parapet, but the large curving roof saves it from being obscured from sight. More prominent than the tower itself are the guard-houses in front of it and the old bastion which contains some Chia Ching bricks, though it evidently has been patched up at a later date.

Here the gate opening is, just as in Hsi Pien men, square and covered with beams and boards. Passing through this we arrive in the small gate-yard, which is a little deeper, though at the same time narrower than in Hsi Pien men. Nor has it any of the picturesque character of the west gate. There is no tree, no growth of any kind, simply a small shed or guard-cabin which serves to accentuate rather than to relieve the impression of dead emptiness. Now and again a carrier with baskets swinging from the ends of a long pole over his shoulder passes through the gate, but rickshaws and carts are quite rare.

The gateway of the outer bastion is also square towards the yard but vaulted towards the outside. The vault, however, is not quite as large as on the Hsi Pien men; consequently the "tower" seems a little more dominant. It is, as usual, erected with thick brick walls over a constructive frame of wooden columns and beams and provided with two rows of loopholes which give it an air of defensive severity. But over the roof is spread a thick carpet of soft and smooth grass. The tower as well as the barbican wall were renewed in the Ch'ien Lung period, probably in the Emperor's 31st year.

Just outside the gate at the corner of the barbican is a place for cattle and mule drivers, a sort of miniature cattle market, where one may sometimes see quite a display of sturdy oxen and drowsy mules. A few steps further east the ground slopes considerably and the wall is supported by a double terrace. As this substructure is now partly broken, its various elements and manner of construction may be observed most clearly, and the wall rising on the successive terrace steps makes a most impressive picture.

The landscape outside Tung Pien men receives a very definite character and beauty from the proximity of the Eastern canal. The moat is actually broadened into a stone-lined canal, and this receives plenty of water through the moat from the north. This is the beginning of the Tung Ho, which was formerly the most important transport line by which the capital was connected with the Grand Canal at Tientsin. The very end of it, on the west side of the gate where it joins the moat of the Inner city, forms a small lake or pond which in summer-time is covered with rushes and lotus and in the winter offers a good opportunity for skating. Large willows and locust trees provide a very effective setting against the background of the broad castle-like corner-tower of the Inner city, and the broken remains of the small tower which stood at the junction between the inner and outer wall. Right in front of the gate the canal is spanned by a fine stone bridge on three arches, decorated with tiger-heads and provided with locks to regulate the flow of water. Here, whenever the weather is fine, one may watch boisterous urchins on the bridge piers and stone embankments washing cotton yarn and newly dyed blue cloth in the mirroring water. And looking farther eastward one sees the brightly painted houseboats with care-free youths and maidens starting on their pleasure cruises to the " Princess's Tomb," or other romantic spots along the banks of the silent old canal.

Sha Wu men (the gate of abundant dust), or Kuang Chü men, is probably the loneliest gate of Peking. It is situated in a rather desolate quarter of the Chinese city on the northern section of its East wall. To reach it one has to pass over wide stretches of open ground where no human abodes hamper the manure traders in their preparations of various brands of fertilizing material.

The gate is small and low, though not quite as inconspicuous as the

Hsi Pien men and Tung Pien men; the barbican is considerably longer than at those gates. The inner tower is a one-storied pavilion, with an open gallery of five spans on the front but no columns on the short sides or at the back. Being partly hidden by the parapet of the bastion it looks quite low, almost like that of Hsi Pien men, and the curving roof is now in a very dilapidated condition with broken ridge and missing hips. After the rains it looks more like a grass-covered terrace than a tiled roof. Yet I should hardly think that this tower is older than the Ch'ien Lung period; it was probably rebuilt, together with the barbican and the outer tower, in the 31st year of Ch'ien Lung. But the bastion on which it stands is mainly constructed of Ming bricks.

The gateway is formed by a large slightly ogival arch (probably also reconstructed in the Ch'ien Lung period) corresponding exactly to the arch of the outer gateway. Both are unusually wide in proportion to the bastions, and it is thus possible to get a good view through the arches into the yard and the outside country.

The barbican is large enough to offer space for several small food shops of a quite picturesque type with open fronts and outside brick-laid seats. There are no trees, no temple, nor any other particularly interesting features, but it is an uncommonly well-proportioned and unspoilt old-fashioned gate-yard. It is just large enough to balance the two low towers, yet not any larger than to allow us to see it all in one glance —walls, shops and towers—it forms a unified picture, which is by no means the case in the larger gate-yards. The whole place seems to have been rebuilt in the 31st year of Ch'ien Lung; the barbican wall is datable to that year, and the towers are clearly not earlier but possibly later.

The outer tower is just as low as the inner one and its roof is no less broken; the eaves are crumbling and parts of the main ridge missing. It has only two rows of loopholes. It makes nevertheless a much finer and stronger impression than the outer towers of the two small gates just examined, because it stands in a freer position. The tower bastion is both deeper and higher than the barbican wall, projecting like a powerful buttress. The parapet of the wall is not continued around the tower but abuts against it with slanting arms on both sides. By this arrangement something is added to the impression of height; the tower is lifted and made to dominate over the adjoining walls.

The broad brick-lined moat in front of the tower is spanned by an old stone bridge with more food vendors' stalls. The road on the other side seems once to have been paved with flagstones, but offers now more obstacles than facility for cart traffic. Very few such vehicles pass through here; the people who move through the gate are mostly on muleback or on foot and are able to make their way in a sunken ditch just as well as over a levelled road. As I once visited this lonely gate on a lucky day a marriage procession came through—a long array of white-clad men following after the brightly decorated bridal chair and carrying gifts on litters and long poles. After it had passed through the gate it was no longer possible for the men to keep even steps; they had to jump over holes and stones and adjust their slow march to the inequalities of the sunken mud road. But such odds are, of course, by no means unfamiliar to the Peking coolies.

Chang I men (the gate of good manners), or Kuang An men, is the gate on the West wall of the Chinese city corresponding to Sha Wu men on the East. It may originally have been approximately of the same size and general appearance, but it was more thoroughly reconstructed in the eighteenth century and has now a remarkably high and elegant inner tower and an almost square barbican (the outer corners are sharply rounded). The outer tower is, however, practically the same as the corresponding one on Sha Wu men. The plan of this gate illustrates as a whole the type of gate composition which became prevalent in the

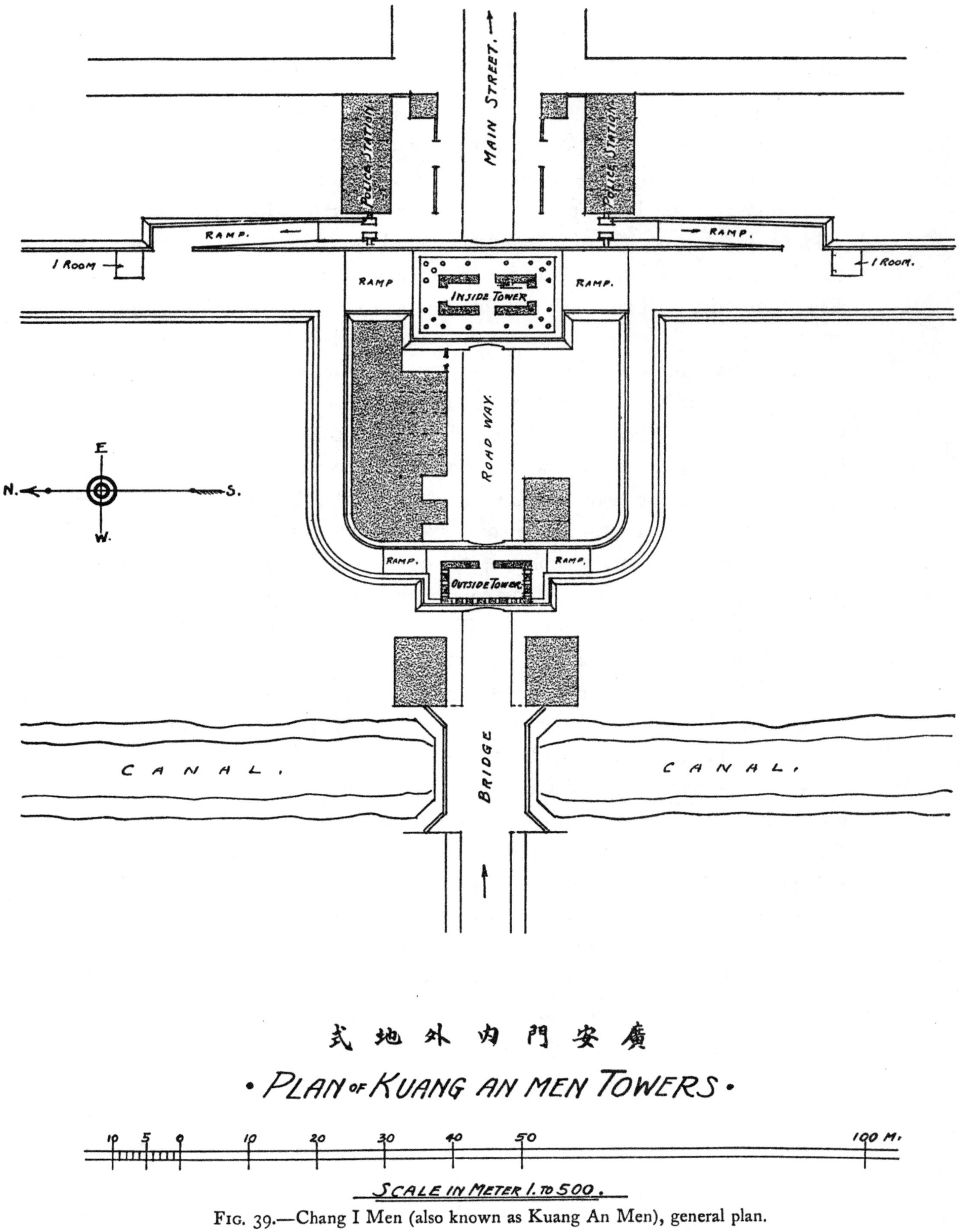

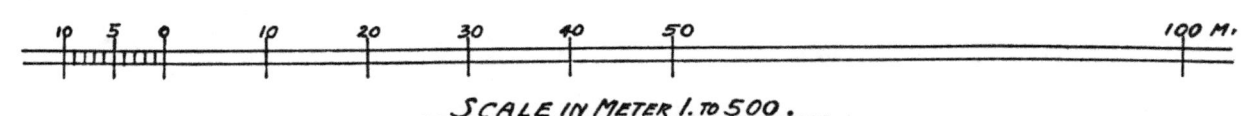

廣安門內外地式

· PLAN OF KUANG AN MEN TOWERS ·

FIG. 39.—Chang I Men (also known as Kuang An Men), general plan.

Ch'ien Lung era, when so many of the gates and so much of the walls were rebuilt. We shall find exactly the same plan in Yung Ting men.

Compared with the older plan disposition, as exemplified in P'ing Tzu men, these later plans have a less fortress-like character and are evidently inferior from a defensive point of view; not simply because the barbican walls have become thinner but also in consequence of their straighter lines. The barbican of P'ing Tzu men is a continuous broad curve attached by short arms to the main wall; the outer bastion projects far out, enabling defenders to rake the curving walls on both sides. And as the entrance to the yard is not under the main tower but at one side, the security of the place is admirably assured. In the later gates the barbican is almost four-cornered, though the two outer corners are rounded, and only the front wall can be raked from the bastion. The entrance is right through this bastion, the road leading straight across the yard. When, furthermore, the inner decorative tower is made about twice as high and prominent as the outer defensive tower one can hardly avoid the conclusion that the old fortification idea has given way to the more peaceful aims of commerce and levying of customs.

The gate-yard of Kuang An men is 34 metres deep and 39 metres wide; the barbican wall that surrounds it is 7 metres thick at the foot and 5 at the top; it is provided with two stone tablets on the outside, both of the 31st year of Ch'ien Lung, so there is no need for hesitation about its date. The paved street which leads right across the yard is lined with small shops mainly dealing in scrap-iron, ropes, and the roughest kind of household pottery, these, together with a few simple articles of food, forming the traditional merchandise of the gate-yards. A few young locust trees and stacks of glazed pottery add splashes of colour to this admirably proportioned and well-preserved gate-vat.

The dominating motive of this gate composition, from whatever side it is seen, is the tall inner tower, for once a real tower, which impresses

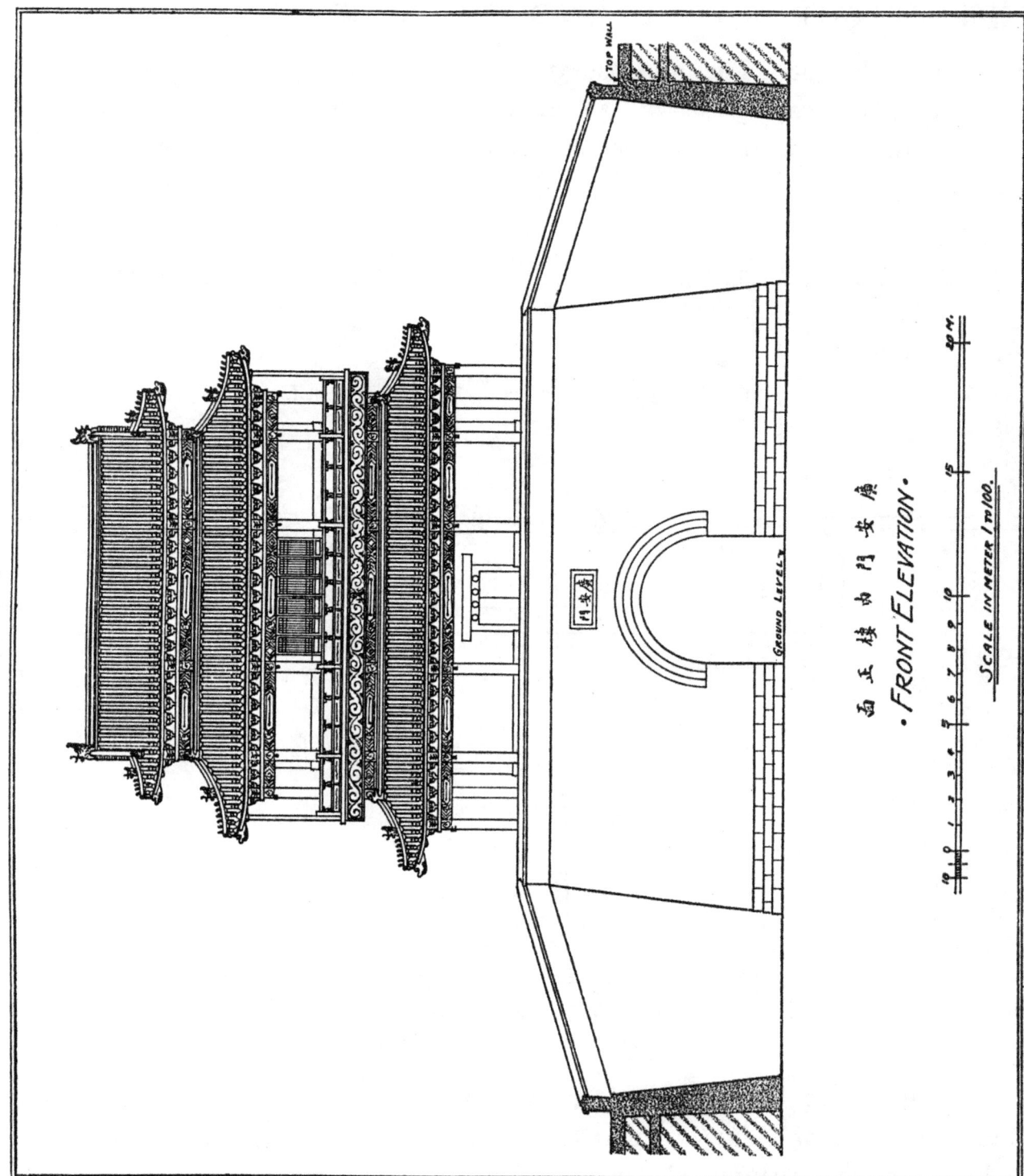

Fig. 40.—Chang I Men, inner tower.

204 THE WALLS AND GATES OF PEKING

us by its height. The dimensions of the walls are 13·8 by 6 metres, and of the outer gallery 18 by 10 metres. The room is thus uncommonly small in proportion to the surrounding gallery. The height of the

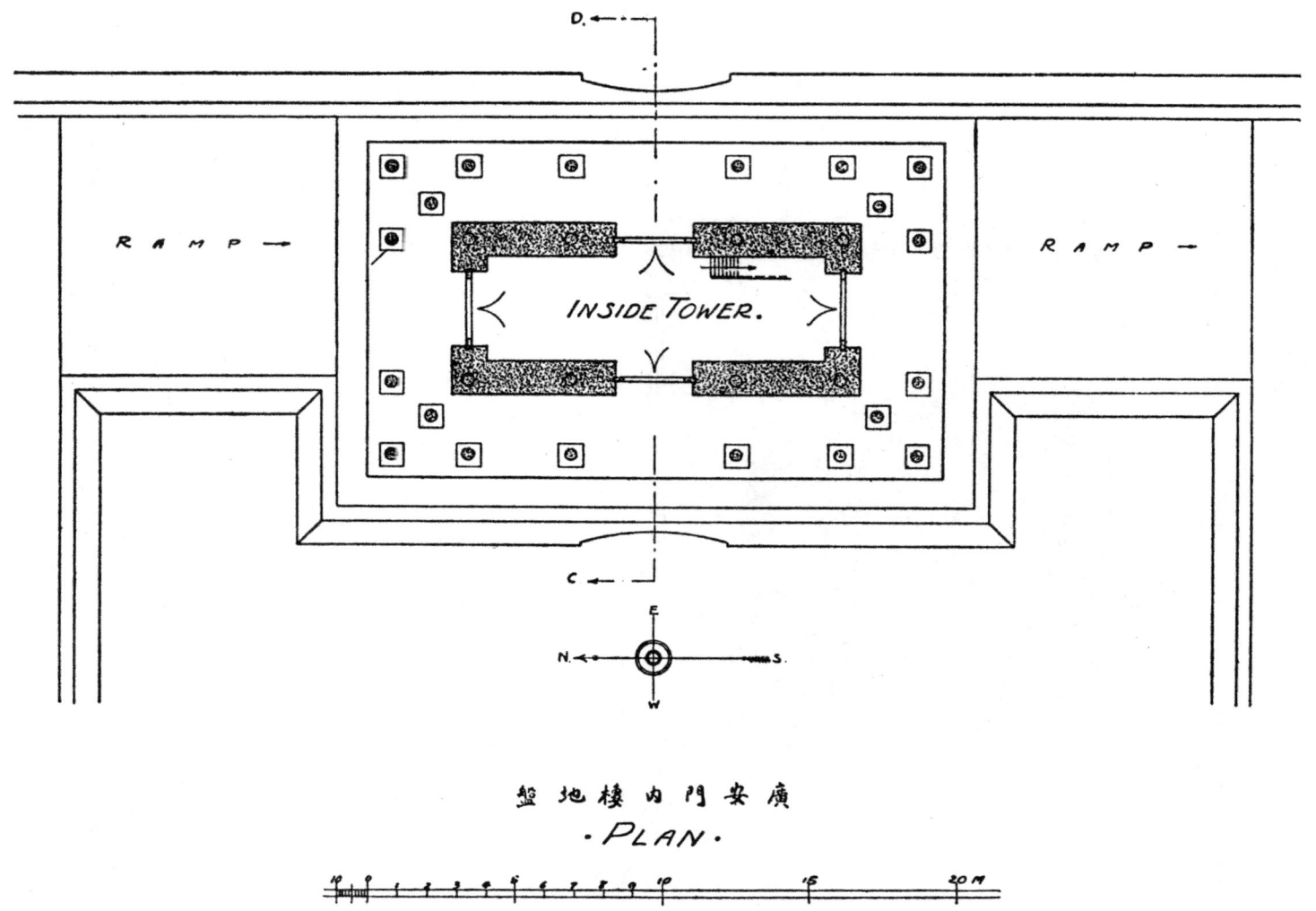

Fig. 41.—Chang I Men, inner tower.

building above the bastion is 17·6 metres and from the ground to the top of the roof ridge 26 metres. It has the usual outward division into three stories, accentuated by the roofs, while there is only one dividing

THE GATES OF THE CHINESE CITY

floor inside, the top story being simply an open loft for the roof-beams. The supporting columns are rather few and slender, and only four are encased on each front in the brick walls. The gallery has 5 by 3 spans of slender columns, and it is doubled only at the corners. The various parts are so well preserved that it almost seems as if some restorations had been made here after Ch'ien Lung's time; only the balustrade of the balcony and the doors of the second story are missing. The painted ornaments are still visible on some of the beams, and the roofs are complete, though overgrown with grass.

The outer tower is only about half as high as the inner; it measures above the bastion 7·8 metres and 16·6 metres from the ground. The plan is 13 by 6·6 metres; the walls are supported by two encased columns

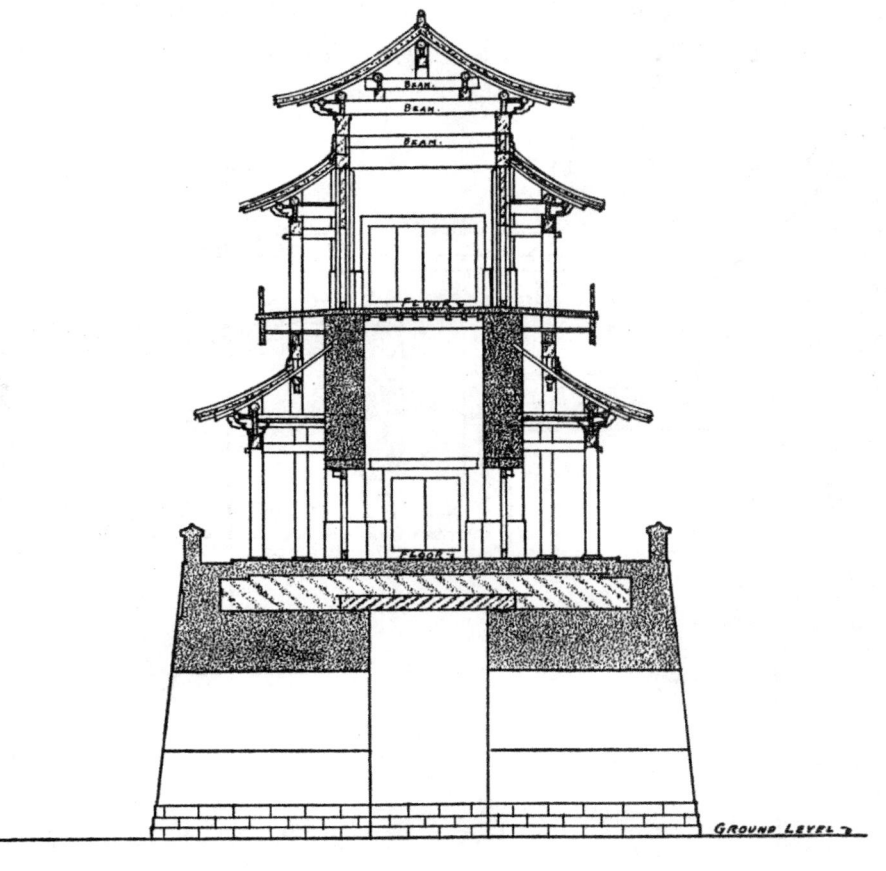

Fig. 42.—Chang I Men, inner tower.

on each side and provided with two rows of loopholes on the front and on the short sides, while the entrance door is at the rear. It is the same simple square brick building as the outer tower of Sha Wu men, and the position on a high bastion to which the wall on both sides reaches up with sloping ramps is also identical. Indeed, these two outer towers form a pair; it is only surprising that the two inner towers do not tally more closely. There must have been some special reason,

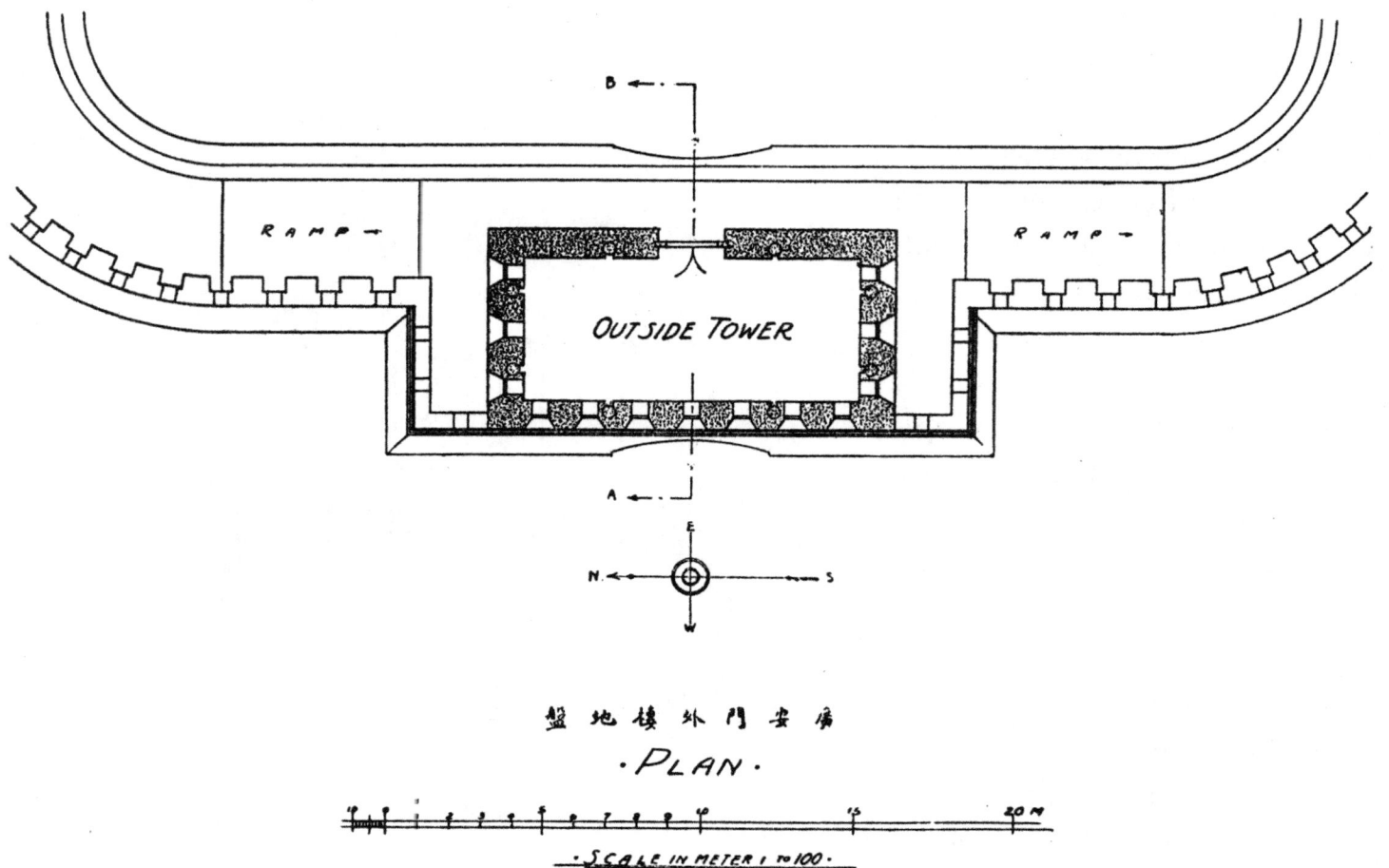

Fig. 43.—Chang I Men, outer tower.

unknown to us, for the rebuilding of the Chang Yi men tower on such a grand scale.

The vaults of the two gateways are very wide and slightly pointed (more so than appears in our drawing). In the middle of them right

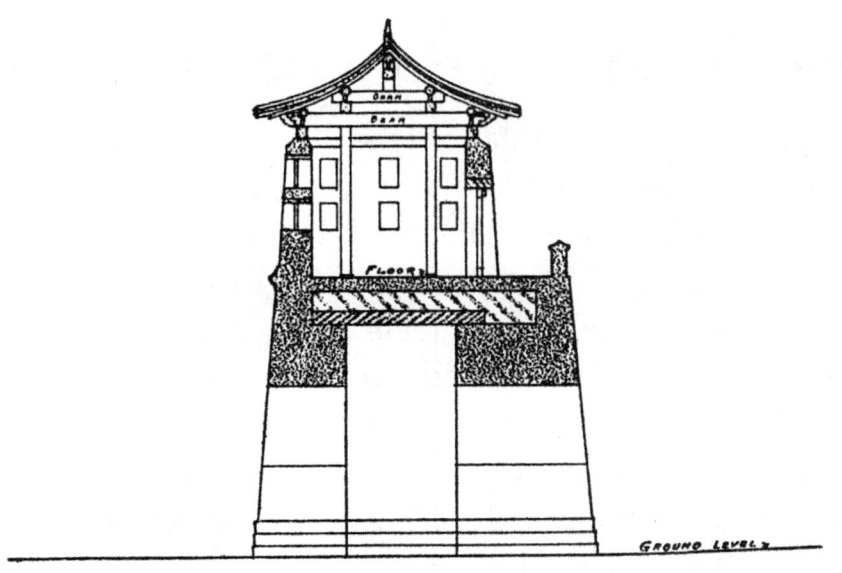

廣安門外樓剖式
· CROSS SECTION ·
ON A.--B.

FIG. 44.—Chang I Men, outer tower.

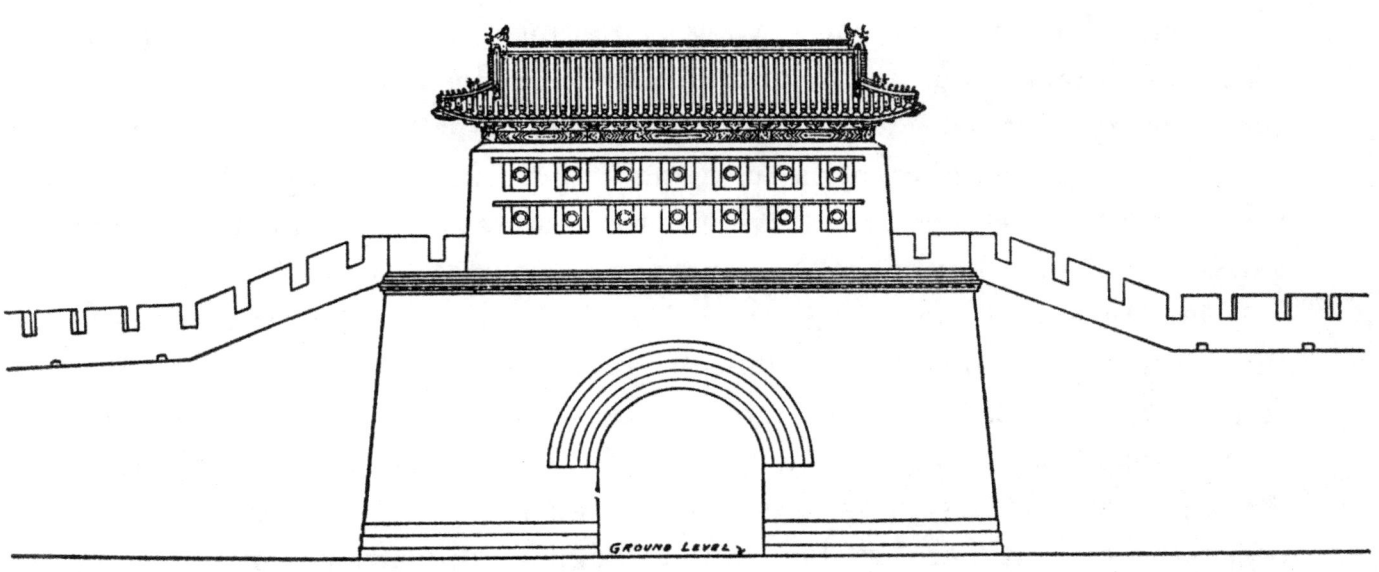

廣安門外樓正面
· FRONT ELEVATION ·

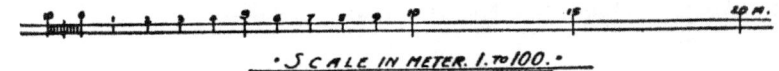

· SCALE IN METER. 1. TO 100. ·

FIG. 45.—Chang I Men, outer tower.

under the towers are, as usual, higher square compartments in which the doors move. The arches are not encased in niches, as on some of the older gates of the inner wall, but laid on the front of the battering bastion wall. They are formed by six to eight bands of alternately standing and lying bricks which, however, are not wedge-shaped and consequently can hardly be called proper voissoires. It is the mortar between the bricks which acts as voissoires, and the strength of the construction depends largely on the quality of the mortar and the care with which the bricks are laid. Most of these arches, which are quite common on the Peking city gates, are rough and uneven, but here at the Chang Yi men they are rather carefully built and have well withstood the test of time.

Of the three gates on the South wall the two outside ones, Yu An men and Tso An men form a pair with closely corresponding towers and barbicans. The middle gate, Yung Ting men, is somewhat larger and more important. Yu An men and Tso An men may well be called the country gates of the capital; they are situated in quarters which retain little or nothing of a city, and their interest depends less on their architectural features than on the natural setting in which they appear.

Yu An men (left peace gate), or Nan Hsi men (south-west gate), is on the whole in a much better state of preservation than Tso An men. It leads out into a landscape of rare beauty where no modern improvements in the shape of railways or motor-cars disturb the perfect country peace. To visit this gate is to witness a charming idyll of old Peking life. In order to reach it one has to travel through city quarters which are like old-fashioned country villages and through fields of oats and kaoliang. It is an excursion which takes one far away, both in time and space, from the modern quarters of the Chinese capital. The inner " tower " is a low one-storied building with pink plastered walls and an open gallery all

THE GATES OF THE CHINESE CITY

around, about 16 metres long and 9 metres broad. It is altogether well preserved and has no doubt been rebuilt in recent times. The bastion on which it stands, however, is of the Ming period, weather-worn and decayed in parts, now bulging under the pressure of tree roots. Ailanthus trees of considerable size grow out of the cracks, forming a screen of foliage in front of the open gallery.

The archway is of the usual construction, described above, slightly ogival and very large in proportion to the bastion and the tower. The view through it into the gate-yard and further on through the vault of the outer bastion into the country is particularly fine when the sunshine filters through the green curtains of the ailanthus and willow trees which hang in front of the dark vaults and recesses. The perfect harmony and quietness of the picture is not disturbed by any hustling traffic. Carts and rickshaws do not often come this way. The solitary peasant who passes through here on a summer day with his baskets of fresh vegetables hanging from the ends of a long pole over his shoulder only serves to enhance the dreamy mood of this out-of-the-world place.

The barbican wall is, at least on its inner side, old and full of holes, but the bastion of the outer tower was renewed, according to the inscriptions on two inserted tablets, in the 51st year of Ch'ien Lung. The building on the terrace is probably later; it looks just as fresh and well preserved as the inner tower and as a matter of fact makes quite a dominating impression, as it seems to be lifted by the slowly rising lines of the parapet over the small sheds and mud houses at its foot. The dimensions of this tower are practically the same as those of the outer towers on Sha Wu men and Chang I men (about 13 by 6 metres), and it has the usual two rows of seven loopholes on the front. The large curving roof is in a better state of preservation than those on any of the previously described gates of the Outer city. It is covered simply with grey tiles and has a single row of small brackets over the ornamental beams under the eaves. The archway is of similar size and construction to that on the inner tower.

The remarkably good effect of this tower depends largely on the appropriate small scale and dinginess of the buildings near by. There is, of course, an ugly modern guard-house, but it is small and partly hidden by the sun sheds of the food-shops and stalls which line the paved road just outside the gate. The narrow moat is spanned by an old stone bridge, but at the sides of the bridge it broadens out, especially after the rains, into shallow ponds. A few steps further south there is a second ditch—or branch moat—spanned by a smaller bridge. The gate thus becomes most intimately linked with the landscape by means of the successive bridges, the small mud houses nestling right up to the wall, and by trees which grow both inside and outside the barbican. The towers simply form the finishing motives in this picturesque composition, which indeed is created more by nature than by man. Its charm and character are infinitely varying, depending on the season and the light, but it is no doubt richest and most enchanting when the summer is ripe and the bulrushes and water-lilies are in bloom. Then the large willows lower their green draperies almost to the dusty road and ailanthus trees sweep the walls with their leafy brooms. If some solitary passer-by comes riding through the gate he is half asleep on his donkey. The air is heavy, the dusty road and stone bridges almost scorchingly hot. Nobody moves who can avoid it, except the children, the dark sunburnt urchins who splash and sport in the muddy water of the moat amongst the white ducks. The Peking summer is here condensed in a picture of exuberant growth around an old gate which forms a perfect link between the decaying city and an idyllic country.

Tso An men (right peace gate), or *Chiang T'sa men* (river swim gate), is architecturally the counterpart of Yo An men, but the general effect of it is different because the adjoining landscape is not so rich and beautiful. To reach this gate one has to make a still longer journey than the one to Yo An men; it is situated furthest away of all the gates from the more fully inhabited central parts of the city. The road down here to the south-east corner leads over an open country partly cultivated with grain and vegetables and partly overgrown with reeds. There is really nothing to remind one of the city except the wall which may be seen at some distance. How many old capitals can afford so much of unbuilt ground and pure country life within their precincts?

The towers and the barbican of Tso An men seem to correspond very closely to those of the south-west gate, but their present state of preservation is not so good. Although probably restored in the 31st year of Ch'ien Lung, the year marked on a tablet close to the outer bastion, they are now much dilapidated and in urgent need of repair. The roofs are actually breaking down at the eaves and the hips and giving way under the pressure of big tufts of grass; plaster is flaking off the walls, doors and parapets are missing. Still worse, during the summer of 1922 one of the ramps on the inside of the wall leading up to the tower bastion, broke down completely. The rain-water had been dripping under the brick coating until it slid off from the mud core and the whole ramp lay in ruins, as may be seen in one of our illustrations. It is the most recent and telling example of how the walls and gate ramps of Peking have been ruined from time to time and of their future fate, if no serious efforts are made to check the threatening destruction at various points.

After what has been said about the towers of Yo An men it is hardly necessary to go into a particular description of the Tso An men towers. They are alike in all their essential features, only, as we have seen, their state of preservation is quite different. The two gate-yards also closely correspond in size and general character, though the Tso An men yard is emptier, with no such beautiful trees as there are in the

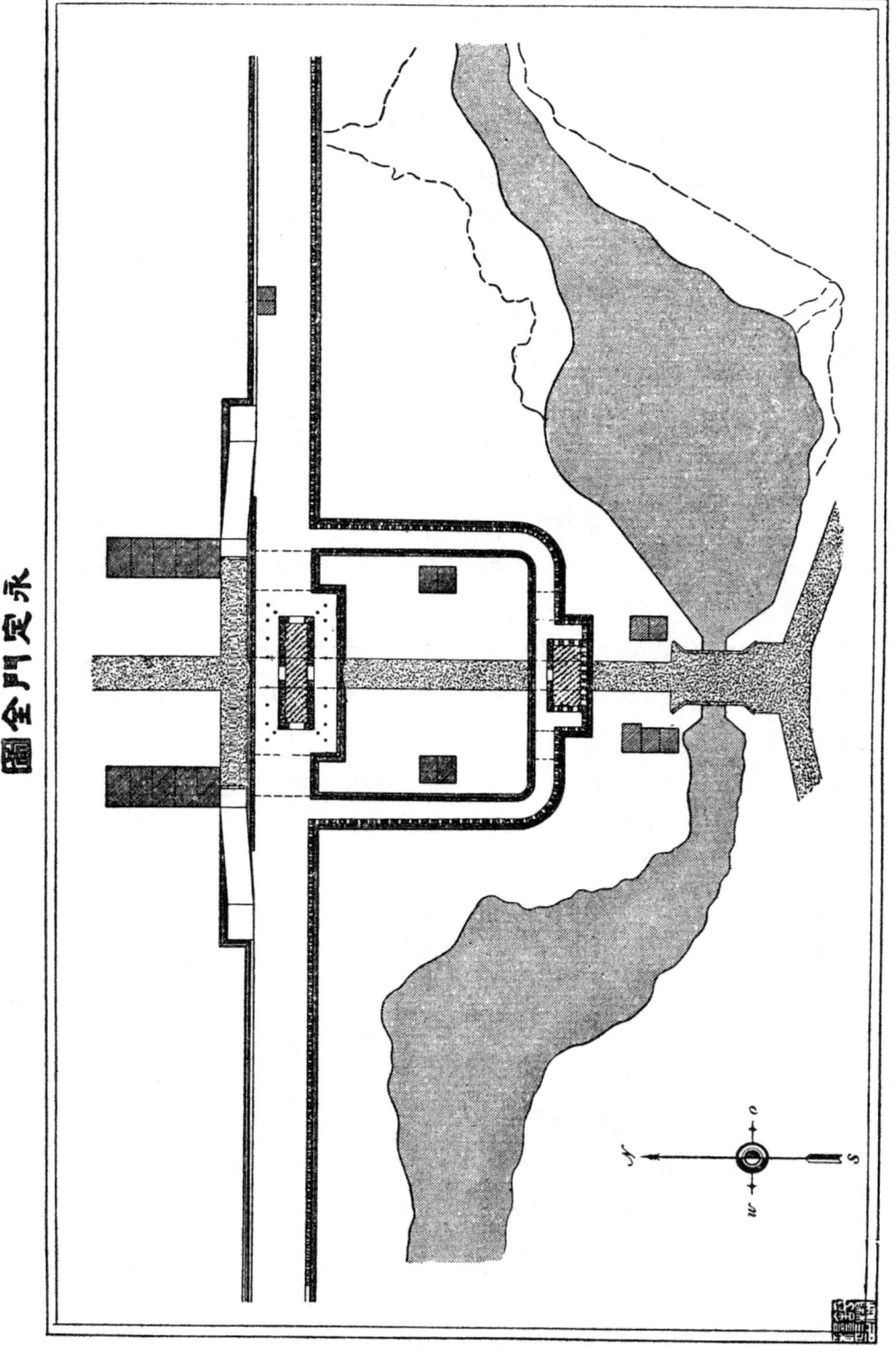

Fig. 46.—Yung Ting Men, general plan.

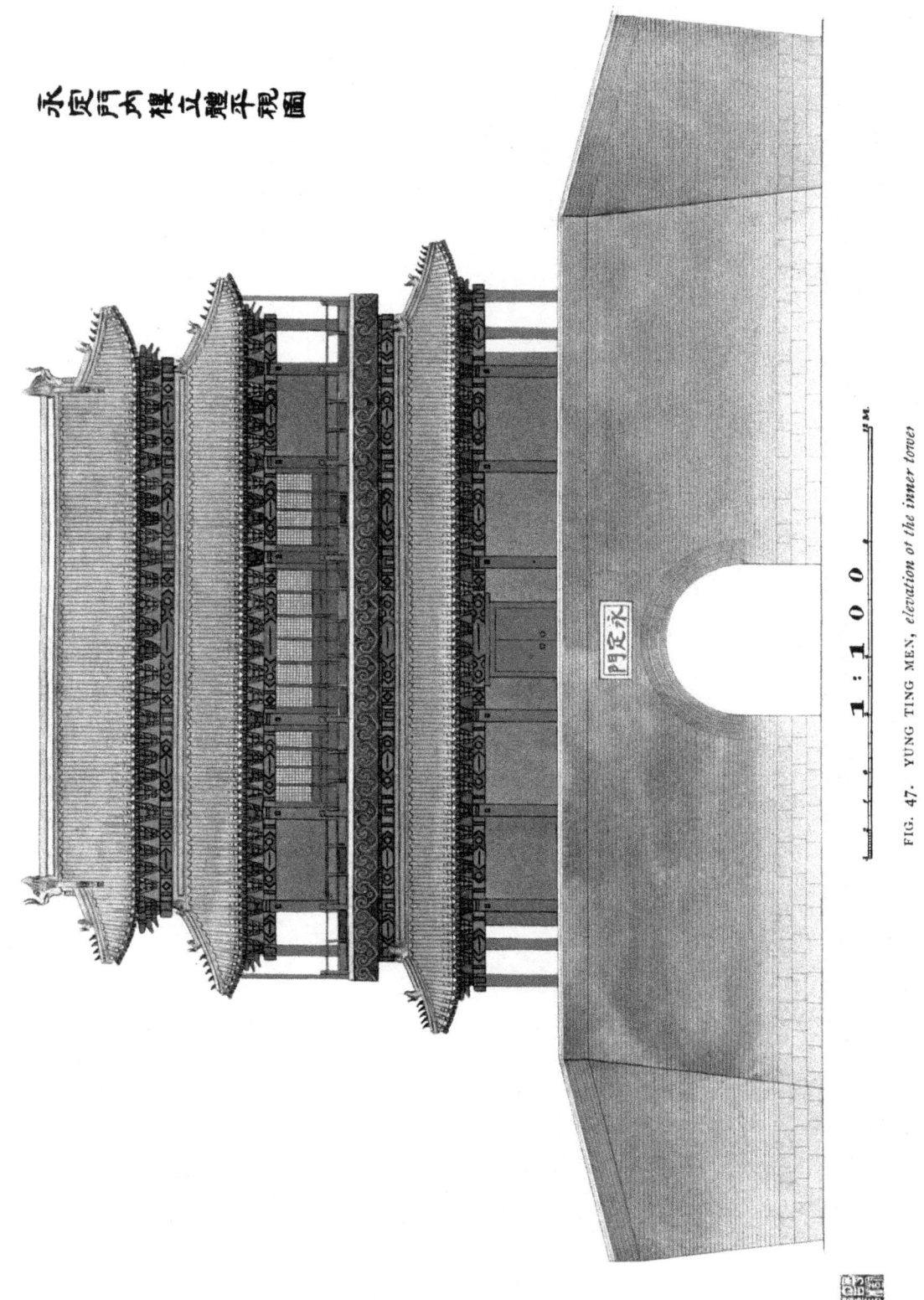

FIG. 47. YUNG TING MEN, *elevation of the inner tower*

other gate; there are simply two old-fashioned small shops, the one occupied by a cart builder, the other by a rope and ironmonger, and an eating place with the usual brick seats and tables under an outside shed. The traffic through this gate is mainly represented by a few solitary donkey-drivers and an occasional Peking cart; the larger transports pass through the gates which are closer to the centre of the capital.

The landscape outside the gate is bare and dusty, almost treeless. The only animating elements in this drab and monotonous picture are the grazing sheep which find a meagre pasture on the banks of the moat and the white ducks which never seem to get tired of pecking and dipping for their food in the savoury mud. Human beings are quite scarce here, and even the children are not so numerous as at the other gates; they are shy and reticent and quite unaccustomed to the visit of a foreigner.

Yung Ting men (the gate of perpetual certainty) is the largest and most important of all the gates on the Outer city wall. It occupies the central position on the South wall at the head of the long street which leads straight down from Ch'ien men, passing between rows of important native shops, and in its southern section between the enclosures of the Temple of Heaven and the Temple of Agriculture. The gate is thus visible at a long distance and makes a very stately impression with its remarkably high and well-restored inner tower. The general aspect and decorative effect of this may be judged from one of our coloured drawings, which, however, represents the gate in a rather too perfect state without the subduing element of Peking dust which is so plentiful at this end of the city when the wind sweeps down from the north.

The age of this tower cannot be very great; it may have been rebuilt in connection with the construction of the little station outside Yung Ting men, which served as the head of the electric railway running between the capital and Ma Chia pu, a village further south which was

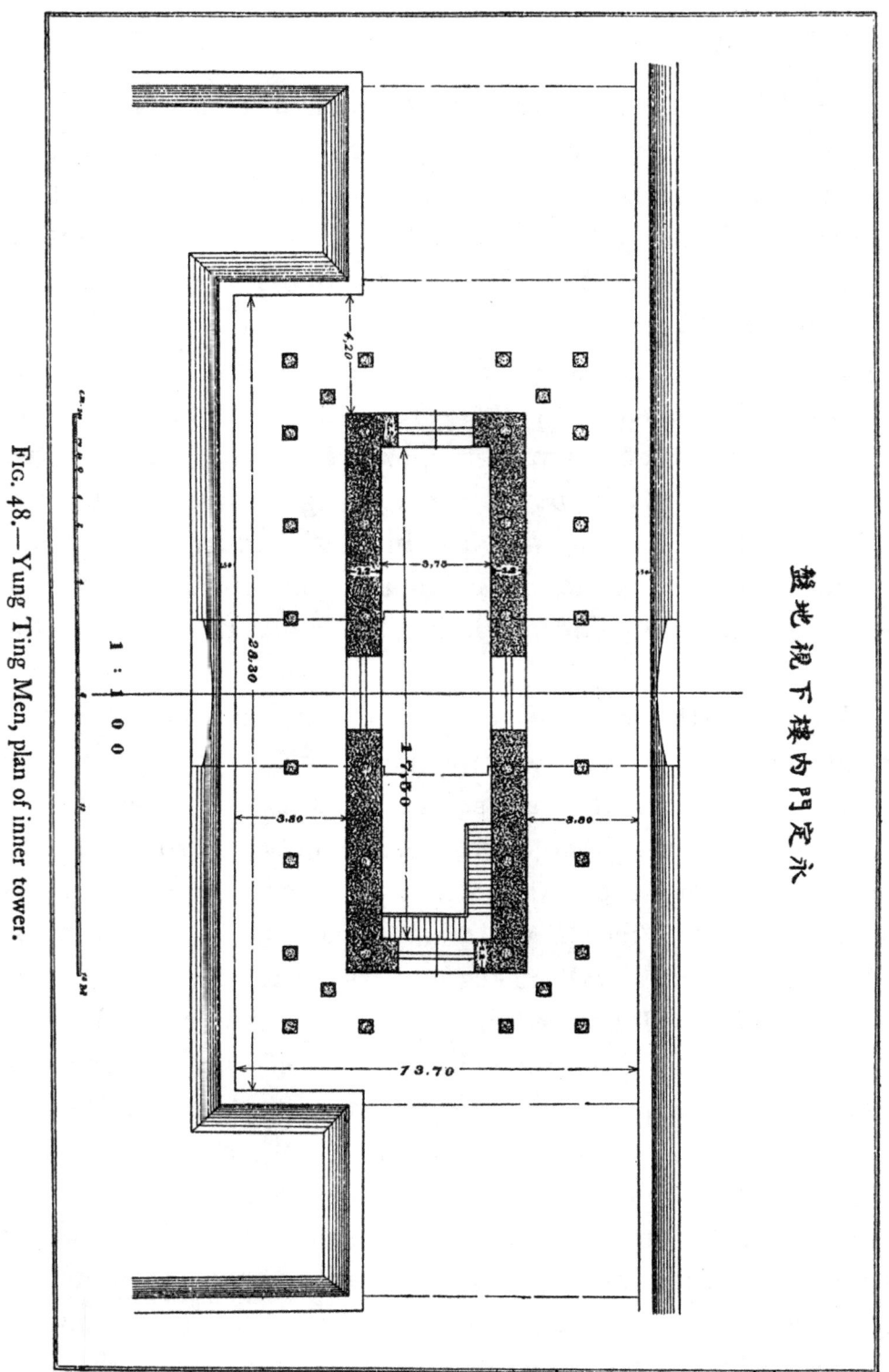

FIG. 48.—Yung Ting Men, plan of inner tower.

THE GATES OF THE CHINESE CITY

the terminal of the Tientsin-Peking line up to 1900. At the end of the Boxer war, after the occupation of the capital by the foreign powers, the station was moved just outside the Temple of Heaven, and about four years later to the place where it now stands. If our assumption is correct, the Yung Ting men tower would be only a little more than

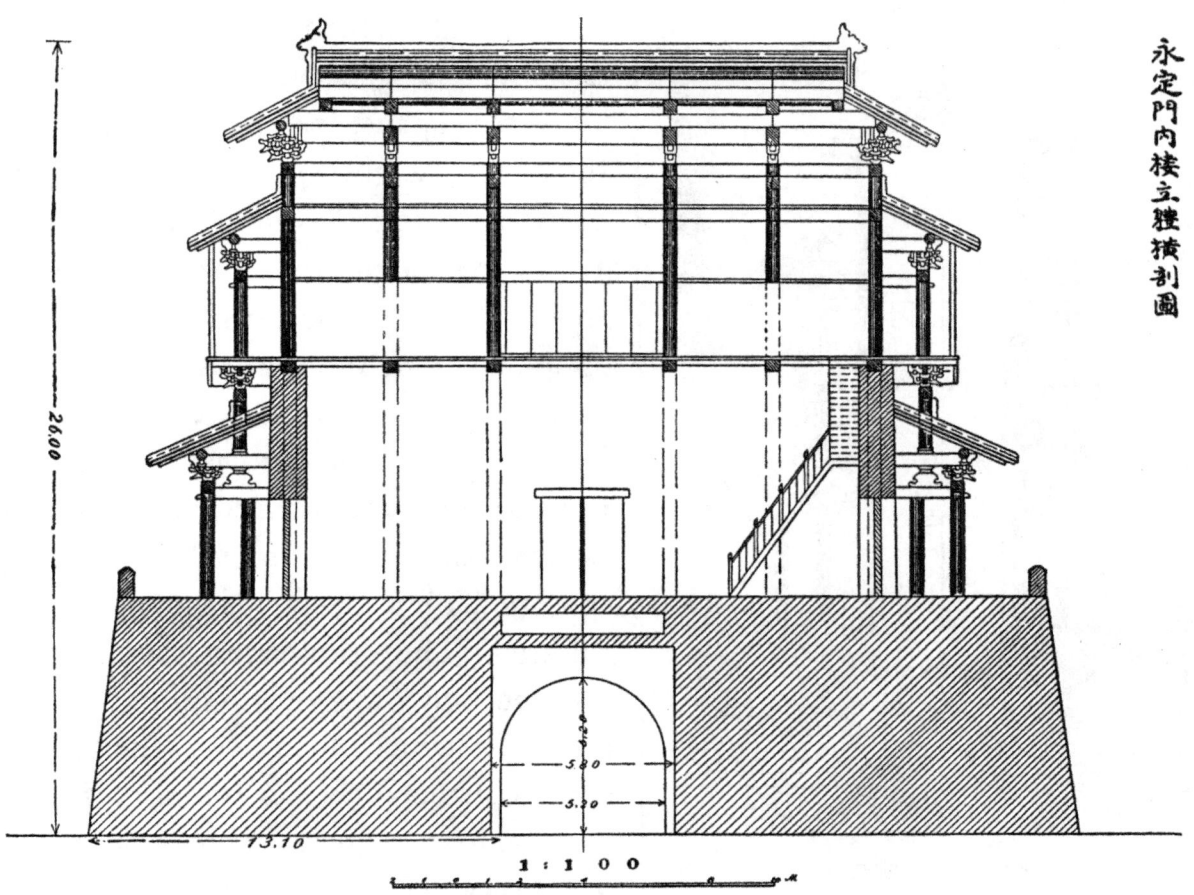

Fig. 49.—Yung Ting Men, plan of inner tower.

a quarter of a century old, and its present state of preservation does not suggest a greater age. The bastions and the barbican were rebuilt in the 31st year of Ch'ien Lung; they enclose a gate-yard of the same shape and proportions as at Chang Yi men, only a little larger. Here the measurements are: depth 36 metres, width 42 metres; thickness of the barbican wall about 6 metres, to which is added about 5 metres at the outer bastion, so that this bastion becomes about 9 metres broad, while the inner bastion measures nearly 15 metres.

The inner tower is of unusual proportions, being very narrow, broad and high. The outer measurements of the walls are 19·8 by 6·1 metres, and of the gallery, which has seven by three spans, 24 by 10·2 metres; the full height is 26 metres, the bastion being 8 and the building 18 metres high. The construction is thoroughly typical, though a little simpler than in the earlier towers. The three successive roofs, which have hardly any curve except at the corners, are carried by columns, beams, and brackets, which by the intermediation of purlins support the rafters. The projecting balcony of the second story is supported by columns which stand on the beams that connect the columns of the outer gallery with the walls, not simply by brackets as in the P'ing Tzu men tower. In addition to its usual balustrade the balcony has at its four corners thin masts or poles to support the hips of the second roof, a feature which is not uncommon on the restored towers. The main roof is carried by two layers of crosswise and lengthwise beams and purlins. The brackets under the eaves of this

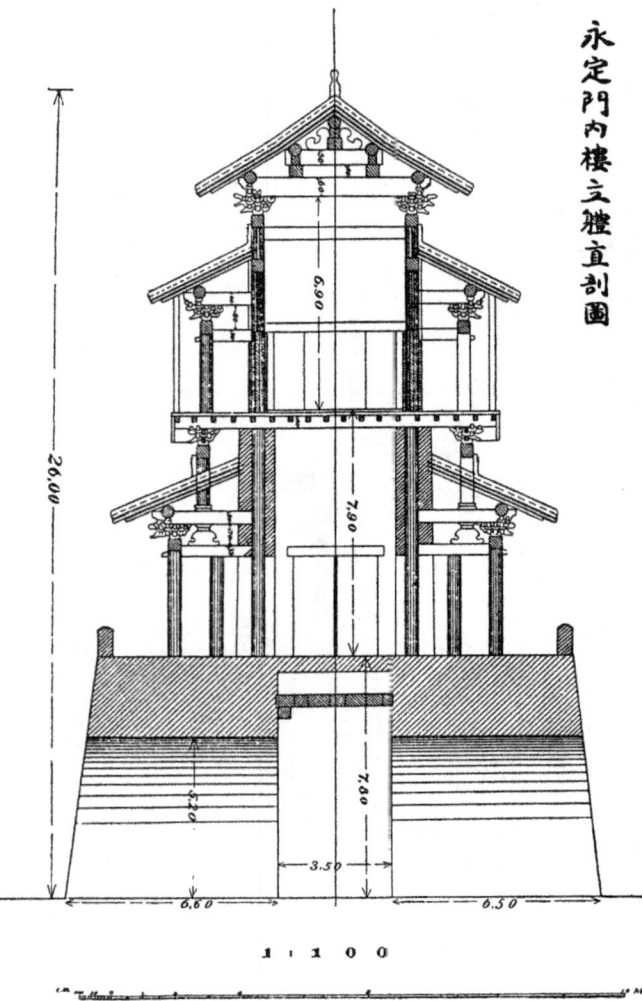

Fig. 50.—Yung Ting Men, cross section of the inner tower.

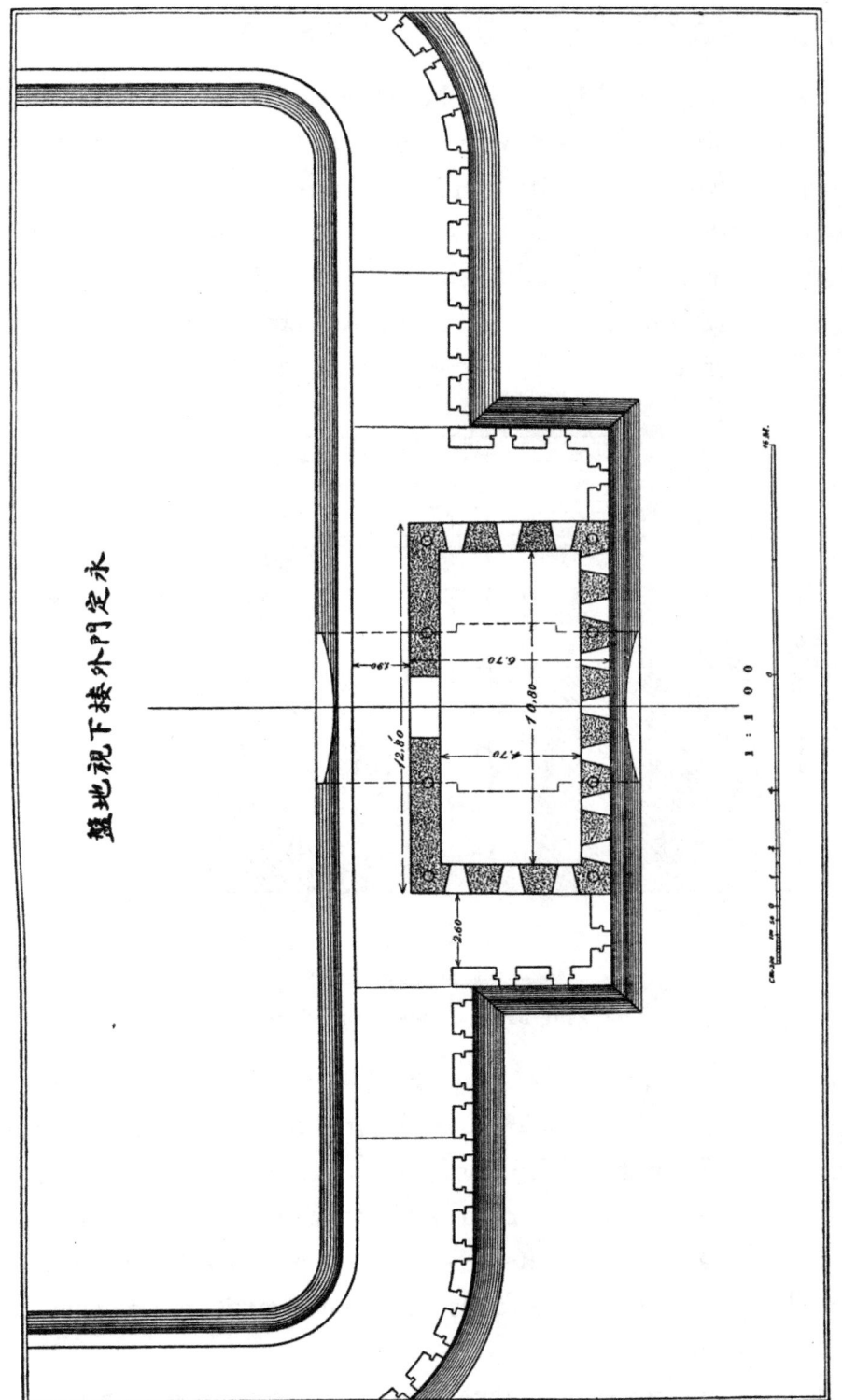

Fig. 51.—Yung Ting Men, plan of outer tower.

roof and the second are tripled, but in the lowest story simply doubled. Their alternating colouring in green and blue as well as the characteristic ornamentation of the beams becomes quite evident from the drawing, and also the fantastic animal heads and the Kuei Lung tzû on the ridges and hips.

The outer tower is practically the same as those on the other larger gates of the Chinese city; it appears quite small in proportion to the inner tower. The front is 12·8 metres long and has two rows of seven

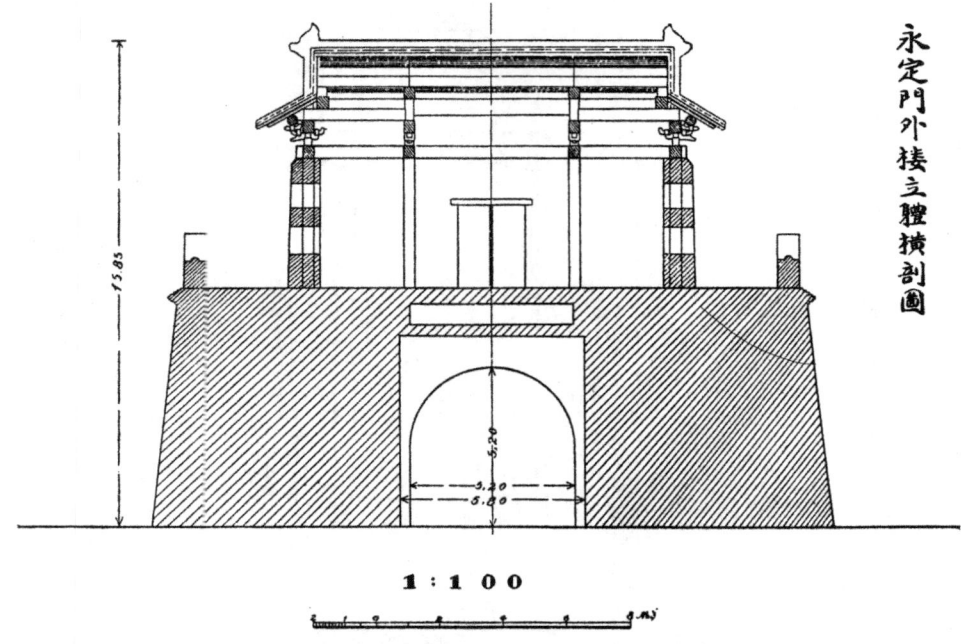

Fig. 53.—Yung Ting Men, cross section of the outer tower.

loopholes, but as the parapet of the barbican wall reaches up over the first row, the appearance of height is again lessened. The actual height of the building is 8 metres, and of the supporting bastion 7·8 metres. It is in good condition, with a complete roof and the ornaments on the beams under the eaves and the painted gun muzzles in the loopholes fully visible. The rear side, towards the gate-yard, is, as usual, a plain brick wall with a double door.

The yard is a picturesque place, with a number of trees and shops.

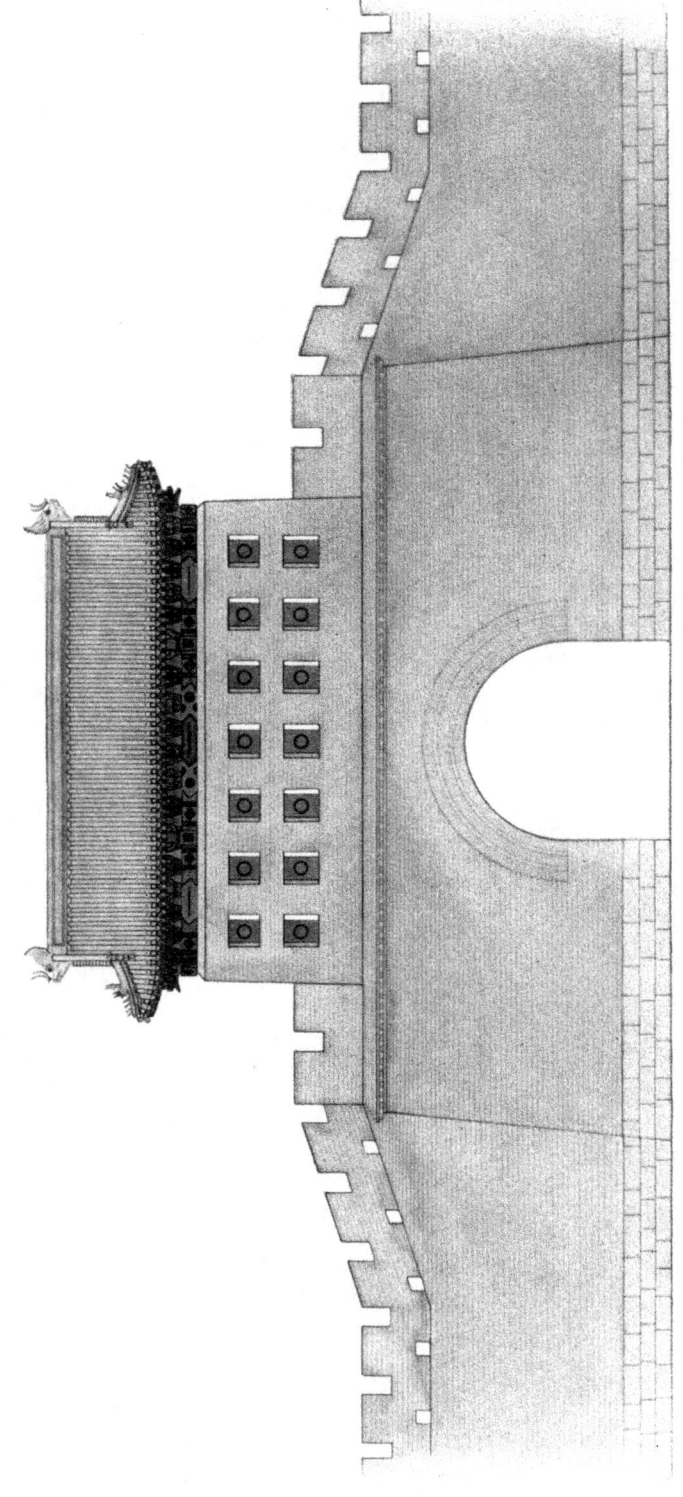

FIG. 52. YUNG TING MEN, *elevation of the outer tower*

A continuous stream of rickshaws, carts, wheelbarrows, camel caravans, and military transports (to the southern barracks), besides carriers with baskets slung on long poles, passes through here . . . stops sometimes at the eating places inside and outside the barbican . . . continues over the broad stone bridge which spans the deep moat, and divides along the two roads which slope down in an easterly and westerly direction from the bridge head. The life on the bridge is often quite animated, and the lively scene gets a very appropriate setting from the old-fashioned shops which line the street on which the bridge abuts. The city life, with all its hustle and bustle, is concentrated here for a moment before it flows out into the suburbs and to the peaceful country beyond.

The most beautiful and complete picture of Yung Ting men may be obtained from the west side, when the whole architectural composition is seen in one view. The moat is quite broad and well framed by bulrushes and weeping willows. The towers and the crenellated wall of the curving barbican stand out in dark silhouette against the clear sky. The lines of the city wall and of the barbican lead up to the main tower, which seems to lift itself on its broad wing-like roofs over the heavy walls and bastions. The reflection in the water is just as distinct as any of the forms above. But when the wind sweeps through the soft branches of the willows the wings of the tower begin to tremble and the crenellated wall to crumble and sway. . . .

How long will they still remain, these wonderful walls and gates, these silent records of Peking's most beautiful and glorious past?

INDEX

		PAGES
AN CHEN MEN	安貞門	23, 38
AN TING MEN	安定門	23, 38, 43, 46, 47, 50, 75, 77, 79, 99, 130, 182, 183, 184, 185, 186
AN TUNG MEN	安東門	17
CHANG CH'IN	張欽	88, 120, 124, 125
CHANG CHIU	張九	122
CHANG CHIU CHIH	張九志	86
CHANG HUAN	張煥	37
CHANG I MEN	彰義門	19, 108, 115, 120, 200, 201, 203, 204, 205, 206, 207, 208, 209, 215
CHANG LOU	張樓	120
CHANG MÊNG CHAO	張孟昭	124
CHANG PAO CH'AO	張寶鈔	69
CHANG TSÊNG SHÊNG	張增盛	121
CHANG YANG HAO	張養浩	18

INDEX

		PAGES
CH'ANG AN	長安	27, 28, 32
CH'ANG CHOW FU	常州府	81
CH'ANG LUN	暢綸	123
CH'ANG MÊNG YANG	常孟陽	121
CH'ANG SHIH YUNG	常世榮	121
CH'ANG TSENG	常增	124
CHAO FÊNG YÜ	趙豐玉	123
CHAO I	趙義	125
CHAO TÊ FU	趙德輔	121
CH'AO YANG MEN	朝陽門	43
CHÊN WU MIAO	真武廟	184, 186
CH'ÊN CHÜ	陳擧	86
CH'ÊN CH'ANG	陳昌	124
CH'ÊN FU	陳福	123
CH'ÊN KUEI	陳貴	124
CH'ÊN, THE RULER	陳王	18
CHÊNG TÊ	正德	60, 78, 88

INDEX

		PAGES
CHÊNG TUNG	正統	40, 41
CHÊNG YANG MEN	正陽門	40, 43, 108, 129, 167
CH'ÊNG HUA	成化	40, 53, 58, 60, 78, 84, 88, 89
CH'ÊNG HUANG MIAO	城隍廟	65
CHI CHOU	冀州	16
CHI SHUI TAN	積水潭	82
CH'I HUA MEN	齊化門	23, 24, 43, 45, 51, 69, 70, 95, 97, 98, 131, 155, 156, 157, 159
CHIA CHING	嘉靖	21, 54, 58, 59, 60, 61, 62, 63, 64, 66, 67, 68, 69, 70, 71, 72, 73, 76, 77, 78, 79, 81, 83, 84, 85, 86, 87, 88, 89, 107, 109, 110, 113, 114, 119, 120, 121, 122, 123, 124, 125, 126, 187, 194, 197
CHIA CH'ING	嘉慶	54, 57, 58, 60, 61, 62, 63, 67, 68, 69, 70, 72, 76, 78, 80, 81, 83, 85, 86, 89, 94, 101, 102, 103, 104, 113, 115, 116, 117, 119, 120, 121, 122, 123, 126, 158
CHIA WU	甲午	68, 81, 89
CHIANG TA SHUN	蔣大順	121
CHIANG TS'A MEN	江擦門	124, 210
CHIANG YÜEH	蔣月	125
CHIEN TÊ MEN	健德門	23, 38

INDEX

		PAGES
CH'IEN LUNG	乾隆	11, 29, 53, 54, 57, 58, 59, 60, 61, 62, 63, 64, 67, 68, 69, 70, 72, 73, 75, 76, 77, 78, 79, 80, 81, 83, 84, 85, 86, 87, 88, 89, 94, 95, 96, 97, 98, 99, 100, 101, 102, 103, 104, 105, 113, 114, 115, 116, 117, 118, 119, 120, 121, 122, 123, 124, 125, 126, 133, 139, 157, 159, 177, 182, 184, 187, 194, 197, 199, 202, 205, 209, 211, 215
CH'IEN MEN	前門	17, 43, 48, 55, 56, 57, 60, 61, 104, 105, 161, 167, 168, 169, 170, 171, 173, 175, 177, 178, 179, 180, 181, 213
CH'IEN MEN TA CHIEH	前門大街	169, 181
CHIH CHÊNG	至正	25
CHIH YÜAN	至元	21, 22, 25, 29
CH'IN SHIH HAUNG TI	秦始皇帝	16
CHING FÊNG MEN	景風門	18
CHING MEN	驚門	131
CHING MEN	景門	129
CH'ING CHOU FU	青州府	3, 4, 59
CH'ING YIN MEN	清音門	17
CHO CHOU	涿州	20
CHOU CHÜN	周鈞	120

INDEX

		PAGES
CHOU HSIN LU	周新廬	120
CHOU HSUEH	周雪	120
CHÜ CHÊNG YAO	居正耀	68
CHU WÊN	朱文	122
CH'U CH'ÊN	楚琛	120
CH'U CHU	楚祝	119
CH'U WU PIN	楚吳濱	126
CHUNG HSIEN WANG	忠獻王	18
CHUNG HUA MEN	中華門	169, 172
CHUNG TU	中都	19, 20, 21, 24
CH'UNG CHÊNG	崇禎	54, 69, 72, 77, 79, 80, 81, 84, 86, 87, 113, 114, 115, 116, 117, 122, 165
CH'UNG CHIH MEN	崇智門	19
CH'UNG JÊN MEN	崇仁門	23, 24
CH'UNG WÊN MEN	崇文門	43
FÊNG I MEN	豐宜門	18
FÊNG SHUI	風水	13, 139, 154

2 G

INDEX

		PAGES
FÊNG TA CHAO	馮大昭	122
FU CH'ÊNG MEN	阜成門	43, 133, 134
FU CHÜ	符居	59
FU HO	傅和	123
FU TIEN	傅典	120
HAI LING WANG	海陵王	18
HAN CH'ANG	韓常	18
HANG CHOW	杭州	13, 21, 39
HAO HUA MEN	灝華門	19
HATA MEN	哈達門	43, 45, 51, 57, 59, 60, 104, 129, 130, 155, 161, 162, 163, 164, 165
HEI YAO CH'ANG	黑窰廠	108
HÊNG SHÊNG KILN	恒盛窰	60
HÊNG SHUN KILN	恒順窰	76
HO I MEN	和義門	23, 24
HO PU NIEN	何卜年	18
HO SHÊNG KILN	和盛窰	85
HO TSUNG	何宗	60

INDEX

		PAGES
HOU LU	侯六	121
HSI CHIH MEN	西直門	24, 43, 45, 51, 83, 84, 100, 131, 150, 151, 152, 153, 154, 156, 158, 159, 183
HSI P'IEN MEN	西便門	115, 119, 189, 190, 191, 192, 193, 194, 195, 196, 197, 199
HSIAO HSI MEN	小西門	108
HSIEH HSIANG	薛香	124
HSIEN FÊNG	咸豐	70, 77, 78
HSIEN HSI MEN	顯西門	17
HSIN SSŬ	辛巳	67, 68, 76, 77, 81, 85, 88
HSING TAI KILN	興泰窰	89
HSING TSAI	行在	39
HSIU MEN	修門	130
HSÜ TA	徐達	23, 37
HSÜAN WU MEN	宣武門	43
HSÜAN YAO MEN	宣耀門	18
HU YUNG CHÊNG	胡永正	121
HUA YÜN LUNG	華雲龍	37

INDEX

		PAGES
HUANG CH'ÊNG	黃城	31
HUI CH'ÊNG MEN	會城門	19
HUNG WU	洪武	23, 25, 37, 38, 39
JÊN CHING	任經	125
JÊN WEI NAN	任威南	68
JÊN WU	壬午	88
JIH HSIA CHIU WEN KAO	日下舊聞考	15, 24
JUI SHÊNG KILN	瑞盛窰	72, 85
JUI SHUN KILN	瑞順窰	71, 73
KAI FÊNG	開封	32
K'AI MEN	開門	131
K'AI YANG MEN	開陽門	17
K'ANG HSI	康熙	54, 58, 165
KAO SHANG YI	高尚義	64, 70, 124
KAO T'ANG CHOU KILN	高唐州窰	84
KUAN TI MIAO	關帝廟	149, 157, 166, 180

INDEX

		PAGES
KUAN YIN	觀音	172, 180
KUANG AN MEN	廣安門	200, 201, 202
KUANG CH'ÊNG KILN	廣成窰	81
KUANG CHÜ MEN	廣渠門	112, 198
KUANG HSI MEN	光熙門	23, 37, 108
KUANG HSÜ	光緒	60, 61, 62, 63, 64, 70, 71, 101, 105, 117, 118, 119
KUANG SHÊNG KILN	廣盛窰	86
KUANG TÁI MEN	光泰門	19
KUEI LUNG TZÜ	夔龍字	10, 139, 218
KUNG CH'ÊN MEN	拱宸門	17
KUNG CH'ÊNG	宮城	31
KUNG PU INSPECTOR FU	工部監督福	83
KUNG PU INSPECTOR KAO	工部監督高	122
KUNG PU INSPECTOR KUEI	工部監督桂	57, 58, 62, 63, 64, 72, 76, 83, 86, 122, 125, 126
KUNG PU INSPECTOR SA	工部監督薩	69, 80, 85, 86
KUNG PU INSPECTOR YUNG	工部監督永	62, 63, 64, 72, 73, 76, 88, 122, 125, 126

INDEX

		PAGES
KUNG SHUN KILN	工順窰	77, 89, 125
KUO MEN	國門	129
LI CHÊNG MEN	麗正門	23, 38, 43
LI CHI WEI	李寄威	59
LI CHIH KANG	李至剛	39
LI CHING	李經	123
LI CH'UNG	李充	121
LI HUAN	李煥	60
LI JÊN	李仁	121
LI LIN	李林	123, 124
LI SHANG KUEI	李尚貴	122
LI TSE MEN	麗澤門	19
LI YÜ PAO	李裕寶	119
LIANG CHANG	梁章	120
LIANG TUNG	梁棟	120
LIAO TUNG	遼東	16

INDEX

		PAGES
LIN KUEI	林貴	68
LIN YUNG SHOU	林永壽	68, 70, 122, 123, 125
LIU CHAO	劉釗	59, 85
LIU CHIN	劉金	119
LIU KAO	劉高	76
LIU LI CH'ANG	琉璃廠	16
LIU MAO	劉茂	121
LIU NENG	劉能	76
LIU SUNG	劉松	76
LO YANG	洛陽	5
LU MING YANG	陸明陽	122, 124
MA CHIA MIAO	馬家廟	108
MA CHIA PU	馬家鋪	213
MAO TZÜ CH'ÊNG	帽子城	106, 110
NAN HSI MEN	南西門	118, 122, 208
NANKING	南京	5, 21, 38

INDEX

PAGES

NAN YANG FU	南陽府	59
NIU CH'I	牛七	120
NIU CH'UNG	牛充	122
O SHIH	兀室	18
PEKING PEI CHING	北京	9, 15, 16, 22, 23, 24, 25, 28, 33, 34, 35, 36, 37, 39, 40, 43, 53, 55, 65, 74, 75, 92, 98, 104, 105, 112, 114, 116, 124, 129, 131, 132, 154, 155, 159, 161, 167, 170, 176, 177, 181, 182, 184, 190, 198, 208, 213, 215, 219
PEI P'ING	北平	38, 39
PEI P'ING LU	北平路	37
PIEN LIANG	汴梁	21
PING SHEN	丙申	68, 89
P'ING TZU MEN	平則門	23, 24, 43, 45, 51, 86, 87, 88, 101, 131, 133, 134, 135, 136, 137, 138, 140, 141, 142, 143, 146, 147, 148, 150, 151, 152, 153, 156, 157, 163, 167, 202, 216
PO YÜN KUAN	白雲觀	20, 24
PU T'IEN KUEI	卜天貴	68
PU T'UNG WEI	卜通威	68

INDEX

		PAGES
SAN HU CH'IAO	三虎橋	108
SAN TOU	三頭	12
SHA WU MEN	沙窩門	114, 126, 198, 200, 206, 209
SHAN SI	山西	5
SHANG HAI	上海	2, 16
SHANG MEN	商門	131
SHANTUNG	山東	3, 11, 59
SHÊN MU CH'ANG	沈木廠	108
SHÊNG MEN	生門	130
SHENSI	陝西	3
SHIH JÊN MEN	施仁門	18
SHIH TSU	世祖	21
SHUANG T'A SSÜ	雙塔寺	24
SHUN CH'ÊNG MEN	順承門	23, 43
SHUN CHIH	順治	58
SHUN CHIH MEN	順治門	45, 51, 56, 63, 103, 104, 129, 130, 161, 165, 166
SHUN T'IEN FU	順天府	39

INDEX

		PAGES
SHUN T'IEN FU CHIH	順天府志	15, 17, 18, 21, 22, 23, 25, 37, 39, 40, 44, 50, 107, 109, 112
SIANFU	西安府	3, 4, 5, 8
SOO CHOW	蘇州	13
SOO CHOW FU	蘇州府	72
SSŬ MEN	死門	130
SU CH'ING MEN	肅清門	23, 37
SUN CH'UAN WEI	孫傳威	59
SŬN HSIN	孫馨	119
SUN LUNG	孫龍	125
SUN PAO	孫寶	87
SUN PIAO	孫標	123
SUN TZU TUNG	孫紫東	59
SUN WÊN KÊ	孫文萵	125
SUNG I	宋義	123
SUNG WÊN MING	宋文明	68
TA CH'ING MEN	大清門	169
TA MING KUNG	大明宮	32

INDEX

		PAGES
TA NEI	大內	32
TA T'UNG CH'IAO	大通橋	41, 42, 112
TAI TU	大都	22
TAI TU LU	大都路	37
T'AI	臺	12, 30
T'AI TSU	太祖	39
T'AI TSUNG	太宗	18
TAIYUANFU	太原府	5
TAN FÊNG MEN	丹鳳門	17
TAN TÊ CHÊNG	譚德政	121
TAO KUANG	道光	53, 54, 58, 70, 71, 76, 77, 78, 80, 83, 84
TÊ SHENG MEN	德勝門	23, 38, 43, 46, 50, 75, 79, 80, 82, 99, 130, 184, 185, 187
TÊ SHUN KILN	德順窯	85
TI TAN	地壇	130
T'IEN CH'I	天啟	112
T'IEN NIEN SSǓ	天寧寺	20
T'IEN TÊ	天德	18

INDEX

		PAGES
TS'AO CH'UN	曹春	69
TS'AO	曹	113
TS'AO JUNG	曹榮	121
TSO AN MEN	左安門	208, 210, 211
TSUNG WANG	宗望	18
TU CH'UNG	杜充	121
TU MEN	杜門	131
TU TI MIAO	土地廟	20
TUAN CHOU	段洲	69
TUAN LI MEN	端禮門	19
TUNG CHIH MEN	東直門	24, 43, 45, 50, 70, 72, 96, 98, 131, 155, 158, 159, 160, 183, 184
TUNG HO CANAL	東河	42, 112, 198
TUNG PIEN MEN	東便門	19, 20, 105, 113, 126, 196, 198, 199
T'UNG CHIH	同治	70, 84
T'UNG CH'IN KILN	通欽窰	72
T'UNG FÊNG KILN	通豐窰	57

INDEX

		PAGES
T'UNG HO KILN	通和窰	59, 67, 68, 78, 85, 86, 123, 124
T'UNG SHUN KILN	通順窰	78
T'UNG T'IEN MEN	通天門	17
T'UNG YÜAN	通元門	19
WAI CH'ÊNG	外城	106
WAN JUI	萬瑞	125
WAN LI	萬曆	15, 54, 60, 62, 64, 67, 68, 69, 71, 72, 73, 76, 77, 79, 80, 81, 83, 84, 85, 86, 87, 88, 89, 112, 121, 124, 187
WANG HSING	王興	120
WANG HUI	王惲	19
WANG JUI	王瑞	89, 121
WEI HSIEN	濰縣	11
WEI SHAO WANG	衛紹王	21
WÊN MING MEN	文明門	22, 23, 43
WU CH'ANG PEI	吳昌培	124
WU CH'I JUNG	吳濟榮	120
WU CHÜ	吳矩	123, 125

INDEX

		PAGES
WU KUN	吳鯤	125
WU LIANG PEI	吳良培	125
WU LING YUNG CHANG	烏陵用章	21
WU SHÊN	戊申	121
WU TZÜ	戊子	62
WU YÜ	吳玉	68
YANG CHIN	楊金	121
YANG CHOU FU	揚州府	72
YANG CH'UN MEN	陽春門	18
YANG CHUNG CHÜ	楊中矩	125
YANG P'EI	楊佩	120
YANG YÜ	楊玉	120
YEH KUO CH'ÊN	葉國珍	37
YEN CHING	燕京	16, 17, 18, 19, 20, 21, 37
YING CH'UN MEN	迎春門	17
YO AN MEN	右安門	208, 210, 211

INDEX

		PAGES
YÜ CH'ÊNG KILN	裕成窰	85
YU CHOU	幽州	16, 17
YÜAN CH'ÊNG	元城	23
YÜAN CHIH	元志	23
YÜAN CH'ÜAN KILN	源泉窰	85
YÜAN I T'UNG CHIH	元壹統志	24, 29
YUNG CH'ÊNG KILN	永成窰	58, 59
YUNG HO KILN	永和窰	85
YUNG HO KUNG	雍和宮	76, 182
YUNG LO	永樂	24, 30, 37, 39, 40, 41, 43, 46
YUNG NIEN HSIEN KILN	永義興窰	89
YUNG SHUN KILN	永順窰	73
YUNG TING GOVERNMENT KILN	永定官窰	70, 72, 73, 81, 83, 85
YUNG TING MEN	永定門	111, 117, 123, 202, 208, 212, 213, 214, 215, 216, 217, 218, 219